Dictionary of Literary Biography • Volume Sixty-nine

Contemporary German Fiction Writers
First Series

Contemporary German Fiction Writers
First Series

7568

Edited by
Wolfgang D. Elfe
University of South Carolina
and
James Hardin
University of South Carolina

A Bruccoli Clark Layman Book
Gale Research Company • Book Tower • Detroit, Michigan 48226

Manufactured by Edwards Brothers, Inc.
Ann Arbor, Michigan
Printed in the United States of America

The illustrations on pp. 28, 30, 32, 33, 38, 39, and 42
are reproduced by permission of René Böll.

Copyright © 1988
GALE RESEARCH COMPANY

Library of Congress Cataloging-in-Publication Data

Contemporary German fiction writers. First series / edited by
    Wolfgang D. Elfe and James Hardin.
        p. cm.—(Dictionary of literary biography; v. 69)
    "A Bruccoli Clark Layman book."
    Includes index.
    ISBN 0-8103-1747-8
    1. German fiction—20th century—Bio-bibliography.
2. Novelists, German—20th century—Biography—Dic-
tionaries. 3. German fiction—20th century—History and
criticism. I. Elfe, Wolfgang. II. Hardin, James N. III. Series.
PT772.C59 1988
833'.914'09—dc19   88-11164
[B]   CIP

Contents

Contents

Plan of the Series

. . . Almost the most prodigious asset of a country, and perhaps its most precious possession, is its native literary product–when that product is fine and noble and enduring.

Mark Twain*

The advisory board, the editors, and the publisher of the *Dictionary of Literary Biography* are joined in endorsing Mark Twain's declaration. The literature of a nation provides an inexhaustible resource of permanent worth. We intend to make literature and its creators better understood and more accessible to students and the reading public, while satisfying the standards of teachers and scholars.

To meet these requirements, *literary biography* has been construed in terms of the author's achievement. The most important thing about a writer is his writing. Accordingly, the entries in *DLB* are career biographies, tracing the development of the author's canon and the evolution of his reputation.

The purpose of *DLB* is not only to provide reliable information in a convenient format but also to place the figures in the larger perspective of literary history and to offer appraisals of their accomplishments by qualified scholars.

The publication plan for *DLB* resulted from two years of preparation. The project was proposed to Bruccoli Clark by Frederick G. Ruffner, president of the Gale Research Company, in November 1975. After specimen entries were prepared and typeset, an advisory board was formed to refine the entry format and develop the series rationale. In meetings held during 1976, the publisher, series editors, and advisory board approved the scheme for a comprehensive biographical dictionary of persons who contributed to North American literature. Editorial work on the first volume began in January 1977, and it was published in 1978. In order to make *DLB* more than a reference tool and to compile volumes that individually have claim to status as literary history, it was decided to organize volumes by topic, period, or genre. Each of these freestanding volumes provides a biographical-bibliographical guide and overview for a particular area of literature. We are convinced that this organization–as opposed to a single alphabet method–constitutes a valuable innovation in the presentation of reference material. The volume plan necessarily requires many decisions for the placement and treatment of authors who might properly be included in two or three volumes. In some instances a major figure will be included in separate volumes, but with different entries emphasizing the aspect of his career appropriate to each volume. Ernest Hemingway, for example, is represented in *American Writers in Paris, 1920-1939* by an entry focusing on his expatriate apprenticeship; he is also in *American Novelists, 1910-1945* with an entry surveying his entire career. Each volume includes a cumulative index of subject authors and articles. Comprehensive indexes to the entire series are planned.

With volume ten in 1982 it was decided to enlarge the scope of *DLB*. By the end of 1986 twenty-one volumes treating British literature had been published, and volumes for Commonwealth and Modern European literature were in progress. The series has been further augmented by the *DLB Yearbooks* (since 1981) which update published entries and add new entries to keep the *DLB* current with contemporary activity. There have also been *DLB Documentary Series* volumes which provide biographical and critical source materials for figures whose work is judged to have particular interest for students. One of these companion volumes is entirely devoted to Tennessee Williams.

We define literature as the *intellectual commerce of a nation:* not merely as belles lettres but as that ample and complex process by which ideas are generated, shaped, and transmitted. *DLB* entries are not limited to "creative writers" but extend to other figures who in their time and in their way influenced the mind of a people. Thus the series encompasses historians, journalists, publishers, and screenwriters. By this means readers of *DLB* may be aided to perceive litera-

---

*From an unpublished section of Mark Twain's autobiography, copyright © by the Mark Twain Company.

ture not as cult scripture in the keeping of intellectual high priests but firmly positioned at the center of a nation's life.

DLB includes the major writers appropriate to each volume and those standing in the ranks immediately behind them. Scholarly and critical counsel has been sought in deciding which minor figures to include and how full their entries should be. Wherever possible, useful references are made to figures who do not warrant separate entries.

Each *DLB* volume has a volume editor responsible for planning the volume, selecting the figures for inclusion, and assigning the entries. Volume editors are also responsible for preparing, where appropriate, appendices surveying the major periodicals and literary and intellectual movements for their volumes, as well as lists of further readings. Work on the series as a whole is coordinated at the Bruccoli Clark Layman editorial center in Columbia, South Carolina, where the editorial staff is responsible for accuracy of the published volumes.

One feature that distinguishes *DLB* is the illustration policy–its concern with the iconography of literature. Just as an author is influenced by his surroundings, so is the reader's understanding of the author enhanced by a knowledge of his environment. Therefore *DLB* volumes include not only drawings, paintings, and photographs of authors, often depicting them at various stages in their careers, but also illustrations of their families and places where they lived. Title pages are regularly reproduced in facsimile along with dust jackets for modern authors. The dust jackets are a special feature of *DLB* because they often document better than anything else the way in which an author's work was perceived in its own time. Specimens of the writers' manuscripts are included when feasible.

Samuel Johnson rightly decreed that "The chief glory of every people arises from its authors." The purpose of the *Dictionary of Literary Biography* is to compile literary history in the surest way available to us–by accurate and comprehensive treatment of the lives and work of those who contributed to it.

The *DLB* Advisory Board

Foreword

Contemporary German Fiction Writers, First Series continues where volume 56 of the *Dictionary of Literary Biography, German Fiction Writers: 1914-1945* leaves off. It covers West German, East German, and Swiss-German authors who experienced Nazi rule and World War II as adults and who, for the most part, firmly established themselves as writers in the first decade after the war. *Contemporary German Fiction Writers*, Second Series deals with authors whose literary fame was established after the mid 1950s—that is, after the two German states had gained sovereignty and the postwar period had come to an end. Austrian writers of the World War II and postwar eras will be treated in a later volume.

The primary bibliography at the beginning of each entry lists the first editions and important revisions of the author's books, along with the first American and first British editions of English translations. Important periodical publications, translations into German, forewords, contributions to collections, and books edited by the author are also listed.

An attempt has been made to render each entry comprehensible to a reader not familiar with German political, economic, and cultural affairs. The same care has been observed in the linguistic area: German words, expressions, titles, and quotations not readily understandable to a native English speaker have been translated into English. Words of German origin that have passed into English are printed in accordance with English rather than German usage; hence, *Weltanschauung* and *Zeitgeist* are capitalized, but *bildungsroman* and *gymnasium* are not. Many of the writers have been productive in more than one literary genre; in these cases, the contributors focus their attention chiefly on the authors' prose fiction. The bibliographies at the end of each essay include secondary literature in both German and English. Where a collection of letters and other papers of an author exists, the location of the collection is given.

As the entries in this volume show, coming to terms with the experience of fascism was a major concern of most postwar German writers and led them to a strong political awareness and, in some cases, to actual involvement in political affairs. The writers were often the conscience of a society that was inclined to forget its recent past. A good example is the Gruppe 47, a loose organization of German writers including Alfred Andersch, Heinrich Böll, Paul Celan, Günter Eich, Wolfgang Hildesheimer, Walter Jens, Wolfgang Koeppen, Hans Werner Richter, and Wolfdietrich Schnurre. The entries also reflect the influence, especially on West German writers, of contemporary foreign literature. Having been cut off from the rest of the world during the Nazi era, they had a strong interest in recent literary developments in other countries, and many of them used their skills to translate contemporary American, English, and French literature into German. Furthermore, the entries shed light on the question: to what extent did the year 1945 constitute a new beginning in German literature and to what degree were pre-1945 literary traditions continued? Finally, consideration is given to the different directions taken in the development of East and West German literature.

The volume, which treats forty-three authors, should be of interest both to the layperson and the expert. Since the lives and works of these writers were profoundly influenced by the turbulent political and socioeconomic realities of twentieth-century Germany, the biographies together with the discussions of the writers' works provide an insight not only into German literature but also into several decades of German history.

—Wolfgang D. Elfe and James Hardin

Acknowledgments

This book was produced by Bruccoli Clark Layman, Inc. Karen L. Rood is senior editor for the *Dictionary of Literary Biography* series. Philip B. Dematteis was the in-house editor.

Production coordinator is Kimberly Casey. Art supervisor is Cheryl Crombie. Copyediting supervisor is Joan M. Prince. Typesetting supervisor is Kathleen M. Flanagan. Laura Ingram and Michael D. Senecal are editorial associates. The production staff includes Rowena Betts, Charles D. Brower, Patricia Coate, Mary Colborn, Mary S. Dye, Sarah A. Estes, Cynthia Hallman, Judith K. Ingle, Maria Ling, Warren McInnis, Kathy S. Merlette, Sheri Neal, Joycelyn R. Smith, and Virginia Smith. Jean W. Ross is permissions editor. Joseph Caldwell, photography editor, and Joseph Matthew Bruccoli did photographic copy work for the volume.

Walter W. Ross and Rhonda Marshall did the library research with the assistance of the staff at the Thomas Cooper Library of the University of South Carolina: Daniel Boice, Kathy Eckman, Gary Geer, Cathie Gottlieb, David L. Haggard, Jens Holley, Dennis Isbell, Jackie Kinder, Marcia Martin, Jean Rhyne, Beverley Steele, Ellen Tillett, Carole Tobin, and Virginia Weathers.

Dictionary of Literary Biography • Volume Sixty-nine

Contemporary German Fiction Writers
First Series

Dictionary of Literary Biography

Alfred Andersch
(4 February 1914-21 February 1980)

Michael Winkler
Rice University

BOOKS: *Deutsche Literatur in der Entscheidung: Ein Beitrag zur Analyse der literarischen Situation* (Karlsruhe: Volk und Zeit, 1948);

Die Kirschen der Freiheit: Ein Bericht (Frankfurt am Main: Frankfurter Verlagsanstalt, 1952);

Piazza San Gaetano: Neapolitanische Suite (Olten & Freiburg im Breisgau: Walter, 1957);

Sansibar oder Der letzte Grund: Roman (Olten & Freiburg im Breisgau: Walter, 1957; London: Harrap, 1964); translated by Michael Bullock as *Flight to Afar* (London: Gollancz, 1958; New York: Coward-McCann, 1958);

Fahrerflucht (Hamburg: Hans Bredow-Institut, 1958); enlarged as *Fahrerflucht: Hörspiele* (Munich: Deutscher Taschenbuch Verlag, 1965);

Geister und Leute: Zehn Geschichten (Olten & Freiburg im Breisgau: Walter, 1958); translated by Christa Armstrong as *The Night of the Giraffe and Other Stories* (New York: Random House, 1964; London: Murray, 1965);

Die Rote: Roman (Olten & Freiburg im Breisgau: Walter, 1960; revised edition, Zurich: Diogenes, 1972); translated by Bullock as *The Red-Head* (London: Heinemann, 1961); translation republished as *The Redhead* (New York: Pantheon, 1961);

Der Tod des James Dean: Eine Funkmontage (St. Gallen: Tschudy, 1960);

Paris ist eine ernste Stadt (Olten: Vereinigung Oltner Bücherfreunde, 1961);

Wanderungen im Norden (Olten & Freiburg im Breisgau: Walter, 1962);

Ein Liebhaber des Halbschattens: Drei Erzählungen (Olten & Freiburg im Breisgau: Walter, 1963);

Bericht, Roman, Erzählungen (Olten & Freiburg im Breisgau: Walter, 1965);

Die Blindheit des Kunstwerks und andere Aufsätze (Frankfurt: Suhrkamp, 1965);

Aus einem römischen Winter: Reisebilder (Olten & Freiburg im Breisgau: Walter, 1966);

Efraim: Roman (Zurich: Diogenes, 1967); translated by Ralph Manheim as *Efraim's Book* (London: Cape, 1970; Garden City: Doubleday, 1970);

Ein Auftrag für Lord Glouster (Baden-Baden: Signal, 1968);

Hohe Breitengrade oder Nachrichten von der Grenze (Zurich: Diogenes, 1969);

Giorgio Bassani oder Vom Sinn der Erzählens: Laudatio (Dortmund: Kulturamt der Stadt, 1969);

Tochter: Erzählung (Zurich: Diogenes, 1970);

Gesammelte Erzählungen (Zurich: Diogenes, 1971);

Mein Verschwinden in Providence: Neun neue Erzählungen (Zurich: Diogenes, 1971); translated by Manheim as *My Disappearance in Providence, and Other Stories* (Garden City: Doubleday, 1978);

Norden, Süden, rechts und links: Von Reisen und Büchern 1951-1971 (Zurich: Diogenes, 1972);

Winterspelt: Roman (Zurich: Diogenes, 1974); translated by Richard and Clara Winston (Garden City: Doubleday, 1978);

Kulturetats, Kulturzensur, by Andersch and others (Munich: Damnitz, 1976);

Öffentlicher Brief an einen sowjetischen Schriftsteller, das Überholte betreffend: Reportagen und Aufsätze (Zurich: Diogenes, 1977);

Einige Zeichnungen: Betrachtungen zu Bildern von Gisela Andersch (Zurich: Diogenes, 1977);

Alfred Andersch

empört euch der himmel ist blau: Gedichte und Nachdichtungen 1946-1977 (Zurich: Diogenes, 1977);

Das Alfred Andersch Lesebuch, edited by Gerd Haffmans (Zurich: Diogenes, 1979);

Ein neuer Scheiterhaufen für alte Ketzer: Kritiken und Rezensionen (Zurich: Diogenes, 1979);

Selected Writings (London: Heinemann, 1979);

Neue Hörspiele (Zurich: Diogenes, 1979);

Studienausgabe in 15 Bänden, 15 volumes (Zurich: Diogenes, 1979);

Der Vater eines Mörders: Eine Schulgeschichte (Zurich: Diogenes, 1980);

Texte und Zeichen: Für Alfred Andersch, compiled by Thomas Scheuffelen (Marbach: Deutsche Schillergesellschaft, 1980);

Flucht in Etrurien: Zwei Erzählungen und ein Beispiel (Zurich: Diogenes, 1981);

Sämtliche Erzählungen (Zurich: Diogenes, 1983).

OTHER: *Europäische Avantgarde,* edited by Andersch (Frankfurt am Main: Verlag der Frankfurter Hefte, 1949);

Joseph Wechsberg, *Ein Musikant spinnt sein Garn,* translated by Andersch (Karlsruhe: Stahlberg, 1949).

Alfred Andersch rose to literary prominence relatively late in life. At the time of Hitler's assumption of power he was eighteen, too young to think seriously of emigration, and too inexperienced for a career in journalism in exile. But he was an idealistic communist and was unwilling to make any compromise with Nazism. His political and artistic sensibilities developed during the decline of the Weimar Republic; they were decisively shaped by the experience of living under the Third Reich and by his disenchantment with Soviet political strategies. Though he considered his early exposure to the American way of life a liberating experience, he became disillusioned with U.S. policies during the Vietnam war. Refusing to turn anticommunist and unable to believe in the claims of capitalist democracy, Andersch came to represent the dilemma of the disaffected intellectual in an apparently well-functioning "administered world." His skill as a novelist was often questioned because of his preference for popular fictional genres over esoteric experimentation. He was not averse to seeking the widest possible readership for his books, on occasion with a "journalistic" instinct for what would sell. But he was an accomplished storyteller whose best work shows a subtle ability to capture human frailty and to portray the complicated situations in which thinking people have to make decisions.

Andersch was born in Munich in 1914 into a solid middle-class family with a diverse background. His mother, Hedwig Watzek Andersch, was of Austrian-Czech descent; the ancestors of his father, Alfred A. Andersch, were Huguenots with roots in East Prussia. Before World War I the elder Andersch was a successful independent merchant and insurance agent. During the war, in which he lost a leg, he rose to the rank of colonel. His political sympathies after the collapse of

Andersch at the ceremony at which he was awarded the Nelly Sachs Prize in Dortmund in 1968 (Ullstein–dpa)

the empire were nationalistic and reactionary; he was one of the founders of an ultraconservative patriotic organization, the Thule Gesellschaft. After the war he was usually out of work. When he died in 1930 of diabetes, his family's circumstances had been severely reduced.

Alfred was the second of three sons. His older brother, Rudolf, became a journalist; his younger brother, Otto, became a graphic designer. All three were given a traditional education in the humanistic state gymnasia; Alfred attended the prestigious Wittelsbacher Gymnasium. (Its principal was the father of Heinrich Himmler, who was to become Hitler's chief of the state police and minister of the interior.) Andersch was an alert student with generally good marks, but in 1928, after only four years, he had to leave school because of failing grades in Greek and mathematics. He was apprenticed to the conservative bookseller and publishing firm of Lehmann. In 1931, after losing his job, he joined the Communist Youth League, becoming its chief organizer for southern Bavaria in

1932. Nazi security agents arrested him during the roundup of communist functionaries at the end of February 1933. He spent over two months at the Dachau concentration camp north of Munich, was released due to the untiring efforts of his mother, was arrested again later that year, and was finally placed under Gestapo surveillance. All of his books were confiscated. He worked as an office employee in his hometown until 1937 and then in the advertising department of a Hamburg company that manufactured photographic paper.

He was drafted in 1940 to serve in the occupation forces in France but was discharged the following year and went to work in an office in Frankfurt am Main. He was reactivated in September 1943 for training in a company of engineers but was declared temporarily unfit for service on medical grounds. Early in April 1944 he was ordered to Denmark as a grenadier; in May he was sent to Italy, where he deserted on 6 June 1944. He was sent to the United States on a Liberty ship and worked at first as a paramedic in the POW camp in Ruston, Louisiana. From 15 April to 15 August 1945 he served on the editorial staff of the camp newspaper, *Der Ruf* (The Call), at Fort Kearney, Rhode Island. He was then transferred to Fort Getty, Rhode Island, where he took reeducation courses in democracy and business administration. He returned to Germany at the end of 1945 and assumed the post of editorial assistant to the novelist Erich Kästner on the staff of the *Neue Zeitung* in Munich.

In collaboration with the writer Hans Werner Richter he started his own journal, *Der Ruf,* on 15 August 1946. After sixteen issues the American military government intervened to soften its cultural and political commentary, and Andersch turned to other projects. His first book, a collection of essays titled *Deutsche Literatur in der Entscheidung* (German Literature in Crisis), appeared in 1948. He instituted the "Evening Studio" of Radio Frankfurt, a program of analysis and discussion he directed from 1948 to 1950. In the latter year he married Gisela Dichgans, a painter; they had three children. From 1951 to 1953 Andersch was supervising editor of feature broadcasts that were coproduced by radio stations in Frankfurt and Hamburg and edited a book series, "studio frankfurt," that published progressive new literature; thereafter he edited a literary journal, *Texte und Zeichen* (Texts and Signs), which ceased publication after sixteen issues.

Flight into freedom and withdrawal into the world of artistic creation are dominant themes in all of Andersch's works, and his personal experiences, re-created with intellectual honesty, are the source of inspiration for his fiction. His second book, *Die Kirschen der Freiheit* (The Cherries of Freedom, 1952), is his most directly autobiographical publication. It is an account of his life beginning with the moment when, as a five-year-old, he sees a group of revolutionaries from the Bavarian Republic of Revolutionary Councils led away to their execution. It is an unemotional report without embellishments, written in a dry, sparse style of lucid recollection, emphasizing the impotent lack of resolve that doomed the German organized labor movement and describing his own disorientation before he escaped from politics into a life of introversion and aesthetic imagination. As an expression of freedom from apathy and powerlessness, Andersch decides to commit an act of private sabotage against the regime: he asserts his independence by deserting from the army. Just before he crosses the no-man's-land that stands between him and the American lines, he sees a cherry tree and tastes the fresh and tart juice "von den wilden Wüstenkirschen meiner Freiheit" (of the wild desert cherries of my freedom).

From 1955 to 1958 Andersch was editor in chief of a Stuttgart broadcast venture called "radio-essay"; his assistants were the poet-critics Hans Magnus Enzensberger and Helmut Heissenbüttel. The themes of resistance, moral courage, intellectual self-examination, and struggle for freedom are given exemplary expression in his first work of fiction, *Sansibar oder Der letzte Grund* (Zanzibar or The Last Reason, 1957; translated as *Flight to Afar*, 1958). In autumn 1937, in the small Baltic seaport of Rerik, Judith Levin, a young Jewish woman whose mother has committed suicide in order not to stand in the way of her daughter's rescue, is waiting for a ship to take her to Sweden. She is joined by Gregor, a young communist instructor who has lost all trust in his party but has agreed to execute its orders one more time. They seek the help of Knudsen, a fisherman who must take care of his mentally ill wife, and of Knudsen's young helper–identified only as "der Junge" (the boy)–who is plotting to run away from his nagging mother and from the boredom of life in a backwater community. Like his hero Huckleberry Finn, the boy dreams of freedom and adventure in the wide world beyond the sea. The fifth principal charac-

ter is a minister who is slowly bleeding to death from a reopened war wound in his leg. He has received orders to remove from his church an expressionist sculpture depicting a young monk that has been officially classified as "degenerate." The safe transport abroad of this work of religious art has become a duty of oppositional solidarity. The statue is recognized as a symbolic icon, representing intellectual freedom. Judith says: "Weil er alles liest, was er will, sollte er eingesperrt werden. Und deswegen muß er jetzt dorthin, wo er lesen kann, was er will" (Because he reads everything he wants to read, he was ordered to be put away. And for that reason he must get to where he can read what he wants). Saving the sculpture unites all the characters in a common purpose. They succeed in moving it to Sweden. Those characters who do not flee perform courageous acts of self-negation: the fisherman returns to Germany to save his wife from the government's euthanasia program; the boy comes back so as not to incriminate his master; instead of going to a hospital, the minister returns and kills the Gestapo officer who has come to arrest him.

The novel is skillfully written as a sequence of thirty-seven short episodes. It blends precise descriptions of persons and atmosphere with interior monologue, combines a gripping plot with penetrating character analysis, and poses a serious ethical dilemma in which a small group of people search for an appropriate response to a profound challenge. These qualities as well as the book's reassuring conclusion made *Sansibar* a success with critics and readers; Andersch received the German Critics' Prize for it in 1958. That year he moved to the village of Berzona in the canton of Ticino in southern Switzerland, and thenceforth devoted himself entirely to writing.

His next novel, *Die Rote* (1960; translated as *The Red-Head*, 1961), tarnished his reputation considerably. Although the work was serialized in the prestigious conservative daily *Frankfurter Allgemeine Zeitung* in 1960 and was made into a movie by the renowned director Helmut Käutner in 1962, it did not fare well with reviewers. They objected to its use of popular literary devices, such as a secret-agent plot to supplement the principal story line, incidents drawn from the repertory of pulp fiction, and stereotyped, one-dimensional characters, and they found its use of language laborious and careless. This criticism is not without justification, but it misses an essential

Cover for Andersch's 1977 collection of essays

point: Andersch had not simply written a pot-boiler around the dual themes of life in a mind-less consumer society and obsession with the Nazi past but had tried to use the conventions of a best-selling genre for educational purposes. He wanted to confront readers with contemporary is-sues, and he knew he needed to retain their atten-tion by making concessions to popular taste. Andersch may have compromised his aesthetic standards, but his attempt to speak to a wider audi-ence than is normally attracted to serious novels signaled neither a loss of artistic integrity nor de-clining ability as an imaginative writer. The com-mercial success of the book, moreover, may have vindicated his purposes: by the late 1980s it had been translated into thirteen languages and sold close to half a million copies in German.

The novel's titular heroine, the red-haired woman, is Franziska Lukas, a thirty-year-old inter-preter who is proficient in five languages and mar-ried to a wealthy sales representative. She ends her frustrating marriage and her love affair with her husband's boss by suddenly leaving both men, although she suspects she is pregnant. With almost no money she runs off to Venice, where she rents a room in a cheap hotel and meets the ho-mosexual Irish officer Patrick O'Malley, who had betrayed his contact under torture when he was captured on a secret mission inside Germany in 1944, and the Nazi bureaucrat Kramer, a brutal fa-natic dedicated to the ideology of racial purity. When O'Malley recognizes Kramer as his former tormentor, he plots revenge. He offers Franziska and Kramer a cruise through the Mediterranean on his motor yacht; she is to become his witness when he offers his unsuspecting victim a poi-soned glass of beer. Horrified, Franziska leaves the yacht before the execution takes place. She meets Fabio Crepaz, an impoverished violinist who had fought against Franco in Spain, been an antifascist partisan in Italy, and is now a disillu-sioned communist with a yearning for the simple life. He offers her refuge in his mother's small house. Franziska takes a lowly job in a factory and decides against ending her pregnancy, al-though she will never return to her husband.

In a revised version of 1972 Andersch changed the end of the novel, opening it to wider and more realistic possibilities. But the revi-sion did not affect its nearly unanimous critical condemnation. Perhaps as a consequence of this rejection, he did not engage again in this type of writing, which challenged a deep-seated critical prejudice against the popularity of the minor genres.

Efraim (1967; translated as *Efraim's Book*, 1970) is a novel within a novel. George Efraim, a German Jew educated in England, is a former journalist. His wife, Meg, a photographer, had told him early in their marriage that she had no in-tention of giving up her affair with his employer, the magazine publisher Keir Horne. Now living in Rome, separated from his wife and having quit his job, Efraim writes a novel. It tells the story of his return to Berlin, where he was sent to discover the fate of Horne's illegitimate daugh-ter Esther, whose mother had been a member of Berlin's elegant society. Efraim obtains little pre-cise information but has reason to believe that Esther was saved by nuns and may have entered a convent. Horne, who could have gotten her out of Germany by adopting her, appears to have known about her rescue all along and perhaps sent the self-righteous Efraim on his mission merely to teach him a lesson in tolerance of other people's weaknesses: Efraim learns what difficult choices were involved in what had appeared to him to be a cowardly act of betrayal. In Berlin Efraim meets Anna Krystek, a former actress from the Soviet sector and still a Marxist with strong convictions. He falls in love with her and wants to take her to Rome, but they separate en route. Efraim goes to London, where Meg informs him that she has left Horne for a film producer. Unable to accept her infidelity any longer, Efraim goes to Rome, where he will give up his lucrative career as a journalist in order to write his novel.

In *Efraim* Andersch re-creates the immediate past of the postwar years and the slowly receding past of the Third Reich in a series of flashbacks and recollections in the form of interior monologues; simultaneously, he reflects on the difficulties of regaining truthful images of the past as his hero seeks to reconstruct the events of his life in the context of recent history. In 1968 Andersch won the Charles Veillon Prize and the Nelly Sachs Prize for *Efraim*.

Andersch projected onto his fictional alter ego, Efraim, his own search for answers about the German past and also his problems with the novel form. He was not at his best when he tried to write in the German tradition of philosophical or lyrical self-analysis, and he does not sound quite convincing in passages of self-absorption and of intellectual dialogue. The styles from which Andersch had learned the most and which he had adapted to his own purposes were those of the American "lost generation," especially Ernest Hemingway, and of Italian verism as practiced by Elio Vittorini, Cesare Pavese, and *film noir* directors such as Vittorio de Sica. He had also read Edgar Allan Poe, Joseph Conrad, and William Faulkner to learn how the crime thriller and the adventure story can be made into high literature; and he had found Franz Kafka and Ernst Jünger to be models for his own expressive intentions. In addition, the skeptical existentialism and defiant attitude of political commitment that characterizes the best of French *résistance* literature had left an indelible mark on his understanding of the role the writer should play in society; Jean-Paul Sartre and Arthur Koestler, whom Andersch admired as writers with an active sense of political responsibility, became his intellectual

mentors. But he resisted the temptation of making imaginative literature a vehicle for the propagation of ideological positions and political programs. Without compromising his basic principles, which included intellectual integrity, democratic tolerance, opposition to dogmatism, and resistance to the abuses of power, Andersch always allowed his characters freedom of choice and an awareness of alternatives.

Andersch tried his hand at many different forms, including radio plays, poems, translations of poetry, travel reports, essays on books and writers, and political commentary. His style ranged from a suggestive impressionism through the analytical precision of informed criticism to open polemic. He continued the kind of literary involvement in issues of the day that had produced such effective radio plays as *Fahrerflucht* (Leaving the Scene of an Accident, 1958) and "In der Nacht der Giraffe" (published in the collection *Geister und Leute* [Ghosts and People], 1958; translated as *The Night of the Giraffe and Other Stories,* 1964), which is about General de Gaulle's role in the Algerian war of liberation. He traveled extensively: in the Scandinavian countries from 1958 to 1961, in 1965 on an expedition to the Arctic Circle with a German television crew, to Rome for ten months in 1962 and 1963, and to Berlin for three months in 1964. But the decade after 1960 was a time of hesitation and uncertainty which did not produce a major work other than *Efraim*. The apparent reason for this crisis was Andersch's increasing disenchantment with American politics and with Europe's inability to find alternatives to Soviet-American confrontation. The saddest event in this resumption of the Cold War for Andersch was the murder of Chilean president Salvador Allende in 1973.

Work on his last novel, *Winterspelt* (1974; translated, 1978), occupied Andersch for three years. It is a complex demonstration of an abstract moral possibility that is an impossibility in real-life circumstances, an exploration of "absolute unrealizable truths." Its basic principle is indicated in the sentence: "Geschichte berichtet, wie es gewesen, Erzählung spielt eine Möglichkeit durch" (History reports how it was, narrative fiction plays with a possibility).

The novel is set around the idyllic village of Winterspelt in the Snow Eifel, the mountainous region southwest of Cologne bordering on Belgium, in early October 1944–a period of military inactivity during which preparations were being made for the last desperate German attack on

Andersch in Paris in 1979

the western front known as the Battle of the Bulge. Five people are involved in a plan to surrender a German infantry battalion to the Americans. Two of them are military men: Major Dincklage, the thirty-four-year-old commander with a bad conscience and the awareness that the defection of his unit will not prevent the continuation of the war; and Captain Kimbrough, whose suspicion of higher authority makes him sympathetic to any sort of defiance, even anarchy. Dincklage seeks the cooperation of three civilians: the art historian Schefold, a Marxist existentialist who agrees to serve as a go-between; the resistance fighter Wensel Hainstock, a communist and concentration camp survivor who alternates his hiding place between a hut in a quarry and a cave where he nurses a barn owl back to health; and the twenty-four-year-old student teacher Käthe Lenk, "eine Intellektuelle, dennoch versessen darauf, abstrakte Ideen in Leben, Theorie in Praxis zu verwandeln, wenn sich ihr

dazu auch nur die leiseste Möglichkeit bot" (an intellectual, but passionately devoted to changing abstract ideas into living reality, to transforming theory into practical acts whenever the slightest possibility offered itself). Hainstock, as a Marxist, does not believe "an den Wert solcher individueller Aktionen" (in the value of such individual actions), and Dincklage knows that his unit will soon be withdrawn from battle anyway. In the end Käthe alone crosses over to the other side. Schefold loses his life as he tries to deliver a message with conditions for the surrender. The plan of subverting military discipline has failed completely, but Schefold does save a work of art, a 1930 painting by Paul Klee titled "polyphon umgrenztes Weiß" (Polyphonously Bounded White), which has become a symbol of passive resistance to authority.

Andersch implicitly suggests numerous parallels between the time *about* and the time *during* which he is writing. Yet the temper and sensibilities of his characters distinctly reflect the mood of the late 1960s. His own attitude of resignation reveals a profound skepticism about both bourgeois humanism and communism. Andersch did not publicly participate in or comment on the student movement of 1968, and he remained reticent throughout the tumultuous years of opposition to Bonn and Washington. His poem "artikel 3 (3)," however, taking its title from the definition of civil liberties in the Basic Law of the Federal Republic of Germany, caused a nationwide controversy when it was published in the newspaper *Frankfurter Rundschau* on 3 January 1976; it was reprinted in the collection *empört euch der himmel ist blau* (rise up in revolt the sky is blue, 1977). The poem is a furious attack on what he saw as the reality of political life during the debates on terrorism and national security that resulted in legislation restricting the political affiliations of civil servants. Andersch's response, no doubt deeply affected by his experiences under the Nazi dictatorship, was an outcry of extreme anguish.

Andersch continued to travel, visiting Mexico in 1972; Spain, Portugal, and Russia in 1975; and France in 1979. He also continued to write, completing his last long story, *Der Vater eines Mörders: Eine Schulgeschichte* (The Father of a Murderer: A School Story, 1980) about the principal who had expelled him from school. By then he was suffering from a circulatory ailment that had required a kidney transplant in 1977. He died at his home during the night of 21 February 1980.

Letters:

Ein Briefwechsel: Alfred Andersch, Konstantin Simonow, Simonov's letters translated by Friederich Hitzer (Berlin: Volk und Welt, 1978);

Arno Schmidt: Der Briefwechsel mit Alfred Andersch (Zurich: Arno Schmidt Stiftung im Haffmans Verlag, 1985);

Einmal wirklich Leben: Ein Tagebuch in Briefen an Hedwig Andersch, 1943 bis 1975, edited by Winfried Stephan (Zurich: Diogenes, 1986).

Biographies:

Erhard Schütz, *Alfred Andersch* (Munich: Beck, 1980);

Volker Wehdeking, *Alfred Andersch* (Stuttgart: Metzler, 1983).

References:

Heinz Ludwig Arnold, ed., *Alfred Andersch* (Munich: text + kritik, 1979);

Alfons Bühlmann, *In der Faszination der Freiheit: Eine Untersuchung zur Struktur der Grundthematik im Werk von Alfred Andersch* (Berlin: Schmidt, 1973);

Hans Geulen, "Alfred Andersch: Probleme der dargestellten Erfahrung des 'deutschen Irrtums,' " in *Gegenwartsliteratur und Drittes Reich,* edited by Hans Wagener (Stuttgart: Reclam, 1977), pp. 205-221;

Gerd Haffmans, Rémy Charbon, and Franz Cavigelli, eds., *Über Alfred Andersch* (Zurich: Diogenes, 1974; revised and expanded, 1980);

Karl Migner, "Alfred Andersch," in *Deutsche Literatur der Gegenwart in Einzeldarstellungen,* volume 1, edited by Dietrich Weber (Stuttgart: Kröner, 1976), pp. 243-259;

Volker Wehdeking, ed., *Zu Alfred Andersch* (Stuttgart: Klett, 1983);

Livia Z. Wittmann, *Alfred Andersch* (Stuttgart: Kohlhammer, 1971).

Papers:

Alfred Andersch's papers are at the Deutsches Literaturarchiv in Marbach am Neckar, Federal Republic of Germany.

Stefan Andres
(26 June 1906-29 June 1970)

Franz-Joseph Wehage
Appalachian State University

BOOKS: *Bruder Luzifer: Roman* (Jena: Diederichs, 1933);

Eberhard im Kontrapunkt: Roman (Cologne: Staufenverlag, 1933);

Die unsichtbare Mauer: Roman (Berlin: Gutenberg, 1934);

El Greco malt den Großinquisitor: Erzählung (Leipzig: List, 1936); edited by Richard C. Clark and Ilse Reiling (Englewood Cliffs, N.J.: Prentice-Hall, 1968);

Vom heiligen Pfäfflein Domenico (Leipzig: List, 1936);

Utz, der Nachfahr (Saar: Hausen, 1936);

Moselländische Novellen (Munich: List, 1937); republished as *Gäste im Paradies: Moselländische Novellen* (Munich: List, 1937);

Der Mann von Asteri: Ein Roman (Berlin: Riemerschmidt, 1939);

Das Grab des Neides: Novellen (Berlin: Riemerschmidt, 1940);

Der olympische Frieden: Erzählung (Leipzig: Reclam, 1940);

Der gefrorene Dionysos: Erzählung (Berlin: Riemerschmidt, 1942); republished as *Die Liebesschaukel: Roman* (Munich: Piper, 1951);

Wir sind Utopia: Novelle (Berlin: Riemerschmidt, 1943); edited by John Michalski (Boston: Heath, 1963); translated by Elita Walker Caspari as *We Are God's Utopia* (Los Angeles: Gateway Editions, 1950); translated by Cyrus Brooks as *We Are Utopia: A Novel* (London: Gollancz, 1955);

Wirtshaus zur weiten Welt: Erzählungen (Jena: Diederichs, 1943);

Italiener (Berlin: Luken & Luken, 1943);

Das goldene Gitter (Berlin: Lüttke, 1943);

Die Hochzeit der Feinde: Roman (Zurich: Scientia, 1947);

Requiem für ein Kind (Hamburg: Ellermann, 1948);

Ritter der Gerechtigkeit: Roman (Zurich: Scientia, 1948);

Tanz durchs Labyrinth: Dramatische Dichtung (Munich: Piper, 1948);

Stefan Andres (Ullstein–Fotoagentur Sven Simon)

Umgang mit Italienern (Berlin: Luken & Luken, 1949);

Die Sintflut: Roman, 3 volumes (Munich: Piper, 1949, 1951, 1959);

Der Granatapfel: Oden–Gedichte–Sonette (Munich: Piper, 1950);

Die Häuser auf der Wolke (Opladen: Middelhauve, 1950);

Main nahezu rhein-ahrisches saar-pfalz-mosel-lahnisches Weinpilgerbuch (Neuwied: Strüder, 1951);

Das Antlitz: Erzählung (Munich: Piper, 1951);

Der Reporter Gottes: Eine Hörfolge in zehn Kapiteln (Frankfurt am Main: Knecht, 1952);

11

Die Rache der Schmetterlinge: Eine Legende (Freiburg im Breisgau: Klemm, 1953);

Der Knabe im Brunnen: Roman (Munich: Piper, 1953);

Die Reise nach Portiuncula: Roman (Munich: Piper, 1954);

Positano: Geschichten aus einer Stadt am Meer (Munich: Piper, 1957);

Toleranz: Die Brücke zwischen Wahrheit und Freiheit (Oldenburg: Scharf, 1958);

Sperrzonen: Eine deutsche Tragödie (Hamburg: Hans Bredow-Institut, 1959);

Die unglaubwürdige Reise des Knaben Titus: Zwei Novellen, edited by Fritz Fröhling (Freiburg im Breisgau: Hyperion, 1960);

Die großen Weine Deutschlands (Frankfurt am Main, Berlin & Vienna: Ullstein, 1960);

Die Verteidigung der Xanthippe: Zwölf Geschichten (Munich: Piper, 1960);

Eine Einführung in sein Werk (Munich: Piper, 1962);

Novellen und Erzählungen (Munich: Piper, 1962);

Der Mann im Fisch: Roman (Munich: Piper, 1963);

Die biblische Geschichte (Munich & Zurich: Droemersche Verlags-Anstalt Knaur, 1965); translated by Michael Bullock as *The Bible Story, Retold by Stefan Andres* (New York: McGraw-Hill, 1966; London: Deutsch, 1966);

Der Taubenturm: Roman (Munich: Piper, 1966);

Gedichte (Munich: Piper, 1966);

Der 20. Juli, Tat und Testament: Eine Rede (Frankfurt am Main: Klostermann, 1966);

Ägyptisches Tagebuch (Munich: Piper, 1967);

Die Mosel, text by Andres, photographs by Hermann Weisweiler (Cologne: Greven, 1968);

Noah und seine Kinder (Munich: Piper, 1968);

Die Dumme: Roman (Munich: Piper, 1969);

Die Versuchung des Synesios: Roman (Munich: Piper, 1971);

Die große Lüge: Drei Erzählungen (Munich: Piper, 1973);

Das Fest der Fischer (Munich: Piper, 1973);

Der Dichter in der Zeit: Reden und Aufsätze (Munich: Piper, 1974);

Gedichte (Munich & Zurich: Piper, 1976);

Die schönsten Novellen und Erzählungen (Munich: Piper, 1982).

OTHER: Günter Giefer, ed., *Wenn der Tag beginnt: Morgengedanken für jedermann*, contributions by Andres (Witten: Eckart, 1956);

Das Buch der Kogge, contributions by Andres (Emsdetten: Lechte, 1958);

Nie wieder Hiroshima, edited by Andres (Lahr: Kaufmann, 1960);

Kurt Hoffman, ed., *Die Wirklichkeit des Mythos: Zehn Vorträge*, contributions by Andres (Munich: Knaur, 1965);

Matthaeus Merian, *Die schönsten Städte der Pfalz, des Rheinlands und Westfalens*, introduction by Andres (Hamburg: Hoffmann & Campe, 1967);

Hannelore Frank, ed., *Fünfzehnmal Sonntag*, contributions by Andres (Stuttgart & Berlin: Kreuz, 1970).

PERIODICAL PUBLICATIONS: "Über die Sendung des Dichters," *Literarische Revue*, 3 (1948): 129-139;

"Eine halblaute Frage," *Merkur*, 3 (1949): 100-103;

"Aquaedukte der Erinnerung," *Welt und Wort*, 5 (1950): 505-506;

"Auf der Via Appia: Gespräch mit einem Kinde," *Deutsche Rundschau*, 76, no. 11 (1950): 976;

"Das drohende Schmutz- und Schundgesetz: Die düsteren Perspektiven," *Das literarische Deutschland*, no. 3 (1950): 2;

"An einen Staatssklavenbildner: Der Fall Johannes R. Becher," *Der Monat*, no. 29 (1951): 487-490;

"Der Dichter und das Jugendbuch," *Das literarische Deutschland*, no. 13 (1951): 7;

"Jugendtage in Schweich," *Merian*, 4, no. 11 (1952): 74-78;

"Der Dichter in dieser Zeit," *Börsenblatt des deutschen Buchhandels*, no. 37 (1952): 177-179;

"Ein Schriftsteller spricht sich aus: Was ich vom Leser fordere," *Standpunkt*, no. 36 (1953): 7;

"Gedanken zum homo publicus," *Die Schau*, no. 8 (1953): 4-5;

"Die Komiks: Eine neue Art des Lesens," *Die Schwarzburg*, no. 6 (1954): 104-106;

"Von der Würde des Schriftstellers," *Deutsche Rundschau*, 79, no. 7 (1954): 698-701;

"Henry D. Thoreau, der Eremit von Walden Pond," *Perspektiven*, no. 10 (1955): 52-71;

"Die Musen von übermorgen," *Frankfurter Hefte*, 16 (1961): 763-773;

"Mythos und Dichtung: Ein Versuch," *Deutsche Rundschau*, 89, no. 12 (1963): 44-53;

"Der Romancier in dieser Zeit," *Deutsche Rundschau*, 89, no. 3 (1963): 30-40.

Stefan Andres owes his reputation as a major twentieth-century German Catholic writer primarily to the great success of his novella *Wir sind Utopia* (We Are Utopia, 1943; translated as *We Are God's Utopia*, 1950). His *Moselländische Novellen* (Novellas about the Moselle River, 1937), which incorporate local settings and childhood experiences, and the nonfiction writings *Die großen Weine Deutschlands* (The Great Wines of Germany, 1960) and *Die Mosel* (The Moselle, 1968) also brought him popular acclaim. Andres's works have been translated into Dutch, Swedish, English, and Polish, and in Germany he was among the most widely read authors during the 1950s and 1960s. As a result of his experience of Nazism, Andres rejects any form of totalitarianism and upholds the freedom of the individual in his speeches, essays, and many of his works of fiction.

Andres's evolution as an author passed through three stages. The early work centers on autobiographical concerns and the clash between tradition and technology. The second stage includes novels and novellas about guilt and atonement, works in which Andres's theoretical statements are applied to history, and novellas and dramas dealing with the Third Reich and the Resistance. The third stage comprises works dealing with events of the late 1950s and the 1960s.

Stefan Paul Andres was born on 26 June 1906 in Breitwies, near Trier. His father owned a mill which had been in the family for several generations. Andres's childhood experiences at the mill became the central theme of *Der Knabe im Brunnen* (The Boy in the Well, 1953), which combines his fantasies with the story of his eight older siblings.

The family moved to nearby Schweich in 1910 after a new dam deprived them of the use of the mill. World War I interrupted the idyll of Andres's childhood. His father's opposition to the war was in stark contrast to his teachers' enthusiasm for it. Andres swayed between these two points of view until he heard Pope Benedict's appeal for peace in 1915; afterward he identified with the pope's call for love and understanding of one's fellowman. After his father's death in 1916 Andres was educated at several Catholic monasteries, and in 1926 he entered a Franciscan monastery with the intention of becoming a monk. During the next two years he realized that he was not ready to accept the isolation of the monastic existence. He left the monastery in 1928

and enrolled at the University of Cologne to study literature and philology. At the same time he was working on his first novel, *Bruder Luzifer* (Brother Lucifer), which was published in 1933. The novel is autobiographical, dealing with a painter's attempt to find a place as a novice in a monastery and his ultimate realization that he is not ready to abandon the world. A similar theme is treated in *Eberhard im Kontrapunkt* (Eberhard in Counterpoint, 1933), in which a young musician searches for his identity as a human being and as an artist.

In 1930, after his fourth semester at the University of Cologne, Andres transferred to the University of Jena, where he met the medical student Dorothee Freudiger. Together they moved to the University of Berlin, where they saw firsthand the growing strength of National Socialists in the increasing numbers of "brown shirts" in the lecture halls. Andres and Freudiger were married in 1932. Because his mother-in-law was Jewish, Andres found himself repeatedly confronted with anti-Semitism and publication restrictions. In 1933, before the publication of *Bruder Luzifer*, Andres received a grant from the Abraham Lincoln Foundation which made possible a prolonged stay in Italy. The tranquillity of the idyllic island town of Anacapri contrasted starkly with the atmosphere in Germany, where, upon his return in 1933, Andres encountered a charged political climate and widespread anti-Semitism, even among his former friends.

In 1934 Andres published his third novel, *Die unsichtbare Mauer* (The Invisible Wall), which draws on his childhood memories of the Moselle area. Mill owners and farmers are forced to give up their land for the construction of a dam. The novel depicts the confrontation between the rural traditions of the farmers and modern technology in a manner reminiscent of Gerhart Hauptmann's naturalistic drama *Vor Sonnenaufgang* (1889; translated as *Before Dawn*, 1909). The impact of industry and technology on a rural area results in tragedy for several people who cannot adjust to the change. The engineers are cynical, callous, and egotistical and lack any awareness of their destruction of the environment. The protagonist, Wendelin, who initiated the construction of the dam, finds himself caught between two extremes which he cannot reconcile and must forfeit his life. Andres clearly shows his sympathies for the people of the Moselle region, yet he also portrays ignorance and other human weaknesses among them.

Drawing by Andres of Positano, the Italian village to which he and his family escaped from the Nazis in 1937 (Gero von Wilpert, Deutsche Literatur in Bildern *[Stuttgart: Kröner, 1965])*

A first reaction to the Third Reich is found in Andres's novella *El Greco malt den Großinquisitor* (El Greco Paints the Grand Inquisitor, 1936), which was completed in Lomnitz in the summer of 1935. The novella is one of Andres's best-known works and by 1944 had been published in thirty-six editions. El Greco is torn between betraying his artistic principles by merely painting the outer appearance of the inquisitor, or remaining true to those principles by depicting the man's inner qualities. Although he is fully aware of his possible persecution by the Inquisition, El Greco finally cannot withdraw from the responsibility of his profession; like Andres, he tries to preserve his independence and artistic integrity in the face of terror and dictatorship. El Greco's decision reflects Andres's view of art as an expression of resistance.

In 1937 a school friend of Andres's wife who had connections with a high-ranking Nazi official made it possible for Andres and his family to escape to Positano, Italy. There, however, Andres found himself surrounded by Italian fascists, and the close proximity to Germany caused him to fear that he might be arrested. In the summer of 1938 he left for Paris, but increasing hostility toward the flood of German immigrants in France convinced him to return to Italy later that summer.

Until 1943 the *Frankfurter Zeitung* found ways to publish Andres's books in Germany and to transfer his royalties to Italy. In the winter of 1942-1943 the Berlin publisher Ulrich Riemerschmidt printed *Wir sind Utopia* and distributed it illegally. It was reprinted in the *Frankfurter Zeitung* in 1943. During the Spanish civil war Paco, a former monk, is brought as a prisoner to the monastery he had entered twenty years before, when his dissatisfaction with the world and his yearning for perfection had driven him to search for a secluded utopian ideal. His expectations had not been fulfilled by the monastic life and he had returned to the world to continue his vain search for his ideal. The lieutenant, who had later had all the monks killed, is plagued by his conscience and, recognizing the priest in Paco, wishes to confess to him. At this moment the lieutenant receives orders to kill all the prisoners because the enemy is rapidly approaching. Paco must decide whether to kill the lieutenant and free the 200 prisoners or die along with them. He remembers the words of his mentor, Father Damiano: "Gott geht nicht nach Utopia! . . . Gott liebt dic Welt, weil sie unvollkammen ist.– Wir sind Gottes Utopia, aber eines im Werden!" (God does not go to Utopia! . . . God loves the world because it is imperfect.–We have to create Utopia on earth!). Paco accepts his priesthood, hears the lieutenant's confession and blesses him, and confers absolution on his fellow prisoners and dies with them. The novella proclaims the redeeming values of Christianity in a world of shattered illusions. The desire for personal perfection is not fulfilled in utopian dreams but in the acceptance of the fragile human condition.

Andres wrote his first novel dealing with contemporary events in 1938, but it was not published until 1947. *Die Hochzeit der Feinde* (The Wedding of the Enemies) depicts, in the story of a German-French wedding which almost fails to take place, the mutual hatred of France and Germany and culminates in an appeal to overcome nationalistic resentments.

Ritter der Gerechtigkeit (Knights of Justice, 1948), set in Italy at the time of the fall of fas-

Andres in the 1950s (Ullstein–Fritz Eschen)

cism in 1943, examines the restoration of order in a collapsing society. The novel draws an initially pessimistic picture of a world in which opportunists swear allegiance while practicing treason, and where principles are betrayed for success and money. Three characters attempt to choose the right path out of this world of corruption and evil. The medical student Fabio Casani, having witnessed the end of fascism in Naples, is searching for new ideals. The Prince di A. realizes that his theoretical Christian idealism and humanism bear no relationship to reality. He finally dies at a hospital for the poverty-stricken, atoning for his guilt. Dino, the prince's nephew, chooses the opposite path: falsely accused of stealing a porcelain horse from his uncle's collection, he becomes a rebel and forfeits his life.

Andres's novels *Der Mann von Asteri* (The Man from Asteri, 1939), *Der gefrorene Dionysos* (The Frozen Dionysos, 1942), and *Die Reise nach Portiuncula* (The Trip to Portiuncula, 1954) share the theme of a guilty person who, at first, does not want to face up to his guilt but finally tries to atone for his sins and to reconcile himself with God and the world.

Andres started writing a trilogy, *Die Sintflut* (The Deluge), in 1940. The first volume, *Das Tier aus der Tiefe* (The Beast from the Deep), appeared in 1949; the second, *Die Arche* (The Ark), followed in 1951, the year after Andres returned to Germany and settled in Unkel, near Bonn; the third, *Der graue Regenbogen* (The Grey Rainbow), was published in 1959. The trilogy received a negative response; the critics were not ready for a satirical approach to the Nazi era. The first volume depicts the gradual development of the "Norm Movement" in Germany and its rise to power under the leadership of Alois Moosthaler, a former professor of Catholic theology. In the second volume Moosthaler is the leader of a dictatorship; he finds an opponent in Lorenz Gutmann, a theology student. In the third volume Moosthaler is assassinated by the Resistance fighter and architect Gabriel Clemens. After Germany has been defeated in war and the era of restoration has been inaugurated, Lorenz and his friends settle in the countryside to lead a simple and self-sufficient life. The story line is interrupted at various points by fifteen legends about Noah recounted by Gabriel Clemens's brother, the former officer Emil Clemens; the biblical legends are analogies to contemporary events.

The trilogy depicts a time in which God has become obsolete and the state has attained absolute power. Although the political system portrayed is based on National Socialism, the trilogy is intended as a critique of any state that assumes a God-like status; the parallels to the Third Reich correspond to historical fact only to a limited degree. At the beginning of *Das Tier aus der Tiefe* Andres says that the work is not a historical novel but an attempt to describe clearly, by means of analogy, what had been obscured by blind partisanship and passionate enthusiasm. The trilogy, he says, refers not so much to the past as to future epochs in which political ideologies will attempt to suppress individualism.

The trilogy does include specific political criticisms. Andres considers the Versailles Treaty, which led to the rise of the Norm movement, a failure. He attacks the army for its blind obedience to the state, German industry for its support of fascism, and the parliamentary democracy of the Weimar Republic for the selfishness of its political parties. Andres also criticizes the Catholic church, which he perceives as an ally of dictatorship.

In 1961 Andres moved to Rome. In a 1966 speech dealing with the attempted assassination

Stefan Andres

Self-portrait of Andres, 1965 (Gero von Wilpert, Deutsche Literatur in Bildern *[Stuttgart: Kröner, 1965])*

of Hitler on 20 July 1944 he agreed with Ernst Jünger that the elimination of a dictator through assassination only produces a new dictator. Nevertheless, Andres voiced his support for the assassination attempt because the actions of the plotters derived from a sense of moral duty based on religious principles and a deep feeling of responsibility for their country.

In the novel *Die Dumme* (The Ignorant Girl, 1969) a naive and honest girl, Lina, becomes the object of exploitation by a West German textile merchant and an East German Marxist. Lina swings like a pendulum between the points of view represented by the two men until she discovers her own direction in life. The new society in the West has, in Andres's view, abandoned Christian values and accepted the ethos of capitalism, while the totalitarian regime in the East is the reincarnation of the Third Reich.

In his last novel, *Die Versuchung des Synesios* (The Temptation of Synesios, 1971), completed nine days before his death in Rome on 29 June 1970, Andres reiterated his criticism of the Catholic church's collaboration with Nazism by demon-

strating how the church should have reacted to the Third Reich. The Neoplatonist Synesios (around 368 to 413), a rich nobleman of the Cyrenaican province (today's Libya), is chosen as bishop despite his belief in Greek philosophy and the fact that he is married. Synesios defends the authority of the church against Andronikos, the tyrannical representative of the imperial government. Andronikos's increasing acts of violence and finally his disregard for the church's right to grant asylum force Synesios to excommunicate him. Synesios and his family are killed, presumably by Andronikos's soldiers.

A novel whose hero is an admirer of Hellenistic culture and classical philosophy can hardly be interpreted as a Christian legend. Synesios appears as an early Christian Becket who, once appointed bishop, defends the authority of the church. Andres is examining the question of a possible compromise between the church and a tyrannical government. Synesios rejects such an arrangement, knowing full well that he will be defeated if it comes to a power struggle. The irony of the novel becomes evident in the fact that Synesios is not a Christian by conviction; rather, he acts according to his conception of his duty and thus puts the church of the twentieth century to shame.

Andres's success as a writer is due in part to his traditional narrative style, which contrasted with the experimental movements in literature after 1945. On the other hand, Andres's oeuvre is imbued with a philosophy that was much needed in the 1950s and 1960s. Andres considered it his obligation to demonstate the possibilities of individual freedom and to revive aesthetic values which had gone through a process of disintegration. His appeal for beauty and spiritual freedom contributed to his popularity.

Letters:

Ein Briefwechsel um Trier geführt zwischen Stefan Andres und W.B. (Trier: Trevirensia, 1946);
Lieber Freund, lieber Denunziant: Briefe (Munich: Piper, 1977).

References:

Claude Andre, "Dichtung im Dritten Reich: Stefan Andres *Die Arche*," Ph.D. dissertation, Bonn University, 1980;
Aloyse Belche, "Mensch und Totalitarismus in der Romantrilogie *Die Sintflut* von Stefan Andres," Ph.D. dissertation, University of Luxembourg, 1964;

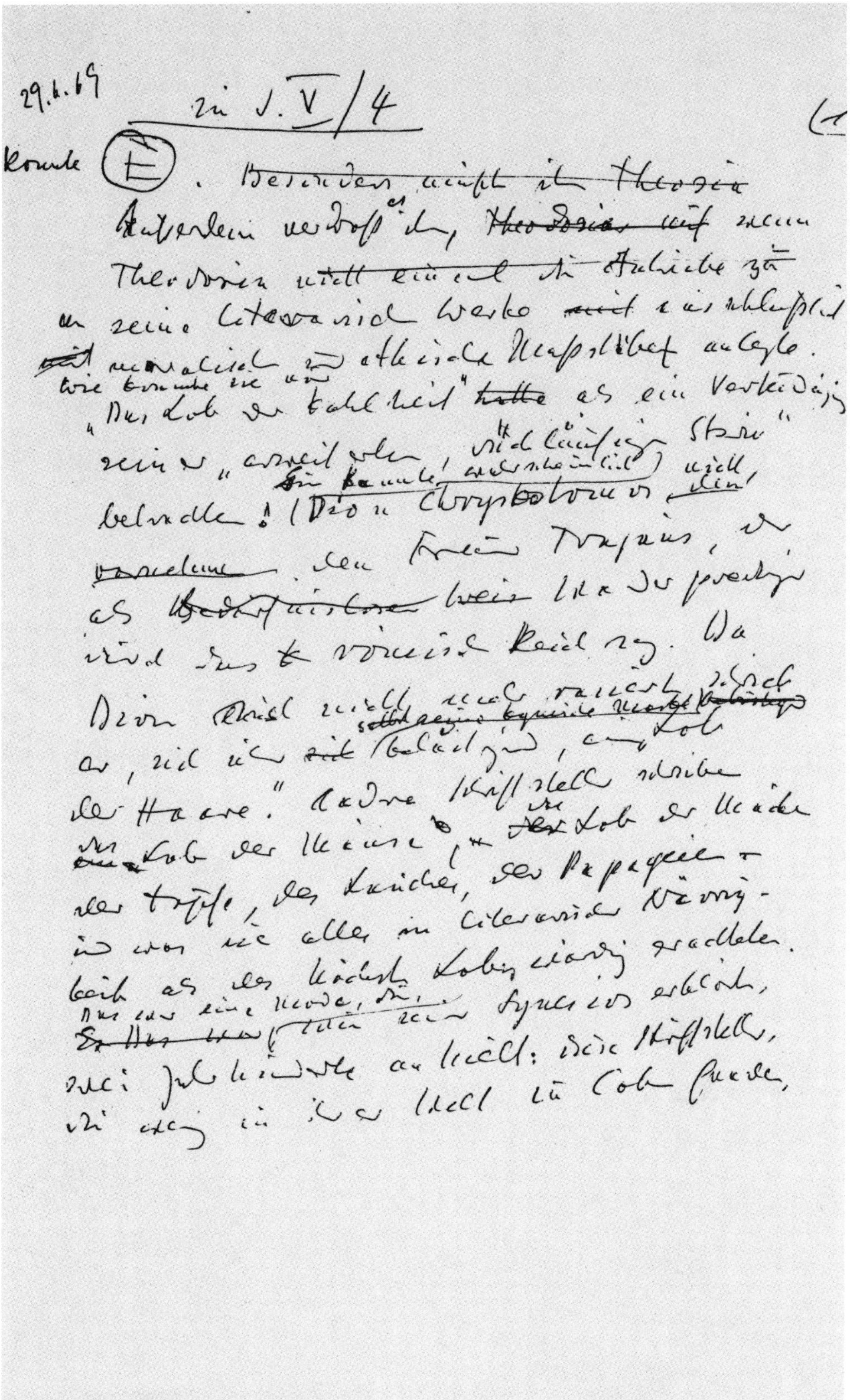

Page from the manuscript for Andres's last novel, Die Versuchung des Synesios *(R. Piper GmbH & Co. KG)*

R. J. Cahill, "Stefan Andres und 'Die Ordnung der Welt,'" Ph.D. dissertation, Boston University, 1955;

Walter Franke, "Stefan Andres 'Wir sind Utopia,'" *Deutschunterricht*, 4, no. 6 (1952): 69-86;

Wilhelm Grosse, *Stefan Andres: Ein Reader zu Person und Werk* (Trier: Spee, 1980);

G. Guder, "Wir sind Utopia," *Modern Languages*, 36 (1954/1955): 22-24;

Karl Josef Hahn, "Dichtung zwischen Drang und Glaube: Zum Werk von Stefan Andres," *Hochland*, 44 (1952): 432-442;

Anton Janko, "The Problem of Faith in the Three Major Novels of Stefan Andres: *Ritter der Gerechtigkeit, Der Mann im Fisch* and *Die Versuchung des Synesios*," Ph.D. dissertation, University of Waterloo (Canada), 1976;

Otto Mann, "Stefan Andres," in *Christliche Dichter der Gegenwart: Beiträge zur europäischen Literatur*, edited by Hermann Friedmann and Mann (Heidelberg: Rothe, 1955), pp. 391-402;

Karl Otto Nordstrand, "Stefan Andres und die 'innere Emigration,'" *Moderna sprak*, 63 (1969): 247-264;

Gottfried Stix, "Wahrheitssuche: Erinnerungen an Stefan Andres," *Neues Hochland*, 64 (1972): 453-467;

Don Carlos Travis, "The Pattern of Reconciliation in the Work of Stefan Andres," Ph.D. dissertation, University of Wisconsin, 1959;

Utopia und Welterfahrung: Stefan Andres und sein Werk im Gedächtnis seiner Freunde (Munich: Piper, 1972);

Karl Günther Werber, "Das Verhältnis von Persönlichkeitsentfaltung und Zeiterlebnis im Werk von Stefan Andres," Ph.D. dissertation, Bonn University, 1959.

Papers:

The Stefan Andres Archive is located at the Stefan Andres Realschule, Stefan-Andres-Straße, 5558 Schweich/Mosel, Federal Republic of Germany.

Ulrich Becher
(2 January 1910-   )

Nancy Anne McClure Zeller

BOOKS: *Männer machen Fehler* (Berlin: Rowohlt, 1931);

Niemand: Ein neuzeitliches Mysterienspiel in 14 Bildern (Mährisch-Ostrau: Kittl, 1934);

Die Eroberer: Geschichten aus Europa (Zurich: Oprecht, 1936);

Reise zum blauen Tag: Verse (St. Gallen: Verlag Buchdruckerei Volksstimme, 1946);

Der Bockerer, by Becher and Peter Preses (Berlin: Aufbau, 1949);

Der Pfeifer von Wien, by Becher and Preses (Munich: Sessler, 1949);

Die Frau und der Tod: Novelle (Berlin: Aufbau, 1949);

Brasilianischer Romanzero (Zurich: Claasen, 1950);

Nachtigall will zum Vater fliegen: Ein Zyklus New Yorker Novellen in vier Nächten (Munich: Weismann, 1950);

New Yorker Novellen (Munich: Weismann, 1950); republished as *Die ganze Nacht* (Reinbek: Rowohlt, 1955);

Samba: Schauspiel in drei Akten (Vienna: Universal-Edition, 1950);

Kurz nach vier: Roman (Hamburg: Rowohlt, 1957; revised edition, Zurich & Cologne: Benziger, 1975);

Spiele der Zeit (Hamburg: Rowohlt, 1957);

Der schwarze Hut (Halle: Mitteldeutscher Verlag, 1957);

Das Herz des Hais: Roman (Reinbek bei Hamburg: Rowohlt, 1960; revised edition, Zurich & Cologne: Benziger, 1972);

Der große Grosz und eine große Zeit: Rede (Reinbek: Rowohlt, 1962);

Spiele der Zeit II (Berlin: Aufbau, 1968);

Murmeljagd: Roman (Hamburg: Rowohlt, 1969); translated by Henry A. Smith as *The Woodchuck Hunt* (New York: Crown, 1977);

Biene, gib mir Honig (Munich: Sessler, 1972);

Das Profil: Roman (Reinbek bei Hamburg: Rowohlt, 1973);

Williams Ex-Casino: Roman (Zurich & Cologne: Benziger, 1973);

SIFF: Selektive Identifizierung von Freund und Feind (Zurich & Cologne: Benziger, 1978);

Ulrich Becher in 1956 (Ullstein)

Franz Patenkindt: Romanze von einem deutschen Patenkind des François Villon in fünfzehn Bänkelsängen (Munich: Universitas, 1980);

Vom Unzulänglichen der Wirklichkeit: 10 nicht so nette Geschichten (Basel: Lenos, 1983).

OTHER: "Eine sehr baltische Geschichte," in *Deutsche Erzähler der Gegenwart: Eine Anthologie,* edited by Willi Fehse (Stuttgart: Reclam, 1959), pp. 43-46;

Ödön von Horvath, *Stücke,* edited by Traugott Krischke, afterword by Becher (Reinbek bei Hamburg: Rowohlt, 1961);

"Auszug von Ulrich Bechers 'Schwarzem Hut,'" in *Interview mit Amerika,* edited by Alfred Gong (Munich: Nymphenburger Verlagsanstalt, 1962), pp. 212-225.

PERIODICAL PUBLICATIONS: "Einigt euch um Gottes willen," *Europa,* no. 13 (28 March 1936);

"Mahn-Sonette," *Das andere Deutschland* (Buenos Aires), 5 (15 September 1942): 14;

"Drohlied der Erschlagenen," *Das andere Deutschland* (Buenos Aires), 5 (November 1942): 21;

"Die sieben stummen Fragen," *Das andere Deutschland* (Buenos Aires), 5 (December 1942): 19-20;

"Zehn Jahre," *Das andere Deutschland* (Buenos Aires), 6 (March 1943): 20-21;

"In der Alpenkatakombe," *Das andere Deutschland* (Buenos Aires), 6 (1 April 1943): 6-9; (15 April 1943): 3-7;

"Ostersegen," *Das andere Deutschland* (Buenos Aires), 6 (15 April 1943): 16;

"Gefallene Kameraden der Freiheit. Zum Gedenken an die ersten Bücherverbrennungen in Europa," *Das andere Deutschland* (Buenos Aires), 6 (1 June 1943): 1-6;

"Krieg der Mirakel," *Das andere Deutschland* (Buenos Aires), 6 (15 July 1943): 5-7;

"Verhör eines Paßlosen," *Das andere Deutschland* (Montevideo), 1 (15 February 1944): 25-26;

"Abendländisches Gelübde," *Das andere Deutschland* (Buenos Aires), 8 (25 April 1944): 12;

"Der große Grosz und eine große Zeit," *Das andere Deutschland* (Buenos Aires & Montevideo), 8 (June 1944): 21-23; (July 1944): 16-19; (August 1944): 21-23; (September 1944): 14-17;

"Die Seine fließt nicht mehr durch Paris: Porträt eines literarischen Kriegsverbrechers," *Freies/Neues Deutschland* (Mexico City), 3 (July 1944): 27-28;

"Das arme Licht," *Aufbau* (New York), 11 (5 January 1945): 20;

"Ahnung und Versprechen: Am 29. August 1939 an Max Hermann-Neisse," *Freies/Neues Deutschland* (Mexico City), 4 (September 1945): 21;

"Ein 'innerer Emigrant': Der Typ Frank Thiess," *Aufbau* (New York), 11 (23 November 1945): 6;

"Väterchen," *Freies/Neues Deutschland* (Mexico City), 4 (November/December 1945): 55-57;

"Ein Nachwort zum Nürnberger Prozeß," *Das andere Deutschland* (Buenos Aires), 8 (1 December 1946): 6-8; (15 December 1946): 8-9;

"George Grosz' Dreißigjähriger Krieg gegen den Krieg," *Das andere Deutschland* (Buenos Aires), 9 (1 January 1947): 14-15;

"Der Rosenkavalier," *Das andere Deutschland* (Buenos Aires), 9 (15 October 1947): 12-14;

"Das Theater–die Welt," *Blätter des Deutschen Theaters in Göttingen,* no. 129 (1957/1958);

"Ein Leben lang Krieg gegen den Krieg: Zum Tod des Malers George Grosz," *National-Zeitung* (Basel), 117 (7 July 1959): 2-3;

"Junge deutsche Dichter für Aufhörer," *Weltwoche* (Zurich), no. 1609 (11 September 1964): 25, 29;

"Es war einmal ein freier Kritiker," *Weltbühne,* 25 (1971): 787-790;

"Roda Roda, der lächelnde Zentaur," *Weltbühne,* 15 (1972): 457-460;

"Abseits vom Rodeo," *Poesie: Zeitschrift für Literatur* (Basel) (December 1975/January 1976): 36.

Although Ulrich Becher's works have not been included in the surveys and anthologies of post-World War II German literature taught in schools, his publishing career has spanned more than fifty years, a longevity attained by few others of his generation–a generation for whom mere survival was often considered a mark of distinction. Becher has survived the vicissitudes of the twentieth century, years of exile, loss of readership, and being out of step with literary fashion. With the renewal of interest in the literature of the Hitler era in general and exile literature in particular, Becher's works are enjoying a revival of interest as well.

Becher was born on 2 January 1910 in Berlin to Richard and Elisa Ulrich Becher. While his immediate family was solidly middle class, the earliest influence on Becher was his maternal grandfather, Martin Ulrich, whom Becher described as a freethinker, a socialist, and an ardent anti-militarist and anti-imperialist. Aside from his grandfather Becher was most influenced by people he met as a teenager in Berlin, where he began several formative relationships, perhaps the foremost being his friendship with the caricaturist Georg Grosz, the self-proclaimed "saddest man in Europe." Becher was the youngest member of the Grosz circle, a group that included the director Erwin Piscator, the poet Max Herrmann-Neisse, the publisher Wieland Herzfelde and his brother, the dadaist photomonteur John Heartfield, and the publisher Ernst Rowohlt.

Becher also visited Das Romanische Café and came under the influence of a completely different set of elders, including the satirist Alexander Roda Roda (pseudonym of Sandór von Rosenfeld), the artists Max Slevogt and Emil Orlik, and "the racing reporter" Egon Erwin Kisch. Grosz and Roda Roda represented two poles of socially aware art: at one extreme was Grosz's focus on the grotesque hypocrisy of capitalists caught in obscene acts; at the other was Roda Roda's gentle satire, the objective of which was edification and reform through laughter. Although Roda Roda's influence became more evident in Becher's later works, his initial publications reflect the influence of Grosz almost exclusively. Becher attended the University of Geneva from 1928 to 1929 and the University of Berlin from 1930 to 1933.

Becher's first book, a collection of short stories entitled *Männer machen Fehler* (Men Make Mistakes, 1931), is a potpourri of styles and themes that testifies to the impact of 1920s experimental art on him. "Joshua war kein Feldherr" (Joshua Was No General) describes the brutal death by beating of an old, half-crazed zither player; the story can be read as an allegory of the brutality of capitalism. Joshua is the artist-clown-outcast seen in much expressionist literature; his milieu is the night life of the bar with its violence and sexual innuendos. Other stories in the collection reveal expressionist or dadaist themes such as the inhumanity of capitalist technology, the saintliness of the poor working man, the conflict of youth with age, art as a political weapon, and reverence for the Dionysian qualities of the arts, especially music. After the publication of *Männer machen Fehler*, Becher became the youngest member of the International P.E.N. Club.

The trial of Grosz and the Malik publishing firm for blasphemy gave Becher the impulse to write his first play, *Niemand* (Nobody, 1934), in 1931. Clearly showing the influence of Grosz, *Niemand* has Christ return to contemporary earth, where he is again rejected by those in authority—in this case the military and the capitalists—for his pacifism and solidarity with the working class. *Niemand* brought Becher the distinction of becoming, at twenty-three, the youngest author to have his books burned by Nazi sympathizers. But his youth created a problem that has continued for the rest of his career: the search for his own literary style. The talented novice was surrounded by expressionists, dadaists, and politically and socially engaged artists who had established themselves at least a decade earlier. Association with them confirmed Becher's own tendencies, but also locked him into the role of eternal disciple or historian of the masters of artis-

tic movements whose glory was already fading when he was finally old enough to be admitted to the inner circle.

Becher, like other exile writers, believed that a writer's career depends on his native tongue; so in 1933 when Grosz and the circle of artists around the Malik firm immigrated to New York, Becher instead followed Roda Roda to Vienna, where he married Roda Roda's daughter, Dana Marie, on 4 November. From Vienna he contributed a few essays to antifascist newspapers in Switzerland and Paris; one essay, "Einigt euch um Gottes willen" (Unite for God's Sake, 1936), which calls for unity between Christians, socialists, democrats, and all friends of peace in the fight against fascism, was reprinted in many socialist exile publications. Becher wrote little of importance while in Austria, but the atmosphere he absorbed there would manifest itself in his postwar publications.

When Hitler invaded Austria in March 1938 Becher took the last unsearched train to Switzerland, where it was still possible to publish for the European market. Becher has described the difficult situation of exiles in Switzerland in his series of essays entitled "In der Alpenkatakombe" (In the Catacombs of the Alps, 1943) for the Buenos Aires journal *Das andere Deutschland* and in his novel *Murmeljagd* (1969; translated as *The Woodchuck Hunt*, 1977). In March 1941 Swiss authorities informed him that, in spite of his mother's Swiss citizenship, they could no longer grant him asylum. Becher finally acquired a passport identifying him as a Czech engineer traveling with an industrial advisory group to Brazil. From mid 1941 to mid 1944 he lived in Rio de Janeiro, or on the outskirts of the city in a pension he called his "jungle farm."

In South America Becher found himself in the professional isolation he had tried so long to avoid. The isolation was magnified not only by the alien culture of South America, but also by his youth, since he had not had time to establish a reputation as a writer. He established new contacts and drew on Continental acquaintances in an attempt to call attention to his works. While in Brazil Becher published essays and poems in the journals that were the only outlets available for his writing; as he had during his Austrian exile, however, he absorbed much atmosphere and developed themes that would become central in his later fiction. In his essays and poems for *Das andere Deutschland* can be found, for example, the comparison of fascism to cancer that becomes the

Expressionistic painting of Becher by his friend George Grosz

central metaphor in *New Yorker Novellen* (New York Novellas, 1950) and in the play *Feuerwasser* (Firewater, 1952; published in *Spiele der Zeit* [Plays of the Time, 1957]).

While Becher supported himself financially with his cultural and political articles, he was developing his basically expressionist literary style in his verse. *Reise zum blauen Tag* (Journey to the Blue Day, 1946) and *Brasilianischer Romancero* (Brazilian Romancero, 1950) are noteworthy for descriptions of the colorful, luxuriant surroundings of the Brazilian jungle. His language began to take on new depths of expression, described by Becher and critics alike as "jungle baroque." The environment he had absorbed was completely unfamiliar to the postwar audience to which he returned, and Becher found it necessary to append ten pages of notes to the 1962 edition of *Brasilianischer Romanzero* to explain the poems' more obscure references to Brazilian legends, customs, and places.

In mid 1944 Becher and his wife were called to New York City to care for Roda Roda, who died of leukemia in August 1945. Becher spent the next three years in New York taking notes, absorbing anecdotes, and writing stories and plays that were published after his return to Europe. His only publications during his stay in New York were essays in the exile journals *DAD*, *Aufbau*, and *Freies Deutschland*. Failing to gain a foothold in New York and seeing that his works were being accepted in Austria and Switzerland, Becher returned to Vienna in 1948. Since 1949 he has lived mainly in Basel, which became his permanent residence in 1954.

The play *Der Bockerer*, written jointly in 1946 by Becher and the Vienna-born actor Peter Preses, was published in Berlin in 1949. *Der Bockerer* tells the story of the seven years of Hitler's "Thousand-Year Reich" in Austria as seen through the eyes of Karl Bockerer, a middle-class butcher and the embodiment of Viennese charm and wit. Becher and Preses show how an in-

Becher in 1965 (courtesy of Benziger Verlag, Zurich)

among West German dramas to receive scholarly attention in the mid 1950s. Drawing on his exile years in South America, Becher depicts the fate of a group of Europeans stranded in a decaying hotel in the interior of Brazil. The music of the samba symbolizes the untapped power and vitality of the Brazilian poor; at the same time, its Dionysian power to intoxicate explains their political impotence. The conflict in *Samba* is the central conflict in most of Becher's work: the protagonist's shift from an exclusive concern with his art to acceptance of personal responsibility in the fight against fascism.

Feuerwasser, which premiered at the Deutsches Theater in Göttingen in 1952, deals with German immigrants in New York. Set in 1946, the play shows the destructive effects of war on peacetime society. Brutality and criminality have become commonplace among the clientele of a Manhattan bar, but Charlie Brown, the bartender, is able to keep order. When threatened by a professional gangster, however, Charlie finds that the only way to save his friends is to sacrifice his own life. As in *Samba*, the basic question is: what can a socially and politically aware individual do, in a world filled with injustice, exploitation, and institutionalized violence, to improve the human condition? In *Feuerwasser* Becher's answer is that the strong individual must be willing, as a last resort, to give up everything, even his life, for the betterment of society. For those incapable of self-sacrifice there is another solution to the problems of living in postwar society: surrender to the intoxication of alcohol, music, and sex.

Becher's play *Mademoiselle Loewenzorn* (published in *Spiele der Zeit II*, 1968) received an award of 3,000 marks from the German Theater Union in Cologne in 1955. This play, like *Feuerwasser*, deals with the transference of wartime murderousness to peacetime society. It opens with a shooting on carnival night in Basel; the remaining scenes are flashbacks that reveal the motivations each of the characters could have had to commit the crime. This time it is not just the battle with fascism but the universal fear and paranoia characteristic of the atomic age which motivate the characters to arm themselves.

In 1957 Becher had a great dramatic disaster: Heinz Hilpert's production of *Der Herr kommt aus Bahia* (The Lord Comes from Bahia) at the Deutsches Theater in Göttingen. The play deals with the fascist leader of a gang of robbers in the interior of Brazil who is murdered while portray-

dividual might have survived the horrors of the time by using his wit, humor, and, when necessary, physical strength to combat the tyranny of fascism. After established theaters refused the play, *Der Bockerer* opened in late 1948 at the Neues Theater in der Scala, a theater started in Vienna by the Austrian Communist party. The play had eighty performances plus a tour, a feat equaled in immediate postwar theater history in the German-speaking countries only by Carl Zuckmayer's *Des Teufels General* (1946; translated as *The Devil's General*, 1962). Due to late-1970s interest in the Hitler era, *Der Bockerer* was revived by the Nationaltheater in Mannheim and added to the repertoires of five other theaters.

Becher's play *Samba* (1950) was written in 1949 in Salzburg and produced in March 1951 at the Theater in der Josefstadt in Vienna; in April 1952 at Boleslaw Barlog's Schloßparktheater in West Berlin; and in December 1954 at the Meiningen Theater in the German Democratic Republic, where Becher's works were almost alone

ing Adolf Hitler in a victory parade at the end of World War II. In 1957 audiences had little tolerance for yet another exploration of the roots of fascism. The revised version of the play, *Makumba*, (published in *Spiele der Zeit II*), tries to explain the Brazilian milieu and to blur the parallels to Nazism by investing the setting with a fairy-tale timelessness. *Makumba* was never produced.

Der Herr kommt aus Bahia was Becher's last dramatic effort until the 1970s, but the end of Becher the dramatist marked the rebirth of Becher the prose writer. Becher had actually begun work on the *New Yorker Novellen* in 1945 while still in exile in New York. The novellas are dedicated to George Grosz, and Grosz's life and art are the major inspiration for both the content and form of the stories. "Nachtigall will zum Vater fliegen" (Nachtigall Wants to Fly to Father) contains an only slightly fictionalized account of Grosz in the alcoholic left-wing artist Theodosi Boem. Becher traces Grosz's development from social caricaturist of 1920s Berlin to the apocalyptic Boschean visionary of the late works–the artist of the "hole," of ominous landscapes, and of the stickmen, called "Hornissenmenschen" (wasp people) in the novella. Becher invests his other protagonist, Hans Heinz Nachtigall, with the psychological problems of Richard Huelsenbeck, another member of the Berlin Dada group. One side of Nachtigall's personality forever wants to return home to his father, who has survived the war; but the American side of his personality, Nightingale (the English translation of *Nachtigall*), fears that his father has turned into one of Boem's "Hornissenmenschen," the fulfillment of Boem/Grosz's apocalyptic vision. "Der schwarze Hut" (The Black Hat) and "Die Frau und der Tod" (Woman and Death) are Grosz graphics translated into prose. The cocktail party scene in "Der schwarze Hut" with its predominantly dark hues (everyone is in mourning) dotted with bright splashes of color is reminiscent of Grosz's early café and street scenes. Grosz's cityscapes appear in the "Times Square" montage of "Die Frau und der Tod," where the reader is caught up in the crowd of revelers celebrating the dropping of the atom bomb on Hiroshima. Also like Grosz, Becher sometimes exaggerates physical or psychological features of his characters to the point of grotesqueness. Many of the characters are given animal traits, a technique used by Grosz in his paintings to indicate dehumanization. Women are more dehumanized than men for, as in expressionism generally and in Grosz's

paintings particularly, they are seen almost exclusively through the eyes of men. They are mere dolls, marionettes, beautiful animals (especially birds), or carnival masks. The only human alternatives for Becher's women are nymphomaniacs, prostitutes, terminally ill Camille figures, vaguely defined and frequently absent wives, or symbols of grace and beauty; Becher's women are not flesh and blood but representatives of various female traits.

From novellas dealing with exile experiences in New York Becher moved to a novel about the events and motivations that led to exile. In *Kurz nach vier* (Shortly after Four, 1957) Zborowsky, a Viennese art professor, is traveling to Rome to visit an old friend. During a sleepless night in noisy, tourist-filled Piacenza his Hemingwayesque past is recounted in cinematic flashbacks which weave together the pre- and postwar Austrian literary scene, the Spanish civil war, and the guerilla warfare of the Yugoslav partisans with the story of Zborowsky's love for Lola Aguirre, who was murdered by Spanish Falangists. But *Kurz nach vier* is more than an adventure-packed love story. Embodied in Zborowsky's odyssey is the dilemma faced by Becher's generation. In contrast to Becher's earlier works, in which separate characters represent the opposing viewpoints, here one character, Zborowsky, contains both sides of the debate. Torn between pacifism and the desire to help destroy the evil of fascism, and between the artist's roles as both member and observer of society, Zborowsky wavers between fight and flight, action and inaction. The double ending of *Kurz nach vier* demonstrates the resulting schism: Zborowsky kills a traitorous friend, but the murder turns out to be a fantasy. Thus Zborowsky purges himself of the need for actual revenge, discards the pistol he has carried since his fighting days, forgives his friend, and ends his personal war "for the time being." Like Zborowsky, Becher has tried to take the middle road, to maintain his integrity both as an artist and as a pacifist by using his art in the fight against fascism. But it is clearly an unsatisfactory choice, because Becher feels compelled to reargue his case with each new work.

Except for seven newspaper articles and one unsuccessful novel, *Das Herz des Hais* (Heart of the Shark, 1960), no new work by Becher appeared until 1969, when his monumental *Murmeljagd* was published. Praised by critics as Becher's masterpiece, *Murmeljagd* contains all the

Cover of Becher's 1978 collection of essays on his friends and enemies

themes of his earlier works. In *Murmeljagd* Becher has gathered forces that were merely "in training" in other works for one gigantic attack on the demons of his past; but if his intent was cathartic, *Murmeljagd* is a failure, because it is not Becher's last work to deal with these themes. Albert Trebla, a socialist, Viennese journalist and former fighter pilot, skis across the Alps to neutral Switzerland after the fall of Austria in 1938. The events of four weeks of his exile are interspersed with flashbacks from forty years of Austrian history: Trebla is as old as the twentieth century, and his biography is a mirror of the history of the country. Convinced that he is the target of a Nazi plot, Trebla rushes headlong from one imaginary trap to another, the victim of the justifiable paranoia of his generation. Trebla identifies with

the woodchuck, the skittish ground dweller who flees at the slightest hint of danger. *Murmeljagd* almost brought long-expected fame to Becher; it was widely reviewed, called worthy of a literary prize, and translated into French and English. But fame did not come; and nothing Becher has written since has received as much attention.

In 1973 Rowohlt published in paperback *Das Profil* (The Profile), an entertaining short novel based on an anecdote Becher had heard from Grosz concerning interviews of Grosz by Richard O. Boyer for the "Profiles" series in the *New Yorker* in 1943. *Das Profil* contains much the same constellation of themes as Becher's New York works, but the solutions given in the novel to the dilemma of the artist in society are less nihilistic, more resigned. Becher seems to have acquired, along with a permanent residence and a secure income, a kind of good-humored resignation about the ineffectuality of the engaged artist. The artist is still a privileged seer who prophesies the peril inherent in a corrupt and exploitative society, but this threat no longer demands immediate personal sacrifice. He has become an antihero, a Cassandra or Don Quixote, with at most a hope that his message will be heard.

Becher's most straightforwardly autobiographical piece of fiction, *Williams Ex-Casino*, was published in 1973. Written simultaneously with *Das Profil*, it shares with the latter work many of the expected themes and viewpoints. But whereas *Das Profil* emphasizes the role of the artist in society, *Williams Ex-Casino* highlights the inescapability of politics in the modern world. Written during a serious illness by a man in his sixties, the novel is also preoccupied with unfulfilled dreams, infirmity, disease, and death. The protagonist is not the daring activist of Becher's early plays but a totally resigned and passive antihero.

After *Williams Ex-Casino* Becher began to publish collections of shorter pieces which had been abandoned at some stage of writing in favor of the longer novels. *SIFF* (1978) is a collection of essays celebrating Becher's friends and foes; most of these essays had previously appeared in newspapers. Becher took up the romance form again with *Franz Patenkindt: Romanze von einem deutschen Patenkind des François Villon in fünfzehn Bänkelsängen* (Franz Godchild: Romance of a German Godchild of François Villon in Fifteen Popular Ballads, 1980). *Vom Unzulänglichen der Wirklichkeit* (On the Shortcoming of Reality, 1983) is a collection of ten short prose works, some of which had appeared elsewhere. Frequent bouts of emphysema and near-pneumonia in recent years have left Becher weak and unable to travel to the theaters which are producing *Der Bockerer*.

Becher's style and themes were fixed by his exile trauma, but he continues to find an audience interested in fascism and its effects. Stylistically, Becher's work has broken no new ground; but his stories provide fascinating glimpses into the nightmarish world of the Hitler exiles, and his storytelling ability ranks with Ernest Hemingway's or Günter Grass's. His work cannot easily be categorized, which has, perhaps, led most critics simply to ignore his half century of writing.

References:

Wolfgang Beck, "Zeit auf den Brettern: Bemerkungen zu Thematik und Technik des Dramatikers Ulrich Becher," *Theater der Zeit,* 12, special addition to no. 3 (March 1957): 8-32;

Lion Feuchtwanger, "Ulrich Becher," *Das Wort,* no. 8 (August 1937): 90-92;

Martin Gregor-Dellin, "Jeder Satz exotisch," *Die Zeit,* 29 August 1969, p. 17;

Paul Huehnerfeld, "Auf der Suche nach dem alten Europa: Die Wege und Irrwege des Schriftstellers Ulrich Becher," *Die Zeit,* 23 May 1957, p. 6;

Herbert Ihering, "Episches und dramatisches Theater," *Sonntag* (East Berlin), 11 (15 January 1956): 11;

Arnold Kuenzli, "Ulrich Becher–Dichter havarierten Europäertums," *National-Zeitung* (Basel), 3 March 1957, pp. 1-2;

Klaus Mann, "Ulrich Becher," *Das Neue Tagebuch,* 5, no. 30 (1937): 719;

Werner Mittenzwei, "Deutsche Dramatik gegen die Atomkriegsgefahr," in *Frieden und Sozialismus* (Berlin: Aufbau, 1969), pp. 201-260;

Alexander J. Seiler, "Europa im Urwald–Urwald Europa: Der Schriftsteller Ulrich Becher," *Weltwoche* (Zurich), 6 January 1961, p. 17;

Nancy Anne McClure Zeller, *Ulrich Becher: A Computer-Assisted Case Study of the Reception of an Exile* (Bern, Frankfurt am Main & New York: Lang, 1983).

Papers:
Ulrich Becher's voluminous papers are stored in his son's cellar in Basel; there are no current plans to donate them to any institution.

Heinrich Böll

(21 December 1917-16 July 1985)

Reinhard K. Zachau
University of the South

BOOKS: *Der Zug war pünktlich: Erzählung* (Opladen: Middelhauve, 1949); translated by Richard Graves as *The Train Was on Time* (London: Arco, 1956; New York: Criterion Books, 1956);

Wanderer, kommst du nach Spa . . . : Erzählungen (Opladen: Middelhauve, 1950); translated by Mervyn Savill as *Traveller, If You Come to Spa . . .* (London: Arco, 1956);

Die schwarzen Schafe: Erzählung (Opladen: Middelhauve, 1951);

Wo warst du, Adam? Roman (Opladen: Middelhauve, 1951); translated by Savill as *Adam, Where Art Thou?* (New York: Criterion Books, 1955); translated by Leila Vennewitz as "And Where Were You, Adam?," in *Adam and The Train: Two Novels* (New York: McGraw-Hill, 1970);

Nicht nur zur Weihnachtszeit (Frankfurt: Frankfurter Verlagsanstalt, 1952); published with *Der Mann mit den Messern,* edited by Dorothea Berger (New York: American Book Co., 1959);

Und sagte kein einziges Wort: Roman (Cologne & Berlin: Kiepenheuer & Witsch, 1953); translated by Graves as *Acquainted with the Night: A Novel* (New York: Holt, 1954); translated by Vennewitz as *And Never Said a Word* (New York: McGraw-Hill, 1978);

Haus ohne Hüter: Roman (Cologne & Berlin: Kiepenheuer & Witsch, 1954); translated by Savill as *The Unguarded House* (London: Arco, 1957); translation republished as *Tomorrow and Yesterday* (New York: Criterion Books, 1957);

Das Brot der frühen Jahre: Erzählung (Cologne & Berlin: Kiepenheuer & Witsch, 1955); translated by Savill as *The Bread of Our Early Years* (London: Arco, 1957); translated by Vennewitz as *The Bread of Those Early Years* (New York: McGraw-Hill, 1976);

So ward Abend und Morgen: Erzählungen (Zurich: Arche, 1955);

Heinrich Böll in 1983 (Ullstein–Poly-Press)

Unberechenbare Gäste: Heitere Erzählungen (Zurich: Arche, 1956);

Irisches Tagebuch (Cologne & Berlin: Kiepenheuer & Witsch, 1957); translated by Vennewitz as *Irish Journal* (New York: McGraw-Hill, 1967; London: Secker & Warburg, 1983);

Im Tal der donnernden Hufe: Erzählung (Wiesbaden: Insel, 1957); edited by James Alldridge (London: Heinemann Educational, 1970);

Abenteuer eines Brotbeutels, und andere Geschichten, edited by Richard Plant (New York: Norton, 1957);

27

Die Spurlosen: Hörspiel (Hamburg: Hans Bredow-Institut, 1957); published with Leopold Ahlsen, *Philemon und Baukis,* edited by Anna Otten (New York: Odyssey, 1967);

Doktor Murkes gesammeltes Schweigen und andere Satiren (Cologne & Berlin: Kiepenheuer & Witsch, 1958); edited by Gertrud Seidmann (London: Harrap, 1963);

Der Wegwerfer: Erzählung (Alfeld-Gronau: Hannoversche Papierfabriken, 1958);

Im Ruhrgebiet, text by Böll, illustrations by Karl Hargesheimer (Frankfurt am Main: Büchergilde Gutenberg, 1958);

Die ungezählte Geliebte (Zollikofen: Privately printed, 1958);

Die Waage der Baleks und andere Erzählungen (Berlin: Union, 1959);

Billard um halb zehn: Roman (Cologne & Berlin: Kiepenheuer & Witsch, 1959); translated by Patrick Bowles as *Billiards at Half-past Nine* (London: Weidenfeld & Nicolson, 1961; New York: McGraw-Hill, 1962);

Der Mann mit den Messern: Erzählungen (Stuttgart: Reclam, 1959); published with *Nicht nur zur Weihnachtszeit,* edited by Berger (New York: American Book Co., 1959);

Der Bahnhof von Zimpren: Erzählungen (Munich: List, 1959);

Aus unseren Tagen, edited by Gisela Stein (New York: Holt, Rinehart & Winston, 1960);

Menschen am Rhein, text by Böll, illustrations by Hargesheimer (Frankfurt am Main: Büchergilde Gutenberg, 1960);

Brief an einen jungen Katholiken (Cologne & Berlin: Kiepenheuer & Witsch, 1961);

Bilanz; Klopfzeichen: Zwei Hörspiele (Stuttgart: Reclam, 1961);

Erzählungen, Hörspiele, Aufsätze (Cologne & Berlin: Kiepenheuer & Witsch, 1961);

Als der Krieg ausbrach; Als der Krieg zu Ende war: Zwei Erzählungen (Frankfurt am Main: Insel, 1962); translated by Vennewitz as "Enter and Exit," in *Absent without Leave: Two Novellas* (New York: McGraw-Hill, 1965); translation republished in *Absent without Leave and Other Stories* (London: Weidenfeld & Nicolson, 1967);

Ein Schluck Erde: Drama (Cologne & Berlin: Kiepenheuer & Witsch, 1962);

Assisi (Munich: Knorr & Hirth, 1962);

Ansichten eines Clowns: Roman (Cologne & Berlin: Kiepenheuer & Witsch, 1963); translated by Vennewitz as *The Clown* (New York: McGraw-Hill, 1965);

Böll as a student in the mid 1930s (Klaus Schröter, Heinrich Böll *[Reinbek: Rowohlt, 1982])*

Hierzulande: Aufsätze (Munich: Deutscher Taschenbuch Verlag, 1963);

1947 bis 1951: Erzählungen (Cologne & Opladen: Middelhauve, 1963); translated by Vennewitz as *Children Are Civilians, Too* (New York: McGraw-Hill, 1970);

Die Essenholer und andere Erzählungen, edited by Fritz Bachmann (Frankfurt am Main: Hirschgraben-Verlag, 1963);

Zum Tee bei Dr. Borsig: Hörspiele (Munich: Deutscher Taschenbuch Verlag, 1964);

Entfernung von der Truppe: Erzählung (Cologne & Berlin: Kiepenheuer & Witsch, 1964); translated by Vennewitz as "Absent without Leave," in *Absent without Leave: Two Novellas* (New York: McGraw-Hill, 1965); translation republished in *Absent without Leave and Other Stories* (London: Weidenfeld & Nicolson, 1967);

Der Rat des Weltunweisen: Roman (Gütersloh: Mohn, 1965);

Frankfurter Vorlesungen (Cologne: Kiepenheuer & Witsch, 1966);

Ende einer Dienstfahrt: Erzählung (Cologne: Kiepenheuer & Witsch, 1966); translated by Vennewitz as *End of a Mission* (New York: McGraw-Hill, 1967); translation republished as *The End of a Mission* (London: Weidenfeld & Nicolson, 1968);

Die Spurlosen: Drei Hörspiele (Leipzig: Insel, 1966);

18 Stories, translated by Vennewitz (New York: McGraw-Hill, 1966);

Aufsätze, Kritiken, Reden (Cologne: Kiepenheuer & Witsch, 1967);

Georg Büchners Gegenwärtigkeit: Eine Rede (Berlin: Friedenauer Presse, 1967);

Hausfriedensbruch: Hörspiel; Aussatz: Schauspiel (Cologne: Kiepenheuer & Witsch, 1969);

Leben im Zustand des Frevels: Ansprache zur Verleihung des Kölner Literaturpreises (Berlin: Berliner Handpresse, 1969);

Geschichten aus zwölf Jahren (Frankfurt am Main: Suhrkamp, 1969);

Böll für Zeitgenossen: Ein kulturgeschichtliches Lesebuch, edited by Ralph Ley (New York: Harper & Row, 1970);

Gruppenbild mit Dame: Roman (Cologne: Kiepenheuer & Witsch, 1971); translated by Vennewitz as *Group Portrait with Lady* (New York: McGraw-Hill, 1973);

Erzählungen, 1950-1970 (Cologne: Kiepenheuer & Witsch, 1972);

Gedichte (Berlin: Literarisches Colloquium, 1972);

Versuch über die Vernunft der Poesie: Nobelvorlesung (Stockholm: Norstedt & Söner, 1973);

Neue politische und literarische Schriften (Cologne: Kiepenheuer & Witsch, 1973);

Die verlorene Ehre der Katharina Blum oder wie Gewalt entstehen und wohin sie führen kann: Erzählung (Cologne: Kiepenheuer & Witsch, 1974); translated by Vennewitz as *The Lost Honor of Katharina Blum: How Violence Develops and Where It Can Lead* (New York: McGraw-Hill, 1975);

Drei Tage im März: Ein Gespräch, by Böll and Christian Linder (Cologne: Kiepenheuer & Witsch, 1975);

Berichte zur Gesinnungslage der Nation (Cologne: Kiepenheuer & Witsch, 1975);

Gedichte: Mit Collagen von Klaus Staeck (Cologne: Labbe und Muta, 1975);

Wie kritisch darf engagierte Kunst sein? (Munich: Presseausschuß Demokratische Initiative, 1976);

Einmischung erwünscht: Schriften zur Zeit (Cologne: Kiepenheuer & Witsch, 1977);

Werke: Romane und Erzählungen, edited by B. Balzer, 5 volumes (Cologne: Middelhauve/ Kiepenheuer & Witsch, 1977);

Missing Persons and Other Essays, translated by Vennewitz (New York: McGraw-Hill, 1977);

Werke: Essayistische Schriften und Reden, Interviews, edited by Balzer, 4 volumes (Cologne: Kiepenheuer & Witsch, 1978);

Hörspiele, Theaterstücke, Drehbücher, Gedichte, edited by Balzer (Cologne: Kiepenheuer & Witsch, 1978);

Mein Lesebuch (Frankfurt am Main: Fischer, 1978);

Eine deutsche Erinnerung: Interview mit René Wintzen (Cologne: Kiepenheuer & Witsch, 1979);

Du fährst zu oft nach Heidelberg und andere Erzählungen (Bornheim-Merten: Lamuv, 1979);

Fürsorgliche Belagerung: Roman (Cologne: Kiepenheuer & Witsch, 1979); translated by Vennewitz as *The Safety Net* (Franklin Center, Pa.: Franklin Library, 1981; London: Secker & Warburg, 1982);

Ein Tag wie sonst: Hörspiele (Munich: Deutscher Taschenbuch Verlag, 1980);

Was soll aus dem Jungen bloß werden? Oder: Irgendwas mit Büchern (Bornheim-Merten: Lamuv, 1981); translated by Vennewitz as *What's to Become of the Boy? or, Something to Do with Books* (New York: Knopf, 1984);

Eine deutsche Erinnerung: Interview mit René Wintzen (Munich: Deutscher Taschenbuch Verlag, 1981);

Warum haben wir aufeinander geschossen?, by Böll and Lev Kopelev (Bornheim-Merten: Lamuv, 1981);

Der Autor ist immer noch versteckt, by Böll and Jürgen Wallmann (Hauzenberg: Pongratz, 1981);

Vermintes Gelände: Essayistische Schriften 1977-1981 (Cologne: Kiepenheuer & Witsch, 1982);

Verantwortlich für Polen? (Reinbek: Rowohlt, 1982);

Das Vermächtnis: Kurzroman (Bornheim-Merten: Lamuv, 1982); translated by Vennewitz as *A Soldier's Legacy* (New York: Knopf, 1985; London: Secker & Warburg, 1985);

Antikommunismus in Ost und West (Cologne: Bund-Verlag, 1982);

Die Verwundung und andere frühe Erzählungen (Bornheim-Merten: Lamuv, 1983); trans-

Böll with his fiancée, Annemarie Cech, in 1942 (Klaus Schröter, Heinrich Böll *[Reinbek: Rowohlt, 1º82])*

lated by Vennewitz as *The Casualty* (New York: Farrar, Straus & Giroux, 1987);

Der Angriff (Cologne: Kiepenheuer & Witsch, 1983);

Bild, Bonn, Boenisch (Bornheim-Merten: Lamuv, 1984);

Katholisch und rebellisch: Ein Wegweiser durch die andere Kirche (Reinbek: Rowohlt, 1984);

Veränderungen in Staech: Erzählungen 1962-1980 (Cologne: Kiepenheuer & Witsch, 1984);

Weil die Stadt so fremd geworden ist (Bornheim-Merten: Lamuv, 1985);

Die Juden von Drove (Berlin: Rütten & Loening, 1985);

Heinrich Böll, on His Death (Bonn: Inter Nationes, 1985);

Frauen vor Flußlandschaft: Roman in Dialogen und Selbstgesprächen (Cologne: Kiepenheuer & Witsch, 1985);

The Short Stories of Heinrich Böll, translated by Vennewitz (New York: Knopf, 1986);

Die Fähigkeit zu trauern (Bornheim-Merten: Lamuv, 1986).

OTHER: Wolfgang Borchert, *Draußen vor der Tür und ausgewählte Geschichten,* afterword by Böll (Hamburg: Rowohlt, 1956);

Ein Artikel und seine Folgen, edited by Böll and Franz Grützbach (Bornheim-Merten: Lamuv, 1982).

TRANSLATIONS: Patrick White, *Zur Ruhe kam der Baum des Menschen nie,* translated by Böll and Annemarie Böll (Cologne: Kiepenheuer & Witsch, 1957);

Bernard Malamud, *Der Gehilfe,* translated by Böll and Annemarie Böll (Cologne: Kiepenheuer & Witsch, 1960);

J. M. Synge, *Ein wahrer Held,* translated by Böll and Annemarie Böll (Berlin: Kiepenheuer & Witsch, 1960);

J. D. Salinger, *Der Fänger im Roggen,* translated by Böll (Cologne: Kiepenheuer & Witsch, 1962);

Salinger, *Franny und Zooey,* translated by Böll and Annemarie Böll (Cologne: Kiepenheuer & Witsch, 1963);

George Bernard Shaw, *Caesar und Cleopatra,* translated by Böll and Annemarie Böll (Frankfurt: Suhrkamp, 1965).

When in the summer of 1972 Heinrich Böll received the news that he had been awarded the Nobel Prize for Literature, he responded with the surprised question: "Was, ich, und nicht Günter Grass?" (Really? I, and not Günter Grass?). This reaction summarizes Böll's assessment of his place in West German postwar literature–sometimes referred to as "Grass-Böll-literature"–and it reflects Böll's competition with Grass, who is generally regarded by critics as the superior writer. Böll's sales figures, however, tell a different story: with 31 million books in print and having been translated into forty-five languages, he is by far the most popular of all modern German writers. In his unpretentious style he became a chronologist of the first forty years of the Federal Republic of Germany. The reader recognizes himself and people he knows in Böll's books; the simple ideas of this modest man influenced the way Germans look at their second republic. Böll became an important public figure in Germany–much against his will: when a poll was conducted in the 1970s to determine the ten most influential people in West Germany, Böll was mentioned in fourth place, after the politicians Helmut Schmidt, Willy Brandt, and Franz Josef Strauß, as the man who "represents our conscience."

Heinrich Theodor Böll was born in Cologne on 21 December 1917, to Victor Böll and his second wife, Marie Hermanns Böll, during the worst famine year of World War I. Böll had two older brothers and three older sisters. His mother was an energetic, domineering woman from a long line of Catholic farmers and brewers. His father's family, Catholics who had preferred emigration to the state religion of Henry VIII, had come centuries earlier from the British Isles. Victor Böll had moved to Cologne from Essen in 1896, at the age of twenty-six, to "move up" socially and, together with an associate, to start his own business as a carpenter and wood sculptor; he worked ambitiously for fifty years, much like Heinrich Fähmel in Heinrich Böll's novel *Billard um halb zehn* (1959; translated as *Billiards at Half-past Nine*, 1961). Victor Böll was a sensitive, nervous man who liked to tell stories to his sons. His tastes were neoclassic; he created the kind of sculptures that were in demand during the second German empire, which he supported enthusiastically. During World War I, however, Victor's enthusiasm for the Kaiser–"der kaiserliche Narr" (the imperial fool)–changed to cynicism. It is clear that Böll inherited his anti-Prussian attitude from his father. But if Böll represented the attitude of the citizens of Cologne as far as Prussia was concerned, his postwar

antiestablishment position did not reflect the prevailing mood at the time.

The Böll family at first lived in an apartment but soon acquired their own home in Cologne-Raderberg, Kreuznacher Straße 49. Böll recalled his childhood years as happy ones, and some critics see his writings as an attempt to reconstruct his lost childhood experiences in the modern technological world. Böll's parents were broad-minded and never forced their children to join the Catholic church. They also allowed them to play with the children of socialists in their neighborhood, something that the professors, attorneys, architects, and bank directors strictly forbade their children. This childhood paradise ended when Böll entered a Catholic elementary school in 1924, while most of his friends entered public school. Böll later attended the Kaiser-Wilhelm-Gymnasium, which made him more aware of social distinctions: he could not understand why the "Reds" could not go with him.

In October 1930 Böll's father lost his business in the Great Depression, and the family had to sell the house and their possessions. This experience brought Böll even closer to his parents, especially when he realized "daß meine Eltern völlig hilflos waren gegenüber diesen Umständen" (that my parents were totally helpless in the face of these conditions). The Bölls had to move several times, the bill collector appeared on numerous occasions, and they were forced to rent out rooms in their apartment. The family was slipping out of the middle class but was not really establishing itself in a new class. These experiences explain why Böll sometimes described himself as proletarian, sometimes as "kleinbürgerlich" (lower middle class).

When Hitler became chancellor in 1933, Böll, in bed with the flu, heard his mother say: "That means war." During his last years at the gymnasium, Böll saw how the Nazis brought the unemployment caused by the Great Depression under control: "Einige Jahre später waren die Arbeitslosen untergebracht, sie wurden Polizisten, Soldaten, Henker, Rüstungsarbeiter–der Rest zog in die Konzentrationslager" (A few years later the unemployed were taken care of: they were given work as policemen, soldiers, executioners, and armament workers–the rest were sent into concentration camps). His parents permitted secret meetings of the illegal Catholic Youth in their apartment, while his teachers tried to remain neutral. Literature became Böll's main interest in those years: he read Bloy, Bernanos,

Böll with his wife and their sons Raimund, Vincent, and René (Klaus Schröter, Heinrich Böll *[Reinbek: Rowohlt, 1982])*

Dickens, Balzac, and the German dramatists Kleist and Hebbel, who were to become his models. He withdrew into reading to the point of neglecting his studies and having to repeat a grade.

After graduating from the gymnasium in 1937 Böll worked in a bookstore in Bonn, where he catalogued collections of old books for ten marks a month. The job brought him into his first contact with banned books such as the works of Freud and Marx. He soon quit, considered becoming a librarian, began writing, and worked as a tutor but essentially did not know what to do. His mother worried: "Was soll aus dem Jungen bloß werden?" (What is to become of the boy?). Everything in those days, Böll later said in an interview, was overshadowed by the prospect of the war that many sensed was coming. Before he could be admitted to a university, Böll had to perform the compulsory labor service to which all high school graduates were called. In the winter of 1938-1939 he dug irrigation ditches and worked in the forests in Hesse. After completion of his labor service he enrolled at the University of Cologne to study German and classical philology and literature. In early 1939 he was called into military service for an eight-week training course. When the war broke out in September,

he was called to active duty as an infantryman and served in France, Poland, and then again in France, where his right hand was wounded when the train in which he was traveling struck a mine. In 1942 Böll married Annemarie Cech. That same year his parents' apartment was destroyed in an air raid; the family was evacuated to Ahrweiler, where his mother died during another air raid. The family was then evacuated to the Bergisches Land, a rural area east of Cologne. In the summer of 1943 Böll was sent to the Crimea, where he was wounded in the leg. Shortly afterward he was struck in the head by a shell fragment and was sent to a hospital in Odessa. The front, however, was rapidly approaching the city, and Böll was quickly released from the hospital. He was transferred to Jassy in Romania; eight days after arriving there he was seriously wounded in the back. He managed to stay in a hospital in Hungary until August 1944. By this time he was trying to evade the army by faking illness. He deserted in February or March 1945. In the confusion of the final days of the war, he was able to rejoin the army in time to be taken prisoner by the Americans on 9 April 1945, thereby guaranteeing that he would obtain the proper army release papers. He was impris-

Böll at work (Klaus Schröter, Heinrich Böll *[Reinbek: Rowohlt, 1982])*

oned in France and Belgium until the fall.

In November 1945 Böll and his family returned to Cologne. His first son, Christoph, who had been born earlier that year, died that winter. Cologne was almost totally destroyed; only 300 buildings were without damage, and there was no transportation, no water, and no electricity. Böll enrolled at the University of Cologne in 1945, not to study but to acquire a ration card. He worked for a while in the family carpentry shop but soon found temporary employment with the statistical office of the City of Cologne; the family was dependent, however, on his wife's income as a middle-school teacher. During this time Böll wrote industriously and in 1947 published two outstanding short stories, "Die Botschaft" (The Message; translated as "Breaking the News") and "Kumpel mit dem langen Haar" (Coal Miner with the Long Hair; translated as "My Pal with the Long Hair"), in the periodical *Karussell.*

These and other stories were printed in newspapers such as the *Rheinischer Merkur* and in Alfred Andersch's magazine *Der Ruf* and were published in book form in 1950 as *Wanderer,*

kommst du nach Spa . . . (translated as *Traveller, If You Come to Spa* . . . , 1956). These stories can be separated into two groups: war stories and stories dealing with the immediate postwar era. The war stories are told in the first person; the narrator is a typical, usually unnamed German soldier who relates Böll's own experiences and dreams of a better world. The latter are normally the unpolitical, middle-class dreams of good books in a quiet home, a family, music, and art. The most common pattern is the fatal outcome; the hero usually does not survive. The mood of these stories is best characterized by a sentence from "Die Botschaft" where the narrator has to tell a woman that her husband has been killed in the war: "Da wußte ich, daß der Krieg niemals zu Ende sein würde, niemals, solange noch irgendwo eine Wunde blutete, die er geschlagen hat" (Then I knew that the war would never be finished, never as long as somewhere a wound was bleeding that it had caused). One of Böll's concerns in these stories was to refute the notion of heroism in war; most men of his generation realized the absurdity of their existence under war conditions.

The tales about the postwar period typically describe returning veterans who do not benefit from the "Wirtschaftswunder" (economic miracle) after the Currency Reform of 1948; these unfortunate men are looking for their niche in the new society. One man counts people crossing a bridge for a statistical office, but he never counts his girlfriend, in order to maintain her "humanity." Such individual forms of resistance constituted a theme which was to become Böll's central message in the next decades.

The stories did not provide enough money to support his family, which by then included three children: Raimund, born in 1947; René, born in 1948; and Vincent, born in 1950. The publication of his first two novels did not change Böll's financial situation significantly, partly because his publisher, Middelhauve, was mainly a publisher of science books and was not interested in promoting literature. In 1949 Middelhauve had published Böll's first book, *Der Zug war pünktlich* (translated as *The Train Was on Time*, 1956), the structure of which closely resembles that of a classical novella. A soldier, Andreas, boards an army train to join a unit in the Ukraine. He travels through Dresden and Krakow, and finally arrives in Lemberg, where two other soldiers take him to an expensive restaurant and a bordello. There he meets the Polish resistance fighter Olina, for whom he develops a platonic affection. Andreas, Olina, and the two other soldiers decide to flee in a general's car, and all are killed when a mortar fired by partisans strikes the vehicle. The tension and atmosphere of the story are created by Andreas's premonition at the beginning of the trip that he will never see Germany again. He knows he will die near Lemberg because his mind goes blank when he thinks of the next town, Stry. This unrealistic element of "fate" gives Böll's style its special quality. The reader is convinced of Andreas's ability to see the future and thus anticipates his death. The novella takes on biblical dimensions: Andreas is seen as Jesus at the Last Supper and as having a Jesus-Mary Magdalene relationship with Olina. He persuades Olina to give up her political undercover war, which he considers immoral and insignificant. In the same way, Andreas is apolitical in his relationship to Nazi Germany. *Der Zug war pünktlich*, with its religious and mystical treatment of the war, shows Böll's own limited understanding during the period 1945 to 1950 of the social aspects and causes of the war. The formal achievement of the novella, however, and its humanistic, antifascist spirit, drew praise. Gert Kalow calls it a "Geniewurf" (stroke of genius), and Theodore Ziolkowski writes: "Never again has Böll written a story of such close perfection and inevitability. . . . It is an artistic tour de force." The success of *Der Zug* can also be seen in the fact that in 1949 Böll was invited to read at a meeting of the Gruppe 47, the major German literary group of the 1950s and 1960s.

Böll's most famous war novel, *Wo warst du, Adam?* (translated as *Adam, Where Art Thou?*, 1955), was published in 1951. Minor characters in earlier chapters become main characters in later ones; except for this aspect, the chapters are not connected and can be seen as independent short stories. The chapter about the building of the bridge at Berczaby, in fact, has been performed separately as a radio play. The Ilona episode is an early treatment of concentration camps in postwar German fiction: when Ilona sings the Litany of the Saints, the camp commander, Filskeit, comprehends the monstrousness of the death camps. The book's main theme is the absurdity of man's existence; the deaths of Feinhals and his parents at his parents' home caused by German artillery fire show that there is no escape from the senselessness of the war. After publication of *Wo warst du, Adam?*, the Gruppe 47 again invited Böll to one of their meetings. He read his humorous story *Die schwarzen Schafe* (The Black Sheep, 1951), for which he received a prize of 1,000 marks and an invitation to attend subsequent meetings.

A third novel about World War II, written at about the same time as *Der Zug war pünktlich* and *Wo warst du, Adam?*, was published in 1982 by Böll's son René under the title *Das Vermächtnis* (translated as *A Soldier's Legacy*, 1985). It takes place in 1943 in France. The commanding officer, Schelling, is trying to find out why his soldiers' food rations are being illegally withheld. When he discovers that Captain Schnecker is partly responsible, Schnecker kills him. As is often the case in Böll's works, the compassionate die and the heartless survive, eventually to play a leading role in postwar society.

In "Die Waage der Baleks" (The Balek Scales, 1952), one of his most popular stories, Böll introduced the overriding concern in his writing, the criticism of postwar materialism. Here, however, he approaches the subject indirectly, setting the story of capitalist exploitation in a provincial Austrian town around 1900. Although the

geseeen haben musste: sie hatte dunkles Haar und ihr Mantel war
so grün wei Gras, das ~~eeeeeee~~ geschoseen ist in einer warmen
Regennacht, er war so grün, dass mir schien, er müsse nach Gras
riechen; ihr Haar war so dunkel, wie Schieferdächer nach einem
Regen sind und ihr Gesicht so weiss wie die wWeisse von Blättern,
durch die es rötlich schimmert -- ~~eeeeeeeeeeeeeeeee~~,
ich sah nur diesen grellgrünen Mantel, sah dieses Gesicht und ich
hatte plötzlich Angst, jene Angst, die Entdecker empfinden mögen,
wenn sie das neue Land betreten haben, wissend, dass eine andere
Expedition unterwegs ist, die vielleicht die Flagge schon ge-
steckt, schon Besitzergriffen hat und die fürchten müssen, die
Qual der langen Reise, die Strapazen, dieses Spiel auf Leben und
Tod könnte umsonst gewesen sein. -- ~~eeeeeeeeeeeeeeeee~~

~~eeeeee~~

~~eeeeeeeeeeeeeeeeeeeeeeeeeeeeeeeeeeeeee~~ Ich liess die Zigarette fallen und lief
die sechs Schritte, die die Breite der Treppe ausmachten ~~een~~
~~eeeeeeeeeeeeeeeeeeeeeeeeeeeeeeeeeeeeeeee~~
~~eeeee~~. Meine Angst war weg, als ich vor ihr stand, ~~eee~~ Ich sagte
~~eeeeeeeeeeeeeeeeeeeeeeeeeeeeeeeeeeeeeeee~~
~~eeeeeee~~ " Kann ich etwas für Sie tun?"
Sie lächelte, nickte ~~eeee~~ und sagte:"Oh, ja, Sie können mir
sagen, wo die ~~eeeee~~gasse ist".
"~~eeeee~~gasse" sagte ich, und es war mir, wie wenn ich im Traum
meinen Namen rufen hörte, ohne ihn als meinen Namen zu erkennen;
~~eee~~ war nicht bei mir, und es schien mir, als begriffe ich, was es
heisst, nicht bei sich zu sein.

Page from the typescript for Böll's 1955 story "Das Brot der frühen Jahre" (courtesy of Viktor Böll)

Dust jacket by Werner Labbé for Böll's 1958 collection of satires

story involves a failed proletarian revolt, it does not advocate revolution.

With the novel *Und sagte kein einziges Wort* (And Said Not a Single Word, 1953; translated as *Acquainted with the Night*, 1954) Böll switched to the publisher Kiepenheuer and Witsch and achieved an immediate breakthrough; this work, still one of his best-known books, made him financially independent. Poverty causes the protagonist, Fred Bogner, to become ill; it drives him away from the one room he shares with his wife, Käte, and their children. He drifts around the city and meets his wife in cheap hotels on weekends. She is ready to leave him, but in the end they are reconciled. The novel is told in alternating first-person narratives by Fred and Käte. Fred is a drinker, has beaten his children, and is beginning to question the authority of the church. He is not ambitious and feels self-pity for being left out, but he wants no part of the new society. The social criticism is explicit; the author especially criticizes the bigoted landlady, Frau Franke, who refuses to give the family another room, maintaining that she needs it as a reception room for Catholic aid committees. There is corruption in the church: the church offices fail to criticize the pharmaceutical industry for advertising contraceptives because the bishop's cousin is the chairman of the association of druggists. The druggist becomes the personification of modern-day society with its cleanliness, contraception, and mindless consumption. Neither Fred nor Käte accepts these values; Fred sees himself as the only righteous one and defends his own way of life. When he gets back together with Käte, she is expecting another child. The novel demonstrates Böll's meticulously realistic style in its description of the world that surrounds Fred Bogner. Most critics agree that the novel is a preparatory stage to Böll's more political works; many critics deplore its peaceful ending, which, as Günter Wirth points out, is inconsistent with the hostility Fred had shown to society.

Haus ohne Hüter (1954; translated as *The Unguarded House*, 1957) uses film techniques, such as rapid cuts between scenes. The story is told in consecutive chapters by two boys, Martin Bach and Heinrich Brielach; the children's perspective adds an element of alienation, allowing the reader to see the adult world in a different light. Both boys have lost their fathers in the war. Martin's mother, Nella, remains caught in a fantasy world after the death of her husband, the poet Rai. Martin is sent to live in luxury with his grandmother, whose wealth comes from the family's inherited business; Böll rarely depicts a "self-made" man. Heinrich, on the other hand, has to earn a living for his family on the black market while still attending school. His mother works in a bakery and later moves in with the baker, as she had with several other "uncles" before. The Brielachs are stigmatized because of their poverty and are ashamed to move their modest belongings in front of their curious neighbors.

The novel gains momentum at the end when Gäseler is introduced. During the war Gäseler, who had disliked Rai, had sent the poet on a reconnaissance mission, knowing that he was ill equipped for it and probably would not survive. Since the war Gäseler has become a conformist representative of the new capitalist system; he is vain and opportunistic, not unlike the devil of

Nella's fantasies. When Nella asks Gäseler to tell her about the war, he reveals himself as a representative of the times: "Ich denke nicht oft daran. Ich versuche, es zu vergessen, und es gelingt mir.... Man muß den Krieg vergessen" (I don't think about it any more. I try to forget it, and I can.... People have to forget the war). But he has not forgotten the names of his Nazi heroes; only the death and suffering have been erased from his mind. Nella responds to Gäseler: "Ohrfeigen an Leute verteilen, die den Krieg vergessen haben" (A box on the ears for all the people who have forgotten the war) and walks away.

Das Brot der frühen Jahre (1955; translated as *The Bread of Our Early Years*, 1957) covers time from about eight o'clock in the morning to about eight o'clock in the evening of a single day in the narrator's life in 1955. Walter Fendrich goes to the train station to meet Hedwig Müller, the daughter of a friend of his father, who is coming to the city to study at the university. Walter has previously found her a room and is to take her there and go back to work. But when he sees Hedwig, his life changes: "Ich sah nur diesen grellgrünen Mantel, sah dieses Gesicht, und ich hatte plötzlich Angst, jene Angst, die Entdecker empfinden, wenn sie das neue Land betreten haben.... Dieses Gesicht ging tief in mich hinein ... es war, als würde ich durchbohrt ohne zu bluten" (I saw only her dazzling green coat, her face, and I was suddenly filled with that fear which explorers have when they enter upon a new land.... Her face went deep into me ... it was as if I had been pierced without bleeding). From this moment on, Walter is a new person. He does not return to his old job, withdraws all his savings from the bank, breaks his engagement to his boss's daughter, and decides to live with Hedwig without the sacrament of the church.

In one of Böll's most beautiful short stories, "Und so ward Abend und Morgen" (And It Became Night and Day, 1955), the relationship between man and woman is symbolized as a cry of a man for company in his lonely life. His wife has stopped talking to him, and on a Christmas evening he makes her say "no" twice and "yes" once—which saves his life.

Böll's treatment of the relationship between the sexes continues in the longer narrative *Im Tal der donnernden Hufe* (In the Valley of the Thundering Hooves, 1957), about the sexual problems of two Catholic boys, Paul and Griff. An atheist girl, Mirzova, helps Paul overcome his anxiety by ex-

posing her breasts; but as a result she has to leave town for a few years to avoid being labeled a prostitute by the narrow-minded townspeople.

In the mid 1950s the Federal Republic of Germany under Chancellor Konrad Adenauer embarked on a rearmament campaign which Böll opposed. Until that time he had been a supporter of Adenauer's Christian Democratic Union (CDU). In response to these developments, Böll "escaped" to Ireland for a few weeks in the summer of 1955. Later, when asked whether Ireland was his second home, he said: "Ich weiß, daß es keine zweite Heimat gibt, entweder man emigriert oder behält seine Nationalität–ich bin Deutscher, schreibe deutsch" (I know there is no such thing as a second homeland; either you emigrate, or you keep your nationality–I am a German, I write in German). Böll was a "Kölner" (a person from Cologne); his idea of "home" was centered in Cologne. He could not represent Prussia or the eastern part of Germany.

In 1956 Böll made a second trip to Ireland. His *Irisches Tagebuch* (1957; translated as *Irish Journal*, 1967) resulting from those trips is not a conventional travelogue; rather, Böll uses travel impressions to make moral and historical points about Ireland and Germany. He continues his criticism of German society in this book in a more subtle form.

Another reason for Böll's escape to Ireland was the attacks on some satirical short stories he published in the 1950s, especially *Nicht nur zur Weihnachtszeit* (Not Only at Christmastime, 1952). The mother in a middle-class family has saved Christmas decorations from the prosperous times before the war and protests whenever anybody tries to take the Christmas tree down; so the family celebrates Christmas every day of the year. When Böll was attacked by the church he responded that he had not intended to denounce Christmas but rather the commercialization of it. In "Der Wegwerfer" (The Disposer, 1951) he criticizes the same commercialism by portraying a mailroom clerk whose job is to throw away junk mail, thereby reducing the work load of the others in the office. The satirical story "Doktor Murkes gesammeltes Schweigen" (Dr. Murke's Collected Silences, 1955) is considered by Cesare Cases one of the finest works of European literature since World War II, and Walter Jens claims that Böll's work culminates in this story. The "philosopher" Bur-Malottke wants to change the word *God* in a tape of one of his notorious radio

Böll and his wife in Red Square, Moscow (Klaus Schröter, Heinrich Böll *[Reinbek: Rowohlt, 1982])*

talks to the phrase "jenes höhere Wesen, das wir verehren" (the higher being whom we revere). The word *God* is cut out of the tape and edited into another program, where an atheist's questions are now answered by Bur-Malottke's "God." What is left is cut-out "silence," and the journalist Murke takes the pieces home in a box. Murke shows the absurdity of the procedure when he lets Bur-Malottke say the phrase "the higher being whom we revere" twenty-seven times; he hates Bur-Malottke because of the latter's opportunism. Böll was criticizing the intellectual climate that left religion out of the economic and political restoration of the 1950s: God got "cut out" of social considerations.

Billard um halb zehn, published in 1959, shows the rise of a middle-class family, the Fähmels, through whose perspective the novel presents fifty years of German history from 1907 to 1958. The novel, however, actually covers only a few hours, from about ten o'clock in the morning to about eight o'clock in the evening on 6 September 1958, the eightieth birthday of Heinrich Fähmel, the day his wife shoots at a politician and symbolically destroys corruption. Böll symbolically contrasts those who have partaken of "das

Sakrament des Büffels" (the sacrament of the buffalo)–the militarists, Nazis, and the power-hungry–to those who have tasted of "das Sakrament des Lamms" (the sacrament of the lamb)–the persecuted, emigrés, and people sensitive to suffering. Böll himself criticized this symbolism later as being too simplistic to portray the horrors and intricacies of German history. The St. Anton Abbey ties the three generations of Fähmels together: the grandfather built it, the son blew it up, and the grandson does not know whether he wants to reconstruct or demolish it. Some critics claimed that the *nouveau roman* and the psychological novel excluded each other and that Böll failed by trying to combine the two. Böll worked out the novel in a meticulous, almost mathematical, way, using a colored chart divided into three levels: the present, the reflective or memory level, and the symbolic. But the resulting novel is too confusing. Johanna Fähmel's attempt to shoot a high government official with a Nazi past fails to enhance the novel's tension. Walter Jens summarized the views of many critics when he observed that the novel form was too long for Böll, and that he should have stayed with the short story.

Page from the manuscript for Böll's 1962 story "Als der Krieg ausbrach" (Hermann Stresau, Heinrich Böll *[Berlin: Colloquium, 1964])*

In 1961, in one of his fiercest essays, "Hast Du was, dann bist Du was" (You Are What You Have), Böll attacked Cologne's Cardinal Frings for his pastoral letter linking the Bonn government's idea of making stocks available to low-income people to the principles of the Christian church: "Die Heiligsprechung des Habenichts von Assisi war wohl ein Irrtum" (The canonization of the have-not Francis of Assisi probably was a mistake). Böll also attacked Chancellor Adenauer for too eagerly forgetting Germany's Nazi past and for his socioeconomic policies as outlined in the statement: "Der Erwerb mäßigen Besitzes für alle ehrlich Schaffenden ist zu fördern [und] ist eine wesentliche Sicherung des demokratischen Staates" (The accumulation of a moderate amount of property by all honest workers is to be furthered [and] is an essential guarantee of the democratic state). Böll asked sarcastically: "Was machen wir da bloß mit dem unmäßigen Besitz des unehrlich Schaffenden?" (What are we to do about [the] immoderate property of the dishonest worker [that is, the capitalist]?). In those years Böll also criticized the change by the Social Democrats to a more capitalist ideology, as reflected in the 1959 Godesberg Program of the Social Democratic Party (SPD). An advocate of socialism and even Marxism, Böll wanted two basic sociopolitical concepts to be expressed in the German party system; he was opposed to a system like that of the United States, where both parties advocate capitalism. In his writings Böll tried to change the course of the SPD. In the early 1960s Böll, together with the artist HAP Grieshaber and others, founded the Christian socialist periodical *Labyrinth*. Here he published his first play, *Ein Schluck Erde* (A Piece of Earth, 1962), about an old man who would like to combine Christianity and communism. In 1960 Böll completed the essay "Karl Marx," which praises the philosopher as a secular saint, and "Assisi," a study of St. Francis. In a 1967 interview with the critic Marcel Reich-Ranicki, Böll confessed his Communist sympathies and wished communism as many years of power as capitalism had already had. He said that if he had not grown up in fascist Germany he would have certainly been a Communist by 1936. Böll also regretted that more Germans had not had the opportunity to become Communists in the 1930s, thereby purifying the political atmosphere.

The *Brief an einen jungen Katholiken* (Letter to a Young Catholic, 1961) reveals that Böll's development toward socialism was related to his disenchantment with the Catholic church. He expresses his disapproval of what he considered the merger of church and government in the Federal Republic at that time. The *Brief an einen jungen Katholiken* started a process that ended with Böll officially leaving the church in 1977 (in Germany this means that he simply stopped paying "church taxes").

In 1962 Böll made his first official trip to the Soviet Union in connection with the new German-Soviet Cultural Exchange Program. At the time he was working on a new book, *Ansichten eines Clowns* (1963; translated as *The Clown*, 1965), one of his most controversial novels. Böll's biographer Klaus Schröter has said that after finishing this book he lost interest in reading Böll for a long time. The novel takes place on one evening in the Bonn apartment of twenty-seven-year-old Hans Schnier, who has left the home of his wealthy parents to earn his living as a clown. Hans is feeling sorry for himself because his girlfriend, Marie, has left him to marry a "Berufskatholik" (professional Catholic). Through phone calls to relatives and friends, Hans learns that Marie is on her honeymoon which will include a visit to the pope. He decides to await her return by singing religious songs at the railroad station while wearing his clown costume. Hans advocates a form of marriage in which the church plays no role and only the mutual consent of the partners matters. With his anarchistic tendencies, it is not surprising that Hans has become a professional clown, entitled, like a medieval court jester, to criticize society.

The novel shows Hans's isolation: he can live only with Marie, and she has left him. Because of his artistic nature, Hans views the living and the dead differently than other people do. His sister Henriette, who died in the war, is alive in his mind, while his mother is dead for him because she adjusts eagerly to the new social conditions and wants to forget. J. D. Salinger's *The Catcher in the Rye* (1951), which Böll and his wife had just translated into German, influenced Böll's writing of the novel; Holden Caulfield's character and his relationship with his sister are clearly reflected in Böll's depiction of Hans.

Ansichten eines Clowns divided the critics into two groups: those who saw it as a lapse in Böll's progress as a writer and those who considered it his best and most straightforward book to that time. Manfred Durzak argued that the novel was an aesthetic dead end for Böll, who had reached his satirical limits. Hans-Joachim Bernhard was of the opinion that the aesthetic balance of the book was disrupted by Böll's subjectivity. But Frank Trommler saw in *Ansichten eines Clowns* a new phase in post-World War II German literary history, characterized by blunt political reasoning instead of formal artistic expression.

The author's detachment from German political life is noticeable in the short novel *Entfernung von der Truppe* (Absent without Leave, 1964). The narrator states that his life as a human being began with his "desertion," his rejection of society. Despite its bleak plot, the story is told in a loose, humorous manner, reminiscent of Laurence Sterne. Böll's effort to experiment with a different style is not completely successful.

In *Frankfurter Vorlesungen* (Frankfurt Lectures, 1966), given at the University of Frankfurt after a long stay in Dugort, Ireland, where he had bought a home, Böll says that love for one's "Heimat" (homeland), memory, and language constitute the human being. Böll criticizes the German rejection of regionalism in the postwar period, pointing out that many important works of art have been created in cities such as Dublin or Prague. Böll's literary position is "engaged": the poet is to analyze the "Abfall der Gesellschaft" (garbage of society) and take the place of a political opposition that no longer exists in West Germany. The Grand Coalition of the CDU and the SPD from 1966 to 1969 confirmed Böll's political fears.

Ende einer Dienstfahrt (1966; translated as *End of a Mission*, 1967), in its depiction of the military as a senseless machine, is reminiscent of *Wo warst du, Adam?* In classical novella form, the book describes the trial of the Gruhls, a father and son who burn the son's army jeep as an act of protest. The case is an embarrassment to the authorities, who play it down by keeping the press out and by giving the case to a lenient judge. The Gruhls are finally sentenced to only six weeks imprisonment. Böll wanted to show that the ruling class understands the danger of the Gruhls' political action; he also wanted to show the goodness of the village people, all of whom support the Gruhls. The critic Jochen Vogt asserted that this support by the villagers reveals too idealized a sense of "Heimat." The novel, he said, excludes the reader who comes from a different background.

In August 1968 Böll happened to be in Czechoslovakia during the Soviet invasion. This event provided an opportunity for him to protest Soviet policies, which increased his political credi-

bility with the right. He campaigned for Willy Brandt and the Social Democrats (SPD) in the national elections of 1969, seeing the victory of the SPD as a unique opportunity to overcome what he considered the authoritarian government Adenauer's CDU had perpetuated. He also welcomed the defeat of the CDU because it had chosen a former Nazi, Kurt Georg Kiesinger, as its candidate for chancellor. Brandt, Böll wrote, was not a Herr (ruler); for the first time a real human being sat in the Chancellery.

In "Epilog zu Stifters *Nachsommer*" (Epilogue to Stifter's *Indian Summer*, 1970; published in *Erzählungen, 1950-1970*, 1972) Böll imitates the language and plots of the nineteenth-century novelist Adalbert Stifter, whose work he admired. Böll, however, destroys the nineteenth-century middle-class world and shows how that society was based on lies.

In 1971 Böll was elected the first German president of the International P.E.N. Club and visited the New York P.E.N. offices. At the time of Böll's election Hans Werner Richter, the founder of the Gruppe 47, said: "Böll can do things that we others cannot even dream of."

When the Swedish Academy awarded Böll the Nobel Prize for Literature in 1972, it especially mentioned *Gruppenbild mit Dame* (1971; translated as *Group Portrait with Lady*, 1973). The publishers called the book Böll's "most comprehensive, encompassing work," a "summation of his previous life and work." The heroine, Leni Pfeiffer, joins other tenants in preventing her relatives from tearing down the Cologne apartment house where she lives. Leni is another of Böll's attempts to combine realism with Christian mythology; she is a "pure" soul, without any interest in the consumer and achievement-oriented society. She is helpful, sensual, a "subversive madonna." She and her son Lev introduce Böll's principle of "Leistungsverweigerung" (rejection of the work ethic), a concept attacking the dehumanization of life under capitalism. Their belief in Leistungsverweigerung makes Leni and Lev the center of a counterculture in the city.

The novel offers another dimension, introduced by an inquiring author who collects information about Leni from the people around her and discovers that she was the lover of a Russian prisoner of war during World War II; the Russian, Boris, is Lev's father. Böll contrasts the purity of the couple with the petty reactions of Leni's friends to her affair and the birth of her illegitimate son. Böll said later that he tried to portray

Böll receiving the Nobel Prize for Literature from King Carl Gustaf of Sweden in December 1972 (Klaus Schröter, Heinrich Böll *[Reinbek: Rowohlt, 1982])*

Leni as a woman "die die ganze Last dieser Geschichte . . . auf sich genommen hat" (who carried the whole burden of German history).

According to Karl Korn, the novel reveals the "archaeology of Cologne's society," especially of the lower classes. Rainer Nägele said *Gruppenbild mit Dame* was "a much more rambling novel than anything Böll had written previously." Theodore Ziolkowski called it a "secular beatification." The novel struck a responsive chord in Germany during the years of student protests. The reception of *Gruppenbild mit Dame* in the United States, however, is typical of Böll's lack of success there. The *Newsweek* reviewer wrote that he would rather read Günter Grass but read Böll out of "a guilty feeling"; *Time* magazine implied that Böll received the Nobel Prize more for his "idealistic tendency" than for his literary qualities. Böll's failure in the United States is puzzling; he is the most popular German author in England, France, Sweden, and the Soviet Union.

After receiving the Nobel Prize, Böll was an important public figure in Germany, praised by the left as the "conscience of his age" and attacked from the right as a writer without any real talent. Those opposed to Böll claimed that the best writers never received the Nobel Prize. Böll responded that he could not afford not to accept the prize, since Germany had not had many people whom the world could look up to.

In 1972 Böll published an article in the magazine *Der Spiegel* defending the terrorist Baader-Meinhof gang, members of which were then on trial. The tabloid *Bild-Zeitung* had already concluded that the group was guilty; Böll's defense of the gang was based on the belief that everybody is entitled to due process. Böll pointed out that former Nazis were being released from jail but predicted that the Baader-Meinhofs would find no mercy. In reaction to this article, the papers controlled by the West German press czar Axel Springer published a letter by Prime Minister Filbinger of the State of Baden-Württemberg asking for Böll's resignation as International P.E.N. president. On 1 June Böll's house was searched by the police, and on 7 June a CDU member of the West German parliament declared people like Böll to be more dangerous than the Baader-Meinhofs. Böll's literary response to these events was *Die verlorene Ehre der Katharina*

Böll in 1973 (Ullstein–Josef A. Slominski)

Blum (1974; translated as *The Lost Honor of Katharina Blum*, 1975), which first appeared in July 1974 in *Der Spiegel;* it was the first work of fiction ever published by the periodical. The first edition of the book, published in August, sold 100,000 copies in a few weeks and 200,000 by the end of the year; the paperback edition sold more than 1 million copies. The novel has been translated into eighteen languages.

Katharina, a housekeeper who has accumulated some wealth through her frugality, loses her reputation through the practices of the *Zeitung.* The *Zeitung* finds out that Katharina fell in love with an army deserter and bank robber, kept him in her apartment overnight, and let him escape the following morning. Without any justification, the *Zeitung* calls him a "terrorist" and Katharina his accomplice. Details about her love life are fabricated and published. Katharina is so enraged that she decides to shoot Tötges, the journalist who is responsible for the stories. Other citizens are equally appalled by the *Zeitung* and ready for revenge against the slander, which Böll describes as "public violence."

As P.E.N. president, Böll played host to Aleksandr Solzhenitsyn after he was exiled from

the Soviet Union in 1974, and later to Wolf Biermann and Lev Kopelev, who were exiled from East Germany and the Soviet Union, respectively. Despite his support for Soviet dissidents, Böll continued to be one of the most popular German writers in the Soviet Union.

In 1977, when the German industrialist Hanns-Martin Schleyer was kidnapped and murdered by terrorists and several terrorists committed suicide in the Stammheim prison, Böll was again accused by conservatives of promoting terrorism. They criticized his 1975 satire *Berichte zur Gesinnungslage der Nation* (Reports on the Attitudinal State of the Nation), which attacks West German bureaucracy because of its surveillance of so-called radicals. They also found fault with his story "Du fährst zu oft nach Heidelberg" (You Go to Heidelberg Too Often, 1977), an indictment of the Berufsverbote (the law that keeps suspected Communists out of government jobs).

In the novel *Fürsorgliche Belagerung* (1979; translated as *The Safety Net,* 1981) the house of the newspaper editor Fritz Tolm is constantly protected by police against a possible terrorist attack. Tolm, a sensitive man, is ready to withdraw into private life and give up his privileged but exposed public position. The same events are recounted from the viewpoints of Tolm, other family members, the guards, and the terrorists, allowing the reader to see the protection system from all sides. Family life is destroyed by the heavy security; there is no privacy for the protected. Finally, after the terrorists burn down the house, the Tolms withdraw into a pastoral idyll in the country.

Böll continued to be involved in political issues, participating in the 1981 Bonn peace demonstration. In 1983 he was made an honorary citizen of the city of Cologne. The local CDU was not opposed to honoring Böll the "great writer" but was opposed to honoring Böll the social critic. In his acceptance speech Böll said it was a mistake to separate the two aspects, asserting that his essays, reviews, and lectures were also literature and had been written with the same kind of moral consciousness as his novels and short stories. Böll called his being regarded as the moral conscience of Germany a sign of the corruption of German society: parliament and press, not a single writer, should constitute the public conscience.

Böll's health had long been poor; diabetes and a liver disorder necessitated several hospital stays, and his smoking aggravated his circulatory

Böll with Aleksandr Solzhenitsyn in 1974 (photograph by Erich Schaake, Cologne)

problems. On 16 July 1985 he died in his house in Langenbroich/Eifel, having been released from the hospital two days before. His last novel, a book about Bonn and its women titled *Frauen vor Flußlandschaft* (Women with River Landscape), was published in August 1985 in an edition of 100,000 copies. Although the novel was not intended as a roman à clef, it is easy to recognize certain politicians on the Bonn scene.

Heinrich Böll's contribution to postwar German literature was considerable. At a time when Germany was discredited and most Germans, including most writers, were ready to withdraw into introspection, he set an example of social commitment. Although he was a regional writer of the lower Rhineland, his home, Cologne, was the spiritual center of West German political power during the Adenauer years. His writing was at its best when he anticipated a political crisis; it became superior when he was drawn into the turmoil of politics. His ability to maintain his roots, his religion, and his idealism throughout his political involvement made him an exemplary figure among postwar West German writers.

Interviews:

Horst Bienek, *Werkstattgespräche mit Schriftstellern* (Munich: Deutscher Taschenbuch Verlag, 1965), pp. 168-184;

"Interview von Marcel Reich-Ranicki," in Heinrich Böll, *Aufsätze, Kritiken, Reden* (Cologne: Kiepenheuer & Witsch, 1967), pp. 502-510;

Im Gespräch: Heinrich Böll mit Heinz Ludwig Arnold (Munich: Boorberg, 1971);

"Ich tendiere nur zu dem scheinbar Unpolitischen: Gespräche mit Heinrich Böll," in Manfred Durzak, *Gespräche über den Roman* (Frankfurt: Suhrkamp, 1976), pp. 128-153.

Bibliographies:

Ferdinand Melius, *Der Schriftsteller Heinrich Böll: Ein biographisch-bibliographischer Abriß* (Cologne: Kiepenheuer & Witsch, 1959);

Werner Lengning, ed., *Der Schriftsteller Heinrich Böll: Ein biographisch-bibliographischer Abriß*, third edition (Munich: Deutscher Taschenbuch Verlag, 1972);

Werner Martin, *Heinrich Böll: Eine Bibliographie seiner Werke* (Hildesheim: Olms, 1975).

Biographies:

Christine Gabriele Hoffmann, *Heinrich Böll* (Hamburg: Dressler, 1977);

Christian Linder, *Heinrich Böll* (Reinbek: Rowohlt, 1978);

Alfred Böll, *Bilder einer deutschen Familie: Die Bölls* (Bergisch-Gladbach: Lübbe, 1981);

Klaus Schröter, *Heinrich Böll: In Selbstzeugnissen und Bilddokumenten* (Reinbek: Rowohlt, 1982).

References:

Heinz Ludwig Arnold, ed., *Heinrich Böll* (Munich: Edition text + kritik, 1982);

Albrecht Beckel, *Mensch, Gesellschaft, Kirche bei Heinrich Böll* (Osnabrück: Fromm, 1966);

Hans-Joachim Bernhard, *Die Romane Heinrich Bölls: Gesellschaftskritik und Gemeinschaftsutopie* (Berlin: Rütten & Loening, 1970);

Hanno Beth, ed., *Eine Einführung in das Gesamtwerk in Einzelinterpretationen* (Kronberg: Scriptor, 1975);

Viktor Böll and Yvonne Jürgensen, *Heinrich Böll als Filmautor: Rezensionsmaterial aus dem Literaturarchiv der Stadtbücherei Köln* (Cologne: City of Cologne, 1982);

Robert A. Burns, *The Theme of Non-Conformism in the Works of Heinrich Böll* (Coventry: University of Warwick, 1973);

Robert C. Conard, *Heinrich Böll* (Boston: Hall, 1981);

Manfred Durzak, *Der deutsche Roman der Gegenwart* (Stuttgart: Kohlhammer, 1971), pp. 19-107;

Hermann Friedmann and Otto Mann, eds., *Heinrich Böll als christlicher Dichter der Gegenwart* (Heidelberg: Rothe, 1955);

Frank Grützbach, ed., *Freies Geleit für Ulrike Meinhof: Ein Artikel und seine Folgen* (Cologne: Kiepenheuer & Witsch, 1972);

Heinrich Herlyn, *Heinrich Böll und Herbert Marcuse: Literatur als Utopie* (Lambertheim: Kübler, 1979);

Walter Jens, *Deutsche Literatur der Gegenwart: Themen, Stile, Tendenzen* (Munich: Piper, 1962);

Manfred Jurgensen, ed., *Böll: Untersuchungen zum Werk* (Bern: Francke, 1975);

Karl Korn, "Heinrich Bölls Beschreibung einer Epoche," *Frankfurter Allgemeine Zeitung*, 28 July 1971;

Enid MacPherson, *A Student's Guide to Böll* (London: Heinemann, 1972);

Materialien zur Interpretation von Heinrich Bölls "Fürsorgliche Belagerung" (Cologne: Kiepenheuer & Witsch, 1982);

Renate Matthaei, ed., *Die subversive Madonna: Ein Schlüssel zum Werk Heinrich Bölls* (Cologne: Kiepenheuer & Witsch, 1975);

Rainer Nägele, *Heinrich Böll: Einführung in das Werk und in die Forschung* (Frankfurt am Main: Athenäum-Fischer, 1976);

Marcel Reich-Ranicki, *In Sachen Böll: Ansichten und Einsichten* (Munich: Deutscher Taschenbuch Verlag, 1971);

James Henderson Reid, *Heinrich Böll: Withdrawal and Re-Emergence* (London: Wolff, 1973);

Klaus Schröter, *Heinrich Böll: In Selbstzeugnissen und Bilddokumenten* (Reinbek: Rowohlt, 1982);

Wilhelm J. Schwarz, *Der Erzähler Heinrich Böll* (Bern: Francke, 1973);

Schwarz, *Heinrich Böll: Teller of Tales,* translated by Alexander Henderson and Elizabeth Henderson (New York: Ungar, 1968);

Jochen Vogt, *Heinrich Böll* (Munich: Beck/edition text + kritik, 1978);

Günter Wirth, *Heinrich Böll: Essayistische Studie über religiöse und gesellschaftliche Motive im Prosawerk des Dichters* (Berlin: Union, 1967).

Papers:

The holdings of the former Böll-Archiv of Kiepenheuer and Witsch and those of the Boston University Library were transferred to the Archives of the City of Cologne on 29 April 1983, when Böll was awarded the honorary citizenship of the City of Cologne; they are administered by a nephew of Böll, Viktor Böll (Literaturarchiv der Stadtbücherei: Köln, Zentralbibliothek, Josef-Hanbrich-Hof, 5000 Köln 1). The former Kiepenheuer and Witsch collection contains all of Böll's printed texts; his manuscripts and letters are in private possession. The former Boston University Library collection contains manuscripts, typescripts, notes, correction sheets, copies of Böll's works, reviews, and articles about Böll; it is described by Robert C. Conard in the *University of Dayton Review*, 10 (Fall 1973): 11-14.

Wolfgang Borchert

(20 May 1921-20 November 1947)

Wulf Koepke

Texas A&M University

BOOKS: *Laterne, Nacht und Sterne: Gedichte um Hamburg* (Hamburg: Hamburgische Bücherei, 1946);

Die Hundeblume: Erzählungen aus unseren Tagen (Hamburg: Hamburgische Bücherei, 1947);

Draußen vor der Tür: Ein Stück, das kein Theater spielen und kein Publikum sehen will (Hamburg & Stuttgart: Rowohlt, 1947);

An diesem Dienstag: Neunzehn Geschichten (Hamburg & Stuttgart: Rowohlt, 1947);

Hundeblumen-Geschichten, edited by Martin F. Cordes (Horgen: Holunderpresse, 1948);

Im Mai, im Mai schrie der Kuckuck (Leipzig: Akademie für Grafik und Buchkunst, 1948);

Das Gesamtwerk, edited with a biographical afterword by Bernhard Meyer-Marwitz (Hamburg & Stuttgart: Rowohlt, 1949); translated by David Porter as *The Man Outside: Prose Works*, introduction by Stephen Spender (Norfolk, Conn.: New Directions, 1952; London: Calder & Boyars, 1966);

Draußen vor der Tür und ausgewählte Erzählungen, afterword by Heinrich Böll (Hamburg: Rowohlt, 1956);

Schischyphusch oder Der Kellner meines Onkels (Stuttgart: Druckspiegel-Verlag, 1959);

Die traurigen Geranien und andere Geschichten aus dem Nachlaß, edited by Peter Rühmkorf (Reinbek bei Hamburg: Rowohlt, 1962); translated by Keith Hamnet as *The Sad Geraniums and Other Stories* (New York: Ecco Press, 1973; London: Calder & Boyars, 1973);

Selected Short Stories, edited by A. W. Hornsey (Oxford: Pergamon Press/New York: Macmillan, 1964);

Selected Readings, edited by Anna Otten (New York: Holt, Rinehart & Winston, 1973).

Wolfgang Borchert (Ullstein)

Wolfgang Borchert rose to instant fame when the Nordwestdeutscher Rundfunk broadcast his radio play *Draußen vor der Tür* (Outside the Door; translated as "The Man Outside," 1952) on 13 February 1947. Suddenly there seemed to be a literary spokesman for the genera- tion of returning soldiers who were suffering from the aftermath of World War II and the rejection of "normal" society. Borchert was identified with Trümmerliteratur, postwar literature describing life in the ruins. He was quite ill at the time and died on 20 November of the same year, one day before the first stage performance of his play in Hamburg.

The legend of his dramatic life and early death added to his popularity, but literary criticism was mostly hostile. Hans Egon Holthusen called the play "saurer Kitsch" (sour kitsch). A new image of Borchert began to emerge in 1962 when Peter Rühmkorf published *Die traurigen Geranien und andere Geschichten aus dem Nachlaß* (translated as *The Sad Geraniums and Other Stories*, 1973), a collection of previously unknown stories which could not be classified as Trümmerliteratur. Since then, more sober scholarship has helped to enhance Borchert's stature as a writer.

Borchert was deeply attached to Hamburg, where he was born in 1921 and lived all his life except for enforced absences during the war. The windy and rainy port city, much of which was left in ruins by air raids in 1943, provides the atmosphere for most of Borchert's works. Borchert's father, Fritz Borchert, was a schoolteacher who had been involved in modernist literary movements after World War I; his mother, Hertha Salchow Borchert, was a popular Low German writer in the 1930s. Borchert's parents were not Nazi enthusiasts; his mother, who wrote radio programs, was denounced by a competitor as an anti-Nazi. Borchert joined the youth movement in 1932, but left when it was taken over by the Hitler Youth. He entered the gymnasium in 1932. He was a happy but unruly and individualistic boy; his grades grew progressively worse, and he left school at the end of 1938, in the middle of the academic year. His parents disapproved of his wish to become an actor, so he worked as an apprentice at the bookstore of Heinrich Boysen. He hated the routine work, but it gave him the chance to read the forbidden expressionist poetry of Benn, Heym, and Trakl. His hero was Rainer Maria Rilke, and he began calling himself Wolff Maria Borchert. He wrote several plays and poems during his two years at the bookstore; except for some poems published by newspapers, this huge output of juvenalia remained unpublished.

Borchert persisted in his wish to be an actor. He took lessons secretly and passed the actor's examination at the end of 1940. He left the bookstore and joined a traveling acting company in Lüneburg, playing light fare in the small towns of eastern Lower Saxony until he was drafted into the army in June 1941. In November, during the first crisis for the Germans at the eastern front, Borchert was sent to Russia. Early in 1942 he was wounded in the left hand and also came down with jaundice and was sent back to Germany. A superior reported that his wound might have been self-inflicted, and Borchert was arrested in May 1942. After some months in the Nuremberg prison, he was brought before a military court. Although he was acquitted, with the help of a courageous lawyer, of the charge of

Borchert's father, Fritz Borchert (Peter Rühmkorf, Wolfgang Borchert *[Reinbek: Rowohlt, 1970])*

wounding himself, the trial brought to light Gestapo reports of utterances Borchert had made against the Nazi regime and the war; the Gestapo had been watching him since 1940. He was sentenced to six weeks imprisonment and Frontbewährung (probation in a special unit at the front). Back in Russia in December 1942, he suffered frostbitten feet, new attacks of jaundice, and possibly spotted fever. After a long convalescence, Borchert was given a leave for Hamburg, where he appeared in September 1943 in cabaret programs.

In November 1943 Borchert was about to be transferred because of illness to duty at a "front theater." During his farewell party he imitated Propaganda Minister Joseph Goebbels–a popular joke in the German army–and was denounced by some of the participants. He was sent to Moabit prison in Berlin, where he had to wait nine months for his trial. Sentenced to nine months in prison, he was again transferred to a special army unit in September 1944. In the spring of 1945 the surviving members of the unit were captured near Frankfurt and sent in trucks

Borchert, age four, with his mother, Hertha Salchow Borchert (Peter Rühmkorf, Wolfgang Borchert *[Reinbek: Rowohlt, 1970])*

Sterne (Streetlight, Night and Stars, 1946), alluding to the well-known "lantern" song sung by children in the fall. These lighthearted poems about Hamburg and its people did not attract much attention. With the prose of his first short story, "Die Hundeblume" (The Dandelion), written in January 1946, Borchert found his own unmistakable voice. Two small volumes of stories appeared in 1947, *Die Hundeblume* and *An diesem Dienstag* (This Tuesday). Other stories written at this time were published after his death in *Das Gesamtwerk* (The Collected Works, 1949) and in Rühmkorf's *Die traurigen Geranien und andere Geschichten aus dem Nachlaß.* These stories may be classified as follows: autobiographical tales of boyhood, stories of outsiders in society, prison stories, war stories (all taking place in Russia during the winter), and stories of postwar life in the ruins of Hamburg. The boyhood stories are recollections of funny incidents. Typical of the "outsider stories" is "Die traurigen Geranien," in which a man shrinks from a woman because of her ugliness, and she recognizes the inevitability of her loneliness. Borchert is best known for the prison stories. "Die Hundeblume" describes the boost in morale enjoyed by a prisoner in solitary confinement when he picks the little yellow weed and keeps it secret from his guards. "Unser kleiner Mozart" (Our Little Mozart) tells of the shock experienced by a group of prisoners when one of their cell mates is taken away for execution. In "Maria, alles Maria" (Mary, All Is Mary) a Polish prisoner attributes the miraculous stay of his execution to the little picture of the Virgin Mary which he carries around with him.

Most of these stories are only a few pages long, with little description or characterization. They tell of seemingly insignificant incidents which reveal truths about the inhumane system of imprisonment and about human nature. Similarly, the war stories avoid heroics and focus on little episodes. "Jesus macht nicht mehr mit" (Jesus Does Not Cooperate Anymore) takes place on a gravedigging detail. "Jesus" was a common nickname for a person too gentle to be a good soldier. This "Jesus" is supposed to lie down in the graves to see if they are long and deep enough–the easiest job on the detail in the Russian winter. Suddenly, he refuses to continue and just walks away. His superior reluctantly says that he will have to report this disobedience. Here is another Jesus suffering for humankind. But is not this suffering and silent rebellion meaningless? Many of Borchert's stories raise questions which

to French prison camps. Borchert escaped from his truck and walked 600 kilometers to Hamburg, sick though he was. He arrived home on 10 May.

Borchert wanted to resume his theater career but was too ill to do so. By the end of 1945 he rarely left his bed. Two hospital stays did not improve his condition. Thus far, his writing had yielded little of real value, mostly poems which he collected in a small volume, *Laterne, Nacht und*

Borchert as a soldier in 1943 (Peter Rühmkorf, Wolfgang Borchert *[Reinbek: Rowohlt, 1970])*

they do not answer. In "An diesem Dienstag" scenes from the front and from a soldier's hometown in Germany on a certain day are contrasted. Their alternation provides graphic pictures of life and death, of illusion and bitter truth.

The largest group of tales, and the group containing the most complex narrative structures, is the postwar stories. One of the longer of these is "Billbrook." Bill Brook, a Canadian soldier, finds out that Hamburg has a district called Billbrook. Out of curiosity he goes there, only to find that it has been destroyed by the bombs. And yet there are people living in these ruins where no life seems possible. Life and death, survival in a landscape of death, is the theme of this story. In one of Borchert's last stories, "Die lange lange Straße lang" (Along the Long Long Street), former lieutenant Fischer walks to the streetcar station. He is starving and has fainted twice. In a stream of consciousness, the street passes by with its images, pieces of overheard conversation and graffiti. All human life is condensed into these fleeting impressions–death and suffering, the insensitivity of most people, and fear that the future will be another march for "progress" which will destroy humanity. Finally, Fischer reaches the yellow streetcar and buys a ticket. But the con-

ductor does not say where they are going, and the passengers do not know whether the conductor, who may be God, is good or evil.

Borchert's protagonists are young men without a home, contemplating suicide but looking for a new meaning in life. They come back from the war and find ruins. Their families may be dead, their wives may have deserted them. At the same time, guilt burdens them. They have the deaths of comrades on their consciences, and these dead men come back in their nightmares and ask: why did we have to die? They never receive an answer. Borchert does not analyze the political situation or discuss the collective guilt of the Germans or the Nazi problem. He just describes the mood of the survivors of 1945: those who are burdened by guilt and those who leave everything behind and have clear consciences, no matter what they did. All of these elements come together in Borchert's play.

Borchert wrote *Draußen vor der Tür* in eight days in January 1947. Convinced that it was, as he subtitled it, *Ein Stück, das kein Theater spielen und kein Publikum sehen will* (A Play That No Theater Wants to Perform and No Audience Wants to See), he had little hope of success. But when it was transmitted on the radio in February,

Borchert with his mother in 1947 (Rosemarie Clausen, Hamburg)

Borchert's generation recognized itself in his protagonist, Beckmann. Borchert's play is melodramatic; it overstates its case. Its shrillness both caused its success and resulted in condemnation by many critics. It is by no means a masterpiece, but some scenes have great power. Beckmann, "the man outside," returns from a prison camp in the Soviet Union. He is a frightful sight: one leg is stiff, and he wears glasses designed to be worn under a gas mask. His wife is living with another man. Beckmann attempts suicide, but the river Elbe rejects him. He is befriended by a young woman, but the ghost of her husband, of whose death Beckmann is guilty, appears to him and frightens him away. He visits his former colonel to unburden himself of his guilt at having caused the deaths of eleven soldiers, but the colonel rebuffs him. Beckmann's attempt to find employment in a cabaret fails; his song is not serene enough. Trying to return to his parents, he is rudely informed by a woman that they have committed suicide. At various points in this drama in the expressionist tradition Beckmann is confronted by "der Andere" (the Other), the "Yea-Sayer," who tells him to go on. But at the end, when Beckmann is alone in the street desperately searching for a reason not to die, the Other has disappeared. The play is framed by a dialogue between an old man in whom nobody believes (God) and a funeral director (Death). God pities his children but cannot help them, while Death has grown fat and cynical with all the work and importance that he is being given.

Draußen vor der Tür is an intense search for meaning. The depiction of God as a weak father who has no power to help his children, the shrill tone, the melodrama, and the sentimentality are designed to make the audience think. Borchert called his play a "Plakat"; in German theater jargon, this means a direct statement of an abstract thesis without poetic transformation into an action. But Borchert underestimated his play; it has not lost its power even today. Borchert said in a letter to the dramatist Carl Zuckmayer of 15 November 1947 that he was still "on his way" to real achievement. He did not have time to reach his goal, but the last short stories provide an idea of what he might have become.

Borchert's sudden fame extended beyond Germany. Some Swiss publishers offered to bring him to Switzerland for better treatment than Germany could offer. There were many bureaucratic

Hans Quest as Beckmann in the premiere of Borchert's play, Draußen vor der Tür *in Hamburg on 21 November 1947–the day after the author's death (Rosemarie Clausen, Hamburg)*

obstacles, and the journey did not take place until September 1947. It was too late. Borchert died after a short stay at a hospital in Basel. In Basel, he wrote only one more text, a manifesto against participation in any future war; it reiterates the phrase "Sag Nein!" (Say No!). While Borchert drew on his war and postwar experiences and described the miseries of the present and the immediate past, he was intensely concerned about the future of humankind. Would society learn from World War II and avoid more slaughter and mass destruction? Not the persons in power, Borchert decided; they do not suffer and do not learn. Only if the common people stop cooperating might there be a change.

Borchert has been called an existentialist, but he was not a philosopher. His pronouncements are usually neither profound nor original. Borchert is convincing when he points out the meaning in seemingly insignificant situations. In "Das Brot" (Bread) a slice of bread that a man steals from his wife's ration threatens to shatter a marriage of thirty-seven years, but the crisis is overcome by the wife's generosity. In some stories people turn from death to life: the old man in "Nachts schlafen die Ratten doch" (The Rats Sleep at Night, You Know) tells a weary boy, in effect, to stop trying to keep the rats away from his brother's corpse, which is buried under the rubble, and start living his own life. In spite of the "nihilist" image he had during his lifetime, most of

Page from the manuscript for Borchert's last work, an antiwar manifesto, written in a hospital in Basel (Peter Rühmkorf, Wolfgang Borchert [Reinbek: Rowohlt, 1970])

Borchert's grave in the Ohlsdorf cemetery

Borchert's stories propose such a new life, which begins in acts of human kindness and decency. Borchert distrusts authorities and does not believe that science guarantees progress. Survival means fighting against the mentality and organization of power and destruction.

In political terms, these ideas may seem simplistic. Borchert was not a political writer. His rebellion, resistance, pacifism, and humanism were spontaneous. He did not write overtly about Auschwitz, Nazis, German guilt, or political institutions. But he did have a message, and his appeal was urgent. He thought that no time should be lost in changing the direction of society. He felt that the old power structures were being reestablished immediately after the total breakdown and that the people in responsible positions had not changed, and he was mortally afraid of the consequences. His fears went beyond the reemergence of Nazism in Germany: he was fighting against the old system under new names.

These are the two points of attraction that make Borchert's stories popular reading and move the audiences of *Draußen vor der Tür*: the fundamental protest against all power structures which destroy life to further their own goals, and the plea to base one's actions on kindness and mutual help. Borchert stands out as the most impressive chronicler of postwar conditions in Germany and of the intense will and hope at the time to start a new life that could really be called "new."

Rühmkorf and other scholars have demonstrated Borchert's artistry, especially in the field of short stories. At his death he was still a young man, more promise than fulfillment, but he was already an accomplished writer with an impressive style and technique; he cannot be dismissed as an insignificant figure who happened to gain notoriety because nobody else was writing in 1947. Borchert's stories are certainly on a level with the best of German postwar short-story writing, such as that of Heinrich Böll and Wolfdietrich Schnurre. *Draußen vor der Tür* was important in the history of the German radio play and in postwar literature in general. Borchert's significance for German literature lies both in his role as an example for postwar writers and in the intrinsic value of his writings.

References:

Reinhard Baumgart, "Wolfgang Borchert, ein Hungerkünstler," in his *Die verdrängte Phantasie* (Neuwied/Darmstadt: Luchterhand, 1973), pp. 173-178;

Kurt J. Fickert, "Some Biblical Prototypes in Wolfgang Borchert's Stories," *German Quarterly*, 28 (1965): 172-178;

Adolf D. Klarmann, "Wolfgang Borchert: The Lost Voice of a New Germany," *Germanic Review*, 27 (1952): 108-123;

Wulf Koepke, "In Sachen Wolfgang Borchert," *Rice University Studies*, 55, no. 3 (1969): 69-91;

Ruth Lorbe, "Wolfgang Borchert: 'Die Küchenuhr,'" *Der Deutschunterricht*, 9, no. 1 (1957): 45-47;

Joseph Mileck, "Wolfgang Borchert's Draußen vor der Tür: A Young Poet's Struggle with Guilt and Despair," *Monatshefte*, 51 (1959): 328-336;

Peter Rühmkorf, *Wolfgang Borchert in Selbstzeugnissen und Bilddokumenten* (Reinbek: Rowohlt, 1961);

Rolf Schulmeister, "Wolfgang Borchert," in *Deutsche Literatur seit 1945 in Einzeldarstellungen*, edited by Dietrich Weber, third edition, volume 1 (Stuttgart: Kröner, 1976), pp. 183-200;

Herbert Seliger, "Wer schreibt für uns eine neue Harmonielehre?" *Akzente*, 2 (1955): 128-138;

Robert Spaethling, "Wolfgang Borchert's Quest for Human Freedom," *German Life & Letters*, 14 (1960/1961): 188-194;

Siegfried Unseld, "An diesem Dienstag," *Akzente*, 2 (1955): 139-148;

Karl S. Weimar, "No Entry No Exit: A Study of Borchert with Some Notes on Sartre," *Modern Language Quarterly*, 17 (June 1956): 153-165;

Rudolf Wolff, ed., *Wolfgang Borchert: Werk und Wirkung* (Bonn: Bouvier, 1984).

Papers:
Wolfgang Borchert's papers are in the possession of his family.

Paul Celan
(Paul Antschel)
(23 November 1920-? April 1970)

James K. Lyon
University of California, San Diego

BOOKS: *Edgar Jené und der Traum vom Traume* (Vienna: Agathon, 1948);

Der Sand aus den Urnen (Vienna: Sexl, 1948);

Mohn und Gedächtnis: Gedichte (Stuttgart: Deutsche Verlags-Anstalt, 1952);

Von Schwelle zu Schwelle: Gedichte (Stuttgart: Deutsche Verlags-Anstalt, 1955);

Sprachgitter (Frankfurt am Main: Fischer, 1959);

Gedichte: Eine Auswahl, edited by Klaus Wagenbach (Frankfurt am Main: Fischer, 1959);

Der Meridian: Rede anläßlich der Verleihung des Georg-Büchner-Preises, Darmstadt, am 22. Oktober 1960 (Frankfurt am Main: Fischer, 1961); translated by Walter Billeter as "The Meridian," in *Paul Celan: Prose Writings and Selected Poems* (Carlton, Victoria, Australia: Paper Castle, 1977), pp. 84-93;

Die Niemandsrose (Frankfurt am Main: Fischer, 1963);

Atemkristall (Paris: Brunidor, 1965);

Gedichte (Darmstadt: Moderner Buch-Club, 1966);

Atemwende: Gedichte (Frankfurt am Main: Suhrkamp, 1967);

Fadensonnen (Frankfurt am Main: Suhrkamp, 1968);

Ausgewählte Gedichte; Zwei Reden (Frankfurt am Main: Suhrkamp, 1968);

Lichtzwang (Frankfurt am Main: Suhrkamp, 1970);

Ausgewählte Gedichte, edited by Klaus Reichert (Frankfurt am Main: Suhrkamp, 1970);

Speech-grille, and Selected Poems, translated by Joachim Neugroschel (New York: Dutton, 1971);

Schneepart (Frankfurt am Main: Suhrkamp, 1971);

Nineteen Poems, translated by Michael Hamburger (South Hinksey, U.K.: Carcanet Press, 1972);

Selected Poems, translated by Hamburger and Christopher Middleton (Harmondsworth, U.K.: Penguin, 1972);

Paul Celan in 1967 (Ullstein–Heinz Köster)

Gedichte: In zwei Bänden, 2 volumes (Frankfurt am Main: Suhrkamp, 1975);

Zeitgehöft: Späte Gedichte aus dem Nachlaß (Frankfurt am Main: Suhrkamp, 1976);

Paul Celan: Poems, selected and translated by Hamburger (New York: Persea, 1980);

Gesammelte Werke in fünf Bänden, 5 volumes (Frankfurt am Main: Suhrkamp, 1983);

Todesfuge (New York: Edition Gunnar A. Kaldewey, 1984);

65 Poems (Dublin: Raven Arts Press, 1985);

Last Poems (San Francisco: North Point Press, 1986).

OTHER: "Ansprache anläßlich der Entgegennahme des Literaturpreises der Freien Hansestadt Bremen," in *Ansprachen bei der
Verleihung des Bremer Literaturpreises an Paul
Celan* (Stuttgart: Deutsche Verlags-Anstalt,
1958), pp. 10-11; translated by Robert Kelly
as "Address on Acceptance of the Prize for
Literature of the Free Hanseatic City of Bremen," *Origin*, third series, no. 15 (1969):
16-17.

TRANSLATIONS: Jean Cocteau, *Der goldene Vor-
hang* (Bad Salzburg & Düsseldorf: Rauch,
1949);
Arthur Rimbaud, *Bateau ivre/Das trunkene Schiff*
(Wiesbaden: Insel, 1958);
Osip Emil'evich Mandel'shtam, *Gedichte* (Frank-
furt am Main: Fischer, 1959);
Jean Cayrol, *Im Bereich einer Nacht: Roman* (Olten:
Walter, 1961);
*Drei russische Dichter: Alexander Block, Ossip Mandel-
stamm, Sergej Jessenin* (Frankfurt am Main:
Fischer, 1963);
Pablo Picasso, *Wie man Wünsche beim Schwanz
packt: Ein Drama in sechs Akten* (Zurich: Ar-
che, 1963);
Paul Valéry, *Die junge Parze/La jeune Parque* (Frank-
furt am Main: Insel, 1964);
William Shakespeare, *Einundzwanzig Sonette*
(Frankfurt am Main: Insel, 1967);
Jules Supervielle, *Gedichte* (Frankfurt am Main: In-
sel, 1968);
Sergei Aleksandrovich Esenin, *Gedichte* (Leipzig:
Reclam, 1970);
René Char, translated by Celan and others (Ber-
lin: Neues Leben, 1973).

PERIODICAL PUBLICATIONS: "Gegenlicht," *Die
Tat* (Zurich) (12 March 1949);
"Gespräch im Gebirg," *Neue Rundschau*, 71, no. 2
(1960): 199-202; translated by Joachim Neugroschel as "Conversation in the Mountains," *Antaeus*, no. 7 (1972): 68-71;
"Ansprache vor dem hebräischen Schriftstellerverband," *Die Stimme* (Tel Aviv), no. 246 (August 1970): 7;
"Geräuschlos hüpft ein Griffel . . . ," *Neue Literatur* (Bucharest), 11 (1980): 63-64.

Paul Celan (pronounced say-*lahn*), whom
George Steiner has called "almost certainly the
major European poet of the period after 1945,"
is known primarily for his verse. Yet his reputation as a lyric poet overshadows a small but significant body of prose works that deserve attention
both for their close links to his poetry and as independent creations.

Paul Antschel, the only child of Jewish
parents, Leo Antschel-Teitler and Friederike
Schrager, was born in Czernovitz (now Chernov-
tsy, U.S.S.R.), capital of the Romanian province
of Bukovina, on 23 November 1920. He grew up
in a multilingual environment. German, the language spoken at home and in some of the
schools he attended, remained his mother tongue
throughout his life, and Vienna was the cultural
lodestar of his youth; but his language of daily
speech was Romanian. Before his bar mitzvah he
studied Hebrew for three years, and by the time
he began a year of premedical studies at the
École préparatoire de Médecine in Tours,
France, in 1938, he was also fluent in French. Returning to Czernovitz shortly before the outbreak
of World War II, he learned Russian at the university and, after Soviet troops occupied Bukovina
in 1940, in the streets. When German troops captured the city in 1941 his parents were deported
and shot, but he survived. After eighteen months
at forced labor for the Germans, he escaped to
the Red Army and returned to Czernovitz, which
was again under Russian control. There, sometime in late 1944, he wrote the remarkable
"Todesfuge" (Death Fugue), perhaps the most
powerful poem ever written on the Holocaust. It
was included in his first two collections of poems,
Der Sand aus den Urnen (The Sand from the Urns,
1948) and *Mohn und Gedächtnis* (Poppy and Memory, 1952).

Leaving Czernovitz in 1945 for Bucharest,
Antschel joined a surrealist circle, became friends
with leading Romanian writers, and worked as a
translator and reader in a publishing house. For
his prose translations from Russian into Romanian—primarily of Lermontov, Simonov, and
Chekhov—and for publication of his own poems,
he used several pseudonyms before transmuting
Ancel, the Romanian form of his surname, into
Celan in 1947.

Sometime between 1945 and 1947 he wrote
a two-page prose fragment that has survived
under the title "Geräuschlos hüpft ein Griffel . . ." (A Stylus Noiselessly Hops . . . , 1980).
This work reveals his indebtedness to surrealism.
In it a noiseless slate pencil or stylus writes under
its own power, first on a slate tablet, which is the
earth, and then on a "Blatt" (leaf or page) in a tree-
top. Further surrealistic sequences show a man in
a room who finds that the window has been

locked by a powerful, unseen external hand, and the same man looking into a mirror, only to see his coat buttons and the carpet transformed into mirrors. At this point the series of dreamlike scenes breaks off.

Late in 1947 Celan went to Vienna, where he joined a circle of leading avant-garde painters, writers, and publishers. His friendship with the painter Edgar Jené gave rise to a brief prose piece, "Die Lanze" (The Lance), which he and Jené wrote jointly early in 1948 and circulated on mimeographed sheets to announce a reading of surrealist texts as part of an exhibition of surrealist painters in Vienna. Like "Geräuschlos hüpft ein Griffel . . . ," "Die Lanze" consists of typical surrealist images: "rainbowfish" flying through the sky, a giant hammer in the air, and waves beating against treetops. It ends with speakers casting nets into the water—an image also found in Celan's early poems. The work contains a dialogue, a format that became a hallmark of his later prose works.

A second prose piece, *Edgar Jené und der Traum vom Traume* (Edgar Jené and the Dream of the Dream, 1948), written at about the same time as "Die Lanze," purports to be a discussion of Jené's paintings but quickly becomes a confessional essay on what happens in the "Tiefsee" (deep sea) of the writer's mind, the "große Kristall der Innenwelt" (huge crystal of the internal world) into which he follows Jené and where he explores his paintings. Aware that language has become false and debased, he seeks to regain a naive view of the world and to recover pristine speech or "truth" that cannot be restored by reason, but only by venturing into the depths of the mind and engaging in dialogue with its "finstere Quellen" (dark sources). With this newfound freedom, he engages Jené's paintings in a dialogue. In the process Celan sketches the contours of "die schöne Wildnis auf der anderen, tieferen Seite des Seins" (the beautiful wilderness on the other, more profound side of existence), the internal world in which most of his poetry takes place, a world of "true" language obscured by lies, an internal darkness that is dispelled only by the light of "true" language. In prose marked by unusual new compound nouns, Celan's many interrogative sentences give one the sense that he wishes to engage his reader in a direct dialogue.

Leaving Vienna in July 1948, he settled in Paris and began studies in German philology and literature. In March 1949 the Swiss journal *Die Tat* published a collection of his brilliant but enig-

matic aphorisms entitled "Gegenlicht" (Counter-Light). These aphorisms appear surrealistic in their subversion of conventional time and of space and object relationships–trees fly to birds, hours jump out of the clock, a woman hates a mirror's vanity. Behind them lies a Kafkaesque awareness that the world makes no sense. For Celan it seems that only in the paradox of new language combinations can the world be made coherent, and only in a dialectic of contradictions can truth be rendered. Hence, an aphorism that juxtaposes a battleship and a drowned man might be read as a pacifist statement: "Man redet umsonst von Gerechtigkeit, solange das größte der Schlachtschiffe nicht an der Stirn eines Ertrunkenen zerschellt ist" (One speaks in vain of justice as long as the largest battleship has not been smashed to pieces on a drowned man's brow).

Celan took his Licence des Lettres in 1950. In 1952 he married the graphic artist Gisèle de Lestrange, with whom he had a son, Eric, who was born in 1955. Though he wrote no original prose for almost ten years, the works Celan chose to translate into German were usually prose. For him each translation was a new linguistic creation, a means of establishing his identity and verifying his existence within language. He never gave up German as his mother tongue, telling a friend, "Only in one's mother tongue can one express one's own truth. In a foreign language, the poet lies." Though all of these translations reflect his unique prose style, one reveals almost more of himself than of the original–his rendering of Jean Cayrol's prose narration for Alain Resnais's *Nuit et Brouillard* (Night and Fog, 1956), a film on the Holocaust that Celan endowed with an authentic Jewish voice for German-speaking viewers.

The address he delivered upon receiving the Bremen Literary Prize in 1958 (translated, 1969) is Celan's most personal prose work. After referring to the Bukovinian landscape of his youth and his acquaintance with Martin Buber's Hasidic tales in this world "in der Menschen und Bücher lebten" (where humans and books lived), the address becomes a discussion of his relationship to the German language, one of the few elements of his spiritual existence he did not lose under the Nazis. This language, he says, "mußte nun hindurchgehen . . . durch furchtbares Verstummen, hindurchgehen durch die tausend Finsternisse todbringender Rede" (had to pass . . . through a frightful muting, pass through the thousand darknesses of deathbringing speech).

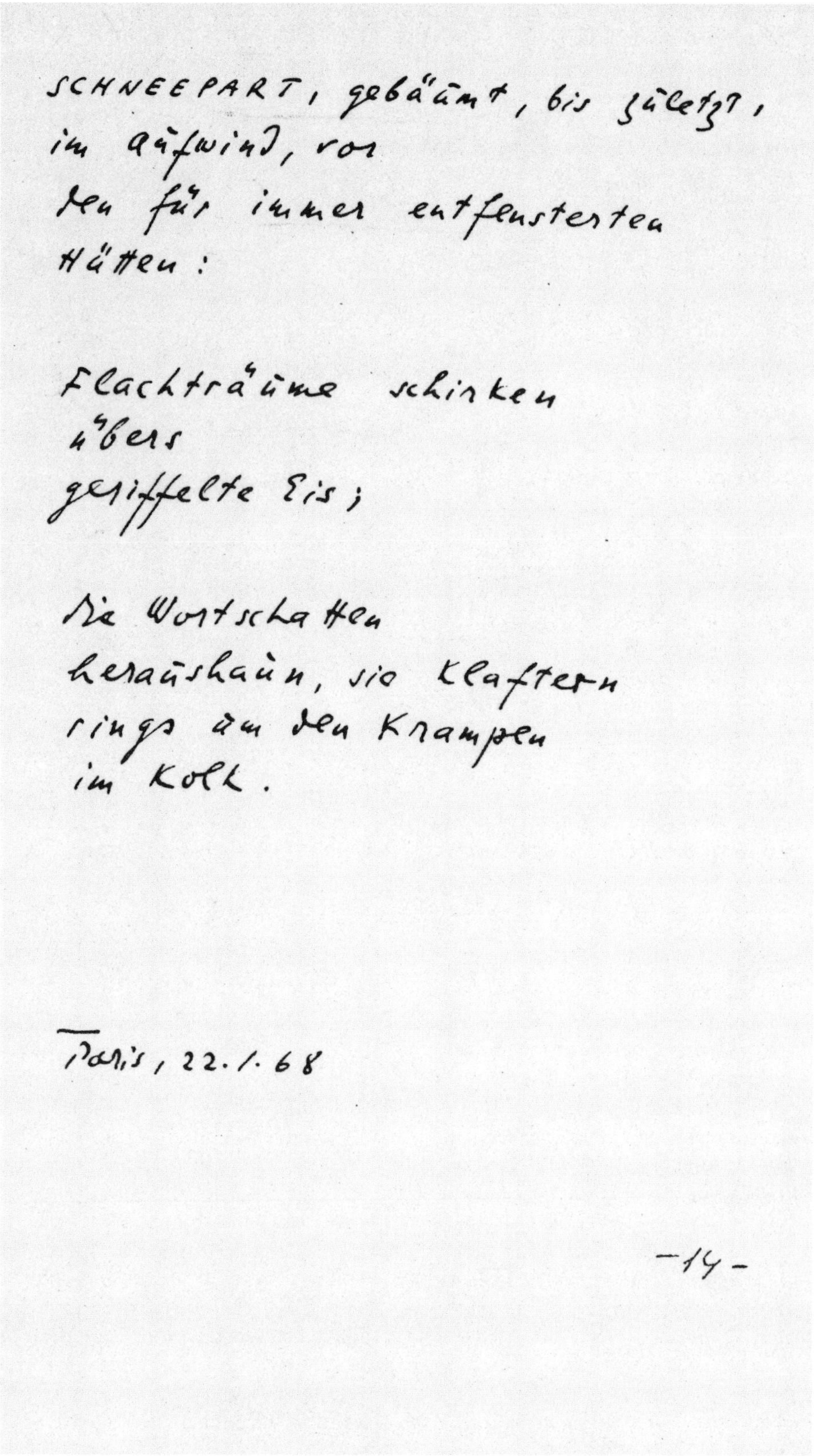

SCHNEEPART, gebäumt, bis zuletzt,
im Aufwind, vor
den für immer entfensterten
Hütten:

Flachträume schirken
übers
geriffelte Eis;

die Wortschatten
heraushaun, sie klaftern
rings um den Krampen
im Kolk.

Paris, 22.1.68

—14—

Manuscript for a poem by Celan (Paul Celan, Gesammelte Werke [Frankfurt am Main: Suhrkamp, 1983])

From its miraculous survival, he now attempts to write "um zu sprechen, um mich zu orientieren . . . um mir Wirklichkeit zu entwerfen" (in order to speak, to orient myself . . . to outline reality). He states his views on poetry as dialogue, as a "Flaschenpost" (message in a bottle) cast out and addressed to "etwas Offenstehendes, auf ein ansprechbares Du vielleicht, auf eine ansprechbare Wirklichkeit" (something that stands open, perhaps an addressable Thou, an addressable reality). But he accomplishes this painful task as one who "mit seinem Dasein zur Sprache geht, wirklichkeitswund und Wirklichkeit suchend" (goes to language with his very being, stricken by and seeking reality). Besides being a statement of personal poetics, this piece stands, like Buber's *Ich und Du* (1923; translated as *I and Thou*, 1937), as an expression of man's need for a relation to an "Other."

In 1959 Celan became a reader in German Language and Literature at L'École Normale Superieure, a position he held until his death. While in the Swiss Alps in July 1959 he was to meet Theodor Adorno at Sils-Maria. Forced to return to Paris before they met, Celan composed "Gespräch im Gebirg" (1960; translated as "Conversation in the Mountains," 1972) the following month; it was a reflection on this missed encounter; he later called it a "Mauscheln" (jabber, schmooze) between himself and Adorno. This most distinctly Jewish of his prose works portrays a meeting in the mountains between "Jud-Klein" (Jew-Small) and "Jud-Groß" (Jew-Big). It opens with involved sentences punctuated with dashes, thought fragments, and repetitions as Jew-Small walks through the Alps reflecting on the landscape, his own Jewishness with which he does not feel at ease, the nature of silence, and, finally, the nature of speech. After meeting Jew-Big, he admits that he came there to talk with someone, and immediately they make a distinction between "Reden" (talk) and "Sprechen" (speech) as they reflect on hearing, remembering, and language. Jew-Small, who dominates the conversation, delivers a long reverie on the Jewish dead and on his love for an ancestral candle as it symbolically burns toward extinction: "Auf dem Stein bin ich gelegen, damals, du weißt, auf den Steinfliesen; und neben mir, da sind sie gelegen, die andern, die wie ich waren, die andern, die anders waren als ich und genauso, die Geschwisterkinder; und sie lagen da und schliefen, schliefen und schliefen nicht, und sie träumten und träumten nicht . . ." (On the stone is where I lay, back then, you

know, the flagstones; and near me, that's where they were lying, the others, who were different from me and the same, the cousins; and they lay there and slept, sleeping and not sleeping, dreaming and not dreaming . . .). Gradually he realizes that in the dialogue with Jew-Big he is meeting himself, that is, encountering and beginning to accept his people, his heritage, and his Jewish identity.

In 1960 Celan traveled to Darmstadt to receive the Georg Büchner Prize from the German Academy of Language and Literature. His acceptance speech, *Der Meridian* (1961; translated as "The Meridian," 1977), is viewed by critics as a statement of poetic theory, but it is also a literary expression of how Celan attempts to make sense of the world. Written as a dialogue with his listeners, it is punctuated by reservations or uncertainties about the poet's craft, leading the listener/reader through a labyrinth of images relating to the poet's quest for speech in an age when speech has become nearly impossible. After an exposition of Büchner's tragedy *Dantons Tod* (1835) and his short story "Lenz" (1839), both of which for Celan pay homage to the "Majestät des Absurden" (majesty of the Absurd) characteristic of our era, he expresses doubts about the existence of literary "art"; before anything else, the contemporary writer must radically question the existence of such art. Writing a poem is a search for an "Ort" (place), perhaps a place that does not exist, a "u-topia." Poetic creations do not enjoy universal, a priori existence but arise only through encounters, through the meeting of a voice with an Other, through dialogue that allows an "I" to orient itself through speech and understand itself through contact with a Thou, an act that enables this "I" to discover the "meridian" that connects it through language to the rest of the world.

Before his suicide sometime in April 1970—he had been missing since the middle of April and his body was found in early May—Celan produced only one more prose work, a brief address delivered to the Hebrew Writers' Association on 14 October 1969 during a trip to Israel; it was published in the Tel Aviv magazine *Die Stimme* in August 1970. In the address Celan expresses gratitude for discovering in Israel an "äußere und innere Landschaft" (external and internal landscape) conducive to creating great poetry. He draws an analogy between these two landscapes: "Ich verstehe . . . den dankbaren Stolz auf jedes selbstgepflanzte Grün, das bereitsteht, jeden der hier vorbeikommt zu erfrischen; wie ich die Freude begreife über jedes neuerworbene, selbsterfühlte Wort, das herbeieilt, den ihm Zugewandeten zu stärken" (I understand ... the grateful pride in every homegrown green thing that stands ready to refresh anyone who comes by; just as I comprehend the joy in every newly won, self-felt word that rushes up to strengthen him who is receptive to it).

Under the heading "Prose," the 1983 edition of Celan's collected works includes three letters he wrote in response to survey questions. Celan wrote brilliant letters; like Rainer Maria Rilke's, they could almost qualify as a separate genre. But so few of them have been published that it is not yet possible to give a general analysis of their style and content.

Creative extensions and elaborations of his poetry, Celan's prose works express the strain of being Jewish, the struggle to reclaim language in a nonpoetic age, and the need for dialogue as a means of connecting oneself with and orienting oneself in the modern world.

Bibliography:
Christiane Heuline, "Bibliographie zu Paul Celan: Werke und Sekundärliteratur," *Zeitschrift für Kulturaustausch*, 3, no. 32 (1982): 245-287.

Biography:
Israel Chalfen, *Paul Celan: Eine Biographie seiner Jugend* (Frankfurt am Main: Suhrkamp, 1979).

References:
Renate Böschenstein-Schäfer, "Anmerkungen zu Paul Celans 'Gespräch im Gebirg,'" *Neue Zürcher Zeitung*, 20 October 1968;

David Brierley, *"Der Meridian": Ein Versuch zur Poetik und Dichtung Paul Celans* (Frankfurt am Main: Lang, 1984);

Beatrice Adrienne Cameron, "Anticomputer: An Essay on the Work of Paul Celan, Followed by Selected Poems in Translation," Ph.D. dissertation, University of California, Berkeley, 1973;

Cameron, "The 'Meridian' Speech: An Introductory Note," *Chicago Review*, 29, no. 3 (1978): 23-27;

Claude David, "Paul Celan, 'Der Meridian,'" *Études Germaniques*, 17 (1962): 101;

Jerry Glenn, "Paul Celan: Edgar Jené and the Dream of the Dream," *Boston University Journal*, 21, no. 1 (1973): 61-63;

Christiane Heuline, "Bibliographie zu Paul Celan," *text + kritik*, 53/54 (second, enlarged edition, July 1984): 100-149;

John E. Jackson, "Die Du-Anrede bei Paul Celan: Anmerkungen zu seinem 'Gespräch im Gebirg,'" *text + kritik*, 53/54 (1977): 62-68;

Jackson, *La Question du moi* (Neuchâtel: Editions de la Baconnière, 1978), pp. 145-240;

James K. Lyon, "Paul Celan and Martin Buber: Poetry as Dialogue," *PMLA*, 86, no. 1 (1971): 110-120;

Hans Mayer, "Lenz, Büchner und Celan: Anmerkungen zu Paul Celans Georg-Büchner-Preis-Rede 'Der Meridian' vom 22.10.1960," *Vereinzelt Niederschläge: Kritik, Polemik* (Pfullingen: Neske, 1973), pp. 160-171;

Dietlind Meinecke, ed., *Über Paul Celan* (Frankfurt am Main: Suhrkamp, 1973);

Peter Horst Neumann, *Zur Lyrik Paul Celans* (Göttingen: Vandenhoeck & Ruprecht, 1968);

Georg-Michael Schulz, "Individuation und Austauschbarkeit: Zu Paul Celans 'Gespräch im Gebirg,'" *Deutsche Vierteljahresschrift für Literaturwissenschaft und Geistesgeschichte*, 53 (1979): 463-477;

George Steiner, "The Loud Silences of Paul Celan," *Jewish Quarterly*, 4 (1980-1981): 49-50;

Steiner, "Songs of a Torn Tongue," *Times Literary Supplement*, 28 September 1984, pp. 1093-1094;

Studies in Twentieth Century Literature, special Celan issue (Fall 1983).

Papers:
The bulk of Paul Celan's manuscripts is in the possession of his widow, Mme Gisèle Celan-Lestrange of Paris. Manuscripts of poems and letters are known to exist in the hands of friends in Europe, Israel, and the United States.

Friedrich Dürrenmatt
(5 January 1921-   )

Roger A. Crockett
Texas A&M University

BOOKS: *Es steht geschrieben: Ein Drama* (Kloster-
berg & Basel: Schwabe, 1947); revised as
Die Wiedertäufer: Eine Komödie in zwei Teilen
(Zurich: Arche, 1967);
Der Blinde: Ein Drama (Berlin: Bühnenverlag
Bloch Erben, 1947);
Pilatus (Olten: Vereinigung Oltner Bücherfreunde, 1949);
Der Nihilist (Horgen: Holunderpresse, 1950); re-
published as *Die Falle* (Zurich: Arche, 1952);
Das Bild des Sisyphos (Zurich: Arche, 1952); translat-
ed by Michael Bullock as "The Picture of Sisyphos," *Mundus Artium*, 1, no. 3 (1968):
53-69;
Der Tunnel (Zurich: Arche, 1952); in *Die Panne
and Der Tunnel*, edited by F. J. Alexander
(London: Oxford University Press, 1967);
translated by Carla Coulter and Alison Scott
as "The Tunnel," *Evergreen Review*, 5, no. 17
(1961): 32-42;
Die Stadt: Prosa I-IV (Zurich: Arche, 1952);
Der Richter und sein Henker (Einsiedeln, Zurich &
Cologne: Benziger, 1952); edited by William Gillis and John J. Neumaier (Cambridge, Mass.: Riverside Press, 1961); edited
by Leonard Forster (London: Harrap,
1962); translated by Cyrus Brooks as *The
Judge and His Hangman* (London: Jenkins,
1954); translated by Theresa Pol as *The
Judge and His Hangman* (New York: Harper,
1955);
*Die Ehe des Herrn Mississippi: Eine Komödie in zwei
Teilen* (Zurich: Oprecht, 1952; revised edition, Zurich: Arche, 1966); edited by Reinhold Grimm and Helene Scher (New York:
Holt, Rinehart & Winston, 1973); translated
by Bullock as *The Marriage of Mr. Mississippi*,
in *The Marriage of Mr. Mississippi: A Play and
Problems of the Theatre: An Essay* (New York:
Grove Press, 1966); German version adapted as filmscript, *Die Ehe des Herrn Mississippi:
Ein Drehbuch mit Szenenbildern* (Zurich: Sanssouci, 1961);

Ullstein–Interfoto

Der Verdacht (Einsiedeln, Zurich & Cologne: Benzi-
ger, 1953); edited by Gillis (Boston: Hough-
ton Mifflin, 1964); edited by Forster
(London: Harrap, 1965); translated by Eva
H. Morreale as *The Quarry* (New York:
Grove Press, 1961; London: Cape, 1962);
*Ein Engel kommt nach Babylon: Eine Komödie in drei
Akten* (Zurich: Arche, 1954; revised, 1958);
translated by William McElwee as *An Angel
Comes to Babylon*, in *An Angel Comes To Baby-
lon and Romulus the Great* (New York: Grove
Press, 1964);

Herkules und der Stall des Augias: Mit Randnotizen eines Kugelschreibers (Zurich: Arche, 1954); radio play revised as stage play, *Herkules und der Stall des Augias: Eine Komödie* (Zurich: Arche, 1963); translated by Agnes Hamilton as *Hercules and the Augean Stables* (Chicago: Dramatic Publishing Co., 1963);

Theaterprobleme (Zurich: Arche, 1955); translated by Gerhard Nellhaus as "Problems of the Theatre," in *Four Plays* (London: Cape, 1964; New York: Grove Press, 1965);

Grieche sucht Griechin: Eine Prosakomödie (Zurich: Arche, 1955); translated by Richard and Clara Winston as *Once a Greek . . .* (New York: Knopf, 1965; London: Cape, 1966);

Die Panne: Eine noch mögliche Geschichte (Zurich: Arche, 1956); in *Die Panne and Der Tunnel*, edited by Alexander (London: Oxford University Press, 1967); translated by Richard and Clara Winston as *Traps* (New York: Knopf, 1960); translation republished as *A Dangerous Game* (London: Cape, 1960); German version adapted as radio play, *Die Panne: Ein Hörspiel* (Zurich: Arche, 1961), adapted as stage play, *Die Panne: Komödie* (Zurich: Diogenes, 1979);

Romulus der Große: Eine ungeschichtliche historische Komödie (Basel: Reiss, 1956; revised edition, Zurich: Arche, 1958); edited by Hugh Frederic Garten (Boston: Houghton Mifflin, 1962; London: Methuen, 1962); translated by Nellhaus as *Romulus the Great*, in *An Angel Comes to Babylon and Romulus the Great* (New York: Grove Press, 1964);

Der Besuch der alten Dame: Eine tragische Komödie (Zurich: Arche, 1956); edited by Paul Kurt Ackermann (Boston: Houghton Mifflin, 1957; London: Methuen, 1961); translated by Patrick Bowles as *The Visit: A Tragicomedy* (New York: Grove Press, 1962; London: Cape, 1962);

Komödien (Zurich: Arche, 1957);

Nächtliches Gespräch mit einem verachteten Menschen: Ein Kurs für Zeitgenossen (Zurich: Arche, 1957); translated by Robert D. Macdonald as *Conversation at Night with a Despised Character: A Curriculum for Our Times* (Chicago: Dramatic Publishing Co., 1957);

Der Prozeß um des Esels Schatten: Ein Hörspiel (nach Wieland—aber nicht sehr) (Zurich: Arche, 1958);

Das Unternehmen der Wega: Ein Hörspiel (Zurich: Arche, 1958); translated by Alfred Schild as

"The Mission of the Vega," *Texas Quarterly*, 5, no. 1 (1962): 125-149;

Das Versprechen: Requiem auf den Kriminalroman (Zurich: Arche, 1958); edited by Forster (London: Harrap, 1967); translated by Richard and Clara Winston as *The Pledge* (New York: Knopf, 1959; London: Cape, 1959);

Abendstunde im Spätherbst: Ein Hörspiel (Zurich: Arche, 1959); translated by Gabriel Karminski as *Episode on an Autumn Evening* (Chicago: Dramatic Publishing Co., 1959);

Stranitzky und der Nationalheld: Ein Hörspiel (Zurich: Arche, 1959);

Der Doppelgänger: Ein Spiel (Zurich: Arche, 1960);

Friedrich Schiller: Eine Rede (Zurich: Arche, 1960);

Frank der Fünfte: Oper einer Privatbank (Zurich: Arche, 1960; revised, 1964);

Gesammelte Hörspiele (Zurich: Arche, 1961);

Die Physiker: Eine Komödie in zwei Akten (Zurich: Arche, 1962); edited by Robert E. Helbling (New York: Oxford University Press, 1965); edited by Arthur Taylor (London: Macmillan, 1966); translated by James Kirkup as *The Physicists* (London: French, 1963; New York: Grove Press, 1964);

Die Heimat im Plakat: Ein Buch für Schweizer Kinder (Zurich: Diogenes, 1963);

Komödien II und frühe Stücke (Zurich: Arche, 1963);

Four Plays, translated by Nellhaus and others (London: Cape, 1964; New York: Grove Press, 1965)—includes *Romulus the Great, The Marriage of Mr. Mississippi, An Angel Comes to Babylon,* and *The Physicists;*

Drei Hörspiele, edited by Henry Regensteiner (New York: Holt, Rinehart & Winston, 1965); includes *Abendstunde im Spätherbst, Der Doppelgänger,* and *Die Panne;*

Theaterschriften und Reden, edited by Elisabeth Brock-Sulzer, 2 volumes (Zurich: Arche, 1966, 1972); translated by H. M. Waidson as *Writings on Theatre and Drama*, 1 volume (London: Cape, 1976);

Der Meteor: Eine Komödie in zwei Akten (Zurich: Arche, 1966); translated by Kirkup as *The Meteor* (Chicago: Dramatic Publishing Co., 1966; London: Cape, 1973);

Vier Hörspiele (Berlin: Volk und Welt, 1967);

König Johann: Nach Shakespeare (Zurich: Arche, 1968);

Play Strindberg: Totentanz nach August Strindberg (Zurich: Arche, 1969); translated by Kirkup as *Play Strindberg* (Chicago: Dramatic Publishing Co., 1970; London: Cape, 1972);

Monstervortrag über Gerechtigkeit und Recht nebst einem helvetischen Zwischenspiel: Eine kleine Dramaturgie der Politik (Zurich: Arche, 1969); translated by John Wood as "A Monster Lecture on Justice and Law Together with a Helvetian Interlude: A Brief Discussion on the Dramaturgy of Politics," in *Friedrich Dürrenmatt: Plays and Essays*, edited by Volkmar Sander (New York: Continuum, 1982), pp. 263-312;

Sätze aus Amerika (Zurich: Arche, 1970);

Titus Andronicus: Eine Komödie nach Shakespeare (Zurich: Arche, 1970);

Der Sturz (Zurich: Arche, 1971);

Porträt eines Planeten (Zurich: Arche, 1971);

Komödien III (Zurich: Arche, 1972);

Gespräch mit Heinz Ludwig Arnold (Zurich: Arche, 1976);

Zusammenhänge: Essay über Israel. Eine Konzeption (Zurich: Arche, 1976);

Der Mitmacher: Ein Komplex. Text der Komödie, Dramaturgie, Erfahrungen, Berichte, Erzählungen (Zurich: Arche, 1976); play republished as *Der Mitmacher: Eine Komödie* (Zurich: Arche, 1978);

Die Frist: Eine Komödie (Zurich: Arche, 1977);

Dürrenmatt: Bilder und Zeichnungen, edited by Christian Strich (Zurich: Diogenes, 1978);

Friedrich Dürrenmatt Lesebuch (Zurich: Diogenes, 1978);

Albert Einstein: Ein Vortrag (Zurich: Diogenes, 1979);

Werkausgabe in 30 Bänden, 30 volumes (Zurich: Diogenes, 1980);

Stoffe I-III (Zurich: Diogenes, 1981);

Friedrich Dürrenmatt: Plays and Essays, edited by Sander (New York: Continuum, 1982);

Die Welt als Labyrinth (Vienna: Deuticke, 1982);

Achterloo: Eine Komödie in zwei Akten (Zurich: Diogenes, 1983);

Die Erde ist zu schön . . . : Die Physiker; Der Tunnel; Das Unternehmen der Wega (Zurich: Arche, 1983);

Minotaurus: Eine Ballade mit Zeichnungen des Autors (Zurich: Diogenes, 1985);

Justiz (Zurich: Diogenes, 1985);

Varlin, 1900-1977 (New York: Claude Bernard Gallery, 1986);

Der Auftrag oder Vom Beobachter des Beobachters der Beobachter (Zurich: Diogenes, 1986).

If Friedrich Dürrenmatt is a household word, it is as a dramatist. Two plays in particular have insured him lasting fame: *Der Besuch der alten Dame* (The Visit of the Old Lady, 1956; translated as *The Visit*, 1962), a success worldwide, including Broadway and the Soviet Union; and *Die Physiker* (1962; translated as *The Physicists*, 1963), which became the most-performed play in German-language theaters in the year following its premiere. On the other hand, his most successful novel is a detective story and, as such, is unjustly relegated to the category of trivial literature. Furthermore, Dürrenmatt does not write lengthy novels; most of his prose works can be read in a single sitting. Finally, his first three published novels were the products of financial necessity. For all these reasons Dürrenmatt the writer of prose fiction stands in the shadow of Dürrenmatt the dramatist.

In actuality, the same pessimistic view of history, the same distrust of absolutes, and the same dominance of coincidence over rational planning which characterize his dramas also pervade his prose. There is a distinctly dramatic quality to Dürrenmatt's prose which is demonstrated by the ease with which it can be adapted as stage play, radio play, and film. *Der Besuch der alten Dame* was itself an adaptation of an earlier prose version. Two of the novels have been filmed, while another began as a successful film before becoming a novel; yet another was adapted from a radio play and later rewritten as a stage play. Then, too, several of the prose works adhere to, or at least approximate, the dramatic unities of time, place, and plot.

Dürrenmatt was born in Konolfingen, Canton Bern, Switzerland, on 5 January 1921 to Pastor Reinhold Dürrenmatt and Hulda Zimmermann Dürrenmatt. He spent his first fourteen years in the village, which he described as "häßlich, eine Häufung von Gebäuden im Kleinbürgerstil" (ugly, a conglomeration of buildings in petit-bourgeois style). Remembering the fields of tall grain, serpentine paths through piles of hay in dark barns, and the cluttered attic of his house, Dürrenmatt characterized the rural setting in which he spent his formative years as labyrinthine.

Dürrenmatt was a daydreamer who preferred the provocative tales of his father and a favorite teacher to the rigorous discipline of the village school. John Bunyan, Karl May, Jules Verne, and the nineteenth-century Swiss novelist Jeremias Gotthelf fired his imagination at an early age, as did his father's stories of Hercules, Prometheus, Daedalus, Theseus, and the Minotaur from Greek mythology. During his school

An der grossen Strasse

15. Juni. 1945.

Am folgenden Morgen, nachdem die Alte mir geholfen, den Vater zu begraben, traf mein Bruder ein, vom schwarzen Wagen hergeführt den ich schon von weitem auf der grossen Strasse über die Hügel habe fahren sehen. Doch konnte es mein Bruder nicht vermeiden, dass ich jenen erblickte, wenn auch nur zwischen zwei Schlägen meines Herzens, der ihn herangeführt, obschon der Bruder mich bei den Schultern gefasst und ins Haus hinaufgeführt hatte, während sich der Wagen wandte und nach den Städten zurückfuhr. Das Gesicht des Mannes aber, welches ich hinter den Scheiben gesehen, kam mir nie mehr aus dem Sinn und es verfolgte mich wie ein Schreckbild, das uns im Traume erschienen ist. Dieses Antlitz war von äusserstem Ebenmass, doch war ihm eine Kälte eigen, dass erstarrte. Ich fühlte damals eine ungeheure Abwehr die in diesen Zügen lag, welche darauf ausging, den Menschen von sich zu weisen, doch stieg schon damals in mir, wenn auch undeutlich die Ahnung auf, dass dieses Wesen solches nur tat, um ganz im Verborgenen wirken zu können und ich halte diese unbewusste Erkenntnis für den Grund, dass ich mich damals so fürchtete, doch war dies nur einen Augenblick der Fall, denn die Umarmung meines Bruders verdeckte gleichsam den Abgrund, der sich dem Knaben geöffnet. So begannen jene Jahre, welche ich mit meinem Bruder im Hause an der grossen Strasse verbrachte, welche von den Städten nach den grossen Wäldern führte, welche noch zum grossen Teil unerforscht waren und die wir von ferne hinter den Hügeln als einen dunklen Streifen zu erblicken vermochten, den Schein der Städte aber sahen wir in klaren Nächten am südlichen Himmel und dann war es oft, als würden sich in jenen Gegenden riesenhafte Brände ausdehnen. Dann geschah es, dass ich stundenlang dorthin schaute, bis ich einschlief, bis am frühen Morgen das Gepolter

Page from the manuscript for an early story by Dürrenmatt (Elisabeth Brock-Sulzer, Friedrich Dürrenmatt [Zurich: Arche, 1960])

days in Konolfingen Dürrenmatt acquired two life-long hobbies: sketching and astronomy. "Ich wuchs in einer christlichen Welt auf, die mich später nicht losließ" (I grew up in a Christian world, which did not release me later), he writes of his relationship to the villagers under his father's pastoral care. Their expectations of him were unrealistically high, he believed; he was tolerated but never quite trusted by his playmates. The results were a revolt against the religiosity of his father and a distrust of organized religions.

In 1935 the Dürrenmatts moved to Bern. The city was an even greater, albeit different kind of labyrinth, and the displaced country boy felt like the minotaur imprisoned in Daedalus's maze. The intellectual but nonconformist teenager's academic woes continued. At his private prep school he became an expert at feigning illness, and he was not above occasionally altering his grade report–"das Humanste, was ich meinen Eltern gegenüber tun konnte" (the most humane thing I could do for my parents). He preferred spending his days at a café reading Lessing, Hebbel, and Nietzsche. Although he had his uncle's private box in the city theater at his disposal, he was less interested in drama than in painting and drawing. After changing schools and finally passing his university qualifying examination (Type A– Older Languages) in 1941, he intended to pursue an art career. But swimming against the current has always been characteristic of Dürrenmatt, and the aspiring young artist was already resisting the trend at the time he was about to begin serious art studies. His pictures were full of wild fantasy, expressionistic at a time when Bern was swept up in impressionism. Artists laughed at his pictures and told him to learn first to sketch apples. Dürrenmatt abandoned his plans to become a professional painter; still, art remains close to the center of his life. He writes of the "Leidenschaft" (passion) he experiences while working out a technical problem on paper or canvas. One night he sketched until 5:00 A.M., discovering only then that he had been freezing in just a pajama top. In 1976 he confessed to Heinz Ludwig Arnold: "Ich habe sehr darunter gelitten, daß ich beim Schreiben nicht dieses unmittelbare Verhältnis zur Materie habe wie beim Zeichnen" (I have long suffered from the fact that I do not have the same immediate relationship to the material in writing that I have in drawing).

Instead of the Art Academy, Dürrenmatt enrolled at the University of Bern for the winter semester 1941-1942 and the following summer

Dürrenmatt circa 1946 (Elisabeth Brock-Sulzer, Friedrich Dürrenmatt: Stationen seines Werkes *[Zurich: Arche, 1970])*

semester. While earning money as a tutor of Latin and Greek, he began a study of German literature. After a difference of opinion with the leading Germanist in Bern, Fritz Strich, and a brief stint with the military, from which he was soon released because of nearsightedness (he had begun saluting mailmen instead of officers), he took up residency in Zurich in the winter of 1942 "mit der Ausrede, dort studieren zu müssen" (with the excuse of having to study there). An infrequent visitor to the lecture halls, Dürrenmatt spent much of his time in an attic room trying to write a comedy. He also frequented the social circle of the artist Walter Jonas; through Jonas he became acquainted with German expressionist literature, especially Heym and Kafka. This bohemian life in Zurich was the fertile soil in which fantastic stories began to grow. On Christmas Eve 1942 he wrote the first of the narratives he would later publish in the collection *Die Stadt* (The City, 1952). "Weihnacht" (Christmas), a 120-word paragraph written in a staccato, subject-verb-object style, is a nightmarish vision of darkness, snow, and emptiness. All but one of the stories in *Die Stadt* were written in the ensuing three years.

From the fall of 1943 until the summer of 1946 Dürrenmatt studied philosophy in Bern, a study he claimed was prompted by the conflict with his father over religion. Plato left a deep impression on Dürrenmatt–the cave allegory recurs in his works–and he was an enthusiastic reader of Kant. Perhaps most influential was Kierkegaard, about whom he planned, but never wrote, a dissertation. Under his name on his door in Zurich Dürrenmatt hung the designation "Nihilistischer Dichter" (nihilistic poet).

The works in *Die Stadt* reflect both the religious conflict and the study of philosophy he undertook to master it. The awkward, choppy sentences of the earliest prose works precisely and effectively express the unrelenting, horrifying images. The sentences fall like rhythmic hammer blows in "Der Folterknecht" (The Torturer), which, along with "Weihnacht," forms the first and most nihilistic of the four divisions of *Die Stadt*. Aptly called by Armin Arnold "one of the bitterest indictments of God in world literature," the barely seven-page-long parable depicts the world as a torture chamber and God as a sadistic torturer who repudiates, with derisive laughter, his own erstwhile human incarnation. "Der Hund" (The Dog) represents a barely disguised repudiation of the extreme religious position taken by Dürrenmatt's father. An ascetic preacher of the Gospel, who has left his wealth and family in order to teach the truth, is followed and ultimately killed by a mysterious black devil-dog. His daughter, who believes in the Gospel but also breaks free to experience the world by making love to the narrator, is able to master the beast. In "Das Bild des Sisyphos" (also published separately, 1952; translated as "The Picture of Sisyphos," 1968) the artist Rotmantel creates a fortune out of nothing by forging and selling a Hieronymous Bosch painting, but to complete the creation ex nihilo he must regain the forgery. In a struggle over the painting, Rotmantel loses everything; the flames which destroy the forgery

consume him and his house as well. If the author is coming to grips with his own nihilistic tendencies here, he seems to be winning the battle: nothingness proves to be infertile ground, in which it is impossible to create anything. "Der Theaterdirektor" describes the rise of a dictator. Though immediately applicable to Hitler, the tale's parabolic nature allows it to be generalized to fit any political system that can, by perverting aesthetic values, convince its citizens to give up their freedom and individuality in the service of an ideology. In "Die Falle" (The Trap; also published separately, 1952), first published in 1950 under the title *Der Nihilist*, a man convinced of the meaninglessness of existence is unable to complete the second half of a murder-suicide: at the decisive moment he is consumed by a desire to live. The protagonist's nightmare preceding the murder is a concentrated dose of pure nihilism in which history is depicted as a progression from a void to Hell's fires. The protagonist's awakening cry, "Wo bleibt die Gnade?" (Where is mercy?), remains unanswered. "Die Stadt" (The City) perhaps best reveals the influence of Kafka but also of Plato (cave allegory) and Kierkegaard. The narrator attempts unsuccessfully to ascertain the truth about his existence in a dimly lit subterranean prison purely through deductive reasoning. Uncertain whether he is a guard or a prisoner, he is afraid to try to walk out, an act which would give an immediate answer. Were he to be stopped, the realization that he is a prisoner would destroy him. On the other hand, his abortive attempts to solve the riddle by reason prevent him from taking a leap of faith and living contentedly in the belief that he is a guard, and thus free. His ramblings end in mid-sentence, sparing the reader further insight into the tortuous mental labyrinth which, according to the subtitle, goes on for fifteen volumes. The protagonist in "Der Tunnel" (also published separately, 1952; translated as "The Tunnel," 1961), the most autobiographical of the stories, attains a degree of personal salvation through faith denied to the narrator in "Die Stadt." Dürrenmatt caricatures himself as an obese student with thick glasses traveling by train from Bern to Zurich. This student, who lives behind a facade of order and barricades his senses by various means against the horror of the world, is suddenly forced to face this horror head-on when the train enters a tunnel which never comes to an end. As recourses to logic fade, the student accepts his fate as God's unalterable will: "Gott ließ uns fallen und so stürzen wir denn auf ihn zu" (God has dropped us, and so we fall toward him). Finally, in "Pilatus" (also published separately, 1949), the collection which began with Christmas ends with the Crucifixion. Contrasted with Christ's suffering is the mental torment of Pilate, on which Dürrenmatt fixes the reader's attention. It is a tragic Pilate, who only partially comprehends the prisoner he is condemning. He recognizes Christ as a god but mistrusts his motives: the humility in the god's eyes is human, not divine, so he must be setting a trap to ensnare humanity. Unable to coax the god out of his disguise, Pilate carries out the sentence on him. Later that day he gazes in horror on the dead face of God, but the resurrection two days later leaves him unmoved. Pilate is the first in a long line of Dürrenmatt characters whose tragic flaw is the inability to recognize and accept God's grace.

Criticism of the early prose varies along a broad spectrum. Hans Bänziger and Murray B. Peppard regard it as weak and mannered; Bänziger feels that the visual images stifle linguistic creativity, while Peppard points to an immature style and the obvious influence of Kafka and Ernst Jünger. Calling the collection the work of a "heavyweight Kafkaist," Timo Tiusanen sees the early prose as a "philosophical and artistic dead end" out of which Dürrenmatt escaped into the theater; nevertheless, he praises "Der Tunnel" as worthy of inclusion in anthologies. Emil Weber, on the other hand, asserts that the narratives of this collection must be taken as seriously as Dürrenmatt's dramas, arguing that the secret core around which they are conceived is his planned but unwritten dissertation on Kierkegaard. Elisabeth Brock-Sulzer writes that the early narratives can stand on their own and that they reveal a sincerity, a poetic and human courage which are hard to find in a modern author. Peter Spycher and Walter Muschg agree that the tales present nightmarish but not nihilistic visions of horror and despair, and they see a transcendent truth behind these visions of a world created but then abandoned by God. Spycher downplays the influence of the expressionists, emphasizing that Dürrenmatt had already developed his own prose style.

Dürrenmatt says in the afterword to the collection that this early prose prefigures his dramas. Like the prose, the dramas are philosophical, and he wrestles with the same problems in both genres: the difficulty of discerning the truth, man's inability to accept divine grace, the supremacy of coincidence over calculation, the nature of justice, and man's responsibility to live in the world rather than try to escape from it.

By the time *Die Stadt* was published in 1952, Dürrenmatt had already achieved fame as a dramatist with four plays and as a prose writer with two serialized detective novels. The first two dramas, *Es steht geschrieben* (It Is Written, 1947) and *Der Blinde* (The Blind Man, 1947), were not as successful as the subsequent two; though containing some humorous passages, they are not primarily comedies. *Es steht geschrieben* is a satirical historical drama about the reign of the Anabaptists in Münster from 1533 to 1536 under "King" Johann Bockelson. The premiere in Zurich on 19 April 1947 was greeted with catcalls. Nevertheless, the drama garnered for Dürrenmatt the first of many literary awards, the Welti-Foundation Prize for Drama. *Der Blinde*, first staged in Basel on 10 January 1948, confronts the healthy, peaceful dream world of a blind duke with the reality of the war-devastated land over which he rules. The governor, a sadistic manipulator, succeeds in destroying the duke's illusion but not his faith. As Armin Arnold states, Dürrenmatt is wrestling with God in this play: by equating faith with blindness he seems to be saying that for anyone who can truly see, there is no just God.

Dürrenmatt's first real comedy, *Romulus der Große* (1956; translated as *Romulus the Great*, 1964), premiered in Basel on 23 April 1949. Out of a sense of justice Romulus, the last emperor of Rome, condemns the corrupt empire to fall by offering no resistance to Odoaker and the Goths. Wanting and expecting death at the hands of the barbarians for his betrayal of Rome, Romulus instead meets a sympathetic Odoaker, like himself a chicken farmer, who pardons and pensions him off. The play is guided by a principle Dürrenmatt would later formulate in conjunction with *Die Physiker* (1962; translated as *The Physicists*, 1963), that a plot has not been completely thought out until it has taken its worst possible turn.

Die Ehe des Herrn Mississippi (1952; translated as *The Marriage of Mr. Mississippi*, 1966), which Dürrenmatt considered a turning point in his career, had its successful premiere in Munich on 26 March 1952. While bringing its author recognition in Germany, it also brought charges from Tilly Wedekind that Dürrenmatt had plagiarized her late husband's comedy *Schloß Wetterstein*

Scene from the premiere of Dürrenmatt's play Es steht geschrieben *at the Schauspielhaus Zürich, April 1947 (Elisabeth Brock-Sulzer,* Friedrich Dürrenmatt: Stationen seines Werkes *[Zurich: Arche, 1970])*

(1910; translated as *Castle Wetterstein*, 1952). Although denying the charge, Dürrenmatt did acknowledge the influence Frank Wedekind had had on him and a whole generation of dramatists. The play is a statement on the immutability of human nature, the author's distrust of ideologies, and the inability of individuals, regardless of how committed they are, to change the world.

On 11 October 1946 Dürrenmatt had married the actress Lotti Geißler, whom he had met while a student in Bern. The couple lived in a four-room converted schoolhouse in Basel, where Lotti was performing at the city theater while Dürrenmatt wrote *Der Blinde* and sketches for Cabaret Cornichon. In 1948 the couple moved into

the "Festi," a villa outside Ligerz in western Switzerland, where they lived until 1952 with Lotti's mother. A son, Peter, was born on 6 August 1948, followed by two daughters: Barbara, born 19 September 1949, and Ruth, on 6 October 1951. It was in this idyllic setting between Lake Biel and the Jura Mountains that Dürrenmatt wrote what would become his most famous prose work, the detective novel *Der Richter und sein Henker* (1952; translated as *The Judge and His Hangman*, 1954). He wrote it, as he readily admits, for the money: his wife was about to give birth, and he needed medical treatment for diabetes. A deal was struck with a semimonthly periodical, *Der schweizersche Beobachter*, for a criminal novel in in-

Georges Wilson as Romulus in a 1964 Paris production of Dürrenmatt's comedy Romulus der Große *(photograph by Lipnitzki)*

stallments. *Der Richter und sein Henker* appeared from December 1950 to March 1951, followed by a sequel, *Der Verdacht* (1953; translated as *The Quarry*, 1961), in the same periodical from September 1951 to March 1952. The second novel, while popular, never approached the sales figures for the first. By 1974 *Der Richter und sein Henker* had sold over a million copies in paperback; by 1981 sales of the Rowohlt paperback edition alone were approaching two million copies.

Common to both novels is Inspector Bärlach, an aging Bern police commissioner who is dying of stomach cancer. The villains in both are amoral, driven by a nihilistic philosophy which places them outside the bounds of good and evil and into the realm of absolute freedom. In *Der Richter und sein Henker* the murder of a policeman becomes the coincidental backdrop for the settling of a forty-year-old score with an international criminal. Gastmann, the latest of his many aliases, had wagered Bärlach long ago that

it was possible to commit crimes which could never be detected. Numerous perfect crimes in the intervening years have shown him to be correct. Now Bärlach punishes his archenemy for the murder of the policeman, a crime which Gastmann did not commit, using the real murderer–another policeman–as his "executioner." In *Der Verdacht* a Nazi concentration camp doctor, reminiscent of the torturer in the early prose, is Bärlach's quarry. Presumed by all the world to be dead, the evil Dr. Emmenberger has been operating a clinic in Zurich, where he secretly continues the sadistic murder of patients with methods he had employed during the war. Confined to bed by cancer, Bärlach has himself admitted to the clinic and tries to overcome Emmenberger in a psychological game, which he ultimately loses. Bärlach is about to become the demonic doctor's next victim, but a series of coincidences results in Emmenberger's death at the hands of a concentration camp survivor. In both novels the amoral villains, though ultimately defeated, are stronger than their idealistic adversary.

These two novels have generated voluminous criticism. Several scholars have pointed to obvious breaches of conventional rules governing detective stories, in particular Bärlach's unorthodox methods. Seeking a literary source, Armin Arnold finds the greatest resemblance between Bärlach and Georges Simenon's Inspector Maigret, while Spycher finds a local model in the Swiss author Friedrich Glauser's detective, Sergeant Studer. Dürrenmatt denies a connection to Glauser, claiming instead the direct influence of Theodor Fontane's novel *Der Stechlin* (1898). To Werner Klose and Manfred Durzak, *Der Richter und sein Henker* is a parable of absolute justice. Klose sees a dialectical process at work in Bärlach, whose sense of justice is perverted in the pursuit of Gastmann. Brock-Sulzer finds this novel to be Dürrenmatt's most autobiographical work, permeated by the people, countryside, and dialect of the Bern uplands. *Der Verdacht* is generally considered the weaker of the two novels. Bänziger finds too much editorializing in it and sees the commissioner not as a hero but as a moralist made alternately tragic and ludicrous. Ulrich Profitlich offers a similar view, placing Bärlach of *Der Verdacht* into that group of Dürrenmatt's protagonists whose heroic intent is genuine but whose deeds are rendered futile by circumstances beyond their control. Finally, Spycher and Günther Waldmann emphasize the religious qual-

Friedrich Domin as Mississippi and Maria Nicklisch as Anastasia in a scene from the premiere of Dürrenmatt's Die Ehe des Herrn Mississippi *in Munich in 1952 (photograph by Steinmetz)*

ity of both novels, which are antirationalistic and show that the world cannot be enlightened through the intellect, that human justice is no match for evil, and that God's plan is not for man to know.

In 1952 the Dürrenmatts moved to Neuenburg. During the two years between *Der Verdacht* and his next published prose work, the novel *Grieche sucht Griechin* (Greek Man Seeks Greek Woman, 1955; translated as *Once a Greek . . .* , 1965), Dürrenmatt wrote several radio plays and the stage play *Ein Engel kommt nach Babylon* (1954; translated as *An Angel Comes to Babylon*, 1964). The latter, which deals with human blindness to divine grace, became one of Dürrenmatt's most highly regarded comedies, but it had a rocky premiere in Munich on 22 December 1953. Dürrenmatt, who liked to have a hand in directing his plays and who habitually made changes in a play after seeing it rehearsed, had placed the direction of *Ein Engel kommt nach Babylon* in the able hands of Hans Schweikert. Delayed by illness, Dürrenmatt arrived in Munich to discover that Schweikert and art director Caspar

Neher had interpreted the play as a satire. It was too late for appreciable changes, and the author perceived the premiere to be a failure. Disillusioned with the theater, he vowed to write no more plays, but four years later he reworked *Ein Engel kommt nach Babylon* into its final, highly successful version.

Grieche sucht Griechin began as an idea for a film which, Dürrenmatt later admitted, seemed ridiculous to him even as he was describing it to the prospective director. As he began to write the story, however, it took shape as something quite unexpected, a fairy-tale prose comedy. As with the detective novels, the immediate need for money prompted the writing of this narrative: his wife required surgery and the prognosis was bad. "Der Vorschuß mußte her," he wrote later. "Ich schrieb das Buch voll böser Ahnungen in wenigen Tagen zu Ende" (The advance was necessary. Full of foreboding I wrote the entire book in a few days). The short novel contains Dürrenmatt's strongest statement on the nature of love and grace. The love of Chloe Saloniki, a former courtesan, is an unexpected windfall

Dürrenmatt with the producer, Franz Peter Wirth, during film-ing of a television play based on Dürrenmatt's novel Der Rich-ter und sein Henker *in August 1956 (Elisabeth Brock-Sulzer,* Friedrich Dürrenmatt: Stationen seines Werkes *[Zurich: Arche, 1970])*

of grace for the naive, moralistic Arnolph Archilochos. It changes his life in such breathtakingly rapid ways–bringing him instant fame and fortune–that he cannot imagine having deserved it. Indeed, he has not deserved it, be-cause grace, according to Dürrenmatt, cannot be earned; one can only become worthy of it after the fact by accepting the gift and using it wisely. This theme is also present in *Ein Engel kommt nach Babylon*, but whereas there Nebuchadnazzar stubbornly refuses his heavenly gift, Archilochos is awakened to the error of his thinking and at-tains a clear vision of the world as it really is. He is saved, even though his pseudomorality caused him to reject Chloe's love when he discovered her past. But in an alternate "Ende für

Leihbibliotheken" (Ending for Lending Librar-ies), he is reunited with Chloe and receives contin-ued education in the nature of absolute love, which accepts unconditionally and in spite of the past.

The tale is set in a romanticized Swiss me-tropolis. The reader is never permitted to forget that he is party to a fairy tale: the president trav-els in a carriage drawn by six white stallions, na-ture mirrors the mood of the protagonist, and the words *Märchen* (fairy tale), *Zauber* (magic), *Wunder* (miracle), and their synonyms appear fre-quently to describe Archilochos's meteoric good fortune. Reinhold Grimm astutely labels the Greek an anti-Job who can no more understand his sudden abundance of blessings than his bibli-cal counterpart could comprehend his incredible misfortune. The narrative defies characterization, asserts Brock-Sulzer; unlike the criminal novels, which represent a flight from literature, it is firmly embedded in literary tradition and resem-bles a medieval allegory. Spycher calls the story one of Dürrenmatt's wittiest, brightest, and most charming tales. Gerhard Knapp, however, says that it exhausts itself in crude situation comedy and plays on words. While Peppard regards the second ending as written tongue in cheek "for sen-timental old maids and aunts who wish to have a gentle moral added to a happy ending," Brock-Sulzer, Spycher, and Heidi Butler-Schmidt de-fend the alternate conclusion as the real one, without which no miracle takes place.

The first of the two dramas for which Dürrenmatt is best known, *Der Besuch der alten Dame*, was written in the same year as *Grieche sucht Griechin*, a year which signals the beginning of his most productive period. Once unjustly branded a whore and driven from her village in disgrace, Claire Zachanassian, now the world's richest woman, returns with a billion francs to buy the murder of Alfred Ill, the perpetrator of the lie. Godlike, impervious to mercy and pity, she possesses, in Dürrenmatt's words, "Distanz zu den Menschen . . . als zu einer käuflichen Ware" (aloofness toward people as toward a purchasable commodity). Ill becomes a hero because he recog-nizes his guilt and is willing to die to atone for it. The people of Güllen are, however, not villains, just poor, hungry, and all too human.

Underlying this most successful drama is a narrative entitled "Mondfinsternis" (Lunar Eclipse), which was written before *Der Besuch der alten Dame* and turned into the play because, once again, Dürrenmatt needed money. Claire

Scene from Dürrenmatt's Ein Engel kommt nach Babylon, *which premiered in Munich in December 1953*
(Archiv Schauspielhaus Zürich)

Zachanassian's forerunner is an aging but ener- getic man named Walt Lotscher, who made his for- tune in Canada and returns to his financially troubled village to exact revenge on the man who had married his fiancée years before. His mo- tivation is much weaker than the injustice which drove Claire back to Güllen, and there is nothing heroic in Mani Döufu, the "victim" of Walt's ven- geance. Tired of life and seeking anything that will give his existence meaning, Mani offers no resistance to the suggestion that he die for the fi- nancial recovery of the village. Feeling no guilt be- cause he has done nothing wrong, Mani remains a static, simpleminded character, and his death lacks the grandeur of Alfred Ill's. Ultimately his death is robbed of all meaning through a final irony: even as he was dying, government officials were en route to announce their plan to infuse

the village with millions of francs and turn it into a resort. "Mondfinsternis" remained unpublished until 1981, when it was included in the volume *Stoffe I-III* (Themes I-III).

Dürrenmatt's fourth major prose work, *Die Panne* (translated as *Traps*, 1960), was published in 1956; a radio play version, which first ap- peared in 1961, was actually written before the narrative. In a short introduction Dürrenmatt raises the question whether there are "noch mögliche Geschichten" (still possible stories) to be written by authors who refuse either to deliver morally useful maxims and higher values or to bare their inner selves to the reader. Fate, he writes, has left the stage and now lurks behind the scenes, while blind chance rules in a technolog- ical society where dams break, nuclear reactors ex-

Ill: Herr Bürgermeister! Womit wollen diese Leute zahlen? Ich frage Sie, womit?

Der Bürgermeister: Jeder muss sich in diesen schweren Zeiten selber durchschlagen.

Ill: Wie ich zu Ihnen Auf dem Wege hieher Traf ich den Sigrist, Herr Bürgermeister. Er sagte mir, Hofbauer wolle eine Bar auftun, eine Bar in Güllen.

Der Bürgermeister: Eine Bar, das ist nun leicht über. Trieb.

Der Bürgermeister: Den guten Leuten ist nicht zu verübeln, dass sie etwas Abwechslung suchen.

Ill: Es stimmt auch, Bürger-

Ill: In diesen schweren Zeiten.

Burg: Um Mitternacht muss er schliessen

Der Bürgermeister: Eben.

Ill: Man kauft neue Schuhe in diesen schweren Zeiten, kauft einen Kognak von 20 Mark und er-öffnet eine Bar. Ich bin nicht blind, Bürgermeister, das alles zielt auf mein Leben.

Man macht Schulden. Diese Schulden wird man einmal bezahlen müssen. Die alte Dame braucht nur zu warten. Auf ihren Zahn von Gold.

Mit den Schulden steigt die Wohl..., der Wohlstand, mit dem Wohlstand die Notwendigkeit mich zu töten, mit der Notwend... Notwendigkeit mich zu töten. Und so wartet jeder, bis mich einer tötet. Ihr alle wartet

Bur: Unsinn. Ill
Ill: Logik, Bürger

Page from the manuscript for Dürrenmatt's Der Besuch der alten Dame *(Elisabeth Brock-Sulzer,* Friedrich Dürrenmatt *[Zurich: Arche, 1960])*

Therese Giehse as Claire Zachanassian, the world's richest woman, in the premiere of Der Besuch der alten Dame *at the Schauspielhaus Zürich, 1956 (Urs Jenny,* Friedrich Dürrenmatt *[Velber: Friedrich, 1965])*

plode, and survival hinges on computers functioning correctly. It is in this arbitrary world of breakdowns, he concludes, where "still possible stories" are to be found. Thus he narrates the story of Alfredo Traps, whose Studebaker's engine failure leads to more catastrophic results than he could have imagined.

The German title, *Panne,* translates as "breakdown" and plays not only on the engine failure which leaves Traps stranded at the home of four retired court officials but also on the communications breakdown which permits him to misinterpret as reality the elaborate artwork his hosts create. Like *Der Besuch der alten Dame,* the tale exposes the dehumanizing effects of the economic boom in postwar Switzerland. But while the people of Güllen are motivated by poverty, Traps's "crime"–he told his boss that the boss's wife was having an affair, knowing that the shock could cause a heart attack–is a result of greed. The re-

tired officials ensnare him in an elaborate parlor game and convince him that he is guilty of the premeditated murder of his boss. Legally Traps is not culpable, and his hosts intend the mock trial merely as an evening's entertainment. That the guest carries out the "death sentence" on himself is a result of the alcohol, the camaraderie, the prosecutor's clever arguments, and Traps's desire to believe that he could have been capable of committing a grandiose crime. The "trial" is interspersed with eating scenes that are among Dürrenmatt's most grotesque, easily outdistancing Bärlach's culinary orgy which concludes *Der Richter und sein Henker.*

Hans Mayer warns against a guilt-and-atonement interpretation of Traps's suicide: far from moralizing about the crimes which every man commits unknowingly during his lifetime, Dürrenmatt is depicting a society devoid of responsibility, in which the writing of tragedy is rendered impossible by the absence of true guilt. Traps is capable of feeling neither guilt nor remorse at his victim's death, Mayer contends; therefore, his suicide is no atonement but a result of confusing the prosecutor's carefully constructed fiction for a reality which gives his humdrum existence a perverse magnificence. Traps's death is merely the last huge "Panne." Spycher disagrees, arguing that the court helps the accused to a recognition of guilt and a desire for atonement. For Knapp, *Die Panne* is Dürrenmatt's ironic statement on the impossibility of artistically representing the problem of guilt and atonement in the modern commercialized, materialistic world; justice according to traditional rules is exposed as a dangerous anachronism. Jan Knopf sees another type of anachronism as the object of Dürrenmatt's scorn: traditional aesthetics, which demands a meaningful, predictable, well-rounded work of art. Against this expectation of perfection Dürrenmatt employs the weapons of coincidence and senselessness.

Dürrenmatt's third detective novel, *Das Versprechen* (translated as *The Pledge,* 1959), began in 1957 as a movie on the subject of sexual crimes against children and was intended as a warning to parents. The film, *Es geschah am hellichten Tag* (English version: *It Happened in Broad Daylight,* 1960), was directed by Lazar Wechsler with the script written by Dürrenmatt in collaboration with Ladislao Vajda. It has been shown in over seventy countries, an apparent success for the pedagogical undertaking. Nevertheless, its author was unwilling to let stand a plot, no matter

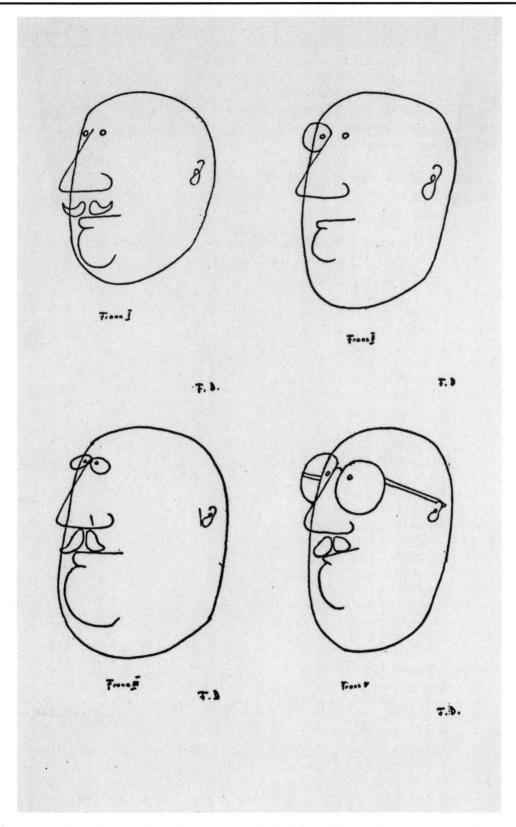

Sketches by Dürrenmatt of characters for his play Frank der Fünfte *(Elisabeth Brock-Sulzer, Friedrich Dürrenmatt: Stationen seines Werkes [Zurich: Arche, 1970])*

how successful, that did not conform to his idea of reality. Thus arose the novel, which appeared in 1958 with the subtitle *Requiem auf den Kriminalroman* (Requiem for a Detective Novel). It is not unusual for Dürrenmatt to change the ending of a story when revising it or adapting it for another medium, yet nowhere does he so radically alter the philosophical statement as in *Das Versprechen*. Whereas police lieutenant Matthäi's logically constructed but unorthodox plan to catch the child murderer by using live bait succeeds in the film, it fails in the novel. It fails not because of any error in planning or hesitancy at the crucial moment but because of the most absurd, incalculable coincidence: the death of the murderer in an automobile accident. Matthäi does not learn why the bait was not taken, and for the detective, who is as sure of his own thoroughness as he is of the predictability of the universe, the result is a gradual descent into insanity.

Matthäi, according to Brock-Sulzer, is a tragic figure who cannot abandon his rational nature simply because fate chooses to be irrational. By taking the absurd seriously, Dürrenmatt has discovered true tragedy, the possibility of which he had denied for the modern day. Armin Arnold, on the other hand, emphasizes not Matthäi's tragic flaw but his stupidity: it is inexcusable for a good detective not to have reckoned with the possibility, no matter how slight, of an accident. Tiusanen sees the novel as Dürrenmatt's answer to the extremists among his other characters: the nihilists who see the world as devoid of justice and the idealists who would establish systems of absolute justice based on the belief in an absolute order in the universe. The cosmos contains chaos *and* order, and both must be taken into account. Spycher calls *Das Versprechen* Dürrenmatt's most mature novel; Brock-Sulzer says it is his most amazing work, in which he demonstrates his mastery of the genre; and Arnold sees in it a more mature narrative technique than in the first two detective novels.

In the fourteen years between *Das Versprechen* and his next published prose work, Dürrenmatt wrote a number of plays. *Frank der Fünfte* (Frank the Fifth, 1960), a musical comedy about a bank run by a group of gangsters, premiered on 19 March 1959 in Zurich under the direction of Oskar Walterlin. The play was not a success; perhaps, as the author contended, the audience misunderstood it. Its inspiration, Dürrenmatt argues, is not in Bertolt Brecht but

in Shakespeare. Frank V, a lover of Goethe and Mörike, is as bad a banker as Richard III is a king, and both are cowardly criminals. The members of the banking family are motivated by fear, mutual mistrust, and the necessity of secrecy.

Die Physiker premiered in Zurich in a three-day gala on 21 February 1962. Kurt Horowitz directed, and Dürrenmatt's friend Teo Otto designed the sets. With Therese Giehse, who had earlier starred as Claire Zachanassian, in the role of the mad doctor Mathilde von Zahnd and with Hans Christian Blech in the role of the physicist Möbius, the drama was a huge artistic and popular success. Written against the backdrop of the Berlin Wall, the cold war, and nuclear saber rattling, *Die Physiker* remains apolitical in that it does not side with either superpower. Instead, it wrestles with the issue of the responsibility of the individual scientist for the ways in which his discoveries are used and with the question of whether problems of global proportions can be solved on the individual level.

In his "Einundzwanzig Punkte zu den 'Physikern'" (Twenty-one Points Concerning the "Physicists"), appended to the play, Dürrenmatt theorizes on the function of chance in his dramaturgy. A plot is only thoroughly thought out when it has taken its worst possible turn, a phenomenon brought about by chance. The more methodically people proceed, the more drastically coincidence can affect them. Möbius had discovered how a force of unparalleled magnitude could be released, and had feared the consequences if the knowledge fell into the hands of the competing superpowers. He had fled into the apparent safety of an insane asylum, where he believed he could work in peace. The coincidence which foils him is that he has fled into the wrong asylum. The doctor is herself mad and power hungry, and she has long ago stolen his secrets.

With *Herkules und der Stall des Augias* (1963; translated as *Hercules and the Augean Stables*, 1963), Dürrenmatt took a satiric swipe at the bureaucracy of Switzerland and the idolization of the Swiss national hero, Wilhelm Tell. In this stage adaptation of his 1954 radio play of the same name, Hercules is a national hero who fails at removing the mountains of manure from the land—not because he lacks the talent to do so but because of an indecisive bureaucracy which thwarts him at every turn.

Dürrenmatt achieved considerable success with *Der Meteor* (1966; translated as *The Meteor*, 1966), which had its first performance on 20 Janu-

Dürrenmatt circa 1960 (photograph by J. H. Bruell)

tors. In September of that year the two successfully staged *König Johann* (1968), Dürrenmatt's adaptation of Shakespeare's *King John*. Philosophical and aesthetic disagreements soon arose, however, among the members of the collective running the theater. Dürrenmatt returned to Zurich in October 1969, having suffered a heart attack as well as the failure of a promising venture. The following month he traveled with his wife to Philadelphia, where he accepted an honorary doctorate from Temple University. They also visited Florida, Mexico, and the Caribbean. The author's impressions are recorded in a somewhat desultory, often critical collection of impressions, *Sätze aus Amerika* (Sentences from America, 1970).

In 1969 and 1970 Dürrenmatt adapted August Strindberg's *Doedsdansen* (1901; translated as *The Dance of Death*, 1912) as *Play Strindberg* and Shakespeare's *Titus Andronicus*. In *Play Strindberg* the theme is Strindberg's, but the product is uniquely Dürrenmatt: a grotesque comedy on the subject of marital tragedies. On 10 November 1970 an original drama, *Porträt eines Planeten* (Portrait of a Planet, 1971), premiered in Düsseldorf. *Porträt eines Planeten* demonstrates the increasing interest of its author in modern experimental theater and the resulting shift to simpler sets, fewer actors, and the concentration of meaning into fewer words. Much more is left to the imagination of the audience and to the skill of the actors. *Porträt eines Planeten* is a tragicomic look at mankind in a series of vignettes, unrelated yet performed by the same actors with the implication of simultaneity. Together the vignettes are a composite portrait of the earth taken by the giant flashbulb of a cosmic camera: an exploding supernova which destroys the solar system. Mankind is forever frozen as it is at the moment of its annihilation, and implicit in the drama is the question whether this is the way the human race would want its final portrait to look.

Delivered as a lecture at the University of Mainz in 1968, Dürrenmatt's *Monstervortrag über Gerechtigkeit und Recht nebst einem helvetischen Zwischenspiel* (1969; translated as "A Monster Lecture on Justice and Law Together with a Helvetian Interlude," 1982) examines the concepts of freedom and justice in capitalism and socialism, systems the author labels "The Wolf Game" and "The Good Shepherd Game," respectively. Central to the essay is a Helvetian Interlude, a critical discussion of Switzerland's role as a wolf disguised as a superlamb and of its "geistige Landesverteidigung" (national defense), which

ary 1966 in Zurich. The play returns to the theme of the inability to recognize and accept divine grace. The famous author Wolfgang Schwitter expects and wants to die, yet he twice rises from the dead, while otherwise healthy individuals around him die as a result of his carelessness and lack of consideration. Dürrenmatt is analyzing the nature of faith: belief cannot be based on empirical evidence, only on trust, so Schwitter, the cynic who has never trusted anyone, cannot have faith even when a miracle happens to him.

In 1968 Werner Düggelin, the newly elected director of the City Theater in Basel, invited Dürrenmatt to join the theater's board of direc-

Dürrenmatt at a rehearsal for his play Die Physiker *at the Schauspielhaus Zürich in 1962 (Elisabeth Brock-Sulzer*, Friedrich Dürrenmatt: Stationen seines Werkes *[Zurich: Arche, 1970])*

Dürrenmatt calls a contradiction in terms, since a nation cannot be defended intellectually.

Dürrenmatt had begun work on the novella *Der Sturz* (The Fall) in 1965, but it was not published until 1971. His fascination with the psychology of the power collective, already treated in *Frank der Fünfte*, had been piqued anew by a month-long trip to the Soviet Union which he took with his wife in the spring of 1964. Already a popular author in Russia because of *Der Besuch der alten Dame*, which was touted there as demonstrating the inherent evil in the capitalist system, Dürrenmatt was feted as an honored guest of the Soviet literary establishment. *Der Sturz* does not mention the Soviet Union by name, but the atmosphere of the Kremlin pervades it. The characters have no names, only letters to denote their order in the power structure. They are the nation's power elite, yet each individual's power is so fragile and contingent on that of the others that protecting and increasing it becomes the pri-

mary occupation of each member of the collective. A series of uncanny coincidences topples a tyrant: the failure of one of the functionaries to attend a meeting–he had forgotten the date–sets in motion a chain reaction of suspicion and fear which leads to the ouster and murder of the Chairman.

Der Sturz could easily have been written as a drama. With its unities of time, place, and plot, its rising action, climax, falling action, and ultimate stoic death of the protagonist, the dramatic narrative superficially resembles a tragedy. Like *Die Panne*, however, *Der Sturz* is governed by chance, not necessity. It is another of those "still possible stories" in which breakdowns–simple miscalculations–determine life or death. The conference room where Dürrenmatt sets his grotesque comedy of errors is located in a world beyond moral imperatives, where the only guiding principle is the instinct to self-preservation, where nothing is inevitable and all is avoidable, and where, ultimately, nothing is learned–a

Portrait of Dürrenmatt by Varlin, 1962

world where comedy, not tragedy, is the only possible medium of expression. The story is more than a mere swipe at the Soviet Politburo; it is a model of reality. In his 1976 conversation with Heinz Ludwig Arnold, Dürrenmatt said that an author "hat unabhängig von der politischen Situation Marksteine zu setzen mit dem Hinweis: es ginge auch so . . . es wäre auch eine Welt denkbar, eine andere Vernunft" (must set milestones independent of politics with the indication: it could also be this way . . . another world would be conceivable, another form of reason).

For his next drama Dürrenmatt returned to a theme which was central to his most successful plays, *Der Besuch der alten Dame* and *Die Physiker:* collaboration. In the epilogue to the second ver-

sion of *Ein Engel kommt nach Babylon* (1958), Dürrenmatt had written: "Dem Plane nach sollte als nächstes Stück der Turmbau selber dargestellt werden: 'Die Mitmacher.' Alle sind gegen den Turm, und dennoch kommt er zustande . . . " (According to plan the next play should describe the construction of the Tower [of Babel] itself: "The Accomplices." Everyone is against the tower, and nevertheless it comes about . . .). This projected sequel to *Ein Engel kommt nach Babylon* was never written. In 1959, however, while spending the summer in Manhattan, Dürrenmatt experimented with the accomplice problem in a prose narrative, "Smithy," which became the prototype for his 1973 play *Der Mitmacher* (The Accomplice, published in 1978). The extreme economy of words in the play's expressionistic staccato dialogue did not appeal to the audience, and a feud broke out between author and director. The result was Dürrenmatt's worst theatrical failure. In 1976 he published the 300-page volume *Der Mitmacher: Ein Komplex*, which, in addition to the drama, contains a series of afterwords to elucidate the text, a diatribe against Bertolt Brecht, and two previously unpublished narratives: "Smithy" and "Das Sterben der Pythia" (The Death of Pythia).

Both "Smithy" and *Der Mitmacher* deal with the collaboration between a vindictive medical scientist and a gangster. Their illicit operation involves an invention called necrodialysis, whereby corpses are dissolved into their component parts and thus disposed of without a trace. Both narrative and play end with the refusal of one of the collaborators to participate further. It is a brief moment of personal heroism, which proves fatal. Although bizarre in its subject matter, "Smithy" is a more conventional story than *Der Mitmacher*, recalling the earlier period in which it was first written. In a fairy-tale episode Smithy, like Arnolph Archilochos before him, receives the unearned love of a beautiful woman. This act of kindness changes his life. When the woman's body is brought to him later for necrodialysis, he repudiates the lucrative business, though it means death at the hands of the gangsters. In contrast to Smithy's sacrifice, which has significance and is indeed heroic, that of his dramatic counterpart fourteen years later is futile. In *Der Mitmacher* the depth and breadth of the corruption in society render the individual powerless against it.

In "Das Sterben der Pythia," an adaptation of the Oedipus saga, coincidence again takes center stage. The oracle at Delphi is corrupt and can

Scene from the premiere of the stage version of Dürrenmatt's Herkules und der Stall des Augias *at the Schauspielhaus Zürich, 1963 (photograph by René Hauri, Zurich)*

be bribed to prophesy anything the customer desires; the oracle can also spout nonsense, according to the mood of the moment. Yet the contrived prophecies concerning Laios, Jocasta, and Oedipus all come true, not through inexorable fate but through a series of coincidences. Anton Krättli has pointed out that in making Oedipus a hapless victim of coincidence, Dürrenmatt has rendered him unfit to be a tragic hero. It is here that the connection to the corrupt world of *Der Mitmacher*–a world devoid of tragedy, and for that matter, of heroes–is established.

Since *Der Meteor* Dürrenmatt has not had a major theatrical success. The critics have not been particularly kind to him, nor has he been

very charitable toward critics. In his 1976 interview by Heinz Ludwig Arnold, Dürrenmatt, apparently still smarting from the devastating failure of *Der Mitmacher*, declares his independence from drama critics in general and from the publication *Theater heute* in particular: "Was geht mich *Theater heute* an?" (What do I care about *Theater heute?*). In the same breath, he laments that what really bothers him is that his theater, the Schauspielhaus Zürich, does not support him against the critics.

On 6 October 1977 the curtain rose at the Schauspielhaus Zürich on Dürrenmatt's first play in four years. *Die Frist* (The Reprieve) was another theatrical failure: a grotesque political comedy in which a dying dictator is kept alive by unconscionable medical means until the leaders of the feuding factions can consolidate power in the hands of a successor. Dürrenmatt, however, thought so highly of it that he included it as the only drama in the 1978 collection *Friedrich Dürrenmatt Lesebuch* (Friedrich Dürrenmatt Reader), which also contains several short stories and a radio play.

One of the narratives in the *Lesebuch*, "Abu Chanifa und Anan ben David," was initially embedded in the lengthy treatise *Zusammenhänge: Essay über Israel* (Connections: Essay on Israel, 1976). Dürrenmatt has long been a vocal supporter of the state of Israel: in 1967, just days after the war with Egypt, he gave a speech in Zurich on Israel's right to exist, and during an official visit to Israel in 1974 he gave a series of lectures on the same topic and was elected a fellow of Ben-Gurion University. "Abu Chanifa und Anan ben David" is a parable of the intertwined histories of a Moslem and a Jewish nation, each of which is personified by a fictional religious leader. It is an uncharacteristically optimistic piece for an author whose prognosis for the human race is gloomy. After centuries of imprisonment together and many more centuries of separation, during which the Son of David wanders Ahasverus-like through Europe, surviving Inquisition, pogrom, and Holocaust, coincidence finally brings Jew and Moslem together again. Each senses intrusion onto his sacred territory, and they engage each other as mortal enemies. At this point Dürrenmatt introduces a beautiful dream, a wish for the future to supersede history: as they stare at each other, their hateful gazes begin to melt as they recognize their God in each other's eyes: "und zum erstenmal formen ihre Lippen, die so lange geschwiegen haben,

Dürrenmatt in 1970 (Ullstein–Karoly Forgacs)

jahrtausendelang, das erste Wort, nicht ein Spruch des Korans, nicht ein Wort des Pentateuchs, nur das Wort: Du" (and for the first time their lips, which had been silent for so long, millennia, form the first word, not a verse from the Koran, not a word from the Pentateuch, only the word: Thou).

The 1970s ended for Dürrenmatt with the formidable task of editing his life's work for a thirty-volume edition. The *Werkausgabe* (Complete Works Edition) contains a few previously unpublished works, but nothing new of significance. Dürrenmatt's prose in the 1980s has consisted of philosophical-psychological pieces of introspection. In 1976 he had described the role of personal experience in his creative process as "dieses Sinken ins Unbewußte, ins Instrumentarium meiner inneren Vorgänge" (this sinking into the unconscious, into the apparatus of my inner processes). These submerged impressions emerge years later in mutated, often fantastic forms. His *Stoffe I-III*, published in 1981, is a fascinating examination of this process. *Stoffe I-III* juxtaposes richly anecdotal autobiography with three previously unpublished narratives in which the reader

can readily recognize numerous points of connection between Dürrenmatt's life and his fiction. It provides revealing psychological insights into the creative process of a successful author.

One of the narratives in *Stoffe I-III* is "Mondfinsternis," the forerunner of *Der Besuch der alten Dame.* In the longest of the tales, "Der Winterkrieg in Tibet" (The Winter War in Tibet), there emerges a theme from the author's earliest childhood: the labyrinth. This theme can be observed by the careful reader of Dürrenmatt in numerous variations from the earliest prose up to the present day: it is the maze of corridors and rooms in the houses of the painter Rotmantel, the detective Bärlach, and the courtesan Chloe Saloniki; the winding streets in "Der Hund," "Die Stadt," and *Grieche sucht Griechin;* and the prison of Abu Chanifa and Anan ben David. Now, for the first time, an entire narrative is built around the theme of the labyrinth. An analysis of the myth of the Minotaur and its wealth of significance for modern times forms a segue between autobiography and fiction. The "Winter War" is being fought as a continuation of the nuclear holocaust which has destroyed most of civilization. The more belligerent survivors carry on a meaningless struggle in the miles of caves under the mountains of Tibet. It is a recreational war of mercenaries, in which the greatest crime is not believing in the existence of the enemy. The narrator, having killed his last enemy in Switzerland and desperately seeking a cause, enlists in the Winter War, a free-for-all in which everybody wears the same white uniforms and it is impossible to distinguish enemy from ally. After years of fighting, the mercenary is reduced to a state in which he is more prosthesis than human: one arm ends in a steel spike, the other in a machine gun, and he is confined to a wheelchair. Yet still he pursues the enemy through the labyrinth, trusting blindly in the Administration and its directives. Only as he is dying from injuries sustained in the final confrontation does he come to the realization, aided by Plato's cave allegory, that the enemy was his own shadow. Like Theseus pursuing the Minotaur, the mercenary had been seeking his enemy in the labyrinth for one final confrontation, which in winning he was doomed to lose: "Vielleicht deshalb, weil Theseus selber der Minotaurus ist und jeder Versuch, die Welt denkend zu bewältigen ... ein Kampf ist, den man mit sich selber führt: Ich bin mein Feind, du bist der deinige" (Perhaps because Theseus is himself the Minotaur, and every attempt to master the world through thought . . . is a battle which we fight with ourselves: I am my enemy, you are yours).

The third story, "Der Rebell" (The Rebel), is the shortest and perhaps the most intriguing. Like a Rodin sculpture, the narrative is constructed with rough edges; in places it is hardly more than an outline with a few sketchy details. Short sentences in telegraph style predominate. Indirect discourse often continues for paragraphs at a time as if to sum up conversations and hasten the narrative along. It has at times a dreamlike quality reminiscent of a Ludwig Tieck fairy tale, of E. T. A. Hoffman, or of Dürrenmatt's earliest prose works. The title is ironic, for the hero is anything but a rebel. He is a reluctant messiah, forced into the role of the liberator promised the people in an ancient prophecy. As he rides into the capital on a donkey he is hailed by the masses, but he is betrayed by the same fickle rabble at the decisive moment. This messiah, however, does not die on a cross. He is imprisoned in a room with mirrors on all four walls, the floor, and the ceiling. Succumbing to insanity, he imagines his thousand mirror images to be an army at his command. He dies, alone and forgotten, while the people continue to live in tyranny and hope for the promised messiah, the rebel.

Dürrenmatt's literary output since *Stoffe I-III* has consisted of a comedy, *Achterloo* (1983), which was unenthusiastically received by critics when it premiered in 1983, and the enthralling narrative *Minotaurus* (1985), which he also illustrated. In *Minotaurus* the reader experiences Daedalus's maze from the perspective of the beast and is quickly drawn into empathy with the naive, childlike creature. The mirrored walls of the labyrinth, which play a prominent part in Dürrenmatt's version of the myth, are an expansion of the device with which he experimented in "Der Rebell." In them the Minotaur sees his thousandfold reflection and believes that he is in control of a vast herd of ruminant creatures which instantly obey his every command. The reader shares the Minotaur's feelings of frustration and betrayal when the mirror images leave him at night, and later his elation at the discovery that there exist creatures unlike those in the glass, warm-blooded and soft to the touch.

Dürrenmatt has long been free from the financial necessity to write, and his international fame is secure. He received honorary doctorates from Hebrew University in Jerusalem and the Uni-

Dürrenmatt and his wife, Lotti Geißler Dürrenmatt, at their home in Neuenburg (photograph by J. H. Bruell)

versity of Nice in 1977, and from the University of Neuchâtel in 1979. He won the Radio Play Award of the Blind War Veterans for *Die Panne* in 1955, the Prix d'Italia for the radio play *Abendstunde im Spätherbst* (1959; translated as *Episode on an Autumn Evening*, 1959) and the Tribune de Lausanne Award for *Die Panne* in 1958, the New York Drama Critics Award for *The Visit* and the Schiller Prize of the City of Mannheim for his previous dramas in 1959, the Grand Prize of the Swiss Writers Foundation in 1960, the Grillparzer Prize of the Austrian Academy of Sciences in 1968, the Grand Prize for Literature of the Canton of Bern in 1969, the Buber-Rosenzweig Medal for Christian-Jewish cooperation in 1977, and the Grand Prize for Literature of the City of Bern in 1979.

Through it all, Dürrenmatt has remained an enigma to critics because it is impossible to categorize him, to identify him with a particular ideology or philosophy. The paradoxes with which he continually confronts his readers are intentional. He does not believe that the problems of society can be resolved through ideologies. In a 1985 interview with Fritz Raddatz in the German weekly *Die Zeit*, Dürrenmatt defined himself as "ein Schriftsteller in Rebellion gegen Ideologien und Gläubige aller Art" (a writer in rebellion against ideologies and believers of all kinds). Yet, he goes on to say, he is no nihilist; without faith he could not survive. Such paradoxes are typical of Dürrenmatt.

Interviews:

Violet Ketels, "Friedrich Dürrenmatt at Temple University: Interview," *Journal of Modern Literature*, 1, no. 1 (1971): 88-108;

Heinz Ludwig Arnold, *Friedrich Dürrenmatt im Gespräch mit Heinz Ludwig Arnold* (Zurich: Arche, 1976);

Dieter Fringeli, *Nachdenken mit und über Friedrich Dürrenmatt: Ein Gespräch* (Breitenbach: Jeger-Moll, 1977);

Fritz Raddatz, "Ich bin der finsterste Komödienschreiber, den es gibt: Ein *Zeit*-Gespräch mit Friedrich Dürrenmatt," *Die Zeit*, no. 34 (23 August 1985): 13-14.

Bibliographies:

Elly Wilbert-Collins, *A Bibliography of Four Contemporary German-Swiss Authors: Friedrich Dürrenmatt, Max Frisch, Robert Walser, Albin Zollinger* (Bern: Francke, 1967);

Johannes Hansel, *Friedrich Dürrenmatt: Bibliographie* (Bad Homburg: Gehlen, 1968).

References:

Armin Arnold, *Friedrich Dürrenmatt* (Berlin: Colloquium, 1969);

Arnold, ed., *Zu Friedrich Dürrenmatt: Interpretationen* (Stuttgart: Klett, 1982);

Heinz Ludwig Arnold, ed., *Friedrich Dürrenmatt I*, second edition (Munich: Beck, 1980);

Arnold, ed., *Friedrich Dürrenmatt II* (Munich: Beck, 1977);

Hans Bänziger, *Frisch und Dürrenmatt* (Bern: Francke, 1960);

Urs Baschung, "Zu Friedrich Dürrenmatts 'Der Tunnel,'" *Schweizer Rundschau*, 68 (1969): 480-490;

Gottfried Benn, Elisabeth Brock-Sulzer, Fritz Buri, Reinhold Grimm, Hans Mayer, and Werner Oberle, *Der unbequeme Dürrenmatt* (Basel & Stuttgart: Basilius, 1962);

Elisabeth Brock-Sulzer, *Dürrenmatt in unserer Zeit: Eine Werkinterpretation nach Selbstzeugnissen* (Basel: Reinhardt, 1968);

Brock-Sulzer, *Friedrich Dürrenmatt: Stationen seines Werkes* (Zurich: Arche, 1960);

Donald Daviau, "Justice in the Works of Friedrich Dürrenmatt," *Kentucky Foreign Language Quarterly*, 9, no. 4 (1962): 181-193;

Daviau, "The Role of *Zufall* in the Writings of Friedrich Dürrenmatt," *Germanic Review*, 47 (November 1972): 281-293;

Manfred Durzak, *Dürrenmatt, Frisch, Weiss: Deutsches Drama der Gegenwart zwischen Utopie und Wirklichkeit* (Stuttgart: Reclam, 1972);

Bodo Fritzen and Heimy F. Taylor, eds., *Friedrich Dürrenmatt: A Collection of Critical Essays* (Normal, Ill.: Applied Literature Press, 1979);

Peter Gontrum, "*Ritter, Tod und Teufel*: Protagonists and Antagonists in the Prose Works of Friedrich Dürrenmatt," *Seminar*, 1 (Fall 1965): 88-98;

Sigrun Gottwald, *Der mutige Narr im dramatischen Werk Friedrich Dürrenmatts* (New York: Lang, 1983);

Walter Hinck, "Ein Bewohner des Labyrinths: Friedrich Dürrenmatts Erzählungen *Stoffe I-III*," in his *Germanistik als Literaturkritik: Zur Gegenwartsliteratur* (Frankfurt am Main: Suhrkamp, 1983), pp. 148-153;

Urs Jenny, *Friedrich Dürrenmatt* (Velber: Friedrich, 1965);

Werner Klose, "Friedrich Dürrenmatt: Der Richter und sein Henker," in *Deutsche Romane von Grimmelshausen bis Walser*, edited by Jakob Lehmann (Königstein: Scriptor, 1982), pp. 339-356;

Gerhard Knapp, *Friedrich Dürrenmatt* (Stuttgart: Metzler, 1980);

Knapp, ed., *Friedrich Dürrenmatt: Studien zu seinem Werk* (Heidelberg: Stiehm, 1976);

Knapp and Gerd Labroisse, eds., *Facetten: Studien zum 60. Geburtstag Friedrich Dürrenmatts* (Bern: Lang, 1981);

Jan Knopf, *Friedrich Dürrenmatt* (Munich: Beck, 1980);

Anton Krättli, "Friedrich Dürrenmatt: Der Koloß von Neuchatel–'wie soll man es spielen? Mit Humor!'–Die Welt als Labyrinth," in his *Zeitschrift: Zürcher Theaterbriefe, Kommentar, Kri-*

tik, *Polemik* (Aarau: Sauerländer, 1982), pp. 123-142;

Hans Mayer, *Dürrenmatt und Frisch: Anmerkungen* (Pfullingen: Neske, 1963);

Murray B. Peppard, *Friedrich Dürrenmatt* (New York: Twayne, 1969);

Ulrich Profitlich, *Friedrich Dürrenmatt: Komödienbegriff und Komödienstruktur: Eine Einführung* (Stuttgart: Kohlhammer, 1973);

Peter Spycher, *Friedrich Dürrenmatt: Das erzählerische Werk* (Frauenfeld & Stuttgart: Huber, 1972);

Timo Tiusanen, *Dürrenmatt: A Study in Plays, Prose, Theory* (Princeton: Princeton University Press, 1977);

Günter Waldmann, "Ideologiekritische Modellanalyse: Dürrenmatts Anti-Detektivroman und die Ideologie religiöser Anti-Aufklärung," in his *Theorie und Didaktik der Trivialliteratur* (Munich: Fink, 1977), pp. 37-49;

Emil Weber, *Friedrich Dürrenmatt und die Frage nach Gott: Zur theologischen Relevanz der frühen Prosa eines merkwürdigen Protestanten* (Zurich: Theologischer Verlag, 1980);

Peter Wyrsch, "Die Dürrenmatt-Story," *Schweizer Illustrierte*, no. 12 (18 March 1963): 23-25; no. 13 (25 March 1963): 23-25; no. 14 (1 April 1963): 23-25; no. 15 (8 April 1963): 23-25; no. 16 (15 April 1963): 37-39; no. 17 (22 April 1963): 37-39.

Günter Eich

(1 February 1907-20 December 1972)

Egbert Krispyn
University of Georgia

BOOKS: *Gedichte* (Dresden: Jess, 1930);

Der Präsident: Neun Szenen (Baden: Merlin, 1931);

Die Glücksritter: Singspiel in fünf Akten (Berlin: Chronos, 1933);

Das festliche Jahr: Ein Lesebüchlein vom Königswusterhäuser Landboten, by Eich and Martin Raschke (Oldenburg: Stalling, 1936);

Katharina (Leipzig: List, 1936);

Abgelegene Gehöfte (Frankfurt am Main: Schauer, 1948);

Untergrundbahn (Hamburg: Ellermann, 1949);

Träume: Vier Spiele (Frankfurt am Main: Suhrkamp, 1953);

Botschaften des Regens: Gedichte (Frankfurt am Main: Suhrkamp, 1955);

Zinngeschrei (Hamburg: Hans Bredow-Institut, 1955);

Die Brandung vor Setúbal (Hamburg: Hans Bredow-Institut, 1957); enlarged as *Die Brandung vor Setúbal; Das Jahr Lazertis: Zwei Hörspiele* (Frankfurt am Main: Suhrkamp, 1963); edited by Robert Browning (New York: Harcourt, Brace & World, 1966); translated by Michael Hamburger as *Journeys: Two Radio Plays* (London: Cape, 1968);

Allah hat hundert Namen: Ein Hörspiel (Wiesbaden: Insel, 1958);

Stimmen: Sieben Hörspiele (Frankfurt am Main: Suhrkamp, 1958);

Der Stelzengänger (Zurich: Spektrum, 1960);

Die Mädchen aus Viterbo: Hörspiel (Frankfurt am Main: Suhrkamp, 1960); edited by Peter Prager (London: Macmillan, 1962; New York: St. Martin's, 1962);

Ausgewählte Gedichte, edited by Walter Höllerer (Frankfurt am Main: Suhrkamp, 1960);

Unter Wasser; Böhmische Schneider: Marionettenspiele (Frankfurt am Main: Suhrkamp, 1964);

Zu den Akten: Gedichte (Frankfurt am Main: Suhrkamp, 1964);

In anderen Sprachen: Vier Hörspiele (Frankfurt am Main: Suhrkamp, 1964);

Anlässe und Steingärten: Gedichte (Frankfurt am Main: Suhrkamp, 1966);

Fünfzehn Hörspiele (Frankfurt am Main: Suhrkamp, 1966);

Festianus, Märtyrer (Stuttgart: Reclam, 1966);

Kulka, Hilpert, Elefanten (Berlin: Literarisches Colloquium, 1968);

Eich in 1960 (Ullstein)

Maulwürfe: Prosa (Frankfurt am Main: Suhrkamp, 1968);

Ein Tibeter in meinem Büro: 49 Maulwürfe (Frankfurt am Main: Suhrkamp, 1970);

Günter Eich, translated by Teo Savory (Santa Barbara, Cal.: Unicorn, 1971);

Nach Seumes Papieren (Darmstadt: Bläschke, 1972);

Günter Eich: Ein Lesebuch (Frankfurt am Main: Suhrkamp, 1972);

Gesammelte Maulwürfe (Frankfurt am Main: Suhrkamp, 1972);

Semmelformen, text by Eich, drawings by Sven Knebel (Zurich: Brunnenturm-Presse, 1972);

Gesammelte Werke, edited by Ilse Aichinger, Susanne Müller-Hanft, and others, 4 volumes (Frankfurt am Main: Suhrkamp, 1973);

Gedichte, selected by Aichinger (Frankfurt am Main: Suhrkamp, 1973);

Günter Eich, selected by Bernd Jentzsch (Berlin: Neues Leben, 1973);

Tage mit Hähern: Ausgewählte Gedichte, edited by Klaus Schumann (Berlin: Aufbau, 1975);

Valuable Nail: Selected Poems of Günter Eich, translated by Stuart Friebert, David Walker, and David Young (Oberlin, Ohio: Oberlin College, 1981).

OTHER: Willi Fehse and Klaus Mann, eds., *Anthologie jüngster Lyrik 1927,* includes poems by Eich, as Erich Günter (Hamburg: Enoch, 1927), pp. 30-37;

"Fis mit Obertönen," in *Hörspielbuch II* (Hamburg: Europäische Verlagsanstalt, 1951), pp. 71-113;

"Rede vor den Kriegsblinden," in *Gestalt und Gedanke: Ein Jahrbuch* (Munich: Bayrische Akademie der schönen Künste, 1953), pp. 37-41;

"Der Stelzengänger," in *Im Rasthaus—32 Erzählungen aus dieser Zeit,* edited by Walter Karsch (Berlin: Herbig, 1954), pp. 71-77;

"Züge im Nebel," in *Moderne Erzähler,* edited by Wilhelm Grenzmann (Paderborn: Schöningh, 1957), pp. 21-31;

Lyrik des Ostens: China, edited by Wilhelm Gundert, A. Schimmel, and Walther Schubring, translations by Eich (Munich: Hanser, 1958);

"Trigonometrische Punkte," in *Mein Gedicht ist mein Messer,* edited by Hans Bender (Munich: List, 1961), pp. 23-24;

Aus dem Chinesischen, translated by Eich (Frankfurt am Main: Suhrkamp, 1973).

PERIODICAL PUBLICATIONS: "Morgen an der Oder," *Die Kolonne: Zeitschrift für Dichtung,* 2, no. 3 (1931);

"Prosafragment," *Die Kolonne,* 2, no. 4 (1931);

"Ein Traum am Edsin-gol," *Die Kolonne,* 3, no. 4 (1932);

"Der sechste Traum," *Neue deutsche Hefte* (1954): 647-652;

"Einige Bemerkungen zum Thema Literatur und Wirklichkeit," *Akzente,* 3 (1956): 313-315;

"Die Macht und die gelenkte Sprache," *Kultur,* 8 (1959-1960): 4-5;

"Darmstädter Rede bei der Entgegennahme des Georg Büchner Preises 1959," *Akzente,* 7 (1960): 35-47;

"Drei Prosastücke: Dem Libanon. Hilpert. In das endgültige Manuskript nicht aufgenommenes Bruchstück einer Memoire," *Neue Rundschau,* 77 (1966): 577-584.

     Though Günter Eich was primarily an author of radio plays and a lyric poet, he occasion-

Woodcut by Karl Rössing for Eich's 1948 poetry volume Abgelegene Gehöfte *(Gero von Wilpert)*

ally also wrote stories. In his final creative phase, prose became his medium of choice. From the time of the currency reform in 1948 through the 1960s, Eich was one of the best-known writers in Germany. At first the public detected in his poetry and radio plays an expression of their own concerns and experiences in the postwar era of chaos and deprivation. As the "economic miracle" unfolded, his writing tended to expose the hypocrisy and smugness which often accompanied this newfound prosperity while the horrors of the Nazi era were conveniently forgotten. Eich's reputation as an uncomfortable voice of the nation's conscience reached a climax in the last

years of his life with the publication of some brief prose texts seen by many readers and critics as an endorsement of the antiestablishment radicalism of the 1960s. But Eich was never a political author. Such activist implications as could be found in his work were reflections of a comprehensive philosophy.

Eich was born on 1 February 1907 in Lebus an der Oder, a small town in eastern Germany; he was the second son of an accountant. During the next ten years the family moved several times and in 1918 settled in Berlin, where the father worked as a tax consultant. In 1925 Eich graduated from a gymnasium in Leipzig and began to

Drawing of Eich by Gerda von Stengel

poetry. After his release in 1946 he settled in Bavaria. The following year he joined the Gruppe 47 (Group 47), a loose association of Germany's leading postwar authors. Two published short stories and some unpublished prose sketches and fragments date from this period. In the 1950s and 1960s Eich wrote, besides poetry, a large number of radio plays which set a standard for the genre. At the 1967 meeting of the Gruppe 47 he read the first of a new type of prose text, which he called a "Maulwurf" (mole). During the following years he devoted himself mainly to the writing of these short pieces. He won the Gruppe 47 Prize in 1950 for his radio play "Geh nicht nach El Kuwehd!" (Do Not Go to Kuwait!), the Bavarian Academy of Fine Arts Prize for Literature and the Prize of the War Blind for Radio Drama in 1952, the Georg Büchner Prize in 1958, and the Schiller Prize in 1968. He died in a Salzburg hospital on 20 December 1972. He is survived by his second wife, the eminent Austrian author Ilse Aichinger, whom he married in 1953; their son Clemens, born in 1954; and their daughter Mirjam, born in 1957.

In a development spanning forty-five years, Eich's philosophical position moved from traditional mysticism to nihilism. At successive stages in this process he saw the universe as structured by various ordering principles, from metaphysics to love. Ultimately he denied all systems, except for the alphabet. As long as Eich adhered to the notion that existence had a meaning, his writing intended to describe people and situations in which this meaning became manifest. He favored the radio play and lyric poetry but also used narrative prose for this purpose. When he reached the point of denying all cosmic order, the allusiveness of verse and the emotional suggestiveness of broadcast voices were no longer usable. Only prosaic monologues could convey an utterly chaotic and fragmented universe in which the arbitrary sequence of the alphabet was the only fixed point of reference.

Eich's first prose work to appear in print, "Morgen an der Oder" (Morning on the River Oder, 1931), bears all the marks of an early effort. The parts of the story are not well integrated, the writing is somewhat overblown, and there are too many abstract nouns. But thematically the brief tale is highly characteristic of Eich's views at this stage. Sleep and death are the interlocking motifs which serve to introduce the romantic mystical notion of man's essential oneness with nature. This unity is indicated by such

study Chinese at the University of Berlin. His interest in the Far East was consistent with a trend in German philosophy and literature since the early nineteenth century; after World War I this preoccupation was reinforced by theosophist and other escapist currents. In 1927 Eich transferred to Leipzig University, where he added economics to his program of studies. During 1929-1930 he took courses in sinology at the Sorbonne in Paris, and during the next two years he again occupied himself with economics. But he did not complete his studies, opting instead to become a full-time writer. Eich's lyric production had started when he went to Berlin University, and in 1929 he wrote his first radio play in collaboration with another young author, Martin Raschke. From then until the outbreak of World War II Eich mainly worked on a serial for Berlin Radio. In the same period, literary journals published a brief prose fragment and two short stories by him. In 1937 Eich married a singer who died shortly after the end of the war. The marriage was unhappy, and Eich did not wish to have it publicized.

During the war Eich served on the Russian front, was made a noncommissioned officer, and was taken prisoner by the Americans in 1945. In a POW camp he resumed his production of lyric

Manuscript of a poem by Eich (Günter Eich, Gesammelte Werke, volume 1 [Frankfurt am Main: Suhrkamp, 1973]) means as the comparison of the protagonist's hunchback with the humps on tree trunks. The idea of a mystical union of all creation reaches a rather macabre climax in the conclusion of the story, when the fishermen decide to use their drowned father's body as bait for eels.

The same journal which published "Morgen an der Oder" printed in its next issue a prose fragment by Eich, which consists of the interior monologue of someone riding on a train. Insofar as a theme is developed, it is the incomprehensibility of the world to a human being who is a small part of creation. The fragment also introduces a recurring theme of Eich's, the identification of reality and dream.

In 1935 a much more ambitious story appeared in *Das innere Reich* (The Inner Realm), a journal that attempted to maintain a degree of ideological independence from the Nazi regime. The story was published in book form in 1936, and again in 1942 in a special edition for the armed forces. *Katharina* deals with the loss of innocence of a young boy. Echoing the biblical myth, awakening sexuality marks the transition from cosmic integration to individuation. Sitting in a tree, the boy at first senses his oneness with the universe like a fragrance that he breathes, but after the girl touches him he notices that the world is visible only in small segments through the foliage. In case these images leave any doubt about the meaning of Eich's tale, he spells it out: "The nebulous unity has split up, and the enigmas of singularity began."

Eich's next prose publication appeared in 1947 and much to his embarrassment became a popular text in anthologies and readers. "Züge im Nebel" (Trains in the Fog) reflects conditions during the first postwar years, when the struggle for survival in the ruins of the Third Reich led to the widespread collapse of ethical standards. A man who robs freight trains is caught by a policeman who turns out to be his younger brother. The overly melodramatic ending stresses the shattering effect of this encounter on both men. There are overtones of the motif of man's responsibility for his fellowmen, which also plays a prominent role in other works by Eich written around this time. Otherwise the story seems to be an attempt to get on the postwar literary bandwagon, which was characterized by plain, even folksy language and veristic plots. This trend has been explained as a reaction to the hollow rhetoric and phony heroics of Nazi literature.

Eich in 1972, the year of his death (Ullstein)

Seven years later another prose work by Eich was included in *Im Rasthaus*, a short-story collection. The title figure of "Der Stelzengänger" (The Stiltwalker) is a man who finds complete fulfillment in advertising shoe polish by walking on stilts with signs bearing the product's name hung around his neck. In the context of Eich's worldview at this stage of his career, the stilts assume symbolic value as a connecting link between the earth and the "higher" spheres alluded to in the shoe polish trade name "Astrol." In this union of the "wonderful earth" and the "pale lunar scythe and the nocturnal clouds" the narrator finds his "everlasting happiness."

By the mid 1960s Eich had completely given up the belief in a meaningfully structured universe, and he started writing the brief absurdist prose pieces, or "Maulwürfe" (Moles), that dominated the output of his final years. They were published in three slender volumes: *Kulka, Hilpert, Elefanten* (Kulka, Hilpert, Elephants, 1968); *Maulwürfe* (1968); and *Ein Tibeter in meinem Büro* (A Tibetan in My Office, 1970). In their avoidance of dialogue and story telling, these texts have hardly anything in common with traditional prose narratives. Consisting of offbeat reflections, observations, and verbal associations, the "Maulwürfe" renounce all pretense of expressing any facet of experiential reality. Instead, they evoke an autonomous universe consisting solely of words and letters structured by alphabetical sequentiality. According to the programmatic Maulwurf "Hilpert," "the connections are unambiguous and verifiable, without any irrationality." But even though the texts distance themselves from the everyday world, reality provides the frame of reference for the reader's reception of these absurd compositions. Consequently, the alphabetic universe postulated by Eich becomes a countermodel of the real world, which it brings into relief. The moles live in their separate underground world, but "over their passages the grass dies out." This indirect effect of sociopolitical criticism was probably the real reason for the hue and cry over the supposed activism of Eich's Maulwürfe, but the critics rationalized their emotional opinions pro and con by reference to the mildly antiestablishment sentiments expressed in some of the works. Long after their topicality has worn off, these texts still stand as a memorable literary-philosophical achievement and a fitting capstone to Eich's career.

References:

Hans Magnus Enzensberger, "In Search of the Lost Language," *Encounter*, 30 (1963): 44-51;

F. M. Fowler, "Günter Eich," in *German Men of Letters*, volume 4, edited by Brian Keith-Smith (London: Wolff, 1966), pp. 89-107;

F. K. Jakobsh, "Günter Eich: Homage to Bakunin," *Germano-Slavica: A Canadian Journal of Germanic and Slavic Comparative Studies* (1974): 37ff;

Joachim Kaiser, "Schmerzen, wo er nicht ist: Eine Antwort auf M. Reich-Ranickis Rezension von Günter Eichs 'Maulwürfen,'" *Die Zeit*, 4 October 1968;

Michael Kohlenbach, *Günter Eichs späte Prosa: Einige Merkmale der Maulwürfe* (Bonn: Bouvier, 1982);

Egbert Krispyn, *Günter Eich* (New York: Twayne, 1971);

Susanne Müller-Hanft, ed., *Über Günter Eich* (Frankfurt am Main: Suhrkamp, 1970);

Marcel Reich-Ranicki, "Kein Denkmalschutz für Günter Eich: Zu den Prosastücken 'Maulwürfe,'" *Die Zeit*, 27 September 1968;

Heinz Schafroth, *Günter Eich* (Munich: Beck, 1976);

Siegfried Unseld, ed., *Günter Eich zum Gedächtnis* (Frankfurt am Main: Suhrkamp, 1973);

Heinrich Vormweg, "Dichtung als Maul-Wurf," *Merkur*, 23 (1969): 85-87.

Papers:

Günter Eich discarded most of his uncompleted projects and his pre-1945 manuscripts, and the originals of many of his later works have also been lost. His literary estate is administered by the Suhrkamp publishing firm, Frankfurt am Main, West Germany.

Max Frisch
(15 May 1911-   )

Wulf Koepke
Texas A&M University

BOOKS: *Jürg Reinhart: Eine sommerliche Schicksals-fahrt. Roman* (Stuttgart: Deutsche Verlags-Anstalt, 1934); revised as *J'adore ce qui me brûle oder Die Schwierigen: Roman* (Zurich: At-lantis, 1943); revised as *Die Schwierigen oder J'adore ce qui me brûle* (Zurich: Atlantis, 1957);

Antwort aus der Stille: Eine Erzählung aus den Ber-gen (Stuttgart & Berlin: Deutsche Verlags-Anstalt, 1937);

Blätter aus dem Brotsack (Zurich: Atlantis, 1940);

Bin oder Die Reise nach Peking (Zurich: Atlantis, 1945);

Marion und die Marionetten: Ein Fragment (Basel: Gryff-Presse, 1946);

Nun singen sie wieder: Versuch eines Requiems (Kloster-berg & Basel: Schwabe, 1946); edited by W. F. Tulasiewicz and K. Scheible (London: Harrap, 1967); translated by David Lom-men as *Now They Sing Again*, in *Contemporary German Theatre*, edited by Michael Roloff (New York: Avon, 1972);

Tagebuch mit Marion (Zurich: Atlantis, 1947); en-larged as *Tagebuch 1946-1949* (Frankfurt am Main: Suhrkamp, 1950); translated by Geof-frey Skelton as *Sketchbook 1946-1949* (New York: Harcourt Brace Jovanovich, 1977);

Santa Cruz: Eine Romanze (Klosterberg & Basel: Schwabe, 1947);

Die chinesische Mauer: Eine Farce (Klosterberg & Basel: Schwabe, 1947; revised edition, Frank-furt am Main: Suhrkamp, 1955; revised again, 1972); translated by James L. Rosen-berg as *The Chinese Wall* (New York: Hill & Wang, 1961);

Als der Krieg zu Ende war: Schauspiel (Klosterberg & Basel: Schwabe, 1949); edited by Stuart Friebert (New York: Dodd, Mead, 1967);

Graf Öderland: Ein Spiel in zehn Bildern (Berlin: Suhrkamp, 1951); revised as *Graf Öderland: Eine Moritat in zwölf Bildern* (Frankfurt am Main: Suhrkamp, 1963); edited by George Salamon (New York: Harcourt, Brace & World, 1966);

Max Frisch in 1986 (Ullstein–Teutopress)

Don Juan oder Die Liebe zur Geometrie: Eine Komödie in 5 Akten (Frankfurt am Main: Suhrkamp, 1953);

Stiller: Roman (Frankfurt am Main: Suhrkamp, 1954); translated by Michael Bullock as *I'm Not Stiller* (London & New York: Abelard-Schuman, 1958; New York: Random House, 1962);

Herr Biedermann und die Brandstifter: Hörspiel (Ham-burg: Hans Bredow-Institut, 1955); adapted for the stage as *Biedermann und die Brandstif-ter: Ein Lehrstück ohne Lehre. Mit einem Nach-spiel* (Frankfurt am Main: Suhrkamp, 1958); edited by Paul Kurt Ackermann (Boston: Houghton Mifflin, 1963; London: Methuen, 1963); translated by Bullock as *The Fire Rais-*

ers: *A Morality without a Moral, with an Afterpiece* (London: Methuen, 1962); translated by Mordecai Gorelik as *The Firebugs: A Learning-Play without a Lesson* (New York: Hill & Wang, 1963);

Achtung: Die Schweiz. Ein Gespräch über unsere Lage und ein Vorschlag zur Tat, by Frisch, Lucius Burckhardt, and Markus Kutter (Basel: Handschin, 1955);

Die neue Stadt: Beiträge zur Diskussion, by Frisch, Burckhardt, and Kutter (Basel: Handschin, 1956);

Homo faber: Ein Bericht (Frankfurt am Main: Suhrkamp, 1957); edited by Ackermann and Constance Clarke (Boston: Houghton Mifflin, 1973); translated by Bullock as *Homo Faber: A Report* (London & New York: Abelard-Schuman, 1959; New York: Random House, 1962);

Ausgewählte Prosa (Frankfurt am Main: Suhrkamp, 1961); edited by Stanley Corngold (New York: Harcourt, Brace & World, 1968);

Andorra: Stück in zwölf Bildern (Frankfurt am Main: Suhrkamp, 1961); edited by H. F. Garten (London: Methuen, 1964); translated by Bullock as *Andorra: A Play in Twelve Scenes* (New York: Hill & Wang, 1964; London: Methuen, 1964);

Stücke, 2 volumes (Frankfurt am Main: Suhrkamp, 1962);

Three Plays, translated by Bullock (London: Methuen, 1962)—includes *The Fire Raisers, Count Oederland,* and *Andorra;*

Mein Name sei Gantenbein: Roman (Frankfurt am Main: Suhrkamp, 1964); translated by Bullock as *A Wilderness of Mirrors* (London: Methuen, 1965; New York: Random House, 1966);

Zürich-Transit: Skizze eines Films (Frankfurt am Main: Suhrkamp, 1966);

Biografie: Ein Spiel (Frankfurt am Main: Suhrkamp, 1967; revised, 1968); translated by Bullock as *Biography: A Game* (New York: Hill & Wang, 1969);

Öffentlichkeit als Partner (Frankfurt am Main: Suhrkamp, 1967);

Three Plays, translated by Rosenberg (New York: Hill & Wang, 1967)—includes *Don Juan; or, The Love of Geometry, The Great Rage of Philip Hotz,* and *When the War Was Over;*

Erinnerungen an Brecht (Berlin: Friedenauer Presse, 1968);

Dramaturgisches: Ein Briefwechsel mit Walter Höllerer (Berlin: Literarisches Colloquium, 1969);

Four Plays: The Great Wall of China, Don Juan; or, The Love of Geometry, Philipp Hotz's Fury, Biography, a Game, translated by Bullock (London: Methuen, 1969);

Rip van Winkle: Hörspiel (Stuttgart: Reclam, 1969);

Der Mensch zwischen Selbstentfremdung und Selbstverwirklichung, by Frisch and Rudolf Immig (Stuttgart: Calwer, 1970);

Wilhelm Tell für die Schule (Frankfurt am Main: Suhrkamp, 1971);

Glück: Eine Erzählung (Zurich: Brunnenturm-Presse, 1972);

Tagebuch 1966-1971 (Frankfurt am Main: Suhrkamp, 1972); translated by Skelton as *Sketchbook 1966-1971* (New York: Harcourt Brace Jovanovich, 1974; London: Methuen, 1974);

Dienstbüchlein (Frankfurt am Main: Suhrkamp, 1974);

Montauk: Eine Erzählung (Frankfurt am Main: Suhrkamp, 1975); translated by Skelton as *Montauk* (New York: Harcourt Brace Jovanovich, 1976);

Stich-Worte, selected by Uwe Johnson (Frankfurt am Main: Suhrkamp, 1975);

Zwei Reden zum Friedenspreis des Deutschen Buchhandels 1976, by Frisch and Hartmut von Hentig (Frankfurt am Main: Suhrkamp, 1976);

Gesammelte Werke in zeitlicher Folge, edited by Hans Mayer and Walter Schmitz, 6 volumes (Frankfurt am Main: Suhrkamp, 1976);

Triptychon: Drei szenische Bilder (Frankfurt am Main: Suhrkamp, 1978); translated by Skelton as *Triptych: Three Scenic Panels* (New York: Harcourt Brace Jovanovich, 1981);

Der Mensch erscheint im Holozän: Eine Erzählung (Frankfurt am Main: Suhrkamp, 1979); translated by Skelton as *Man in the Holocene: A Story* (New York: Harcourt Brace Jovanovich, 1980);

Erzählende Prosa 1939-1979 (Berlin: Volk und Welt, 1980);

Stücke, 2 volumes (Berlin: Volk und Welt, 1981);

Blaubart: Eine Erzählung (Frankfurt am Main: Suhrkamp, 1982); translated by Skelton as *Bluebeard* (New York: Harcourt Brace Jovanovich, 1984; London: Methuen, 1984);

Forderungen des Tages (Frankfurt am Main: Suhrkamp, 1983).

OTHER: Robert S. Gessner, *Sieben Lithographien*, annotations by Frisch (Zurich: Hürlimann, 1952);

Markus Kutter and Lucius Burckhardt, *Wir selber bauen unsere Stadt: Ein Hinweis auf die Möglichkeiten staatlicher Baupolitik*, foreword by Frisch (Basel: Handschin, 1956);

Bertolt Brecht, *Drei Gedichte*, afterword by Frisch (Zurich, 1959);

"Nachruf auf Albin Zollinger, den Dichter und Landsmann, nach zwanzig Jahren," in Albin Zollinger, *Gesammelte Werke*, volume 1 (Zurich: Atlantis, 1961), pp. 7-13;

Teo Otto, *Skizzen eines Bühnenbildners: 33 Zeichnungen*, texts by Frisch, Kurt Hirschfeld, and Oskar Wälterlin (St. Gallen: Tschudy, 1964);

Alexander J. Seiler, *Siamo italiani/Die Italiener: Gespräche mit italienischen Arbeitern in der Schweiz* (Zurich: EVZ Verlag, 1965), pp. 7-10;

Gody Suter, *Die großen Städte: Was sie zerstört und was sie retten kann*, preface by Frisch (Bergisch Gladbach: Lübbe, 1966);

Andrei D. Sakharov, *Wie ich mir die Zukunft vorstelle: Gedanken über Fortschritt, friedliche Koexistenz und geistige Freiheit*, postscript by Frisch (Zurich: Diogenes, 1969).

PERIODICAL PUBLICATIONS: "Was bin ich?," *Zürcher Student*, 10 (1932/1933): 9-11;

"Prag, die Stadt zwischen Ost und West," *Neue Zürcher Zeitung*, 23 April 1933, p. 2;

"Kleines Tagebuch einer deutschen Reise," *Neue Zürcher Zeitung*, 30 April 1935, p. 5; 7 May 1935, p. 6; 20 May 1935, p. 6;

"Ein Roman, zweimal besprochen," *Neue Zürcher Zeitung*, 22 November 1940;

"Blätter aus dem Brotsack: Neue Folge," *Neue Zürcher Zeitung*, 23 December 1940, p. 5; 25 December 1940, p. 2; 27 December 1940, p. 4; 29 December 1940, p. 1; 30 December 1940, p. 4;

"Albin Zollinger: Zu seinem Gedächtnis," *Neue Schweizer Rundschau*, 9 (1941/1942): 464-467;

"Über Zeitereignis und Dichtung," *Neue Zürcher Zeitung*, 22 March 1945, p. 7;

"Stimmen eines anderen Deutschland? Zu den Zeugnissen von Wiechert und Bergengruen," *Neue Schweizer Rundschau*, 13 (1945/1946): 537-547;

"Kleines Nachwort zu einer Ansprache von Thomas Mann," *Zürcher Student*, 25 (1947): 57-59;

Frisch in 1957 (photograph by Fritz Eschen, Berlin)

"Drei Entwürfe zu einem Brief nach Deutschland," *Die Wandlung*, 2 (1947): 478-483;

"Judith: Ein Monolog," *Die Neue Zeitung*, 25 August 1948, p. 3;

"Friedrich Dürrenmatt: Zu seinem neuen Stück 'Romulus der Große,'" *Die Weltwoche*, 6 May 1949, p. 5;

"Orchideen und Aasgeier: Ein Reisealbum aus Mexico. Oktober/November 1951," *Neue Schweizer Rundschau*, 20 (1952/1953): 67-88;

"Unsere Arroganz gegenüber Amerika," *Neue Schweizer Rundschau*, 20 (1952/1953), 584-590;

"Begegnung mit Negern: Eindrücke aus Amerika," *Atlantis*, 26 (1954): 73-78;

"Brecht als Klassiker," *Dichten und Trachten: Jahresschau des Suhrkamp Verlages*, 5 (1955): 35-37;

"Brecht ist tot," *Die Weltwoche*, 24 August 1956, p. 5;

"Die große Wut des Philipp Hotz: Sketch," *Hortulus*, 8 (1958): 34-62;

"Öffentlichkeit als Partner," *Börsenblatt für den deutschen Buchhandel*, 14 (1958): 1331-1334;

"Das Engagement des Schriftstellers heute," *Frankfurter Allgemeine Zeitung*, 14 November 1958, p. 8;

"Erinnerungen an Brecht," *Kursbuch*, 7 (1966): 54-79;

"Politik durch Mord," *Die Weltwoche*, 26 April 1968, pp. 49, 51;

"Die Schweiz als Heimat! Dankrede für die Verleihung des Großen Schillerpreises," *Nationalzeitung Basel*, 19 January 1974, pp. 1, 6;

"Notizen von einer kurzen Reise nach China 28. 10.- 4.11.1975," *Der Spiegel*, 9 February 1976, pp. 110-132;

"Ohnmächtiger Poet," *Süddeutsche Zeitung*, 1 September 1981.

One of the most respected writers in the German language, Max Frisch achieved recognition as a playwright after World War II and made his mark with experimental narrative prose, notably the novel *Stiller* (1954; translated as *I'm Not Stiller*, 1958). He has maintained his reputation as an author of integrity and high standards who is not afraid to experiment with new forms. Frisch is an independent, politically involved writer who is particularly concerned about conditions in his native Switzerland. His works are characterized by a unique blend of autobiographical and fictional elements and a striving for sincerity and truth. Intimate human relations, especially between man and woman, are at the center of Frisch's works, but he never forgets the social and political dimensions of such seemingly private affairs. He is a very modern writer, full of contradictions, with sharp insight into contemporary life. He is more concerned about the truth and relevance of his writing than about harmony and "form." He constantly reworks his oeuvre–especially his plays, which exist in different versions, frequently with differing endings. While born and reared in Switzerland and loyal to it, Frisch has also lived in Rome, Berlin, and New York and has traveled widely. His writing conveys both the openness of the wide world and the solidity of conservative Switzerland.

Frisch was born in Zurich in 1911 to Franz and Lina Wildermuth Frisch. His father was an architect; his mother's family had immigrated to Switzerland from Württemberg. As a teenager he wrote several plays that were neither published nor performed. In 1930 Frisch began the study of German literature at the University of Zurich but left school after his father died in 1933 and became a free-lance journalist, mainly for the *Neue Zürcher Zeitung* and the *Frankfurter Zeitung*. His first extended trip took him to Italy, Czechoslovakia, Hungary, Yugoslavia, Turkey, and Greece. While making a living through his articles for Swiss and German papers he wrote his first novel, *Jürg Reinhart* (1934), the tragedy of a young man embroiled in a passionate love affair and undergoing a painful process of maturation. It is a novel written in the popular tradition of the bildungsroman, whose classical Swiss model was Gottfried Keller's *Der grüne Heinrich* (1879-1880; translated as *Green Henry*, 1960). Prominent in Frisch's novel, and in his story about a young man's attempt to conquer a mountain, *Antwort aus der Stille* (Answer from the Silence, 1937), is closeness to nature. Both works betray the "heroic" atmosphere prevalent in the 1930s, even in democratic countries. Frisch's reports on his trip to Nazi Germany in 1936 are rather ambivalent.

In 1936 Frisch enrolled at the Eidgenössische Technische Hochschule in Zurich to study architecture. He had grown increasingly disenchanted with writing, and in 1937 he burned all of his manuscripts. During World War II he served intermittently in the Swiss army, usually as a border guard on the Austrian or Italian frontiers. Frisch could not keep his vow never to write again; in 1940 he published a diary from his military service, *Blätter aus dem Brotsack* (Pages from the Knapsack). The diary form emerged as a basic constituent of Frisch's narrative style. *Blätter aus dem Brotsack* is largely nonpolitical and reveals little understanding of the true nature of the war.

Frisch received his degree in 1941 and opened his own architectural firm. He married Gertrud Anna Constance von Meyenburg on 30 July 1942; they had three children. He won a competition for a big new public outdoor swimming pool in Zurich, the Freibad Letzigraben, which was built from 1947 to 1949 under his supervision. He pursued his writing career with equal vigor. In 1943 he published a revision of *Jürg Reinhart* titled *J'adore ce qui me brûle oder Die Schwierigen* (I Love That Which Burns Me; or, The Difficult Ones). It was followed in 1945 by *Bin oder Die Reise nach Peking* (Am; or, The Trip to Peking), a conversation between a young man and his imaginary alter ego during a journey to China. Two features stand out in these works: Frisch's proximity to surrealism, and the feeling of having to escape from conditions and places which threaten to become prisons for the self.

In 1944 the dramaturge and leading spirit of the Schauspielhaus in Zurich, Kurt Hirschfeld, invited Frisch to assist at rehearsals and write for the theater. The Schauspielhaus offered first performances of the plays of exile writers, such as Bertolt Brecht, as well as of the Western avant-garde. The influx of prominent German emigrés provided exceptional talent and high standards. Thus the Schauspielhaus was an ideal place for young writers like Frisch or Friedrich Dürrenmatt to find inspiration for their own work. Frisch's first play, *Santa Cruz*, was written in 1944 but not performed until 1946; it was published in 1947. In *Santa Cruz* the arrival at their home of a vagabond each had known in the past leads a cavalry captain and his wife to think about opportunities they have missed and alternative lives they might have led. The play was not an immediate success, but his next two works, *Nun singen sie wieder* (1946; translated as *Now They Sing Again*, 1972) and *Die Chinesische Mauer* (1947; translated as *The Chinese Wall*, 1961), hit the nerve of the time. The surrealistic *Nun singen sie wieder* was written in January 1945 and premiered in March of that year. Its subtitle is *Versuch eines Requiems* (Attempt at a Requiem), and its prevailing mood is one of sorrow and mourning. The dead and the living both appear on-stage but cannot communicate with each other. Three aspects of the war stand out in the play: the German killing of Russian civilians, the Allied bombing of German cities, and the support that so many Germans gave the Nazis. Frisch does not mention Jews or concentration camps. He may have been too scrupulous in trying to be neutral; he did not want to accuse, only to express his sorrow and his conviction that a truly new beginning had to be made. Therefore, he distributes blame equally among the participants in the war. The main issue raised in the play is that of Nazi "nihilism": the disillusionment of young Germans who become Nazis not because they believe in the party's ideas but because they have grown disenchanted with the ideals of German humanism. For them, Goethe and Schiller have not stood the test of time. These young cynics kill because there is no reason not to. This image of the intellectual Nazi as nihilist has proven to be popular and durable in fiction, plays, and films about the period.

Frisch's message was well received by his audiences, especially in Germany. There was widespread longing for radical renewal and a new beginning, and an acceptance by many Germans of shame and responsibility. Frisch's play appeared at about the same time as plays on similar themes by Thornton Wilder, Jean-Paul Sartre, Jean Anouilh, and T. S. Eliot. Along with Carl Zuckmayer's *Des Teufels General* (1946; translated as *The Devil's General*, 1962) and Wolfgang Borchert's radio play *Draußen vor der Tür* (Outside the Door, 1947; translated as *The Man Outside*, 1952), *Nun singen sie wieder*, although written by an "outsider" living in comfortable Switzerland, became part of German Trümmerliteratur (literature from the ruins).

Die chinesische Mauer, which premiered in October 1946, is an allegorical farce expressing grotesque humor on the question of the survival of humankind. Set in China in 200 B.C. but including characters from other eras and places, it is one of the first reactions to the atomic bomb. It is also an inquiry into the question whether history and the life of the individual are predetermined repetitions of the same patterns, or whether humanity or the individual can really change and make a new beginning. The answer is a pessimistic one: the overthrow of the Chinese dictatorship merely replaces one violent regime with another. "Der Heutige" (the Modern Man), with his knowledge of the fatal consequences of such violence, is unable to stop the destruction. Love is merely a faint hope; truth is drowned out by propaganda and false pretenses; historical figures such as Napoleon will appear again and again. In his later versions, Frisch even toned down the faint hope of the first version. The play became a grim indictment of the destructive nature of government.

Als der Krieg zu Ende war (When the War Was Over, 1949), the third of Frisch's plays on the postwar situation, is the most realistic one. A German woman and a Russian officer fall in love while the Russians occupy the woman's house in Berlin in 1945; the officer is transferred and leaves. The woman recognizes the groundlessness of her prejudices against "Bolsheviks" and also the guilt of her husband, who had taken part in the attack on the ghetto in Warsaw. The lovers cannot speak to each other except through a Russian soldier of Jewish extraction who knows Yiddish. In the end the woman's communication with her husband, the guilty soldier, is cut off; there is nothing left for them to say to each other. The Marxist Brecht objected to this play because he felt that it merely touched on social and political issues instead of focusing on them and

Scene from the premiere of Frisch's Biedermann und die Brandstifter *at the Schauspielhaus Zürich, 1958*

thus remained too much a private love story. The play once more demonstrates Frisch's reluctance to be ideological. In its attempt to escape the alternatives of the cold war, *Als der Krieg zu Ende war* is a typical product of its time. It tries to undercut the stereotypes of propaganda with human realities and individual truths.

As a neutral Swiss, Frisch was invited to writers' congresses and other public events in both West and East, and he traveled widely to attend first performances of his plays. Thus he gained firsthand experience of the growing separation of East and West Germany between 1945 and 1949 and of the Communist takeovers of Czechoslovakia and other countries. These experiences form part of his *Tagebuch 1946-1949* (1950; translated as *Sketchbook 1946-1949*, 1977), his first publication with the new Suhrkamp Verlag in Frankfurt, which was his publisher from then on. The diary contains three main elements: the description of Frisch's experiences in postwar Europe, his thoughts on life and art, and sketches for most of the works he was to write until the early 1960s.

Of Frisch's next three plays only one is open to a direct political interpretation. *Biedermann und die Brandstifter* (translated as *The Fire Raisers*, 1962), was first written as a radio play, *Herr Biedermann und die Brandstifter*, in 1952 (published in 1955), following a sketch in the *Tagebuch 1946-1949*. The stage version followed in 1958. The plot remains the same: the hair-lotion manufacturer Gottlieb Biedermann is bullied into allowing two vagrants to move into the attic of his house; the vagrants, who are actually terrorists, fill the attic with gasoline tanks and finally ask Biedermann for matches to destroy the entire city. Biedermann is a brutal capitalist, but he has a guilty conscience because he dismissed the real inventor of his hair oil, who then committed suicide. The destruction of this idyllic capitalist city–including Biedermann and his wife, who die in the blaze–is due to Biedermann's cowardice. This parable is open to several contradictory political interpretations: it may refer to the Communist takeover of Eastern European countries, the Nazi seizure of power, terrorism in general, or the inner weakness of capitalist society. Frisch endorsed the last of these interpretations through an afterpiece set in hell for the stage version. Like Dürrenmatt's *Der Besuch der alten Dame* (1956; translated as *The Visit*, 1962), *Biedermann und die Brandstifter* contains a chorus, a parody of Greek tragedy. Frisch points out that the events in the play are not Schicksal (fate) and thus inevitable; they are rather Zufall (chance) or the fault of the people themselves.

Frisch's play *Graf Öderland* (1951; translated as *Count Oederland*, 1962) is the story of a public prosecutor who dreams of freedom and a life beyond the bureaucratic order. He becomes the legendary anarchist Graf Öderland, overthrows the government, and becomes the head of a new one. At the end it is not clear whether the prosecutor's adventures as Graf Öderland were real or a dream. The play points to a central dilemma of contemporary society: the complexity and rigidity of order provokes more and more violent outbreaks in the name of freedom. One of the least "finished" of Frisch's works even in its last version, the play has never been popular with audiences.

The recipient of a Rockefeller Foundation grant, Frisch spent 1951 and 1952 in the United States and Mexico working on the play *Don Juan oder Die Liebe zur Geometrie* (1953; translated as *Don Juan; or, The Love of Geometry*, 1967) and on a novel which underwent many changes until it appeared in the fall of 1954: *Stiller*. He was separated from his wife in 1953; they were divorced in 1959.

Don Juan offers a new version of one of Europe's most artistically productive myths. Don Juan is a mathematician; he loves geometry. But women are attracted to him. To escape the fatal repetition of events–seduction, duels with husbands or fathers, and so forth–Don Juan stages his own "death" and descent into hell. But the rest of his life is not what he expected: he only exchanges the repetition of seduction for the repetition and boredom of married life.

Stiller turns an implausible plot into an authentic picture of life in Switzerland in the early 1950s. Anatol Ludwig Stiller, a struggling sculptor, is torn between his wife Julika, a dancer suffering from tuberculosis, and his lover Sibylle, the wife of a public prosecutor. Stiller disappears and returns to Switzerland from America six years later with a forged passport in the name of James White. He is recognized and arrested at the border; he is suspected of having worked for the Communists in Switzerland because he had fought as a volunteer in the Spanish civil war. In

Portrait of Frisch by Varlin, 1958 (Oeffentliche Kunst-sammlung Basel Kunstmuseum. Inv. G. 1959. 6)

prison in Zurich Stiller's attorney confronts him with his past: friends, relatives, dental and military records, his wife. Claiming not to be Stiller, the prisoner tries to establish his American identity with sensational stories from Mexico and the United States but convinces nobody except his guard. The novel is largely told through Stiller's journal, jotted down in seven notebooks he keeps during his confinement. These notebooks leave the defense attorney bewildered and angry but establish a relationship of trust with the prosecutor Rolf, Sibylle's husband. When the court rules that he is indeed Stiller, Stiller stops writing. It is the prosecutor who describes, in an epilogue, Stiller's attempt to start a new life with Julika, which ends in failure and Julika's death after an operation. The book ends anticlimactically with the words "Stiller blieb in Glion und lebte allein" (Stiller remained in Glion and lived alone).

Stiller is characterized by irony and parody. Many passages echo well-known works of literature, from Thomas Mann's *Der Zauberberg* (1924; translated as *The Magic Mountain*, 1927) and Ernest Hemingway's *For Whom the Bell Tolls*,

Scene from the premiere of Andorra, *Frisch's play about anti-Semitism, at the Schauspielhaus Zürich, 1961*
(Schauspielhaus Zürich)

(1940) to Frisch's own previous works; Frisch declares such parodies and "repetitions" or "reproductions" to be inevitable. The narrative structure is complex, as it is Stiller who records what the other characters say about the former Stiller and how they react to the present Stiller/White. Stiller likes to blur the line between reality and fiction, so that it will never be quite clear what he really did and saw in America. Archetypal figures abound; the influence of C. G. Jung's psychology is evident. The central statement in the book is the commandment "Du sollst dir kein Bildnis machen" (Thou shalt make no image). Stiller warns his visitors not to see him as Stiller; but he seems to see them as stereotypes, not as individuals. The book makes it clear that problems cannot be solved through development, through an inner change of the person; hence, it is a destructive parody of the bildungsroman and a final farewell to the illusions of youth contained in Frisch's earliest works. *Stiller* is a novel about the disillusionment of middle age. Stiller fits neither into the order and love of tradition of Switzerland nor into the isolation and ahistoric life of the United States, although at the end he lives in Switzerland as if he were in America.

In 1955 Frisch abandoned architecture to embark on a career as a full-time writer. That

year he won the Schleussner-Schüller Prize from the Hessian radio network and the Wilhelm Raabe Prize from the city of Brunswick.

Homo faber: Ein Bericht (1957; translated as *Homo Faber: A Report,* 1959) is the first-person account of Walter Faber, a Swiss engineer working for UNESCO, and of how he was confronted with his repressed past: his Jewish-German girlfriend Hanna and their daughter, Sabeth, whom he loves incestuously. The title is both a play on Faber's name and a Latin term meaning "technological man." This new kind of man, represented by Walter Faber, is shown not to be an advance on homo sapiens. The novel is the report of a man who begins to realize that he may die and who wants to exclude death from his life–as Americans do, according to Frisch. In this last period of his life, characterized by a growing awareness of human existence, he not only comes into contact with his own past failures and their long-term consequences but also begins to see the truth of nontechnological realities–especially the myth of Oedipus, which he is fated to repeat in reverse. In 1958 Frisch was awarded the Georg Büchner Prize by the German Academy of Literature, the Literature Prize of the City of Zurich, and the Veillon Prize of Lausanne. Around this time he moved to Rome, where he lived until 1965.

The sketch for Frisch's greatest success on the stage, *Andorra* (1961; translated, 1964), can be found in the *Tagebuch 1946-1949*. The play is an indictment of anti-Semitism. Anti-Semitism, according to Frisch, is a projection, the creation of a "Bildnis" (image) of another person. The boy Andri is mistakenly thought to be a Jew. He dreams of being a normal citizen of Andorra–a fictional country modeled on Switzerland, with no connection to the real Andorra–but is constantly confronted with stereotypical prejudices: the Jew is intelligent but has no feelings; the Jew cannot be a good craftsman but must be a salesman, because he always thinks about money; he cannot be a good soccer player; cannot be patriotic, and so forth. Finally, Andri accepts this image and declares himself to be a Jew. At this point it is revealed that he is not Jewish after all, but the illegitimate son of the teacher Can, who invented the story of Andri's Jewishness to conceal his true parentage. But Andri does not believe the truth about his origins; and when the neighboring country, a totalitarian state, invades Andorra and demands a Jewish sacrifice, he dies willingly.

Andorra is not only a play about prejudice; it also shows the destructive nature of politically convenient lies, such as Can's lie about Andri's background. The twelve scenes of the play are separated by monologues by some of the characters, who appear in a witness box and comment on Andri's death; except for the priest, they all proclaim their innocence and goodwill. Frisch is saying that even catastrophic events do not lead to a change in people; the expectation that World War II would change history was an illusion. Although Frisch was sympathetic to socialist ideals, he was not willing to concede that even socialism would change people. Like Brecht, whom he had met in 1947, Frisch uses the devices of Epic Theater to bring his audiences to the awareness of social evils; but unlike Brecht, Frisch has no real hope that these evils can be remedied. In 1962 Frisch received the Great Art Prize of Rhineland-Westphalia.

The novel *Mein Name sei Gantenbein* (Let My Name Be Gantenbein, 1964; translated as *A Wilderness of Mirrors*, 1965) returns to the theme of escape. The unnamed narrator imagines different roles that he might play, giving them different names. The most extended role is that of Theo Gantenbein, who pretends to be blind. Thus Gantenbein is a role in a double sense: an imag-

Frisch in 1966 (Ullstein–Gertrude Fehr)

ined persona who lives by role playing. Gantenbein and the other aliases of the narrator, Felix Enderlin and Frantisek Svoboda, live in a world of make-believe, of games and imagination; a world which may be created or canceled at any time. The novel represents an impossible attempt to find out the best way of life before living it. In 1965 Frisch won the Schiller Prize of Baden-Württemberg and the Jerusalem Prize. That year he moved back to Switzerland.

The imaginary characters of *Mein Name sei Gantenbein* are trying to avoid the inevitability of fate. Frisch dwelt on this possibility of thwarting fate in two further works. In 1966 he published *Zürich-Transit*, the script of a film project that was not realized. Returning by plane to Zurich, Theo Ehrismann reads in the newspaper that he has died in a car accident. Instead of interrupting the funeral and revealing his identity as he at first intended to do, he merely observes his wife, his relatives, and his friends from a distance. People he meets on the street, believing that he is dead, fail to recognize him. After withdrawing money from the bank and paying a nighttime visit to his home, where his family is asleep but he is recognized by his dog, he disappears into the Orient; Zurich, his former home, has become a mere transit station. In the comedy *Biografie: Ein Spiel* (1967; translated as *Biography: A Game,* 1969) Kürrmann, a dying professor of behavioral science, is given the opportunity to live his life over again and alter past events under the direction of a Registrator (Recorder). The experiment reveals that the alternative lives would have been no more satisfactory than his actual one. Kürrmann is selfish and opportunistic but stubbornly clings to useless principles. Most of all, he cannot establish a lasting relationship with a woman–not with his black American girlfriend; not with his first wife, who commits suicide; not with his present wife, Antoinette. In this play Frisch reveals his horror of the one definite and inevitable ending. He used to say that he found plays, including his own, boring; he only liked rehearsals, where everything was still open.

Frisch took part in the political struggles of the late 1960s and early 1970s in speeches and essays, in his *Tagebuch 1966-1971* (1972; translated as *Sketchbook 1966-1971*, 1974), and in two little books on Switzerland. The *Tagebuch 1966-1971*, however, is not merely a political document. It does record conflicts and revolts in Europe and the issues arising from the Vietnam War; but it also dwells heavily on the problem of aging and death, and contains literary items such as sketches and notes of encounters with other writers. There are long passages on the United States, New York in particular. He married Marianne Oellers in December 1968; this marriage ended in divorce a few years later.

In 1971 Frisch published *Wilhelm Tell für die Schule* (William Tell for Schools), a reformulation of the myth of Tell and the foundation of Switzerland. The hero is depicted as a dim-witted murderer; the Austrian administration appears progressive compared to the stubborn and narrowly provincial conservatism of the Swiss peasants; the Austrian "atrocities" are shown to be either normal legal practice or mere fabrications. Frisch does not claim that his version is the truth; he is merely showing how implausible the official Swiss legend is.

Frisch, who lived in Berlin in the early 1970s, questioned Swiss attitudes during World War II in his *Dienstbüchlein* (Service Booklet, 1974). Remembering his military service between 1939 and 1945, Frisch describes the rigid class system in the Swiss army and the shallow basis of Swiss patriotism. While the Swiss, according to Frisch, were determined to defend themselves

Frisch in 1976 (Ullstein–Gerd Pfeiffer)

should the Germans try to invade Switzerland, they had no clear political ideals to fight for and no understanding of National Socialism. Frisch's own *Blätter aus dem Brotsack* had contained a good deal of criticism of the organization of the Swiss army, but within the context of a moderate yet unquestioned Swiss patriotism. There is hardly any mention of the Germans or the Italians in the earlier book, in which Frisch does not look beyond the Swiss borders. It is just this attitude that Frisch attacks in his *Dienstbüchlein:* self-centered Switzerland never asked what was really at stake in the war; therefore, the war did not bring any social change for Switzerland, only added wealth. Even the *Dienstbüchlein* is very discreet about Switzerland's shameful handling of the refugee problem; it merely mentions the existence of internment camps. But this matter was still so sensitive in the 1970s that even these mild comments caused harsh criticism of the book in Switzerland. In 1974 Frisch received the Great Schiller Prize.

Frisch's works since the mid 1970s reflect his preoccupation with aging, death, and the past. One of his most harmonious, unpretentiously satisfying stories is *Montauk* (1975; translated, 1976). The narrator, Max, recounts a weekend spent near Montauk, Long Island, with a young American woman named Lynn. This uneventful yet fulfilling weekend, which is not intended to lead to a lasting relationship between the couple, gives Max, a famous writer, an opportunity to reflect on his experiences with women, on his two wives, on the writer Ingeborg Bachmann (with whom Frisch had lived during his years in Rome), on his problems with his daughter, on a problematic friendship with a rich Swiss man, and on himself as writer and man. The seemingly simple style of the story, the smile which accompanies the entire episode, hides the deep melancholy of aging. The writer takes stock of himself and begins to say farewell to his manhood.

In 1978 Frisch published *Triptychon: Drei szenische Bilder* (translated as *Triptych: Three Scenic Panels*, 1981). Though intended for the stage, it is not really a play but three "scenic pictures" reminiscent of medieval altar paintings. There is no "action." The first picture depicts the embarrassed mourners at a widow's reception after the funeral. In the second picture a group of dead people stand before the river of the underworld and ruminate about their unfinished lives on earth. Regrets, reproaches, repetitive formulas, and unpleasant memories prevail. The last scene is devoted to the regrets of Roger, who cannot stop thinking about his love for the dead Francine. A horror story of futility and of total lack of communication, *Triptychon* was not successful when it premiered in Vienna in 1981. It is melancholy, bitter, and pessimistic.

Not much more comforting is Frisch's story *Der Mensch erscheint im Holozän* (1979; translated as *Man in the Holocene*, 1980). Mr. Geiser, a retired industrialist in his seventies, lives alone in an isolated valley in the Ticino. Torrential rains which disrupt traffic on the only road to civilization cause Geiser to reflect on nature and the human race. He immerses himself in the geological and early human history of the region and finally becomes fascinated by dinosaurs, cutting out information on them from books and pasting the clippings on the walls. In a moment of panic Geiser tries to see if he could escape through a mountain pass should the valley really be cut off. The road and electricity are soon restored, but

Geiser has drifted into a new frame of mind. He does not answer the doorbell or the telephone, and his daughter, who finally comes to see him, considers him senile, a danger to himself. Geiser has discovered that humankind is merely an episode in nature and may be on its way out.

Frisch's story *Blaubart* (1982; translated as *Bluebeard*, 1984) returns to more familiar themes. Felix Schaad, a specialist in internal medicine, is accused of murdering one of his former wives, a prostitute. After a year of imprisonment, he is tried and acquitted. The experience causes him to start his own introspective investigation of his guilt or innocence. When he finally decides that he is morally guilty, the real murderer has been found, and his confession is rejected. A suicide attempt by means of a car crash is unsuccessful. Schaad ends as a failure.

After *Montauk* Frisch's works reveal few good memories. The past seems heavy; former relationships cast shadows of reproach over the present; loneliness pervades the atmosphere. While in *Montauk* numerous quotes from Frisch's earlier works indicate self-acceptance, the past has become threatening in the last works. Old age and death are dominant themes, but even more prevalent may be regret of the past–one's own and that of the human race. And there is little to look forward to. Even the short moments of bliss that occasionally appeared in Frisch's earlier works are lacking in the late ones.

Frisch's work shows a remarkable continuity. It has an unmistakable style, discernible since the early 1940s, and several central themes which reappear in ever new contexts: reality and imagination, the problem of determinism, the difficulty of relations between man and woman, life in familiar but confining Switzerland as opposed to life in vast lands such as America, personal and social responsibility, and the quest for self-fulfillment and truth. Frisch never seems satisfied; he is always open to new experiences. He prefers an open structure for his works: the mosaic of diaries and notebooks, plays that experiment with different endings. Frisch's work fights valiantly against an inevitable fate; it is a constant search for alternatives. Frisch takes his responsibilities as a writer seriously–perhaps too seriously. There is the element of Überforderung (demanding too much) in his own efforts as well as in those of his protagonists. He is trying to achieve the impossible. Disquieting, always surprising, controversial, rarely completely satisfying himself or his readers, he is one of the most highly regarded writers of the age.

Letters:
"Briefwechsel zwischen Karl Schmid und Max Frisch," in Karl Schmid, *Unbehagen im Kleinstaat* (Zurich: Artemis, 1977), pp. 255-268.

Interviews:
Horst Bienek, "Max Frisch," in *Werkstattgespräche mit Schriftstellern* (Munich: Hanser, 1962), pp. 21-32;

Alfred A. Häsler, "Wir müssen unsere Welt anders einrichten: Gespräch mit Max Frisch," in his *Leben mit dem Haß: 21 Gespräche* (Reinbek: Rowohlt, 1969), pp. 40-46;

Peter Andre Bloch and Bruno Schoch, "Gespräch mit Max Frisch," in their *Der Schriftsteller und sein Verhältnis zur Sprache, dargestellt am Problem der Tempuswahl* (Bern: Francke, 1971), pp. 68-81;

Rolf Kieser, "An Interview with Max Frisch," *Contemporary Literature*, no. 1 (1972): 1-14;

Heinz Ludwig Arnold, "Gespräch mit Max Frisch," in his *Gespräche mit Schriftstellern* (Munich: Beck, 1975), pp. 9-73;

Rudolf Ossowski, ed., *Jugend fragt–Prominente antworten* (Berlin: Colloquium, 1975), pp. 116-135.

References:
Heinz Ludwig Arnold, ed., *Max Frisch* (Munich: text + kritik, 1975);

Hans Bänziger, *Frisch und Dürrenmatt*, sixth edition (Bern: Francke, 1971);

Bänziger, *Zwischen Protest und Traditionsbewußtsein: Arbeiten zum Werk und zur gesellschaftlichen Stellung Max Frischs* (Bern: Francke, 1975);

Thomas Beckermann, ed., *Über Max Frisch I* (Frankfurt am Main: Suhrkamp, 1971);

Begegnungen: Eine Festschrift für Max Frisch zum siebzigsten Geburtstag (Frankfurt am Main: Suhrkamp, 1981);

Marianne Biedermann, *Das politische Theater von Max Frisch* (Lampertheim: Schäuble, 1974);

John T. Brewer, "Max Frisch's *Biedermann und die Brandstifter* as the Documentation of an Author's Frustration," *Germanic Review*, 46 (1971): 119-128;

Michael Butler, *The Novels of Max Frisch* (London: Wolff, 1976);

Mary E. Cook, " 'Countries of the Mind': Max Frisch's Narrative Technique," *Modern Language Review*, 65 (1970): 820-828;

Erna M. Dahms, *Zeit und Zeiterlebnis in den Werken Max Frischs: Bedeutung und technische Darstellung* (Berlin: de Gruyter, 1976);

Martin Esslin, "Max Frisch," in *German Men of Letters*, edited by Alex Natan, volume 3, second edition (London: Wolff, 1968), pp. 307-320;

Wolfgang Frühwald and Walter Schmitz, eds., *Max Frisch: Andorra/Wilhelm Tell. Materialien, Kommentare* (Munich: Hanser, 1977);

Hans Geulen, *Max Frischs Homo faber: Studien und Interpretationen* (Berlin: de Gruyter, 1965);

Heinz Gockel, *Max Frisch: Gantenbein. Das offenartistische Erzählen* (Bonn: Bouvier, 1976);

Tildy Hanhart, *Max Frisch: Zufall, Rolle und literarische Form. Interpretationen zu seinem neueren Werk* (Kronberg: Scriptor, 1976);

Walter Hinck, "Abschied von der Parabel: Frisch," in his *Das moderne Drama in Deutschland* (Göttingen: Vandenhoeck & Ruprecht, 1973), pp. 170-180;

Walter Hinderer, " 'Ein Gefühl der Fremde': Amerikaperspektiven bei Max Frisch," in *Amerika in der deutschen Literatur: Neue Welt. Nordamerika. USA*, edited by Sigrid Bauschinger, Horst Denkler, and Wilfried Malsch (Stuttgart: Reclam, 1975), pp. 353-367;

Gerhard vom Hofe, "Zauber ohne Zukunft: Zur autobiographischen Korrektur in Max Frischs Erzählung *Montauk*," *Euphorion*, 70 (1976): 374-397;

Manfred Jurgensen, *Max Frisch: Die Dramen* (Bern: Francke, 1968);

Jurgensen, *Max Frisch: Die Romane* (Bern: Francke, 1972);

Jurgensen, ed., *Frisch: Kritik–Thesen–Analysen* (Bern: Francke, 1977);

Hellmuth Karasek, *Max Frisch* (Munich: dtv, 1976);

Rolf Kieser, "Man as His Own Novel: Max Frisch and the Literary Diary," *Germanic Review*, 47 (1972): 109-117;

Kieser, *Max Frisch: Das literarische Tagebuch* (Frauenfeld: Huber, 1975);

Gerhard P. Knapp, ed., *Max Frisch: Aspekte des Bühnenwerks* (Bern: Lang, 1979);

Knapp, ed., *Max Frisch: Aspekte des Prosawerks* (Bern: Lang, 1978);

Hans Mayer, *Über Friedrich Dürrenmatt und Max Frisch*, second edition (Pfullingen: Neske, 1977);

Doris F. Merrifield, *Das Bild der Frau bei Max Frisch* (Freiburg: Hecksmann, 1971);

Marian E. Musgrave, "The Evolution of the Black Character in the Works of Max Frisch," *Monatshefte*, 66 (1974): 117-132;

Jürgen H. Petersen, *Max Frisch* (Stuttgart: Metzler, 1978);

Gertrud B. Pickar, *The Dramatic Works of Max Frisch* (Frankfurt am Main & Bern: Lang, 1977);

Gerhard F. Probst and Jay F. Bodine, eds., *Perspectives on Max Frisch* (Lexington: University Press of Kentucky, 1982);

Albrecht Schau, ed., *Max Frisch: Beiträge zur Wirkungsgeschichte* (Freiburg: Becksmann, 1971);

Walter Schmitz, ed., *Materialien zu Max Frischs Biedermann und die Brandstifter* (Frankfurt am Main: Suhrkamp, 1979);

Schmitz, ed., *Materialien zu Max Frischs Stiller*, 2 volumes (Frankfurt am Main: Suhrkamp, 1978);

Schmitz, ed., *Max Frisch: Homo faber. Materialien, Kommentar* (Munich: Hanser, 1977);

Schmitz, ed., *Über Max Frisch II* (Frankfurt am Main: Suhrkamp, 1976);

M. E. Schuchmann, *Der Autor als Zeitgenosse: Gesellschaftliche Aspekte in Max Frischs Werk* (Frankfurt am Main & Bern: Lang, 1979);

Eduard Stäuble, *Max Frisch: Gesamtdarstellung seines Werks,* fourth edition (St. Gallen: Erker, 1971);

Horst Steinmetz, *Max Frisch: Tagebuch; Roman; Drama* (Göttingen: Vandenhoeck & Ruprecht, 1973);

Alexander Stephan, *Max Frisch* (Munich: Beck, 1983);

Ulrich Weisstein, *Max Frisch* (New York: Twayne, 1967);

Ernst Wendt and Walter Schmitz, eds., *Materialien zu Max Frischs Andorra* (Frankfurt am Main: Suhrkamp, 1978);

Monika Wintsch-Spieß, *Zum Problem der Identität im Werk Max Frischs* (Zurich: Juris, 1965).

Gerd Gaiser
(15 September 1908-9 June 1976)

Penrith Goff
Wayne State University

BOOKS: *Die Plastik der Renaissance und des Frühbarock in Neukastilien* (Tübingen: Druckerei Bölzle, 1938);

Reiter am Himmel: Gedichte (Munich: Langen-Müller, 1941);

Zwischenland: Erzählungen (Munich: Hanser, 1949);

Eine Stimme hebt an: Roman (Munich: Hanser, 1950);

Die sterbende Jagd: Roman (Munich: Hanser, 1953); translated by Paul Findlay as *The Last Squadron* (New York: Pantheon, 1956); translation republished as *The Falling Leaf* (London: Collins, 1956);

Das Schiff im Berg: Aus dem Zettelkasten des Peter Hagmann (Munich: Hanser, 1955);

Einmal und oft: Erzählungen (Munich: Hanser, 1956);

Gianna aus dem Schatten: Novelle (Munich: Hanser, 1957);

Ansprache an die Tübinger Jungbürger (Tübingen, 1957);

Aniela: Erzählung (Munich: Hanser, 1958);

Schlußball: Aus den schönen Tagen der Stadt Neu-Spuhl (Munich: Hanser, 1958); translated by Marguerite Waldman as *The Final Ball* (New York: Pantheon, 1960); translation republished as *The Last Dance of the Season* (London: Collins, 1960);

Moderne Kunst: Eine Einführung (Munich: Knorr & Hirth, 1958);

Damals in Promischur (Olten: Vereinigung Oltener Bücherfreunde, 1959);

Gib acht in Domokosch: Erzählungen (Munich: Hanser, 1959);

Sizilianische Notizen (Munich: Hanser, 1959);

Revanche: Erzählungen (Stuttgart: Reclam, 1959);

Am Paß Nascondo (Munich: Hanser, 1960); edited by K. Bullivant (London & Toronto: Harrap, 1960);

Klassiker der modernen Malerei von Matisse bis Miró (Munich: Knorr & Hirth, 1962);

Alte Meister der modernen Malerei von Cézanne bis Bonnard (Munich: Knorr & Hirth, 1963);

(Ullstein–Ursula Röhnert)

Aktuelle Malerei: Von Arp bis Wols (Munich: Knorr & Hirth, 1963);

Moderne Malerei von Cézanne bis zur Gegenwart (Munich: Knorr & Hirth, 1963);

Gerd Gaiser: Eine Auswahl aus seinen Erzählungen, edited by Theo Stollenwerk (Frankfurt am Main: Diesterweg, 1963);

Gazelle, grün: Erzählungen und Aufzeichnungen (Munich: Hanser, 1965);

Der Mensch, den ich erlegt hatte: Erzählungen (Munich: Goldmann, 1965);

Vergeblicher Gang (Baden-Baden: Signal, 1967);

Flug über Schwarzwald und Schwabenland: Bodensee, Oberrhein, Neckartal, Oberschwaben (Braunschweig: Westermann, 1968);

Merkwürdiges Hammelessen: Erzählungen (Frankfurt am Main: Fischer, 1971);

Der Motorradunfall: Erzählungen (Munich: Heyne, 1972);

Umgang mit Kunst: Konzept, Mittel, Kommunikation (Tübingen: Katzmann, 1974);

Alpha und Anna: Geschichten einer Kindheit, edited by Benno Mascher (Basel: Reinhardt, 1975);

Ortskunde (Munich: Hanser, 1977);

Mittagsgesicht (Ostfildern: Schwaben Verlag, 1983).

OTHER: Carl Näher, *Reutlingen: Aufnahmen*, text by Gaiser (Lindau: Thorbecke, 1953);

Konrad Helbig, *Tempel Siziliens: Sechsundzwanzig Bildtafeln*, afterword by Gaiser (Frankfurt am Main: Insel, 1963);

Matthaeus Merian, *Die schönsten Städte Baden-Württembergs: Aus den Topographien*, introduction by Gaiser (Hamburg: Hoffmann & Campe, 1966);

Schwäbische Alb, contributions by Gaiser and Hermann Baumhauser, photos by Albrecht Brugger and others (Stuttgart & Aalen: Theiß, 1976).

Gerd Gaiser grew up in the upheaval surrounding World War I, came of age in the year of the stock market crash, and fought in World War II. His career–really only an avocation–as a writer flourished after the war, bringing a number of distinctions: the Fontane Prize in 1951, the Prize for Literature from the Bavarian Academy of Fine Arts in 1955, election to the prestigious Academy of Arts in Berlin in 1956, the Immermann Prize in 1959, and the Wilhelm Raabe Prize in 1956 and 1960. In the turbulent 1960s his nostalgic conservatism and the gentle restraint of his prose had little appeal, and his popularity went into a decline from which it has not recovered. Gaiser's work includes one of Germany's finest war novels; many of his other tales are sensitive reflections of postwar moods and concerns, particularly skepticism toward the new affluent society.

Gerhard Gaiser was born in 1908 in Oberriexingen, Württemberg, to Hermann Gaiser, a Protestant minister, and Julie Lachenmann Gaiser. At first he intended to follow in his father's footsteps, but after attending seminaries in Urach and Schöntal he decided to pursue his true inclination and study art. He attended art academies in Stuttgart, Königsberg, and Dresden, and received his Ph.D. in art history from the University of Tübingen in 1934 with a dissertation titled *Die Plastik der Renaissance und des Frühbarock in Neukastilien* (The Sculpture of the Renaissance and Early Baroque in New Castile, 1938). During his years of study he had traveled much in the Baltic and Danube regions and in his favorite lands, France, Italy, and Spain.

He married Elisabeth Schmidt in 1935 and taught art until the outbreak of the war. From 1939 until 1945 he served in the air force as a fighter pilot. He was stationed in Romania, the Helgoland Bay, and Italy, where he was captured by the British. After the war he worked as a laborer and as a free-lance artist but returned to teaching in 1949 at the Friedrich List Gymnasium in Reutlingen. In 1959 he married Irene Widmann. He became Professor of Fine Arts at the Pedagogical Institute in Reutlingen in 1962.

Gaiser failed as an artist but succeeded as a writer, even though, as he put it in an autobiographical sketch published in the story collection *Revanche* (1959), "Das Malen erscheint mir als das Schönste und Freudevollste auf der Welt. Von den Freuden das Malens habe ich mir einen Begriff; Freuden eines Schriftstellers kann ich mir indessen durchaus nicht vorstellen. Schreiben verzehrt" (Painting seems the most beautiful and joyful thing in the world. I understand the joys of painting. On the other hand, I cannot even imagine the joys of a writer. Writing consumes). He had written for as long as he could remember, though not with the idea that others would read his work. His attitude toward writing, even after he became established, remained modest, even ambivalent: "Der Schreibtisch ist nicht meine Welt. Trotzdem und deshalb könnte ich, ohne zu schreiben, das Leben nicht ertragen" (The desk is not my world. In spite of that and because of it I could not bear life without writing). But writing remained a sideline, pursued only in the time left after teaching; and if that was sometimes less than he would have liked, at least he was spared the professional writer's problem "einen Bogen einspannen zu müssen, wenn ich im Grunde nichts zu schreiben hätte" (of having to put paper in the typewriter even when I really had nothing to write).

Gaiser mentions as influences on his development his governess Anna–a genius at storytelling–and a Spanish shoeshine man who gave him a pocket edition of Cervantes's *Novelas ejemplares*. His upbringing in the parsonage was by no means narrow: in addition to the Bible, Pindar and Horace were on the library bookshelves. Another important factor was his love of travel and new landscapes, especially areas spared the refinements of modern civilization. He loved the mountains, particularly areas unsuited to human habitation, and wine-growing valleys where Romance languages were spoken. These predilections are reflected throughout his writing.

Gaiser's first book, *Reiter am Himmel* (Riders Against the Sky, 1941), a collection of poems in free verse, gives full expression to his love of unspoiled nature and his admiration for country people with their roots in the land. Gaiser's participation in the flight from urban industrial culture of the German youth movement of the 1920s shaped his attitude toward modern civilization. In this poetry, though, there is also, as Marcel Reich-Ranicki has pointed out, the rhetoric of the Nazi blood-and-soil ideology. Gaiser published no further poetry and repudiated this early writing as "half-baked" beginner's work, produced in a period of ideological turmoil when a politically naive visionary could easily be ensnared.

Gaiser's next book, five stories published under the title *Zwischenland* (The Land in Between, 1949), reflects the postwar upheaval. The soldier coming home from the war is a familiar figure in the literature of the time. Gaiser's soldiers return to find that they cannot simply resume the old life; they miss the excitement of war, and, not knowing what they want, they drift aimlessly. Their primary concern is how to continue their interrupted lives. Those who would try to take up the past find that history has been altered by the war; those who would forget the past feel that whatever new society emerges must be based on sound old values of marriage, family ties, and faithfulness.

The title, *Zwischenland*, indicates a "land beyond" the chaotic world of reality, a world of dreams in which one can rest from the frustrations, hardships, and struggles of the real world. But brief contacts with the "land between" are not mere escapes–they bring insight and inspiration and renew inner strength. In "Das Wasser verbirgt sich im Berg" (The Water Hides in the Mountain) the wounded soldier Tom Andernoth, bone weary and discouraged, is reunited with his family in a dream and is spurred on by the dream to reach home as quickly as possible.

Drawing of Gaiser by G. J. Widmann

The theme of the returning soldier is given a broad treatment in Gaiser's first novel, *Eine Stimme hebt an* (A Voice Begins, 1950). The importance of the novel lies not so much in its realistic portrayal of the soldier's situation as in the soul-searching of the protagonist, Oberstelehn, who resolves that this war, unlike World War I, must lead to a more meaningful life. His first attempts to find such a life are frustrated by incidents which seem to bear out the cyclic nature of history. But the book concludes on a hopeful if unconvincing note: Oberstelehn attains the insight that the recurrence of history includes both good and evil, and that one can preserve from the past what is meaningful and reject what is not.

Gaiser's experiences as a fighter pilot provided the material for his second novel, *Die sterbende Jagd* (The Dying Hunt, 1953; translated as *The Last Squadron*, 1956), which was quickly acclaimed by critics as one of the best novels about the war. Again, the theme of unchanging history is struck: Gaiser points to the survival of medieval chivalry in the "jousting" of a squadron of fighter pilots in Norway. The pilots, only a few of whom the reader knows by name, form a collective hero. Proud that they are an elite and quickened by the thrill of battle, they begin to feel doubts when they realize that they are hopelessly outnumbered and that their destruction will end a tradition which has extended from the Middle Ages. The contrast between permanent, beautiful nature and transient civilization is also a theme, with nature represented by the fixed elitist social order and civilization by democracy with its petit-bourgeois, bungling bureaucracy. The novel elegizes a vanishing elite and acknowledges with taciturn irony the triumph of democracy.

The nature/civilization polarity is the central theme of *Das Schiff im Berg* (The Ship in the Mountain, 1955). This novel caused Gaiser much difficulty (the original manuscript was three times as long as the finished book) because its characters include not just people but rock formations, vegetation, and meteorological phenomena. It is not even a novel in the conventional sense but a history of a mountain in the Swabian Alb, based on the notes of a fictitious geologist, Peter Hagmann. The vastness, power, and permanence of nature are contrasted with man's puniness. The chronicle of the mountain reveals the pattern in human events to be cyclic rather than progressive—civilizations rise and fall; war brings development in the form of fortifications, but peace brings back the shepherds. Yet the most recent developments—the radical changes wrought in the mountain by modern developers—show the irreversible inroads of civilization upon nature. The simple way of life of the inhabitants has changed to a materialistic one; nature is valued only for the income to be derived from her. Gaiser's view of history in this novel is more pessimistic than in his previous work; it is symbolized in Hagmann's decision to give up trying to find a meaningful pattern which would serve as a guide to the future.

Gaiser's most strident criticism of postwar affluent society is contained in his best-known novel, *Schlußball* (1958; translated as *The Final Ball*, 1960). Its thirty chapters are reports given alternately by six living and four dead characters. Their views of events culminating in a homicide and a suicide on the evening of a dance provide a hologram of the lives and thinking of the citizens of Neu-Spuhl. The name of the town (New Spuhl) suggests a break with the past. Built on the rubble of the old town of Spuhl, Neu-Spuhl is not a city in the traditional sense; it is an outcropping of industrialization–Gaiser calls it "Ausschlag" (a rash)–and most of its populace reflect postwar conformity and pride in material possessions. A few stand outside this society: a lame girl who cannot participate and who becomes a canny critic of the people around her; Mrs. Förckh, who is gradually alienated from her husband by his growing business success and the lifestyle it brings with it; Mrs. Andernoth and her daughter Diemuth, whose nonconformity causes her continual problems with her schoolmates; and in particular the teacher, Soldner, who tries to instill in his pupils more fulfilling values than those of their parents. Whereas the rest of the people of Neu-Spuhl believe in a life of ease, these outsiders scorn comfort, convinced that struggle produces strength and enriches life. But they cannot exist in this world, nor can they combat it effectively. Mrs. Förckh's estrangement from her husband is symptomatic of the general spiritual crisis that ensues when material values displace humane ones: success has broken down the closeness which the Förckhs had known in needier times; there is no longer any communication, and Mrs. Förckh is driven to suicide. Soldner is ineffective at broadening his pupils' outlook. His nonconformity is underscored by his lack of formal qualifications for his post, but it is not so much this lack as it is the influence of the wealthy, who suspect him of subversive activity, which forces him to leave his job.

The stories in *Am Paß Nascondo* (On the Nascondo Pass, 1960) are set in a mythical landscape. Critics speculated that Gaiser was writing about the contemporary German political situation, but the landscape is actually an amalgam of European elements, with suggestions of the Balkans and the Romance countries as well as the two Germanies. In the title story, the citizens of Vioms enjoy the comforts of civilization and live the shallow lives of petty ambition and materialism Gaiser had portrayed in *Schlußball*. The narrator, who finds that culture repugnant, is at first attracted to Calvagora, a rural community with a less comfortable but more wholesome way of life. But he rejects Calvagora because of its stifling authoritarian regime. Life in Promischur, on the periphery of Vioms, also proves unsatisfactory. After he has accepted death as the completion rather than the negation of life he goes to Nascondo, a surreal "Zwischenland" where death fuses with life.

Gaiser's approach to writing was strongly influenced by his background as a painter. Even after he had established himself as a writer, he felt himself to be primarily a painter and to be doing in prose what he did with paint: "Auch schreibend versuche ich nichts anderes als in Bildern zu begreifen, was uns gestaltlos und unbewältigt umgibt" (Also as a writer all I try to do is grasp in pictures those things which surround us inchoate and uncontrolled). Gaiser said that he did not begin a work with a plan or even an idea. He spoke of poetic inspiration in terms of his experience as an artist: as the painter begins with a color or juxtaposition of colors or forms, with figuration coming later, so the writer may begin with a word or an outcry–the rhythmic intonation of a single sentence could lead to a story. For Gaiser writing did not spring from a need to communicate but was triggered by language itself. The measured cadences of the Bible, read aloud daily in the parsonage, impressed him deeply as a boy; hearing language became an experience for him well before he learned the magic of reading and writing. Gaiser has been criticized for his highly individual literary style, but more often he is praised for his ability to capture nuances of colloquial language and for his linguistically inventive, accurately detailed, graphic descriptions of nature.

Gaiser's outlook is conservative. He sees nature as a grand and powerful force which is disinterested in human fates. In the course of his career his optimistic view of the cyclic nature of history dissipated. He was resigned to the inexorable deterioration of human relationships and values brought about by modern industrial civilization, but he was nostalgic over the loss of primal ties to nature and to one's fellow human beings. The material of his tales is not the sensational incidents–these are always underplayed–but the inner search for the meaning of life.

Interview:
Horst Bienek, *Werkstattgespräche mit Schriftstellern* (Munich: Hanser, 1962), pp. 208-220.

Bibliography:
Siegfried Dangelmayr and Hannelore Quenel, "Gerd-Gaiser-Bibliographie. Mit Anmerkungen von Norbert Feinäugle," in *Gerd Gaiser zum Gedenken*, edited by the Vereinigund der Freunde der Pädagogischen Hodschule Reutlingen (Reutlingen: Pädagogische Hochschule, 1983), pp. 1-35.

References:
David Bronsen, "Unterdrückung des Pathos in Gerd Gaisers *Die sterbende Jagd*," *German Quarterly*, 38 (1965): 310-317;

Thomas A. Buesch, "The Poetic Language of Gerd Gaiser," *German Quarterly*, 45 (1972): 57-69;

Keith Bullivant, *Between Chaos and Order: The Work of Gerd Gaiser* (Stuttgart: Heinz, 1980);

Peter Demetz, *Postwar German Literature* (New York: Pegasus, 1970), pp. 172-178;

Ian Hilton, "Gerd Gaiser," in *German Men of Letters*, volume 4, edited by B. Keith-Smith (London: Wolff, 1967), pp. 111-138;

Clemens Hohoff, *Gerd Gaiser: Werk und Gestalt* (Munich: Hanser, 1962);

E. Hülse, *Möglichkeiten des modernen deutschen Romans* (Frankfurt am Main: Diesterweg, 1962), pp. 161-190;

Walter Jens, "Gegen die Überschätzung Gerd Gaisers," in *Deutsche Literaturkritik der Gegenwart*, volume 4, edited by H. Mayer (Stuttgart: Goverts, 1972);

Otto Keller, *Gerd Gaiser: Am Paß Nascondo* (Munich: Oldenbourg, 1965);

Marcel Reich-Ranicki, "Der Fall Gerd Gaiser," in his *Deutsche Literatur in West und Ost: Prosa seit 1945* (Munich: Piper, 1963), pp. 55-80;

Anna Regula Schaufelberger, *Das Zwischenland der Existenz bei Gerd Gaiser* (Bonn: Grundmann, 1974).

Ernst Glaeser
(29 July 1902-8 February 1963)

Richard Critchfield
Texas A&M University

BOOKS: *Überwindung der Madonna: Drama* (Potsdam & Berlin: Kiepenheuer, 1924);

Jahrgang 1902 (Berlin: Kiepenheuer, 1928); translated by Willa and Edwin Muir as *Class 1902* (London: Secker, 1929); translation republished as *Class of 1902* (New York: Viking, 1929);

Fazit: Ein Querschnitt durch die deutsche Publizistik (Hamburg: Enoch, 1929);

Frieden (Berlin: Kiepenheuer, 1930); revised as *Die zerstörte Illusion* (Munich, Vienna & Basel: Desch, 1960);

Der Staat ohne Arbeitslose: Drei Jahre Fünfjahresplan, by Glaeser and Franz Carl Weiskopf (Berlin: Kiepenheuer, 1931); translated as *The Land without Unemployment: Three Years of the Five-Year Plan* (New York: International Publishers, 1931; London: Lawrence, 1932);

Das Gut im Elsaß: Ein Roman (Berlin: Kiepenheuer, 1932);

Die Apotheke am Neckar, as Anton Ditschler (Berlin: Kiepenheuer, 1933);

Der letzte Zivilist (Paris: Europäischer Merkur, 1935); translated by Gwenda David and Eric Mosbacher as *The Last Civilian* (New York: McBride, 1935);

Das Unvergängliche: Erzählungen (Amsterdam: Querido, 1936);

Die Sühne: Erzählung (Zurich, 1938);

Das Jahr (Zurich: Weltwoche, 1938);

Wider die Bürokratie? (Kassel: Schleber, 1947);

Kreuzweg der Deutschen: Ein Vortrag (Wiesbaden: Limes, 1947);

Die deutsche Libertät: Ein dramatisches Testament in zwei Aufzügen und mit einem Nachwort (Kassel: Schleber, 1948);

Köpfe und Profile: Staatsmänner des In-und Auslands (Zurich: Scientia/Vienna: Gallus/Berlin: Nauck, 1952);

Das Kirchenfest: Erzählungen (Zurich: Scientia/Berlin: Nauck/Vienna: Gallus, 1953);

Glanz und Elend der Deutschen: Roman (Munich, Vienna & Basel: Desch, 1960); translated by

Ernst Glaeser in 1958 (Ullstein)

Mosbacher as *The Shady Miracle* (London: Secker & Warburg, 1963);

Die Lust zu gefallen (Wiesbaden: Verlag für Wirtschaftspublizistik, 1960);

Auf daß unsere Kinder besser leben (Frankfurt am Main: Ner-Tamid-Verlag, 1961);

Was ist mit der Jugend heute los? (Vienna: Evangelischer Pressverband, 1964).

OTHER: "Der Pächter auf dem Werth: Ein Kapitel aus einem unvollendeten Roman," in *Das Ufer: Ein Buch rheinischer Dichtungen*, edited by Otto Doderer (Siegburg: Gericke, 1928);

Ulrich Becher, *Die Eroberer: Geschichten aus Europa*, preface by Glaeser (Zurich: Oprecht, 1936).

With the publication in 1928 of his novel *Jahrgang 1902* (translated as *Class 1902*, 1929) Ernst Glaeser became one of the most important writers in the waning years of the Weimar Republic. The novel was an immediate success and was translated into twenty-five languages; Ernest Hemingway characterized it as a "damned good book." *Jahrgang 1902* was almost as successful as the classic antiwar novel of the time, Erich Maria Remarque's *Im Westen nichts Neues* (1929; translated as *All Quiet on the Western Front*, 1929). Glaeser's other highly successful novel, *Der letzte Zivilist* (1935; translated as *The Last Civilian*, 1935), was written during his exile from Nazi Germany and published in Paris. Like *Jahrgang 1902*, *Der letzte Zivilist* quickly became known to an international audience; it was translated into twenty-four languages.

Glaeser was born on 29 July 1902 to Hans G. and Ruppel Glaeser in the small town of Butzbach in Hesse; his father was a judge. He studied at the Universities of Freiburg and Munich. From 1928 to 1930 he worked as a Dramaturg (dramatic adviser) at the Neues Theater in Frankfurt am Main, as literary editor of a southwestern German radio station, and as a journalist for the *Frankfurter Zeitung* and other papers. He entered the literary scene of the Weimar Republic as a leftist and pacifist who, like many other writers of the period, was impressed and attracted by the promises of the new Soviet state. In 1930 he was a member of the German delegation to the Second International Congress for Revolutionary Literature in the Soviet city of Kharkov. In 1931 Glaeser and the Communist writer Franz Carl Weiskopf published *Der Staat ohne Arbeitslose: Drei Jahre Fünfjahresplan* (translated as *The Land without Unemployment: Three Years of the Five Year Plan*, 1931). Because of his pacifist stand in *Jahrgang 1902* and his alleged Communist leanings, his books were burned when the National Socialists came to power in Germany in 1933. Glaeser left the newly founded Third Reich that year and went first to Prague and then to Locarno, Switzerland.

During the following six years Glaeser frequently expressed a desire to return to Germany, even though the fascist state stood for everything he was supposedly against. In 1939 he did return. In 1941 Glaeser was sent to Sicily to edit the army newspaper *Der Adler im Süden* (The Eagle in the South); his detractors have pointed out that the once celebrated pacifist and leftist now employed his great talents to glorify the war and Hitler. He married Mathilde Schmidt in 1946. In the postwar years Glaeser tried to justify his activities in the Third Reich by arguing that he was then an "innerer Emigrant" (a writer who lived in Nazi Germany in a state of isolation and was alienated by Hitler's policies). During the early 1950s he lauded Konrad Adenauer, the first chancellor of the Federal Republic of Germany, who was deeply committed to a democratic Germany. Glaeser's biography reveals a writer who adapted his political stand to the changing political climate of Germany.

Contradictory and controversial though Glaeser's career as a writer may be, his novels *Jahrgang 1902* and *Der letzte Zivilist* have secured him a firm place in the literature of the Weimar Republic and in German exile literature. *Jahrgang 1902* is an excellent novel, which–even though it was written for pacifists and foes of German nationalism in the late 1920s–is still quite readable and instructive in the 1980s. It is highly autobiographical: its setting is a small German town and its hero, E., was born in the same year as Glaeser. The story begins in the last months before the outbreak of World War I and continues through the war years. Perhaps more than anything else the novel is a moral indictment of German society at the turn of the century. Glaeser poses the question: who was really responsible for the war? The answer is given by a French boy whom the storyteller meets in a Swiss resort at the beginning of the hostilities: "La guerre, ce sont nos parents, mon ami" (The war is our parents, my friend). The focal point of the novel's criticisms and protests is the parents of the generation born at the beginning of the century, particularly the Germans who were deluded by the promises of Kaiser Wilhelm II and by the illusions of Germany's righteousness and mission as an emerging world power.

As the novel unfolds, the dubious values and inhuman aspects of German society in the years leading up to the war are portrayed. Glaeser depicts a society permeated by intolerance and anti-Semitism. At school E. meets a Jewish boy, Leo Silberstein, who is tormented by both his fellow pupils and his teacher. The sexual prudishness and secretiveness of the parents of E.'s generation are responsible for E.'s anxieties about the mysterious world of sex. His initia-

Glaeser in 1932 (Ullstein–Lotte Jacobi)

tion into this forbidden sphere traumatizes him; it is not until years later that he overcomes this trauma through his relationship with a gentle and wise woman. The novel presents almost a complete spectrum of German society of the time, ranging from an anti-Semitic teacher to a militaristic sports instructor and an arrogant and petty government official. *Jahrgang 1902* also documents with great skill a key turning point in the consciousness of sensitive young Germans who, during and after the war, came to condemn the mores and political policies of prewar Germany. Glaeser and kindred souls were painfully aware that many of these problems were growing worse during the Weimar Republic.

In the novel *Frieden* (Peace, 1930) Glaeser dealt with a subject that intrigued and perplexed other major German authors of the period: the unsuccessful German revolution of 1918. The revolution began in Kiel as a sailor's revolt against the Kaiser and the military. In 1919 the Communists tried to bring about a proletarian revolution in Germany. Some critics have felt that Glaeser's novel centers too much on the general anger and protests of the people and neglects the organized struggle of the Communists.

The 1930s also saw the publication of the story *Die Apotheke am Neckar* (The Pharmacy on the Neckar, 1933), written under the pseudonym Anton Ditschler, and the novels *Das Gut im Elsaß* (The Farm in Alsace, 1932) and *Der letzte Zivilist.* The thread which runs through all of these works, as well as the earlier story "Der Pächter auf dem Werth" (The Farmer on the Island, 1928), is a highly idealized, if not romanticized image of nature. In *Das Gut im Elsaß* life in the country appears as a refuge for the simple people as well as for the intellectuals, the last domain of freedom in a constantly changing and threatening political world.

A second ideal expressed in Glaeser's work of the 1930s, especially after 1933, is that of Heimat (homeland). *Der letzte Zivilist*, Glaeser's second truly successful novel, takes place during the Weimar Republic and ends as the National Socialists come to power. Bäuerle, the novel's main character, is a German-American whose parents had been financially ruined and politically persecuted and had immigrated to the United States in the late nineteenth century. Bäuerle's love of his homeland compels him to return to Germany after World War I. For Bäuerle, who sees himself as a "utopian democrat," the defeat of Germany in World War I was synonymous with the destruction of the Prussian spirit with its aggressive militaristic and nationalistic tendencies. Through Bäuerle, who lives with his daughter Irene not far from the small town of Siebenwasser, the reader sees that the National Socialists have already become a dangerous force in the Weimar Republic by the end of the 1920s. They have involved the town officials of Siebenwasser in their activities, and they intimidate those who attempt to leave the movement or who fall into disfavor. Nazi accusations precipitate the suicide of Hans, the father of the child expected by Irene. Seeing that Germany is once again becoming a nation of uniformed soldiers, Bäuerle and his daughter return to the United States. In this novel, as in many works by exile writers, the Weimar Republic is criticized for its political and moral impotence and its inability to thwart the growth of National Socialist movement. When the novel first appeared in Germany in 1946 it was embraced by a politically disillusioned public as an appeal for democracy and pacifism. Some years later, however, after the emotional trauma of the war years had subsided, critics found Glaeser's views on democracy and freedom, as articulated by Bäuerle, overly romantic and ill suited to the realities of modern industrial society. Bäuerle's return to Germany is really a return to the countryside and the ideal of the farmer, who, separated from the corruption and vice of the city, lives on the land in a virtual state of "natural freedom."

The novel's title indicates that Bäuerle is "the last civilian" in a society of soldiers; at the same time it refers to Bäuerle's uniqueness in an age of mass society in which the integrity and autonomy of the individual are constantly threatened and undermined. For the romantic Glaeser, freedom can only exist in the sphere of nature, which lies beyond the social and political strife of the cities. Glaeser's simplistic idealization of nature reflects the illusions of a writer who was trying to escape the realities of the twentieth century.

Glaeser's last novel, *Glanz und Elend der Deutschen* (1960; translated as *The Shady Miracle*, 1963), is set in the years of the Wirtschaftswunder (economic miracle) when West German society and industry were rebuilt at an astonishing pace. The novel treats the problem of Vergangenheitsbewältigung (overcoming the legacy of the Third Reich). This novel is also highly autobiographical: the central character, the architect Ferdinand von Simmern, wrote a successful novel which was burned by the Nazis, immigrated to Switzerland, returned to the Third Reich, and wrote for a German army newspaper. Glaeser's hero is surrounded by former Nazis who have gained prominence in industry in postwar Germany. While he attempts to fight the corruption he finds about him, the other main figures try to forget their past as well as their present shady dealings by indulging in sexual escapades.

Many critics felt that the characters in *Glanz und Elend der Deutschen* were overdrawn and had little to do with the real people of the time. Still, the novel is of interest to students of Glaeser's work, particularly with regard to its autobiographical aspects. Von Simmern, like Glaeser, is haunted by his past, a past for which he attempts to atone by combating the corruption about him. Glaeser, who died in Mainz on 8 February 1963, will be remembered above all for his early works *Jahrgang 1902* and *Der letzte Zivilist*.

References:

Gilbert Badia and Rene Geoffroy, "Ernst Glaeser, ein Antisemit? Eine kritische Untersuchung des in der Emigration gegen Ernst Glaeser erhobenen Vorwurfs des Antisemitismus," *Exilforschung*, 1 (1983): 283-301;

Ulrich Becher, "Der Fall Ernst Glaeser," *Die Weltbühne*, 2 (1947): 105-108;

Thomas Koebner, "Ernst Glaeser: Reaktion der 'betrogenen' Generation," in *Zeitkritische Romane des 20. Jahrhunderts*, edited by Hans Wagener (Stuttgart: Reclam, 1975), pp. 192-219;

Ludwig Marcuse, "Zum 50. Geburtstag des Jahrgangs 1902," *Der Monat*, 4 (1952): 98-99;

Edna Carolyn McCown, "Ernst Glaeser: Between the Fronts: A Study of His Work," Ph.D. dissertation, State University of New York, Stony Brook, 1982;

Marcel Reich-Ranicki, "Ernst Glaeser: 'Glanz und Elend der Deutschen,'" in his *Deutsche Literatur in West und Ost* (Munich: Piper, 1966), pp. 288-294;

Erwin Rotermund, *Zwischen Exildichtung und Innerer Emigration: Ernst Glaesers Erzählung 'Der Pächter.' Ein Beitrag zum literarischen 'Niemandsland' 1933-1945 und zur poetischen Vergangenheitsbewältigung* (Munich: Fink, 1980);

Sigrid Schneider, "Der letzte Zivilist," in her *Das Ende Weimars im Exilroman: Literarische Strategien zur Vermittlung von Faschismustheorien* (Munich: Saur, 1980), pp. 53-124;

Schneider, "Von der Verfügbarkeit des Geistes: Über Ernst Glaeser," in *Deutschsprachige Exilliteratur: Studien zu ihrer Bestimmung im Kontext der Epoche 1930-1960*, edited by Wulf Koepke and Michael Winkler (Bonn: Bouvier, 1984), pp. 179-192.

Albrecht Goes
(22 March 1908-   )

Alfred D. White
University of Wales College of Cardiff

BOOKS: *Verse* (Stuttgart: Published by the author, 1932);

Die Hirtin: Ein vorweihnachtliches Spiel (Munich: Kaiser, 1934);

Der Hirte: Gedichte (Leipzig: Kulturpolitischer Verlag, 1935);

Heimat ist gut: Zehn Gedichte (Hamburg: Verlag der Blätter für der Dichtung, 1935);

Lob des Lebens: Betrachtungen (Stuttgart: Deutsche Verlagsanstalt, 1936);

Vergebung: Ein Frauenspiel (Munich: Kaiser, 1937);

Mörike (Stuttgart: Cotta, 1938; revised, 1954);

Über das Gespräch (Berlin: Furche, 1938; enlarged edition, Hamburg: Furche, 1954);

Der Zaungast: Ein Evangelienspiel (Munich: Kaiser, 1938);

Begegnungen (Berlin: Furche, 1939);

Leuchter und Laterne: Eine Erzählung auf Christtag (Berlin: Wichern, 1939);

Der Nachbar (Berlin: Fischer, 1940);

Der Weg zum Stall: Ein Krippenspiel für Kinder (Munich: Lempp, 1940);

Die guten Gefährten: Prosastücke (Stuttgart: Cotta, 1942; enlarged, 1961);

Auf der Flucht: Ein Gespräch zu Weihnachten 1945 (Stuttgart: Häbich, 1946);

Schwäbische Herzensreise (Stuttgart: Hatje, 1946);

Rede auf Hermann Hesse (Berlin: Suhrkamp, 1946);

Ein erster Schritt, by Goes, Hermann List, and Kurt Müller (Stuttgart: Gundert, 1946);

Goethegedichte–jetzt (Stuttgart: Günther, 1946);

Die Herberge (Berlin: Suhrkamp, 1947);

Da rang ein Mann mit ihm (Munich: Kaiser, 1947);

Von Mensch zu Mensch: Bemühungen (Berlin: Suhrkamp, 1949);

Der Mensch von unterwegs: Ein Gespräch für die Christnacht in unseren Tagen (Hamburg: Wittig, 1949);

Die fröhliche Christtagslitanei (Munich: Kaiser, 1949);

Gedichte, 1930-1950 (Frankfurt am Main: Fischer, 1950);

Unruhige Nacht (Hamburg: Wittig, 1950); edited

Albrecht Goes (S. Fischer Verlag, Frankfurt am Main)

by Waldo C. Peebles (New York: American Book Co., 1955); edited by A. E. Hammer (London: Macmillan, 1965); translated by Constantine Fitzgibbon as *Unquiet Night* (Boston: Houghton Mifflin, 1951); translation republished as *Arrow to the Heart* (London: Joseph, 1951);

Christtag: Sieben Betrachtungen (Hamburg: Furche, 1951);

Unsere letzte Stunde: Eine Besinnung (Hamburg: Furche, 1951);

Im Dornburger Licht: Rede, gehalten an der Goethe-Feier (Olten: Vereinigung Oltner Bücherfreunde, 1952);

Freude am Gedicht: Zwölf Deutungen (Frankfurt am Main: Fischer, 1952);

Vertrauen in das Wort: Drei Reden (Frankfurt am Main: Fischer, 1953);

Freundschaft und Entfremdung (Mainz: Eggebrecht Presse, 1953);

Krankenvisite: Sechs Anreden (Hamburg: Furche, 1953);

Heilige Unruhe (Stuttgart: Evangelisches Verlagswerk, 1954);

Das Brandopfer (Frankfurt am Main: Fischer, 1954); edited by Alan P. Robinson (London: Harrap, 1958); translated by Michael Hamburger as *The Burnt Offering* (New York: Pantheon, 1956; London: Gollancz, 1956);

Worte zum Sonntag (Hamburg: Furche, 1955);

Das dreifache Ja: Rede zum Volkstrauertag (Frankfurt am Main: Fischer, 1956);

Ruf und Echo: Aufzeichnungen 1951-1955 (Frankfurt am Main: Fischer, 1956);

Genesis: Bilder aus der Wiener Genesis (Hamburg: Wittig, 1956);

Der Neckar (Königstein: Langewiesche-Brandt, 1957);

Goethes Mutter: Rede zum 150. Todestag von Catharina Elisabeth Goethe (Frankfurt am Main: Der Goldene Brunnen, 1958);

Hagar am Brunnen: Dreißig Predigten (Frankfurt am Main: Fischer, 1958);

Ein überfließend Maß: Predigt (Hamburg: Furche, 1958);

Worte zum Fest (Hamburg: Furche, 1959);

Wagnis der Versöhnung: Drei Reden–Hesse, Buber, Bach (Leipzig: Kochler & Amelang, 1959);

Stunden mit Bach (Hamburg: Furche, 1959);

Ravenna (Munich: Knorr & Hirth, 1960; London: Wolff, 1963);

Die Roggenfuhre: Ein Evangelienspiel (Munich: Kaiser, 1962);

Gehe, leide, warte: Drei Geschenke aus Israel (Hamburg: Gesellschaft für christlich-jüdische Zusammenarbeit, 1962);

Die Weihnacht der Bedrängten: Ein Zyklus von Gedichten und Betrachtungen (Hamburg: Furche, 1962);

Aber im Winde das Wort: Prosa und Verse aus 20 Jahren (Frankfurt am Main: Fischer, 1963);

Erkennst du deinen Bruder nicht? (Munich: Verlag Mensch und Arbeit, 1964);

Das Löffelchen: Eine Erzählung (Frankfurt am Main: Fischer, 1965); edited by Christoph

E. Schweitzer (New York: Appleton-Century-Crofts, 1968); translated by E. William Rollins and Harry Zohn as "The Boychik," in *Men of Dialogue: Martin Buber and Albrecht Goes,* edited by Rollins and Zohn (New York: Funk & Wagnalls, 1969);

Im Weitergehen: Fünfzehn Versuche (Munich & Hamburg: Siebenstern, 1965);

Dichter und Gedicht: Zwanzig Deutungen (Frankfurt am Main & Hamburg: Fischer, 1966);

Nachtgespräche (Hamburg: Wittig, 1966);

Der Knecht macht keinen Lärm: Dreißig Predigten (Hamburg: Wittig, 1968);

Der ungeteilte Mensch (Hamburg: Wittig, 1970);

Erster und letzter Besuch: Geschrieben im Gedanken an Karl Barth (Hamburg: Wittig, 1970);

Kanzelholz: Dreißig Predigten (Hamburg: Siebenstern-Taschenbuch, 1971);

Dunkler Tag, heller Tag: Erwägungen (Hamburg: Siebenstern-Taschenbuch, 1973);

Tagwerk: Prosa und Verse (Frankfurt am Main: Fischer, 1976);

Ein Winter mit Paul Gerhardt (Neukirchen-Vluyn: Neukirchener Verlag, 1976);

Lichtschatten du: Gedichte aus fünfzig Jahren (Frankfurt am Main: Fischer, 1978);

Besonderer Tage eingedenk: Ansprache zur Eröffnung einer Ausstellung in der Deutschen Bibliothek und andere Erwägungen (Frankfurt am Main: Buchhändler-Vereinigung, 1979);

Das Brandopfer; Das Löffelchen; Mit einem Nachwort von Albrecht Goes (Frankfurt am Main: Fischer, 1980);

Hebel der Ratgeber: Rede (Lörrach: Hebelbund, 1981);

Noch und schon: Zwölf Überlegungen (Stuttgart: Radius, 1983);

Christtagswege (Stuttgart: Radius, 1984);

Das mit Katz (Frankfurt am Main: Privately printed, 1984);

Erzählungen, Gedichte, Betrachtungen (Frankfurt am Main: Fischer, 1986);

Den Anderen im Wort zu finden: Albrecht Goes im Gespräch mit Hans-Rüdiger Schwab (Frankfurt am Main: Fischer Taschenbuch, 1988).

OTHER: Christian Wagner, *Blühender Kirschbaum: Gedichte und Prosa,* afterword by Goes (Munich: Langen-Müller, 1943);

Eduard Mörike, *Gedichte: Feldauswahl,* selected by Goes (Stuttgart: Cotta, 1945);

Goethe-Gedichte, selected by Goes (Stuttgart: Günther, 1947);

Maria im Rosenhag: Madonnen-Bilder altdeutscher und altniederländischer Maler, introduction by Goes (Königstein: Langewiesche, 1959);

Das Sankt Galler Spiel von der Kindheit Jesu, adapted by Goes (Frankfurt am Main: Fischer, 1959);

Mörike, *Werke in einem Band,* selected by Goes (Hamburg: Hoffmann & Campe, 1963);

Mozarts Briefe aus Paris, introduction by Goes (Frankfurt am Main: Trajanus Presse, 1963);

Waldemar Augusting, *Alle unsre Tage: Hausbuch für christliche Eheleute,* with seven addresses for special days by Goes (Hamburg: Furche, 1963);

Paul Gerhardt, *Gedichte,* selected by Goes (Frankfurt am Main: Fischer, 1969);

Wolfgang Amadeus Mozart, *Briefe,* edited by Goes (Frankfurt am Main: Fischer Taschenbuch, 1979).

PERIODICAL PUBLICATION: "Das mit Katz," *Deutsches Allgemeines Sonntagsblatt,* no. 2, 13 January 1985, p. 26.

Goes in 1953 (Ullstein)

Albrecht Goes (rhymes roughly with *verse*) is best known as the author of a few short stories describing vital moments of human contact and religious experience. *Unruhige Nacht* (1950; translated as *Unquiet Night,* 1951) was translated into fifteen languages and has sold 165,000 copies in the German edition. *Das Brandopfer* (1954; translated as *The Burnt Offering,* 1956) was translated into eleven languages, *Das Löffelchen* (1965; translated as "The Boychik," 1969) into five. A fourth story, *Das mit Katz* (The Business with Katz, 1984), however, has only been privately printed and published in one newspaper. In these poetic yet concrete narrations, with their skilled use of rhetorical and structural devices and different registers of language, Goes grasps a problem of fundamental evil: the persecution and murder of the innocent under Hitler. He sees Christian renewal, not existentialist despair, as the answer to the political situation. Though largely disregarded by the academic world, the stories deserve attention as documents of a particular phase of the history of German literature and of Vergangenheitsbewältigung (Germans' coming to terms with the legacy of Hitler).

Born in 1908 in Langenbeutingen, Württemberg, the second son of Eberhard and Elisabeth Panzerbieter Goes, Albrecht Goes was to follow five generations of his family and his elder brother into the Lutheran ministry. His mother died when he was three. Goes grew up amid rich family memories of such figures of Swabian culture as the poet Ludwig Uhland and the philosopher David Friedrich Strauß. A child who liked to be alone and do things for himself, he took all the parts in the puppet theater that was his favorite toy at the age of nine. While living with relatives in Berlin and attending the Steglitz gymnasium from 1915 to 1919 he became a keen hiker and nature lover and an accomplished pianist. After a short time at Göppingen with his father, who had remarried (Goes has two half sisters; his two half brothers were killed in World War II), the mathematically gifted, literary-minded child was educated from the age of thirteen at Schöntal and Urach seminaries; at the university and the famous theological college in Tübingen, where he drew attention by wearing the open-air shorts and blouse of the Jugendbewegung (youth movement) and not the sober attire of a budding minister; and at the University of Berlin. He was ordained in 1930 by his father. The young curate took his vocation seriously as a ministry of comforting. In 1933 he married Elisabeth Schneider, an official's daughter; three daughters were born to the marriage.

Hitler's rise found Goes inclined, like many idealists at the time, to dream that National Socialism would bring advances. Disillusionment followed; in 1934 he wrote a troubled letter to Martin Buber, one of many Jewish thinkers and writers whose works he had studied. After a series of curacies, Goes became pastor of Gebersheim, a village near Stuttgart, in 1938. His time there was interrupted by service in World War II as a private from 1940 to 1942 and as an army chaplain, mainly in hospitals behind the eastern front, from 1942 to 1945. At home his wife quietly helped those persecuted by the regime. In the war he experienced the heights and depths of human nature, humiliations and small triumphs, meetings and sudden partings, "die Welt der Gewalt und der Grausamkeit, und die winzige, wunderbare Möglichkeit des Menschen" (the world of violence and cruelty, and the tiny, wondrous opportunities to be a human being). Those experiences provided the material for his best stories. He was entirely, if impotently, opposed to Hitler's aggressions.

In 1953 Goes took indefinite leave from his parish and moved to Stuttgart. His utterances on politics show a critical liberal stance with leanings toward pacifism. He has preached on the need for international reconciliation, pleaded the cause both of those who resisted Hitler and of those who obeyed to the end, and been prominent in bodies aiming to reconcile Germans and Jews after 1945.

Though a firm Lutheran, Goes is familiar with the teachings of Judaism and Roman Catholicism. The Word shows itself most importantly for him, as for Buber, in dialogue and conversation, as the title of his collection of essays *Von Mensch zu Mensch* (From Man to Man, 1949) shows. A member of the Deutsche Akademie für Sprache und Dichtung (Literary Academy) in Darmstadt, the Verband deutscher Schriftsteller (German Writers' Union), the International P.E.N. Club, and the Akademie der Künste (Academy of Arts), he was awarded the Hamburg Lessing prize in 1953, the Großes Bundesverdienstkreuz (a high West German decoration) in 1959, the Heinrich Stahl prize of the Jewish community in West Berlin in 1962, and an honorary doctorate of theology in 1974.

Since 1932 he has regularly published reflective, unpretentious, restrainedly moralizing verse influenced by Hölderlin, Rilke, and Mörike.

From about 1934 to 1959 he wrote modest dramas on religious themes for amateur church groups. From 1936 on, in the respected *Frankfurter Zeitung* (a bastion of liberalism in Hitler's Germany) and later in other organs and in book form, he has busily published essays and contemplations on many religious, cultural, and general subjects. Often, in keeping with Buber's advice not to withhold himself, he bares part of his own inner life in order to shed light on others' problems. He analyzes the work of kindred spirits in music and literature–including Mozart, Bach, Mörike, Goethe, Thomas Mann, and Hermann Hesse (whom he helped to restore to Germans' awareness after 1945)–with great erudition, commitment, and sensitivity.

Goes's published work before 1945 clearly belongs to the "Inner Emigration"; it makes no concessions to Nazi thought, largely by avoiding all areas where conflict was likely. His concentration on Mörike, a poet whose work fiercely resisted nationalistic misinterpretations, was a statement in itself; and he wrote at least one poem–"Gelöbnis" (Vow)–which, if circulated, could have earned him the death penalty. After 1945 he published sermons and other directly religious works and achieved modest fame as a television preacher on the program "Das Wort zum Sonntag" (The Word for Sunday). His writings breathe sincere love of his neighbor and appreciation of the divinely inspired beauty of nature and art, especially the kindly and canny people, humorously wise writers, and gentle landscapes of Swabia. His trust in God–his watchword is "Fürchte dich nicht" (fear not)–has often made him underplay life's inevitable unhappiness. Man, he contends, may be cruel, but God is kind and nature is forgiving. Worldly life is insecure; life with and under God is secure. He appeals to a conservative readership, often preaching to them and demanding of them an effort at deeper spirituality.

Amid this oeuvre the short stories stand out by the starkness of their themes and the depth of Goes's response to the challenge of evil. He wrote the first two when Germans were still preoccupied with rebuilding their country and taking up the threads of lives interrupted by the war. Many had not fully grasped the enormity of the wartime crimes; under Konrad Adenauer, who was chancellor from 1949 to 1963, West Germany was more concerned about avoiding future Hitlerian temptations than reckoning with the recent past. German writers who had tackled recent history in fictional form tended to concentrate on ordinary Germans' troubles and not to empathize with those whom Germans had persecuted; Goes and a few others avoided this narrowness of view because a wider belief, such as Christianity or Marxism, informed their approach. Even so, the attempt by such writers to use the goodness of a few Germans (Christians or Communists) to justify the German people as a whole was later considered a distortion. Goes and others wrote honestly of a small sector of personal experience in Hitlerian Germany, but later writers showed more insight into mass psychology.

In *Unruhige Nacht* a military chaplain spends a night skillfully and sympathetically feeling his way into the mind of Baranowski, a deserter sentenced to be shot, whom he must help to make his peace with God. The man's life, he finds, was bereft of love; his desperate search for some relationship, his urge to realize human feelings, was never understood by others, least of all by the military machine. Before his death he can be shown, and respond to, the love and warmth of which he has been deprived; terror is held at bay during his last moments by human dialogue, which has sacramental character. During a hectic twenty-four hours the chaplain meets men of various degrees of commitment to fascism: the entirely brutal, who give themselves away by bureaucratic or cynical ways of talking about the execution; the indifferent; those with some shreds of decency left; the forcedly cheerful; and the really good men amid the degradation, who, like the chaplain, preserve their humanity even in slavery and do the dictator's foul work in silence because they see no way of improving matters by rebelling. If Ernst, a minister serving as an officer, were to refuse his duty of commanding the firing squad, he would at best be demoted to a position giving him less chance to exercise decency. He and the chaplain are distinguished from the committed Hitlerians only "dadurch, daß wir nie, zu keiner Stunde gutheißen, was nicht gut ist. . . . wir sind hineinverstrickt, der Hexensabbat findet uns schuldig . . ." (because we never, not even for a single hour, call evil good. . . . we are all ensnared in this witches' sabbath, . . . we are all guilty . . .). But in a conciliatory ending that has been criticized as weakening the story's impact the narrator, in a plane in the symbolic blue sky, gathers renewed confidence in the final outcome of the struggle of good and evil and is strengthened to return to

Dust jacket by Martin Kausche for Goes's 1954 novel about a woman who tries to help the persecuted Jews in her small town

the world's storms; and a sensitive young officer and his fiancée exemplify earthly love, a true contact of two human beings which bears some relation to divine love.

In *Das Brandopfer* the setting is the home front; the protagonist is a butcher's wife who, designated as the sole supplier of meat to Jews in the town, develops sympathy and solidarity with the persecuted minority, which never loses its dignity in suffering the taunts of the SS and the threat of imminent "resettlement." Frau Walker is inspired by her helpless customers first to small acts and words of kindness, then, at the climax—when a pregnant Jewish woman has given her a baby carriage which she will not survive to use—to try to sacrifice herself. By not taking shelter from an air raid she risks becoming the "burnt offering" of the title; but she is saved by a Jew, whose presence is rather too coincidental. God does not desire such a self-sacrifice but intends for her to survive to bear witness to the power of individual renewal by bearing the scars of fire on her face and by telling the story of Nazi cruelty to the narrator, an active listener who lets her experience work on him. "Kann man sagen: unser Gespräch? *Sie* hatte gesprochen, aber wenn Zuhören eine andere Form von Sprechen ist, dann *war* es ein Gespräch" (Conversation, I suppose, is the wrong word; she had done the talking, but if listening is a different form of speaking, it was a conversation indeed). The reader, like the narrator, is intended to perceive the fire not as destructive and diabolical but as an agent of mankind's purgation and renewal. Senseless death and terror are insignificant beside the triumphant assurance of human communication with the transcendent. Fragmentary as the instances of this communication are, they outweigh the inhumanity and sacrilegiousness of the Nazis.

Das Löffelchen, shorter but more densely packed with symbolism than the previous stories, came too late to repeat their popular success. Stefan is a Jew recruited by the bluff, humane surgeon in charge of an army hospital to maintain its complex heating system, which is vital to the patients' welfare in the Russian winter. He is loved by the staff, but when the SS hears of his presence he is arrested. (Goes hints that the SS would give disabled German soldiers equally short shrift.) Stefan is taken off to be shot; his young son Leib, unaware, happily accompanies him, proudly wearing in his belt a silver spoon which had been given to his father in recognition of his helpfulness. The ensuing meal, at which the medical officers drink wine together in solemn silence, and the narrator, the chaplain, breaks his glass and so sheds his own blood, is meant to have transcendent importance. Goes again illustrates extremes of human behavior: the callous SS men who call to fetch Stefan with cynical jokes and the hospital staff forgetting all else in their anxiety to settle a new batch of patients. Such digressions, and the anticipation of the climax at the outset, rob the story of tension; it resembles a series of stylized diary entries.

Das mit Katz concerns a lieutenant, left (improbably) to his own devices in Berlin in early 1945 while a foot wound heals, who is able to dissuade Katz, a renegade Jew, from continuing to betray Jews who had gone underground to escape

deportation. Luckily the lieutenant is a theology student who uses his biblical knowledge to extract a binding oath from Katz; otherwise he would have been forced to kill him to save other Jews and would have faced the wrath of Katz's "große Beschützer" (high-up protectors). In this story Goes has left abstract principles and symbolism behind: the narration is sparse and to the point, the plot anecdotal, the intention simply to show that some moral dilemmas can be solved by a little thought and goodwill.

These are war stories claiming verisimilitude and historical relevance, but also religious literature embodying a spiritual intuition and a moral approach to the manifold problems of guilt which the reader may or may not share. Goes cannot forget his Christian creed and the commandment to love his neighbor, though he refuses to censor "immoral" scenes out of his works; in *Unruhige Nacht,* for example, because of overcrowding, the officer and his fiancée sleep together in the very room where the chaplain is reading Baranowski's file. His narrators feel that they must confront and oppose a miasmic, menacing world; they are people with moral convictions but no political sophistication who suddenly see their world convulsed by political evil and tyranny and are forced to be accomplices of brute destructive force. In military prison, field hospital, butcher's shop, or the garden hut where a fleeing Jew hides they meet the designated victims of the system and become aware of the inhumanity of a cause which has warped German idealism into torture and slaughter. Outwardly continuing to play their roles in the system, they remain detached from Nazism and, as far as they think it feasible, exercise private compassion, trying to discern hidden chances of growth and regeneration. Only by not opposing the tyranny can they go on helping. Such stresses endow them—insofar as the reader is told about their postwar years—with an urgent moral tone unusual in the apathetic peacetime world.

Socially the moral process leads to nothing. Frau Walker has changed nothing and can point to no achievement that would set her apart from other postwar Germans. The chaplain of *Das Löffelchen* is unable to forget his wartime experience, but only by chance is he impelled to write it down and communicate his spiritual shock. Political activity, even resistance to tyranny, is irrelevant to Goes's pursuit of contacts between individuals and of a personal religious renewal. The causes of Hitlerism and the war are not men-

Oil painting of Goes by Kurt Weinhold, 1954 (Schiller-Nationalmuseum, Marbach am Neckar)

tioned. A reader who does not share Goes's (and Buber's) belief that authentic human encounter is a self-transcendence of the individual, a breakthrough to an order of value more valid than the empirical world, must see the stories as inadequate: the chaplain merely offers the condemned man an opiate; Frau Walker expresses irrationally, by her attempted self-sacrifice, insights that she is not competent to deal with rationally. In *Das Brandopfer*, especially, Goes is caught between naturalistic attempts at psychological analysis and a transcendence which remains shadowy and alien, is invoked rather than given artistic life, and is imposed on a nonmetaphysical framework rather than existing from the outset. The religious viewpoint is not sufficiently integrated into setting and narrative to convince the non-believing reader that there is a metaphysical dimension at all or to carry him along with Goes's intentions. In *Unruhige Nacht*, on the other hand, as in Heinrich Böll's almost contemporary novel *Das Brot der frühen Jahre* (1955; translated as *The Bread of Those Early Years*, 1957), the narrator-protagonist adopts a matter-of-fact attitude to Christianity, the habitual basis for interpreting all his experience. The many stray remarks and unobtrusive symbols of these stories, unlike those in *Das Brandopfer*, are integrated into everyday material existence. Goes's belief that society's outcasts are loved by God comes across more strongly in the routine of the Lutheran chaplain than in Frau Walker's isolated, unrepeatable, dramatic, nonsectarian gesture.

Goes's popularity comes from his making it easy for the reader. His works provide cheap comfort for Germans who did not go out of their way to oppose Hitler. The reader, without having undergone the spiritual experiences of these figures, can nevertheless identify with them—"Yes, I too was against Nazism but could never risk showing it"—or can see his fellow Germans as people who, if at all decent, were passive victims of a tyranny forced on them. Böll, on the other hand, continually stresses how many Germans have a Nazi past and refuses to allow easy self-forgiveness. The international acceptance of Goes's stories may betoken a corresponding readiness abroad to pardon the German nation on the basis of statements of contrition made by a minority. The origins of Nazism in German history and politics, and the need for evidence and judgment before pardon, are easily forgotten when Goes evokes the universal themes of original sin and redemption. He writes of a reading he gave in The Hague: "Sprach ich von Deutschland, von deutscher Schuld? Ja. Aber die Versuchung, wir wußten es wohl, ist in allen Ländern" (Did I speak of Germany, of German guilt? Yes. But the temptation, as we well knew, is in all countries).

Goes clearly has no wish to whitewash German crimes. On the contrary, he sees himself as working to keep their memory alive: the victims can only forget German guilt if Germans do not. But he truly believes that he must stress the transcendent good which is to be salvaged from earthly catastrophe. Goes in his stories (some of his sermons and reflections show another side of him) is a good example of the "unpolitical German" who, eyes fixed on his higher strivings, believes political activity is beneath him and leaves it to inferior people—only to be puzzled when the result is an inferior political system.

References:

Albrecht Goes: Zu seinem sechzigsten Geburtstag (Frankfurt am Main: Fischer, 1968);

Willy Bourgoignie, "Auf der Suche nach reiner Menschlichkeit: Der schwäbische Dichter Albrecht Goes," *Studia Germanica Gandensia*, 7 (1965): 255-286;

Edward McInnes, "Abandonment and Renewal: Reflections on the Novellas of Albrecht Goes," *Forum for Modern Language Studies*, 7 (1971): 183-190;

Erwin K. Münz, "Albrecht Goes," in *Christliche Dichter der Gegenwart*, edited by Hermann Friedmann and Otto Mann (Heidelberg: Rothe, 1955), pp. 415-425;

Alan R. Robinson, "Am I My Brother's Keeper?," in *The Literary and Pastoral Mission of Albrecht Goes* (Cardiff: University of Wales Press, 1973);

E. William Rollins, "Albrecht Goes, Man of Dialogue: The Personal and Literary Relationship of Goes to Buber," Ph.D. dissertation, Vanderbilt University, 1968;

Rollins and Harry Zohn, eds., *Men of Dialogue: Martin Buber and Albrecht Goes* (New York: Funk & Wagnalls, 1969);

Werner Zimmermann, "Albrecht Goes: Unruhige Nacht," in his *Deutsche Prosadichtungen der Gegenwart: Interpretationen für Lehrende und Lernende*, third edition (Düsseldorf: Schwann, 1956), pp. 143-158.

Rudolf Hagelstange

(14 January 1912-5 August 1984)

H. M. Waidson
University College of Swansea (University of Wales)

BOOKS: Ich bin die Mutter Cornelias (Nordhausen: Haacke, 1939);

Es spannt sich der Bogen (Leipzig: Rupert, 1943);

Venezianisches Credo (Verona: Officina Bodoni, 1945; Wiesbaden: Insel, 1946);

Renée Sintenis, by Hagelstange, Carl Georg Heise, and Paul Appel (Berlin: Aufbau, 1947);

Strom der Zeit: Gedichte (Wiesbaden: Insel, 1948);

Mein Blumen-ABC: Verse (Berlin: EOS-Verlag, 1949);

Das Vergängliche: Für Harald Kreutzberg (Burgdorf: Berner Handpresse, 1950);

Meersburger Elegie (St. Gallen: Tschudy, 1950);

Die Elemente: Gedichte zu den Mosaiken von Frans Masereel (Winterthur: Reinhart, 1950; Verona: Officina Bodoni, 1950);

Balthasar: Eine Erzählung (Wiesbaden: Insel/St. Gallen: Tschudy, 1951);

Ewiger Atem (Olten: Vereinigung Oltner Bücherfreunde, 1952);

Der Streit der Hirsche: Festgabe für Emil Junker, Riehen, zum 60. Geburtstag (Olten: Vereinigung Oltner Bücherfreunde, 1952);

*bibliography revised by *DLB* staff

Ballade vom verschütteten Leben (Wiesbaden: Insel, 1952); translated by Herman Salinger as *Ballad of the Buried Life*, introduction by Charles W. Hoffmann (Chapel Hill: University of North Carolina Press, 1962);

Zwischen Stern und Staub: Gedichte (Wiesbaden: Insel, 1953);

Es steht in unserer Macht: Gedachtes und Erlebtes (Munich: Piper, 1953);

Politik und Persönlichkeit Ernst Reuters: Gedenkrede zur 1. Wiederkehr seines Todestages (Berlin-Friedenau: Bürgermeister Reuter-Stiftung, 1954);

Die Beichte des Don Juan: Dichtung (Olten: Vereinigung Oltner Bücherfreunde, 1954);

Die Nacht (Zurich: Europa, 1955);

Verona (Munich: Knorr & Hirth, 1957);

Griechenland (Berlin: Rembrandt, 1957); translated as *Greece* (Berlin: Rembrandt, 1957);

How Do You Like America? Impressionen eines Zaungastes (Munich: Piper, 1957);

Der moderne Mensch und sein Körper (Düsseldorf & Oberhausen: VVA-Druck, 1957);

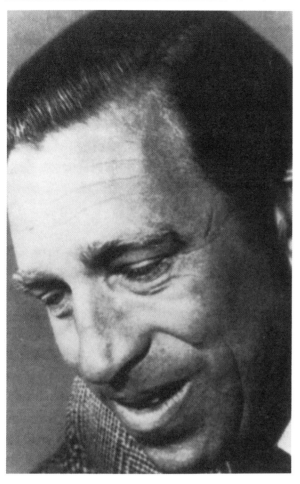

Rudolf Hagelstange

Wo bleibst du, Trost . . . Eine Weihnachtserzählung (Cologne & Olten: Hegner, 1958);

Offen gesagt: Aufsätze und Reden (Frankfurt am Main: Ullstein, 1958);

Das Lied der Muschel (Munich: Piper, 1958);

Die Nacht Mariens: Ein Weihnachtsbuch (Zurich: Arche, 1959); republished as *Stern in der Christnacht: Eine Weihnachtsgabe* (Zurich: Arche, 1965);

Spielball der Götter: Aufzeichnungen eines trojanischen Prinzen (Hamburg: Hoffmann & Campe, 1959);

Viel Vergnügen (Hannover: Fackelträger, 1960);

Römische Brunnen (Munich: Knorr & Hirth, 1960);

Huldigung: Droste, Eichendorff, Schiller (Wiesbaden: Insel, 1960);

Römisches Olympia: Kaleidoskop eines Weltfestes (Munich: Piper, 1961);

Die schwindende Spur (Starnberg: Keller, 1961);

Laudatio auf Jakob Hegner (Erlangen: Merkel, 1961);

Lied der Jahre: Gesammelte Gedichte 1931-1961 (Frankfurt am Main: Insel, 1961; enlarged edition, Hamburg: Hoffmann & Campe, 1964);

Reise nach Katmandu (Olten: Vereinigung Oltner Bücherfreunde, 1962);

Sport und Demokratie (Kiel: Landessportverband Schleswig-Holstein, 1962);

Deutschland im Farbbild, by Hagelstange and Wolfgang Martin Schede (Frankfurt am Main: Umschau, 1962);

Corazón: Gedichte aus Spanien (Hamburg: Hoffmann & Campe, 1963);

Olympische Impressionen (Stuttgart: Olympischer Sportverlag, 1963);

Die Puppen in der Puppe: Eine Russlandreise (Hamburg: Hoffmann & Campe, 1963);

Fabeln des Aesop: Nacherzählt (Ravensburg: Maier, 1965);

Zeit für ein Lächeln: Heitere Prosa (Hamburg: Hoffmann & Campe, 1966);

Der schielende Löwe oder How Do You Like America? (Hamburg: Hoffmann & Campe, 1967);

Ein beispielhaftes Lebenswerk: Laudatio auf Giovanni Mardersteig (Mainz: Gutenberg-Gesellschaft, 1968);

Ägäischer Sommer (Hamburg: Hoffmann & Campe, 1968);

Der Krak in Prag: Ein Frühlingsmärchen (Hamburg: Hoffmann & Campe, 1969);

Altherrensommer: Roman (Hamburg: Hoffmann & Campe, 1969);

Alleingang: Sechs Schicksale (Hamburg: Hoffmann & Campe, 1970);

Es war im Wal zu Askalon: Dreikönigslegende (Munich: Piper, 1971);

Ein Gespräch über Bäume (Munich: Bruckmann, 1972); translated by Salinger as "A Conversation about Trees," *Dimension,* 6, no. 1 (1973): 106-131;

Gast der Elemente: Zyklen und Nachdichtungen 1944-1972, edited by Heinrich Hahne (Cologne: Kiepenheuer & Witsch, 1972);

Venus im Mars: Liebesgeschichten (Cologne: Kiepenheuer & Witsch, 1972);

Der General und das Kind (Cologne: Kiepenheuer & Witsch, 1974);

Die Weihnachtsgeschichte (Munich: Fabbri & Praeger, 1974);

Reisewetter (Munich: List, 1975);

Der große Filou: Die Abenteuer des Ithakers Odysseus (Munich: List, 1976);

Tränen gelacht: Steckbrief eines Steinbocks (Munich: List, 1977);

Hagelstange in 1947 (Ullstein)

Ausgewählte Gedichte (Munich: List, 1978);
Und es geschah zur Nacht: Mein Weihnachtsbuch (Munich: List, 1978);
Von großen und kleinen Tieren: Lustig-listige Fabeln (Würzburg: Popp, 1978);
Der sächsische Großvater (Munich: List, 1979);
Die letzten Nächte (Gütersloh: Mohn, 1979);
Mein Bodensee-Brevier (Constance: Stadler, 1979);
Spiegel des Narziß: Spiel in fünf Bildern (Munich: List, 1980);
Der Bodensee (Zurich: Atlantis, 1981);
Das Haus oder Balsers Aufstieg (Munich: List, 1981);
Flaschenpost (Munich: List, 1982);
Menschen und Gesichter (Munich: List, 1982);
Der Niedergang: Von Balsers Haus zum Käthe-Kollwitz-Heim (Munich: List, 1983);
Hausfreund bei Calypso (Munich: List, 1983);
Eisenbahngeschichten mit Pfiff (Munich: List, 1985).

OTHER: *Deutschland: Mitteldeutschland und der Osten, wie er war. Ein Bildband von deutscher Landschaft, ihren Städten, Dörfern und Menschen,* edited by Harald Busch, introduction by Hagelstange (Frankfurt am Main: Umschau, 1955); translated as *Germany: Countryside, Cities, Villages, and People* (New York: Hastings House, 1956);
Angelo Poliziano, *Die Tragödie des Orpheus,* translated by Hagelstange (Wiesbaden: Insel, 1956);
Frans Masereel, *Gesang des Lebens,* edited by Hagelstange (Hannover: Fackelträger, 1957);
Giovanni Boccaccio, *Die Nymphe von Fiesole,* translated by Hagelstange (Wiesbaden: Insel, 1957);
Ein Licht scheint in die Finsternis: Ein Weihnachtsbuch, edited by Hagelstange (Gütersloh: Rufer, 1958);
Phantastische Abenteuererzählungen: Eine Sammlung der spannendsten Erzählungen aus aller Welt, edited by Hagelstange and Jens Carstensen (Munich: Bardtenschlager, 1961);
Pablo Neruda, *Die Höhen von Macchu Picchu,* translated by Hagelstange (Hamburg: Hoffmann & Campe, 1965);
Das große Weihnachtsbuch für die Familie, compiled by Hagelstange and Monika Achtelik (Munich: Moderne Verlags-GmbH, 1969);
Fünf Ringe: Vom Ölzweig zur Goldmedaille, compiled by Hagelstange (Munich: Bruckmann, 1972).

Rudolf Hagelstange was acclaimed as a lyric and narrative poet during the first years after World War II and has been widely read as a novelist, short-story writer, and essayist since the 1960s. His poetry is often idealistic, advocating positive values in spite of the somber moods that life in his times often called forth. His novels and stories are fluent narratives, frequently unconventional and unexpected in their emphasis, reflecting their author's liberal approach to contemporary problems.

Hagelstange was born in Nordhausen on 14 January 1912 to Wilhelm Hagelstange, a merchant, and Helene Struchmann Hagelstange. He attended the Humanistisches Gymnasium at Nordhausen and studied German language and literature at the University of Berlin from 1931 to 1933. Hagelstange traveled in the Balkans after leaving the university and was on the staff of the *Nordhäuser Zeitung* from 1936 until he was called into the army in 1940. He married Karola Dittel in 1939; they had five children. During World War II he was an editor of army newspapers in France and Italy.

Hagelstange in 1959, the year he won the Großes Bundesverdienstkreuz (Ullstein–Ursula Röhnert)

Some of the poems in Hagelstange's first collection, *Es spannt sich der Bogen* (The Bow is Drawn, 1943), assert a faith in the transcendence of mind and spirit. Other poems invoke nature, autumn, or scenes in Italy or France. The poet has here an easy fluency in regular rhythms and rhymes and turns from one setting to another without a sense of effort; there are parallels with some of Rainer Maria Rilke's work.

In Venice in 1944 Hagelstange wrote the poems of *Venezianisches Credo* (Venetian Creed), which were circulated in secret. This cycle of thirty-five sonnets led to his being acclaimed as a poet with a voice of his own that pioneered a spirit of resistance to National Socialism when the volume was published in 1945. As Heinrich Hahne says in his edition of poetic cycles by Hagelstange, *Gast der Elemente* (Guest of the Elements, 1972): "These poems are deeply enmeshed in the living conditions of their time. They were also the only important literary work which took issue fundamentally with the political circumstances and were understood and acknowledged, after the great void, as a valid and suffi-

cient answer." The sonnets are preceded by a quotation from Friedrich Schiller, an indication that the poet is taking Schiller's concepts of freedom and ethical idealism as criteria for the judgment of Germany's current situation. Passion and blind strength have no validity as guidelines, these sonnets say; the true law is that of "Geist" (mind or spirit). There must be faith that right will eventually triumph over wrong. To justify his existence, man must bring light out of darkness. Freedom is the breath of our life. Death has attacked so many; who will build a new world from this chaos, a world without hatred and violence?

At the end of the war Hagelstange was taken prisoner by the Americans. He returned to Nordhausen in September 1945, but left the Russian zone of occupation in 1946 and moved to West Germany–first to Westphalia, then near Lake Constance, and finally, in 1968, to Erbach in the Odenwald area of the state of Hessen.

The collection *Strom der Zeit* (The River of Time, 1948) contains a sequence of sixteen poems, "Der Fischzug" (The Haul of Fish), which mourns the loss of a town's thousand-year heritage in its overnight destruction and the shortage of food and goods after a past of plenty. The protagonist sees himself as a child of a merciless era, but he can still respond to the goodness of the land and the rivers. In spite of threatening forces, he believes that renewal is replacing destruction and that nothing can dishonor a free man.

Hagelstange's poetic explorations at this time led him to write longer poems in elegiac or ballad style. *Meersburger Elegie* (Meersburg Elegy, 1950) looks back with longing to a past of greater happiness and to a fulfillment that is associated with the heroes and gods of classical Greece as well as with myths of other cultures. It is autumn: the immediate past is one of ruin and destruction. Hagelstange conjures up a colorful panoramic vision of past and present, and a sensitive awareness of threats of destruction.

The extended narrative poem *Ballade vom verschütteten Leben* (1952; translated as *Ballad of the Buried Life*, 1962) made considerable impact when first published and combines a compelling story (it was written originally for radio) with lively and resonant free verse. The poem is based on a news report (which was later revealed to be a hoax) that Polish workers had found six German soldiers who had been trapped in a giant food storage bunker for the six years since the end of the war; only two had survived.

Cover of Hagelstange's 1979 account of the last nights in the life of Jesus

Hagelstange shows how the initial pleasure at finding a vast store of food and drink soon turns to nightmare when the men realize that they cannot escape. A young man takes his own life, as does an older man who is oppressed by feelings of guilt for his actions as a guard in a concentration camp. A third man falls ill, but his religious convictions sustain him until his death, while a fourth dies without grace. Of the two who are alive when release comes, one collapses and dies at the great moment, while the survivor is only half alive. The imprisonment may be seen as a symbol of Germany's position after the war or of the fate of mankind.

In *Zwischen Stern und Staub* (Between Star and Dust, 1953), a further collection of lyric poems, there is an assertion of traditional values in "Ein Frühling" (A Springtime) and a reminder of human limitations in "Glück des Weisen" (The

Wise Man's Happiness). In "Das Wort" the word is a knife that can be thrown; but the word becomes flesh when used in a poem in "Auf die Feder in der Hand des Dichtenden" (On the Pen in the Hands of the Poet). The phrase which gives the collection its title occurs in "Urlaub" (Leave), a poem of autumn and the anticipation of spring: human beings are "between star and dust."

In the later 1950s Hagelstange began to move away from poetry. The collection of essays *Offen gesagt* (Speaking Frankly, 1958) contains sympathetic studies of Ernst Reuter and of the novelist Theodor Plievier and moderate reactions to the economic and social recovery of the Federal Republic, war guilt and anti-Semitism, abstract art, and East-West relations. Hagelstange had already shown that the world of the Greek classics was significant to him, and in 1959 he retold the story of the Trojan War in a style that was attractive to readers of his time. *Spielball der Götter* (Plaything of the Gods, 1959) is a prose account based on *The Iliad*. It is narrated by Paris, who looks back to his past and alternates episodes from his earlier life with an account of the war, which is now in its tenth year. Paris's idyllic life with Oenone is interrupted by Priam's insistence on his taking up a princely role at Troy, and his relationship with Helena further links his destiny with those leading figures whose lives are the concern of the gods. Near the end Paris writes a long letter to Helena and includes in it an imagined reply from her: "Er [Menelaos] haßt ihn weit mehr, weil dieser Paris Grazie hat, die mehr ist als Kraft; weil er Witz hat, der liebenswürdiger ist als Zorn; weil dieser Paris glücklicher zu machen versteht, als er selbst es auch nur zu erstreben für angebracht hielte" (He [Menelaos] hates him much more because this Paris has grace which is more than strength; because he has wit which is more endearing than anger; because this Paris knows how to give greater happiness than he himself would consider it suitable to aim at).

Hagelstange traveled widely as a lecturer and reader of his own works. He received many awards, including the Südverlag Prize for Lyric Poetry in 1950, the Berlin Critics' Prize in 1952, an award from the Schiller Foundation in 1955, the Villa Massimo Prize in 1957, the Julius Campe Prize in 1958, and the Großes Bundesverdienstkreuz (Grand Federal Service Cross) in 1959. During the 1960s, 1970s, and early 1980s his major energies were devoted to prose.

Aquatint drawing of Hagelstange by Oskar Kreibich

The novel *Altherrensommer* (Indian Summer, 1969) centers upon the personal problems of two Germans who meet on a cruise from Genoa to the Far East. Oliver Kitz has taken the trip to liberate himself from a liaison with an older woman. Thomas Theodor Thannhausen, an author, has a love affair with a young Asiatic woman, but decides to take his life when he realizes that his health is declining. Out of a sense of duty Thannhausen had remained with his wife in spite of growing disharmony between them; he now feels that he waited too long to separate from her.

Two volumes of short stories that Hagelstange published in the early 1970s are set during World War II. *Alleingang* (Going It Alone, 1970) relates the fates of six characters and the suffering they undergo under National Socialism. The stories of Ernst Katz ("Ernst"), who lives most of his life in a mental hospital, and of Fritz Hammer ("Lebenslauf" [Career]), who is pressed by his father into joining the SS, are striking; indeed, all the stories in this collection are convinc-

ing in their realism. The thirteen stories of *Venus im Mars* (1972) depict soldiers, mainly officers, in their relationships with women of occupied countries; sometimes they are seeking easy entertainment, and at other times they find an experience at a deeper level. In all instances it is taken for granted that these relationships can and should flourish, in spite of political and wartime circumstances. "Die letzte Nacht" (The Last Night) is an effectively tense narrative; a married woman's series of transient love affairs during the war seems to be the working out of a predestined pattern.

The novel *Der General und das Kind* (The General and the Child, 1974) has as its central figure Ernst Kaluschke, who becomes a professional soldier in the Bundeswehr (new Federal army) and has attained the rank of general by the time he retires in 1957. He and his wife move to a different town, where Kaluschke and a younger woman have an affair which results in a child. The background of the novel is that of the professional and business class, where prosperity is taken for granted; the approach of this group to the relationships of the general with his wife and his mistress succeeds in avoiding bitterness and the passionate expression of emotions.

Der große Filou (The Great Rogue, 1976), a retelling of *The Odyssey*, is less complex in its narrative form than *Spielball der Götter*. There is relatively little introspection; the story unfolds chronologically, and its hero is fully at home in his relationships with the gods, a confident manager of his sailors, and able to count on the loyalty of his Ithacan servants.

One of the last prose works Hagelstange was able to complete before his death in Hanau on 5 August 1984 is a family novel in two volumes. The first volume, *Das Haus oder Balsers Aufstieg* (The House; or, Balser's Rise, 1981), presents sharply defined characters against a realistic evocation of a small German town at the beginning of the twentieth century. In 1908 Carl Balser, a medical doctor who is interested in socialism and the arts, moves with his family into a house that he has had designed and built. His marriage to Anna, thirteen years younger than he, has been arranged between himself and his father-in-law, and the wife's role is one of subordination to her husband. There are four children: two daughters, Ilse and Margret; the handicapped Hans; and the lively and intelligent Carl. World War I does not bring any major disasters to the family. The second volume, *Der Niedergang* (The

Hagelstange in 1982 (Ullstein–Binder/Thiele)

nally turned into a home for the orphans of railway workers.

Rudolf Hagelstange's contribution to the literature of his time was varied and considerable. He first made a name for himself as a poet, writing not only short lyric poems but also longer narrative poems and cycles. Prose took the place of poetry as his dominant mode of self-expression in the 1950s. His novels and short stories, inventively conceived and fluently written, have attracted many readers.

References:

R. C. Andrews, "Two German War Poets. Rudolf Hagelstange, Hans Egon Holthuren," *German Life and Letters, New Series,* 4 (1950-1951): 115-122;

Maurice Collerille, "Rudolf Hagelstange," *Etudes Germaniques,* 8 (1953): 45-46;

Rolf Hellmut Foerster, "Rudolf Hagelstange," in *Handbuch der deutschen Gegenwartsliteratur,* edited by Hermann Kunisch, second edition, volume 1 (Munich: Nymphenburger Verlagshandlung, 1969), pp. 262-263;

Hans Fromm, "Die Ballade als Art und die zeitgenössische Ballade. Erörterungen an Rudolf Hagelstanges *Ballade vom verschütteten Leben,*" *Deutschunterricht,* 8, no. 4 (1956): 84-99;

Charles W. Hoffmann, "Rudolf Hagelstange's Saga of Dust and Light: *Ballade vom verschütteten Leben,*" *Germanic Review,* 33 (1958): 143-154;

Franz Lennartz, "Rudolf Hagelstange," in *Deutsche Schriftsteller des 20. Jahrhunderts im Spiegel der Kritik,* volume 2 (Stuttgart: Kröner, 1984), pp. 654-656.

Papers:

A Hagelstange archive has been established at Deutsches Literaturarchiv, Marbach am Neckar, Federal Republic of Germany.

Downfall, 1983), opens with the establishment of the Weimar Republic. The younger Carl becomes head of the family after his father's death in 1926. The family and their friends are for the most part opposed to National Socialism, though Margret's husband comes to an acceptance of the regime which she does not share. Carl, a lawyer, is allowed to go on working during the 1930s, though he is suspected of disloyalty by the Gestapo. In 1945 he finds himself in the Russian Zone. At first he hopes to be able to obtain congenial work there, but he flees to the West in 1950. He, like Ilse and Margret, fails to find stability in his personal relationships. The family's house is fi-

Stephan Hermlin
(Rudolf Leder)
(13 April 1915-)

Richard Critchfield
Texas A&M University

BOOKS: *Zwölf Balladen von den großen Städten* (Zurich: Morgarten, 1945);

Wir verstummen nicht: Gedichte aus der Fremde, by Hermlin, Jo Mihaly, and Lajser Ajchenrand (Zurich: Posen, 1945);

Der Leutnant Yorck von Wartenburg (Singen: Oberbadische Druckerei und Verlagsanstalt, 1946);

Die Straßen der Furcht (Singen: Oberbadischer Verlag, 1947);

Ansichten über einige neue Schriftsteller und Bücher, by Hermlin and Hans Mayer (Wiesbaden: Limes, 1947); revised as *Ansichten über einige Bücher und Schriftsteller* (Berlin: Volk und Welt, 1947);

Reise eines Malers in Paris (Wiesbaden: Limes, 1947);

Zweiundzwanzig Balladen (Berlin: Volk und Welt, 1947);

Russische Eindrücke (Berlin: Kultur und Fortschritt, 1948);

Die Zeit der Gemeinsamkeit: Erzählungen (Berlin: Volk und Welt, 1949); translated by Joan Becker as *City on a Hill: A Quartet in Prose* (Berlin: Seven Seas, 1962);

Mansfelder Oratorium, text by Hermlin, music by Ernst H. Meyer (Leipzig: Peters, 1951);

Die erste Reihe (Berlin: Neues Leben, 1951);

Die Zeit der Einsamkeit (Leipzig: Insel, 1951);

Der Flug der Taube (Berlin: Volk und Welt, 1952);

Der Kampf um eine deutsche Nationalliteratur (Berlin: Deutscher Schriftstellerverband, 1952);

Die Sache des Friedens: Aufsätze und Berichte (Berlin: Volk und Welt, 1953);

Ferne Nähe (Berlin: Aufbau, 1954);

Wo stehen wir heute? (Berlin: Kongreß-Verlag, 1956);

Dichtungen (Berlin: Aufbau, 1956);

Nachdichtungen (Berlin: Aufbau, 1957);

Begegnungen 1954-1959: Essays und Reden (Berlin: Aufbau, 1960);

Gedichte (Leipzig: Reclam, 1963);

Gedichte und Prosa (Berlin: Wagenbach, 1965);

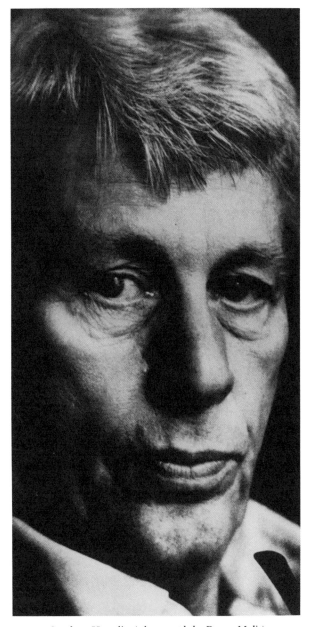

Stephan Hermlin (photograph by Roger Melis)

Balladen, selected by Sina Witt (Leipzig: Insel, 1965);

Hermlin (right), Anna Seghers, and Adolf Hennecke departing for the World Peace Congress in Vienna in 1952 (Zentralbild)

Die Städte, selected by Alfred Karnein (Munich & Esslingen: Bechtle, 1966);

Erzählungen (Berlin & Weimar: Aufbau, 1966; enlarged, 1970);

Scaranelli: Ein Hörspiel (Berlin: Wagenbach, 1970);

Stephan Hermlin, selected by Bernd Jentzsch (Berlin: Neues Leben, 1973);

Lektüre 1960-1971 (Berlin: Aufbau, 1973);

Die Argonauten (Berlin: Kinderbuchverlag, 1974);

Städte-Balladen (Leipzig: Reclam, 1975);

Gesammelte Gedichte (Munich: Hanser, 1979);

Abendlicht (Berlin: Wagenbach, 1979); translated by Paul F. Dvorak as *Evening Light* (San Francisco: Fjord Press, 1983);

Aufsätze, Reportagen, Reden, Interviews, edited by Ulla Hahn (Munich: Hanser, 1980);

Lebensfrist (Berlin: Wagenbach, 1980);

Arkadien (Leipzig: Reclam, 1983);

Äußerungen 1944-1982 (Berlin: Aufbau, 1983);

Bestimmungsorte (Berlin: Wagenbach, 1985).

OTHER: *Auch ich bin Amerikaner: Dichtungen amerikanischer Neger*, translated by Hermlin (Berlin: Volk und Welt, 1948);

Fritz Cremer, *Sieben Lithographien aus dem Zyklus "Ungarische Vision 1956,"* edited by Hermlin (Berlin: Die Nation, 1958);

Attila József, *Gedichte*, edited by Hermlin (Berlin: Volk und Welt, 1960);

Franz Carl Weiskopf, *Gesammelte Werke*, edited by Hermlin (Berlin: Dietz, 1960);

Ungarische Dichtungen aus 5 Jahrhunderten, edited by Hermlin and G. M. Vajda (Budapest: Corvina, 1970);

Paul Eluard, *Trauer schönes Anlitz*, translated by Hermlin (Berlin: Volk und Welt, 1974).

PERIODICAL PUBLICATIONS: "Gesang vom Künftigen: Zum 100. Todestag Friedrich Hölderlins," *Neue Schweizer Rundschau*, 12 (1944-1945): 390-401;

"Wo bleibt die junge Dichtung: Rede auf dem Schriftstellerkongreß," *Aufbau*, 11 (1947): 340-343;

"Stalin," *Aufbau*, 12 (1949): 1063-1069;

"Deutsches Tagebuch in Ost und West," *Aufbau*, 9 (1951): 836-844;

"Paul Eluard: Kämpfer gegen den Tod," *Neue Deutsche Literatur*, 1 (1953): 150-156;

Hermlin (with cigarette) at the German Writers Congress in Berlin, January 1956. Others pictured are (clockwise from lower left) Johannes R. Becher, Hans Marchwitza, Willi Bredel, Kuba (Kurt Barthel), Eduard Claudius, Alfred Kurella, and Michael Tschesno-Hell (photograph by Gerhard Kiesling, Berlin).

"Die Kommandeuse," *Neue Deutsche Literatur,* 10 (1954): 19-28;

"Methoden des Autors, Methoden der Kritik," *Neue Deutsche Literatur,* 3 (1955): 129-132;

"Über Heine," *Sinn und Form,* 1 (1956): 78-79;

"Frederico Garcia Lorca," *Aufbau,* 5 (1957): 157-159;

"Diskussionsbeitrag zum internationalen Kolloquium," *Neue Deutsche Literatur,* 3 (1965): 104-109;

"Wortmeldung: Schriftsteller über Erfahrungen, Pläne und Probleme," *Neue Deutsche Literatur,* 1 (1971): 41-42;

"Mein Friede," *Neue Deutsche Literatur,* 1 (1976): 3-9; *Akzente,* 1 (1976): 1-7;

"Rede auf dem VIII. Schriftstellerkongreß der DDR," *Neue Deutsche Literatur,* 8 (1978): 67-71.

Stephan Hermlin first gained acclaim in postwar German literary circles with the publication of *Zwölf Balladen von den großen Städten* (1945). These "twelve ballads of the great cities" of Europe, and other works which followed in the next five years, showed Hermlin to be both a poet of great sensitivity and vision and an adroit adapter of earlier poetry. In one of the earliest appraisals of Hermlin's poetry, the noted critic Hans Mayer praised *Zwölf Balladen von den großen Städten* not only for its aesthetic quality but also for its prophetic visions of a new social order and, above all, for its expressions of hope in one of Germany's darkest hours.

Drawing on German and French traditions, particularly on the German expressionist Georg Heym and the French surrealists Louis Aragon and Paul Eluard, Hermlin wrote poetry during World War II and the immediate postwar years which remains unique. He has also written several short stories and a major autobiographical work and has distinguished himself as a translator. In addition, he has been instrumental in promoting a dialogue between writers and scientists of German-speaking countries about political oppression in Poland and the prospects for peace in the nuclear age.

Hermlin was born Rudolf Leder on 13 April 1915 in Chemnitz (today Karl-Marx-Stadt). He was one of two sons of a wealthy textile merchant. Reared in a cultured atmosphere, he attended a Swiss boarding school and later a gymnasium in Berlin. Although his family was not religious, when he was thirteen Leder wished to become a monk. He was, as he has stated in an interview, a seeker whose path would ultimately lead to communism, and in 1931, at the age of sixteen, he became a member of a Communist youth organization. From 1933 to 1936 he took part in the Communist resistance movement in Berlin against the Nazi regime. In 1936 he went into exile. During the next two years he lived for brief periods in Egypt, Palestine, and England and fought with the Republican forces against Franco in Spain. In 1938 he immigrated to France; he joined the French army in 1940.

During the years of the French Resistance, in which he was active, Leder became acquainted with Eluard and Aragon, representatives of the late stages of French surrealism, the poetry of the Resistance. From 1944 to 1945 he was interned in Switzerland. After his return to Germany in 1945, at which time he adopted the pseudonym Stephan Hermlin, he collaborated

Hermlin (right) at a 1974 conference in Berlin honoring Pablo Neruda. Others pictured include (from right to left) Hermann Kant, Seghers, Kurt Stern, Franz Fühmann, and Paul Wiens (Frank Wagner, Anna Seghers [Leipzig: VEB Bibliographisches Institut, 1980]).

Drawing of Hermlin by Walter Arnold

with Hans Mayer in a series of broadcasts for the American-sponsored Radio Frankfurt called "Neue Bücher" (New Books), the purpose of which was to familiarize the German public with the major literary and intellectual events of the time; under the Third Reich the German people had been denied access to the works of many important authors of the period. Hermlin's contributions to the program demonstrated that he was not only a poet of great promise but also a perceptive critic capable of appreciating and discussing with equal understanding and insight James Joyce's *Ulysses* (1922), John Steinbeck's *The Grapes of Wrath* (1939), and the poetry of T. S. Eliot.

In 1947 Hermlin moved to East Germany; he resides in the East Berlin suburb of Niederschönhausen with his wife, Irina Belokoneva, a Soviet citizen, and their son Andrej. He received the Heinrich Heine Prize in 1948 and 1972 and the National Prize of the German Democratic Republic (GDR) in 1975; nonetheless, he has often been punished for his criticism of official literary policies. In 1962 he was dismissed from his post as secretary of the Section for Literature in the Academy of Arts, and in 1979 he was excluded from the Writers' Association of the GDR. In addition, Hermlin was a staunch supporter of the songwriter Wolf Biermann, whose songs were anathema to the Communist authorities and who now lives in the West. Hermlin's own ballads and poems, particularly those written during and immediately after World War II, were often criticized and rejected by East German critics, who found them too decorative and esoteric.

In the early years after the founding of the GDR in 1949, Hermlin was prodded by Communist critics to write poetry that could be easily understood by the majority of the people. His attempts to do so may have stifled his creativity as a poet, for in 1958 he published his last poem. Dedicated to the German Communist poet Johannes R. Becher, who was himself a spokesman for the doctrine of literary accessibility, the poem bore the appropriate title "Der Tod des Dichters" (The Death of the Poet). West German critics have noted correctly that the poem shows Hermlin at his worst; his gifts as a stylist and a poet of great expressive power are all but absent. As John Flores has said, "The career of Stephan Hermlin, once a gifted political poet, remains truncated, bearing grim testimony to the fatal impact of restrictive ideological demands." However severely Hermlin's late poems may be judged, it re-

Hermlin in 1984 (Ullstein–Marianne Fleitmann)

mains true that he introduced surrealism into German poetry. Perhaps his greatest achievement as a poet was to adapt the tone and poetic means of Heym to the hopeful and committed spirit of the French Resistance and the Communist cause. Hermlin's early and best poems reflected a dialectic of despair and hope, of pessimism and optimism, and of cowardice and courage that has, to an extent, been continued in his short stories.

The stimulus for writing his first short story was, Hermlin has stated, his reading of "An Occurrence at Owl Creek Bridge" (1892) by Ambrose Bierce. The result was *Der Leutnant Yorck von Wartenburg* (1946). Like its American model, the story portrays the last minutes in the life of a condemned man who, in a hallucinatory state, experiences his liberation. In his hallucination Lieutenant Yorck von Wartenburg, one of the conspirators in the attempt to assassinate Hitler on 20 July 1944, is freed shortly before his execution and escapes to the Red Army, and Germany frees itself from fascism in a popular uprising. Hermlin is describing in these passages the course German history should have taken in the last year of the war. As Yorck von Wartenburg is led to his actual execution, the images he has experienced in his hallucination give him the courage to face death. In this story Hermlin masterfully interweaves two levels of reality and two levels of time. He also adapts the surrealistic tendency to portray dreams, visions, and hallucinations to his own needs in the story *Reise eines Malers in Paris* (Journey of a Painter in Paris, 1947), in which the central figure experiences in a dreamlike setting the Spanish civil war, an internment camp, and the struggle of the Chinese Communists.

Hermlin's own struggle against fascism had made him keenly aware of the weakness of the individual who is isolated from his countrymen. In *Die Zeit der Gemeinsamkeit* (The Time of Community, 1949) he depicts a time of intense solidarity and community in the heroic revolt of Jewish resistance groups in the Warsaw ghetto against the Germans. In *Die Zeit der Einsamkeit* (The Time of Solitude, 1951), on the other hand, he treats the problem of individual isolation. The story, which takes place in occupied France, begins as a tale of cruelty and inhumanity. The Jewish wife of Neubert, a German immigrant, is sexually abused by a French policeman; in a case of mistaken identity, the police also torture Neubert. While Neubert is not the fugitive they seek, he does murder his wife's tormentor. Neubert has isolated himself from his former comrades and their struggle against fascism. His torture and the rape of his wife, who eventually dies, rekindle his desire to fight against the force of barbarity and inhumanity. Neubert ultimately breaks out of his isolation and rejoins the struggle against the Germans and their French underlings. Both *Die Zeit der Gemeinsamkeit* and *Die Zeit der Einsamkeit* depict individuals in extreme situations from which there is no escape other than violence. Hermlin's heroes commit their lives to a struggle against overwhelming odds; in so doing, they dedicate themselves to a better future.

In 1951 Hermlin also published the nonfictional work *Die erste Reihe* (The First Rank), a series of portraits of young German resistance fighters who fought against the Nazis; a year later the book had sold 200,000 copies. In the preface to the work Hermlin writes: "Allzu wenig ist bisher über diesen Kampf gesprochen worden. Er ist ein wichtiges Stück unserer Geschichte.... Daß es diese Jugend gab, ist nicht nur bedeutsam für die deutsche Jugend, sondern für die Jugend aller Länder" (All too little has been said about this struggle. It is an important part of our history.... The very fact that there were these

young people is not only important for German youth, but for the youth of all countries).

On the other hand, Hermlin had little positive to say about the East German workers who rebelled against their Soviet occupiers in 1953. In his "Die Kommandeuse" (1954) he denigrates the main participants in the uprising as former Nazis and common criminals; the title figure, a former SS commander, emerges as a negative heroine par excellence. While the work was understandably attacked in the West, it was also criticized in the GDR: Hermlin had violated one of the key tenets of socialist realism, the official literary doctrine in the GDR and many other socialist countries which calls for the portrayal of only positive heroes and heroines. Hermlin was only partially successful in his attempts in the early postwar years to adapt his writing to suit Communist critics and official versions of history.

In 1979 a major autobiographical work appeared in which Hermlin's genius and gifts as a writer are once again apparent. *Abendlicht* (translated as *Evening Light*, 1983) tells with great skill the origins, struggles, hopes, and defeats of an individual, his political party, and his time. Hermlin recalls his childhood in the comfort and security of an upper-middle-class family, his eventual politicalization and conversion to communism in the turbulent years of the Weimar Republic, and his struggle against fascism. In this memoir Hermlin sometimes writes in a factual and direct manner; with regard to his life as a Communist, he says: "Ich war nicht besser und nicht schlechter als die Bewegung, der ich angehörte, ich teilte ihre Reife und Unreife, ihre Größe und ihr Elend" (I was no better or worse than the movement to which I belonged, I shared its maturity, its greatness and its misery). On the other hand, Hermlin's style in *Abendlicht* is at times marked by a tendency to depict dreamlike settings and visions in long, unpunctuated sentences reminiscent of his early and best poetry: "Damals als ein schräges Licht auf El Gesira ruhte und ich Tauben essend die rubinbesetzten Dolche in den Gürteln feiernder Scheichs betrachtete als der feine unendliche Regen auf die Hecken in Marienbad und auf meinen Bruder und mich fiel ... " (At the time when the slanting light shone on El Gesira and feasting on doves I gazed at the ruby-inlaid daggers in the belts of the celebrating sheiks when the fine unending rain fell on the hedges in Marienbad and on my brother and me ...); this passage continues for almost two pages. *Abendlicht* is thus in

Covers for two of Hermlin's works of the late 1970s and the mid 1980s

part an oneiric and highly lyrical work. Stylistically, it is one of the best prose pieces Hermlin has written. It is also a penetrating work in which Hermlin deals sympathetically with the illusions of Germans and foreigners at the beginning of Nazi rule in Germany, and scathingly with those businessmen who profited from the Third Reich. With *Abendlicht* Hermlin has once again become one of the more intriguing writers in the GDR.

Interviews:
Günther Gaus, "Im Gespräch mit Stephan Hermlin," *Freibeuter*, 22 (1984): 1-10;
Silvia Schlenstedt, "Gespräch mit Stephan Hermlin," *Weimarer Beiträge*, 30 (1984): 1884-1897.

Bibliography:
Maritta Rost and Rosmarie Geist, eds., *Stephan Hermlin Bibliographie* (Leipzig: Reclam, 1985).

References:
Hans Peter Anderle, *Mitteldeutsche Erzähler: Eine Studie mit Proben und Portraits* (Cologne: Wissenschaft und Politik, 1965), pp. 174-176;
Uwe Berger, "Der Flug der Taube," *Aufbau*, 1 (1953): 81-84;
Volker Braun, "Zu Hermlin, die Einen und die Anderen," *Sinn und Form*, 4 (1975): 737;
Werner Brettschneider, *Zwischen literarischer Auto-*

nomie und Staatsdienst: Die Literatur der DDR (Berlin: Schmidt, 1972), pp. 196-199;

Manfred Durzak, "Versuch über Stephan Hermlin," *Akzente,* 3 (1976): 256-267;

Durzak, "Der Zwang der Politik: Georg Kaiser und Stephan Hermlin," *Monatshefte,* 68 (Winter 1968): 373-386;

Margund Durzak, "Ambrose Bierce und Stephan Hermlin: Zur Rezeption der amerikanischen Short Story in Deutschland," *Arcadia,* 1 (1976): 38-66;

Beate Ehlert, "Dichterische Ich-Konstanten im Geschichtsprozeß: Über Stephan Hermlins autobiographische Utopie der Stille: *Abendlicht,*" *Jahrbuch zur Literatur in der DDR,* 3 (1983): 73-87;

Wolfgang Ertle, *Stephan Hermlin und die Tradition* (Bern: Lang, 1977);

John Flores, *Poetry in East Germany: Adjustments, Visions and Provocations 1945-1970* (New Haven: Yale University Press, 1971), pp. 27-71;

Bernhard Greiner, "Autobiographie im Horizont der Psychoanalyse: Stephan Hermlins *Abendlicht,*" *Poetica,* 14 (1982): 213-249;

Theodore Huebner, *The Literature of East Germany* (New York: Ungar, 1970), pp. 98-105;

Hanjo Kesting, "Der Worte Wunden bluten heute nur nach innen: Der Lyriker Stephan Hermlin," *Merkur,* 35 (1981): 1157-1165;

Günter Kunert, *Liebes- und andere Erklärungen: Schriftsteller über Schriftsteller* (Berlin: Aufbau, 1974), pp. 130-134;

Georg Laschen, *Lyrik in der DDR: Anmerkungen zur Sprachverfassung des modernen Gedichts* (Frankfurt am Main: Athenäum, 1971), pp. 59-74;

Hans Mayer, *Deutsche Literatur und Weltliteratur* (Berlin: Rütten & Loening, 1957), pp. 649-654;

Elke Mehnert, "Zu einigen Aspekten der Antikerezeption Stephan Hermlins," *Weimarer Beiträge,* 31 (1985): 621-629;

Martha Nawarth, "Methoden des Autors—Methoden der Kritik: Einwände gegen Stephan Hermlins *Kommandeuse,*" *Neue Deutsche Literatur,* 3 (1955): 127-133;

J. Fritz Raddatz, *Traditionen und Tendenzen: Materialien zur Literatur in der DDR* (Frankfurt am Main: Suhrkamp, 1972), pp. 146-157;

Jürgen Rühle, *Literatur und Provokation* (Cologne: Kiepenheuer & Witsch, 1960);

Silvia Schlenstedt, "Die Sprache der Kunst: Zu Stephan Hermlins Essays," *Weimarer Beiträge,* 30 (1984): 1898-1907;

Klaus Werner, "Bilder von Leben, Sterben und Widerstand: Versuch über Hermlins Erzählungen," *Weimarer Beiträge,* 31 (1985): 602-620;

Hubert Witt, ed., *Stephan Hermlin: Texte, Materialien, Bilder* (Leipzig: Reclam, 1985).

Stefan Heym
(Helmut Flieg)

(10 April 1913-   )

Inge Dube
Northwestern University

BOOKS: *Nazis in the U.S.A.: An Exposé of Hitler's Aims and Agents in the U.S.A.* (New York: American Committee for Anti-Nazi Literature, 1938);

Hostages: A Novel (New York: Putnam's, 1942); translated into German by Heym as *Der Fall Glasenapp: Roman* (Leipzig: List, 1958); English version republished as *The Glasenapp Case* (Berlin: Seven Seas, 1962);

Of Smiling Peace (Boston: Little, Brown, 1944);

The Crusaders (Boston: Little, Brown, 1948; London: Cassell, 1950); translated into German by Heym and Werner von Grünau as *Der bittere Lorbeer: Roman unserer Zeit* (Munich: List, 1950); German version also published as *Kreuzfahrer von heute: Roman unserer Zeit* (Leipzig: List, 1950);

The Eyes of Reason: A Novel (Boston: Little, Brown, 1951); translated into German by Ellen Zunk as *Die Augen der Vernunft: Roman* (Leipzig: List, 1955);

Tom Sawyers großes Abenteuer, by Heym and Hanus Burger (Halle: Mitteldeutscher Verlag, 1953);

Goldsborough: A Novel (Leipzig: List, 1953; New York: Blue Heron Press, 1954); translated into German by Heym as *Goldsborough: Roman* (Leipzig: List, 1954); German version republished as *Goldsborough oder Die Liebe der Miss Kennedy* (Leipzig: List, 1960);

Die Kannibalen und andere Erzählungen, translated into German by Zunk and Heym (Leipzig: List, 1953); original English version published as *The Cannibals and Other Stories* (Berlin: Seven Seas, 1958);

Offene Worte: So liegen die Dinge (Berlin: Tribüne, 1953);

Forschungsreise ins Herz der deutschen Arbeiterklasse: Nach Berichten 47 sowjetischer Arbeiter (Berlin: Tribüne, 1953);

Reise ins Land der unbegrenzten Möglichkeiten: Ein Bericht (Berlin: Freier deutscher Gewerkschafts-

Stefan Heym (Ullstein–dpa)

bund, Bundesvorstand und Zentralvorstand der Gesellschaft für deutsch-sowjetische Freundschaft, 1954);

Im Kopf–sauber: Schriften zum Tage (Leipzig: List, 1954);

Keine Angst vor Russlands Bären: Neugierige Fragen und offene Antworten über die Sowjetunion (Düsseldorf: Brücken, 1955);

Offen gesagt: Neue Schriften zum Tage (Berlin: Volk und Welt, 1957);

Das kosmische Zeitalter: Ein Bericht (Berlin: Tribüne, 1959); translated as *The Cosmic Age: A Report* (New Delhi: People's Publishing House, 1959); republished as *A Visit to Soviet*

Science, bound with Charles Bettelheim, René Dumont, K. S. Gill, D. D. Kosambi, Leo Huberman, and Paul M. Sweezy, *China Shakes the World Again*, under the title *Socialism: 1959* (New York: Marzani & Munsell, 1959);

Schatten und Licht: Geschichten aus einem geteilten Land, translated into German by Helga Zimnik and Heym (Leipzig: List, 1960); original English version published as *Shadows and Lights: Eight Short Stories* (London: Cassell, 1963);

Die Papiere des Andreas Lenz, translated into German by Zimnik (Leipzig: List, 1963); republished as *Lenz oder Die Freiheit: Ein Roman um Deutschland* (Frankfurt am Main, Vienna & Zurich: Büchergilde Gutenberg, 1963); original English version published as *The Lenz Papers* (London: Cassell, 1964; Berlin: Seven Seas, 1968);

Casimir und Cymbelinchen: Zwei Märchen (Berlin: Kinderbuchverlag, 1966); enlarged as *Cymbelinchen oder Der Ernst des Lebens: Vier Märchen für kluge Kinder* (Munich: Bertelsmann, 1975);

Uncertain Friend: A Biographical Novel (London: Cassell, 1969); translated into German by Heym as *Lassalle: Ein biographischer Roman* (Munich: Bechtle, 1969);

Die Schmähschrift oder Königin gegen Defoe, translated into German by Heym (Zurich: Diogenes, 1970); original English version published in *The Queen against Defoe, and Other Stories* (New York: Hill, 1974; London: Hodder & Stoughton, 1975);

Der König David Bericht (Munich: Kindler, 1972); translated as *The King David Report* (New York: Putnam's, 1973);

Fünf Tage im Juni: Roman (Munich, Gütersloh & Vienna: Bertelsmann, 1974); translated as *Five Days in June: A Novel* (London: Hodder & Stoughton, 1977; Buffalo, N.Y.: Prometheus, 1978);

Das Wachsmut Syndrom (Düsseldorf: Claassen, 1975);

Erzählungen (Berlin: Der Morgen, 1976);

Die richtige Einstellung und andere Erzählungen (Munich: Bertelsmann, 1976);

Collin (London: Hodder & Stoughton, 1979); translated into German by Heym (Munich: Bertelsmann, 1979);

Wege und Umwege: Streitbare Schriften aus fünf Jahrzehnten, edited by Peter Mallwitz (Munich: Bertelsmann, 1980);

Ahasver (Munich: Bertelsmann, 1981); translated as *The Wandering Jew* (New York: Holt, Rinehart & Winston, 1984);

Atta Troll: Versuch einer Analyse (Munich: Bertelsmann, 1983);

Münchner Podium in den Kammerspielen '83: Reden über das eigene Land Deutschland (Munich: Bertelsmann, 1983);

Schwarzenberg (Munich: Bertelsmann, 1984);

Reden an den Feind (Munich: Bertelsmann, 1986).

OTHER: *Auskunft: Neue Prosa aus der DDR*, edited by Heym (Munich, Gütersloh & Vienna: Bertelsmann, 1974);

Auskunft 2: Neuste Prosa aus der DDR, edited by Heym (Munich: Verlag Autoren Edition, 1978).

The works of Stefan Heym are widely read in both parts of Germany and abroad. Since the beginning of his literary career in 1942 his major themes have been unconditional antifascism and the improvement of the human condition through democratic socialism. Almost all of Heym's more than thirty published prose works concern themselves in some fashion with Germany.

In his writings Heym has always tried to tell the truth as he sees it and to fight against violence and injustice. According to the critic Peter Mallwitz, "Heym ist lebendige Kritik seiner Zeit. Sein Leben ist Polemik im aufklärerischen Sinn sozial-revolutionärer Vorfahren" (Heym is living criticism of his time. His life is polemics in the enlightenment tradition of his social-revolutionary predecessors).

Heym was born Helmut Flieg on 10 April 1913 in the industrial town of Chemnitz (now Karl-Marx-Stadt), Germany, to Daniel Flieg, a businessman, and Else Primo Flieg. His critical social conscience was aroused early by reactionary teachers. The publication of an antimilitaristic poem, "Exportgeschäft" (Export Business), in 1931 in a liberal Chemnitz newspaper resulted in his expulsion from the local Staatsgymnasium. Flieg was sent to Berlin, where he passed the Abitur (high school examination) in 1932. These traumatic events, in the course of which a newspaper called Flieg a "parasite" who was helping to spread Marxist ideas in the schools, were decisive for his future development. He had felt harassment and social injustice from an early age; since he enjoyed the material comforts of a middle-class home, the social injustices around him became all

Cover of the 1978 reprint of the German version of Heym's first novel, published in English in 1942 as Hostages

the more salient. He felt compassion particularly for the grossly mistreated working class.

Until Hitler's seizure of power in 1933, Flieg studied German literature and journalism at Berlin University and wrote poems for the prestigious weekly *Die Weltbühne*. Soon after the burning of the Reichstag building on 27 February 1933 Flieg's younger brother came to Berlin to warn him that the Gestapo had been looking for him in Chemnitz. Flieg's father was arrested instead; he committed suicide after his release. Flieg fled over the mountains to Czechoslovakia. "Nichts nahm ich mit mir als meinen Haß" (I took nothing with me but my hatred), he writes about his forced departure from his native land. This hatred for National Socialism and fascism

constitutes the point of departure of the literary career of Stefan Heym, the name Flieg assumed as a safety precaution during his exile in Czechoslovakia.

The Czech capital had become a haven for refugees from Germany. It was in Prague literary circles that Heym first heard discussions of socialist realism, the new teachings from the Soviet Union which were supposed to enable the writer to portray the truth about reality. Politically, the young Heym sympathized with the small Socialist Workers Party of Germany (SAP), which aimed at establishing communism by democratic means.

In Prague Heym learned that two scholarships from the University of Chicago were available for German students persecuted by Hitler. As a Jew Heym qualified, and in 1935 a Jewish fraternity secured one of the scholarships for him. Several Czech newspapers collected the money for his ticket to America. To repay the editors who had financed his journey Heym sent back a series of articles from the United States. The young German immigrant observed his adopted country with a keen and critical eye. He also became politically active: at meetings, street corners, and on the radio he warned Americans and German-Americans of the dangers of National Socialism.

After a year of study in the German Department of the University of Chicago, Heym earned a B.A. degree; another grant allowed him to earn his M.A. in German literature a year later. His master's thesis on Heinrich Heine's *Atta Troll* (1847) deals with the issue of the task of the writer/journalist. (In 1983 the German publishing house Bertelsmann printed a limited edition of the thesis on the occasion of Heym's seventieth birthday.)

Equipped with two degrees and an excellent command of English, Heym set out to find a job. Christmas 1936 found him selling copies of *Gone with the Wind* for the Carson, Pirie, Scott department store in Chicago. In February 1937 Heym accepted an offer to go to New York to become chief editor of *Das deutsche Volksecho*, the successor of the Communist newspaper *Der Arbeiter*. For the next two years he wrote prolifically in German and English about the threat of fascism and about his vision of a true democracy for Germany. His first book, *Nazis in the U.S.A.: An Exposé of Hitler's Aims and Agents in the U.S.A.* (1938), was written at this time. Heym also wrote for the Communist periodicals *Das Wort* in Moscow and *Die neue Weltbühne* in Prague; his articles dealt critically, from a leftist perspective, with American political and economic life. After the *Volksecho* ceased publication in 1939, Heym found work as a salesman for a printing company, a job which left him time to pursue his literary career. His first novel, *Hostages* (1942), was written in English in 1941 and 1942. (A German edition was published in 1958 in Leipzig under the title *Der Fall Glasenapp.*) Putnam's, the publisher, sold the film rights to Paramount before the novel was printed. In a review in the *New York Times*, Orville Prescott called the book one of the best of its kind of the year. Soon after its publication *Hostages* hit the best-seller list and the young writer was freed from his financial worries.

Hostages is set in the Gestapo-beleaguered Prague of 1941. The German lieutenant Glasenapp drowns himself in the river behind a tavern; but since suicide is an entirely unacceptable, decadent weakness for a Nazi his death is disguised as murder by the Gestapo leader Reinhardt. As suspects in the Glasenapp "murder" all patrons and employees of the tavern are taken hostage and sentenced to death. The two leading characters among the hostages are the Czech freedom fighter Janoshik, who is tortured to death, and the skilled worker Breda, the first of Heym's searching intellectual heroes. The gruesome Gestapo methods are described in minute detail. In the end Reinhardt is forced to recognize the superior strength of those he tried to eliminate, for they possess the courage of despair and an ideal to fight for.

This first novel is basically a work of ideas; the characters remain somewhat shapeless and vague. The theme of National Socialist atrocities is transcended by another message: the working class must unite to fight its oppressors. Socialist realism is not yet displayed in this work: there are long passages of inner monologue and stream-of-consciousness typical of the fiction of the early twentieth century.

In 1942 Heym legally changed his name to his pseudonym. The following year he was drafted into a small propaganda intelligence unit of the United States Army; shortly afterward he became an American citizen. His military training took place at three different posts in the United States; the last was Camp Sharpe, Pennsylvania, where, together with a small group of European journalists and writers, he was trained by a young lieutenant named Hans Habe in the art of psychological warfare. On 4 March 1944, before his embarkation to Europe, Heym married the

American journalist Gertrude Gelbin. A few days after D-Day, his unit landed in Normandy. From there the intelligence unit followed the army through France and into Germany.

During his training Heym had been working on his second novel, which was published in 1944 under the title *Of Smiling Peace*. It is the only one of his novels that has not been translated into German. Based on Habe's experiences in Africa, *Of Smiling Peace* is a historical novel with a strong element of suspense. The plot concentrates on some American and French soldiers and a group of high-ranking Nazis. The worst of the latter is Major von Liszt, who–like Reinhardt in *Hostages*–embodies the viciousness of an evil system. American and German ideologies receive equal attention in the novel. Some American critics disapproved of the author's tendency to give the enemy too many interesting traits: Liszt is a much more alive and fascinating character than his main American counterpart, Bert Wolff, a highly idealistic German-American antifascist who fights his own war against National Socialism.

When Habe asked him to write a strongly anti-Communist article for *Die neue Zeitung* in Munich in 1945, Heym, who by then had been commissioned a lieutenant, could no longer reconcile his duties as an American soldier with his ideological convictions. He gained his release from the army and returned to New York. It took him three years to write the monumental novel *The Crusaders* (translated into German as *Der bittere Lorbeer* [The Bitter Laurel], 1950). Despite his publisher's pessimism concerning the success of yet another war novel, Heym's epic reached the best-seller list shortly after it was published in September 1948. Along with Norman Mailer's *The Naked and the Dead* and Irwin Shaw's *The Young Lions*, both of which appeared in the same year, *The Crusaders* became one of the most-read novels about World War II.

Heym draws a panoramic and partially autobiographical picture of the war in Europe in almost a thousand pages. The novel follows a small American propaganda intelligence unit from Normandy across France to Germany. The army is portrayed as a corrupt institution, most of whose members are only interested in feathering their own nests. The Americans, who are not soldiers at heart, are waging a war without knowing precisely what they are fighting for. For some, the reasons are idealistic; for others, they are political or economic. The thesis of the novel, according to

Malcolm Cowley's review in the *New Republic*, is a sound one: that some of the evils being fought against existed in the American army and nation themselves. Heym's intentions in this novel were threefold: he wanted to write a historical novel about war and the "terrible finality of the silence of the dead," as he states in the epilogue; he needed a catharsis to free himself from the devastating experience of war; and he used the novel as a vehicle for his ideology—one of the heroes, Yates, envisions a future world in which socialism will prevail.

Overall, *The Crusaders* was warmly received by American reviewers; the portrayal of wrongdoing and corruption in the army was welcomed by leftist intellectuals, who applauded the fight of a few courageous soldiers against the moral cowardice and profiteering of their fellow Americans. Most socialist reviewers were jubilant about the depiction of the army as a corrupt capitalist institution. For the staunch Communist Alexander Abusch, however, the message was not unequivocal enough: the doubting and wavering Yates was not the "positive hero" prescribed by socialist realism. Yates and the novel's other protagonist, Bing, are erring and suffering individuals, not Communist paragons.

Between 1948 and 1951 Heym made several trips to Europe. In Prague he did research on the Communist takeover of 1948, which he presented in a favorable light in his novel *The Eyes of Reason* (1951; translated into German as *Die Augen der Vernunft*, 1955). Appearing at the beginning of the McCarthy era, this novel was much less enthusiastically received than the previous one.

In 1949 and 1950 he visited Pennsylvania to observe a bitter coal strike, even delivering a truckload of goods to the suffering miners. After intensive studies of the situation Heym wrote a novel about the strike. By the time he finished it the political situation had deteriorated; the Korean War was imminent, and, in Heym's opinion, America was on a path toward fascism. Feeling that his leftist views and recently published prosocialist book put him in danger of becoming a victim of Sen. Joseph McCarthy's witch-hunt, and with little hope of getting his novel about the coal strike published in America, he decided to leave the country. In 1953 he was granted political asylum by the German Democratic Republic (GDR). As a gesture of protest Heym sent his World War II Bronze Star medal to President Eisenhower. After almost two decades he had returned to his native land—the Communist part of which, in his opinion, held the only hope for the future. His novel about the coal strike, *Goldsborough*, was published in English in Leipzig in 1953; the following year a German translation by Heym was published in Leipzig.

More than any earlier work of Heym's, *Goldsborough* observes the guidelines of socialist realism. The author sides with the striking Pennsylvania miners against the cruel and corrupt mining company bosses and also against the demoralized miners' union representatives as he reveals the workers' slowly awakening sense of solidarity in their fight against the depravity of the Establishment. The "positive hero," Carlisle Kennedy, leader of the wildcat strike, fits the pattern envisioned by socialist realism. The work is highly dramatic in structure; the characters reveal themselves mainly through dialogue.

Shortly after Heym's arrival in the GDR a collection of ten short stories about America, *Die Kannibalen und andere Erzählungen* (1953), appeared in Leipzig in German; its original English version, *The Cannibals and Other Stories*, was not published until 1958. Heym continued to write in English because he believed that English forced him to think more clearly than German. *Die Kannibalen und andere Erzählungen* presents an entirely negative view of America.

The workers' uprising against the Communist regime which began on 17 June 1953 forced Heym to critically evaluate East German socialism. The novel *Fünf Tage im Juni* (translated as *Five Days in June*, 1977) is an analysis of the causes of the uprising. The reaction of the Communist authorities to the work was a sobering blow to Heym, who had to realize that even the sincerest criticism was not welcome in the socialist state: *Fünf Tage im Juni* was not allowed to be published in the GDR. The novel finally appeared in West Germany in 1974. The West German *Süddeutsche Zeitung* called it a didactic work about the contradictions in the socialist system. The novel placed Heym once more—this time unintentionally—in the position of a dissident and cost him his high position in East Germany. He accepted this state of affairs with equanimity. In his opinion, the idea of the revolution had not failed; it had been carried out in the wrong way.

In the novel *Die Papiere des Andreas Lenz* (The Papers of Andreas Lenz, 1963; original English version published as *The Lenz Papers*, 1964) Heym uses the Baden riot of 1848 to address the issue of freedom and dictatorship in a revolution.

The year 1965 brought new confrontations with the party politburo. As a result, Heym was blacklisted, and for a number of years only his earlier books could be published in the GDR.

In 1969 Heym's wife died after a long illness. Two years later he married Inge Hohn, a story editor for the East German DEFA film studios, and adopted her fifteen-year-old son.

As Heym had no intention of leaving the GDR, three options were open to him: he could remain silent, he could write according to the party line, or he could publish in the West. After pleading in vain with East German authorities to accept fair criticism, he chose to publish outside the GDR. His biographical novel *Uncertain Friend*, about the nineteenth-century socialist Ferdinand Lassalle, was published in London in 1969 in its original English version, and in German the same year in Munich under the title *Lassalle*. Publication of the novel in East Germany was denied. Heym was fined 300 marks for ignoring the GDR stipulation not to have the book published in the West.

The novel develops Lassalle's ideas of a socialist society, which he hoped to bring about through peaceful means, and also portrays his complex, charismatic personality. At the age of forty Lassalle falls in love with the young daughter of the Protestant ambassador to the Bavarian court. The relationship is doomed not only because Helene von Dönningen is almost twenty years younger than Lassalle and already engaged but because her father is fiercely opposed to the "jüdischer Hausierer mit Demagogenallüren" (Jewish peddler with the allures of a demagogue). To spare Helene the hostility she would encounter because of their relationship, Lassalle parts from her until he can realize his political goals. Helene loses trust in Lassalle and promises her father that she will never see him again. Lassalle tries desperately to win her back, but becomes the victim of his own outdated code of honor: he challenges Helene's fiancé to a duel and is fatally wounded.

Lassalle is juxtaposed with the monumental figure of Bismarck, who is portrayed as an arrogant Junker interested only in exploiting Lassalle's ideas for the benefit of the monarchy. Under the pretense of sympathy for the working class, Bismarck enters a coalition with Lassalle, only to turn on him and have him prosecuted by the courts. But despite all adversity, Lassalle has begun the struggle of the working class against the monarchy. (The novel's English title derives from a letter to Marx in which Friedrich Engels called Lassalle, whose version of socialism differed from Engels and Marx's, an "uncertain friend" who would become an enemy in the future.)

Die Schmähschrift oder Königin gegen Defoe (English version published in *The Queen against Defoe, and Other Stories*, 1974) was published in 1970 in Switzerland. It describes Daniel Defoe's anonymous publication of a pamphlet about the suppression of an uncomfortable truth, his exposure as its author, and his resulting arrest and punishment. Heym, no doubt conscious of the similarity between Defoe's situation and his own, condemns those who persecuted Defoe.

In 1972 Heym's *Der König David Bericht* (translated as *The King David Report*, 1973) appeared in Munich. A political parable about the misuse of power, the book tells how the historian Ethan is not allowed to reveal his findings concerning King David's life since they would destroy the illusions about a great ruler. The novel was highly acclaimed in the West; Heinrich Böll praised its imaginative qualities and the irreverence with which Heym interprets the biblical texts.

In 1973 and 1974, during a period of detente, *Der König David Bericht*, *Lassalle*, and *Die Schmähschrift* were published in the GDR; East German citizens were, however, not considered mature enough to be exposed to *Fünf Tage im Juni*. This relatively liberal period did not last long; the hard-liners soon prevailed again, and in 1977 Heym was expelled from the writers' union of the GDR. With stoic patience he adapted once more to the changed climate. His journalistic works became fewer and were replaced by interviews and speeches in western news media viewed by many East Germans. Today Heym is hoping for another softening of the party line under which the East German population would be allowed to read the constructive criticism of *Fünf Tage im Juni*.

One day, Heym anticipates, the East Germans might also be allowed to face the disclosure of the Stalinist past of the GDR, and the various attempts to block out that past as portrayed in his novel *Collin*, published in 1979 by Hodder and Stoughton in London and in German translation the same year in Munich. The East German writer Collin, forbidden to write about atrocities committed by Communists in Mexico and Spain, takes refuge in psychosomatic illness. When he recognizes the truth about the Communist system

Heym in 1978 (Ullstein–Binder/Thiele)

and his own cowardice, deception, and sins of omission, he dies of a heart attack.

The novel *Ahasver* (translated as *The Wandering Jew*, 1984), published in 1981 in Munich, treats the Ahasver legend in a fresh and highly unconventional manner. Ahasver had been condemned to permanent restless wandering because he had denied Christ refreshment on his way to the cross. He is to be freed only when he meets Christ again and is forgiven. Heym's Ahasver, however, is not the symbolic figure of the Jewish fate but the incarnation of the revolutionary principle; he strikes Christ because he is enraged by Christ's passivity and willingness to accept suffering. In a witty, irreverent fashion Heym does not hesitate to let God Himself appear, or to portray a bucolic, staunchly anti-Semitic Luther, or to have a dispute about Ahasver's existence in modern times carried out in a correspondence between Professor Leuchtenträger of the Hebrew University in Jerusalem and Professor Beifuss of the Institute for Scien-

tific Atheism in East Berlin. For each historical period the exact tone of the time is found, from Luther's German of the sixteenth century to the artificial, stilted GDR party jargon. The critic Toni Meissner calls *Ahasver* "ein amüsantes, phantasmagorisches Spiel mit Dogmen und Legenden, Ideologien und Philosophien" (an amusing, phantasmagorical play with dogmas and legends, ideologies and philosophies). This novel expresses more strikingly than any other of Heym's works his idealism and his unbending belief in the necessity of improving the state of mankind. (A West German newspaper carried a report in early 1988 that *Ahasver* was to be published in East Germany by the publishing house Der Morgen in the last quarter of the year.)

The concept of the novel *Schwarzenberg* (1984) is equally ingenious: at the end of World War II, due to an error, the little German town of Schwarzenberg becomes a neutral territory with no government. Left to their own devices, the Schwarzenbergers found an idyllic miniature republic; but conflicts soon arise. Should the Americans be asked to occupy Schwarzenberg? In the end the Soviets invade and the utopia is destroyed. This novel reflects Heym's lifelong endeavors to find a solution for society's problems through an ideal form of government.

Unconditional antifascism and a democratic form of socialism are Stefan Heym's unchanging goals. He calls himself not an opponent but a critic of the GDR and still considers it to be a fascinating place for a writer. Politics and literature are inseparable for Heym, who is a member of the small but significant freedom movement in the GDR. He claims to harbor no bitterness toward those who ban his books in his own country but continues to protest against all forms of injustice. He has also found ways to reach his audience, both in the West and, most important to him, in the GDR.

References:

Beiträge zu einer Biographie: Eine Freundesausgabe für Stefan Heym zum 60. Geburtstag am 10. April 1963 (Munich: Kindler, 1973);

Paul Dickson, "Das Amerikabild in der deutschen Emigrantenliteratur seit 1933," Ph.D. dissertation, University of Munich, 1951, pp. 181-190;

Otto Ernst, "Stefan Heyms Auseinandersetzung mit Faschismus, Militarismus und Kapitalismus: Dargestellt an den Gestalten seiner Romane," Ph.D. dissertation, University of Jena, 1965;

Hans Habe, *Im Jahre Null* (Munich: Heyne, 1977), pp. 12-13, 143;

Wolfgang A. Luchting, "Das Erlebnis des Krieges im amerikanischen Roman über den 2. Weltkrieg," Ph.D. dissertation, University of Munich, 1956, pp. 409ff, 536ff;

Peter Mallwitz, ed., *Stefan Heym–Wege und Umwege: Streitbare Schriften aus fünf Jahrzehnten* (Munich: Bertelsmann, 1980);

Reinhard Konrad Zachau, "Stefan Heym in Amerika: Eine Untersuchung zu Stefan Heyms Entwicklung im amerikanischen Exil (1935-1952)," Ph.D. dissertation, University of Pittsburgh, 1978;

Jack Zipes, "Die Freiheit trägt Handschellen im Land der Freiheit: Das Bild der Vereinigten Staaten von Amerika in der Literatur der DDR," in *Amerika in der deutschen Literatur*, edited by Sigrid Bauschinger (Stuttgart: Reclam, 1975), pp. 324-352.

Wolfgang Hildesheimer

(9 December 1916-   )

Patricia H. Stanley
Florida State University

BOOKS: *Lieblose Legenden* (Stuttgart: Deutsche Verlags-Anstalt, 1952; revised edition, Frankfurt am Main: Suhrkamp, 1963);

Das Ende einer Welt: Funk-Oper, text by Hildesheimer, music by Hans Werner Henze (Frankfurt am Main: Frankfurter Verlagsanstalt, 1953);

Paradies der falschen Vögel (Munich: Desch, 1953);

Die Eroberung der Prinzessin Turandot (Weinheim/ Bergstraße: Deutscher Laienspiel Verlag, 1954); revised as *Der Drachenthron: Komödie in drei Akten* (Munich: Desch, 1955);

Ich trage eine Eule nach Athen, und vier andere von Paul Flora illustrierte Geschichten (Zurich: Diogenes, 1956);

Begegnung im Balkanexpreß (Hamburg: Hans Bredow-Institut, 1956); published with *An den Ufern der Plotinitza* (Stuttgart: Reclam, 1968);

Spiele, in denen es dunkel wird (Pfullingen: Neske, 1958);

Herrn Walsers Raben (Hamburg: Hans Bredow-Institut, 1960); enlarged as *Herrn Walsers Raben; Unter der Erde: zwei Hörspiele* (Frankfurt am Main: Suhrkamp, 1964);

Die Verspätung: Ein Stück in zwei Teilen (Frankfurt am Main: Suhrkamp, 1961);

Nocturno im Grand Hotel: Eine Fernseh-Komödie, edited by Karl O. Nordstrand (Lund: Gleerup, 1961);

Vergebliche Aufzeichnungen; Nachtstück (Frankfurt am Main: Suhrkamp, 1963);

Betrachtungen über Mozart (Pfullingen: Neske, 1963);

Das Opfer Helena; Monolog: Zwei Hörspiele (Frankfurt am Main: Suhrkamp, 1965); "Das Opfer Helena," translated by Jacques-Leon Rose as *The Sacrifice of Helen* (University Park: University of Pennsylvania Press, 1968);

Tynset (Frankfurt am Main: Suhrkamp, 1965);

Wer war Mozart?; Becketts "Spiel"; Über das absurde Theater (Frankfurt am Main: Suhrkamp, 1966);

Wolfgang Hildesheimer (Suhrkamp-Verlag, Frankfurt am Main)

Interpretationen: James Joyce, Georg Büchner; Zwei Frankfurter Vorlesungen (Frankfurt am Main: Suhrkamp, 1969);

Mary Stuart: Eine historische Szene (Frankfurt am Main: Suhrkamp, 1971);

Zeiten in Cornwall (Frankfurt am Main: Suhrkamp, 1971);

Masante (Frankfurt am Main: Suhrkamp, 1973);

Hauskauf: Hörspiel (Frankfurt am Main: Suhrkamp, 1974);

Theaterstücke; Über das absurde Theater (Frankfurt am Main: Suhrkamp, 1976);

Biosphärenklänge: Ein Hörspiel (Frankfurt am Main: Suhrkamp, 1977);

Mozart (Frankfurt am Main: Suhrkamp, 1977); translated by Marion Faber as *Mozart* (New York: Farrar, Straus & Giroux, 1982; London: Dent, 1983);

Exerzitien mit Papst Johannes; Vergebliche Aufzeichnungen (Frankfurt am Main: Suhrkamp, 1979);

Marbot: Eine Biographie (Frankfurt am Main: Suhrkamp, 1981); translated by Patricia Crampton as *Marbot* (New York: Braziller, 1983; London: Dent, 1983);

Mitteilungen an Max über den Stand der Dinge und anderes (Frankfurt am Main: Suhrkamp, 1983);

Endlich allein: Collagen (Frankfurt am Main: Suhrkamp, 1984);

Das Ende der Fiktionen: Reden aus fünfundzwanzig Jahren (Frankfurt am Main: Suhrkamp, 1984);

Der ferne Bach (Frankfurt am Main: Insel, 1985);

Nachlese (Frankfurt am Main: Suhrkamp, 1987);

The Collected Stories of Wolfgang Hildesheimer, translated by Joachim Neugroschel (New York: Ecco Press, 1987).

OTHER: *Mozart-Briefe*, edited by Hildesheimer (Frankfurt am Main: Insel, 1975).

TRANSLATIONS: Anne Piper, *Jack und Jenny* (Hamburg: Krüger, 1955);

Djuna Barnes, *Nachtgewächs* (Pfullingen: Neske, 1959);

Carlo Goldoni, *Die Schwiegerväter* (Munich: Desch, 1961);

Richard Brinsley Sheridan, *Die Lästerschule* (Munich: Desch, 1962);

Edward St. John Gorey, *Ein sicherer Beweis* (Zurich: Diogenes, 1962);

Gorey, *Die Draisine von Untermattenwaag* (Zurich: Diogenes, 1963);

Gorey, *Eine Harfe ohne Saiten oder Wie man einen Roman schreibt* (Zurich: Diogenes, 1963);

Gorey, *Das Geheimnis der Ottomane: Ein pornographisches Werk* (Zurich: Diogenes, 1964);

George Bernard Shaw, *Die heilige Johanna* (Frankfurt am Main: Suhrkamp, 1965);

Gorey, *Das unglückselige Kind* (Zurich: Diogenes, 1967);

Shaw, *Helden* (Frankfurt am Main: Suhrkamp, 1969);

Gorey, *La Chauve-souris dorée* (Zurich: Diogenes, 1969);

Samuel Beckett, "Wie die Geschichte erzählt wurde," in *Günter Eich zum Gedächtnis*, edited by Siegfried Unseld (Frankfurt am Main: Suhrkamp, 1973);

William Congreve, *Der Lauf der Welt* (Frankfurt am Main: Insel, 1986).

Trained as a painter and graphic artist, Wolfgang Hildesheimer became a writer on 18 February 1950 when his studio was so cold that he could not paint. Moving closer to the stove, he picked up a pad and pencil intending to sketch, but instead began to write a story. The next day he wrote another, "und so wurde ich allmählich Schriftsteller, denn wenn man einmal mit dem Schreiben angefangen hat, scheint es schwer, wieder damit aufzuhören, selbst wenn man will, und ich habe seitdem schon mehrmals gewollt" (And so I gradually became a writer, because when one has once begun writing it seems to be difficult to put a stop to it, even if one wants to, and I have wanted to many times since then). A number of literary prizes and honors attest to the critical success of his second career: the Hörspielpreis der Kriegsblinden (Radio Play Prize of the War Blinded) for "Das Opfer Helena" (published, 1965; translated as *The Sacrifice of Helen*, 1968) in 1955, the Bremer Literaturpreis (Literature Prize of Bremen) and the Büchner Prize for the novel *Tynset* (1965) in 1966, the Premio Verinna-Lorenzon by the Principia di Cosenza for the biography *Mozart* (1977) in 1980, and the Literaturpreis der Bayerischen Akademie der Schönen Künste (Literature Prize of the Bavarian Academy of Fine Arts) for *Marbot* (1981) in 1982. In May of that year he received an honorary doctorate from the Justus-Liebig University in Gießen.

The writer continues to practice art, however. He illustrated "Vergebliche Aufzeichnungen" (Vain Sketches, 1963), *Zeiten in Cornwall* (Times in Cornwall, 1971), and *Mitteilungen an Max über den Stand der Dinge und anderes* (Communicating with Max on the State of Things and Other Matters, 1983) with surrealistic pen-and-ink drawings. *Endlich allein* (Finally Alone, 1984) is a limited edition of thirty-two mostly surrealistic collages created between 1971 and 1983. Additionally, he exhibits drawings and collages in galleries on the Continent and in England and Ireland.

Born in Hamburg in 1916 to Jewish parents–Arnold Hildesheimer, a chemist, and Hanna Goldschmidt Hildesheimer–Wolfgang Hildesheimer attended schools in several German cities until 1933 when the family moved to England in the

Illustration by Hildesheimer for his autobiographical monologue, Mitteilungen an Max über den Stand der Dinge
und anderes

face of increasing persecution. After Hildesheimer completed his high school education in Sur-
rey, the family moved in 1934 to Palestine. From
1934 to 1937 Hildesheimer studied cabinetmak-
ing, drawing, and furniture and stage design in
Jerusalem; he continued his education in drawing and stage design in London from 1937 to
1939. After traveling in France, Switzerland, and
Italy in 1939, he returned to Palestine; from
1940 to 1942 he was employed as an English
teacher at the British Institute in Tel Aviv, and
from 1943 to 1946 he served as public information officer for the British government in Jerusalem. His first marriage, which had taken place in

Palestine around 1940, ended in 1945 or 1946. In 1946 he was appointed simultaneous translator for the War Crimes Tribunal in Nuremberg, and at the conclusion of the trials in 1949 he edited the proceedings. Later that year he settled in the Bavarian village of Ambach am Starnbergersee as a free-lance painter.

His early short stories were published in newspapers and journals throughout Germany; most were collected as *Lieblose Legenden* (Loveless Legends, 1952). Included is "Das Atelierfest" (The Studio Fête), which is probably Hildesheimer's most frequently anthologized story.

Hildesheimer's fiction is literature of the absurd. He is Germany's foremost exponent of this genre and its basic premise: life affirms nothing; reality has no guidelines. The plot of a Hildesheimer story is "absurd" in the sense that the unlikely events depicted are treated by the characters with dignity and composure, as if they were expected. A hallmark of his writing is the elegant prose with which he makes the point that the world's unreasonableness is best accepted with equanimity, although one should employ ingenuity to adapt to it. In "Das Atelierfest" the narrator, a painter, is interrupted by a visit from his patroness and a friend as he is about to begin a new painting after a long dry period. He accepts the interruption without demur, even when his friend telephones acquaintances and organizes a party. The apartment is soon filled with people, and the painter is wedged into a corner next to a carpenter who has installed new windowpanes. The painter takes a hammer from the carpenter's pocket, carefully hammers a hole in the wall, and climbs through it into the bedroom of his sleepy middle-aged neighbors. He persuades them to put on robes and climb through the hole to join the party; they do not return, and he takes over their apartment. The party never ends. The painter moves a wardrobe in front of the hole to dampen the noise; when he complains to the landlord, the latter, too, joins the party. This story is paradigmatic of Hildesheimer's depiction of the absurd: the narrator does not interpret the events, and he is passive—he gives up his life-style (and his wife) rather than protest to his guests or eject them.

Paradies der falschen Vögel (Paradise of False Birds, 1953) is a picaresque novel in the tradition of Defoe's *Moll Flanders* (1722). A superficially amusing story of Balkan intrigue and art forgery on a grand scale, it is also an indictment of that segment of society that can afford to buy art but

does not know what art is. The narrator, a painter, becomes a victim of his uncle's chicaneries when the uncle declares him dead after a border incident and then sells forgeries of his paintings at a handsome price. The nephew concocts a plot to halt his uncle's career and executes it with the help of his former tutor, another dealer in forged paintings. The prose here is refined, witty, and filled with character sketches that convey the narrator's polite but biting scorn.

In 1953 Hildesheimer married Silvia Dillman and moved to Munich. In 1957 they moved to Poschiavo, a village in the canton of Graubünden in Switzerland. Although they have no children of their own, Hildesheimer's wife has two daughters from a previous marriage, and the couple has several grandchildren.

Early in the 1950s Hildesheimer was invited to join Gruppe 47, the association founded in 1947 by Hans Werner Richter, a writer and publisher, to encourage and assist writers and promote the publication of postwar literature. Hildesheimer remained a member of the group for the rest of its twenty-year existence. During this period he wrote a number of Hörspiele (radio plays), a popular form of entertainment while Germany was rebuilding its theaters. Some of these radio plays also became stage plays. *Die Eroberung der Prinzessin Turandot* (The Conquest of Princess Turandot, 1954) appeared first as a radio play, then as a television play in 1954; in 1955 it was performed on stage as *Der Drachenthron* (The Dragon's Throne, 1955) and marked Hildesheimer's debut in the theater. At the beginning of Hildesheimer's version of the fairy tale of the Chinese princess who will only marry the prince who can answer three questions she poses, Turandot has already disposed of nineteen princes; her father presents yet another, the Prince of Astrachan, who answers her questions and wins her heart as well. But he refuses her marriage proposal and announces that he is an imposter, an adventurer who conquers princesses and then leaves them. The real Prince of Astrachan arrives with an army and takes the city, and Turandot is forced to accept him as her husband. Sophisticated dialogue and sudden plot shifts create an externally amusing play, but this is not a comedy. According to Hildesheimer, everyone expects a happy ending from a Märchen (fairy tale) and will wonder why this tale lacks one; the stimulation of such reflection is the goal the author seeks.

Hildesheimer about the time he wrote Marbot: Eine Biographie, *winner of the literature prize from the Bavarian Academy of Fine Arts (Ullstein-dpa)*

"Das Opfer Helena," originally a radio play, became a stage play in 1959. Hildesheimer's version of events leading to the Trojan War is superficially an urbane comedy of manners and morals. The beauteous Helen seduces the young prince Paris, her houseguest; she plans to carry him off to a lonely island where they will live in ideal love and avert the war planned by her husband, Menelaos, who expected Paris to seduce Helen. Aboard the getaway ship, Paris reveals that they are headed for Troy and war after all: he knew that a seduction would occur and has already prepared his warriors for battle. Helen cannot dissuade him from his plan. The Trojans lose the war and Menelaos brings Helen home. She has lost faith in mortals and resigns herself to passive acceptance of their way of life. Like *Die Eroberung der Prinzessin Turandot* this play is not a comedy but a melancholy drama that invites reflection.

Spiele, in denen es dunkel wird (Plays in Which It Grows Dark, 1958) is a collection of three works: *Pastorale, oder die Zeit für Kakao* (Pastorale; or, Time for Cocoa), *Landschaft mit Figuren* (Land-

scape with Figures), and *Die Uhren* (The Clocks). *Pastorale* was produced on the stage in 1958; the other two plays, originally radio plays, were adapted and performed theatrically in 1959. Natural light fades and then returns at the end of each play; characters frequently mention time but pay no heed to the fact that hours pass in the space of minutes; the highly stylized characters speak to themselves rather than to each other. In *Pastorale* two brothers in their sixties, with imposing professional titles, behave like children and have a nurse who is to bring them cocoa at four. In *Landschaft* three people posing for a portrait in Act I are lifeless models in Act II; they are motivated by a music box to climb into shipping crates when they are sold. In *Die Uhren* a man and a woman living in indolence quarrel like children over small decisions; they collect clocks instead of becoming parents, and finally mimic the chiming of their clocks. These plays are obviously theater of the absurd, and some critics noted a resemblance to the work of Samuel Beckett and Eugene Ionesco. Hildesheimer explained his absurdist outlook in a talk, "Über das absurde Theater," given during an international conference at Erlangen in 1960 and published in various collections. Theater of the absurd, Hildesheimer says, is a symbolic ceremony in which the viewer takes the role of a questioner; the play represents the world that, instead of remaining silent, gives "Ersatzantworten" (substitute answers) that reveal nothing more than that there are no real answers. Life cannot be understood or interpreted; the viewer who waits for meaning waits in vain. He should realize and accept his alienation. Rather than feel himself mocked by the absurdity of the dramatic situation on stage, he should mock the object of the situation–that is, life itself.

Three plays of the early 1960s reveal a more sophisticated approach to the absurd. In *Herrn Walsers Raben* (Mr. Walser's Ravens, 1960), a radio play, Walser turns his interfering relatives into ravens; in *Die Verspätung* (The Delay, 1961), a stage play, a frustrated scientist claims that man is descended from a bird he has just identified; and in *Unter der Erde* (Under Ground, 1964), a radio play, a couple finds a wonderful underground cavern in their garden in which time ceases to exist, and, for a moment, they recapture mutual trust.

Hildesheimer's first important novel, *Tynset*, was published in 1965. It was preceded by *Nachtstück* (Night Piece, 1963), a play, and "Monolog" (1965), a radio play; both works derive from material in the novel. The narrator, a nameless insomniac, fantasizes a trip to the Norwegian village of Tynset; but in the course of the night, during which he is plagued by memories of incidents from his past, he realizes that he does not want to leave his home or even his bed: for he can reach the only goal he seeks, "Nichts" (Nothingness), simply by focusing his telescope beyond the moon. The incidents from the narrator's past mingle with impersonal stories based on objects in his house in a highly structured literary adaptation of the musical rondo. Four of the stories are literary equivalents of musical forms: a fugue, a toccata, and two cadenzas. The novel is literature of the absurd–the monologue of an individual alienated in a world of "Ersatzantworten,"–but the writing is often lyrical and evocative, prose poetry of a high order.

Hildesheimer began translating literature from German into English in 1945 with a poem of Stefan George which appeared in a Jerusalem newspaper. In 1946 his translation of Franz Kafka's story "Elf Söhne" was published in England as "Eleven Sons." He took up this craft again in the 1950s, translating Anne Piper's novel *Early to Bed* (1951) into German as *Jack und Jenny* in 1955 and Djuna Barnes's *Nightwood* (1936) as *Nachtgewächs* in 1959 (a phrase from *Nightwood* turns up in *Tynset*). In the 1960s he translated plays by Richard Brinsley Sheridan, Carlo Goldoni, and George Bernard Shaw and stories by Edward St. John Gorey and Samuel Beckett. One of his most ambitious projects is the "Anna Livia Plurabella" section of James Joyce's *Finnegans Wake* (1939), published in his *Interpretationen* in 1969.

Another interest is Wolfgang Amadeus Mozart. Hildesheimer's speech commemorating Mozart's 200th birthday in 1956, published in the journal *Merkur* in October of that year as "Aufzeichnungen über Mozart" (Sketches of Mozart), developed into the essay "Wer war Mozart?" (Who was Mozart?, 1966). Hildesheimer attacks extant biographies and attempts a sketch based on Mozart's letters and manuscript scores and on deductions of his own.

Published in the same volume with "Wer war Mozart?" are two theoretical essays: one is based on Beckett's play *Endgame* (1957), and the other is the Erlangen talk "Über das absurde Theater." Hildesheimer is the only theorist of the absurd in German; his theory is contained in the Erlangen talk and in two talks, "Die Wirklichkeit des Absurden" (The Reality of the Absurd) and "Das absurde Ich" (The Absurd I), given at the University of Frankfurt in 1967 and published in 1969 in *Interpretationen*. Although he uses the work of Beckett, Ionesco, Ilse Aichinger, and Günter Eich to formulate his theories, his own stories best exemplify the genre in German. He defines the absurd by saying that "das Absurde bedeutet die Vernunftwidrigkeit der Welt, indem sie dem Menschen die Antwort auf seine Frage verweigert" (the absurd indicates the unreasonableness of the world in refusing to give man an answer to his question). His justification for the absurd is based on a statement by the German theorist Theodor Adorno that after Auschwitz poetry is no longer possible; Hildesheimer replies that *only* poetry and absurdist prose, which in its intensity and brevity resembles poetry, are possible after Auschwitz. In the prose of Beckett, the narrator reveals himself in his tragic, comic, even ridiculous dimensions: "Und unter der Lächerlichkeit scheint die Verzweiflung durch, objektivierte Verzweiflung, denn der Erzähler betrachtet sich ja nicht als Einzelfall–er ist es auch nicht, der Leser ist in derselben Situation" (And under the ridiculousness despair comes through, objectified despair, because the narrator does not regard himself as exceptional–and he isn't, the reader is in the same situation).

The play *Mary Stuart* (1971) may best exemplify Hildesheimer's formulation of the absurd. As servants prepare the queen for her execution, they pluck jewels from her hair and costume; the doctor fondles one of the ladies in waiting; venal conversations flow in simultaneous dialogue around the praying queen; in short, as the stage directions state, the boundaries between parody and–literally–bloody earnestness are eradicated. The executioner eats his sausage, changes his clothes, massages his muscles, checks his axe, and even handles the queen as if she were another piece of equipment. The queen herself interrupts her prayers from time to time for essentially petty accusations. Her last prayer, in Latin, competes not only with the simultaneous prayer of the Protestant cleric but with discordant music from a small band. Although the play is set in the sixteenth century, the society depicted is a replica of the contemporary society described by Martin Esslin in *The Theatre of the Absurd* (1961): "The madness of the times lies precisely in the existence, side by side, of a large number of unreconciled beliefs and attitudes–conventional morality, for example, on the one hand, and the values of advertising on the other; the conflicting claims of science and religion; or the loudly proclaimed striving of all sections for the general interest when in fact each is pursuing very narrow and selfish particular ends."

Zeiten in Cornwall is an autobiographical account of Hildesheimer's return to the village of Mousehole in Cornwall after a twenty-five-year absence. Hildesheimer had lived there for a semester when he was twenty-one, while studying art in London. The book alternates vivid, detailed pictures of Cornwall in the present with vignettes of student life in London and Mousehole. The tone of the earlier, shorter autobiographical piece, "Vergebliche Aufzeichnungen," was melancholy; *Zeiten in Cornwall* has an equally reflective quality, but the presence of narratives offers a lightening counterpoint. Both works reveal Hildesheimer's ability to create memorable verbal images.

Masante (1973), a sequel to *Tynset*, is set in Meona, a settlement on the edge of a desert; the narrator lives in a run-down bar owned by Maxine, an alcoholic, and her husband Alain. Guests stop a short while in Meona before going into the desert and seldom return. The narrator left his home, Cal Masante, in Urbino, Italy, to die in the desert. The novel ends when he sets out on foot, haunted, as he was in *Tynset*, by his memories. Like the *Decameron* and Goethe's *Unterhaltungen deutscher Ausgewanderten* (Conversations of German Emigrants, 1795), *Masante* contains a number of stories; these are told by Maxine and her husband. Because of the range of material in these stories, one critic has labeled this novel a poetic encyclopedia.

Hauskauf (House Purchase, 1974) is a radio play for two male voices: A, the seller of a house; and B, the potential purchaser. Wind sounds punctuate most of the scenes, and B is so intent on knowing A's feelings about the wind in the first scene that the reader will anticipate (correctly) that the house in question is unimportant to the plot. Both men are fifty-four and are interested in exploring remote regions; both live alone and express satisfaction that they will leave behind no one to inherit a poisoned earth or, worse, become one of the poisoners. The men are so similar, in fact, that they could be twins; the critic Heinz Puknus conjectures that the dialogue is really a split monologue. If so, the narrator is attempting to convince himself of the validity of remaining at home, a variation of the theme in *Tynset* and *Masante*. The play ends with

*Hildesheimer, summer 1985 (photograph copyright ©
Bodo Zoege)*

B admiring the built-in closets in the great room. He has agreed to buy the house, freeing A to travel if he wishes.

Mozart (1977) was preceded in 1975 by Hildesheimer's edition of a volume of the composer's letters. The biography is a strong contribution to Mozart research. It is difficult enough to imagine the subjective life of a genius of our own century, Hildesheimer says in the foreword. How, then, are we to imagine the thoughts and desires of a genius in the Age of Absolutism? Biographers have usually indulged in wishful thinking; they have portrayed Mozart as they want him to be. Even his letters do not give us insight, for Mozart described himself as he thought he should be or as he wanted others to see him, but almost never confessed how he felt. In his biography, which does not proceed in chronological order, Hildesheimer uses a wide range of documents, other biographies, and memoirs of persons who knew Mozart. Hildesheimer speculates frequently in the course of the work; but his speculations are founded on such detailed knowledge of Mozart's household and milieu that the background comes alive and encourages the reader to speculate along with him.

The radio play *Biosphärenklänge* (Sound of the Spheres, 1977) takes place in a living room as a couple awaits a luncheon guest. The man reports a feeling of impending doom for everyone on earth, and he tries to explain this feeling to his wife while also describing an accompanying sound which is inaudible to her. By the end of the play she hears the sound and so does the audience: it is a very high, obnoxious G. It is the sound of the spheres, the sound of the approaching end. This sound seems to be a metaphor for pollution or nuclear fallout. All around the couple there is death: the telephone line is already dead, the electricity does not function, a dead bird lies on the ground outside and another falls dead, dogs howl, children who pass the house on their way home do not reach their destination, and the guest does not arrive. The high G finally becomes so obtrusive that the couple agree that they have nothing more to say, and the play ends.

Marbot: Eine Biographie (1981) records the life of the art historian and critic Sir Andrew Marbot. Born in 1801 in England, he committed suicide in 1830 in the hills surrounding Urbino, but his body was never found. He traveled widely and conversed with Goethe, Delacroix, Berlioz, Byron, Wordsworth, Coleridge, and De Quincey; many of these conversations, as well as entries about paintings from Marbot's notebooks, are recorded in the book. Marbot is credited with attempting for the first time to explore the relationship between the work of art and its motivation in the artist's unconscious. In reality, however, Marbot never existed: the book is a fictional biography. The fact that it won the literature prize of the Bavarian Academy of Fine Arts speaks for the quality of the art criticism in the work. The book is a biography of ideas rather than of a life, and as such it is richly rewarding.

Mitteilungen an Max über den Stand der Dinge und anderes is an autobiographical monologue directed at the Swiss writer Max Frisch; it was origi-nally part of a collection of essays honoring Frisch on his seventieth birthday in 1981. The text is untranslatable because of the wordplays and numerous quotations from poetry, philosophy, and philology that would mean little to a non-German reader. This book reveals Hildesheimer's broad range of intellectual interests and his ability to manipulate German syntax into complex, colorful prose. The benign pessimism underlying this prose places Hildesheimer among the philosophical writers of post-World War II Germany; he is an articulator of man's unavoidably alienated condition.

Hildesheimer's early affinity for art forgers, literal manipulations of light and dark, and frankly absurd situations matured into the elegantly simple plots of *Hauskauf* and *Biosphärenklänge*, which are all the more despairing for their starkness, and his formidable intellect is finally fully revealed in the works *Marbot* and *Mozart*, which set a new standard for biography as a genre.

Bibliography:
Volker Jehle, *Wolfgang Hildesheimer: Eine Bibliographie* (Frankfurt am Main: Lang, 1984).

References:
Heinz Ludwig Arnold, ed., *Wolfgang Hildesheimer* (Munich: text + kritik, 1986);
Heinz Puknus, *Wolfgang Hildesheimer* (Munich: Beck, 1978);
Dierk Rodewald, *Über Wolfgang Hildesheimer* (Frankfurt am Main: Suhrkamp, 1971).

Papers:
The Hildesheimer-Archiv in Reutlingen, West Germany, contains manuscripts, articles about Hildesheimer, all references to him in newspapers and magazines, and some material that Hildesheimer is withholding from examination until after his death. The archivist is Volker Jehle. The mailing address is Kantstrasse 58, D-7410 Reutlingen, West Germany.

Hans Egon Holthusen

(15 April 1913-   )

Mark E. Cory
University of Arkansas at Fayetteville

BOOKS: *Rilkes Sonette an Orpheus: Versuch einer Interpretation* (Munich: Neuer Filser-Verlag, 1937);

Klage um den Bruder: Sonette (Hamburg: Ellermann, 1947);

Hier in der Zeit: Gedichte (Munich: Piper, 1949);

Der späte Rilke (Zurich: Arche, 1949); translated by J. P. Stern as *Rainer Maria Rilke: A Study of His Later Poetry* (Cambridge, U.K.: Bowes & Bowes, 1952; Philadelphia: West, 1977);

Die Welt ohne Transzendenz: Eine Studie zu Thomas Manns "Doktor Faustus" und seinen Nebenschriften (Hamburg: Ellermann, 1949);

Der unbehauste Mensch: Motive und Probleme der modernen Literatur (Munich: Piper, 1951; revised, 1955; revised edition, Munich: Deutscher Taschenbuch Verlag, 1964);

Labyrinthische Jahre: Neue Gedichte (Munich: Piper, 1952);

Ja und Nein: Neue kritische Versuche (Munich: Piper, 1954);

Autor und Leser: Rede zur Eröffnung der Frankfurter Buchmesse (Munich: Piper, 1955);

Totenreden für Gottfried Benn, by Holthusen, Oskar Söhngen, and Clemens Graf Podewils (Wiesbaden: Limes, 1956);

Das Schiff: Aufzeichnungen eines Passagiers (Munich: Piper, 1956); translated by Robert Kee and Susi Hughes as *The Crossing* (London: Deutsch, 1959);

Gutachten der Akademie der Künste zum Entwurf eines Denkmals des unbekannten politischen Gefangenen (Berlin: Akademie der Künste, 1956);

Der spielende Mensch in der Arbeitswelt: Vortrag (Celle: Pohl, 1957);

Das Schöne und das Wahre: Neue Studien zur modernen Literatur (Munich: Piper, 1958);

Deutsche Literatur seit 1945 (Aarau: Privatdruck der Literarischen und Lesegesellschaft Aarau, 1958);

Rainer Maria Rilke in Selbstzeugnissen und Bilddokumenten (Reinbek: Rowohlt, 1958); translated by W. H. Hargreaves as *Portrait of Rilke: An Il-*

Hans Egon Holthusen in 1957 (Ullstein)

lustrated Biography (New York: Herder & Herder, 1971);

Kritisches Verstehen: Neue Aufsätze zur Literatur (Munich: Piper, 1961);

Avantgardismus und die Zukunft der modernen Kunst (Munich: Piper, 1964);

Plädoyer für den Einzelnen: Kritische Beiträge zur literarischen Diskussion (Munich: Piper, 1967);

Kritische Versuche: Ausgewählte Essays (Darmstadt: Moderner Buch-Club, 1968);

Indiana Campus: Ein amerikanisches Tagebuch (Munich: Piper, 1969);

Eduard Mörike in Selbstzeugnissen und Bilddokumenten (Reinbeck: Rowohlt, 1971);

Kreiselkompaß: Kritische Versuche zur Literatur der Epoche (Munich: Piper, 1976);

Amerikaner und Deutsche: Dialog zweier Kulturen (Munich: Callwey, 1977);

Chicago: Metropolis am Michigansee (Munich: Piper, 1981);

Sartre in Stammheim: Zwei Themen aus den Jahren der großen Turbulenz (Stuttgart: Klett-Cotta, 1982);

Opus 19: Reden und Widerreden aus fünfundzwanzig Jahren (Munich: Piper, 1983);

Gottfried Benn: Leben, Werk, Widerspruch 1886-1922 (Stuttgart: Klett-Cotta, 1986).

OTHER: *Ergriffenes Dasein: Deutsche Lyrik, 1900-1950*, edited by Holthusen and Friedhelm Kemp (Ebenhausen: Langewiesche-Brandt, 1953); enlarged as *Ergriffenes Dasein: Deutsche Lyrik des zwanzigsten Jahrhunderts* (Ebenhausen: Langewiesche-Brandt, 1957);

"Gedenkworte," in *Totenreden für Gottfried Benn* (Wiesbaden: Limes, 1956), pp. 15-21;

"Die Einheit der modernen Welt," in *Mensch im Zwiespalt der Zeit: Versuch einer Diagnose*, edited by Max Bleibnihaus (Nuremberg: Glock & Litz, 1958);

"Das lyrische Kunstwerk," in *Deutsche Philologie im Aufriß*, edited by Wolfgang Stammler (Berlin: Schmidt, 1962), pp. 1399-1428;

"Unwiederbringliche Stadt," in Eberhard von Cranach-Sichart, *Die Reise nach Wertheim: 2 Erzählungen* (Berlin: Evangelische Verlagsanstalt, 1966);

Gottfried Benn, *Weinhaus Wolf; Die Stimme hinter dem Vorhang*, epilogue by Holthusen (Stuttgart: Reclam, 1967);

"Rainer Maria Rilke 1875-1926," in *Die großen Deutschen: Deutsche Biographie*, volume 4, edited by Hermann Heimpel and others (Berlin: Propyläen, 1967), pp. 464-477;

Eduard Friedrich Mörike, *Gedichte*, edited by Holthusen (Frankfurt am Main: Fischer, 1968);

"Porträt eines jungen Mannes, der freiwillig zur SS ging," in *War ich ein Nazi: Politik-Anfechtung des Gewissens*, edited by Ludwig Marcuse (Munich: Rütten & Loenig, 1968), pp. 39-89;

"Aussichten einer Akademie in dieser Stunde," in *Internationales Jahrbuch für Literatur: Ensemble 1* (Munich: Deutscher Taschenbuch Verlag, 1969), pp. 249-261;

"Versuch über einen Reisetag," in *Ensemble*, edited by C. G. Podewik and Heinz Piontek (Berlin: Deutscher Taschenbuch Verlag, 1969);

"German Literature and the Experience of Nazism," in *Literature and Western Civilization*, edited by David Daiches and Anthony Thoolby (London: Aldus Books, 1972), pp. 315-338;

Information und Imagination, edited by Holthusen (Munich: Piper, 1973);

Rudolf Alexander Schröder, *Ausgewählte Gedichte*, afterword by Holthusen (Frankfurt am Main: Suhrkamp, 1978).

PERIODICAL PUBLICATIONS: "Der Aufbruch: Aufzeichnungen aus dem polnischen Kriege," *Eckart*, 16, no. 3 (March 1940): 75-77; no. 4 (April 1940): 104-107;

"Ist Europa am Ende?," *Universitas*, 8 (September 1953): 465-470;

"Vollkommen sinnliche Rede," *Akzente*, 2 (1955): 346-356;

"Das unmögliche Geschäft des Gedichts," *Merkur*, 9 (March 1955): 295-298;

"Ernst Jünger," *Universitas*, 10 (June 1955): 605-611;

"Die Lust am Englischen," *Hochland*, 49 (1957): 475-479;

"Literatur ohne Kritiker: Anmerkungen zu einem 'Lexikon der Weltliteratur im 20. Jahrhundert,' " *Hochland*, 53 (1960): 79-83;

"Die literarische Opposition," *Süddeutsche Zeitung*, 26 November 1960;

"Geschichte einer Emigration," *Merkur*, 14 (December 1960): 1204-1208;

"Eine deutsche Schaubude in Amerika: Theorie und Praxis des 'Goethe House,' " *Der Monat*, 15 (January 1963): 24-33;

"1014 Fifth Avenue: Als Leiter des New Yorker Goethe-Hauses: Ein Erfahrungsbericht," *Frankfurter Allgemeine Zeitung*, 24 October 1964;

"Jens Dampf in allen Gassen: Walter Jens 'Republikanische Reden' gegen die Republik," *Die Welt*, 23 July 1977;

"Einer, dem auf Erden nicht zu helfen war," *German Studies Review*, 1 (February 1978): 72-90;

"Windige Stadt: Versuch über Chicago," *Merkur*, 33 (January 1979): 65-79;

"Kontrapunktisches Denken: Zu Friedrich Sengles *Biedermeierzeit*," *Merkur*, 37 (April 1983): 332-337;

"Warum ich die Akademie verließ: Ein offener
Brief an Günter Grass," *Die Welt*, 7 April
1984, p. 17;
"Heimweh nach Geschichte: Postmoderne und
Posthistorie in der Literatur der Gegenwart," *Merkur*, 38 (December 1984): 902-
917.

Hans Egon Holthusen's repeated invocation
to "meine Brüder in Apoll" (my brothers in
Apollo) and his long-standing affiliation with the
journal *Merkur* give rise to the suggestion that
this classically oriented poet, critic, essayist, and
novelist operates within a tradition defined at
least in part by heroic proportions and expectations. Mercury-like, Holthusen has served for decades as a messenger between the cultures of
Germany and America, all the while striving to mediate in both quasi-political and scholarly capaci-
ties between a traditional aesthetic and an
increasingly radical definition of literature. His
place in modern German letters is anchored no
less by a modest amount of superior poetry than
by the meticulously crafted essays collected, as of
1988, in eight volumes. Holthusen's best-known
title, *Der unbehauste Mensch* (The Homeless Man,
1951), captured the imagination of a generation
of postwar readers, but today it ill defines one
whose home in contemporary belles lettres is by
all indications remarkably secure.

The eldest of five children of Johannes
Holthusen, a Lutheran pastor, and Alma Hagel-
stein Holthusen, Hans Egon Holthusen was born
in 1913 in Rendsburg, Schleswig-Holstein. He
came of age in exceedingly turbulent times. As a
student at the Andreanum Gymnasium in Hildesheim, he flirted with radical intellectual causes
and identified with Marxist political methods. By
1933, however, Holthusen had jettisoned Marxism; that year he joined the SS. In "Porträt eines
jungen Mannes, der freiwillig zur SS ging" (Portrait of a Young Man Who Volunteered for the
SS, 1968), Holthusen reflects that his motives issued from a mixture of parental nationalism, intellectual curiosity, indiscriminate reliance upon
radical solutions to contemporary social and economic problems, and a naive fascination with the
trappings of power. It was a short-lived attraction. By 1937, while still a student, Holthusen
had quit the SS. He had by then pursued
Germanistik (German philology) for six years at
the Universities of Tübingen, Berlin, and Munich
and had defended his dissertation on Rilke's

Sonette an Orpheus (1923; translated as *Sonnets to Orpheus*, 1936).

The years 1937 to 1939 saw Holthusen's
first publications in periodicals such as *Neue
Rundschau, Hochland*, and *Eckart*, as well as brief editorial employment with the Goethe Institute in
Munich, but war swept aside these early efforts
to establish a literary career. In contrast to his earlier affiliation with the SS, Holthusen's active military service was as a common soldier with duty
on both fronts. His brother Walter fell in 1942, a
trauma transmuted into one of Holthusen's most
influential works, the cycle of sonnets *Klage um
den Bruder* (Lament for My Brother, 1947). After
three years in Russia, Holthusen returned in
1945 to Munich, where he was attached to a translator unit. The disaffection which had led to his
resignation from the SS in 1937, compounded by
the events of the intervening years—not the least
of which was the harassment of his father, who
died in 1938, as a member of the Bekennende
Kirche (Confessional Church)—led Holthusen
into association with the April 1945 putsch attempted by the resistance movement "Frei-
heitsaktion Bayern" (Bavarian Freedom Action).

Cleared without detention in the denazification proceedings, Holthusen was free to resume his literary career immediately after the
war. The poem for which he is best known, "Tabula rasa," appeared in 1945, followed by
"Heimkehr" (Coming Home) in the first issue of
Merkur in 1947. Over the next several years
Holthusen worked with extraordinary energy
both on the poems which were collected in 1949
in the volume *Hier in der Zeit* (Here in This
Time) and on the many essays which established
him as the most frequent single contributor to
Merkur and as one of the most influential postwar voices in German letters.

During the following three decades
Holthusen participated in a program of international travel and intellectual exchange that may
be unparalleled in postwar history. An Anglo-
American connection was established by encounters with W. H. Auden in 1945 and T. S. Eliot in
1946; these two poets, along with Rilke, Wilhelm
Lehmann, and Gottfried Benn, are the most
often cited in Holthusen's oeuvre. In 1951
Holthusen undertook a lecture tour of England
and Holland, and in 1953 he was one of four Germans invited to participate in Harvard's International Summer Seminar. This first experience in
America led to visiting professorships at Northwestern University in 1959 and at the University

of Chicago in 1960. The breadth of Holthusen's intellectual and cultural associations, plus his own considerable status as a poet and as a member since 1956 of the Berlin Academy of Arts, led to his appointment in 1961 as director of the New York Goethe House. Holthusen's three-year directorship brought an extraordinary level of activity to 1014 Fifth Avenue, including presentations by Germany's premier authors, musicians, artists, and critics. Holthusen moved with great diplomatic skill between the émigré community and guests from Germany, radicals and conservatives, and the other factions on the German-American intellectual scene. Although he declined a second term to resume writing in Munich, he returned to the United States as a visiting professor at the University of Pittsburgh in 1965 and at Indiana University in 1967. In 1968 he accepted a tenured position on the faculty of Northwestern University. At about the same time he was elected president of the Bavarian Academy of Fine Arts, a post which involved many of the same diplomatic skills he had manifested as director of the Goethe House. Holthusen divided his time between Evanston and Munich until he stepped down as president of the Bavarian Academy in 1974, after which he continued to spend one semester at Northwestern and the balance of each year traveling or in Munich. He retired from Northwestern in 1981 to become a fellow of the newly founded Wissenschaftskolleg (Institute for Advanced Study) in Berlin; a year later he returned to Munich and full-time writing. Awards and honors conferred on Holthusen include the Prize for Literature from the Confederation of German Industry in 1954, the Cultural Prize of the City of Kiel in 1956, the Bavarian Prize for Literature (Jean Paul-Preis) in 1983, and the Bavarian Order of Merit and the Schleswig-Holstein Art Prize in 1984. Two important collections of essays, *Sartre in Stammheim: Zwei Themen aus den Jahren der großen Turbulenz* (Sartre in Stammheim: Two Themes from the Years of the Great Turbulence, 1982) and *Opus 19: Reden und Widerreden aus fünfundzwanzig Jahren* (Opus 19: Addresses and Rebuttals of 25 Years, 1983), have appeared since Holthusen's "retirement," and in 1986, at seventy-three, he completed the first volume of an extensive critical biography of Benn. He has been married twice: on 5 June 1950 to Lore Schäder and on 28 October 1952 to Inge Havemeier; he has a son and a stepdaughter.

Holthusen's earlier poetry and many of his essays have as their common source the collision of German classical humanism with World War II. The young Germanist's fascination with Rilke, which produced a dissertation, two monographs, and several essays, has unmistakable reflections in Holthusen's own poetry: a resonant lyricism and a classical lexicon prepared to discover new beauty in nature, in loneliness, and in questions of transcendental values. In the first elegy of his "Trilogie des Krieges" (War Trilogy), included in *Hier in der Zeit*, this spirit collides with the invasion of Poland in 1939:

> Plötzlich war es den Völkern unmöglich, einander
>   zu dulden,
> Und eine Stunde September, eine Stunde im späte-
>   ren Sommer,
> Heiß und träg und wie immer, eine Stunde der
>   Hirten und Jäger
> (Goldgrün kräuselt sich das Moos, in den Wäldern
>   roch man die Sonne,
> Feiner, sahniger Schweiß bedeckte die Hände der
>   Menschen),
> Diese beliebige Stunde war die Stunde entsetzlicher
>   Reife.

> (Suddenly it was impossible for people to tolerate
>   each other,
> And one September hour, one late summer hour,
> Hot and lazy and as always an hour for shepherds
>   and hunters
> [Greengold curled the moss, in the woods one
>   smelled the sunshine,
> Fine, creamy perspiration covered one's hands],
> This arbitrary hour was the hour of terrible
>   harvest).

The popularity of these poems and the cycle of sonnets dedicated to Holthusen's brother obviously had to do with the comfort they gave many readers attempting to deal with their own losses, but beyond that thematic solace there is a reassertion of strict aesthetic form over personal and, by extension, national chaos. The remaining poems in *Hier in der Zeit* turn gradually away from the immediate experiences of war to a more general, even existential anguish. The final poem in the collection goes beyond this anguish to turn images of shipwreck and defeat into an affirmation of Christian faith:

> Gib mir, o Herr, am Strande der reinen
>   Entbehrung
> Süßem Zusammenbruch auf den Kieseln der Unbill,
> Und meine Seele, veratmend und langsam
>   getröstet,
> Möge sich endlich stillen und lösen wie eine
> Beere im dunkelnden Wein der Geduld.

(Grant me, O Lord, on the shores of pure privation
Sweet shipwreck on the coarse gravel of injustice,
That my breathless soul might gradually find solace
And sustenance, and dissolve like a
Berry in the darkening wine of patience).

The image of the labyrinth, symbolizing man's fruitless wandering in a worldly garden ungraced by faith, is the starting point for Holthusen's second collection of poems, *Labyrinthische Jahre* (Labyrinthine Years, 1952). The first eight poems, grouped as "Acht Variationen über Zeit und Tod" (Eight Variations on Time and Death), reflect a continuum on several levels with the later poems in *Hier in der Zeit*. But the dominant influence is now less Rilke than Eliot, who also figures repeatedly in essays by Holthusen.

The second group of poems in *Labyrinthische Jahre* shifts in tone and theme away from echoes of Eliot to a celebration of the beauty of nature. Poems such as "April," "Sommermorgen im Wallis" (Summer Morning in Valais), "Früh im Herbst" (Early in the Fall), and "Ende September" are strongly reminiscent of the Naturmagie (magical nature) of Lehmann. There is no absolute sanctuary in nature in these poems, however, no escape from reminders of one's own mortality, of the fragile quality of love, or of the readiness of barbarism to shatter short-lived tranquillity. These reminders figure even more prominently in the last cycle of poems in the collection, poems which also become more abstract and more universal in their reach. There are references to Marx and Mao and a smiling Buddha, and the landscape broadens to include China as well as Europe. When Holthusen turned his creative efforts away from poetry after the publication of *Labyrinthische Jahre*, he was at the apogee of a steady development from his earliest models and most immediate personal experiences to a mature and sophisticated lyrical statement.

The attention paid Holthusen's poetry has paled beside the influence of his essays. As of 1988 he had composed well over sixty essays, many of which have been collected in widely discussed volumes whose titles have become part of the grammar of contemporary German literary and cultural criticism: *Der unbehauste Mensch, Ja und Nein* (Yes and No, 1954), *Das Schöne und das Wahre* (The Beautiful and the True, 1958), and *Kritisches Verstehen* (Critical Understanding, 1961). His ability to render broad contemporary intellec-

tual issues immediately accessible contributed to a well-deserved reputation as "Stichwortgeber der Epoche" (keywordsmith of the epoch). More than mere verbal facility, this talent as "keywordsmith" flows from a classical education, an acute sense of style schooled by a passion for some of the finest writers in the Western tradition, and an uncompromisingly humanistic value system. As an essayist Holthusen joins a limited brotherhood of twentieth-century German writers, including Benn, Thomas Mann, Hermann Broch, and perhaps Ernst Jünger, who have elevated the essay to a literary art form.

It would be difficult to find in these essays the same kind of clear thematic and stylistic development that characterizes Holthusen's poetry. There are gradually developing critical assessments of major figures such as Rilke, Benn, and Eliot, but some of the later essays reverse or modify positions taken in earlier treatments of the same author—for example, "Thomas Mann und die Nachwelt" (Thomas Mann and Posterity) in *Kreiselkompaß* (Gyro-Compass, 1976) as compared with the early and vehement review of Mann's *Doktor Faustus* (1947; translated as *Doctor Faustus*, 1948), *Die Welt ohne Transzendenz* (World without Transcendence, 1949). Some of the essays are devoted to an exchange with Hans Magnus Enzensberger that started in 1960; a sizable number to largely ceremonial occasions recognizing significant milestones in the career of friends, fellow poets, and patrons; and still others to reviews of contemporary American writers, including Katherine Anne Porter, Mary McCarthy, Truman Capote, and James Baldwin.

The most extensive critical treatment of Holthusen's essays, a 1980 dissertation by John Joseph Rock, identifies three general thematic categories: essays that deal with the relationship between beauty and art, those that deal with the twentieth-century tendency toward the politicization of literature, and those that deal broadly with intercultural (primarily German-American) relations. In the first category Rock lists "Versuch über das Gedicht" (An Essay on Poetry), "Über den sauren Kitsch" (On Sour Kitsch), "Gott als Tabu" (God as Taboo), and "Das Schöne und das Wahre in der Poesie" (The Beautiful and the True in Poetry). In these and the many other essays in this category Holthusen is concerned primarily with probing the difference between aesthetic and philosophical truth. One of the distinguishing features of his critical approach to Rilke, in fact, has been his willingness to embrace

Holthusen in 1972 (Ullstein–Karoly Forgacs)

Rilke's lyrical achievement while rejecting his concept of an interpersonal love which claims to be independent of the other person. Similarly, Holthusen can celebrate the elegant aesthetic truths in Benn's poetry while distancing himself from the latter's conceptual position, which is considerably at odds with Holthusen's Christian beliefs. This distinction is most clearly framed in "Das Schöne und das Wahre": "Das Wahre, das in einer Poesie zum Leuchten kommt, ist offenbar von grundsätzlich anderer Art als das Wahre, das in der naiven, in der wissenschaftlichen, der philosophischen oder der theologischen Rede ergriffen werden soll. Es ist ein Wahres, das nur im Schönen oder durch das Schöne hindurch erscheint" (The True revealed in poetry is manifestly of a different order than the True accessible through lay, scientific, philosophical or theological discourse. It is a True that is only revealed in or through the Beautiful).

Rock's second category includes the well-known essays "Günter Grass als politischer Autor," "Thomas Mann und die Nachwelt," and "Literatur und Rechtfertigung" (Literature and Justification). To these should be added the powerful "Utopie und Katastrophe: Der Lyriker Hans Magnus Enzensberger 1957-1978" and "Sartre in Stammheim: Literatur und Terrorismus" in *Sartre in Stammheim*. In these essays Holthusen defends the venerable tradition of the political poem, of socially engaged, relevant literature, but castigates the subversion of literature by ideology, whether of the right or the left. In the first essay of the volume *Plädoyer für den Einzelnen* (Plea for the Individual, 1967), "Poesie und Politik: Überlegungen zum Problem des literarischen Engagements" (Poetry and Politics: Reflections on the Problem of Literary Engagement), Holthusen writes: "Das politische Gedicht kann, wenn es gut ist, ein Zeugnis überparteilicher Menschlichkeit sein in der blinden, haßerfüllten, von moralischen Ironien genarrten Sphäre des politischen Parteiergreifens" (The political poem, if it is good, can be a testimonial to nonpartisan humanity in the blind, hate-filled sphere of foolishly competing, morally confused political ideologies). Although open since adolescence to a variety of political ideas, Holthusen takes a clearly conservative posture in these essays, whether criticizing *Doktor Faustus* in 1949 or Enzensberger and Jean-Paul Sartre in 1982. A consistent theme is an exasperation with authors and critics who are too eager to attack the Federal Republic or the United States as authoritarian or even fascist. In resisting what he feels is an unwarranted ideological bent in the criticism of the 1970s, he has, in "Rilke-Finsternis–vorübergehend" (Rilke-Eclipse–Temporarily), defend-fended Rilke against charges of proto-fascism and denied, in "Einer, dem auf Erden nicht zu helfen war" (One Who Was Not To Be Helped on This Earth), that Heinrich von Kleist was a victim of an inhospitable, bourgeois age. *Sartre in Stammheim* contains Holthusen's most forceful indictment of antiestablishment literary figures. Decrying "das pseudopolitische Blendwerk der enzensbergerschen Revolutionstheorie" (the pseudopolitical hocus-pocus of Enzensberger's theory of revolution), Holthusen caps his long-standing debate with one of the chief West German antiauthoritarian prophets of the 1960s by defending the poetic truth of Enzensberger's long poem *Der Untergang der Titanic: Eine Komödie* (1978; translated as *The Sinking of the Titanic*, 1980) while disputing the political legitimacy of its apocalyptic vision of Western Europe. Although milder in his treatment of Sartre, whose visit to the terrorist Andreas Baader in Stammheim prison in 1974 forms the starting point for a brilliant essay on terrorism and literature, Holthusen is uncompromising in condemning the exploitation of literature to serve anarchy in the name of revolution. Sartre's advocacy of terrorism in *Les Mouches* (1943; translated as *The Flies*, 1946) made sense in occupied France, but "der altgewordene Protagonist der antifaschistischen Generation" (the aging protagonist of the antifascist generation) was tempted, according to Holthusen, into applying once legitimate categories of thought to a completely new and different situation: terrorism aimed at undermining neither a fascist state nor an occupying power but one of the most stable and democratic of countries.

Holthusen's willingness to defend the Federal Republic and to preserve in postwar German society the classical values of its bourgeois heritage has been a major factor in his success as a cultural diplomat and as a professor of German at American universities. This voice resonates strongly in the third category of essays, those with an intercultural theme, such as "Unter amerikanischen Intellektuellen" (Among American Intellectuals), "Die Einheit der modernen Welt" (The Unity of the Modern World), "Deutscher Geist im Urteil der Welt" (German Culture in World Opinion), "Amerikaner und Deutsche–Dialog zweier Kulturen" (Americans and Germans–Dialogue between Two Cultures), and the monograph *Indiana Campus: Ein amerikanisches Tagebuch* (Indiana Campus: An American Diary, 1969). The last work relates Holthusen's experience of the American student protest movement of the late 1960s. He saw the students in Germany and the United States wrestling with a common dilemma: "Ihr Problem, so könnte man sagen, war ein Übermaß an revolutionärer Phantasie bei gänzlicher Abwesenheit einer revolutionären Situation" (Their problem, one could say, was an excess of revolutionary imagination in the total absence of a revolutionary situation). The contrast between these dispassionate observations on the protests of the 1960s and the intensity of the essay on Sartre speaks eloquently about the costs to society of the metamorphosis of protest into terrorism.

In the middle of his career–as measured from the dissertation on Rilke in 1937 to the critical biography of Benn in 1986–Holthusen ventured into prose fiction with a novel entitled *Das Schiff: Aufzeichnungen eines Passagiers* (The Ship: Notes of a Passenger, 1956; translated as *The Crossing*, 1959). The novel consists of nineteen entries in the diary of a postwar Atlantic crossing by a German poet named Hans. Retreating from an unhappy affair with an American girl, Hans finds himself surrounded by a bevy of Sweet Briar women bound for study and adventure in Europe. He is drawn into an affair with Mercy, while his Italian cabin mate scouts for wealth among Mercy's friends. Dining room, railing, deck, and corridor provide more opportunity for intellectual discussion than for romance, however, and Hans and Mercy part before the docking at Southampton. Less grotesque than Katherine Anne Porter's *Ship of Fools* (1962), less intellectual than Thomas Mann's *Der Zauberberg* (1924; translated as *The Magic Mountain*, 1927), Holthusen's novel attempts something of the same microcosmic view of an international community in transition. It fails because the intellectual partners are too unevenly matched, their exchanges rooted in European sophistication on the one side and American naivete on the other.

Part of the narrator's fascination with Mercy and her friends, in fact, is based on their lack of sophistication, especially as expressed in their American slang idiom. Another part is based on the same uncomplicated openness Holthusen would later celebrate in *Indiana Campus*, which at times strongly echoes the fictional premises of *Das Schiff*. In both works there is a curiously masculine loneliness, the longing of an older, more experienced intellect for the physical and emotional vitality represented by intelligent American coeds.

Holthusen's lifelong passion for truth and dedication to aesthetic style have earned him a formidable reputation but a fickle audience. His insistence on preserving traditional values, his delight in drawing upon a reservoir of classical images and phrases, and his critical scrutiny of some of the greatest names in the canon of modern German literature have their cost with readers seeking trendy commentary or superficial analysis. His disdain for antiestablishment causes, whether Gruppe 47 or the Baader-Meinhof gang, has led some to underestimate his open-mindedness and intellectual curiosity. It is precisely his strength, however, not to seek popularity at the expense of principle and to resist following the oscillations of public opinion. With the shift in the 1980s toward more conservative popular attitudes, the later essays may yet find the resonance that *Der unbehauste Mensch* or *Kritisches Verstehen* had with earlier readers.

References:

Helmuth deHaas, "Hans Egon Holthusens Lyrik," *Merkur*, 5 (August 1951): 776-787;

Peter Demetz, "Der Kritiker Holthusen: Wandlungen und Motive," *Merkur*, 14 (March 1960): 277-283;

Michael Hamburger, "Essay über den Essay," *Akzente*, 12 (1965): 291-292;

Rudolf Hartung, "Im Kreuzfeuer der Kritik: Hans Egon Holthusens *Schiff* und frühere Aufzeichnungen," *Der Monat*, 9 (January 1957): 66-71;

Klaus Günther Just, "Hans Egon Holthusen," *Universitas* (1959-1960): 382;

Werner R. Lehmann, "Zu Ehren Holthusens," *Neue Deutsche Hefte*, 31 (1984): 790-795;

John Joseph Rock, "Toward Orientation: The Life and Work of Hans Egon Holthusen," Ph.D. dissertation, Pennsylvania State University, 1980;

Werner Ross, "Aus der großen Turbulenz gerettet: Ein Meister des Versuches. Zu zwei neuen Prosabänden von Hans Egon Holthusen," *Die Welt*, 19 March 1983;

Herman Salinger, "Hans Egon Holthusen: The Panther and the Prophet," *Poetry*, 82 (1953): 335-341;

Albert von Schirnding, "Glaukon gibt Antwort: Hans Egon Holthusens neues Buch *Sartre in Stammheim*," *Merkur*, 37 (April 1983): 337-343.

Walter Jens

(8 March 1923-   )

Jochen Richter
Allegheny College

BOOKS: *Das weiße Taschentuch: Erzählung,* as Walter Freiburger (Hamburg: Hansischer Gildenverlag, 1947);

Nein: Die Welt der Angeklagten. Roman (Hamburg: Rowohlt, 1950);

Der Blinde (Hamburg: Rowohlt, 1951); edited by Harry Bergholz (New York: Holt, 1959); translated by Michael Bullock as *The Blind Man* (New York: Macmillan, 1954; London: Deutsch, 1954);

Vergessene Gesichter: Roman (Hamburg: Rowohlt, 1952);

Der Mann, der nicht alt werden wollte: Roman (Hamburg: Rowohlt, 1955);

Die Stichomythie in der frühen griechischen Tragödie (Munich: Beck, 1955);

Hofmannsthal und die Griechen (Tübingen: Niemeyer, 1955);

Ahasver: Hörspiel (Hamburg: Hans Bredow-Institut, 1956); edited by A. A. Wolff (London: Macmillan/New York: St. Martin's Press, 1964);

Ilias und Odyssee: Nacherzählt (Ravensburg: Maier, 1956);

Das Testament des Odysseus (Pfullingen: Neske, 1957);

Statt einer Literaturgeschichte (Pfullingen: Neske, 1957; enlarged, 1962; revised, 1978);

Moderne Literatur, moderne Wirklichkeit (Pfullingen: Neske, 1958);

Die Götter sind sterblich: Tagebuch einer Griechenlandreise (Pfullingen: Neske, 1959);

Deutsche Literatur der Gegenwart: Themen, Stile, Tendenzen (Munich: Piper, 1961);

Zueignungen: 11 literarische Porträts (Munich: Piper, 1962; revised, 1963);

Herr Meister: Dialog über einen Roman (Munich: Piper, 1963);

Melancholie und Moral: Rede auf Wolfgang Koeppen (Stuttgart: Goverts, 1963);

Literatur und Politik (Pfullingen: Neske, 1963);

Euripides; Büchner (Pfullingen: Neske, 1964);

Von deutscher Rede (Bremen: Angelsachsen-Verlag,

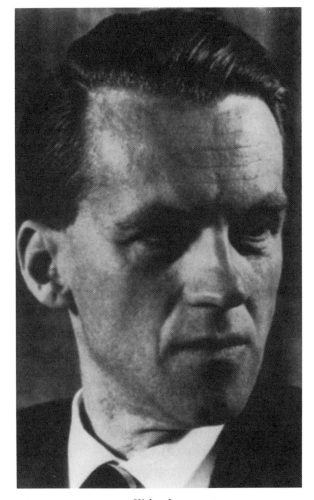

Walter Jens

1966; enlarged edition, Munich: Piper, 1969);

Der Besuch des Fremden: A Radio Play/Vergessene Gesichter: A Play Adapted from His Own Novel, edited by Wolff (London, Melbourne & Toronto: Macmillan/New York: St. Martin's Press, 1967);

Die Verschwörung (Grunwald: Norstar, 1969); republished with *Der tödliche Schlag* (Munich: Piper, 1974);

Bericht über eine Messe (Stuttgart: Mühlrain-Verlag, 1969);

Antiquierte Antike? Perspektiven eines neuen Humanismus (Münsterdorf: Hansen & Hansen, 1971);

Am Anfang der Stall, am Ende der Galgen: Jesus von Nazareth, seine Geschichte nach Matthäus (Stuttgart: Kreuz, 1972);

Fernsehen—Themen und Tabus: Momos 1963-1973 (Munich: Piper, 1973);

Der Fall Judas (Stuttgart: Kreuz, 1975);

Der Ausbruch: Libretto (Tübingen: Rotsch, 1975);

Republikanische Reden (Munich: Kindler, 1976);

Eine deutsche Universität: 500 Jahre Tübinger Gelehrtenrepublik, by Jens, Inge Jens, and Brigitte Beekmann (Munich: Kindler, 1977);

Zur Antike (Munich: Kindler, 1978);

Ort der Handlung ist Deutschland: Reden in erinnerungsfeindlicher Zeit (Munich: Kindler, 1981);

Die kleine große Stadt, Tübingen (Stuttgart: Theiss, 1981);

In Sachen Lessing (Stuttgart: Reclam, 1983);

Momos am Bildschirm, 1973-1983 (Munich: Piper, 1984);

Kanzel und Katheder (Munich: Kindler, 1984);

Rolf Escher (Stuttgart: Belser, 1984);

Dichtung und Religion, by Jens and Hans Küng (Munich: Kindler, 1985);

Festgabe zum 70. Geburtstag für Heinrich Albertz (Stuttgart: Radius-Verlag, 1985);

Roccos Erzählung (Stuttgart: Radius-Verlag, 1985);

Die Friedensfrau (Munich: Kindler, 1986);

Theologie und Literatur, by Jens and Küng (Munich: Kindler, 1986);

Anfang und Ende: Die Offenbarung des Johannes (Stuttgart: Reclam, 1987).

OTHER: "Der Telefonist: Hörspiel," in *Hörspielbuch* (Frankfurt am Main: Europäische Verlagsanstalt, 1957), pp. 45-80;

Griechische Klassiker, translated by Johann Heinrich Voss, Eduard Mörike, and others, edited by Jens (Munich, Vienna & Basel: Desch, 1959);

Eugen Gottlob Winkler, edited by Jens (Frankfurt am Main: Fischer, 1960);

Thomas Mann, *Buddenbrooks*, edited by Jens (Frankfurt am Main: Fischer, 1960);

"Der Besuch des Fremden: Hörspiel," in *Sechzehn deutsche Hörspiele*, edited by Hansjörg Schmitthenner (Munich: Piper, 1962), pp. 185-218;

Wolfdietrich Schnurre, *Kassiber*, afterword by Jens (Frankfurt am Main: Suhrkamp, 1964);

Jens circa 1960 (courtesy of the author)

Hans Mayer zum 60. Geburtstag, edited by Jens (Reinbek: Rowohlt, 1967);

Die Bauformen der griechischen Tragödie, edited by Jens (Munich: Fink, 1971);

Der barmherzige Samariter, edited by Jens (Stuttgart: Kreuz, 1973);

Assoziationen, edited by Jens (Stuttgart: Radius-Verlag, 1978);

Um Nichts als die Wahrheit, edited by Jens (Munich: Piper, 1978);

Warum ich Christ bin, edited by Jens (Munich: Kindler, 1979);

Aeschylus, *Die Orestie: Agamemnon; Die Choephoren; Die Eumeniden*, translated by Jens (Munich: Kindler, 1979);

Literatur und Kritik, edited by Jens (Stuttgart: Deutsche Verlag-Anstalt, 1980);

Frieden, edited by Jens (Stuttgart: Kreuz, 1981);

Bruno Kreisky, *Politik braucht Visionen*, edited by Jens (Königstein: Athenäum, 1982);

Euripides, *Der Untergang*, translated by Jens (Munich: Kindler, 1982);

In letzter Stunde, edited by Jens (Munich: Kindler, 1982);

Literatur in der Demokratie, edited by Jens (Munich: Kindler, 1983);

Vom Nächsten: Das Gleichnis vom barmherzigen Samariter heute gesehen, edited by Jens (Munich: Deutscher Taschenbuch Verlag, 1984);

Studentenalltag, edited by Jens (Munich: Droemer, 1985);

Rhetorik und Theologie, edited by Jens (Tübingen: Niemeyer, 1986).

PERIODICAL PUBLICATION: "Der Teufel lebt nicht mehr, mein Herr! Ein Totengespräch zwischen Lessing und Heine," *Die deutsche Bühne,* 5 (1979): 57-63.

For some critics Walter Jens is a second-rate author who owes his reputation to his prominence as critic, philologist, essayist, and professor of rhetoric rather than to the merit of his literary work; but Jens unquestionably occupies a prominent place in German postwar literature. The richness and diversity of his talents have made him a mediator between genres and cultures. His declared goal is to overcome the narrow confines of traditional literature and to find a synthesis between the sciences and the arts. He is considered a *poeta doctus,* a learned writer, who emphasizes his roots in the rationalist, democratic, and humanist tradition. The fact that most of his books had more than one edition and are also selling well as paperbacks indicates that he reaches a large audience. In addition, he has been awarded several prizes for literary excellence, among them the German-Swedish Culture Prize of the City of Stockholm in 1964, the prestigious Lessing Prize of the Hansestadt Hamburg in 1968, and the Heinrich Heine Prize of the City of Düsseldorf in 1981. His books have been translated into ten languages. Jens has an especially strong following in France, whereas he is virtually unknown in the United States.

Jens was born in Hamburg on 8 March 1923. His father, Walter Jens, was the president of a bank, and his mother, Anna Martens Jens, was a schoolteacher with socialist leanings. He grew up in a liberal, antifascist atmosphere. A severe case of asthma kept him from having to join the Hitler Youth or the German army. He attended the excellent and progressive Johanneum in Hamburg, where he noticed very early the marked discrimination against his Jewish classmates.

In 1941 Jens began to study Germanistik (German language and literature) at the University of Hamburg, but soon switched to the University of Freiburg, where he studied classics. He disagreed with the kind of literature the National Socialists offered as models and could not accept the strong interference of nationalist ideology in the field. Classics, on the other hand, was relatively free of political intrusion. In 1944 he received the Ph.D. for his dissertation "Die Stichomythie in Sophocles' Tragödien der Mannesjahre" (Stichomythia in Sophocles' Later Tragedies). His oral defense took place in a bomb shelter and was disrupted by an air attack. In 1946 Jens found work in the classics department at the University of Tübingen. He wrote his Habilitationsschrift (inaugural dissertation), "Libertas bei Tacitus," in 1949. On 10 February 1951 he married Dr. Inge Puttfarken; they have two sons, Tilman, born in 1954, and Christoph, born in 1965. Jens was appointed full professor in 1963.

Jens's first publication, a short parabolic narrative entitled *Das weiße Taschentuch* (The White Handkerchief) which appeared in 1947 under the pseudonym Walter Freiburger, describes two days in the life of the student O., who is on leave from prison. The prison represents a state which forces the inmates to submit to its totalitarian rule. Deprived of white handkerchiefs, the inmates have lost all hope of surrendering to a better outside force. Although the rulers of the prison are depicted as evil and demonic, individuals like O. also have to accept responsibility for their miserable condition because they had originally supported the evil powers. The prison represents fascist Germany and O. stands for the abused individual who is forced to conform to a totalitarian system without hope for escape. Although the historical references are unambiguous, the parabolic structure of the story allows for a more universal interpretation: there will always be oppressed and powerless people without white handkerchiefs. With its excessive pathos and neoexpressionistic style, the narrative can only be considered a preliminary exercise.

The novel *Nein: Die Welt der Angeklagten* (No: The World of the Accused, 1950) firmly established Jens's literary renown. It has been translated into eight languages, and several German editions have been issued. One year after its publication Jens was awarded the French Prize of the *Amis de la Liberté.* Twenty-two years after the last war, one power is ruling the earth. Society is di-

Fragment of a manuscript by Jens (by permission of the author)

vided into three classes: accused, witnesses, and judges. The supreme judge has chosen Walter Sturm, a former professor, as his successor. Sturm must either accept the position or die. He rejects the offer and is immediately executed. The final chapter shows the planet Earth thirty years later: "Gestalten lebten auf ihm. Früher nannte man sie: die Menschen" (Figures lived on it. In the past they were called: humans). The parabolic character of this negative utopian novel is obvious: again, fascist Germany serves as a model, and Sturm is the typical intellectual who did not dare say his "no" when it would have mattered. The reader is urged to learn the lesson before it is too late. The central theme of the novel is the destruction of the individual and his humanity by an inhumane system. Jens has said that Kafka's view of the world as a trial and of the machine as a metaphor for life influenced his writing of the novel; the short, precise, and paratactic narrative style can be traced to Hemingway. As is often the case in Jens's fiction, the protagonist shares such features as his first name, his profession, and some of his experiences with his author. In the year the novel was published Jens joined the Gruppe 47, the most influential literary organization in postwar Germany.

In the short novel *Der Blinde* (1951; translated as *The Blind Man*, 1954) the teacher Heinrich Mittenhaufen learns that he will be blind for the rest of his life. He tries to solve his crisis through a game given to him by a Jewish friend; the game had enabled the friend to survive in a concentration camp. The game consists of black polished blocks which were carved in a concentration camp. The blocks represent houses, streets, and people, allowing the players to create an imaginary world. In the concentration camp the blocks were used to overcome the hopelessness of the inmates and enabled the players to survive. Mittenhaufen, however, uses the game to isolate himself and to escape from his painful reality. He breaks the three rules connected with the game: One is only allowed to play (1) if no other help is available, (2) if one hopes to live again, and (3) if one creates a future which can later be transformed into reality. A fourth and most important rule is added later: One is not allowed to play the game alone. When Mittenhaufen finally recognizes the rules, the game loses its escapist quality, and he is able to accept help from his family. He learns that he was blind in his relationship with his family and his responsibilities to society while he still had the use of his eyes. Only as a blind man does he recognize his failings; "Ich bin immer blind gewesen. Ihr hättet es mir früher sagen müssen" (I have always been blind. You should have told me earlier). The paradox, that he was blind when he still had the use of his eyes and that he has learned to see only by going blind, reveals the parabolic character of the narrative. Mittenhaufen may be seen as a personification of recent German history: only by understanding and accepting the past and by learning the new game of democracy can postwar Germany break out of its isolation and resignation. On another level the novel reflects the dilemma of the artist, who must choose between retreat into his own imaginary world and his responsibility to society. The style of the novel is precise and clear; but the game does not function very convincingly, and the introduction of several concentration camp survivors to save one blind man appears artificial.

Der Blinde was followed by a longer novel, *Vergessene Gesichter* (Forgotten Faces), in 1952. Ten retired French actors living in a home for aged actors spend their time reminiscing, playing roles, and trying to cover up their isolation and loneliness. They miss the days when they were stars and everything centered around them. They are extreme individualists and soloists who cannot act as a team; only in their final performance, the "Play of Death and the Sick Man," do they act in unison. Jens seems to be suggesting new forms of art and social behavior in which soloists would be replaced by the team. Unfortunately the novel only strings together impressionistic dialogues and misses the opportunities offered by the themes of role-playing and identity.

The complex novel *Der Mann, der nicht alt werden wollte* (The Man Who Did Not Want to Grow Old, 1955) is the first attempt by Jens to realize his concept of *poeta doctus*. The narrator Friedrich Jacobs, a retired professor of literature, tries to find out why one of his former students, the author Wolfgang Bugenhagen, has committed suicide. His investigation forms the first level of the novel, the life and death of Bugenhagen form the second level, and the third is supplied by fragments of Bugenhagen's work. Through analysis of this work, Jacobs finds the root of the crisis in Bugenhagen's inability to overcome time and in his feelings of being an epigone oppressed by tradition and history; his suicide was a desperate attempt to achieve freedom. His crisis mirrors the crisis of modern art and is paralleled by a crisis in Jacobs's scientific method. Although

Charcoal drawing of Jens by Oskar Kreibich

Jacobs tries to remain detached and objective, he becomes increasingly involved in his investigation. As he does so, literature and literary analysis, which are two distinct modes of perception, are united. Jens demonstrates this process stylistically: Jacobs's dry and abstract prose again and again gives way to vivid and concrete language. Jens adds two epilogues to the novel. The first, by a fictitious teacher named Obergefell, condemns Bugenhagen's work as mediocre, paranoid, and unworthy of Jacobs's treatment. The other epilogue, written by Jens in his own name, mediates between Obergefell's harsh judgment and Jacobs's enthusiasm. With this novel Jens has abandoned the traditional form of narration and is trying to obliterate the difference between text and analysis.

Das Testament des Odysseus (Odysseus's Last Will, 1957) is Jens's first attempt to reinterpret a myth from a modern perspective. Odysseus appears as a pacifist and a melancholic sage, a writer whose life has been destroyed by a senseless war. The celebrated adventures of his return voyage to Ithaca are only stories he tells the ailing Priam, whom he befriended after the fall of

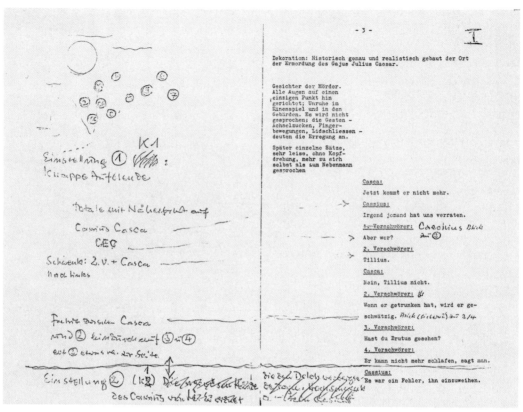

Typescript annotated by Jens for his teleplay Die Verschwörung *(by permission of the author)*

Jens and director Franz Josef Wild preparing for the 1969 broadcast of Die Verschwörung *(photograph by Will McBride)*

Jens in 1978 (Ullstein–Wolfgang Timmermann)

pose the twentieth century with the heroic ancient world. This task can only be achieved because the gods and myths are mortal; thus, each period can reinterpret them.

Herr Meister: Dialog über einen Roman (Herr Meister: Dialogue about a Novel, 1963) continues his experimentation with the novel form and takes the crisis of the genre as its main theme. The author appears as the writer A., as the professor of literature B., and as himself. A., looking for a subject for a new novel, sends plot outlines, summaries, and fragments to B., who critiques them and offers countersuggestions. In the process, the main character changes from a melancholic professor to a black man living in the United States, then to Martin Luther, Hamlet, and finally Odysseus. In the correspondence between A. and B. the entire history of the genre of the novel is discussed, and the critical role of B. comes to dominate the exchange. At the end the project is aborted; no novel has been written. Instead, A. and B. decide to permit Walter Jens to publish their correspondence. The fictitious dialogue about a novel that was never written explores the relationships among reality, art, and interpretation. The real problems of the author, Jens, are translated into fiction and at the same time commented on and analyzed. Most critics consider the novel a failure. Jens reached a dead end with *Herr Meister*, and he is too keen a literary critic not to recognize the fact. He has not written another novel.

After 1945 radio plays became a popular and accepted genre for German writers. Seven of Jens's plays were broadcast between 1951 and 1957, but only three appeared in print. *Der Besuch des Fremden* (The Visit of the Stranger, broadcast 1952, published 1967) analyzes the situation of the German intellectuals who refused to serve in Hitler's totalitarian regime. Professor Hartmann returns after sixteen years of exile to find that his daughter and son-in-law have been killed in an Allied air raid. Although Hartmann feels pity for the victims, he insists that his decision to oppose Hitler was the only correct one: if all had followed his example, no one would have had to die. As in his novel *Nein: Die Welt der Angeklagten*, Jens asserts his conviction that the only acceptable response to Hitler's barbarism is an unequivocal "No." *Ahasver* (1956) describes the suffering of the Jewish surgeon Albrecht Busch, who flees fascist Germany but does not find acceptance in France, Switzerland, or postwar Germany. Only shortly before his death does

Troy. He does not kill the suitors, as Homer reports; on the contrary, fearing a civil war, he does not return to Penelope, who has remarried. Although Jens has some problems concerning the motivation of Helena in her role as a warmonger, he uses the first-person narrative successfully to condemn war and to plead the case of the outcast, the defeated and homeless antihero. The novel skillfully exploits the tension between the expected heroic epic and modern pacifism.

A trip through Greece which ends in divided Germany is the subject of the diary *Die Götter sind sterblich* (The Gods Are Mortal, 1959). Jens freely mixes history and fiction and presents a sequence of reinterpretations of ancient myths. Myth, he says, is "vielleicht die einzige, die letzte und unverlierbare Sprache, in der wir uns noch verständigen können. Auch in Chicago ist Apollon zu Hause" (perhaps the only, the last and the never-lost language, in which we can still communicate. Apollo is at home in Chicago as well). The purpose of the book is to decipher the ancient myths for the present day and to juxta-

Cover for Jens's 1982 translation of Euripides' The Trojan Women

he experience the feeling of belonging and love he has sought all his life. The play was one of the earliest literary efforts to confront the problem of relations between Jews and Germans. The title of the play is taken from one of the names given the Wandering Jew in medieval legend. In "Der Telefonist" (The Operator, 1957) Karl Hentig, a telephone operator, decides to join the plot to assassinate Hitler on 20 July 1944. For the first time, Jens fully utilizes the technical possibilities of the radio play. The use of the telephone, sound effects depicting the atmosphere in a switchboard center, radio announcements, and shifting of time levels are employed to indict the fascist dictatorship and to memorialize those who sacrificed themselves.

During the 1960s television began to replace radio in importance, and Jens took an imme-

diate interest in the new medium. From 1963 to 1985 he wrote a weekly column of television criticism for the newspaper *Die Zeit* under the pseudonym Momos. He has also written television plays. In "Die rote Rosa" (Red Rosa), shown in 1963, Jens tries to rehabilitate the image of Rosa Luxemburg, the prominent leftist politician who was murdered in 1919. In a trial at which Luxemburg herself appears, both her nationalist murderers and the leftist supporters who deserted her are found guilty. The play, which has not been published, demonstrates how history is falsified by ideologies. Its success could be measured by the vehement protests from both left and right.

In 1967 Jens was appointed to a newly created chair for rhetoric at the University of Tübingen; he also served as a guest lecturer at the University of Stockholm, from which he received an honorary degree in 1969. In the same year his second teleplay, *Die Verschwörung* (The Conspiracy, 1969), was shown on German television. Another reinterpretation of a historical event, the play suggests that Julius Caesar carefully planned and staged his own assassination with the intent of immortalizing himself. By presenting well-known historical events and mythical or biblical subjects in a new light and from a different perspective, Jens "alienates" his material and forces his readers or spectators to reflect upon the role of history and tradition.

In the television play *Der tödliche Schlag* (The Deadly Blow, 1974) Jens establishes parallels between the destruction of Troy and the possible destruction of the world in the atomic age. Philoktet, who was replaced ten years previously as commander of the Greek army, is recalled to save the army from defeat. He tries to convince the Greeks of the immorality and senselessness of the destruction of Troy, but fails because of the machinations of the cold, cynical power-politician Odysseus.

In the 1970s Jens's work was dominated by scholarly productions, including translations, collections of essays and speeches, and editions of works by other authors. During this period he revealed a strong interest in biblical subjects, presenting them from a historical and social perspective and taking a critical view of dogmatic approaches. In *Der Fall Judas* (The Judas Case, 1975) he presents a case for the reevaluation of the Christian belief concerning the role of Judas. In Jens's opinion, Judas's treason, which is the *conditio sine qua non* for the Christian concept of salvation, is an act of the utmost faith which deserves sanctification rather than vilification. The petition to beatify Judas is denied and its advocates, the Franciscan Bertholt B. and the theologian Ettore P., like Judas before them, are vilified and persecuted. Implicit in this treatise is severe criticism of the Christian dogmatism that has led to the persecution of the Jews, because the traitor Judas has always been presented as the typical Jew.

In 1976 Jens was elected president of the West German section of P.E.N.; he held the office until 1982, when he was made honorary chairman of the organization. In 1979 he was awarded the Tübingen medal by his own university. That honor was obviously connected with his book *Eine deutsche Universität: 500 Jahre Tübinger Gelehrtenrepublik* (A German University: 500 Years of Scholarly Republic at Tübingen, 1977). Jens calls the book a *roman vrai*, but although he narrates the history of the city and the University of Tübingen in an entertaining way, the historical facts and essayistic reflections outweigh the fictional episodes by such a wide margin that the book cannot be considered a novel. The scholar dominates the poet—a fact which is also obvious in the annoying frequency of unnecessary Latin and Greek words.

Jens's television play "Der Teufel lebt nicht mehr, mein Herr! Ein Totengespräch zwischen Lessing und Heine" (The Devil No Longer Lives, Sir! A Dialogue between the Dead Lessing and Heine) was televised in honor of Lessing's 250th birthday in 1979. It also provided an opportunity for the Lessing Prize winner Jens to define his own position once more and to defend it against his critics. When the romantic poet Heine speaks of inspiration and genius, the *poeta doctus* Lessing responds: "Aber so seid Ihr nun einmal, Ihr Künstler. Spielt das Genie aus gegen das Talent, das Gebären gegen das Machen, das Entstehen gegen die Imitation. Schön, dann bin ich eben kein Künstler.... Sagt einmal, ist Euch noch nie der Gedanke gekommen, es könne Schriftsteller geben—so Handwerker wie mich, keine großen Poeten—Artisten, denen über einem Gedicht, nehmt Sappho oder Horaz, nicht minder vortreffliche Verse einfielen als Euch über dem Näschen einer angebeteten Schönheit?... Das ist Poesie an der Grenze des Philosophierens, mein Freund. Das Gedicht als Gedanke. Die Formel, die ins Bild gesetzt ist" (There you go again, you artists. Playing genius against talent, creation against craft, origination against imitation. Fine, then I should not be called an artist.... Tell me,

did you never think there could be writers—craftsmen like I am, no great poets—artisans who, while reading a poem by Sappho or Horace, for example, write poetry no less excellent than yours when you look at the cute nose of your adored beauty?... That is poetry at the threshold of philosophy, my friend. The poem as thought. The formula shaped into an image).

In the 1980s Jens's work has shown a marked tendency toward the theoretical. He concentrates his efforts in four areas: literary criticism, rhetoric, theology, and work for world peace. The literary criticism, mainly extending toward television, is intended to teach critical viewing and found its expression in two collections: *Fernsehen—Themen und Tabus* (Television—Themes and Taboos, 1973) and *Momos am Bildschirm* (Momos in Front of the TV Monitor, 1984). Both collections show Jens's commitment toward the artistic, political, and moral values of rationalism. A similar commitment is obvious in the two volumes of collected essays and speeches *Ort der Handlung ist Deutschland* (The Place of the Action is Germany, 1981) and *Kanzel und Katheder* (Pulpit and Lectern, 1984). The common theme of most of these works is an effort to combine art and science within a social context. As the title of the last collection suggests, Jens also continues to explore biblical and theological themes. He edited a collection of essays about the parable of the Good Samaritan, *Vom Nächsten: Das Gleichnis vom barmherzigen Samariter heute gesehen* (About Your Neighbor: The Parable of the Good Samaritan Seen Today, 1984). With the theologian Hans Küng, he published *Dichtung und Religion* (Fiction and Religion, 1985), a dialogue which tries to bridge the two academic disciplines. Again with Küng as coauthor, he published *Theologie und Literatur* (Theology and Literature, 1986); the same year he edited *Rhetorik und Theologie* (Rhetoric and Theology). In 1987 he published a reinterpretation of the Book of Revelation, *Anfang und Ende: Die Offenbarung des Johannes* (Beginning and End: The Revelation of St. John). Finally, he has continued his strong commitment to peace, which was already evident in his first narrative, *Das weiße Taschentuch*. He edited a volume of essays, *In letzter Stunde* (In the Last Hour, 1982), advocating disarmament and wrote two modern adaptations of Greek plays dealing with peace: *Der Untergang* (The Destruction, 1982) is based on Euripides' antiwar play *The Trojan Women*; *Die Friedensfrau* (1986) uses Aristophanes' *Lysistrata* as a source. Together with a small volume offering

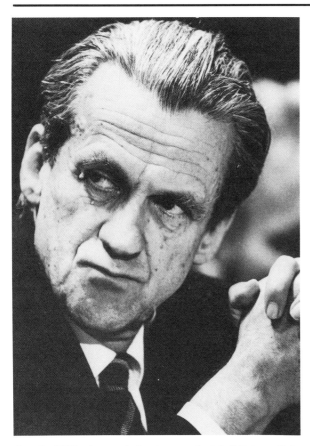

Jens in 1983, the year before he won the Adolf Grimme Prize from the Deutsche Volkshochschulverband and the medal for arts and sciences of the City of Hamburg (Ullstein–AP)

texts to be used in Ludwig van Beethoven's *Fidelio*, called *Roccos Erzählung* (Rocco's Tale, 1985), the two adaptations are the only literary works Jens has produced in the 1980s. Nevertheless, he is an important contributor to modern German literature precisely because of his rare capability to combine the theoretical with the creative. Like Lessing, his model, Jens carries on the business of enlightenment as poet and scholar. In 1981 he was awarded the prestigious Heinrich Heine Prize of the City of Düsseldorf, followed in 1984 by the Adolf Grimme Prize of the Deutsche Volkshochschulverband. The prize, however, which best expresses Jens's unique contributions is the 1984 medal for art and sciences of the City of Hamburg, because it has been his lifelong goal to combine these two modes of thinking and expression as *poeta doctus*.

Bibliographies:

Jürgen Kolbe, "Walter Jens," in *Deutsche Literatur der Gegenwart in Einzeldarstellungen*, edited by Dietrich Weber, third edition, volume 1 (Stuttgart: Kröner, 1976), pp. 338-357;

Manfred Lauffs, "Walter Jens," in *Kritisches Lexikon zur deutschsprachigen Gegenwartsliteratur*, edited by Heinz Ludwig Arnold, volume 3 (Munich: Edition text + kritik, 1978).

References:

Heinz Ludwig Arnold, *Als Schriftsteller leben* (Reinbek: Rowohlt, 1979), pp. 97-116;

H. W. Bähr, "Grenzen des Romans? Zu dem neuen Buch von Walter Jens," *Universitas*, 12 (1963): 1359-1361;

Kurt Batt, "Groteske und Parabel," *Neue Deutsche Literatur*, 7 (1964): 57-66;

Friedhelm Baukloh, "Noch einmal: Der Spiegelmensch," review of *Der Mann, der nicht alt werden wollte, Frankfurter Hefte*, 1 (1956): 63-64;

Ulrich Berls, "Walter Jens als politischer Schriftsteller und Rhetor," Ph.D. dissertation, University of Tübingen, 1984;

Manfred Durzak, *Der deutsche Roman der Gegenwart* (Stuttgart: Kohlhammer, 1971), pp. 274-296;

Hans Magnus Enzensberger, Review of *Herr Meister, Der Spiegel*, 2 October 1963, p. 92;

Ivo Frenzel, "Typologie des Schriftstellers," review of *Statt einer Literaturgeschichte, Frankfurter Hefte*, 2 (1958): 145-146;

Karl August Horst, "Walter Jens oder die Bestimmung des Unbestimmbaren in der Literatur," *Merkur*, 15 (1961): 587-590;

Gottfried Just and others, *Walter Jens: Eine Einführung* (Munich: Piper, 1965);

Joachim Kaiser, "Walter Jens," in *Schriftsteller der Gegenwart*, edited by Klaus Nonnenmann (Freiburg im Beisgau: Olten, 1963), pp. 177-182;

Thilo Koch, *Ähnlichkeit mit lebenden Personen ist beabsichtigt: Begegnungen* (Reinbek: Rowohlt, 1972), pp. 283-293;

Herbert Kraft, "Das literarische Werk von Walter Jens," in *Lexikon der deutschsprachigen Gegenwartsliteratur*, edited by H. Wiesner (Munich: Nymphenburger Verlagshandlung, 1981), pp. 247-249;

Gerhard F. Kramer, "Lessingpreis für Walter Jens," in *Jahrbuch der Akademie der Künste in Hamburg* (Hamburg, 1968), pp. 200-209;

Manfred Lauffs, " 'Meister' Jens: Dialog über einen 'Dialog über einen Roman,' " *Wirkendes Wort*, 2 (1980): 92-107;

Lauffs, *Walter Jens* (Munich: Beck, 1980);

Cornel Meder, "Walter Jens oder Die Entwicklung eines Poeta doctus," Ph.D. dissertation, University of Luxembourg, 1966;

Hans Schwab-Felisch, Review of *Der Blinde, Der Monat*, 40 (1952): 426-427;

Heinrich Vormweg, "Walter Jens und ein Ende?," *Merkur*, 18 (1964): 879-884;

Jürgen P. Wallmann, "J in A und B," *Der Monat*, 183 (1963): 83-86;

Helmut Wiemken, "Soziale Utopien: Bemerkungen zu Büchern von George Orwell und Walter Jens," *Deutsche Universitätszeitung*, 12 (1954): 14-17.

Hermann Kasack
(24 July 1896-10 January 1966)

Michael Winkler
Rice University

BOOKS: *Das schöne Fräulein: Ein Stück in acht Szenen* (Munich: Roland, 1918);

Der Mensch: Verse (Munich: Roland, 1918);

Die Heimsuchung: Eine Erzählung (Munich: Roland, 1919; revised edition, Berlin: Die Schmiede, 1922);

Die tragische Sendung: Ein dramatisches Ereignis in zehn Szenen (Berlin: Rowohlt, 1920);

Die Schwester: Eine Tragödie in acht Stationen (Berlin: Rowohlt, 1920);

Die Insel: Gedichte (Berlin: Rowohlt, 1920);

Der Gesang des Jahres (Potsdam: Kiepenheuer, 1921);

Stadium: Eine Gedicht-Reihe (Potsdam: Kiepenheuer, 1921);

Vincent: Schauspiel in fünf Akten (Potsdam: Kiepenheuer, 1924);

Wolf Przygode (Berlin: Privately printed, 1927);

Echo: Achtunddreißig Gedichte (Berlin: Rabenpresse, 1933);

Tull der Meisterspringer (Leipzig & Vienna: Schneider, 1935);

Der Strom der Welt: Gedichte (Hamburg: Ellermann, 1940);

Das ewige Dasein: Gedichte (Berlin: Suhrkamp, 1943; enlarged edition, Frankfurt am Main: Suhrkamp, 1949);

Die Stadt hinter dem Strom (Berlin & Amsterdam: Bermann-Fischer, 1949; Frankfurt am Main: Suhrkamp, 1949; revised, Frankfurt am Main: Suhrkamp, 1956); translated by Peter de Mendelssohn as *The City beyond the River* (London, Toronto & New York: Longmans, Green, 1953);

Hermann Kasack in 1935 (Ullstein)

Der Webstuhl: Erzählung (Frankfurt am Main: Suhrkamp, 1949); enlarged as *Der Webstuhl; Das Birkenwäldchen: Zwei Erzählungen* (Stuttgart: Reclam, 1957);

Oskar Loerke: Charakterbild eines Dichters (Mainz: Verlag der Akademie der Wissenschaften und der Literatur, 1951);

Das große Netz: Roman (Berlin & Frankfurt am Main: Suhrkamp, 1952);

Fälschungen: Erzählung (Frankfurt am Main: Suhrkamp, 1953);

Aus dem chinesischen Bilderbuch (Frankfurt am Main: Suhrkamp, 1955);

Mosaiksteine: Beiträge zur Literatur und Kunst (Frankfurt am Main: Suhrkamp, 1956);

Das unbekannte Ziel: Ausgewählte Proben und Arbeiten (Frankfurt am Main: Suhrkamp, 1963);

Wasserzeichen: Neue Gedichte (Frankfurt am Main: Suhrkamp, 1964).

OTHER: *Elegien,* edited by Kasack (Potsdam: Kiepenheuer, 1920);

Friedrich Hölderlin, *Hymnische Bruchstücke aus der Spätzeit,* edited by Kasack (Hannover: Banas, 1920);

Klabunds Literaturgeschichte: Die deutsche und die fremde Dichtung von den Anfängen bis zur Gegenwart, edited by Kasack and Ludwig Goldscheider (Vienna: Phaidon, 1930);

Oskar Loerke, *Tagebücher, 1903-1939,* edited by Kasack (Heidelberg: Schneider, 1955);

Loerke, *Reden und kleinere Aufsätze,* edited by Kasack (Mainz: Verlag der Akademie der Wissenschaften und der Literatur, 1957);

Loerke, *Das Goldbergwerk: Erzählungen,* edited by Kasack (Stuttgart: Reclam, 1965);

Loerke, *Der Bücherkarren,* edited by Kasack (Heidelberg: Schneider, 1965).

Hermann Kasack was a poet and, for a brief period late in his life, a novelist. Unwilling or unable to accept the challenges of an era dominated by politics, Kasack responded to the irrationalities of the world as did other writers with strong conservative and metaphysical inclinations: by withdrawing into refined melancholy and asocial meditation. His writing was intended to be the sublime antithesis to the disorders of contemporary society; as the symbolic evocation of a cosmic order it was meant to provide spiritual consolation. For a few years during the early 1950s his first novel was considered a work of international stature that rivaled the philosophical fiction of French existentialism. It was read widely and praised as a compelling surrealistic portrayal of life under a modern dictatorship. But its popularity gave way to attitudes ranging from respectful neglect to resolute criticism when a new

generation of writers sought answers about the immediate past without turning to metaphysical speculation.

Kasack was born in 1896 in Potsdam, the provincial capital of Brandenburg and the traditional summer residence of Prussian royalty. It was an attractive town of nearly 60,000 inhabitants, unmarred by modern industry and supported primarily by the massive presence of the bureaucracy. His father, Richard, was a physician with the respected title of Sanitätsrat in the state health service; his mother, Huguenel, came from an old family of landowners. He graduated from the most prestigious of the local high schools, the Humanistische Gymnasium, in 1914, and enrolled at the University of Berlin to study German literature, philosophy, and economics. During World War I he spent two years in Brussels in the civilian service of the military administration, then resumed his studies in Munich, where he joined the circle around the young editor Wolf Przygode. In November 1917 he met the poet Oskar Loerke, who was to be his most supportive friend until Loerke's death in 1941.

In 1920 Kasack became a reader for the recently founded publishing firm of Gustav Kiepenheuer, which favored the work of new authors. He soon became the company's director, an appointment that did not guarantee financial security but did help him extend his contacts among young writers. Also in 1920 he married Maria Fellenberg, the daughter of a high school professor. The couple had two children, Renate, born in 1924, and Wolfgang, born in 1927. On 1 May 1926 Kasack became a reader for Germany's most prominent publishing house, S. Fischer in Berlin, which published works by virtually all of the established names in German and world literature. But a year later he resigned from the position to establish himself as a dramatist and poet.

Kasack wrote for the stage, gave lectures, and reviewed books; he also wrote a number of Hörspiele (radio plays) dealing with cultural and political issues, none of which has been published. In 1927 he began a drama about the Sacco-Vanzetti trials, "Die Verurteilten" (The Condemned), but it was never completed. His work attracted the attention of the Nazis, and in 1933 he was forbidden to engage in any public activities. Three years later he was allowed to publish some of his poems and stories in the literary journal *Neue Rundschau,* and he was free to travel both in Germany and Italy. But with the exception of a short children's story, *Tull der Meisterspringer*

Kasack at work on his first novel, Die Stadt hinter dem Strom *(drawing by Oskar Kreibich)*

(1935), no book of his was printed from 1933 until 1940. His wife's work as a masseuse supported the family until he succeeded Loerke in 1941 as the principal reader for what by then was the German branch of S. Fischer. The firm had been reorganized after various maneuvers by the Ministry of Propaganda had failed to dismantle it, and Peter Suhrkamp had been appointed its director on 1 January 1937. He was removed on 1 July 1942, and Kasack was named his successor. In 1949 Kasack resigned to devote himself again to writing. He assumed a role of leadership in the German P.E.N Center, of which he was a founding member, and in the Academy of Sciences and Literature in Mainz. In 1953 he accepted the presidency of the German Academy for Language and Literature in Darmstadt, a position he held for ten years. But a steadily deteriorating eye ailment forced him to retire in 1963. He died in Stuttgart three years later, a respected member of the literary community. Even then, however, he was held in esteem more for his service in helping literature to resist contamination by Nazi ideology than for his own poetry and prose.

Kasack thought of himself primarily as a lyric poet; his view of life found its most conge-nial expression in the subtly suggestive language and carefully controlled order of refined verse. Over the years this view became more and more a dispassionate and stoic one that eschewed topicality and the politicization of poetry in favor of a gentle, quiet, almost anonymous evocation of permanent forces in nature. Kasack, like many conservative Europeans of the 1920s, was attracted to the quietism and contemplative pessimism of Eastern philosophy; the simplicity and restraint of the Taoist and Buddhist traditions were important influences on his development. Retreating from the insecure imitations of expressionist rhetoric that characterized his first works, he trained himself to become a disciplined observer. He also taught himself to see everything as subject to a larger purpose and ultimately as part of an unfathomable cosmic design.

This tendency to regard the phenomena of this world as symbolic representations of a higher order encouraged his inclination toward abstract allegory. His early plays, especially, seek to reduce specific dramatic confrontations to a set of antagonistic principles for which perennial relevance is claimed. Kasack was never at ease with those requirements of the stage which call for differentiated characterization and "natural" dialogue. This infatuation with high-minded oratory was theatrically fashionable during Kasack's formative years as a writer, but his reluctance to base his dramatic presentations on the insights of precise social analysis continued far beyond the few years after World War I when he was directly influenced by expressionism. It characterizes his entire oeuvre, most notably the novels he published after 1945.

At the end of Hitler's regime the literature of religious meditation produced a number of significant works, of which Kasack's first novel, *Die Stadt hinter dem Strom* (1949; translated as *The City beyond the River,* 1956), was the most widely acclaimed example. It was translated into eight languages and found an appreciative readership in all European countries. The book originated in a dream of his own death Kasack had had in 1942. He had immediately started writing the novel and had completed the first twelve chapters in 1944. After an interruption of over a year, which resulted in at least a partial change in the novel's direction, he finished the last eight chapters in 1946. The scholar Dr. Robert Lindhoff, whose work as a research assistant in an academic institute is concerned with cuneiform tablets, is invited to the realm of the dead for a temporary

Kasack in 1956 (Ullstein–Fritz Eschen)

visit so that he may expand his knowledge of the past; after an unspecified period of time he will be free to return to his former life. Crossing a bridge by train and then continuing his journey by streetcar, he enters the ruined city that is the habitat of the dead. Their peculiar state of existence is supervised by an anonymous bureaucracy that has many similarities to the hierarchy of officials in Franz Kafka's *Das Schloß* (1926; translated as *The Castle*, 1930). But Lindhoff, in contrast to Kafka's protagonist K., does succeed in establishing contact with the highest administrative authority, the Prefect, who informs him by loudspeaker of his commission: he is to become the archivist and chronicler of the City of the Dead, recording its customs for posterity and investigating the life stories of its inhabitants.

Lindhoff wanders through a landscape that is reminiscent in a surrealistically deformed way of life in Berlin during the last years of the war. But reality was to outdistance even the most gruesome images of an allegorical nightmare world: when the first pictures of the extermination camps were released Kasack revised his manuscript to include the victims of the gas chambers and their murderers in his narrative. He also had a chance to confront the question of responsibil-

ity and guilt; his protagonist, however, is unable to assume the role of judge and withdraws into his official function of reporter. Thus the author fails to come to terms with sociopolitical realities of his time. His fictional descent into the underworld ends with an attempt to find an explanation in a realm of transcendent order. He introduces a circle of thirty-three Weltenwächter (World Guardians), who are the protectors of the Golden Scales of the World and are charged with bringing about "a rebirth of the forces of the mind." The crimes of the Third Reich, though they are not condoned, are ultimately justifiable because they are part of a cyclical scheme that moves toward a harmonious balance of good and evil. The law of life and death requires that room be made for new rebirths: "Damit für die andrängenden Wiedergeburten Platz geschaffen wurde" (Thereby place is created for the crowding reborn).

This conclusion, which subsumes Nazi crimes under a universal process of destruction and regeneration, was an intellectual capitulation on Kasack's part. Nevertheless, readers in Germany's destroyed cities could emotionally identify with his images of life in a nether world. They also accepted his metaphysical consolations, which seemed to promise a return to normalcy that would reveal the old cultural and educational traditions as still valid and would relegate the Nazi dictatorship to the role of a brief interlude. Kasack was awarded the Fontane Prize of Berlin in 1949.

Profound skepticism about modern society as a collectivist technological civilization, a search for eternal values, and metaphysical probings into the meaning of death and human existence also characterize Kasack's other books from the postwar era. *Das große Netz* (The Great Net, 1952) is the most ambitious of them. But it did not succeed in capturing popular imagination to the same degree as did George Orwell's *Nineteen Eighty-four* (1949; translated into German, 1950) and the earlier *Brave New World* (1932) by Aldous Huxley, which was not available in German until 1953. Like these two novels, *Das große Netz* is a realistic science-fiction allegory. Here, a seemingly benign alien force–a film company shooting a movie about the decline of the West–takes over an unsuspecting community and in the end dominates a whole country. The methods of this centrally directed power combine persuasion and coercion in a gradual process of infiltration that enslaves an innocent–or at least careless–people.

While Kasack lacks the political urgency that motivated his British colleagues, it is easy to see that he has similar intentions. He is primarily concerned with German circumstances, but his portrayal of a paradigmatic subversion is devoid of historical specifics and is counterbalanced by an almost serene attitude of mental superiority; as a result, it failed to convince readers of its relevance to their own experiences. It did not contribute to a clearer understanding of the Cold War, nor did it elicit more than superficial comparisons with the practices of Hitler's propaganda and control apparatus. The book about the invisible net in which everybody is caught was read less as a provocative parable of seduction than as an elaborate and, after a while, tedious sermon on man's need for spiritual guidance.

False values are the concern of Kasack's last work of prose fiction, *Fälschungen* (Falsifications, 1953). It is the story of a wealthy industrialist and art-and-crafts collector, Clemens Sandberg, who commissions a young art historian to prepare a catalog of his treasures. He especially values his furniture, all of it apparently handmade by master craftsmen of earlier centuries. When he is informed by a blackmailer that for years he has been sold fakes, he is profoundly shaken in his conviction that there is an innate superior quality to things of the past which the expert cannot fail to perceive. In the end he has copies made of all his objets d'art and summons a group of professional connoisseurs to judge which pieces are genuine and which will be thrown into the fire.

Sandberg comes to the resigned conclusion that even real works of art must eventually fade and disintegrate and that this decline is in accord with a higher justice than that which attributes value to earthly things. The realization that he has built on sand is expressed in the statement: "Man kann das Gesicht der Welt nicht unverändert durch die Jahrhunderte tragen, und man soll es auch nicht" (It is impossible and not even desirable to keep things unchanged through the centuries). Even with reference to antique furniture this is hardly an insight that required the invention of an elaborate plot and a final auto-da-fé. The novel, furthermore, with its predi-

lection for artistic luxury and its concern with the vagaries of aristocratic wealth, offended readers who had lost most of their worldly possessions in the war.

It had become obvious by this time that Kasack had reached the limits of his abilities as a writer of "philosophical" fiction; he had also not succeeded in expanding his public beyond the culturally conservative readers of his own generation who responded to his message on ideological grounds. It is not surprising, therefore, that he went back to editorial work, preparing Loerke's diary notes and reviews for publication by the Academy for Language and Literature. He also collected his own essays on literature and art under the title *Mosaiksteine* (Mosaic Stones, 1956). And he returned to writing poems about what Loerke had called "das tragische Wunder unseres Hierseins" (the tragic miracle of our existence in this world). His style had become rather formal, somewhat didactic, and often severely controlled. The title of his last book, the poetry collection *Wasserzeichen* (Watermarks, 1964), has at least three implications: the height to which a flood had risen, the fleeting and changeable surface of life, and the symbolic permanence of poetry as a series of "watermarks in paper" that can be seen only when they are held up to the light.

References:

Wolfgang Kasack, ed., *Leben und Werk von Hermann Kasack* (Frankfurt am Main: Suhrkamp, 1966);

Herbert Schütz, *Hermann Kasack: The Role of the Critical Intellect in the Creative Writer's Work* (Bern & Frankfurt am Main: Lang, 1972).

Papers:

The Deutsches Literaturarchiv in the Schiller-Nationalmuseum in Marbach am Neckar, West Germany, has some Kasack materials from the period after 1945; Kasack destroyed most of his personal papers during the Third Reich. The Deutsche Akademie für Sprache und Dichtung, Darmstadt, West Germany, has official documents of Kasack's activities as its president from 1953 to 1963.

Marie Luise Kaschnitz

(31 January 1901-10 October 1974)

Ruth-Ellen B. Joeres
University of Minnesota

BOOKS: *Liebe beginnt: Roman* (Berlin: Cassirer, 1933);

Elissa: Roman (Berlin: Universitas, 1937);

Griechische Mythen (Hamburg: Goverts, 1943);

Menschen und Dinge 1945: Zwölf Essays (Heidelberg: Schneider, 1946);

Gedichte (Hamburg: Claassen & Goverts, 1947);

Totentanz und Gedichte zur Zeit (Hamburg: Claassen & Goverts, 1947);

Gustave Courbet: Roman eines Malerlebens (Baden-Baden: Klein, 1949); republished as *Die Wahrheit, nicht der Traum: Das Leben des Malers Courbet* (Frankfurt am Main: Insel, 1967);

Zukunftsmusik: Gedichte (Hamburg: Claassen & Goverts, 1950);

Ewige Stadt: Rom-Gedichte (Krefeld: Scherpe, 1951);

Das dicke Kind und andere Erzählungen (Krefeld: Scherpe, 1952);

Engelsbrücke: Römische Betrachtungen (Hamburg: Claassen, 1955);

Das Haus der Kindheit (Hamburg: Claassen, 1956);

Neue Gedichte (Hamburg: Claassen, 1957);

Der Zöllner Matthäus (Kassel: Bärenreiter-Verlag, 1958);

Die Umgebung von Rom (Munich & Ahrbeck: Knorr & Hirth, 1960);

Lange Schatten: Erzählungen (Hamburg: Claassen, 1960); translated by Kay Bridgwater as *Lange Schatten–Long Shadows* (Munich: Hueber, 1966);

Ein Gartenfest (Hamburg: Hans Bredow-Institut, 1961);

Liebeslyrik heute (Mainz: Akademie der Wissenschaften und der Literatur, 1962);

Dein Schweigen–meine Stimme: Gedichte 1958-1961 (Hamburg: Claassen, 1962);

Hörspiele (Hamburg: Claassen, 1962);

Wohin denn ich: Aufzeichnungen (Hamburg: Claassen, 1963);

Ich lebte (Offenbach am Main: Kumm, 1963);

Der Deserteur: Erzählungen und Gedichte (Lübeck & Hamburg: Matthiessen, 1964);

Marie Luise Kaschnitz (Ullstein)

Überallnie: Ausgewählte Gedichte 1928-1965 (Hamburg: Claassen, 1965);

Das Tagebuch des Schriftstellers (Mainz: Akademie der Wissenschaften und der Literatur, 1965);

Ein Wort weiter: Gedichte (Hamburg: Claassen, 1965);

Ferngespräche: Erzählungen (Frankfurt am Main: Insel, 1966);

Caterina Cornaro; Die Reise des Herrn Admet: Hörspiele. Mit einem autobiographischen Nachwort (Stuttgart: Reclam, 1966);

Beschreibung eines Dorfes (Frankfurt am Main: Suhrkamp, 1966);

Tage, Tage, Jahre: Aufzeichnungen (Frankfurt am Main: Insel, 1968);

Vogel Rock: Unheimliche Geschichten (Frankfurt am Main: Suhrkamp, 1969);

Die fremde Stimme: Hörspiele (Munich: Deutscher Taschenbuch Verlag, 1969);

Steht noch dahin: Neue Prosa (Frankfurt am Main: Insel, 1970);

Aufbruch wohin, edited by Friedrich Bentmann (Karlsruhe: Volksbund für Dichtung, Scheffelbund, 1970);

Nicht nur von hier und heute: Ausgewählte Prosa und Lyrik, edited by Wilhelm Borgers (Hamburg & Düsseldorf: Claassen, 1971);

Zwischen Immer und Nie: Gestalten und Themen der Dichtung (Frankfurt am Main: Insel, 1971);

Gespräche im All: Hörspiele (Frankfurt am Main & Hamburg: Fischer, 1971);

Kein Zauberspruch: Gedichte (Frankfurt am Main: Insel, 1972);

Eisbären: Ausgewählte Erzählungen (Frankfurt am Main: Insel, 1972);

Orte: Aufzeichnungen (Frankfurt am Main: Insel, 1973);

Das alte Thema (Düsseldorf: Eremiten-Presse, 1973);

Gesang vom Menschenleben: Gedichte (Düsseldorf: Eremiten-Presse, 1974);

Gedichte, edited by Peter Huchel (Frankfurt am Main: Suhrkamp, 1975);

Der alte Garten: Ein modernes Märchen (Düsseldorf: Claassen, 1975);

Ein Lesebuch 1964-1974, edited by Heinrich Vormweg (Frankfurt am Main: Suhrkamp, 1975);

Der Tulpenmann: Erzählungen, edited by Hans Bender (Stuttgart: Reclam, 1976);

Seid nicht so sicher! Geschichten, Gedichte, Gedanken (Gütersloh: Mohn, 1979);

Selected Later Poems of Marie Luise Kaschnitz, translated by Lisel Mueller (Princeton: Princeton University Press, 1980);

Gesammelte Werke in sieben Bänden, edited by Christian Büttrich and Norbert Miller, 5 volumes published (Frankfurt am Main: Insel, 1981-1985);

Eines Mittags, Mitte Juni (Düsseldorf: Claassen, 1983);

Jennifers Träume: Unheimliche Geschichten (Frankfurt am Main: Suhrkamp, 1984);

Florens: Eichendorffs Jugend (Düsseldorf: Claassen, 1984).

OTHER: "Spätes Urteil" and "Dämmerung," in *Vorstoß: Prosa der Ungedruckten*, edited by Max Tau and Wolfgang von Einsiedel (Berlin: Cassirer, 1930), pp. 125-151;

"Biographie zu Guido von Kaschnitz-Weinberg," in Guido von Kaschnitz-Weinberg, *Ausgewählte Schriften*, edited by Helga von Heintze, volume 1 (Berlin: Mann, 1965), pp. 228-239;

"Gedächtnis, Zuchtrute, Kunstform," in *Das Tagebuch und der moderne Autor*, edited by Uwe Schultz (Munich: Hanser, 1965);

"Martin, We Want a Lesson," in *Dichter erzählen Kindern*, edited by Gertrud Middelhauve (Cologne: Middelhauve, 1966), pp. 71-82;

Franz Grillparzer, *Medea*, edited by Kaschnitz (Frankfurt am Main: Ullstein, 1966);

Josef von Eichendorff, *Gedichte*, edited by Kaschnitz (Frankfurt am Main: Fischer, 1969).

PERIODICAL PUBLICATIONS: "Judith: Ein Gespräch," *Die Gegenwart*, 1, no. 18/19 (1946): 29-31;

"Vom Wortschatz der Poesie," *Die Wandlung*, 4 (1949): 618-623;

"Vom Ausdruck der Zeit in der lyrischen Dichtung," *Der Deutschunterricht*, 2 (1950): 63-71;

"Rede zur Verleihung des Georg-Büchner-Preises," *Jahrbuch der deutschen Akademie für Sprache und Dichtung 1955* (1956): 83-87;

"Das Besondere der Frauendichtung," *Jahrbuch der deutschen Akademie für Sprache und Dichtung 1957* (1958): 59-63.

Marie Luise Kaschnitz is one of the few women writers to have received considerable respect from the predominantly male West German critical establishment: she was the only woman Horst Bienek apparently thought worthy of including in his 1962 series of interviews with German writers; almost all of the admiring journal and newspaper articles on her have been written by men; and the seven-volume collection of her works which began appearing in 1981 is being edited by two men. Since 1984, the tenth anniversary of her death, critics have been discussing and analyzing her work from a feminist perspective.

Marie Luise von Holzing-Berstett was born in Karlsruhe on 31 January 1901, the third daughter and the third of four children of Max Freiherr von Holzing-Berstett, a Prussian general, and his wife, the former Elsa von Seldenek. She spent her early years primarily in Berlin and Potsdam, although there were frequent visits to the family estate in Bollschweil, a village near Freiburg that was to play an important role in her creative life and in whose cemetery she and her husband are buried. Her education was typical for girls in that era. She did not attend a university but trained in 1917 as a book dealer in Weimar and then worked for a short time later that year at the O. C. Recht publishing house in Munich. During 1924-1925 she was employed by an antiquarian bookstore in Rome; in December 1925 she married Guido von Kaschnitz-Weinberg, an assistant at the German Archeological Institute there. Their daughter, Iris Costanza, was born in Rome in 1928. Stays in Freiburg, Königsberg, and Marburg between 1932 and 1941–in the latter year they settled in Frankfurt–and travels to Italy, Yugoslavia, Greece, Turkey, Hungary, and North Africa from 1937 until the outbreak of World War II were occasioned by Guido von Kaschnitz-Weinberg's teaching positions and research trips. She spent the years 1953 to 1956 in Rome, where her husband served as director of the Archeological Institute. The family returned to Frankfurt when Kaschnitz-Weinberg retired in 1956; he died in 1958 from a brain tumor. Kaschnitz lived in Frankfurt for the rest of her life. She died on 10 October 1974 while visiting her daughter in Rome.

In her speech accepting the prestigious Büchner Prize in 1955, Kaschnitz provided a rare look at her motivation for writing. At that time she was best known for her poetry; her important prose works had not yet appeared. The reserve typical of her writing and her life is evident in the speech. She describes her insecurity at being given an award in the name of Georg Büchner, who died young and left behind a small but brilliant body of work, and understates the significance of her own achievements. She speaks of her writings as being, in contrast to Büchner's, "oft vom künstlerischen Spieltrieb bestimmt" (frequently determined by an artistic motive of play), as "Herumversuchen auf vielen literarischen Gebieten" (a testing ground in many literary areas), as marked by "keine große Linie, keinen inneren Zusammenhang aus einer unverrückbaren Gesinnung heraus" (no greatline, no inner connection to a firm and lasting philosophy). Her self-description is not entirely negative; although she was called "die Trümmerdichterin" (the poet of the ruins) because of her poems depicting Germany immediately after World War II, she views her work less as a portrayal of chaos than as "die Sehnsucht nach einer neuen Ordnung" (the yearning for a new order), "ein Ausdruck des Heimwehs nach einer alten Unschuld oder der Sehnsucht nach einem aus dem Geist und der Liebe neu geordneten Dasein" (an expression of the longing for an old innocence or the yearning for a new existence based on intellect and love). In her prose she has attempted "den Blick des Lesers auf das mir Bedeutsame zu lenken, auf die wunderbaren Möglichkeiten und die tödlichen Gefahren des Menschen und auf die bestürzende Fülle der Welt" (to direct the reader's attention toward that which is meaningful to me, the wonderful possibilities and the deadly dangers of human beings and the alarming fullness of the world).

This mix of "wonderful possibilities and deadly dangers" is manifested in Kaschnitz's poetry and prose in her concern for other people and her need to identify herself against the background of a world that revealed both its worst and its most splendid sides to her. One critic has noted that her writing responded above all to the events occurring around her. Two of those events–World War II and the death of her husband–were major turning points in her life.

Despite Kaschnitz's view of her work as disparate and without inner connection, certain principal themes emerge. The search for self that became the central focus of her writings after 1958 is reflected throughout in covert and overt autobiographical references. The need for self-definition is frequently manifested in a concern with childhood: not a nostalgic looking back but an often painful, even terrifying baring of the fears and agonies of a child. In her post-World War II writings there is a growing focus on the individual in an alien world; an individual characterized less as male or female–there is little that is gender-specific in Kaschnitz's writings–than as a lone human being faced with expanding technology, war, and impersonalization. Kaschnitz's writing, never tendentious or preachy, is marked by a certain classical distance; but her intimate connection with the world in which she lives is never absent. Her Büchner Prize speech describes her lyric poetry as neither hermetic nor surrealistic, neither incomprehensible nor removed; its goal is to communicate with "Menschen . . . freilich solchen, die die Mühe des Ungewohnten und nur langsam zu Begreifenden nicht scheuen" (human beings . . . who, however, do not shy away from the strain of the unusual, of that which can only be slowly grasped). Her work, like a Flemish painting, is marked by a precise attention to detail; her eye is that of a painter who considers color, nuance, and composition.

*Kaschnitz in 1933, the year her first book was
published (Ullstein)*

Kaschnitz's earliest writings were prose–two short stories published in an anthology and her only two full-fledged novels–but she did not come into her own as a prose writer until the appearance of the so-called Aufzeichnungen (sketches) of her last years. The novels, *Liebe beginnt* (Love Begins, 1933) and *Elissa* (1937), were ignored by critics until their reprinting in the first volume of the collected works in 1981. Yet they provide significant evidence of the Kaschnitz style and philosophy: the acquiescence of the female protagonist in *Liebe beginnt*, who, like Kaschnitz herself, chooses to subordinate herself to a man, sublimating whatever rebellious impulses she might feel; the interest in myth in *Elissa*, a retelling of the story of Dido and Aeneas in which Elissa/Dido does not die but goes off with an earlier teacher and lover, while Aeneas remains a marginal figure; an investigation of the sister relationship, also in *Elissa*, in which two sisters divide the traits of the archetypal female, one graceful and obedient, the other wild, awkward, and untamed. In both works the male figures, al-though not central, dominate the lives of the female protagonists. These are novels of mental and physical confinement, of an obedient bowing to authority by the female characters and by an author who is almost entirely traditional in her approach.

Between 1939 and 1945 Kaschnitz reworked several Greek myths, wrote a biography of the nineteenth-century French realist painter Gustave Courbet, and prepared her first volume of poetry. Except for the collection of myths, which was published in 1943, the works did not appear until after 1945 and were preceded by a volume of twelve essays, *Menschen und Dinge 1945* (People and Things 1945, 1946), that constituted Kaschnitz's moral and philosophical reaction to the war. Typically for her, it is a detached response; Hitler, for example, is never mentioned. Kaschnitz presents her own reckoning with the horror and provides suggestions for the desperately needed moral rebuilding. In her last work, *Orte* (Places, 1973), she reiterated the philosophy that imbues this small text. As the years passed and she found herself more and more confronted with questions of guilt on both a personal and collective level, she concluded that her own guilt involved her method of survival during the war: distancing, an involvement with ideas, a musing on universal moral problems rather than on the horror around her.

A turning to form as a way to thwart chaos can be found in Kaschnitz's first volume of poetry, *Gedichte* (Poems, 1947). Traditional rhyme patterns predominate; nature images, memories of childhood, and visions of her years in Italy far outweigh the few poems included under the heading "Dunkle Zeit" (Dark Times). There is a sense of isolation and distancing, although never of a nostalgic need to return to the past–the poems about her youth are filled with images of fear and death. The volume acknowledges an awareness of terror, but tries through rigid form and traditional themes to provide a counterforce to that chaos.

The biography of Courbet (1949), in contrast, concentrates less on his painting than on his social concerns. It is a history of France in the days of the Commune, and in its stress on Courbet's social criticism it is an example of the "inner emigration"–a phrase referring to those German writers who remained in Germany during the war but did not support National Socialism, choosing instead not to publish at all or to inject subversively critical elements into what they did write.

With the publication of *Das dicke Kind und andere Erzählungen* (The Fat Child and Other Stories, 1952) Kaschnitz joined the trend toward the short story and revealed considerable talent in the genre. This volume of succinct and vivid tales was followed by several other collections; but no other story had the impact of the title story in this first anthology, and Kaschnitz included it in many of the other collections. Typical of her work in its mix of reality and dream, its autobiographical overtones, and its sense of myth, "Das dicke Kind" is the story of an unattractive child who appears on the doorstep of the narrator; the latter is immediately both repulsed by and attracted to her. The descriptions of the child's triumph through struggle–in contrast to her graceful sister, who succeeds effortlessly–and of the narrator's growing involvement with the child recall motifs from Kaschnitz's earlier writings and also reveal the identification between character and author that would increasingly mark her work. Ten years after the first appearance of this tale Kaschnitz admitted that she was the fat child, and that autobiography was an essential part of all her work.

In 1955 Kaschnitz published *Engelsbrücke: Römische Betrachtungen* (The Bridge of Angels: Roman Observations). These sketches go far beyond the travelogue that their title implies; there are also elements of the diary, the essay, and the commentary. Kaschnitz introduced here a form that she spent the rest of her life developing, a form that resembled Max Frisch's and Luise Rinser's diaries and Wolfgang Koeppen's miniature prose pieces but was ultimately unique. Pieces on her life in Rome are supplemented by accounts of current political events and dreams, literary impressions, and thoughts on a variety of subjects. The sense of the fragmentary and immediate provides a vivid mirror of her life in a new and often confusing world.

Kaschnitz's continuing investigation of self and persistent involvement with childhood are evident in *Das Haus der Kindheit* (The House of Childhood, 1956). In this short prose work a freelance reporter born in the same year as Kaschnitz discovers a museum in which one's childhood can be explored, and in 126 diarylike entries relates her experiences there. The issues of aging, the search for identity, and coming to grips with one's past are dealt with; autobiographical overtones are again unmistakable. The narrator, who is clearly in a time of crisis, seems confined and controlled by men both in the museum and in the world outside, and the final impression is one of impotence and a sense of being lost. This is a transitional work, published in the year in which Kaschnitz's husband fell ill, and its oppressive tone reveals fear and uncertainty.

The volumes of poetry that appeared after 1947 differ considerably from the first collection. They show a move away from the classical sonnet often employed in the earlier poems and away from rhyme to a freer, less definable, less predictable form. There are also changes in theme: Kaschnitz tries to deal with the horrors of the war and the agonies of the postwar world, to come to terms with the issue of guilt, and to define the roles of the poet and the aging woman. As in her early poetry, Kaschnitz remains concrete and accessible, convinced of the need for communication. Her final poem, written a month before her death, confirms a belief in the cyclical process: "Alte Bäume sterben/Und neue wachsen in die neue Zeit" (Old trees die/And new ones grow into the future).

The death of Kaschnitz's husband introduced a new focus into her writing. Of the works to appear within the first years after 1958, the most revealing is *Wohin denn ich* (Where Do I Go Now?, 1963), a volume similar in form to *Engelsbrücke*, yet imbued with Kaschnitz's new sense of loss and need to reorient herself. It is an intensely personal work, best understood in connection with a volume of poetry published the previous year, *Dein Schweigen–meine Stimme* (Your Silence–My Voice). Both works deal with the subject of a dependent woman faced suddenly with an unwanted independence. The earlier search for identity, in stories like "Das dicke Kind" or "Das Haus der Kindheit," was involved with an increasingly distant past; here it is the present–the aging process, the state of being alone–that must be comprehended. And there is survival, the possibility of a continued productive existence: the figure in the prose work agrees to go on a reading tour, and the book of poetry ends with the line "Was willst du, du lebst" (What do you want, you are alive).

By 1962 Kaschnitz had been awarded several literary prizes; had been made a member of the Academy of Sciences and Literature in Mainz; had been given the guest chair for poetry at the University of Frankfurt, where she presented lectures on European writers from Shakespeare to Beckett during the summer semester of 1960; and had spent 1961 as a guest at the Villa Massimo in Rome before leaving on a reading tour of West Germany and Brazil. Although the struggles depicted in *Wohin denn ich* and *Dein Schweigen–meine Stimme* were effectively over for her, her later volumes of sketches continue to reflect her sense of loss and her need to investigate her past as a tool for understanding the present. Perhaps her most brilliantly constructed effort along these lines is *Beschreibung eines Dorfes* (Description of a Village, 1966), a study of Bollschweil. Kaschnitz provides a history of the village that is also a portrayal of the process of writing the history; the twenty-one brief chapters represent the days of work needed for the project. There are multiple levels of meaning and projections of thought and memory. She dips into the past for information, enlightenment, and political or social comment, but never loses sight of the present. Parallels are extensive: the aging, changing village; the aging, changing author/narrator; the aging, changing world. There is, in

contrast to many of her other writings, a deliberately impersonal tone: she never describes her own former house, for example, but refers to it only by its street number. The book was made into a film, with Kaschnitz narrating; the latest edition is heavily illustrated with photographs of Bollschweil today, underlining the graphic quality of the work. It is a stunning text replete with the new emphasis on the inevitable passage of time, on aging, and on death that was to characterize Kaschnitz's remaining work. In 1967 she was awarded the Orden Pour le merité.

Kaschnitz wrote several *Hörspiele* (radio plays) from the 1950s to the early 1970s; mostly based on biblical legends, they represent her only venture into dramatic form. Aside from the appearance in 1971 of *Zwischen Immer und Nie* (Between Always and Never), a collection of her Frankfurt lectures and several critical essays, the works of her final years continued the stylistic tradition of *Engelsbrücke* and *Wohin denn ich. Tage, Tage, Jahre* (Days, Days, Years, 1968) and her final work, *Orte* (Places, 1973), bear the descriptive subtitle *Aufzeichnungen* (Notes); *Steht noch dahin* (Still Remaining, 1970) shares the incompleteness of *Beschreibung eines Dorfes* in its sense of plans yet to be carried out, stories yet to be written. The narrator of the 1968 and 1973 works is a female who bears considerable resemblance to Kaschnitz; in *Steht noch dahin* the narrator switches back and forth from male to female and speaks sometimes in the first, sometimes in the third person. Dreams, fantasies, and the problems of present-day life constitute the subject matter of all three works.

Tage, Tage, Jahre is a diary with a frame story: the narrator has heard that a new construction project may cause her Frankfurt apartment building to be torn down. Within this atmosphere of impending doom there are reflections on age, destruction, and change in the world around her and in herself; she must make a decision as to whether she will have an operation to replace the disintegrating bone in her hip. The diary moves between reality and dream; there is also political commentary in which the narrator takes sides against the excesses of progress and technology. The conclusion is positive: the hip will be reconstructed, the building will not be torn down.

Orte takes a more abstract look at life and death; the places of the title are not just physical locations but also memories and illusions. There is a sense of ending, with discussions of the past and of the future she will not live to see; the major impression is that of an old woman who must make way for others. In an ironic twist, this examination of the self concludes as she departs without leaving footprints.

The gentility of Marie Luise Kaschnitz's writing grew naturally out of her upbringing and her life. As the product of a transitional age, caught, as she says in *Orte*, between the first German women's movement of the nineteenth century, which was in decline by the time she was born, and the second wave of feminism that began when she was an old woman, she was not apt to leave footprints, not easily able to assert a self. She emerged from a tradition of well-to-do, upper-middle-class life, from a set of values that defined a limited woman's role for her. It is thus all the more remarkable that she produced the brilliant body of forceful work that she did, creating a literary form to define and describe herself as well as writing exceptional works in the established genres of lyric poetry and the short story. She not only mirrored the dilemma of a German woman in the first half of the twentieth century but also had a great deal to say about the universal issues of aging, change, and self-definition. Aside from a few dissertations and two monographs, however, literary criticism about Marie Luise Kaschnitz has been mostly limited to reviews and articles that do not consider her within her specific context as a woman during a troubled period of German history. It is clearly time for a reexamination of her writing from a variety of new perspectives.

Interview:

Horst Bienek, *Werkstattgespräche mit Schriftstellern* (Munich: Hanser, 1962), pp. 33-46.

Bibliographies:

Elsbeth Linpinsel, *Kaschnitz-Bibliographie* (Hamburg & Düsseldorf: Claassen, 1971);

Elsbeth Pulver, "Marie Luise Kaschnitz," in *Kritisches Lexikon zur deutschsprachigen Gegenwartsliteratur*, edited by Heinz Ludwig Arnold (Munich: Edition text + kritik, 1978-   ).

References:

Anita Baus, *Standortbestimmung als Prozeß: Eine Untersuchung zur Prosa von Marie Luise Kaschnitz* (Bonn: Bouvier, 1974);

Hans Bender, "Das Gedicht hat kein Alter," *Merkur*, 20, no. 220 (1966): 679-683;

Friedrich Bentmann, "Marie Luise Kaschnitz als Dichterin der Breisgauer Heimat zu ihrem 70. Geburtstag," *Ekkhart-Jahrbuch der Badischen Heimat* (1971): 63-74;

Anthony Bushell, "A Darkening Vision: The Poetry of Marie Luise Kaschnitz," *Neophilologus*, 65 (1981): 272-278;

Alan Corkhill, "Eschatologische Symbolik und Autobiographie als Interpretationsschlüssel zu Marie Luise Kaschnitz' kurzem Prosawerk 'Schiffsgeschichte,'" *Literatur in Wissenschaft und Unterricht*, 10 (1977): 184-193;

Corkhill, "Rückschau, Gegenwärtiges und Zukunftsvision: Die Synoptik von Marie Luise Kaschnitz' dichterischer Welt," *German Quarterly*, 56 (Winter 1983): 386-395;

Ingeborg Drewitz, "Marie Luise Kaschnitz," *Frankfurter Hefte*, 3 (October 1975): 55-62;

Kasimir Edschmid, "Huldigung für Marie Luise Kaschnitz," *Jahrbuch der deutschen Akademie für Sprache und Dichtung 1955* (1956): 74-80;

Joan Louise Curl Elliott, "Character Transformation through Point of View in Selected Short Stories of Marie Luise Kaschnitz," Ph.D. dissertation, Vanderbilt University, 1973;

Elisabeth Endres, "Marie Luise Kaschnitz," in *Neue Literatur der Frauen*, edited by Heinz Puknus (Munich: Beck, 1980), pp. 20-24;

Robert Foot, *The Phenomenon of Speechlessness in the Poetry of Marie Luise Kaschnitz, Günter Eich, Nelly Sachs and Paul Celan* (Bonn: Bouvier, 1982);

Philippe Forget, *Zur frühen Lyrik von Marie Luise Kaschnitz: 1928-1939. Vergehen und Weiterbestehen als Lebensgrund der Kreatur* (Nancy: Mémoire de Maitrise, 1974);

Walter Helmut Fritz, "Marie Luise Kaschnitz: Dein Schweigen—meine Stimme. Gedichte 1958-1961," *Neue deutsche Hefte*, 9, no. 90 (1962): 121-122;

Reinhold Grimm, "Ein Menschenalter danach: Über das zweistrophige Gedicht 'Hiroshima' von Marie Luise Kaschnitz," *Monatshefte*, 71, no. 1 (1979): 5-18;

Theodor Heuss, "Dank an M. L. Kaschnitz," *Jahrbuch der deutschen Akademie für Sprache und Dichtung 1955* (1956): 80-82;

Wolfgang Hildesheimer, "Ein Haus der Kindheit," *Merkur*, 11, no. 107 (1957): 86-89;

Erich Hock, "Zeitgenössische Lyrik im Unterricht der Oberstufe: Marie Luise Kaschnitz und Hans Egon Holthusen," *Wirkendes Wort: Sam-*

melband IV (Düsseldorf: Schwann, 1962), pp. 207-214;

Eberhard Horst, "Marie Luise Kaschnitz: Ein Wort weiter," *Neue deutsche Hefte,* 13, no. 1 (1966): 129-131;

Peter Huchel, Epilogue to Kaschnitz's *Gedichte* (Frankfurt am Main: Suhrkamp, 1975), pp. 139-140;

Interpretationen zu M. L. Kaschnitz: Verfaßt von einem Arbeitskreis. Erzählungen (Munich: Oldenbourg, 1969);

Sigrid Jauker, "Marie Luise Kaschnitz: Monographie und Versuch einer Deutung," Ph.D. dissertation, University of Graz, 1966;

Ruth-Ellen B. Joeres, "Mensch oder Frau? Marie Luise Kaschnitz' 'Orte' als autobiographischer Beweis eines Frauenbewußtseins," *Der Deutschunterricht,* 38, no. 3 (1986): 77-85;

Joeres, "Records of Survival: The Autobiographical Writings of Marieluise Fleißer and Marie Luise Kaschnitz," in *The Faith of a (Woman) Writer,* edited by Alice Kessler-Harris and William McBrien (Westport, Conn.: Greenwood, 1988);

Maria Koger, "Die Rom-Gedichte der Marie Luise Kaschnitz: Ein Thema und seine Variationen," *Recherches Germaniques,* 5 (1975): 217-242;

Lotte Köhler, "Marie Luise Kaschnitz," in *Deutsche Dichter der Gegenwart: Ihr Leben und Werk,* edited by Benno von Wiese (Berlin: Schmidt, 1973), pp. 153-167;

Dietrich Krusche, "Kommunikationsstruktur und Wirkpotential: Differenzierende Interpretation fiktionaler Kurzprosa von Kafka, Kaschnitz, Brecht," *Der Deutschunterricht,* 26, no. 4 (1974): 110-122;

Siegfried Lenz, "Eignung zum Opfer: Über Marie Luise Kaschnitz' Erzählungen: Ferngespräche 1967," in his *Beziehungen, Ansichten und Bekenntnisse zur Literatur* (Hamburg: Hoffmann & Campe, 1970), pp. 226-232;

Fritz Martini, "Auf der Suche nach sich selbst: Zu Marie Luise Kaschnitz' Erzählungen 'Ferngespräche,' " in *Gedichte und Interpretationen,* volume 6: *Gegenwart,* edited by Walter Hinderer (Stuttgart: Reclam, 1982), pp. 60-70;

Ursula Matter, "Tragische Aspekte in den Erzählungen von Marie Luise Kaschnitz," Ph.D. dissertation, University of Zurich, 1979;

Johannes Pfeiffer, "Marie Luise Kaschnitz: Christine," in his *Was haben wir an einer Erzäh-*

lung? Betrachtungen und Erläuterungen (Hamburg: Wittig, 1965), pp. 122-133;

Richard Plant, "The Strange Poetic World of Marie Luise Kaschnitz," *American German Review,* 32, no. 4 (1966): 15-16;

Elsbeth Pulver, *Marie Luise Kaschnitz* (Munich: Beck Verlag/edition text kritik, 1984);

Marcel Reich-Ranicki, "Marie Luise Kaschnitz: 'Ferngespräche,' " in his *Literatur der kleinen Schritte: Deutsche Schriftsteller heute* (Munich: Piper, 1967), pp. 225-233;

Johanna Christiane Reichardt, *Zeitgenossin: Marie Luise Kaschnitz: Eine Monographie* (Frankfurt am Main, Bern, New York & Nancy: Lang, 1984);

Reiner Reiners, "Tradition und Moderne in der Lyrik von Marie Luise Kaschnitz," *Schriften der Theodor-Storm-Gesellschaft,* 14 (1965): 40-57;

Werner Ross, "Dreimal Altern: Jean Améry; Robert Neumann; M. L. Kaschnitz," *Merkur,* 23, no. 4 (1969): 386-390;

Ekkehart Rudolph, *Protokoll zur Person: Autoren über sich und ihr Werk* (Munich: List, 1971), pp. 85-93;

Rudolf Schäfer, "Beschreibung einer Beschreibung oder Das Einundzwanzig-Tage-Werk der Marie Luise Kaschnitz," in his *Germanistik und Deutschunterricht: Zur Einheit von Fachwissenschaft und Fachdidaktik* (Munich: Fink, 1979), pp. 191-224;

Uwe Schweikert, ed., *Marie Luise Kaschnitz* (Frankfurt am Main: Suhrkamp, 1984);

Hans Schwerte, "Marie Luise Kaschnitz," in *Die deutsche Lyrik 1945-1975: Zwischen Botschaft und Spiel,* edited by Klaus Weissenberger (Düsseldorf: Bagel, 1981), pp. 97-109;

Adelheid Strack-Richter, *Öffentliches und privates Engagement: Die Lyrik von Marie Luise Kaschnitz* (Frankfurt am Main & Bern: Lang, 1979);

Fritz Usinger, "Marie Luise Kaschnitz," in his *Welt ohne Klassik: Essays* (Darmstadt: Roether, 1960), pp. 131-147;

Heinrich Vormweg, "Über Marie Luise Kaschnitz: 31.1.1901-10.10.1974," *Merkur,* 29 (1975): 857-860;

Jürgen P. Wallmann, "Marie Luise Kaschnitz," in his *Argumente: Informationen und Meinungen zur deutschen Literatur der Gegenwart* (Mühlacker: Stieglitz, 1968), pp. 152-160;

Peter Wapnewski, "Gebuchte Zeit: Zu den Aufzeichnungen der Marie Luise Kaschnitz," in his *Zumutungen: Essays zur Literatur des 20.*

Jahrhunderts (Düsseldorf: Claassen, 1979), pp. 255-262;

Dietmut E. Wolter, "Grundhaltungen in Gedichten der Marie Luise Kaschnitz," *Der Deutschunterricht*, 28, no. 6 (1976): 108-114;

Susanne Woodtli, "Marie Luise Kaschnitz," *Reformatio*, 16 (1967): 3-11.

Papers:

The literary estate of Marie Luise Kaschnitz is located in the Deutsches Literaturarchiv in the Schiller-Nationalmuseum in Marbach am Neckar, West Germany.

Irmgard Keun
(6 February 1905-5 May 1982)

Ritta Jo Horsley
University of Massachusetts–Boston

BOOKS: *Gilgi, eine von uns: Roman* (Berlin: Universitas, 1931);

Das kunstseidene Mädchen: Roman (Berlin: Universitas, 1932); translated by Basil Creighton as *The Artificial Silk Girl* (London: Chatto, 1933);

Das Mädchen, mit dem die Kinder nicht verkehren durften (Amsterdam: de Lange, 1936); translated by Leila Berg and Ruth Baer as *The Bad Example* (New York: Harcourt, Brace, 1955); translation republished as *Grown-ups Don't Understand* (London: Parrish, 1955);

Nach Mitternacht: Roman (Amsterdam: Querido, 1937); translated by James Cleugh as *After Midnight* (New York: Knopf, 1938; London: Secker, 1938);

Kind aller Länder: Roman (Amsterdam: Querido, 1938);

D-Zug dritter Klasse: Roman (Amsterdam: Querido, 1938);

Bilder und Gedichte aus der Emigration (Cologne: Epoche, 1947);

Ferdinand, der Mann mit dem freundlichen Herzen: Roman (Düsseldorf: Droste, 1950);

Scherz-Artikel (Berlin: Schleicher & Schüll, 1951);

Die kleine Reise, by Keun, H. Dramsch, and others (Cologne: Franz, 1953);

Wenn wir alle gut wären: Kleine Begebenheiten, Erinnerungen und Geschichten (Düsseldorf: Fladung, 1954); revised and enlarged edition, edited by Wilhelm Unger (Cologne: Kiepenheuer & Witsch, 1983);

Blühende Neurosen; Flimmerkisten-Blüten (Düsseldorf: Droste, 1962).

Irmgard Keun at the age of twenty-one (Ullstein)

OTHER: "Begegnung in der Emigration," in *Joseph Roth und die Tradition: Aufsatz und Materialiensammlung*, edited by David Bronsen (Darmstadt: Agora, 1975), pp. 36-38.

The works of Irmgard Keun present a remarkable literary document of German life and times from the late Weimar Republic to the postwar period. Keun's novels interweave ironic insights into the psychology of the middle and lower middle classes with vivid depictions of Depression-era Cologne and Berlin, pubs in Nazi-dominated Frankfurt, European hotels frequented by refugees, and the rubble of the postwar years. The seemingly innocent observations of her naive but bright and spirited young female protagonists reflect Keun's own incisive criticisms of conventional middle-class values and patriarchal attitudes toward sexual mores. Like her characters, Keun displayed courage and honesty in the face of social and political repression; her novels reflect the personal tragedy of her life under fascism and in exile, while providing a clear-sighted critique of the culture of her era.

Born in Berlin in 1905 to affluent and liberal-minded parents, Keun spent her later childhood in Cologne. Her father, Eduard Keun, the director of an oil refinery, encouraged his daughter's independence and intellectual development. While she recalled her mother, Elisa Charlotte Haese Keun, as "stark hausfraulich eingestellt, auf eine sehr schauerliche Weise" (quite domestically inclined, in a very horrible way), her literary portrayals of mother-daughter bonds are usually warm ones; Keun remained devoted to both parents throughout her life. When asked in 1982 what she thought about women's emancipation, Keun replied: "Das war ich ja immer im Grunde genommen. Ich tat doch immer, was ich wollte" (Basically I was always emancipated. I always did what I wanted to). At sixteen Keun attended a school for actors in Cologne; she went on to perform professionally in Hamburg and Greifswald but soon realized that the theater was not what she wanted for a career. Keun published her first story in the *Basler Nationalzeitung* and was encouraged to continue writing by Alfred Döblin. In October 1932 she married Johannes Tralow, a novelist, dramatist, and director.

Her first novel, published in 1931, went through six editions (30,000 copies) the first year and made Keun famous overnight. Set against the background of the increasing unemployment and political volatility of Depression-era Cologne, *Gilgi, eine von uns* (Gilgi, One of Us) portrays an appealingly ambitious, emancipated young stenotypist who sets out to improve her situation through hard work and initiative. Gilgi's optimistic beliefs in individual self-sufficiency and survival of the fit-

test are shaken first when she learns that she had been adopted and again when she falls in love with a charming but impractical bohemian intellectual, Martin Bruck. Her quest for her true mother and thus her own identity brings her into contact with both poor and wealthy classes and increases her appreciation of the power of economic and social forces. Dismissed from her job because of worsening economic conditions, pregnant and unable to obtain an abortion, but with deepened self-knowledge, Gilgi finally leaves Martin to regain her independence and raise her child.

In this novel the narrow moralizing and materialism of the German middle class are sharply satirized. The narrator notes of Gilgi's family: "Der vollkommene Mangel an Unterhaltung kennzeichnet das Anständige, Legitimierte der Familie. . . . Die Langeweile ist die Gewähr für das Stabile ihrer Beziehungen, und daß man sich nichts zu sagen hat, macht einander unverdächtig" (The total absence of conversation typifies the decency, the legitimacy of the family. . . . Boredom is the guarantee of the stability of their relations, and the fact that they have nothing to say to each other makes everyone seem safe and unsuspected). Keun illuminates the hypocritical morality of the bourgeoisie: its daughters are urged to display their physical attributes in the hope of attracting wealthy suitors but reprimanded for spending the night with them. By contrast, Gilgi's attitude is: "Warten ist furchtbar unmoralisch, weil's so sinnlos ist. Man darf sich doch seine Wünsche nicht fortlügen" (Waiting is terribly immoral, because it's so senseless. You mustn't just lie your wishes away). Gilgi's realistic, unsentimental approach to sexuality typifies her coolly observing, common-sense perspective; such matter-of-fact, detached attitudes were a hallmark of the "Neue Sachlichkeit" (New Objectivity) literary style of the mid and late 1920s.

Keun's heroine encounters such problems as sexual harassment and the necessity for women to use their sexuality in the competition for employment. But the most serious social issue treated in *Gilgi, eine von uns* is that of legalized abortion; Keun shows how the effects of Paragraph 218, the antiabortion law, were particularly disastrous in the context of the Depression and widespread unemployment. The novel was filmed in 1932 under the title *Eine von uns* and was translated into seven languages.

Keun's second novel, *Das kunstseidene Mädchen* (1932; translated as *The Artificial Silk*

Girl, 1933), again recounts the struggle of a young office worker in late Weimar Germany to rise beyond her origins; but in contrast to Gilgi, Doris models her dreams and behavior on the romantic world of the cinema and gives up her job as a secretary in her quest to become a star. She announces her intention to record her experiences and impressions, not as a diary but "wie Film, denn so ist mein Leben und wird noch mehr so sein" (like a film, for that's what my life is like and will be even more). Her first attempt to achieve a glamorous existence–as a theater extra in her hometown–ends when she acts on a compulsion both sensual and social and "exchanges" her shabby raincoat for an elegant fur hanging in the lobby. Fated through this act to lead a fugitive, underground existence, Doris flees to Berlin, where she seeks her fortune amid the glitter and misery of a world in turmoil. Her encounters with men of various stations and political attitudes read like a series of episodes in a film scenario. Doris's story ends without a definite resolution; destitute, she nonetheless continues to reject the bourgeois path of "respectable" but exploitative office work and takes refuge in the waiting room of the Zoo train station. Her experiences and feelings have made her an outsider to her former social and economic class: "Aber das ist es ja eben, ich habe keine Meinesgleichen, ich gehöre überhaupt nirgends hin" (But that's just it, I don't have any of my own kind, I don't belong anywhere at all). Recognizing that the most likely option left her may be prostitution, Doris does attain a degree of disillusionment about her dream of stardom and glamour: "Auf den Glanz kommt es nämlich vielleicht gar nicht so furchtbar an" (Maybe the glamour isn't so terribly important at all, you see). For Doris the belief in the bourgeois virtues of diligence and thrift that inspired Gilgi has been replaced by the insight that her fantasy of glamour and luxury only serves to mask the underlying desperation, chaos, and corruption of her society.

Doris's lively first-person narrative provides a vivid panorama of Depression-era Berlin, as well as allowing the reader a critically distanced view of Doris herself. Drawing largely on the clichés of popular films for her values and images, Doris combines a social, political, and cultural naivete, a comical pretension to sophistication, and a sharp, unsentimental feel for economic and psychological realities. Her innocence and honesty lend her observations a kind of "Narrenfreiheit" (fool's freedom); this affinity to

the picaro figure is underscored by her rapidly shifting fortunes, her extralegal status, and the novel's episodic structure and open-ended conclusion. A precise registering of external details and an often comical blending of the spiritual with the material mark *Das kunstseidene Mädchen* as another novel of Neue Sachlichkeit, as does the objectification of feelings and relationships: Doris speaks of her heart as a gramophone and, conversely, loves her stolen fur as a close friend. The cool nonchalance of her generation concerning relations between the sexes is also typical of New Objectivity, yet Doris's recognition that her body must serve as her capital does not prevent her from evolving her own morality: she will only sleep with a man out of economic need or true desire. Moreover, the mask of objective detachment is broken through whenever Doris admits her susceptibility to deeper emotions, such as love and pain at her own and others' suffering. Doris's decision to write of her life sprang from a vague sense of herself as a person of particular sensitivity, in whom "Großartiges vorgeht" (magnificent things transpire). Her struggle to record her experiences and impressions using the conceptual and linguistic materials of her limited background and the popular culture is both brilliantly comical and critically reflective of its time and place. Like its predecessor, the novel reveals a poignant longing for self-understanding and communication on the part of its protagonist. *Das kunstseidene Mädchen* echoed Keun's first success and was translated into seven languages, including English; but a simplified and commercialized 1959 film version bore little resemblance to the original, and a dramatic revue produced in Bremen in 1973 was similarly far removed from the seriousness and complexity of the novel.

The liberal treatment of sexual morality and irreverence toward traditional values in these two novels led the Nazis to ban them as un-German and immoral "Asphalt-Literatur" (defined by the critic Gerd Roloff as literature of "intellectual nihilism" which does not embrace values of "the volkish, ethical, or religious common life"). In the spring of 1933 they were placed on the precursors of the Nazi blacklist and were soon removed from the publishing house and bookstores and destroyed. Keun displayed a typical, though foolhardy, courage and defiance of authority when she attempted to sue for the income lost through the regime's confiscation of her books. Afterward she was closely observed by the Gestapo and was eventually brought in and interrogated; it appears that she was released only because of her father's influence and financial intervention.

Offered support by the Dutch publisher Allert de Lange, Keun left Germany in the spring of 1936 and settled in Ostende on the Belgian seacoast. A novel manuscript which she had completed and left behind in Germany, "Der hungrige Ernährer" (The Hungry Breadwinner), has never been found. In Ostende she encountered other German and Austrian émigrés, among them Egon Erwin Kisch, Ernst Toller, Stefan Zweig, Hermann Kesten, and Joseph Roth. Her husband chose to stay in Germany, and they were divorced in May 1937. Keun became the companion of Roth, a well-known Austrian novelist, and traveled with him to Brussels, Amsterdam, Paris, Wilna, Salzburg, Vienna, Warsaw, and Lemberg. Both wrote novels during their exile, constantly struggling to scrape together enough money to survive.

Das Mädchen, mit dem die Kinder nicht verkehren durften (The Girl with Whom the Children Were Not Allowed to Associate, 1936; translated as *The Bad Example*, 1955) is told by a high-spirited preadolescent girl who, with her friends, plays pranks on hypocritical and authoritarian teachers, neighbors, and relatives in petit-bourgeois Cologne at the end of World War I. The child's seemingly naive perspective gives the narrative a quality of disillusioning humor; speaking the truth as she sees it, this bright tomboy punctures conventions of respectability and patriotism and often reaps punishments she does not understand or deserve. In addition to the convincing presentation of a child's thoughts and feelings and the satire of adult arrogance and misunderstanding, the novel provides a description of the hunger and suffering of the populace in the late phases of the war. It was reprinted several times after 1945 and was translated into four languages. It received an enormous audience response when it was read over German radio in 1948.

Based on her firsthand observation of the early years of National Socialist rule, Keun's *Nach Mitternacht* (1937; translated as *After Midnight*, 1938) again employs a young, culturally and politically naive narrator as the lens through which to view the brutality and stupidity of the totalitarian regime, as well as the responses of the petite bourgeoisie and intellectuals to the fascist culture of denunciation and terror. Keun shows how completely the private lives of nineteen-year-old

Sanna and her friends and family are shaped by the underlying political forces in this account, which begins in a Frankfurt pub and ends a little over twenty-four hours later with the escape of Sanna and her lover Franz across the border. Through Sanna's recollections and reflections, however, a much wider time span and geographic locus are incorporated into the novel. Once again the artfully naive, precisely observing perspective creates a satire that is humorous and deadly serious by turns.

In Sanna's Aunt Adelheid, a Cologne shopkeeper, Keun creates one of the novel's most effective caricatures. A petty, selfish, cruel woman, who, despite her exaggerated unpleasantness, is shown to be typical of many, Adelheid finds in National Socialism the chance to rise above her neighbors; by eager participation in all officially sponsored activities and by threatened or actual denunciation of rivals (including Sanna), she attains a status and wields power otherwise denied her. Sanna has escaped this web of terror and the enmity of her aunt by fleeing to Frankfurt, where her stepbrother Algin Moder, a once popular liberal writer out of favor in the current cultural climate, lives with his wife Liska. In Algin Keun presents the type of intellectual who attempted to accommodate to the Nazi expectations despite his convictions; his complement is the journalist Heini, still anti-Nazi but convinced of the impossibility of taking effective action against the regime. Other types Sanna encounters in Frankfurt are the wealthy Jewish merchant Aaron, who still believes that he is better off under the National Socialists than he would have been under the Communists, and the naively unpolitical, sentimental Jewish doctor Breslauer, who must finally plan to flee. A visit to Frankfurt by Hitler offers Keun an opportunity for further satirizing Nazi pomposity and the worshipful enthusiasm of the populace.

Nach Mitternacht was translated into six languages between 1937 and 1939 and was reprinted in Germany three times between 1956 and 1965. Its republication in 1980 was widely reviewed in the more important German newspapers, and a film version was produced in 1981. In its economical, precise, and critical depiction of "deutsche Wirklichkeit" (German reality), as Klaus Mann put it in 1937, the novel is generally considered one of Keun's strongest and most important works.

In 1938 Keun published *Kind aller Länder* (Child of all Countries), a fictionalized account of exile life. The narrative largely follows the course of her own travels with Roth. The narrator is ten-year-old Kully, whose father, a writer, had to leave Germany with his wife Annchen and their daughter because of his criticism of the regime. Although the father has been compared to Roth, Keun suggested in *Bilder und Gedichte aus der Emigration* (Images and Poems from Emigration, 1947) that he was partially modeled on a Viennese journalist she had encountered in Ostende, "der Entdecker des Versatzwertes von Frau und Kind" (the discoverer of the pawn value of wife and child) who would leave his wife and child virtually captive in their hotel room for weeks while he traveled about Europe trying to raise money to pay the bill. Kully's naive trust and healthy common sense assure her psychic survival despite the chaos of exile existence and her parents' strained relationship. The kaleidoscopic series of impressions of life in exile through a child's puzzled perspective evokes at times an almost comic sense of absurd, endless movement without direction, every arrival soon superseded by a new departure. Again Keun's gift for precise observation provides a vivid, realistic portrait of the times without falling into sentimentality or pathos. The last section offers interesting glimpses of a European view of America. The novel was translated into Dutch in 1939 and reprinted in Germany in 1950 and 1981.

D-Zug dritter Klasse (Express Train, Third Class, 1938), also written and published during Keun's exile, is the humorous and suspenseful story of seven travelers who share a compartment in a train from Berlin to Paris during the time of the Third Reich. Once again Keun presents variations on the motif of flight, of transition from a no-longer-tenable reality to an uncertain future. The main focus is on Lenchen, a young woman who has acquired three fiancés out of her "feminine" fear of offending and is desperately hoping for "ein neues Leben" (a new life). Although the backdrop of Nazi Germany plays a much smaller part than in *Nach Mitternacht*, the events and characters of this novel are, as always with Keun, subtly shaped by their particular social and historical context. The novel was published in Amsterdam and translated into Danish in 1938; it was first published in Germany in 1946.

After a year and a half as his companion, Keun left Roth early in 1938. Roth had become intolerably jealous and increasingly ill, depressed, and alcoholic; he died in a Paris hospital on 27 May 1939. Without money or visa, Keun found herself trapped in Amsterdam when the Nazis occupied the Netherlands in May 1940. She obtained a false passport with the help of a German officer and returned to Germany under the name of Charlotte Tralow. She spent the five years until the end of the war in anxious and dangerous illegality and anonymity, unable to write. Her survival was aided by rumors in the world press that she had committed suicide along with some of her fellow exiles; had she been identified, she would have been executed for working against Hitler while outside Germany.

In 1947 Keun published the small volume *Bilder und Gedichte aus der Emigration*, in which she described the first half year of her exile, much of which was spent in Ostende in conversations with other émigré authors, and her experience as Roth's companion. The reminiscences offer insight into the situation of writers and intellectuals deprived by exile of a nourishing social and cultural context. Keun says that by 1938, having already said what she had to say about Germany and limited for political and tactical reasons in what she could write about the countries of her exile, she feared that she might never produce another book.

After the war Keun wrote feuilletons and light satirical pieces for the radio, journals, and newspapers, in particular the Düsseldorf *Der Mittag*. Her last novel, *Ferdinand, der Mann mit dem freundlichen Herzen* (Ferdinand, the Man with the Friendly Heart, 1950), draws on her years of struggle and deprivation following the war. Employing a male protagonist-narrator for the first time, *Ferdinand* presents an often satirical review of types and conditions in the period immediately before and after the currency reform of 1948. Like his female precursors, Ferdinand Timpe is a naive but perceptive outsider, in this case a returning soldier and jack-of-all-trades with a sensitive, unassertive nature and natural sympathy for the underdog. Ferdinand, something of a male counterpart to Lenchen in *D-Zug dritter Klasse*, becomes engaged without really wanting to and spends most of the novel thinking about how to free himself without hurting his fiancée, Luise. But with the dawn of a more stabilized era and the prospect of a more advantageous match, Luise casts him off without further ado. Ferdinand, adrift and without deeper ties elsewhere, feels "at home" only in the presence of his mother, Laura, an imperturbable Earth-Mother figure.

Ferdinand describes the scarcity of food, housing, clothing, and amenities after the war, and the measures people took to obtain what they needed. Black market operators, militarists, profiteers, and superficially denazified fascists are some of the types that are critically exposed in the novel. The destructive effects on the human psyche of military discipline and the prisoner-of-war camp are also portrayed. Appealing charlatans such as the advice giver and the color therapist pander to the hunger for human contact and meaning in an empty, superficial society. The eccentricity of many of the characters and episodes suggests the grotesque distortions and displacements of postwar existence, but too many such scenes and characters are not adequately developed or integrated into the almost nonexistent plot. *Ferdinand* was translated into Dutch, Danish, and French and was reprinted in Germany in 1960 and 1981. The novel did not attain the same critical or popular success as the earlier works, however, notwithstanding Hermann Kesten's high praise of it in his foreword to the first edition.

Wenn wir alle gut wären: Kleine Begebenheiten, Erinnerungen und Geschichten (If We All Were Good: Little Occurrences, Reminiscences and Stories), a collection of short satirical pieces and anecdotes from the postwar years, including the previously published *Bilder und Gedichte aus der Emigration,* appeared in a small edition in 1954. The satirical sketches show Keun's superb knowledge of human nature, humorous perspective, and sensitivity to the spoken idiom; among the more effective are those capturing the efforts of former small-time Nazis to adapt to postwar conditions. In 1983 an enlarged edition appeared which also included "Briefe aus der inneren Emigration" (Letters from the Inner Emigration); written from 1946 to 1948, these letters provide moving documentation of the bitter conditions in Germany during the immediate postwar years and a sense of their personal and artistic cost for writers like Keun.

Although her earlier books began to be reprinted in the 1950s, Keun failed to recapture the success or regain the literary public she had once enjoyed. The loss of many friends and fellow writers, the years of constant fear and deprivation, the continuing pressure to write simply to survive, and finally the conservative cold war era surely all played a role in her withdrawal from literary activity. Keun had a daughter in 1951, but instead of marrying she remained with and cared for her parents. After their deaths she became increasingly isolated. She wrote no more after the beginning of the 1960s and disappeared from the literary scene, living a marginal, impoverished existence until her works were rediscovered and republished in the more progressive atmosphere of the 1970s and she became the subject of interviews and articles. Her last years were spent in Cologne amid renewed recognition; in 1981 she was awarded the first Marieluise Fleißer Prize of the City of Ingolstadt.

Invited to write her autobiography, Keun chose the title "Kein Anschluß unter dieser Nummer" (No Connection under this Number), but no trace of a manuscript has been found. The outsider-consciousness that had given Keun's novels so much of their brilliance may finally have made it seem futile to try to connect to the present or future. In an interview published shortly before her death Keun spoke of the feeling, which obsessed her during her later years, of a constant need to flee, to leave her present situation for an unknown destination. This pattern of flight, uprootedness, separation, and an uncertain future, which can also be traced throughout the novels, reflects the shaping of her life by historical events. Keun met her final illness, a lung tumor, with characteristic defiance, ignoring medical advice to limit her use of tobacco and alcohol. Her death on 5 May 1982 forever silenced one of Germany's most outspoken and clear-sighted critics, a courageous and trenchant observer of her society through some of its most tormented decades.

Letters:
Ich lebe in einem wilden Wirbel: Briefe an Arnold Strauss, 1933-1947, edited by Gabriele Kreis and Marjory S. Strauss (Düsseldorf: Claassen, 1988).

Interviews:
David Bronsen, *Joseph Roth: Eine Biographie* (Cologne: Kiepenheuer & Witsch, 1974), pp. 69-477;
" 'Woanders hin! Mich hält nichts fest': Irmgard Keun im Gespräch mit Klaus Antes," *die horen,* 27 (Spring 1982): 61-75.

Bibliographies:
Dietrich Steinbach, "Irmgard Keun," in *Kritisches Lexikon zur deutschsprachigen Gegenwartsliteratur,* edited by Heinz Ludwig Arnold (Munich: Edition text + kritik, 1985), pp. 1-11;

Ritta Jo Horsley, "Irmgard Keun," in *Women Writers of Austria, Germany and Switzerland: An Annotated Bio-Bibliographical Guide*, edited by Elke Frederiksen (Westport, Conn.: Greenwood Press, forthcoming).

References:

Elfriede Jelinek, " 'Weil sie heimlich weinen muß, lacht sie über Zeitgenossen': Über Irmgard Keun," *die horen*, 25 (Winter 1980): 221-225;

Hermann Kesten, "Irmgard Keun," in his *Meine Freunde, die Poeten* (Munich: Desch, 1959), pp. 423-434;

Volker Klotz, "Forcierte Prosa: Stilbeobachtungen an Bildern und Romanen der Neuen Sachlichkeit," in *Dialog: Festgabe für Josef Kunz*, edited by Rainer Schönhaar (Berlin: Schmidt, 1973), pp. 244-271;

Ursula Krechel, "Irmgard Keun: Die Zerstörung der kalten Ordnung: Auch ein Versuch über das Vergessen weiblicher Kulturleistungen," *Literaturmagazin*, 10 (1979): 103-128;

Leo Lensing, "Cinema, Society, and Literature in Irmgard Keun's *Das kunstseidene Mädchen*," *Germanic Review*, 60 (Fall 1985): 129-134;

Irene Loriska, *Frauendarstellungen bei Irmgard Keun und Anna Seghers* (Frankfurt am Main: Haag + Herchen, 1985);

Klaus Mann, "Deutsche Wirklichkeit," *Die Neue Weltbühne*, no. 17 (1937): 526-528;

Gerd Roloff, "Irmgard Keun–Vorläufiges zu Leben und Werk," *Amsterdamer Beiträge zur neueren Germanistik*, 6 (1977): 45-68;

Gert Sautermeister, "Irmgard Keuns Exilroman *Nach Mitternacht*," *die horen*, 27 (Spring 1982): 48-60;

Jürgen Serke, "Irmgard Keun," in his *Die verbrannten Dichter* (Weinheim: Beltz & Gelberg, 1977), pp. 162-175;

Hans-Albert Walter, "Das Bild Deutschlands im Exilroman," *Neue Rundschau*, 77, no. 3 (1966): 437-458;

Livia Z. Wittmann, "Erfolgschancen eines Gaukelspiels: Vergleichende Beobachtungen zu *Gentlemen Prefer Blondes* (Anita Loos) und *Das kunstseidene Mädchen* (Irmgard Keun)," *Carleton Germanic Papers*, 11 (1983): 35-49;

Wittmann, "Der Stein des Anstoßes: Zu einem Problemkomplex in berühmten und gerühmten Romanen der Neuen Sachlichkeit," *Jahrbuch der internationalen Germanistik*, 14, no. 2 (1982): 56-78.

Papers:

A small collection of Keun's papers is administered by Freifrau von der Recke, Theodor Heusse Ring 28, 5 Cologne 1, West Germany.

Hans Hellmut Kirst

(5 December 1914-   )

Gunther J. Holst
University of South Carolina

BOOKS: *Wir nannten ihn Galgenstrick: Roman* (Munich: Desch, 1950); translated by Richard and Clara Winston as *The Lieutenant Must Be Mad* (New York: Harcourt, Brace, 1951; Leeds, U.K.: Morley, 1972);

Sagten Sie Gerechtigkeit, Captain? Roman (Munich: Desch, 1952); revised and republished as *Letzte Station Camp 7: Roman* (Munich: Desch, 1966); translated by J. Maxwell Brownjohn as *Last Stop Camp 7* (New York: Coward-McCann, 1969; London: Collins, 1969);

Aufruhr in einer kleinen Stadt: Roman (Munich, Vienna & Basel: Desch, 1953);

Null-acht fünfzehn: Roman, volume 1: *Die abenteuerliche Revolte des Gefreiten Asch* (Munich, Vienna & Basel: Desch, 1954); republished as *08/15 in der Kaserne: Die abenteuerliche Revolte des Gefreiten Asch* (Munich, Vienna & Basel: Desch, 1955); volume 2: *Die seltsamen Kriegserlebnisse des Soldaten Asch* (Munich, Vienna & Basel: Desch, 1954); republished as *08/15 im Krieg* (Munich, Vienna & Basel: Desch, 1955); volume 3: *08/15 bis zum Ende: Der gefährliche Endsieg des Soldaten Asch* (Munich, Vienna & Basel: Desch, 1955); translated by Robert Kee as *Zero Eight Fifteen: A Novel*, volume 1: *The Strange Mutiny of Gunner Asch: A Novel* (London: Weidenfeld & Nicolson, 1955); republished as *The Revolt of Gunner Asch* (Boston: Little, Brown, 1956); volume 2: *Gunner Asch Goes to War: Zero Eight Fifteen II, a Novel* (London: Weidenfeld & Nicolson, 1956); republished as *Forward, Gunner Asch!* (Boston: Little, Brown, 1956); volume 3: *The Return of Gunner Asch: A Novel* (London: Weidenfeld & Nicolson, 1957; Boston: Little, Brown, 1957);

Die letzte Karte spielt der Tod: Roman der Spionage (Munich, Vienna & Basel: Desch, 1955); translated by Brownjohn as *The Last Card* (New York: Pyramid, 1967); republished as *Death Plays the Last Card* (London: Fontana, 1968);

Gott schläft in Masuren: Roman (Munich, Vienna & Basel: Desch, 1956);

Mit diesen meinen Händen: Roman (Munich, Vienna & Basel: Desch, 1957);

Keiner kommt davon: Bericht von den letzten Tagen Europas (Munich, Vienna & Basel: Desch, 1957); translated by Richard Graves as *The Seventh Day* (Garden City: Doubleday, 1959); republished as *No One Will Escape: A Novel* (London: Weidenfeld & Nicolson, 1959);

Kultura 5 und der Rote Morgen: Roman (Munich, Vienna & Basel: Desch, 1958);

Glück läßt sich nicht kaufen: Roman (Munich, Vienna & Basel: Desch, 1959);

Fabrik der Offiziere: Roman (Munich, Vienna & Basel: Desch, 1960); translated by Kee as *Officer Factory: A Novel* (London: Collins, 1962); republished as *The Officer Factory* (Garden City: Doubleday, 1963);

Kameraden: Roman (Munich, Vienna & Basel: Desch, 1961); translated by Brownjohn as *Brothers in Arms: A Novel* (London: Collins, 1965; New York: Harper & Row, 1967);

Die Nacht der Generale: Roman (Munich, Vienna & Basel: Desch, 1962); translated by Brownjohn as *The Night of the Generals: A Novel* (London: Collins, 1963; New York: Harper & Row, 1963);

Bilanz der Traumfabrik: Kritische Randnotizen zur Geschichte des Films (Munich: Brickmann, 1963);

Null-Acht-Fünfzehn heute: Roman (Munich, Vienna & Basel: Desch, 1963); translated by Brownjohn as *What Became of Gunner Asch* (London: Collins, 1964; New York: Harper & Row, 1964);

Aufstand der Soldaten: Roman des 20. Juli 1944 (Munich, Vienna & Basel: Desch, 1965); translated by Brownjohn as *Soldiers' Revolt* (New York: Harper & Row, 1966); translation republished as *The 20th of July* (London: Collins, 1966);

Die Wölfe: Roman (Munich: Desch, 1967); translated by Brownjohn as *The Wolves* (New York:

Hans Hellmut Kirst (courtesy of the author)

Coward-McCann, 1968); republished as *The Fox of Maulen* (London: Collins, 1968);

Kein Vaterland: Roman (Munich: Desch, 1968); translated by Brownjohn as *No Fatherland* (New York: Coward-McCann, 1970); republished as *Undercover Man* (London: Collins, 1970);

Deutschland, deine Ostpreußen: Ein Buch voller Vorurteile (Hamburg: Hoffmann & Campe, 1968);

Soldaten, Offiziere, Generale: Die Tragödie der Soldaten (Munich, Vienna & Basel: Desch, 1969);

Faustrecht: Roman (Munich: Desch, 1969); translated by Brownjohn as *The Adventures of Private Faust* (New York: Coward, McCann & Geoghegan, 1971); republished as *Who's in Charge Here?* (London: Collins, 1971);

Heinz Rühmann: Ein biographischer Report (Munich: Kindler, 1969);

Das Udo-Jürgens-Songbuch, by Kirst, David Hamilton, and Heinz Edelmann (Munich: Junker, 1970);

Held im Turm: Roman (Munich: Desch, 1970); translated by Brownjohn as *Hero in the Tower* (New York: Coward, McCann & Geoghegan, 1972; London: Fontana/Collins, 1974);

Verdammt zum Erfolg: Roman (Munich, Vienna & Basel: Desch, 1971); translated by Brownjohn as *Damned to Success* (New York: Coward, McCann & Geoghegan, 1973); republished as *A Time for Scandal* (London: Collins, 1973);

Verurteilt zur Wahrheit: Roman (Munich: Desch, 1972); translated by Brownjohn as *A Time for Truth* (New York: Coward, McCann & Geoghegan, 1974; London: Collins, 1974);

Gespräche mit meinem Hund Anton (Munich: Desch, 1972);

Verfolgt vom Schicksal: Roman (Munich: Desch, 1973);

Alles hat seinen Preis: Roman (Hamburg: Hoffmann & Campe, 1974); translated by Brownjohn as *Everything Has Its Price* (New York: Coward, McCann & Geoghegan, 1976); republished as *A Time for Payment* (London: Collins, 1976);

Die Nächte der langen Messer: Roman (Hamburg: Hoffmann & Campe, 1975); translated by Brownjohn as *The Nights of the Long Knives* (New York: Coward, McCann & Geoghegan, 1976; London: Collins, 1976);

Generalsaffären: Roman (Munich: Bertelsmann, 1977); translated by Brownjohn as *The Affairs of the Generals* (New York: Coward, McCann & Geoghegan, 1979);

Die Katzen von Caslano (Hamburg: Hoffmann & Campe, 1977);

Null-acht fünfzehn in der Partei: Roman (Munich: Bertelsmann, 1978); translated by Brownjohn as *Party Games* (New York: Simon & Schuster, 1980);

Der Nachkriegssieger: Roman (Munich: Bertelsmann, 1979);

Hund mit Mann: Bericht über einen Freund (Munich: Bertelsmann, 1979);

Der unheimliche Freund (Munich: Heyne, 1979);

Ausverkauf der Helden: Roman (Munich: Bertelsmann, 1980); translated by Brownjohn as *Heroes for Sale* (London: Collins, 1982);

Eine Falle aus Papier (Munich: Heyne, 1981);

Geld, Geld, Geld (Munich: Heyne, 1982);

Bedenkliche Begegnung (Munich: Heyne, 1982);

Ende '45 (Munich: Bertelsmann, 1982);

Die gefährliche Wahrheit (Munich: Heyne, 1984);

Die seltsamen Menschen von Maulen: Heitere Geschichten aus Ostpreußen (Munich: Blanvalet, 1984);

Blitzmädel (Munich: Blanvalet, 1984);

Das Schaf im Wolfspelz (Herford: Busse Seewald, 1985);

Der unheimliche Mann Gottes: Eine heitere Erzählung aus Ostpreußen (Munich: Blanvalet, 1987).

Hans Hellmut Kirst, internationally one of the most successful German authors after 1945, achieved his breakthrough with his trilogy *Null-acht fünfzehn* (1954-1955; translated as *Zero Eight Fifteen*, 1955-1957), about the picaresque adventures of Gunner Asch in the German army just prior to and during World War II. His immense popularity among the general reading public in Germany and abroad is no doubt primarily due to those of his forty-odd novels and tales—some of which were slightly changed and republished under different titles—that are set against the backdrop of the Nazi period, World War II, and the immediate postwar years. A professional soldier from 1933 to 1945, Kirst has been called "der berufsmäßige Epiker des deutschen Soldatenstandes" (the professional novelist of the German soldier class). His books have been printed in more than 250 editions and translated into 28 languages. With sales of around 12 million copies and even his early books being reprinted constantly, his success continues unabated.

Kirst was born on 5 December 1914 in Osterode in East Prussia, then the easternmost province of Germany, now part of the U.S.S.R. and Poland, to Johannes and Gertrud Golldack Kirst. His father, a policeman, was transferred frequently within the remote reaches of that part of the province called Masuria, a land of 3,000

Publisher's advertisement for two of Kirst's three novels written in the early 1950s

lakes, abundant forests, wild animals, and rich agriculture; the countryside and the people of this region are featured in several of Kirst's books. At the Kaiser-Wilhelm-Gymnasium in Osterode Kirst was, by his own admission, not a particularly good student except in German, geography, and history. He worked for a short time as an accountant on a large agricultural estate, counting eggs and sacks of rye. In 1933, following his father's suggestion, he joined the army; but he never became a member of the National Socialist party. At the end of the war in 1945 he was a first lieutenant serving as an instructor in the history of war at an air force war school. After the war Kirst settled in Munich, where he worked as a laborer in road construction and in a nursery and flower shop. In 1947 he became a film critic for the *Münchner Mittag*, now the *Münchner*

Merkur. Fascinated by the medium of film, he continued to free-lance for the paper for twenty-two years; he still occasionally critiques films on television. On 14 December 1962 he married Ruth Mueller; they have an adopted daughter, Beatrice.

Kirst designates himself as a journalist rather than as an author. This preference is reflected in his attitude toward his writing and in his work habits. He attributes ninety percent of his enormous success to sheer diligence and will power. In an interview for his old newspaper in 1980 he said: "Ich verstehe mich nicht als Künstler, sondern als Handwerker" (I do not consider myself an artist, but rather a craftsman). Over the years he has developed a routine that separates work and family life both mentally and physically. He maintains a bachelor apartment on the top floor of a building with a spacious roof garden to keep him close to nature even in Munich; the apartment is filled with books and the African art objects he collects. His wife and daughter live on Lake Starnberg outside Munich, where he joins them in the intervals between projects. In his apartment he works according to habits that were formed in the immediate postwar years when the daylight hours had to be devoted to the menial tasks of survival: he starts writing in the evening and–when things are going well–continues until dawn. Kirst values his privacy both in Munich and during the time he spends with his family. At the few social events he attends, he prefers to be on the sidelines observing, rather than in the center of attention. He is at once fascinated and astounded by his international success. At times he has the feeling that he is an American author more than a German one because it is in the United States that his books have enjoyed the most printings and the best reviews. German literary critics have applied the term "Unterhaltungsliteratur" (literally: entertainment literature) to his novels, following a tendency to equate a very large readership such as Kirst enjoys with lack of first-rate literary quality. In fact, Kirst is, in the critic Armin Mohler's words, a "full-blooded storyteller" who makes no pretense of artfulness in his literary technique. His strength lies in his honest, authentic treatment of the individual soldier and the military machine in which he is caught up. In 1964 he was awarded the Golden Palm of Bordighera for his novel *Null-Acht-Fünfzehn heute* (Zero Eight Fifteen Today, 1963; translated as *What Became of Gunner Asch*, 1964); a year later he received the Edgar

Allan Poe Award of the Mystery Writers of America for *Die Nacht der Generale* (1962; translated as *The Night of the Generals*, 1963). In 1966 he became a member of the German P.E.N. Club and was the first German writer to be made a member of the American Authors Guild. In 1968 he received an honorary membership in the Mark Twain Society for *The Wolves* (1968; translation of *Die Wölfe*, 1967), and in 1979 he was voted into the P.E.N. Club of Liechtenstein.

Kirst maintains that his success carries with it an obligation. A central theme in many of his books is the attempt to come to grips with the burden of World War II and of the Nazi regime which "seduced" him. In a 1980 interview with the *Münchner Merkur* he says that "der Schlüssel zu meinen Büchern ist die Empörung, die ich empfand, als ich erkannte, wie wir belogen worden waren" (the key to my books is the outrage I felt when I realized how we had been lied to). The seductiveness of the regime is a problem that still occupies him. For himself and his fellow East Prussians he attributes it in part to the fact that eighty percent of them had always voted for nationalist issues and candidates; there were few socialists and no Communists in that area bordering in part on the U.S.S.R. National Socialism was considered to represent a combination of "national" and "social" concerns in the best sense. And, given the condition of Germany in the Weimar Republic, the first few years under Hitler were indeed rather seductive. Having been closed off until 1945 as though living "under a giant glass dome," Kirst threw himself into the task of dealing with the events of those years by writing about them: "Man mußte sein Weltbild ändern" (We had to change our picture of the world). He worries that Germany has drawn too few lessons from the mistakes of the past, "als ob es dieses grauenhafte Dritte Reich nie gegeben hätte" (as though this horrible Third Reich had never existed). He is also worried about a lack of acceptance of the basic concepts of tolerance and compromise. He considers his writing a sort of personal atonement which he underlines by designating all Polish royalties from sales of the *Null-acht fünfzehn* trilogy for Warsaw war orphans and by forgoing all proceeds from his Israeli editions. In this personal way he attempts to honor the memory of the first and of the main victims of Nazi aggression.

Many of Kirst's books may be called military novels, as distinguished from war novels such as Erich Maria Remarque's *Im Westen nichts Neues*

Die große Roman-Trilogie von Hans Hellmut Kirst

»NULL-ACHT FÜNFZEHN«

1. Band: 08/15 in der Kaserne. 400 Seiten
2. Band: 08/15 im Krieg.   432 Seiten
3. Band: 08/15 bis zum Ende. 400 Seiten

Kartoniert je DM 5.80, Ganzleinen je DM 9.80

GESCHENK-KASSETTE 08/15

Alle drei Bände in Ganzleinen DM 29.40

Der Roman NULL-ACHT FÜNFZEHN hatte gleich nach seinem Erscheinen wie eine Brisanzbombe eingeschlagen und einen wahren Wirbelsturm der öffentlichen Meinung hervorgerufen. Über Nacht wurde 08/15 zum meistdiskutierten deutschen Roman und zum Bestseller der Gegenwart. Seit vielen Monaten ist 08/15 auf der Straße, in der Familie, auf der Arbeitsstätte, in der Weltpresse und im Rundfunk unentwegt Diskussionsthema Nummer 1.

Mit Humor und Witz, aber auch mit erbarmungsloser Ironie hat HANS HELLMUT KIRST im Zeichen der Wiederaufrüstung in aller Welt eines der brennendsten Themen unserer Zeit angeschnitten: das schikanöse Drillsystem 'des Kasernenhofs; er hat Korruption, Selbstsucht und Endsiegerheldentum von Kasernenhofstrategen im Frontbereich angeprangert und die chaotischen Zustände auf den Rückmarschwegen und in der Heimat, die Umwertung aller Werte während der Wochen des Zusammenbruchs bis zum bitteren Ende der furchtbarsten aller Kriege faszinierend geschildert. So wurde 08/15 die aufsehenerregende große Romantrilogie unserer Zeit mit dem weithin vernehmbaren Ruf: Nie wieder Krieg!

Millionen und aber Millionen haben miterlebt und mitgelitten, was HANS HELLMUT KIRST in diesen drei Romanen so packend und lebenswahr dargestellt hat, daß unzählige Leser spontan urteilten: „Das ist nicht nur ein Roman, das ist ein wahrheitsgetreuer Tatsachenbericht, denn *genau so war es!".* — »NULL-ACHT FÜNFZEHN« wird in 17 Sprachen übersetzt!

Der größte deutsche Romanerfolg seit 1945

VERLAG KURT DESCH

WIEN · MÜNCHEN · BASEL

Advertisement for Kirst's trilogy about the adventures of a German soldier in the years before and during World War II

(1929; translated as *All Quiet on the Western Front,* 1929). They are set in the German army before and during World War II, but even those involving military action, such as the second and third volumes of the *Null-acht fünfzehn* trilogy, only incidentally describe battle scenes. Their main themes are individual conscience, survival in a relentless military machine designed to crush all individuality, and the abuses and corruption permeating this machine. His first novel, *Wir nannten ihn Galgenstrick* (We Called Him Gallows-Rope, 1950; translated as *The Lieutenant Must Be Mad,* 1951), is an unequivocal attack on the excesses of German militarism. Lieutenant Strick, a highly decorated artillery officer, has spent three years on the Russian front and is being transferred to a local command on the home front. At the railhead in Russia, seriously wounded soldiers—among them one he knows well—are removed

from a freight car over his protest, and the car is loaded with crates marked "Secret." Strick becomes suspicious when the same car is unloaded at his own destination, a small town in Franconia. The crates turn out to contain scarce food supplies and luxury items destined for the black market. In a daring move in concert with Gareis, a civilian inspector of the Geheime Feldpolizei (Secret Military Police) he has the transport officer, who is a major and a Nazi party member, arrested. This action immediately pits him against all but one of the officers in his command, foremost among them the commanding officer, Colonel Müller, who runs his little fiefdom with hollow clichés and an insistence on proper form and etiquette, and Captain Wolf, a corrupt quartermaster who is in league with the transport officer and makes sure that the officers' mess and club are well stocked with items withheld from the troops. Lieutenant Rabe, a young, idealistic innocent untouched by the corruption and excesses around him, initially disapproves of Strick's methods, but in the end he sides with him. Strick, appointed political action officer by the regional command, takes on one after the other of his fellow officers and finally becomes involved in the abortive officers' uprising of 20 July 1944. He escapes punishment only with the help of the incorruptible Inspector Gareis.

In this first novel, which is somewhat uneven in characterization and narrative line but marked by vivid imagery, Kirst lays the groundwork for the characters, actions, and themes of the *Null-acht fünfzehn* trilogy, which, when it was published in 1954 and 1955, brought him international success but caused controversy at home. The first volume, *Die abenteuerliche Revolte des Gefreiten Asch* (The Adventurous Revolt of Gunner Asch, 1954; republished as *08/15 in der Kaserne* [In the Barracks, 1955]; translated as *The Strange Mutiny of Gunner Asch,* 1955), has been called by Fred Hepp "die bittere Ballade vom Kasernenhof" (the bitter ballad of the drill field). Kirst turns the designation for a weapon, the 08/15 machine gun, into a symbol for a military system whose goal of perfection can only be reached by relentless insistence on doing everything by rote until all is devoid of meaning and people are dehumanized. At this point living tradition becomes empty form; language is reduced to formulae and human beings to ciphers in a rigid, self-perpetuating military machine. As Mohler points out, a unique feature of Kirst's military novels is the central role of a consistently anarchic

Page from the manuscript for Kirst's novel Fabrik der Offiziere, *published in 1960 (courtesy of Special Collections, Mugar Memorial Library, Boston University)*

character in a nation traditionally averse to anarchism. These heroes have lost all idealism; they merely want to survive. In *Wir nannten ihn Galgenstrick* Lieutenant Strick, a "realist from experience," has lost his ideals after three years in the giant slaughterhouse of the Russian front.

It is friendship, not idealism, that triggers the "mutiny" of PFC Asch, a friendship he resists fiercely because it interferes with his sole aim of not being crushed by the relentless machinery of the army system. When a sensitive young recruit, Johannes Vierbein, is about to be driven to suicide because he has been singled out for unconscionably brutal treatment by the first sergeant, Asch decides to throw sand into the machinery and get even with the system and its worst representatives. But it is not so much sympathy for Vierbein—who ultimately turns out to be the perfect result of the molding process—as it is anger at his own loss of dignity that drives Asch to obstruction. He does thwart the system, but—ironically—is promoted to corporal (a noncommissioned officer rank in the German army). Despite the efforts of decent officers such as Lieutenant Wedelmann and Major Luschke, the battalion commander, the system remains intact. (Some of its vestiges survive the war to resurface in *Null-Acht-Fünfzehn heute,* which depicts the modern Bundeswehr [army of the Federal Republic of Germany].)

In the second part of the trilogy, *Die seltsamen Kriegserlebnisse des Soldaten Asch* (The Singular War Experiences of Soldier Asch, 1954; republished as *08/15 im Krieg* [In the War, 1955; translated as *Gunner Asch Goes to War*, 1956], Asch is an artillery sergeant on the Russian front, where he tries to survive without loss of limbs or self-respect. He has been assigned as an aide to Lieutenant Wedelmann, who is the temporary battery commander. An idealist who mistakes National Socialism for Germany and Hitler for an honorable man, Wedelmann wants to fight a clean war and, like Asch, wants to save lives rather than see them sacrificed needlessly. The regimental commander, Luschke, who is now a colonel, has the same goals. An officer of the honorable old Prussian school, he is a bit of an anachronism; but he has no illusions regarding the nature of the war and those who started it: "Ja, Herr Oberleutnant—ein Krieg ohne Ehre. Mit Berechnung vom Zaun gebrochen. Mit den Methoden eines Zuhälters geführt! Voller Verachtung für Menschenleben—für fremde wie für eigene. Angefeuert durch besoffen machendes

Kirst in 1971, the year his detective novel Verdammt zum Erfolg *was published (Ullstein–Interfoto)*

Pathos. Geschürt mit den billigen Phrasen von Ruhm. Das Heldentum der Amokläufer und ein Vaterland für Größenwahnsinnige. Und das ist das Gift, an dem die ganze Menschheit erkranken wird. Rettungslos" (Yes, Lieutenant, a war without honor. Conducted with the methods of a pimp! Full of contempt for human life—that of the others as well as ours. A war incited by intoxicating pathos. Fired by the cheap clichés of glory. The heroism of those running amuck, a fatherland for megalomaniacs. And that is the poison that will infect the entire humanity. Without a cure).

Asch and Wedelmann have a common enemy in their own ranks: Captain Witterer, a well-connected glory hound, who has been sent to gain experience at the front so that he can be promoted to a staff position. He takes over the battery, runs it "by the book," and finally, by an act of cowardice, causes the needless deaths of the best gun crew in the battery—the crew commanded by Vierbein, who had turned out to be an exemplary leader of men. The death of Vierbein disabuses Wedelmann of the remainder of his idealism. Colonel Luschke promotes him to command the battalion and orders him and Asch to "take care" of Witterer. The novel ends with a brief exchange between Asch and Kowalski, another veteran survivor:

> Für dieses Deutschland will ich nicht sterben, sagte der Wachtmeister Asch.
> Wer fragt dich denn danach? wollte Kowalski wissen.
> Es muß ein anderes Deutschland geben, für das es sich zu sterben lohnt.
> Mensch! sagte Kowalski. Vielleicht gibt es sogar einmal ein Deutschland, in dem es Spaß macht zu leben!

> (I don't want to die for this Germany, said Sgt. Asch.

> So who asks *you?* Kowalski wanted to know.
> There's got to be another kind of Germany worth dying for.
> Hey, guy, said Kowalski. Maybe someday there will even be a Germany in which it is fun to *live!*)

The third part of the trilogy, *08/15 bis zum Ende* (Until the End, 1955; translated as *The Return of Gunner Asch,* 1957), opens with some of the remnants of Luschke's division, among them Asch's battery, surrounded by American troops; Asch is now a lieutenant, Luschke a major general, and Wedelmann a captain. A mysterious Colonel Hauk and his adjutant, Lieutenant Greifer, assume command of the troops and order a breakout in which twenty soldiers are killed and many more are wounded. It turns out that Hauk and Greifer ordered the breakout so that they could get to some truckloads of valuable cargo an equally corrupt quartermaster had hidden for them. Once more Asch survives and manages to join Luschke and Wedelmann. The novel ends in the same garrison town where the trilogy started. General Luschke convenes a court-martial as the American troops advance on the town and has Greifer hanged for murder. To get their hands on Colonel Hauk, Asch and Wedelmann take over the barracks, which are now a prisoner-of-war camp. On the drill field, the symbol of agony for generations of soldiers, Hauk is killed in a machine-pistol duel by Major Hinrichsen, who commanded the breakout. Hinrichsen, the central tragic figure of the novel, stands for the entire army. An idealistic, small-town nationalist, he turned into a believer in Hitler and the National Socialist cause. His entire family dead, he finally

sees how cruelly he was betrayed by the system he fought for courageously and fairly: "Wir, röchelte er, wir, die wir uns um Sauberkeit bemüht haben–soweit ein Krieg überhaupt etwas mit Sauberkeit zu tun hat–, wir sind betrogen worden. . . . Sie düngten ihre Sucht nach Erfolg, ihre Lust an der Macht, ihren Ehrgeiz, Geschichte zu schreiben, mit dem Blut ihrer Soldaten, mit der Asche ihrer Opfer" (We, he said, his voice a death rattle, we who strove to be clean and decent–as much as a war can have anything to do with decency–we were betrayed. . . . They fertilized their craze for success, their lust for power, their ambition to make history, with the blood of their soldiers and the ashes of their victims). Asch agrees, and adds that the disaster was also caused by the German willingness to be degraded to herd animals by the butcher's command for discipline and to accept all sorts of perverted ideals: "Gott schütze uns vor diesen deutschen Selbstmördern!" (God save us from Germans bent on such suicide!).

Although Kirst does not consider *Null-acht fünfzehn* his best work, it stands as a unique account of the German soldier, who fought impossible odds not only at the front but also within his own political and military system. After serial publication of the first volume in a Cologne periodical, the magazine received a flood of letters from veterans saying "that's exactly the way it was," many of them adding "and it should never be that way again."

All three parts of the trilogy were made into movies, the first in 1954 with the title *08/15,* the other two in 1955 as *08/15 an der Front* and *8/15 in der Heimat.* The screenplays were written by Ernst von Salomon; the director was Paul May. The accent was decidedly on the military and comic aspects and less on the connection between the military and political elements stressed in the novels. Kirst was not unhappy with the first film; he called the second "still somewhat bearable"; but he bitterly condemned every aspect of the third film and repeatedly protested against it publicly. He was also critical of two subsequent films based on his novels, *Fabrik der Offiziere* (1960), directed by Frank Wismar, and *The Night of the Generals* (1967), an English-French coproduction directed by Anatole Litvak, with Peter O'Toole, Omar Sharif, Tom Courtenay, and Donald Pleasance.

In *Gott schläft in Masuren* (God Sleeps in Masuria, 1956) Kirst calls on his experience as an accountant on a large estate, his knowledge of

Kirst in 1987 (Ullstein–Teutopress)

village life, and his father's job as a rural policeman. The novel presents an array of Masurian characters in the rural atmosphere of the village of Maulen at the beginning of the Nazi period in 1933. Thiele, an experienced policeman, is transferred to Maulen to clear up a murder. An idealist who believes in the strict primacy of the law, he is pitted against Leberecht, the master of a large estate, who virtually owns the village. Thiele finds out that Leberecht is trying to preserve Maulen as the last paradise on earth where people live in harmony with each other and with nature. If God can sleep in peace anywhere in the world, Leberecht says, He will sleep in Maulen. Leberecht reigns firmly but benignly by the force of his personality and his shrewdness. Anticipating the Nazi takeover, he tries to combat it by setting up a local party organization and appointing his own people to key positions. Gradually these individuals are consumed by their ambitions and filled with a sense of their own importance, they turn against their benefactor. Leberecht barely manages to avert a catastrophe and bring his people back in line, but only because the murdered man turns out to have been

an early Nazi and all the current ones are implicated in his death. Thiele, disillusioned by the way traditional law enforcement is perverted by the new forces, covers up the murder, resigns from the police, and joins with Leberecht to try to avert the worst excesses of the regime. But the novel closes on a pessimistic note. Leberecht says: "Ich spüre, wie eine Zeit auf uns zukriecht, die uns ersticken wird. Der Druck, der uns umgibt, wächst immer mehr. . . . Wir denken nicht mehr an uns; viele beginnen, nur noch an sich zu denken. . . . Anstelle der Gemeinsamkeit tritt die Organisation. Wir sollen zu Zahlen werden, Thiele, zu Karteikarten, zu Dünger. Und wofür, Thiele? Wofür?" (I can feel a time creeping toward us, that will choke us to death. The pressure that surrounds us is growing bigger and bigger. . . . We don't think of each other anymore; many of us are starting to think only of ourselves. . . . The organization is taking the place of communality. We are intended to be turned into numbers, Thiele, into index cards, fertilizer. And what for, Thiele? What for?). Ultimately the criminal drive for supreme power will engulf even this remote paradise, and God will no longer be able to sleep in Maulen.

Three of Kirst's novels involve the events of 20 July 1944, culminating in the unsuccessful attempt on Hitler's life by the German resistance, which included officers up to the rank of field marshal as well as civilians. These novels, written from 1960 to 1964, were republished in 1969 under the title *Soldaten, Offiziere, Generale: Die Tragödie der Soldaten* (Soldiers, Officers, Generals: The Tragedy of the Soldiers). Kirst considers the first of the three, *Fabrik der Offiziere* (1960; translated as *Officer Factory*, 1962), his most important novel. It is set at an officers candidate school at the beginning of 1944. The commander, Major General Modersohn, is an officer of the old Prussian school–extremely self-disciplined and steeped in the principles of decency, morality, right, and freedom. One of the officer candidates, Hochbauer, is a fanatical Nazi who commands his own group of loyalists. A young officer with anti-Nazi tendencies is deliberately killed in a mine explosion by Hochbauer and his friends, who conspire to make it look like an accident. Modersohn orders the newly assigned Lieutenant Krafft to investigate. Krafft, convinced of Hochbauer's guilt, relentlessly pressures the latter until he commits suicide. But Krafft uses the occasion of the eulogy for Hochbauer to indict the lies and perversions of the regime. Because Modersohn backs him, both are accused of high treason and–like the men of the 20th of July–are executed. In this novel Kirst applies many of the effective elements of *Null-acht fünfzehn* but in a more mature way and toward more clear-cut and more forcibly presented themes: virtue versus corruption, soldier versus Nazi. The main characters are fleshed out by a unique device: each is portrayed by skillfully interspersed curricula vitae. These, according to the satirist Robert Neumann, present a cross section of the German nation, bringing about some extraordinary insights. He characterizes the *Officer Factory* as a section of the German resistance movement and a superlative praise of soldierly virtues.

Die Nacht der Generale (1962; translated as *The Night of the Generals*, 1963) combines the elements of a thriller with biting criticism of the military system and blind obedience, and contrasts theoretical with actual heroism and patriotism. One of the major characters, Colonel Grau of the Abwehr (German military counterintelligence), headed by Admiral Canaris, one of the most prominent members of the resistance, denigrates the conspiracy to assassinate Hitler as coming too late: "Jetzt noch Hitler töten, heißt einen Kadaver umbringen. Denn seine Niederlage ist besiegelt. Der Widerstand der Offiziere wäre bei Kriegsausbruch oder noch vor drei, selbst vor zwei Jahren eine historische Tat gewesen–jetzt ist es nur noch Notwehr" (To kill Hitler at this point means killing a cadaver. His defeat is sealed. At the outbreak of the war or three or even two years ago the resistance of the officers would have been a historical act–now it is no more than self-defense). The suspense of the novel is sustained on two converging levels, that of a criminal investigation and the military resistance against Hitler. The plot of the novel, in which Grau, while deeply involved in the resistance movement, doggedly pursues his investigation of the murders of two women–with the evidence pointing at a general–merges with events surrounding the assassination attempt. During the last twenty-four hours leading up to the attempt, the actions of the fictional characters as well as those actually involved at the various headquarters in Paris are chronicled almost minute by minute. Kirst uses the novel to condemn all but a few of the German generals, whom Grau calls "Lakaien und Arschkriecher" (lackeys and asskissers). Some consider it their duty to believe in Hitler. Others have contempt for Hitler and yet do not hesitate to make thousands of soldiers die

for him. Yet others are nothing but glorified drill sergeants, training their soldiers to die a so-called hero's death; the casualties of their divisions are nothing but laurel leaves from which they wind a wreath for themselves. And there are generals of such atrocious abnormality as General Tanz, his name–which means dance–reminiscent of the dance of death: "Dieser Tanz personifizierte den Krieg–einen Krieg, der nichts anderes war als ein sinnloses, hemmungsloses, grausames Blutbad. Wer sich dem Krieg hingibt wie einem Laster, dem man rettungslos verfallen kann, der ist gezeichnet–nicht anders als einer, der die Pest in sich hat, die Syphilis oder sonst eine alles zerstörende Seuche. So war das wahre Gesicht dieses Mannes, . . . nichts anderes als die Fratze des Krieges. Der Blutrausch unter der eisernen Maske: die Lust der Vernichtung. Vielleicht: die Hölle" (This Tanz personified war–a war that was nothing but a senseless, unrestrained, cruel bloodbath. Whoever submits to war as to a vice to which one can become hopelessly addicted, is a marked man–no different from someone carrying within him the plague, syphilis or any kind of pestilence that destroys all. That was the true face of this man, . . . nothing but the grotesque grimace of war. Hidden behind the iron mask was the frenzy of spilling blood: the lust for destruction. Perhaps: hell itself). Tanz, whose lust for blood made him murder the two women, also has a hand in crushing the resistance. He survives the war and continues to use his extraordinary military skills in the postwar organization of the East German army. Colonel Grau has been arrested by Tanz and shot in connection with the assassination attempt on Hitler, but his pursuit of the murderer is carried on with policemen from Poland, France, and East and West Germany all cooperating. Kirst here pays tribute to those professionals whose devotion to justice transcends national borders and political ideologies. He also uses this part of the novel for a biting criticism of the revival in some quarters of the old militarism and the attempt at whitewashing the monstrous failings of the military under the sign of the swastika.

Aufstand der Soldaten (1965; translated as *Soldiers' Revolt*, 1966) is a novelized history of the attempt on Hitler's life and the horrible revenge taken on the conspirators after it failed. A brief foreword points out that the book is based on fact; that names, dates, and events are real; and that much of the dialogue has been taken verbatim from official documents. It is a novel primarily because the central character, Captain Count von Brackwede, is fictional. Brackwede resembles in many respects one of the actual heroes of the 20 July conspiracy, Lieutenant Count Fritz-Dietlof von der Schulenburg, who, along with at least 200 others, paid for his dedication with his life. When Count von Brackwede, after days of torture to make him implicate his coconspirators, appears before the notorious Roland Freisler, presiding judge of the so-called Volksgerichtshof (people's court), Kirst has him express in the defiant words of the actual Count von der Schulenburg the motive of those trying to do away with Hitler: "Wir haben diese Tat auf uns genommen, um Deutschland vor einem namenlosen Unglück zu bewahren. Ich bin mir klar, daß ich daraufhin gehenkt werde. Aber ich bereue meine Tat nicht und hoffe, daß sie ein anderer, in einem glücklicheren Augenblick, durchführen wird" (We have taken this deed upon ourselves, in order to save Germany from an indescribable disaster. It is clear to me that I will be hanged as a consequence. But I do not regret what I have done, and hope that someone else, in a luckier moment, will succeed). In a postscript Kirst gives a brief sketch of Schulenburg, a symbol of the longed-for new Germany. The book is dedicated to him and his comrades in spirit and ultimate suffering.

Die Wölfe, set in Maulen, encompasses the entire Nazi period from 1933 to its catastrophic end in 1945 as the Soviet army is about to sweep through. Like all of Kirst's novels about that time, it deals with the question of how an individual can survive in the face of overwhelming force and power. Its hero is Alfons Materna, a cunning idealist who attempts to defeat the "pack of wolves"–the Nazis–first by using their own tactics against them and finally by joining the resistance. The novel provides an answer to Leberecht's anguished question at the end of *Gott schläft in Masuren*. The individual is indeed turned into a cipher, a cog in a brutal machine running amuck, fertilizer for a grandiose scheme of European domination that ends in total conflagration. The strength of this sprawling novel lies in Kirst's exuberant talent for storytelling and seemingly inexhaustible imagination. *Die Wölfe* combines elements of a regional novel–a colorful portrayal of the Masurian countryside and village life and its spate of characters–with a sociopolitical documentary and a fast-paced, action-packed adventure story. With all its humorous episodes, it never loses sight of the fact that the individual

who opposes this brutal system is engaged in a grim life-and-death struggle.

Kirst's deep love of his home, forever lost to him, is expressed in *Deutschland, deine Ostpreußen* (Germany, Your East Prussians, 1968). A quote by Hansgeorg Buchholtz heading the first chapter reflects the sentiments that prompted Kirst to write the book: "Land des Lichts . . . über deinen Geheimnissen kreisen die Möwen, aus dir gibt es keine Rückkehr. Meine Seele ist dir verfallen. Ich gehöre dir" (Land of light . . . the seagulls are circling over your secrets. There is no return from you. My soul is yours forever. I belong to you). Among the best of Kirst's writings, the thirty chapters of this book deal with a great variety of topics: history, the customs and quirks of the people, their prodigious feats of eating and drinking, their love of life, the seasons of this land of lakes, forests, and fields. There are excursions about the famous and not-so-famous sons and daughters of the province that produced such notables as the philosopher Immanuel Kant and the writer E. T. A. Hoffmann. Kirst manages a sustaining humor and a light touch throughout. Some delightful short stories deal with unforgettable Masurian characters such as Materna, the hero of *Die Wölfe*, who grows the biggest potatoes in the village and outwits the Nazis at their own game. *Die seltsamen Menschen von Maulen: Heitere Geschichten aus Ostpreußen* (The Strange People of Maulen: Amusing Stories of East Prussia, 1984) is a funny, irreverent account of the people of Masuria, of whom the writer Siegfried Lenz says: "Und sie besaßen eine Seele, zu deren Eigenarten blitzhafte Schläue gehörte und schwerfällige Tücke, tapsige Zärtlichkeit und eine rührende Geduld" (And they had a soul whose characteristics included lightninglike cunning and ponderous deviousness, clumsy tenderness and touching patience).

In addition to doing penance for having been led astray under the swastika banner, Kirst writes to warn against any resurgence of militarism and extremist political ideologies in Germany. These sentiments are expressed not only in his military novels but also in many detective novels which serve as a framework for social criticism. Kirst credits four months of intensive research at the Bundeskriminalamt (Office of the Federal Investigative Police) in Wiesbaden for giving him valuable insight into the social fabric and the techniques of detectives. He applied his knowledge in several novels; the first was *Verdammt zum Erfolg* (1971; translated as *Damned to Success*,

1973), which has been called a "study of the symptoms of Germany's illness.... An undisguised picture of the new power structure, of the mendacity of big business, and the disastrous confusion of the young generation." This sociological aspect and a fine irony lift his detective novels above most works in that genre.

Given his apparently inexhaustible imagination and his wealth of memories, Hans Hellmut Kirst will, in all likelihood, continue to look for answers to the persistent questions raised by the destructive twelve-year reign of the Nazis and their perversion of traditional German values.

Interview:
Liselotte Denk, Interview with Kirst, *Münchner Merkur*, 20/21 September 1980.

Reference:
Heinz Puknus, ed., *Hans Hellmut Kirst: Der Autor und sein Werk* (Munich: Bertelsmann, 1979).

Papers:
Mugar Memorial Library, Boston University, has a collection of Kirst manuscripts.

Wolfgang Koeppen
(23 June 1906-)

Michael Winkler
Rice University

BOOKS: *Erleben und Streben: Dichtungen* (Radolfzell: Heim-Verlag, 1929);

Eine unglückliche Liebe: Roman (Berlin: Cassirer, 1934);

Die Mauer schwankt: Roman (Berlin: Cassirer, 1935); republished as *Die Pflicht: Roman* (Berlin: Universitas, 1939);

Tauben im Gras: Roman (Stuttgart & Hamburg: Scherz & Goverts, 1951);

Das Treibhaus: Roman (Stuttgart: Scherz & Goverts, 1953);

Der Tod in Rom: Roman (Stuttgart: Scherz & Goverts, 1954); translated by Mervyn Savill as *Death in Rome: A Novel* (London: Weidenfeld & Nicolson, 1956; New York: Vanguard, 1961);

Nach Rußland und anderswohin: Empfindsame Reisen (Stuttgart: Goverts, 1958);

Amerikafahrt (Stuttgart: Goverts, 1959);

New York: Mit einem autobiographischen Nachwort (Stuttgart: Reclam, 1959);

Reisen nach Frankreich (Stuttgart: Goverts, 1961);

Romanisches Café: Erzählende Prosa (Frankfurt am Main: Suhrkamp, 1972);

Jugend (Frankfurt am Main: Suhrkamp, 1976);

Die elenden Skribenten: Aufsätze, edited by Marcel Reich-Ranicki (Frankfurt am Main: Suhrkamp, 1981);

Gesammelte Werke in sechs Bänden, edited by Reich-Ranicki, Dagmar von Briel, and Hans-Ulrich Treichel, 6 volumes (Frankfurt am Main: Suhrkamp, 1986).

Wolfgang Koeppen belongs to that generation of German novelists whose careers started just as Hitler came to power. The formative life experiences of Koeppen and writers such as Stefan Andres, Emil Belzner, Martin Kessel, Ernst Kreuder, and Horst Lange occurred during the years of the Weimar Republic, but political circumstances prevented them from developing their skills as writers when their need to give literary expression to their concerns was most urgent. Forced into virtual silence during the Third Reich, they expected a social and moral regeneration of Germany after the war and worked toward that goal in their writings. They were keen observers of daily life and especially of political developments during the crucial early years of the Federal Republic; and they eagerly adopted the techniques of the exemplary works of modern

Wolfgang Koeppen (Ullstein–Horst Tappe)

world literature in order to return German writing to international standards.

Their artistic productivity reached a first peak and also a serious crisis toward the end of the 1950s, in Koeppen's case as a result of his profound disappointment with the course of German reconstruction. He had also become uncertain about his ability to help shape the public mind through literature. The feeling that his work had been futile strengthened a persistent inclination to consider all justifications of serious art with deep skepticism. Ultimately, his self-doubt led to silence. But for as long as it could be balanced by a sense of purpose it helped inspire a style of prose fiction that many critics consider the most accurate literary image of life in West Germany during the decade after 1945.

Koeppen was born in 1906 in the old university town of Greifswald in Pomerania, near the Baltic Sea. The illegitimate child of a working-class woman, he grew up in poverty. In 1913 he was sent to Ortelsburg (Masuria) to live with a bachelor uncle who was an architect and mathematician and the owner of an extensive library. In this environment Koeppen developed an interest in literature, art, and the theater; but he did not get along with his uncle, even though both were

opposed to World War I. He also admired his uncle's staunch democratic convictions, which he found incompatible with the man's stern sense of discipline. During his first years in high school Koeppen often got into difficulties with his teachers and quarreled with his peers over their conservative patriotism. He was an avid reader, deeply impressed by the works of Kafka, and had begun to write by the time he was fifteen: an essay of his on literary expressionism was printed in his hometown newspaper in 1921. Shortly thereafter he ran away and became a cook's helper on an oceangoing ship. For five years he worked at a variety of odd jobs in Hamburg, Greifswald, and Berlin, pursuing irregular university studies at the same time. James Joyce's *Ulysses* (1922) had a profound impact on him and became an important influence on his style. In 1926 he finished his first longer manuscript. Its title is representative of much youthful writing of this time: "Memoiren eines Neunzigjährigen" (Memoirs of a Ninety-Year-Old); it is the work of a restless and rootless drifter without hope of ever enjoying the benefits of social stability.

While studying in Würzburg, Koeppen worked as a literary advisor, assistant to the director, and actor at the local theater. But when he was not given an opportunity to direct on his own, he returned to Berlin in 1928, established contacts with the modernist theater group of Erwin Piscator, and became a contributor to the literary-cultural page of the prestigious *Berliner Börsen-Courier*. Under the editorial supervision of the famed critic Herbert Ihering he wrote reviews of films, plays, and books and, for the first time, felt that he had prospects of a literary career. A long prose piece entitled "Ein Leuchtturm und tausend Lampen" (A Lighthouse and a Thousand Lamps), describing the filming of the movie *FP I antwortet nicht* (FP I Does Not Answer), was published by his newspaper on 1 October 1932. This article brought Koeppen to the attention of Max Tau, the artistic director of the Bruno Cassirer Verlag, a small literary publishing company. With an advance from his prospective publisher and plans for a novel, he went on a trip to Sicily but returned without a manuscript. The *Börsen-Courier* was closed by the Nazis on 1 January 1934; Koeppen immigrated to Holland during the latter part of that year, living in The Hague with friends of the late Austrian poet and playwright Hugo von Hofmannsthal.

The following years were a period of intense literary creativity. They were also a time of disappointment over the negative and neglectful reactions to his first two novels. *Eine unglückliche Liebe* (An Unhappy Love), published in the fall of 1934, received almost no encouraging criticism; *Die Mauer schwankt* (The Wall Is Shaking) was virtually unnoticed when it appeared in 1935.

Eine unglückliche Liebe is the story of a seemingly hopeless love between Sibylle, a cabaret actress who works with a troupe of emigré artists, and Friedrich, a struggling middle-class writer. They take a trip together through Italy, and in Venice they come to accept the boundaries that separate them. The novel ends with an allusive homage to Thomas Mann's *Der Tod in Venedig* (1912; translated as *Death in Venice*, 1925), which serves as a stylistic model for Koeppen's prose, and its conclusion introduces a veiled note of political commentary: Friedrich is commissioned to travel to Ragusa, the Yugoslav town where the dramatist Ernst Toller had publicly denounced Hitler's representatives at the P.E.N. Club meeting of 27-30 May 1933.

This subtle signal of Koeppen's opposition to Nazism is easily overlooked, which led to the accusation in a notorious article by the critic Fritz Raddatz in the 12 October 1979 issue of liberal weekly *Die Zeit* that Koeppen and other writers of his generation had sought too easy an accommodation with the Third Reich, that they retreated into an attitude of nonpolitical aloofness from the events of the day. This charge was shown to be ill-founded in a sharp reply by Marcel Reich-Ranicki in the conservative daily *Frankfurter Allgemeine Zeitung* (18 October 1979), but it allowed an old suspicion to resurface. Although Koeppen seems in his early novels to abstain from social analysis and concern with immediate public issues, he did write about the problems of his time, albeit indirectly and unpolemically.

Die Mauer schwankt is a novel in three parts whose principal characters are the architect Johannes von Süde–the narrator usually refers to him as "der Baumeister"–and his two sisters, Emilie and Mary. When Mary's husband, the unsuccessful actor and theater director Reinhold Marr, is fatally wounded during a trip through the Balkans in the summer of 1914 in what the authorities claim was a duel over a woman, Johannes goes to Istria to investigate. He is jailed on suspicion of espionage and mistreated by his captors. His love affair with a Swedish revolutionary, Orloga Haukson, ends with her murder–presumably by rival anarchists, more likely by local police agents. Johannes returns home and is transferred to a provincial garrison town near the Russian border of East Prussia, where his ever-more-lonely life is ordered by the virtues expected of an imperial civil servant: disciplined efficiency and a strict sense of duty. Occasional encounters with the poor make him question his patrimony of obedience and self-denial but he does not give up his attitude of controlled superiority. His town is destroyed in the war, and he is entrusted with the task of its reconstruction after the Russian advance has been repelled. While his sisters are fully absorbed by their wartime duties–Emilie as a surgeon's nurse, Mary as an office helper–Johannes has premonitions that his work may be futile. More and more he fears that the foundations of his world have eroded irreparably. He experiences the outbreak of revolution at the end of the novel with both skeptical anxiety and hopeful anticipation.

A long third novel, tentatively entitled "Die Jawanggesellschaft" (The Jawang Society) and nearly completed in 1938, was never published. Koeppen brought it with him when he clandestinely returned to Berlin that year to regain his direct contact with the German language. His old publisher, a Jew, had been forced to liquidate his business. Koeppen did find a publisher who was willing to distribute the unsold copies of *Die Mauer schwankt* under the title *Die Pflicht* in 1939; but after Hitler's invasion of Poland he disappeared from public attention altogether. Avoiding military service, he worked mostly as a scriptwriter and story consultant for the movies, activities he considered a form of passive resistance. By the end of the war he had permanently moved to Bavaria, first to the small town of Feldafing on Lake Starnberg and then to Munich, where he had his first direct encounters with the problems of German reconstruction. He had hoped that total defeat would lead to a radical new beginning, but he soon saw that the German people would not envision a fundamentally different future.

Koeppen was practically unknown to the reading public when a semblance of a normal cultural life was reinstituted after 1945. The manuscripts of all of his unpublished writing had been burned in the destruction of his apartment during an air raid in 1943, and he saw no justification for having his earlier works republished. A small circle of friends, however, encouraged him to resume writing; the most helpful among them was Henry Goverts, who became his publisher in the 1950s.

Tauben im Gras (Pigeons in the Grass, 1951) is a kaleidoscopic sequence of scenes depicting life in Munich during one day in 1948. As in Joyce's *Ulysses*, the lives of a representative variety of ordinary people unfold simultaneously and then intertwine toward the end of the day. These lives form the mosaic of "normal" existence under the American occupation. Koeppen uses the associative technique of interior monologue and a montage structure reminiscent of the works of John Dos Passos and of Alfred Döblin's *Berlin Alexanderplatz* (1929; translated as *Alexanderplatz, Berlin*, 1931) to bring his characters together in a world whose dismal destructiveness they are powerless to change. There is a teacher who has become dependent on drugs to alleviate his anxieties after refusing to be inducted into the military, a doctor who makes a precarious living by selling his own blood, a movie star who thinks of nothing but chances for new glamour, and his wife who has no purpose in life but to entertain at parties while her child is being brutalized by the religious fanaticism of a nanny. There are also two writers, the German Philipp, who has lost his capacity for love even though his wife is sincerely devoted to him, and Edwin, a homosexual American aesthete who falls into the hands of merciless toughs. Other American characters include the black former soldier Washington Price, who dreams of owning a bar in Paris where he will not be ostracized because his girlfriend, Carla, is white. Carla's son becomes the innocent victim of an act of revenge for the murder of a porter who had befriended another black soldier, Odysseus Cotton. Kate, a young teacher and admirer of Edwin's who was to meet the visiting writer in a hotel lobby after a lecture, mistakenly follows Philipp to his room, where she rebuffs his deceiving advances and convinces him that he cannot forever avoid life's obligations. In a gesture of symbolic significance, Kate silently returns the family jewelry that Philipp's wife had given her, in an act of gratuitous generosity, just hours before. As the midnight bells toll, another typical day comes to an end, a day whose events are told in a tone of resigned sadness rather than satirical outrage.

The same melancholy mood prevails in *Das Treibhaus* (The Hothouse, 1953), a portrait of Bonn in the early 1950s. It is a roman à clef; prominent politicians of the time can easily be identified behind their fictional disguises. The central figure is a member of the parliamentary opposition, Representative Keetenheuve, an introspective intellectual, hesitant, full of scruples, uncompromising, a loner. His much younger wife, with whose burial the novel opens, had died an alcoholic because she could not come to terms with the experience of war. Keetenheuve, unable to live with the intrigues and betrayals of his colleagues, eventually succumbs to the pressures of life in politics. He had started his postwar career with great expectations and progressive attitudes, trying to be faithful to the ideals that had sustained him during his life as an antifascist in exile. But he had returned to Germany as an officer in the enemy's army, an act that his detractors used to disparage his patriotism. When Keetenheuve refuses to compromise his opposition to German rearmament, he is excluded from power and offered the post of ambassador to Guatemala, where he can indulge in his hobby of translating the poems of Baudelaire. Knowing that acceptance of this offer would mean total capitulation, he sees no solution but to take his own life by jumping off a bridge.

Das Treibhaus caused a scandal, especially in Bonn. Koeppen was subjected to vilification from the political right, indignant criticism from the cultural establishment, and rebukes from the left. This hostility was due to the fact that he had captured, as no writer before him, the murky atmosphere of the German capital during the early years of the Adenauer era. This period of internal restoration also saw West Germany's rise to economic dominance in Europe and to a measure of international respectability as America's most reliable ally in the cold war. The Germans needed reassurance that they were moving in the right direction, not criticism of their leaders. Koeppen had touched on many raw nerves and festering wounds; he was denounced in milder terms as a sentimentally foolish moralist who had failed to recognize the chances for a new start and in less restrained expressions of censure as a sanctimonious vilifier of public relations whose commitment to Western democracy was questionable.

This reaction of aggressive self-righteousness may have been inevitable, but it is still surprising to see how vigorously it was directed against Koeppen. For his book, written with a stylistic flexibility that uses for each situation and character their appropriately different nuances of language, is, in its total effect, a restrained work, a lamenting of missed opportunities rather than an impassioned attack on the government.

The reception of his most subtle novel did not discourage Koeppen from publishing a new book the next year. *Der Tod in Rom* (1954; translated as *Death in Rome*, 1956) touched on a different set of national taboos. Its principal concern is the continued existence of Nazi ideology. The scene is a family reunion in Rome, where Gottlieb Judejahn, an SS general who had escaped justice and now serves as the military advisor to an Arab sheik, seeks to buy illegal arms for his employer. His brother-in-law Pfaffrath, formerly a prominent Nazi functionary and at present a respected lord mayor and member of a Christian-conservative party, joins him, as do their sons, both of whom are victims of a fanatical education in an Ordensburg (a military school reserved for the Nazi elite). But Adolf, Judejahn's son, has become a priest to atone for the sins of his father; Siegfried is an avant-garde musician, homosexual because of his traumatic youth, and the composer of a twelve-tone symphony that is successfully performed by the emigré conductor Kürenberg, a former concentration camp inmate whom Judejahn had wanted to purge from the cultural life of Germany. The story is told in a series of short interlocking episodes, partially in imitation of William Faulkner's introspective technique of recalling the past in spontaneous associations. Its climactic moment involves Judejahn in a last murder: believing that he has committed an act of "Rassenschande" (racial disgrace) by sleeping with the barmaid Laura, whom he mistakenly believes to be Jewish, he tries to kill her but inadvertently shoots Kürenberg's wife, who *is* Jewish and steps forward just as he pulls the trigger. He flees under the delusion that he has fulfilled his personal commitment to the Final Solution, collapses, and dies as his son administers the last rites.

The novel has weaknesses: its characters are somewhat overdrawn and tend toward stereotype, its situations seem contrived, and its parodistic allusions to Thomas Mann are feeble. Nevertheless, the West German critical response was again overly harsh and showed an unwillingness to face the political and artistic issues the novel had raised. It had become customary by this time to denigrate Koeppen as a misguided negativist or to give him no more than lukewarm approval. Koeppen's novels were ignored in the German Democratic Republic, where not even those aspects of his work that could be considered congenial to socialism were discussed. A principal reason for this neglect may have been the

underlying current of fatalism and existentialist moralism in Koeppen's books that was inimical to the facile optimism propagated in the other new German state.

When the producers of a film, *Der gläserne Turm* (The Glass Tower, 1957), completely revised Koeppen's script over his protest, he withdrew from the movie industry and from writing novels as well. With the help, both financial and psychological, of Alfred Andersch, who worked as a program director for the South German Broadcasting Network in Munich, Koeppen undertook a series of extensive trips abroad. He went to Spain in 1958 and broadcast his impressions of the country in a highly acclaimed radio essay; then he traveled through the Soviet Union, the United States, and France, each time describing his observations in succinct and suggestive reports. Within a short time each of these books became a respectable commercial success and amassed nearly unanimous critical praise. Honors came to their author in the form of literary awards, among them the Georg Büchner Prize of the German Academy in Darmstadt in 1962, the Literature Prize of the Bavarian Academy of the Arts in 1964, the Immermann Prize of the City of Düsseldorf in 1967, and the Andreas Gryphius Prize of the Artists' Guild in 1971, and membership in prestigious cultural organizations. The most personally satisfying recognition may have been his election as honorary Stadtschreiber (city writer) of Bergen-Enkheim, a suburb of Frankfurt, for the year 1974-1975. This position, to which no duties are attached, is a revival of the post of magistrates' secretary; it provides a house and a comfortable salary and allows the holder complete artistic independence and active participation in the life of the community.

Koeppen's response was the completion of his first novel in twenty-two years, the autobiographical *Jugend* (Youth, 1976), published by the Suhrkamp Verlag, which had collected some of his short stories in 1972 under the title *Romanisches Café* and had also reissued his earlier novels.

Jugend received critical praise but did not enjoy commercial success. It is a sparse, almost taciturn book, devoid of nostalgic evasions and self-serving recollections, but precise and unremitting in its evocation of ambience, its reliance on telling nuances, and its attention to detail. Koeppen uses an unfailing exactness of observation together with precise psychology and controlled stream-of-consciousness technique. His purpose is the recollection of a past that is personal and at the same time of exemplary relevance. The novel includes a succinct portrait of his mother and an appraisal of Prussian provincial society as seen through the eyes of one of its outcasts.

Jugend did not turn out to be the first step in a return to regular literary activity by Koeppen. He did grant interviews and participate in public readings, notably on 14 April 1978 in Zurich's Kongreßhaus to honor the 100th birthday of Robert Walser, but his reclusive avoidance of the demands of a public career did not change. A collection of his essays and occasional criticism, written between 1952 and 1981 and titled *Die elenden Skribenten* (The Miserable Scribblers), appeared in 1981. A six-volume collection of his works (1986) contains all of his previously published fictional prose and travel reports as well as his essayistic and critical writing, including the entire corpus of his book reviews.

References:

Ulrich Greiner, ed., *Über Wolfgang Koeppen* (Frankfurt am Main: Suhrkamp, 1976);

Klaus Haberkamm, "Wolfgang Koeppen, 'Bienenstock des Teufels'–Zum naturhaft mythischen Geschichts- und Gesellschaftsbild in den Nachkriegsromanen," in *Zeitkritische Romane des 20. Jahrhunderts,* edited by Hans Wagener (Stuttgart: Reclam, 1975), pp. 241-275;

Manfred Koch, *Wolfgang Koeppen: Literatur zwischen Konformismus und Resignation* (Stuttgart: Kohlhammer, 1973);

Jean-Paul Mauranges, *Wolfgang Koeppen–Littérature sans frontière* (Bern, Frankfurt am Main & Las Vegas: Lang, 1978);

Thomas Richner, *Der Tod in Rom: Eine existentialpsychologische Analyse von Wolfgang Koeppens Roman* (Zurich & Munich: Artemis, 1982);

Bernhard Uske, *Geschichte und ästhetisches Verhalten: Das Werk Wolfgang Koeppens* (Frankfurt am Main, Bern, New York & Nancy: Lang, 1984).

Ernst Kreuder

(29 August 1903-24 December 1972)

Reinhard K. Zachau
University of the South

BOOKS: *Die Nacht der Gefangenen: Erzählungen* (Darmstadt: Wittich, 1939);

Das Haus mit den drei Bäumen: Erzählungen (Gelnhausen-Gettenbach: Pfister & Schwab, 1944);

Die Gesellschaft vom Dachboden: Erzählung (Hamburg & Stuttgart: Rowohlt, 1946); translated by Robert Kee as *The Attic Pretenders* (London: Putnam's, 1948);

Schwebender Weg; Die Geschichte durchs Fenster: Zwei Erzählungen (Stuttgart & Hamburg: Rowohlt, 1947);

Die Unauffindbaren: Roman (Stuttgart, Hamburg, Berlin & Baden-Baden: Rowohlt, 1948);

Zur literarischen Situation der Gegenwart (Mainz: Akademie der Wissenschaften und der Literatur, 1951);

Herein ohne anzuklopfen: Erzählung (Hamburg: Rowohlt, 1954);

Georg Büchner: Existenz und Sprache (Mainz: Akademie der Wissenschaften und der Literatur, 1955);

Das Geheimnis von Hartlot-Riff (Hamburg: Agentur des Rauhen Hauses, 1955);

Sommers Einsiedelei: Gedichte (Hamburg: Wegner, 1956);

Agimos oder Die Weltgehilfen: Roman (Frankfurt am Main: Europäische Verlagsanstalt, 1959);

Das Unbeantwortbare: Die Aufgaben des modernen Romans (Mainz: Akademie der Wissenschaften und der Literatur, 1959);

Zur Umweltssituation des Dichters (Mainz: Akademie der Wissenschaften und der Literatur, 1961);

Spur unterm Wasser: Erzählung (Frankfurt am Main: Europäische Verlagsanstalt, 1963);

Dichterischer Ausdruck und literarische Technik (Mainz: Akademie der Wissenschaften und der Literatur, 1963);

Tunnel zu vermieten: Kurzgeschichten, Grotesken, Glossen, Erzählungen (Darmstadt: Gesellschaft Hessischer Literaturfreunde, 1966);

Hörensagen: Roman (Freiburg, Basel & Vienna: Herder, 1969);

Ernst Kreuder (Ullstein—Ursula Röhnert)

Der Mann im Bahnwärterhaus: Roman (Munich & Vienna: Langen-Müller, 1973);

Luigi und der grüne Seesack und andere Erzählungen (Frankfurt am Main: Fischer Taschenbuch, 1980).

In 1946 Ernst Kreuder's *Die Gesellschaft vom Dachboden* (The Society of the Attic; translated as *The Attic Pretenders*, 1948) was hailed as the most important book to appear in postwar German literature, but today his work has been all but forgotten. The 1960s and 1970s were not kind to the author sometimes referred to as a "modern Novalis." Kreuder's romantic insight into nature, however, may prove attractive to the German ecol-

206

ogists of the 1980s; his time might still come, just as Hermann Hesse suddenly became popular in the 1960s.

Kreuder was born in Zeitz on 29 August 1903 but spent his formative years in Offenbach, where he attended the Oberrealschule (high school). After a brief period as a bank clerk Kreuder attempted in 1921 to join the French Foreign Legion, but the physical examination in Griesheim found him unsuitable for service. He then supported himself as a construction and transportation worker and studied philosophy, literature, and criminology at Frankfurt University. His first literary works–a poem, essays, and stories–appeared in 1924 in the *Frankfurter Zeitung*. In 1926-1927 Kreuder hiked with the poet Hanns Ulbricht through Yugoslavia and Greece; the journey ended prematurely in a hospital in Salonika after they contracted malaria. In Mainz Kreuder and some friends who admired Hanns Henny Jahnn's plays and novels and Ludwig Klage's philosophy of nature formed a literary circle called "Die Animalisten" (The Animalists). From 1927 to 1932 Kreuder worked again as an unskilled laborer. He then joined the staff of the satirical periodical *Simplizissimus* in Munich, but the Nazis destroyed the publishing house and forced the paper to close in March 1933. He married Irene Matthias ("with five marks in my pocket") in 1934 and rented an abandoned water mill, "Kaisersmühle," near Darmstadt, where he lived until his death. There he started writing entertaining short detective stories that are sometimes referred to as revolver stories. They appeared in newspapers and magazines such as *Die Gartenlaube* and *Neue Badische Landeszeitung*, enabling Kreuder to lead a modest and inconspicuous life as an unpolitical writer. The stories portray dreamers who have no social ambition; their escapism proves to be a virtue and enables them to survive difficult times in a manner similar to Kreuder's own withdrawal into "inner exile." The stories were published in two collections, *Die Nacht der Gefangenen* (The Night of the Prisoners, 1939) and *Das Haus mit den drei Bäumen* (The House with the Three Trees, 1944).

In 1938 Kreuder, encouraged by his writer friends Horst Lange and Oda Schaefer, started work on his first long novel, *Die Unauffindbaren* (The Unfindable Ones). But before he could complete the manuscript he was conscripted into the army, serving as an antiaircraft gunner in the Ruhr from 1940 to 1945. The thought that he would leave nothing worthwhile behind if he

Passport photo of Kreuder in 1926 (Christoph Stoll and Bernd Goldmann, eds., Ernst Kreuder: Von ihm, über ihn *[Mainz: Von Hase & Koehler, 1974])*

died in the war was unbearable to Kreuder. But he survived and, after three months of imprisonment by the Americans at Sinzig, returned to the Kaisermühle and began writing again. He was fascinated by the surprising lushness of nature in his home valley, which had been untouched by the war. He wrote three stories in 1945, *Die Gesellschaft vom Dachboden*, "Schwebender Weg" (Suspended Road), and "Die Geschichte durchs Fenster" (The Story through the Window), after which he reworked the manuscript for *Die Unauffindbaren*.

The seven dreamers in *Die Gesellschaft vom Dachboden* find a meeting place among old boxes, bird cages, and other junk in the attic of a department store. The motto of their society is "Wacht auf! Reißt die Brandmauern eurer Gewohnheiten nieder! Macht die Augen auf und träumt! . . . " (Wake up! Tear down the walls of your habits! Open your eyes and dream! . . .). They find a secret map on their attic wall which tells of a treasure and directs them to a hollow tree which will contain a message with further information. A beautiful girl, Clothilde, who has been locked up by her evil mother, appears; she eventually changes her name to Liane. They find the treasure and buy a steamship with it. The story ends with the narrator in his cabin writing: "Schicht um Schicht mich aus mir entfernend, schrieb schneller, das atemlose Verlieren trat ein, verloren war ich schon nicht mehr bei mir, eine Beute von Gesichten und Stimmen, fiel ich in eine andere Welt" (and I started to remove myself from my inner self, layer after layer, wrote faster, the drifting began, I was no longer lost with myself, I became prey to visions and voices, fell into another world). According to Kreuder, anyone can become such a dreamer. His society revolts against everyday life, against stale normality, against stupidity and a lack of fantasy. The men play with junk, create a childlike antiworld, and live a Jean Paulean life as romantic outsiders.

Die Gesellschaft vom Dachboden was Kreuder's only literary success; it was also Germany's first international literary success after World War II. The first German book translated into English after the war, it influenced the reception of Germany's new literature; Edwin Muir praised it in the London *Observer* as a type of literature not seen in Germany for a hundred years. Wilhelm Emrich asserts that nobody outside Germany knew much about the "inner emigration," and that such antisocial attitudes, with anarchic and pacifist tendencies, had not been suspected of existing in Germany. Alfred Andersch, one of the foremost German critics in 1945, praised Kreuder's book as a "masterpiece" that fulfilled every expectation one might have for a new beginning in literature. Andersch recognized Kreuder as a successor to the romantic writers but in the tougher and more stringent tradition of Flaubert, which, he claims, leads to Hemingway and goes beyond the provincialism of Jean Paul or Wilhelm Raabe.

"Schwebender Weg" deals with a soldier's problems in returning to life in peacetime after World War I and focuses on the extinction of the self as a possible solution: man must give himself up and become one with nature. Different time levels coexist in a magical multidimensionality in the novel, which demonstrates Kreuder's conviction that man is incapable of changing, that he keeps returning to the rim of the volcano to wait for another destructive eruption; but Kreuder hopes to find some natural order through literature. Several critics linked Kreuder with Novalis's romantic mysticism; the romantic label removed

Ernst and Irene Kreuder circa 1930 (Christoph Stoll and Bernd Goldmann, eds., Ernst Kreuder: Von ihm, über ihn *[Mainz: Von Hase & Koehler, 1974])*

him even further from the emerging realism of the 1950s and its proponents, the Gruppe 47, and made his books difficult to sell.

"Die Geschichte durchs Fenster" explains the role of art in helping man overcome difficult times such as war through Novalis's poem "Wenn nicht mehr Zahlen und Figuren" (If No Longer Numbers and Figures). A writer, looking for justification for continuing his work after a brutal war, questions the value of art since it was incapable of preventing the barbarism and terror of the war. He decides, however, that it is not art that failed, but man, and a final negative example demonstrates clearly that art is necessary for man's survival: a painter goes mad after he gives up painting. "Schwebender Weg" and "Die Geschichte durchs Fenster" were published together in 1947, even though Kreuder's publisher, unable to recognize the surrealistic elements in the stories, believed the literary experiments to be the products of insanity.

Die Unauffindbaren, which finally appeared in 1948, is Kreuder's longest book. Gilbert Orlins, a real estate broker in a fictitious America which has little in common with the real one, disappears one day. Orlins has joined the "Unauffindbaren," a secret club of nonconformists who also call themselves "Wiederträumer" (redreamers) and fight the law-and-order mentality of the technocrats, opting for a liberating irrationality. Orlins recognizes the shallowness of his former life and sees that he may only find himself by going back to his childhood and youth. Changed, he returns to his wife and family. This apparently simple plot, however, is hidden in such a maze of figures and adventures that only the most determined readers will follow it. The style is not surrealistic: everything remains plausible and natural. At times one seems to be reading a fantastic detective novel. The message of the book seems to be expressed by another character, a scholar, who says to his daughter before he vanishes: "Über eine grüne Leiter komme ich einst zu dir" (Over a green ladder I will come back to you some day). The path to true reality leads over a "green ladder"; the author sees nature's spirituality pervading all beings.

In 1949 Kreuder was elected a member of the Mainz Academy of Letters, which gave him a forum from which to enunciate his theory of the role of the writer in modern society. Kreuder advocated an uncompromising elitism; a writer should have nothing to do with political and commercial reality, and no political events should be depicted in literature. "Flucht aus der Wirklichkeit" (escape from reality), representing the "unbelievable," is the objective. The poet is to liberate man from alienation and bring him back to nature. In his academy contributions Kreuder advocated a sensualism such as that which he found in the works of Novalis: "Eine Landschaft soll man fühlen wie einen Körper" (A landscape should be felt as if it were a body).

Although excluded from the Gruppe 47, Kreuder earned considerable literary fame during the 1950s, becoming a member of the Darmstadt Academy for Language and Literature and the German P.E.N. Club and making extensive lecture tours in Germany and abroad. In 1953 he was awarded the Büchner Prize. He enjoyed the friendship of famous writers such as Jahnn, Alfred Döblin, and Arno Schmidt. Even so, Kreuder often did not earn more than an unskilled worker; his books were never best-sellers. His income derived mainly from short stories, of which he wrote several hundred for the most prestigious West German newspapers. Some of these stories have been collected in the volume *Tunnel zu vermieten* (Tunnel for Rent, 1966).

The topic of falling out of reality is continued in Kreuder's story *Herein ohne anzuklopfen* (Enter without Knocking, 1954). Collins, the hero, jumps from a train and climbs over a wall into a mental institution, where he refuses to give his name. He wants to forget his role as a member of society because it restricts his possibilities as an individual. A character named "Kreuder" also appears. This story is more farcical than the somber earlier books; it is like an Italian comedy in which everybody takes everybody else's role. Collins eventually loses his hidden self, his "metaphysical source of existence," when he resigns himself to a solitary life away from the mental institution and achieves the desired state of anonymity. The story represents Kreuder's ultimate negation of society and escape from reality.

Agimos oder Die Weltgehilfen (Agimos; or, The World Assistants, 1959) concerns another secret association. *Agimos* stands for Akademie der gilbenden und modernen Speichen (Academy of Yellowing and Decaying Spokes); its members claim to be "world assistants" whose mission is to save the world. The founder, Dr. Frederick, collects the biographies of outcasts and wants to publish their stories as models for the people. The club's secret headquarters is in an abandoned brewery in an imaginary Balkan country inspired by the novels of Karl May. Detective plots, assassinations, chases, and other subplots are combined to create a chaotic world similar to that depicted in Clemens Brentano's *Godwi* (1801). The novel advocates striving for mystical union with nature in order to really see and feel the earth.

The fate of one of the female figures in *Agimos* inspired Kreuder to write his next book, *Spur unterm Wasser* (Trace under Water, 1963). Patricia, the American wife of the literary historian Ertini, runs away while on a tour of Greece. Ernesto, the narrator, is asked by the husband to look for her and finds her on the island of Trikkeri. The couple is reunited and returns to Bavaria, where they hide in the woods. The tale starts out as a detective story, but Kreuder complicates matters by having the narrator record its conclusion before he can know it. The story seems to drift along without any master plan.

Hörensagen (Hearsay, 1969), the last novel published during Kreuder's lifetime, uses multiple perspectives to reflect his preoccupation with

Etching of Kreuder by Eberhard Schlotter

writing. A writer, Bins, tells the narrator fragments of a story, and later the narrator tries to reconstruct the fragments. In the story a group of friends develops a drug that allows people to get rid of the profit motive and to be more sensitive to art and especially nature; and a bank robber, Luis, plans a "Phrasearium," an institute to rid language of political and cultural clichés. The story moves from Germany to Brazil, Argentina, and Yugoslavia; there are quotes from international literature, especially the works of Pablo Neruda. *Hörensagen* appeared at the height of the student revolts, and Heinrich Böll, in his review of the book, pointed to a connection between Kreuder's society with its wonder drug and the hippies who tried to create their own world. But for the political and progressive students of the 1960s, Kreuder's romantic mysticism was too irrational.

The irrationality becomes even more obvious in his last novel, published after his death under the title *Der Mann im Bahnwärterhaus* (The Man in the Signal House, 1973). In the novel, set in present-day Germany, the unnamed narrator meets people of the past who cannot die. The orig-

inal, more appropriate title, "Diesseits des Todes" (On This Side of Death), was rejected by the publisher. Kreuder introduces the ideas of a Japanese thinker named Zenij who wrote on the relativity of time and space. The narrator talks with his father, who died seven years earlier; the narrator's experiences in the war, as well as a past visit to a dead friend in Ireland, come back repeatedly. Memories and experiences are mixed together in dreamlike fashion. At the center of the book lies the idea that nature has to be preserved. The novel, finished the day before Kreuder's death, ends with the words of the fictional editor of the narrator's papers: "Vielleicht meldet er sich einmal wieder" (Perhaps we will hear from him again).

On 24 December 1972 Kreuder died at his home after suffering from bronchitis and circulatory problems. He knew that he was dying and liked the idea that he would not get older than the poet Gottfried Benn.

References:

Alfred Andersch, "Scheinwerfer auf einen Seiltänzer," *Der Ruf,* 13 (1946-1947): 13-14;

Heinrich Böll, "Untergrund im Widerstand," *Frankfurter Rundschau,* 29 November 1969;

Hans-Günther Cwojdrak, "Ein Erzähler am Scheideweg," *Neue Deutsche Literatur,* 11 (1954): 138-140;

Karlheinz Deschner, *Talente, Dichter, Dilettanten: Überschätzte und unterschätzte Werke in der deutschen Literatur der Gegenwart* (Wiesbaden: Limes, 1964), pp. 157-185;

Wilhelm Emrich, "Nachruf auf Ernst Kreuder," *Jahrbuch der Akademie der Wissenschaften und der Literatur* (1974): 86-91;

Hans J. Fröhlich, "Ernst Kreuder," *Jahresring 73/74* (1973): 218-222;

Peter Härtling, "Ernst Kreuder's 'Gesellschaft vom Dachboden,' " *Die Welt der Literatur,* 28 May 1964;

Angelika Mechtel, *Alte Schriftsteller in der Bundesrepublik: Gespräche und Dokumente* (Munich: Reihe Roter Schnitt, 1972), pp. 65-67;

Luise Rinser, "Geheimnis des Alltäglichen: Zu Ernst Kreuders Roman 'Die Unauffindbaren,' " *Die Neue Zeitung,* 19 March 1949, p. 9;

Christoph Stoll and Bernd Goldmann, eds., *Ernst Kreuder: Von ihm, über ihn* (Mainz: Von Hase & Koehler, 1974).

Papers:
The Deutsches Literaturarchiv in Marbach, West Germany, has most of Kreuder's manuscripts, as well as letters from Gottfried Benn, Heinrich Böll, Alfred Döblin, Hermann Hesse, Wilhelm Lehmann, Thomas Mann, and Arno Schmidt.

Kurt Kusenberg

(24 June 1904-3 October 1983)

David B. Dickens
Washington and Lee University

BOOKS: *Rosso fiorentino* (Strasbourg: Heitz, 1931);

A Propos: Das komplizierte Dasein, as Simplex (Berlin: Weltkunst-Verlag, 1932);

La Botella und andere seltsame Geschichten (Stuttgart & Berlin: Rowohlt, 1940);

Der blaue Traum und andere sonderbare Geschichten (Stuttgart & Berlin: Rowohlt, 1942);

Herr Crispin reitet aus (Münster: Der Quell, 1948);

Das Krippenbüchlein (Stuttgart: Hatje, 1949);

Die Sonnenblumen und andere merkwürdige Geschichten (Hamburg: Rowohlt, 1951);

Mal was andres: Eine Auswahl seltsamer Geschichten (Reinbek: Rowohlt, 1954); republished as *Mal was andres, and Other Stories,* edited by Marie Burg (London: Harrap, 1965);

Mit Bildern leben: 27 Kapitel über Malerei und Maler (Munich: Piper, 1955);

Wein auf Lebenszeit und andere kuriose Geschichten (Hamburg: Rowohlt, 1955);

Wo ist Onkel Bertram? Geschichten (Reinbek: Rowohlt, 1955);

Lob des Bettes: Eine klinophile Anthologie (Reinbek: Rowohlt, 1956);

Das vergessene Leben (Gütersloh: Bertelsmann-Lesering, 1958);

Im falschen Zug und andere wunderliche Geschichten (Reinbek: Rowohlt, 1960);

Nicht zu glauben: Eine Auswahl kurioser Geschichten (Reinbek: Rowohlt, 1960);

Zwischen unten und oben und andere Geschichten (Reinbek: Rowohlt, 1964);

Alles für die Gäste: Märchen und Humoresken, Satiren und Grotesken (Lübeck & Hamburg: Matthiesen, 1964);

Der ehrbare Trinker: Eine bacchische Anthologie

Kurt Kusenberg (Ullstein–Karin Vogel)

(Reinbek: Rowohlt, 1965);

Gesammelte Erzählungen (Reinbek: Rowohlt, 1969); republished as *Mal was andres: Phantastische Erzählungen* (Reinbek: Rowohlt, 1983); "Kuriose Zeche," translated by Dickens as "Old Tippling," in *On Being Foreign: Culture Shock in Short Fiction*, edited by Tom J. Lewis and Robert E. Jungman (Yarmouth, Maine: Intercultural Press, 1986), pp. 51-53;

Gespräche ins Blaue (Ebenhausen: Langewiesche-Brandt, 1969);

The Sunflowers and Other Stories, translated by George Bird (London: Chatto & Windus, 1972);

So ist das mit der Malerei: Eine Galerie zuhause (Hamburg: Hoffmann & Campe, 1971);

Man kann nie wissen: Eine Auswahl merkwürdiger Geschichten (Reinbek: Rowohlt, 1972);

Zucker und Zimt: ff. Gereimtheiten, by Kusenberg, Carl Amery, and Eugen Oker (Ebenhausen: Langewiesche-Brandt, 1972);

Heiter bis tückisch: 13 Geschichten (Reinbek: Rowohlt, 1974);

The Restless Bullet (London: Royal College of Art, 1975);

Villa bei Nacht (Zurich: Sanssouci, 1986).

OTHER: Pablo Picasso, *48 Lithographien*, edited by Kusenberg (Munich: Piper, 1953);

Werner Gilles, *Bilder aus Ischia*, introduction by Kusenberg (Baden-Baden: Klein, 1953);

Lob der Faulheit: Ein Almanach für Manager und solche die es nicht werden wollen, edited by Kusenberg (Frankfurt am Main: Bärmeier & Nikel, 1955);

Metta Victoria Victor, *Tagebuch eines bösen Buben*, translated by J. Botstiber, edited by Kusenberg (Reinbek: Rowohlt, 1964);

Jean Eiffel, *Heitere Schöpfungsgeschichte für fröhliche Erdenbürger*, translated by Kusenberg, H. M. Ledig-Rowohlt, and Martin Peters, foreword by Kusenberg (Reinbek: Rowohlt, 1965);

"Warum ich nicht wie E. T. A. Hoffmann schreibe," in *Fünfzehn Autoren suchen sich selbst: Modell und Provokation*, edited by Uwe Schultz (Munich: List, 1967), pp. 72-83;

"Wie mit der Lupe," in *Motive: Deutsche Autoren zur Frage: Warum schreiben Sie?*, edited by Richard Salis (Tübingen & Basel: Erdmann, 1971), pp. 214-218; translated by Egon Larsen as "As with a Magnifying Glass," in *Motives: 46 Contemporary German Authors Discuss Their Life and Work*, edited by Larsen (London: Wolff, 1975), pp. 139-143;

Jacques Prévert, *Gedichte und Chansons*, translated by Kusenberg (Reinbek: Rowohlt, 1971);

"Nekrolog auf einen Miniaturisten," in *Vorletzte Worte: Schriftsteller schreiben ihren eigenen Nachruf*, edited by Karl Heinz Kramberg (Frankfurt am Main: Bärmeier & Nikel, 1974), pp. 78-79.

PERIODICAL PUBLICATIONS: "Über den Unsinn," *Merkur*, 1 (1947): 956-957;

"Nirgends zeigt sich Sinn: Ein Selbstporträt," *Welt und Wort*, 9 (1954): 268;

"Über die Kurzgeschichte," *Merkur*, 19 (1965): 830-838.

Although Kurt Kusenberg's short stories never received unanimous acclaim from German critics, an indication of their popularity lies in the number of times admirers have translated them into other languages or included them in anthologies for beginning and intermediate students of German. His international reputation rests on the quality of his work and owes little to critical endorsement.

Kusenberg was born in 1904 in Göteborg, Sweden, the son of a German engineer and textile company representative whose work took him to various countries. In 1906 he was transferred to Lisbon, Portugal, where Kusenberg spent his early childhood. Italian and Brazilian illustrated magazines and the stories of an elderly seamstress employed by the family provided stimuli to Kusenberg's imagination; he said later that he did not stop reading fairy tales until he was twenty. From 1914 to 1922 he attended secondary schools in Wiesbaden, Bühl, and Baden-Baden. He studied art and art history at the Universities of Munich, Berlin, and Freiburg, from the last of which he received his Ph.D. degree in 1928. His dissertation, a study of the Italian Renaissance artist Giovanni Battista di Jacopo, was published in French in 1931. Kusenberg observed with sly satisfaction that his research had required him to visit museums in Italy, France, England, and Spain.

After brief employment as an art dealer in Berlin he became art critic for the Berlin newspaper *Vossische Zeitung* and also worked for the journal *Weltkunst*. From 1935 to 1943 he was deputy chief editor of the cultural magazine *Koralle*.

In 1943, as he relates in a brief autobiographical sketch, "steckte man mich in eine Uniform; ... Ich war ein friedlicher Soldat, den man in Frieden ließ; wo immer ich hinkam, wurde nicht geschossen" (they stuck me in a uniform. I was a peaceable soldier whom they left in peace, and wherever I went there was never any shooting). Taken prisoner at war's end at the Brenner Pass, he spent two years in an American labor camp near Naples. His comment about this period of his life is characteristic of him: "Nie hätte ich auf eigene Kosten mich so lange in Süditalien aufhalten können" (Never could I have afforded to enjoy southern Italy for so long on my own resources alone).

After a brief period as a free-lance writer in Bühl and Munich, Kusenberg went to Hamburg in 1958 to join the editorial staff of the Rowohlt publishing firm. He founded and edited Rowohlts Monographien, a series of monographs devoted to major figures of world culture; the association with Rowohlt lasted until his death in 1983. Kusenberg's first marriage, which occurred around 1941, ended in divorce; a daughter, Brigitte, was born in 1943. In 1954 he married Beate Möhring, who died in 1985. There were two children of the second marriage, a daughter, Barbara, born in 1955, and a son, Sebastian, born in 1958.

Kusenberg's work includes radio plays, television and film scripts, translations, introductions, and reworkings of the work of others. It is his short stories, however, that he considered his most significant accomplishment. They were collected in the volumes *La Botella und andere seltsame Geschichten* (La Botella and Other Strange Stories, 1940), *Der blaue Traum und andere sonderbare Geschichten* (The Blue Dream and Other Singular Stories, 1942), *Herr Crispin reitet aus* (Mr. Crispin Rides Forth, 1948), *Die Sonnenblumen und andere merkwürdige Geschichten* (The Sunflowers and Other Remarkable Stories, 1951), *Wein auf Lebenszeit und andere kuriose Geschichten* (Wine for Life and Other Curious Stories, 1955), and *Im falschen Zug und andere wunderliche Geschichten* (On the Wrong Train and Other Odd Stories, 1960); apparently dissatisfied with the 1948 collection, he never allowed it to be reprinted. He culled the other six volumes, each of which contains nineteen stories, for a collected edition of eighty-six stories in 1969. Two previously unpublished stories, "Urlaub" (Vacation) and "Das Haus" (The House), appeared in the 1974 paperback anthology *Heiter bis tückisch* (Cheerful to Malicious).

Extremely short and most often humorous, but simultaneously subtle in their elusive suggestiveness of more profound themes, these stories have defied critics' efforts to place them in a category or tradition; Kusenberg himself called them nonsense tales devoid of meaning. Since 1980 there has been a tendency to term them "fantastic," but so restrictive a label fails to do them justice.

Kusenberg's background in art and art history reveals itself in a number of stories. "Der verschwundene Knabe" (The Boy Who Vanished) tells of a boy who learns that he can enter and leave a Flemish landscape painting at will; one day he decides to remain in the painting. The story illustrates the need for retaining the power of imagination. In "Der letzte Pinselstrich" (translated as "The Finishing Touch") a painter of extremely realistic scenes discovers that figures are mysteriously leaving his completed paintings; one day he comes upon an entire colony of these vanished people. He learns that only by withholding the final touch from his work can he confine them to his paintings.

The southern locales of his childhood in Lisbon, his research as a student in Spanish and Italian museums, and his vacations in Italy also appear frequently, both realistically and as the fictitious country of Paturia, which is the scene of "Kuriose Zeche" (translated as "Strange Reckoning"), "Nach Hause" (Homeward Bound), and "Es war kein Schornsteinfeger" (It Was No Chimney Sweep). In "La Botella" a ship and a southern coastal port in a bottle suddenly become real. "Obst und Südfrüchte" (Fruit and Tropical Fruit) hints at a tender and tastefully erotic love story that is never told but merely implied; another love story with a southern setting is "Eine Hotelgeschichte" (translated as "A Hotel Story"). "Die Himmelsschänke" (The Taproom of Heaven) reworks the story of the Italian lovers Romeo and Juliet; characteristically for Kusenberg, it has a happy ending celebrated in the mysterious transcendental power of wine. In "Eine Partie Goleta" (A Game of Goleta), which takes place in a country that might be Italy, a tennislike game is used to settle disputes between feuding families. In "Zwischen unten und oben" (Between Downstairs and Upstairs), however, the exotic turns out to be fatally dangerous.

Many other stories reflect what Kusenberg called his commitment to language. Some appear to result from pursuing a figure of speech to its utterly logical but often absurd conclusions, such as "Das muß man mit in Kauf nehmen" (You must take that in the bargain) in "Der Dazukauf" (The Supplemental Purchase); "Auf diesem Bild kann man so richtig spazierengehen" (This painting seems so real that you could go for a walk in it) in "Der verschwundene Knabe"; and "Es hatte mich seit je gelüstet, einem wirklich dummen

Menschen zu begegnen" (I had always wanted to meet a really stupid person) in "Ein dummer Mensch" (A Stupid Person). This fascination with language is also revealed in puns, plays on words, and suggestive names. There is delightful language-play, consisting of puns and the use of educational jargon and pompous language, at the heart of "Eine Schulstunde" (A School Lesson). In "Ordnung muß sein" (We Must Have Order) the "Es war einmal" (Once upon a time) of the first line yields almost imperceptibly to the dense bureaucratic jargon of an infuriatingly detailed government questionnaire that probes deeply into citizens' private lives.

Language is one of many ordering devices human beings employ to impose a meaningful structure upon their existence. Order is a central theme of Kusenberg's stories. He deals with many forms of order: time, the clock, and the calendar in "Herr Tietze," "Ein fremder Vogel" (A Strange Bird), and "Herr G. steigt aus" (Mr. G. Leaves His Carriage); justice and the law in "Fünfhundert Drachentaler" (Five Hundred Dragon-Dollars); religion in "Herr über Nichts" (Master of Nothing); science and technology in "Nihilit" (Nihilite), "Es" (It), "Die ruhelose Kugel" (The Restless Bullet), and "Eine schwierige Maschine" (A Complicated Machine); the family and settled married life in "Ein schönes Hochzeitsfest" (translated as "A Lovely Reception"), "Mal was andres" (Something Different), "Lästiger Besitz" (Onerous Ownership), "Wer ist man?" (Who Are We?), "Das Bootshaus" (The Boathouse), and "Der Gang in den Berg" (The Walk into the Mountain); and the world of business and economics in "Der Dazukauf," "Eine Begegnung" (An Encounter), and "Die Forderungen" (The Claims).

Entire ethical, moral, and religious systems underlie "Die gläserne Stadt" (translated as "The Glass Town"), "Die Sonnenblumen" (The Sunflowers), and "Villa bei Nacht" (Villa by Night). Stories such as "Der große Wind" (The Great Wind) and "Picknick am Strand" (Picnic on the Beach) show how futile man's efforts to bring order to the weather have been. The order we expect when we sit down for a glass of wine is violated in "Kuriose Zeche"; the order we anticipate when we rent a room for the night is disrupted in "Das ungastliche Gasthaus" (translated as "The Inhospitable Hostelry"). We expect the pages of a book to reflect order, but they do not in "So soll ein Buch nicht sein" (A Book Should Not Be Like This); and when we rise in the morning we ex-

pect to see only one sun in the sky, not two as in "Kein Tag wie jeder andere" (A Day Unlike any Other). Even in extortion, robbery, and murder there are certain patterns we have come to accept as constituting a norm, but in "Ein Brief aus China" (A Letter from China), "Fünfhundert Drachentaler," and "Meine Diebe" (translated as "My Thieves") Kusenberg demonstrates how mistaken this belief in a prevailing order actually is. The harder his characters strive for order, for an explanation of why things are as they seem to be, the more elusive or intangible the ordering principle becomes–until the reader finally realizes that Kusenberg has rejected it entirely.

In place of order as the governing feature of the universe, Kusenberg installs its opposite: chance. When this substitution is acknowledged, his stories, instead of being only humorous, absurd, fantastic, or puzzling, suddenly make a great deal of sense. Much of his thought recalls the urbane skepticism of Voltaire, who attacked the rationalism and ordered universe of Leibniz. In "Ein gewisses Zimmer" (A Certain Room) Kusenberg says: "[Es] ließe sich sagen, daß schlechthin Alles mit Allem zusammenhängt, doch das stimmt nicht ganz" ([It could be] stated flatly that everything is related to everything else, but that isn't entirely true). The story clearly satirizes cause-and-effect rationalism. Such an approach to Kusenberg's thought enables the reader to find a great deal of meaning in these stories, particularly in one that initially appears to be opaque or even disjointed, such as "Die Sonnenblumen." At first this story's random events appear to yield no sense whatsoever. But that is precisely Kusenberg's argument: that there *is* no sense to the world, and that we are foolish to place our trust in any system or ordering force that lays claim to imposing meaning upon existence.

The brief war scene with which "Die Sonnenblumen" concludes leads to another facet of Kusenberg's Weltanschauung. It is clear from a number of stories, such as "Der friedliche Herzog" (The Peaceable Duke), "Die Pantoffel" (The Slippers), and "Leute aus dem Wald" (The People from the Forest), that Kusenberg is a pacifist. "Im Grunde ist keine Tageszeit für den Krieg geeignet" (All in all, no time of day is appropriate for war), he says in "Fast eine Schlacht" (Almost a Battle). War represents destructive chaos or disorder at its worst, involving the deliberate taking of life–and life itself is the greatest accident of chance that we know. It is because he so enjoys "liebte die Schönheit dieser Welt so innig" (the beauty of this world) that the young Indian at the beginning of "Die Sonnenblumen" refuses to become a sacrificial victim to an ancient god.

Enjoyment of life is a frequent theme in Kusenberg's stories. In "Wo ist Onkel Bertram?" (Where Is Uncle Bertram?), "Der Kutscher" (The Coachman), "Im falschen Zug" (On the Wrong Train), and "Auf dem Sterbelager" (On the Deathbed) there also appears to be an echo of Jean-Paul Sartre's concept of authentic existence. Other tales stress the more immediate pleasures life has to offer in eating and drinking: "Wein auf Lebenszeit" (Wine for Life), "Drei Männer im Park" (Three Men in the Park), "Ist die schwarze Köchin da?" (Is the Black Cook Here?) and "Ein schönes Hochzeitsfest" are outstanding examples. The subject of wine-drinking receives serious and extended attention in Kusenberg's anthology *Der ehrbare Trinker* (The Honest Drinker, 1965).

Kusenberg admitted his admiration of the prose of the nineteenth-century Swiss writer Gottfried Keller. Much of Keller's work is similar to Kusenberg's in its robust affirmation of life and–in the story "Kleider machen Leute" (Clothes Make the Man, 1872) in particular–in the role played by chance. Keller found important elements of his outlook in the teachings of the atheistic philosopher Ludwig Feuerbach, for whom there was no God and no afterlife. Feuerbach's ideas, transmitted through Keller, go far to explain many of the questions that arise in Kusenberg's stories.

Kusenberg was accused of not being *engagé* as a writer. But in a 1965 essay about the short story he observed that "selbst einer heiteren Kurzgeschichte muß man anmerken, daß ihr Autor die geistigen wie die politischen Um-schichtungen der letzten fünfzig Jahre in sich nachvollzogen hat–auch wenn mit keinem Wort davon die Rede ist" (Even in a humorous short story it is possible to see that the author has assimilated the intellectual and political regroupings of the last fifty years–even if he doesn't mention them with a single word). Close reading of Kusenberg's work, especially of the war stories, shows how well this observation applies to him, and refutes the charge that he was not *engagé*. "Der Hefekuchen" (The Yeast Cake) comments allegorically about Germany in the years from 1933 to the restoration of sovereignty after World War II; it is a subtle parable and by no means just an insignificant fairy tale. "Der

Zerstörer" (The Destroyer) depicts Hitler's rise to power: a senseless vandal destroys not only "das väterliche Gut" (the national patrimony) but foreign property as well with his "ruchlose Spitzhacke" (infamous pickaxe); the word *Spitzhacke* suggests *Hakenkreuz* (swastika). "Die Belagerung" (The Siege) is far more than a story about a medieval city under siege: here it is possible to see divided Germany and Berlin during the blockade of 1948-1949. (In naming his city Tottenburg, Kusenberg evokes the miniature of Count Kraft von Toggenburg in the Heidelberg Codex, an illustrated collection of medieval German poetry, in a way that again brings Berlin to mind.) The 1940 tale "Jedes dritte Streichholz" (translated as "One Match in Three") appears to anticipate the 1982 conflict between England and Argentina over the Falkland Islands. As Kusenberg says: "Schriftsteller erfinden nichts. Sie verarbeiten entweder Dinge, die sich zuge-tragen haben, oder sie plaudern vorzeitig Dinge aus, die sich zutragen werden" (Writers invent nothing. Either they rework things that have already happened, or they prematurely let slip things that will happen).

The subtleties of the war stories are matched by Kusenberg's subtle use of other writers and their works. Thus "Wo ist Onkel Bertram?" evokes Goethe, the oriental poetry of his *West-östlicher Divan* (1819), and his late love for Marianne Jung. There are delightful echoes of Novalis's novel *Heinrich von Ofterdingen* (1802) in "Der Gang in den Berg," while the wild party of "Ein schönes Hochzeitsfest" recalls a scene in the novel *Der abenteuerliche Simplicissimus Teutsch* (1669) by Johann Jakob Christoffel von Grimmelshausen.

Least successful are Kusenberg's fairy tales in the tradition of German romanticism. He excluded all of them except two, "Schlechte Schüler" (Poor Pupils) and "Zwist unter Zauberern" (Squabble Between Sorcerers), from the 1969 collected edition of his stories.

The sole major examination of Kusenberg's stories in English is a Ph.D. dissertation, Jean E. Pearson's "The Fantastic Short Stories of Kurt Kusenberg" (1980). Pearson is more concerned, however, with establishing a genre and fixing Kusenberg within a tradition than she is with the meanings of the stories. Thousands of readers continue to enjoy Kusenberg; perhaps someday critical examination of his considerable achievement will yield a more complete picture of a writer who has much more to offer than enjoyment alone.

References:

David B. Dickens, "Kurt Kusenberg: How Amazing It is to Be Happy," *West Virginia University Philological Papers,* 29 (1983): 59-69;

Manfred Durzak, "Kurt Kusenberg: Heiter bis tückisch–Thurber," in *Die deutsche Kurzgeschichte der Gegenwart: Autorenporträts, Werkstattgespräche, Interpretationen,* edited by Durzak (Stuttgart: Reclam, 1980), pp. 475-477;

Martin Gregor-Dellin, "Umgang mit Nonsense," *Merkur,* 19 (1965): 897-900;

Karl Heinz Kramberg, "Die Verwandlungen des Erzählers Kurt Kusenberg," *Merkur,* 23 (1969): 587-589;

Jean E. Pearson, "The Fantastic Short Stories of Kurt Kusenberg," Ph.D. dissertation, Cornell University, 1980;

V. O. Stomps, "Kurt Kusenberg," in *Schriftsteller der Gegenwart: Dreiundfünfzig Porträts,* edited by Klaus Nonnenmann (Olten & Freiburg im Breisgau: Walter, 1963), pp. 204-209;

Ludowice Vicari, "I Racconti Brevi di Kurt Kusenberg," Ph.D. dissertation, University of Milan, 1978.

Papers:

Kurt Kusenberg's literary estate is in the possession of his daughter Barbara in Hamburg.

Elisabeth Langgässer

(23 February 1899-25 July 1950)

Erika A. Metzger
State University of New York at Buffalo

BOOKS: *Der Wendekreis des Lammes: Ein Hymnus der Erlösung* (Mainz: Grünewald, 1924);

Triptychon des Teufels: Ein Buch von dem Haß, dem Börsenspiel und der Unzucht (Dresden: Jess, 1932);

Grenze: Besetztes Gebiet. Ballade eines Landes (Berlin: Morgenland, 1932);

Proserpina: Welt eines Kindes (Leipzig: Hesse & Becker, 1933; revised edition, Hamburg: Claassen & Goverts, 1949);

Die Tierkreisgedichte (Leipzig: Hegner, 1935);

Gedichte (Hamburg: Ellermann Dürerpresse, 1935);

Der Gang durch das Ried: Ein Roman (Leipzig: Hegner, 1936);

Rettung am Rhein: Drei Schicksalsläufe (Salzburg & Leipzig: Müller, 1938);

Das unauslöschliche Siegel: Roman (Hamburg: Claassen & Goverts, 1946);

Der Laubmann und die Rose: Ein Jahreskreis (Hamburg: Claassen & Goverts, 1947);

Der Torso (Hamburg: Claassen & Goverts, 1948);

Kölnische Elegie (Mainz: Grünewald, 1948);

Das Labyrinth: Fünf Erzählungen (Hamburg: Claassen & Goverts, 1949);

Märkische Argonautenfahrt: Roman (Hamburg: Claassen, 1950); translated by Jane Bannard Greene as *The Quest* (New York: Knopf, 1953);

Geist in den Sinnen behaust (Mainz: Grünewald, 1951);

Mithras: Lyrik und Prosa, with an essay by Luise Rinser, edited by Otto F. Best (Frankfurt am Main & Hamburg: Fischer, 1959);

Gesammelte Werke, edited by Wilhelm Hoffmann, 5 volumes (Hamburg: Claassen, 1959-1964);

Das Christliche der christlichen Dichtung: Vorträge und Briefe, edited by Hoffmann (Olten & Freiburg im Breisgau: Walter, 1961);

Ausgewählte Erzählungen (Düsseldorf: Claassen, 1979);

Gedichte (Frankfurt am Main: Ullstein, 1981);

Märkische Argonautenfahrt (Frankfurt am Main, Berlin & Vienna: Ullstein, 1981);

(Ullstein)

Saisonbeginn. Erzählungen, edited by Elisabeth
　　Hoffmann and Helmut Meyer (Stuttgart:
　　Reclam, 1981);
Three German Stories (London: Oasis, 1984);
Hörspiele, edited by Franz Pelgen (Mainz: Hase &
　　Köhler, 1986).

OTHER: *Herz zum Hafen: Frauengedichte der Gegen-
　　wart*, preface by Langgässer and Ina Seidel
　　(Leipzig: Voigtländer, 1933).

Historians of literature routinely group
Elisabeth Langgässer with German religious writ-
ers of the first half of the twentieth century who
had their roots in expressionism, such as Werner
Bergengruen, Rudolf Alexander Schröder,
Gertrud von le Fort, and Reinhold Schneider.
Langgässer herself rejected this classification.
Like Ernst Barlach, she wanted to be seen as a
writer whose work took the secular world fully
into account. Her chief concern was to appeal to
her readers as kindred souls and "co-mystics."
Among German women writers she is one of the

most distinctive in articulating an encompassing
view of the concerns of modern women. National
Socialism silenced her during most of the years
after 1933: it was only in the short time left to
her after World War II that she experienced appreciation by a wide audience.

Hermann Broch was one of the many admirers of her work; Langgässer quotes in English
from a letter she received from an editor of Pantheon Books in 1947: "Broch regards your novel
[The Indelible Seal] in many respects as the most
important book of the last years. The American
public must read it in order to understand the
metaphysical background of the present-day
world crisis." Thomas Mann praised her as the
most significant German writer after 1945. Heinz
Piontek spoke of her writing as "literary prose of
the highest order: incandescent and ethereal,
earthly and winged, sensuous and spirit-borne."

Critics gradually began to see that her work
was more comparable to that of Franz Kafka, Robert Musil, Franz Werfel, and Hermann Hesse
than to that of traditional Christian writers of the
1930s and 1940s. For Langgässer, art is "ein
Arkanum und ein Geheimnis" (an arcanum and
a secret), and among her contemporaries she saw
in James Joyce, Graham Greene, Pablo Picasso,
Henri Matisse, Otto Dix, Thomas Mann, Thornton Wilder, Arnold Schönberg, and Paul
Hindemith the same creative impulses that
guided her. Christianity became more and more
for her the paradoxical element in writing:
"Denn zu dieser Welt der Künste, des Ästhe-
tischen oder der Literatur liegt das Christentum
quer; es liegt quer zu ihnen und transzendiert
sie" (For Christianity is in opposition to this
world of the arts, the aesthetic, or literature; it opposes them and transcends them). She took it
upon herself to reveal an experience of the
world that often defies rational investigation.

Elisabeth Maria Langgässer was born in
1899 in the provincial town of Alzey in the region of Rhenish Hesse. With the authors Stefan
George, Kasimir Edschmid, and Carl Zuckmayer,
who also came from this part of Germany, she
shared a great admiration for the landscape of
the Rhineland and for the history of its civilization, which reaches back to Roman times. Much
of Langgässer's prose and many of her poems
use her early impressions of the Rhineland.
She once said in a letter: "Eine brennende
schöpferische Unruhe überfällt mich, sobald der
Zug den Limes bei Hanau überschneidet–eine
tiefe schöpferische Ruhe nimmt mich auf, sobald

Vergehender Frühling

Abgeblüht ist schon das weisse
Ackerfarnkraut, und das Zelt,
Welches die Larve, die leise,
Lila umsäumte, zerfällt.
Löwenzahn löschte die Lampe,
Lerkensporn sankte geschwind,
Brennessel trat vor die Rampe,
Schwalbenflug schreibt in den Wind
– Blass wie auf brüchiger Seide –
Lobe das Urbild und scheide!

Dulde Verwandlung und eile
Von der Erscheinung zum Sinn.
Fürchte dich nicht vor der Feile
Emsiger Grillen: Ich bin,
Wie überm Grab des Osiris,
Flügelblitz – jeglichem Ort,
Wo sich mit Schwertern der Iris
Hingang des Frühlings durchbohrt.
Schmerz nicht und Abschied vermeide.
Neugeboren liebe und leide!

Manuscript for Langgässer's poem "Vergehender Frühling" (Albert Soergel and Curt Hohoff, Dichtung und Dichter der Zeit *[Düsseldorf: Bagel, 1961-1963])*

ich das Ried vor mir liegen sehe: braun, horizontal gegliedert und erhöht in Pappeln, Weiden und dem Wormser Dom" (A burning creative restlessness attacks me as soon as the train passes the Limes at Hanau–a deep creative repose enfolds me, as soon as I see the marshlands before me, brown, horizontal and elevated through poplars, willows, and the cathedral at Worms).

Langgässer was raised as a Catholic. She described her father, Eduard Langgässer, an architect and government surveyor, as "von jener Sorte total assimilierter Juden, die das Nationale eher über- als untertrieben" (of the type of totally assimilated Jews who tended rather to overstate than understate their [German] nationalism). Her mother was Eugenie Dienst Langgässer. Langgässer's father died young in 1909; this event and later World War I and the French occupation of parts of the Rhineland were formative experiences for Langgässer. After her father's death Langgässer, her mother, and her younger brother moved to Darmstadt, where Langgässer attended the Viktoria-Schule. Following her Abitur (school-leaving examination) in 1918, she studied at a teachers' college for a year, thereafter working in Groß-Steinheim, then Grieshein, near Darmstadt, as a primary-school teacher. During this period Langgässer published many book and theater reviews in newspapers and poems and stories in small journals.

In 1924 the Mainz publishing house of Matthias Grünewald, which was interested in young, avant-garde Catholic writers, published her first book. *Der Wendekreis des Lammes* (The Tropic of the Lamb) is a collection of poems celebrating the most solemn feasts of the church calendar which in style and structure shows strong kinship with early German expressionism.

In 1926 Langgässer started work on her first novel, *Proserpina,* which draws strongly on her childhood experiences and is the story of a delicate and precocious girl. Like the Proserpina of mythology, who lived alternately with Demeter and Pluto, she is under the spell of opposed aspects of her own being: sensuality and imagination. With the death of her father, the girl's childhood is abruptly ended. Langgässer shows modern life as a background for the continual reenactment of myth. Even in a world that no longer believes in or even knows of them, myths survive and influence human lives, especially the lives of those gifted with special sensibilities. For the manuscript of *Proserpina* Langgässer was awarded the Literary Prize of the Association of

Women Citizens in 1931; Alfred Döblin was a member of the selection committee. The book was not published until 1933, by which time it had become "mit Anklängen an das kollektive 'Unterbewußte' aufgeputzt" (embellished with allusions to the collective "unconscious"), as the author later sarcastically remarked. She had the original version published in 1949. Shortly after *Proserpina* was first published she also wrote many poems, some of which were incorporated in *Die Tierkreisgedichte* (Zodiac Poems, 1935).

In January 1929 Langgässer moved with her newborn illegitimate child, Cordelia, to Berlin, where she hoped to find wider acceptance of her work and better conditions for writing. Between the wars Berlin was the most exciting city in Germany for many artists, and Langgässer's talents flourished there. She joined a group of postexpressionist writers called Die Kolonne (The Column, after a journal edited by Martin Raschke between 1929 and 1932). She became acquainted with many influential authors, including Wilhelm Lehmann, Oskar Loerke, Ina Seidel, Gottfried Benn, Horst Lange, Oda Schaefer, Jochen Klepper, Günter Eich, and Peter Huchel. She also met several women poets, whose works she and Seidel included in *Herz zum Hafen* (The Heart as Haven, 1933), one of the earliest German anthologies of women's poetry edited by women.

In 1932 Langgässer's powerful collection *Triptychon des Teufels: Ein Buch von dem Haß, dem Börsenspiel und der Unzucht* (The Devil's Triptych: A Book of Hate, Money, and Perversion), containing the stories "Mars," "Merkur," and "Venus," was published. Here the reader finds investigations of the truly evil side of human nature with which Langgässer tried again and again to come to terms. Without renouncing her Christian faith or embracing the psychological models of either Freud or Jung, Langgässer was seeking a reconciliation of the conceptions of "soul" and "psyche" that were then on an intellectual collision course. Her stories, which are set in the period between 1920 and 1930, are concerned with the complexity and irrationality of human passions and the beauty and brutality of their manifestations. Langgässer's intent is neither to moralize religiously nor to analyze in terms of clinical psychology but simply to present the reader with a complex and disturbing phenomenon. The stories depict mythical powers garbed as modern men: soldiers and officers personify Mars, the god of war; bankers and an innkeeper represent

Mercury, the god of merchants, money, and thievery. The women are either destroyed by these forces, as is the case with Johanna, the innkeeper's pregnant wife in "Mars," or, like the prostitutes in "Venus," they take revenge for their constant humiliation in a male-dominated world. Only Marie-Geneviève in "Venus," the compassionate widow of a French officer who kills himself, represents mercy and hope in this hellish postwar world. By adopting an orphan who may be her husband's child, she exhibits the quality that Langgässer considers lacking in many modern women: the ability to increase the substance of love. Two other stories, "Mithras" and a second "Venus," were written for this collection but not included; they were published posthumously in 1951 and 1973, respectively. "Mithras" received much attention when it finally appeared because it showed that Langgässer had rejected the ideology of the National Socialists in 1930.

In 1935 Langgässer married Wilhelm Hoffmann, a philosopher and theologian. The couple had three daughters, Annette, Barbara, and Franziska.

Langgässer's novel *Der Gang durch das Ried* (Journey through the Marshes, 1936) deals with a young soldier who returns from World War I suffering from amnesia. During his wanderings he stays with a farmer's family and becomes involved with life in the country. He almost finds his identity when he plays a glass harmonica, but because he cannot face the truth about himself—an unspecified guilt—he resigns himself to accepting the identities that others give him. Langgässer realistically portrays contemporary conditions from the viewpoint of the people who must endure them, people who do not understand the causes of these conditions and experience such phenomena as Germany's runaway inflation as mythical occurrences. The novel employs symbolic and stylistic techniques that show the influence of Kafka and Joyce. After its publication Langgässer was forbidden by the Nazis to publish any further works on grounds that she was "half-Jewish."

Langgässer continued to write in spite of the prohibition. In her collection of stories *Rettung am Rhein* (Rescue on the Rhine, 1938), published in Austria, she displayed a new confidence in the power of faith, love, and sacrifice in spite of circumstances. Each of the three stories centers on a miraculous instance of people willing to help each other in critical moments. "Die Prophezeiung" (The Prophecy), in which a gypsy

Langgässer circa 1933

girl saves a tow-horse driver from being lynched, vividly depicts the economic and social changes connected with the rechanneling of the Rhine River in the early nineteenth century. "Der gerettete Obolus" (The Rescued Coin) sets an incident of home-front life during World War I in mythic, magical terms; the wondrous return home of a farmer believed dead is linked to the ability, miraculous in those times, of women in desperate need to overcome their fixation on themselves and to act humanely. In "Das erfüllte Versprechen" (The Fulfilled Promise) the dark prophecy of the first story—that the waters of the Rhine will recede, St. Martin will ride down from his place on the roof of the cathedral, and the Moors will enter Mainz—comes true. The river has been regulated, which causes the cathedral to become structurally unsound and in urgent need of restoration; and French African troops occupy Mainz after the war is lost. In the economic crisis following the war two families learn from a wise priest that they must modify their earthly wishes and submit to God's will for the sake of the larger interest of rebuilding the community.

During World War II–the "eintönige Hungerjahre" (monotonous hunger years), as Langgässer called this time–she was recruited to work in a factory. Her short story "An der Nähmaschine" (Sitting at the Sewing Machine) describes the experience. As the Nazis' persecutions worsened, Langgässer's oldest daughter, Cordelia, was sent to a concentration camp on the grounds that her natural father had been Jewish and her mother half-Jewish. Faced with such enormous psychological burdens and suffering from malnutrition, Langgässer fell ill several times during the war. In early 1946 Langgässer heard from the Red Cross that Cordelia, who had been critically ill and unable to contact her mother due to the postwar social crisis, had survived and was living in Sweden.

During these years Langgässer wrote two major cycles of poems, *Der Laubmann und die Rose* (The Leafman and the Rose, 1947) and *Kölnische Elegie* (Cologne Elegy, 1948). She believed that she had created a new poetic form that achieved a fusion of the ancient world of nature and myth and its transformation through the Christian religion. Langgässer saw her poems less as lyrical than as part of a liturgy.

Das unauslöschliche Siegel (The Indelible Seal, 1946), Langgässer's first postwar novel, was reprinted four times by 1953. It signals the author's new approach to the problem of faith and guilt in modern man. She had hoped that the end of the war would bring about a complete reorientation of cultural life, especially in literature; she was deeply disappointed to see that German artists seemed content to fill the void following the collapse of the Third Reich by returning to the forms and concerns flowing from expressionism, relics of a world that she had long since left behind. She strove to redefine novelistic form; according to Anthony W. Riley, "In a nutshell, this new form . . . involves the total rejection of traditional narrative techniques: the complete absence of logical and consistent psychological development of the persons in the novel, the lack of the continuity of a 'straight' or 'rectilinear' plot or story in the conventional sense of the word, but instead a three-dimensional 'cosmos.' "

For the first time, Langgässer deals with the fate of the Jews in Germany in the figure of the main character, Lazarus Belfontaine, a baptized Jew who, because of the acuity with which he perceives evil in the world, is uncertain whether he

Dust jacket designed by Hans Hermann Hagedorn for Langgässer's 1948 collection of stories set in the Nazi period

has received the grace of faith. The only person in whom he can confide is a blind beggar, Jean, whom he encountered on the day of his baptism, which he underwent for the sake of an advantageous marriage. Every year, on the anniversary of this day, the beggar has returned. The novel opens in 1914, seven years after Belfontaine's baptism. He is wealthy but frustrated by the smug corruption of his fellow citizens and the spiritual emptiness of his life. The beggar's failure to appear precipitates Belfontaine's revulsion with his life, and he leaves it behind in a quest for Jean that leads him to France. There he is interned during World War I. Upon his release Belfontaine enters into a bigamous marriage with Suzette, with whom he lives at Senlis. Belfontaine is confronted with numerous manifestations of the Devil, who evoke his despair through their nature and their deeds. By virtue of the inalienable contract with God that his baptism symbolizes, despite the worldliness of the reasons for which it was accepted, Belfontaine realizes that even his tormented faith is a state of true grace and escapes the sin of denying God that would commit his soul to the Devil. The ghastly murder of Suzette by a lover in the late 1920s is the final event in the novel, which has reached its fulfillment in Belfontaine's affirmation of his faith. A brief epilogue tells how he returned to Germany and survived the horrors of the concentration camps of World War II to emerge as a legendary holy man to whom healing powers are attributed, the new personification of the saintly beggar he had set forth to seek.

Langgässer's unorthodox view of an embattled faith in *Das unauslöschliche Siegel,* and the formidable power of evil depicted in the novel, have made the book highly controversial for Catholic critics. There is little disagreement, however, that the work shows her at the full height of her powers as a writer. The complex and highly symbolic action is consistently projected into the real world, redeemed from excessive abstraction by vivid and compelling description and by dialogues of genuine intellectual tension. Langgässer knew that her novel was controversial. As she wrote in a letter in 1947, it was detested by "den lieben Vernunftanbetern in jeder Form und den dürren Rationalisten, von Antisemiten ihrer geistigen Struktur nach und schnaubenden Konvertiten" (our beloved worshippers of reason, by the dry rationalists, by crypto-antisemites and overzealous converts to Catholicism). She felt especially hurt when she was criticized for not accepting the traditional concept of faith. But she was encouraged that artists like Hermann Broch felt the novel's "Atmosphäre der Verruchtheit" (atmosphere of evil) and saw in *Das unauslöschliche Siegel* "das erste Beispiel eines gültigen Surrealismus" (the first example of a valid surrealism).

Langgässer's collections of stories *Der Torso* (1948) and *Das Labyrinth* (1949) analyze the reality of evil during the time of terror in Germany from 1933 to 1945. In "Saisonbeginn" (Season's Start) she shows with subtle and bitter irony the irreconcilability of the anti-Semitism of those years, even in its milder forms, with Christianity by juxtaposing a roadside placard excluding Jews from a resort with a crucifix on which Christ is proclaimed to be "King of the Jews." The everyday world of the Hitler years is characterized by little acts of betrayal and resistance; it was a time when each individual was damaged like a plaster statue long buried in the soil. Langgässer hoped to create a new tradition of the German short story based on American models. The style and content of most of her works in this genre reflect the disillusionment and search for new beginnings of the postwar period. Children, innocent of both the danger they are in and the grace that saves them, as in "Der Erstkommunionstag" (First Communion), represent the only glimpse of hope.

Psychic and spiritual redemption, the establishment of wholeness in the relations of human beings among themselves and with God, became the overriding concern of Langgässer's last novel, *Märkische Argonautenfahrt* (translated as *The Quest,* 1953), begun in 1945 and published posthumously in 1950. The title refers to her years in Berlin and shows her admiration for two authors closely associated with the Mark of Brandenburg, in which Berlin lies: Heinrich von Kleist and Theodor Fontane. She prepared to write the novel by visiting a Benedictine convent near Berlin to study the life of the nuns. That the visit was a deeply moving experience is reflected in the extraordinarily compelling descriptions of the region and its people. Langgässer was haunted and puzzled by the question of how survivors of the war could face life again and rebuild their world and themselves. In the novel seven men and women, unknowing pilgrims, set out on foot from Berlin during the summer of 1945 for Anastasiendorf, a (fictional) convent in the southwestern area of the Mark which shall be for them, as the name (from the Greek *anástasis,* raising up) indicates, a place of resurrection. Some ironically compare their difficult journey with the quest of Jason and the Argonauts for the Golden Fleece. The pilgrims' dialogues are the main structural elements in the novel, and the interweaving of their stories creates a complex tapestry of differing points of view. Langgässer felt that she faced insurmountable problems in writing the novel. She confided to Broch: "Der neue Roman . . . bringt mich fast um. Er ist pure Existenz, pure Aussage eines metaphysischen Sachverhalts. Ein riesiges Bezugssystem, ein einziger Transformator, der schreckliche Spannung umzusetzen sucht. In was umzusetzen? Ich weiß es nicht. Ich tappe vollkommen im Dunkel. Immer wieder versuche ich, alles gleichzeitig auszusagen" (The new novel . . . is almost killing me. It is pure existence, pure expression of a metaphysical phenomenon. A gigantic system of relationships, a single transformer that seeks to transmute terrible energy. Transform into what? I don't know. I am groping entirely in the dark. Time and again I try to express everything simultaneously).

Each of the pilgrims faces unique moral and psychological obstacles in the quest for spiritual purification that will make the creation of a new life on earth possible. The architect Hauteville and Lotte Corneli, the wife of a composer, are isolated in mourning by the deaths of loved ones. An elderly Jewish couple, Arthur and Levi Jeschower, cannot believe that they are no longer persecuted, as an understanding of that fact would force them to cope with the meaning of their wondrous survival. Friedrich am Ende, whose idealism was deformed into nihilism on the battlefield, now seeks only Nirvana, while an actor, Beifuß, suffers an oppressive sense of spiritual emptiness. In the figure of Irene von Dörfer Langgässer incorporated many experiences of her daughter Cordelia in Auschwitz. In the course of their journey, some try to flee from their spiritual torment by attempts to find happiness in purely physical terms–in desperate love affairs, for example. It becomes clear to all, however, that at the end of the quest they must deliver themselves to God, who, as one of the characters puts it, "ist zum Fallensteller geworden" (has laid a trap) of inward redemption for them into which their fates have inexorably led them. The problem in the novel is how each person tries to overcome the emptiness of life after World War II: Lotte Corneli wants to force her husband's return through satanic mysteries; Irene von Dörfer, returning from her hell of memories, finds peace in Christ; Beifuß is killed when he attempts to protect Irene from rape. His words "O Eitelkeit. Alles ist eitel" (O Vanity, everything is vanity) could also be seen as Langgässer's mourning the fate of the world. She then shifts the scene from the monastery back to Berlin, telling the story of two orphans who become victims of the postwar epidemic of crime. In the course of this last chapter, the reader also finds out that Lotte Corneli's husband returned from the war after all and that her brother is able to begin a new life in Berlin. The book closes with entries from the diaries of Father Mamertus, reporting on the pilgrimage and its participants. In *Märkische Argonautenfahrt* Langgässer suggests that history, myth, and the doctrine of salvation are all expressions of a divine Providence motivated by love and mercy, whose purpose is the redemption of humanity through the grace of a

Cover for a 1986 collection of Langgässer's radio plays

conscious and enlightened faith. The individual must constantly strengthen this faith by testing it in the crucible of existence. In her essay on the reality of Christianity and its poetic expression, *Geist in den Sinnen behaust* (Spirit at Home in the Senses, 1951), Langgässer sees the spreading of this truth as the mission of the modern novelist: "Kein moderner Dichter ist denkbar ohne die ausdrückliche oder unausdrückliche Frage nach dem metaphysischen Sinn des Daseins und ohne die immer wiederholte Nachprüfung seiner Selbstaussage . . . ; und selbst dort, wo ein Mensch wie James Joyce oder Sartre, an den äußersten Rand der Verneinung getrieben und von dem schillernden Sog des Nihilismus fasziniert ist, muß er, wie die Dämonen der Schrift, als Gegengott von dem Gott Jesu Christi ungewollt Zeugnis geben" (No modern poet is conceivable who does not ask, explicitly or implicitly, what is the metaphysical meaning of life and who does not time and again reflect on his works in this light . . . ; and even there, where a person like James Joyce or Sartre, driven to the utmost edge of negation, is fascinated by the gleaming tide of nihilism, he must, like the demons of the Scriptures, bear involuntary witness as an anti-God to the God Jesus Christ).

Langgässer's health seemed to improve when she and her family moved to Rheinzabern in the Rhineland in 1948. There, however, she died in 1950 of multiple sclerosis and was buried in Darmstadt. She had been elected a member of the Academy of Sciences and Literature in Mainz shortly before her death, and she received the Büchner Prize for Literature posthumously.

Langgässer's works remain meaningful because of her courageous assertion of hope for redemption in a pluralistic universe whose many claims she could subsume into her own faith. She displayed the rare quality of respecting those who did not share her ideas, a quality that distinguishes many of her literary characters and gives them a peculiar forcefulness. As Heinz Politzer wrote, one will no longer "be able to ignore the radicalism and the consistency with which Elisabeth Langgässer has given her mystical experience a suprarealistic framework and a metapsychological foundation hitherto unknown in the history of the German novel."

Letters:

. . . soviel berauschende Vergänglichkeit: Briefe 1926-1950, edited by Wilhelm Hoffmann (Hamburg: Claassen, 1954).

Bibliography:

Anthony W. Riley, *Elisabeth Langgässer: Bibliographie mit Nachlaßbericht* (Berlin: Duncker & Humblot, 1970).

References:

Eva Augsberger, *Elisabeth Langgässer: Assoziative Reihung, Leitmotiv und Symbol in ihren Prosawerken* (Nuremberg: Carl, 1962);

Ehrhard Bahr, "Metaphysische Zeitdiagnose: Hermann Kasack, Elisabeth Langgässer und Thomas Mann," in *Gegenwartsliteratur und Drittes Reich: Deutsche Autoren in der Auseinandersetzung mit der Vergangenheit,* edited by Hans Wagener (Stuttgart: Reclam, 1977);

Bernhard Blume, "Zur Metaphorik von Elisabeth Langgässers Roman *Das unauslöschliche Siegel," Euphorion,* 48 (1954): 71-89;

Margaret Burrows Brearley, "The Image of Childhood in the Novels of Elisabeth Langgässer," Ph.D. dissertation, University of Connecticut, 1982;

Konstanze Fliedl, "Roman als Heilsgeschichte: Elisabeth Langgässers *Märkische Argonautenfahrt,"* Ph.D. dissertation, University of Vienna, 1983;

Eberhard Horst, "Christliche Dichtung und moderne Welterfahrung: Zum epischen Werk Elisabeth Langgässers," Ph.D. dissertation, University of Munich, 1956;

Ernst Johann and Heinrich Schirmbeck, *Elisabeth Langgässers Darmstädter Jahre: Ein Rückblick* (Darmstadt: Liebig, 1981);

Agnes Körner-Domandi, "Langgässer, Elisabeth (1899-1950)," in *Modern German Literature: A Library of Literary Criticism,* 2 volumes (New York: Ungar, 1972), pp. 80-84;

J. P. J. Maassen, *Die Schrecken der Tiefe: Untersuchungen zu Elisabeth Langgässers Erzählungen. Im Anhang: Erstdruck der "Venus II"-Novelle* (Leiden: Universitaire Pers, 1973);

Anthony W. Riley, " 'Alles Außen ist Innen': Zu Leben und Werk Elisabeth Langgässers unter der Hitler-Diktatur. Mit einem Erstdruck des frühen Aufsatzes 'Die Welt vor den Toren der Kirche' (um 1925)," in *Christliches Exil und christlicher Widerstand,* edited by Wolfgang Frühwald and Heinz Hürten (Regensburg: Pustet, 1987), pp. 186-224;

Riley, "Elisabeth Langgässer and Juan Donoso Cortés: A Source of the 'Turm-Kapitel' in *Das unauslöschliche Siegel," PMLA,* 83 (May 1968): 357-367;

Riley, "Elisabeth Langgässers frühe Hörspiele (Mit bisher unbekanntem biographischem Material)," in *Literatur und Rundfunk 1923-1933,* edited by Gerhard Hay (Hildesheim: Gerstenberg, 1975), pp. 361-386;

Riley, "Nachwort," in Elisabeth Langgässer, *Grenze: Besetztes Gebiet. Ballade eines Landes* (Olten & Freiburg im Breisgau: Walter, 1983), pp. 125-141;

Luise Rinser, *Magische Argonautenfahrt: Eine Einführung in die gesammelte Werke von Elisabeth Langgässer* (Hamburg: Claassen, 1959);

Heinrich Schirmbeck, "Das Dilemma Elisabeth Langgässers," *Frankfurter Hefte,* 32, no. 8 (1977): 50-58;

Harry Steinhauer, "Submerged Heroism: Elisabeth Langgässer's Story 'Untergetaucht,'" *MLN,* 74 (1959): 153-159;

Mary Beth Stocky, "The Radio Plays of Elisabeth Langgässer: A Historical, Biographical Approach," Ph.D. dissertation, State University of New York at Buffalo, 1987.

Papers:
Elisabeth Langgässer's papers have been loaned by the Archives of Dr. Wilhelm Hoffmann, administered by Frau Barbara Grüttner-Hoffmann, Langgässer's daughter, to the Deutsches Literaturarchiv in the Schiller-Nationalmuseum, Marbach am Neckar, West Germany. They may be consulted there, but authorization to make photocopies must be given by Frau Grüttner-Hoffmann.

Hermann Lenz
(26 February 1913-   )

Michael Winkler
Rice University

BOOKS: *Gedichte* (Hamburg: Verlag der Blätter für die Dichtung Heinrich Ellermann, 1936);

Ländiche Volkshochschularbeit, by Lenz and Peter Furth (Braunschweig: Westermann, 1947);

Das stille Haus: Erzählung (Stuttgart: Deutsche Verlags-Anstalt, 1947);

Das doppelte Gesicht: Drei Erzählungen (Stuttgart: Deutsche Verlags-Anstalt, 1949);

Die Abenteurerin (Stuttgart: Deutsche Verlags-Anstalt, 1952);

Der russische Regenbogen: Roman (Darmstadt, Berlin-Spandau & Neuwied: Luchterhand, 1959);

Nachmittag einer Dame (Neuwied, Berlin-Spandau & Darmstadt: Luchterhand, 1961);

Spiegelhütte (Cologne & Olten: Hegner, 1962);

Die Augen eines Dieners: Roman (Cologne & Olten: Hegner, 1964);

Verlassene Zimmer: Roman (Cologne & Olten: Hegner, 1966);

Andere Tage: Roman (Cologne & Olten: Hegner, 1968);

Im inneren Bezirk: Roman (Cologne & Olten: Hegner, 1970);

Der Kutscher und der Wappenmaler: Roman (Cologne: Hegner, 1972);

Dame und Scharfrichter: Erzählung (Cologne: Hegner, 1973);

Stuttgart deine Straßen: Spaziergänge mit Hermann Lenz (Schwieberdingen & Stuttgart: Rüber & Denzel, 1975);

Neue Zeit: Roman (Frankfurt am Main: Insel, 1975);

Der Tintenfisch in der Garage: Erzählung (Frankfurt am Main: Insel, 1977);

Wie die Zeit vergeht (Frankfurt am Main: Corvus, 1977);

Das doppelte Gesicht: Drei Erzählungen (Frankfurt am Main: Suhrkamp, 1978);

Tagebuch vom Überleben und Leben: Roman (Frankfurt am Main: Insel, 1978);

Die Begegnung: Roman (Frankfurt am Main: Insel, 1979);

Constantinsallee: Roman (Frankfurt am Main: Insel, 1980);

Der innere Bezirk: Roman in drei Büchern (Frankfurt am Main: Insel, 1980);

Zeitlebens: Gedichte, 1934-1980 (Munich: Schneekluth, 1981);

Erinnerung an Eduard: Erzählung (Frankfurt am Main: Insel, 1981);

Ein Fremdling: Roman (Frankfurt am Main: Insel, 1983);

Der Letzte: Erzählung (Frankfurt am Main: Suhrkamp, 1984);

Der Wanderer (Frankfurt am Main: Insel, 1986).

PERIODICAL PUBLICATION: "Der Ausgestopfte Steppenwolf: Meine Besuche in Dichterhäusern," *Jahrbuch der Deutschen Schillergesellschaft*, 25 (1981): 525-532.

Hermann Lenz is virtually unknown outside Germany–none of his books has been translated–and even in the German-speaking world he has never had a large readership. But he has always enjoyed the support of a small but steadily increasing group of admirers who sustained him during the many years before his work found general critical recognition. His position in postwar German fiction is now secure and is based on the totality of his creative output rather than on a single great success.

His life is entirely given to his writing; he scrupulously guards his privacy and abstains from involvement in nonliterary issues. Therefore, Lenz is known mainly through his novels, many of which are strongly autobiographical. But his books reveal only remembrances, thoughts, and emotions that have been transformed into fiction. This artistic metamorphosis of the raw material of daily existence into the lucid cohesion of finely stylized narration is the only manner in which Lenz has been able to respond to the often intolerable indignities of his personal life and the collective experiences of his generation; he has found it impossible to confront the moral and political issues of his time without the distancing mediation of literary form. His mode of resistance to the pressures of the totally politicized world of Nazi Germany was retreat into his innermost self. This withdrawal did not lead to emotional narcissism, despair, or intellectual paralysis, but engendered a creative strength which found expression in the evocation of an idealized historical reality. Lenz's style has been called a contemporary variant of mid-nineteenth-century "magic realism."

Hermann Lenz was born in Stuttgart and, excepting his years as a student in Tübingen, Munich, and Heidelberg and his military service, he lived there, and until 1924 in nearby Künzelsau, for over sixty years. His family had deep roots in the Neckar region of Swabia. Lenz grew up in a middle-class environment as the son of a conservative high-school teacher and officer, Hermann Friedrich Lenz, and his wife Elise. His relatives came mostly from the rural and suburban middle class; they included shopkeepers, artisans, and members of the less ambitious academic professions. His studies, first of theology in Tübingen and then of art history, German literature, and classical archaeology in Munich and Heidelberg, were not satisfying to him, and he was not suffi-

ciently motivated to follow in his father's footsteps and prepare for a career in the higher school service. By the age of twenty-four he had come to consider himself a failure in all his practical endeavors, and was also uncertain about his future as a poet. A small volume of his verse had been printed in 1936 but there was little prospect of further publications when, in January 1938, he returned to Munich without much interest in obtaining a degree. It was not long before he was drafted for military service.

Fin-de-siècle Vienna and the courts of his native Württemberg during the Biedermeier period before the 1848 revolutions are Lenz's favorite settings; Hugo von Hofmannsthal and the Swabian poet Eduard Mörike are his stylistic models. These preferences are apparent in his first novel, *Das stille Haus* (The Quiet House, 1947), preliminary versions of which were written in 1938 and published in the *Neue Rundschau*. In this novel Lenz establishes all of the major themes and theses and types of protagonists found in his later works. His work thereafter is a continuous retelling of his principal concerns.

The "quiet house" is both the city home of a young Viennese nobleman, Stephan Clary, and the abode he erects within himself as a refuge from the turbulence of the world outside. He is the talented and sensitive child of an old aristocratic family. His father, a diplomat in the service of the disintegrating monarchy, detests the emergence of the new power constellations and reacts with melancholy cynicism. His marriage can no longer be held together, and as he faces the loneliness of old age his only solace is his vivacious daughter, a young woman of unusual inner resources and simple practicality. The son, who is incapable of facing the challenges of an active existence, attaches himself to his mother, who has become content with the small pleasures that an idyllic life of genteel moderation can provide. It has become impossible for Stephan to develop his dormant talents, especially his capacity for admiration, friendship, and love, and at the end of the novel he has slipped quietly into the solitary role of an elegant outsider who will quickly perish under a new social order.

It is mostly Lenz's young female characters who are sufficiently resourceful to survive in a hostile world, but even they have no illusions about their future. Such is the case with the former medical student Tamara Lasowskaja in *Der russische Regenbogen* (The Russian Rainbow, 1959), who lives through the degradations of a displaced person during World War II, first in the fighting at the front, then in a forced labor camp. After she is liberated, she is not elated at her newfound freedom and safety, nor is she persuaded that people have learned much from their demeaning experiences. She does not expect the symbolic rainbow of conciliatory forgiveness to brighten the sky for very long.

A female character is also at the center of a trilogy of novels–*Nachmittag einer Dame* (Afternoon of a Lady, 1961), *Im inneren Bezirk* (In the Inner District, 1970), and *Constantinsallee* (Constantine Avenue, 1980), all republished as *Der innere Bezirk* (The Inner District, 1980)–that trace the development of a diplomat's daughter, Margot von Sy. At the beginning she is on the verge of committing suicide, as her mother did, but her will to live is restored by her father. He had belonged to the circle of confidants of the last king of Württemberg and became a military attaché in the Nazi regime to disguise his true loyalties; he is now involved in a futile conspiracy against Hitler. The story of his daughter's refusal to conform to the mores of the majority is told in three stages–1935 to 1938, 1938 to 1947, and 1948 and after.

Lenz describes his own life and the history of his family in a series of four novels in which he appears as Eugen Rapp. *Verlassene Zimmer* (Deserted Rooms, 1966) is the story of his maternal grandparents. Their lives as owners of a small tavern are uneventful and are guided by the unobtrusive conservatism of a country town and by the habits of honest self-appraisal. Julius Krumm, the grandfather, had been a rifle maker before machine production forced him into semiretirement and he has continued, through times of war and revolution, to be devoted to a past that is represented by the benign and popular figure of the last king of Württemberg. Resigned to the fact that his own life will end in obscurity and eschewing any self-deceptive illusions, he commits all his resources to the education of his daughter, Eugen's mother, a talented pianist.

Andere Tage (Other Days, 1968) is told from the perspective of Eugen's younger sister. She is as alert and perspicacious as he, but has a more robust ability to live with things as they are. By having Margret Rapp describe and react to the gradual awakening of his own sensitivities, Lenz objectifies his perspectives. The novel juxtaposes Eugen's growing uncertainties with the hardening views of his father, who eventually becomes an active supporter of Hitler. The historical era depicted is that of the Weimar Republic, from the time of its postrevolutionary consolidation in 1919 until the Nazis officially take over the government of Germany in 1933. It is a time that severely tests family loyalties and, in the end, brings about Eugen's withdrawal into the private world of poetic imagination. But as yet he feels no assurance about his vocation.

In *Neue Zeit* (New Age, 1975) the daily humiliations of living under fascism in Munich have brought Eugen close to despair. He has fallen in love with a fellow art student, Johanna Trautwein, who is officially classified as half-Jewish and is in constant danger of being deported. The novel relates his experiences as an infantry soldier in the occupation of France, on the Russian front, in Poland, and again in France, where he becomes an American prisoner of war soon after D day. The final volume, *Tagebuch vom Überleben und Leben* (Diary of Survival and Life, 1978), chronicles his life from his return to Stuttgart in 1946 until the early summer of 1948. He has now made a firm commitment to the profession of writing–with all its risks and hardships as well as its gratifications. The novel tells of his search for Johanna, of their married life in the attic of his parents' house, of his difficulties with publishers, and at last of his growing sense of self-confidence.

Lenz's autobiographical books are not sweeping re-creations of historical events; they offer no more than that small segment of life with which the author is intimately familiar. Lenz makes no attempt to see the rise of Nazism, for example, in a broader context than that established by his immediate circumstances, and he does not try to analyze it. This limitation contradicts the apologies made on his behalf by admirers who speak of his extraordinary ability to portray the subtleties of the public mind. Lenz's world is not a cross-section of the German people but a small subgroup, whose peculiarities he describes with a precise sense of locale and psychological nuance.

His own disposition is a moderately idiosyncratic conservatism that values privacy, orderliness, service, and cultural continuity. To this orientation, the Nazis represent a type of sordidness that appeals to people who are lacking in self-esteem but is abhorrent to those with a strong sense of individuality. The fictional characters that personify Lenz's own preferences almost invariably become reclusive eccentrics who are cognizant of the decay around them and seek to escape into a private sphere of aesthetic nostalgia.

Significant expressions of acclaim have come to Lenz only in his later years. He has traditionally been criticized for concentrating on too narrow a slice of German life, for painting too moderate a picture of the fascist mentality and of the elements that brought the Nazis to power, for suggesting too helpless an alternative, and for refusing to admit that there is anything positive about the modern world. But since the Suhrkamp Verlag acquired the rights to his books in 1975 and brought them out in paperback editions, his posture of eclectic individualism has been reappraised and found less wanting. The award of the Georg Büchner Prize by the German Academy for Language and Literature in 1978 is indicative of a general shift in Germany's cultural temper away from experimentation and aggressive innovation toward conservative forms of realistic narrative and a more tolerant, even apologetic and forgetful view of an ever farther receding past.

References:

Arthur Häny, "Die Lust der Betrachtung: Zum Roman 'Die Begegnung' von Hermann Lenz," *Schweizer Monatshefte*, 60, no. 6 (1980): 512-515;

Helmut Kreuzer and Ingrid Kreuzer, eds., *Über Hermann Lenz: Dokumente seiner Rezeption (1947-1979) und autobiographische Texte* (Munich: Fink, 1981);

Rainer Moritz, " 'Den Nachsommer einwirken lassen': Hermann Lenz und Adalbert Stifter," *Vierteljahresschrift. Adalbert-Stifter-Institut des Landes Oberösterreich*, 33 (1984): 61-74;

Kurt Scheel, "Kein Vorbild: Hermann Lenz zum 70. Geburtstag," *Merkur*, 37 (1983): 239-241.

Joachim Maass

(1 September 1901-15 October 1972)

Dieter Sevin
Vanderbilt University

BOOKS: *Johann Christian Günther: Kleines dramatisches Gedicht in sieben Bildern* (Frankfurt am Main: Englert & Schlosser, 1925);

Bohème ohne Mimi (Berlin: Fischer, 1930);

Der Widersacher: Roman (Berlin: Fischer, 1932);

Borbe: Erzählung (Berlin: Rabenpresse, 1934);

Die unwiederbringliche Zeit: Roman (Berlin: Fischer, 1935);

Auf den Vogelstraßen Europas: Lehrgang einer Leidenschaft (Hamburg: Broschek, 1935);

Stürmischer Morgen: Chronik einer deutschen Künstlerjugend (Bremen: Schünemann, 1937);

Ein Testament: Roman (Hamburg: Goverts, 1939); translated by Erika Meyer as *The Weeping and the Laughter* (New York: Wyn, 1947);

The Magic Year, translated by Meyer (New York: Bermann-Fischer, 1944; London: Barrie & Rockliff, 1964); original German version published as *Das magische Jahr: Ein Roman* (Stockholm: Bermann-Fischer, 1945);

Des Nachts und am Tage: Gedichte (Hamburg: Hamburgische Bücherei, 1948);

Die Geheimwissenschaft der Literatur: Acht Vorlesungen zur Anregung einer Ästhetik des Dichterischen (Berlin: Suhrkamp, 1949);

Der unermüdliche Rebell: Leben, Taten und Vermächtnis des Carl Schurz (Hamburg: Claassen & Goverts, 1949);

Der Fall Gouffé (Berlin: Fischer, 1952); translated by Michael Bullock as *The Gouffé Case* (New York: Harper, 1960; London: Barrie & Rockliff, 1960);

Schwierige Jugend: Aufzeichnungen eines Moralisten (Frankfurt am Main: Fischer, 1952);

Carl Schurz: Ein Leben für die Freiheit (Frankfurt am Main: Steuben-Schurz-Gesellschaft, 1952);

Schwarzer Nebel (Hamburg: Hans Bredow-Institut, 1956);

Kleist, die Fackel Preußens: Eine Lebensgeschichte (Vienna, Munich & Basel: Desch, 1957); revised as *Kleist: Die Geschichte seines Lebens* (Bern & Munich: Scherz, 1977); translated

Joachim Maass (Ullstein)

by Ralph Manheim as *Kleist: A Biography* (New York: Farrar, Straus & Giroux, 1983);

Die Zwillingsbrüder oder Das Leben nach dem Tode (Munich: Theaterverlag Desch, 1958);

Zwischen Tag und Traum: Ein Lesebuch (Vienna, Munich & Basel: Desch, 1961);

Die Stunde der Entscheidung: Drei Dramen (Munich, Vienna & Basel: Desch, 1965);

Jaquemars schwierige Jugend: Erzählungen (Frankfurt am Main & Hamburg: Fischer, 1965);

Der Schnee von Nebraska (Munich, Vienna & Basel: Desch, 1966).

OTHER: *Völkische Poesie und moderne Lyrik Portugals*, translated and edited by Maass (Heidelberg: Groos, 1925);

"Der Fall de la Roncière," in *Vier Fernsehspiele,* edited by Heinz Schwitzke (Stuttgart: Cotta, 1960);

Das Junge Europa: Erzählungen junger Autoren, introduction by Maass (Vienna: Desch, 1962);

Martin Beheim-Schwarzbach, edited by Maass and Rudolf Maack (Hamburg: Christians, 1968).

In 1935 Hermann Hesse called Joachim Maass one of the most talented among the younger generation of German novelists. Maass belongs to the generation of exile authors who left Germany in opposition to the Nazi regime. Unlike Thomas Mann and Bertolt Brecht, who were already well-established authors at the time of their emigration, Maass was just emerging as a prose writer when he decided to leave for the United States. After an unsuccessful homecoming in the early 1950s, he returned to Germany only for brief visits.

The third and youngest son of a well-to-do merchant family–his brother Edgar became a well-known historical novelist–Maass attended a private preparatory school in Hamburg. In 1920, abandoning his plans to study law, he reluctantly became an apprentice with his father's business firm, which sent him to Portugal in 1922. There he discovered his love for literature and began writing lyric poetry, much of which remained unpublished. He returned to Hamburg after a year and resigned from the firm to become a freelance writer. His first book, a volume of translations of Portuguese folk songs, was published in 1925. During the 1920s Maass wrote several dramas, including *Kain* (Cain), *Die Zwillingsbrüder* (The Twin Brothers, published in 1958, first performed in 1960 in Vienna) and *Heinrich der Vierte* (Henry the Fourth).

From the beginning Maass's literary concerns dealt with the conflict of morality and immorality, of the dark, demonic, and destructive forces versus the light, conciliatory, and constructive ones, conflicts he foresaw and feared for his own times. Cain, for instance, denies the existence of God (as the Nazis were ultimately to do) and kills his own brother; consequently, he is marked forever.

While trying to establish himself as an author Maass made a living writing reviews and literary essays, first for the Hamburg newspaper *Hamburger Fremdenblatt* and then, after moving to Berlin, for the *Vossische Zeitung.* In 1930 he published his first novel, *Bohème ohne Mimi* (Bohème without Mimi), which was followed by *Der*

Widersacher (The Adversary) in 1932 and two minor novels in 1934 and 1935. These early works were no lasting accomplishments, but they were successful enough that Maass was able to live off his royalties from them. In 1937 he gave up his work as a journalist to concentrate on what he considered his real calling as a writer of prose fiction.

By this time the Nazis were in power in Germany, and it became increasingly difficult for Maass, with his keen sense of justice and decency, to cope with developments in his country which he felt to be immoral. He had visited the United States in 1936 to find a place of refuge for his lifelong Jewish friends, Dr. Lothar Luft and his wife Marie Renée. As for himself, he was extremely reluctant to leave Germany, not only because of his affection for the country but also because of his keen awareness of what exile would mean to his career: loss of the cultural environment which nurtured him; loss of the language, which he called "the magic instrument" for his art; loss of the readership he had just begun to attract; and most of all, loss of possibilities for publication.

Ironically, it was his first successful novel, and one of his best, that significantly influenced his decision to leave the country. *Ein Testament* (1939), an allegory of the rise to power of the Nazis and of the situation in 1938, contains strong warnings against the criminal policies of the regime. The title reflects Maass's motivation for writing the book: to leave to the German people his "last will and testament" when he went into exile. Maass intended the novel to reach the intellectuals in Nazi Germany. In his essay "Von ihm selber" (About Himself, 1957) he says that he wished to place his own strongly held values– "Reinheit, Klarheit, Geist und Liebe zum Menschen und seiner sittlichen Würde" (Purity, clarity, intellect and the love for man and his ethical dignity)–against those advocated by the Nazis. Even though he disguised its message by cloaking it as a detective novel–the influence of Dostoyevski's *The Brothers Karamazov* (1879-1880) is evident–Maass could not be sure that the Nazi censors would not eventually unlock its real meaning.

The need to circumvent censorship accounts for the complex structure and plot of *Ein Testament,* which has Maass's hometown Hamburg as its locale. As the story progresses, the reader is gradually introduced to divergent points of view on the murder of a well-to-do businessman that

Maass in 1939 (Ullstein)

are presented by the narrator and the main characters involved in the investigation. The interacting, multiple perspectives provoke the critical reader to interpret the novel and to recognize that the murder is really an allegory of the demise of the Weimar Republic and the murderer none other than Adolf Hitler. That such a book could be published in 1939 in Nazi Germany is evidence of Maass's skill as an author.

An excellent English translation of *Ein Testament* appeared in 1947 as *The Weeping and the Laughter*. The American reception, however, was quite subdued. One reason seems to have been that the book was not addressing the general public but the German intellectual of 1938; its complex style and allegorical structure limited its appeal for the American reader.

Maass's hesitation to leave Germany led to a sudden and unprepared departure in 1939 after Nazi storm troopers searched his apartment. In the United States he was initially supported by the National Carl Schurz Association, which also helped him find a job as a lecturer in German language and literature at Mount Holyoke College in the fall of 1940. The early years in this new environment were not especially productive from a lit-

erary point of view. His first novel written in exile, *Das magische Jahr*, appeared in English translation as *The Magic Year* in 1944. Its almost fifty-page-long preface gives a vivid account of the circumstances under which he started to write again in the United States, detailing his feelings of isolation, loneliness, and frustration about the events in Europe. A desperate feeling of resignation common to exile authors becomes strikingly clear as Maass describes his realization that his chances for publication in his original language have been cut off indefinitely.

Das magische Jahr itself is a charming piece of nostalgic, autobiographical prose fiction, full of longing for a lost youth in Maass's beloved Hamburg. Thomas Mann, writing in support of its acceptance for publication, succinctly and adroitly summarized the essence of the book in an October 1944 letter: "The literature of the German emigration has been enriched by a beautiful, important, highly artistic prose work, in which Maass has fulfilled all the expectations that he aroused in his earlier work, *A Last Will and Testament*. Already the prelude to *The Magic Year*, which plays in America, in a lonely wintery farmhouse..., is remarkably original and fascinates the reader not only by the strangeness of the present situation, but also by the importunate memories of the hero's late experiences in his homeland, which has 'awakened' to gruesome insanity. And seldom has the recherche du temps perdu, this descent into the depth of childhood, been with a richer poetic harvest than in the many pages overflowing with life, which then follow. The images of memory, colourful, uncanny, grotesque, tragic enchanting images against the background of the great harbor city of Hamburg crowd upon each other; each one surpasses the previous one in its intensive dream-reality; I did not find a single 'empty spot,' not a single weak scene in the whole book." Mann concludes his letter by emphasizing Maass's "sensitivity toward evil, which prevails without the use of any such pretentious words as morality, religion, humanity"; rather, the reader experiences this sensitivity by feeling it "as a passive suffering power, as a profound, tender, and invincible 'No.'"

The small publisher Bermann-Fischer in New York followed Mann's recommendation, and *The Magic Year* appeared at the end of 1944. Reviews in the major newspapers were generally positive. The *New York Times* (21 December 1944) said: "It is interesting as a study of childhood and of German life, and it is written with impressive skill. Mr. Maass is a deft and original writer with a distinctive manner all his own." The *Chicago Sun Book Week* (24 December 1944) echoed this view, speaking of "superb literary charm . . . , the polished work of a sensitive, keen, poetic craftsman." But the sales figures were low, and Maass abandoned his plans to expand the volume into a trilogy.

One reason for the novel's meager success must be sought in the limited financial resources of the small Bermann-Fischer publishing house, which did little to promote the book in the United States but decided instead to have the original German version published by its Swedish branch as soon as the war was over. Another reason for its limited appeal in America, however, is the subject matter and structure of the novel, which was not written with the American reading public in mind. The only possible readers Maass might have hoped for were his fellow exiles, although the preface does try to provide a background for the general reader.

The end of the war and of the Nazi dictatorship in Germany opened new opportunities for Maass. With Richard Friedenthal he became coeditor of the old, revered literary journal *Neue Rundschau,* which was being revived in New York. Maass welcomed this chance for a forum and hoped to have an impact in his home country, which, as he saw it, needed help in finding a new direction. His many essays for the journal concentrate on authors who had been out of favor with the Nazis and, for the most part, were still living in exile during the immediate postwar years, such as Heinrich and Thomas Mann, Franz Werfel, and Carl Zuckmayer. He also wrote about Stefan Zweig, an old friend and benefactor who had committed suicide in Brazil in 1942 out of despair over the continued successes of the Hitler regime.

The combined responsibilities of editing, most of which was done in New York while Friedenthal lived in London, and teaching did not permit Maass to work on a larger project. The resulting restlessness led to his resignation as editor of the *Neue Rundschau* in 1949. He felt a new confidence in his creative energies; the possibility of once again having his works published for a German-speaking readership must have given him the necessary uplift and motivation.

His novel *Der Fall Gouffé* (1952; translated as *The Gouffé Case,* 1960) brought the long-hoped-for success not only in the German-speaking countries but worldwide. Similar to *Ein Testament,* the

basic plot consists of a murder case that remains unsolved in spite of the efforts of the police. The crime is committed in Paris, but Maass's experiences in exile are strongly reflected, since much of the action takes place in the United States. The search for the murderer leads the brother-in-law of the murdered Gouffé halfway around the world to Saratoga Springs, New York, and Monterey, California. The demonic female character Gabriele Bompard is modeled after a German immigrant Maass had met in California. Like all the male characters in the novel, Maass seems to have fallen prey to her erotic temptation. Even Gouffé's brother-in-law, who suspects her as an accomplice in the murder, is not immune to her magnetism.

Into this suspenseful plot Maass interweaves his real concern: the working of the great powers of the soul—intellect and sensuality, rationality and eroticism—in men and women. A basic ethical dimension characteristic of all of Maass's works is the underlying and integrating component in this novel: once again, Maass is dealing with the struggle of the dark and demonic against the good and moral powers in the world.

One reason for the enormous success of *The Gouffé Case*—aside from the book's appeal as a grimly realistic detective novel—was that Maass was, for the first time, addressing a broad reading public. While definitely speaking to the readers of the German-speaking countries, the book does not limit itself to them. The $50,000 Maass received for the film rights gave him a new freedom. In 1952 he resigned from his position at Mount Holyoke College and returned to Germany to devote himself to his literary endeavors.

As it turned out, Maass was unable to adjust to postwar Germany. Not having been there during the war, he could not understand the intense desire of most Germans to forget the past and concentrate on rebuilding their country. Maass's moral sense was deeply offended; he missed the outcry against what had happened. Also, he failed to receive the welcome in literary circles and the publishing world that he had hoped for. He had left the country too early in his career and had been forgotten. Furthermore, Maass's novels tended to address his readers' feelings of guilt in connection with recent history—but the readers preferred to suppress those feelings. He returned to the United States in 1954. Maass's works were not republished in Germany until the late 1950s and became best-sellers only in the 1960s. He visited Germany only once more, in

*Dust jacket designed by Brigitte B. Fischer for Maass's first
novel written in exile*

1961, to receive a literature prize from the Bavarian Academy for the Fine Arts.

Maass settled in New York in a common-law marriage with Marie Renee Luft, whose husband Lothar Luft had died. He did not attempt to write another major novel but went back to the genre of his early years, the drama, and achieved a modest success with the *Die Zwillingsbrüder*. He also wrote a fascinating literary biography of the great neurotic nineteenth-century German poet Heinrich von Kleist (1957). A personal affinity drew Maass to Kleist, who did not feel at home anywhere in the world, was unable to accept societal demands, and had a deep sense of justice that he expressed in the novella "Michael Kohlhaas" (1810). From about 1965 until his death in 1972, Maass could not leave his New York apartment or write because of his worsening diabetes and emphysema. Many German newspapers reviewed and praised his oeuvre at the time of his death.

Bibliography:
Gitta Schaaf, *Joachim Maass* (Hamburg: Christians, 1970).

References:
Jeremy Brooks, Review of *The Gouffé Case*, *Guardian*, 30 December 1960, p. 4;
Ronald Hayman, Review of *The Gouffé Case*, *New Statesman*, 10 December 1960, p. 944;
Patricia Hicks, Review of *The Weeping and the Laughter*, *New York Times*, 9 November 1947, p. 20;
Wendall Johnson, Review of *The Magic Year*, *Chicago Sun Book Week*, 24 December 1944, p. 3;
Harry W. Pfund, Review of *The Magic Year*, *New York Times Literary Supplement*, 31 December 1944, p. 5;
Dieter Sevin, "Der implizite Leser als Formelement des Exilromans am Beispiel von Joachim Maass' Ein Testament," in *Schreiben im Exil: Zur Ästhetik der deutschen Exilliteratur 1933-1945*, edited by Alexander Stephan and Hans Wagener (Bonn: Bouvier, 1985), pp. 212-223;
Sevin, "Joachim Maass: Exil ohne Ende," *Colloquia Germanica*, 14 (1981): 1-25;
Sevin, "Den Kindern des Geistes und der Nacht: 'Ein Testament' von Joachim Maass oder der Weg ins Exil," in *Das Exilerlebnis*, edited by Donald G. Daviau and Ludwig M. Fischer (Columbia, S.C.: Camden House, 1982), pp. 322-331;
Marguerite Young, Review of *The Magic Year*, *New York Times Literary Supplement*, 31 December 1944, p. 5.

Papers:
Joachim Maass's papers are in the Deutsches Literaturarchiv in Marbach am Neckar, West Germany. Copies of most papers are in the Joachim Maass Collection in the library of the State University of New York at Albany.

Hans Erich Nossack

(30 January 1901-2 November 1977)

Wulf Koepke
Texas A&M University

BOOKS: *Gedichte* (Hamburg: Krüger, 1947);
Nekyia: Bericht eines Überlebenden (Hamburg: Krüger, 1947);
Interview mit dem Tode (Hamburg: Krüger, 1948); republished as *Dorothea: Berichte* (Hamburg: Krüger, 1950);
Der Untergang (Frankfurt am Main: Suhrkamp, 1948); edited by Edgar Lohner (New York: Harcourt, Brace & World, 1966);
Die Rotte Kain: Schauspiel in drei Akten (Hamburg: Krüger, 1949);
Die Begnadigung (Zurich: Bösch, 1955);
Spätestens im November: Roman (Berlin: Suhrkamp, 1955); translated by Ruth Hein as *Wait for November* (New York: Fromm, 1982);
Der Neugierige (Munich: Langen/Müller, 1955);
Die Hauptprobe: Eine tragödienhafte Burleske mit zwei Pausen (Hamburg: Wegner, 1956);
Spirale: Roman einer schlaflosen Nacht (Frankfurt am Main: Suhrkamp, 1956); partially republished as *Unmögliche Beweisaufnahme* (Frankfurt am Main: Suhrkamp, 1959); translated by Michael Lebeck as *The Impossible Proof* (New York: Farrar, Straus & Giroux, 1968);
Über den Einsatz (Mainz: Akademie der Wissenschaften und der Literatur, 1956);
Begegnung im Vorraum: Zwei Erzählungen (Olten: Vereinigung Oltner Bücherfreunde, 1958);
Der jüngere Bruder: Roman (Frankfurt am Main: Suhrkamp, 1958);
Freizeitliteratur: Eine Fastenpredigt (Mainz: Akademie der Wissenschaften und der Literatur, 1959);
Nach dem letzten Aufstand: Ein Bericht (Frankfurt am Main: Suhrkamp, 1961);
Ein Sonderfall: Schauspiel (Neuwied & Berlin: Luchterhand, 1963);
Sechs Etüden (Frankfurt am Main: Insel, 1963);
Menschliches Versagen: Rede bei der Verleihung des Wilhelm-Raabe-Preises 1963 (Braunschweig: Kulturamt, 1963);
"Es ist schade um die Menschen": Ansprache zur Eröffnung der Frankfurter Buchmesse im Oktober

Hans Erich Nossack (Suhrkamp Verlag, Frankfurt am Main)

1963 (Frankfurt am Main: Börsenverein des deutschen Buchhandels, 1963);
Das kennt man: Erzählung (Frankfurt am Main: Suhrkamp, 1964);
Das Testament des Lucius Eurinus (Frankfurt am Main: Suhrkamp, 1965);
Das Mal und andere Erzählungen (Frankfurt am Main: Suhrkamp, 1965);
Die schwache Position der Literatur: Reden und Aufsätze (Frankfurt am Main: Suhrkamp, 1966);
Das Verhältnis der Literatur zu Recht und Gerechtigkeit (Mainz: Akademie der Wissenschaften und der Literatur, 1968);

Der Fall d'Arthez: Roman (Frankfurt am Main: Suhrkamp, 1968); translated by Lebeck as *The d'Arthez Case* (New York: Farrar, Straus & Giroux, 1971);

Dem unbekannten Sieger: Roman (Frankfurt am Main: Suhrkamp, 1969); translated by Ralph Manheim as *To the Unknown Hero* (London: Alcove Press, 1974; New York: Farrar, Straus & Giroux, 1974);

Pseudoautobiographische Glossen, selected by Christof Schmid (Frankfurt am Main: Suhrkamp, 1971);

Romanfiguren, by Nossack and others (Mainz: Hase & Koehler, 1971);

Die gestohlene Melodie: Roman (Frankfurt am Main: Suhrkamp, 1972);

Bereitschaftsdienst: Bericht über eine Epidemie (Frankfurt am Main: Suhrkamp, 1973);

Der König geht ins Kino: Eine Geschichte (Frankfurt am Main: Insel, 1974);

Um es kurz zu machen: Miniaturen, selected by Schmid (Frankfurt am Main: Suhrkamp, 1975);

Ein glücklicher Mensch: Erinnerungen an Aporée. Roman (Frankfurt am Main: Suhrkamp, 1975);

Dieser Andere: Ein Lesebuch mit Briefen, Gedichten, Prosa, edited by Schmid (Frankfurt am Main: Suhrkamp, 1976).

OTHER: "Übersetzen und übersetzt werden," in *Übersetzen: Vorträge und Beiträge vom internationalen Kongreß literarischer Übersetzer in Hamburg 1965*, edited by Rolf Italiander (Frankfurt am Main: Athenäum, 1965), pp. 9-19;

"Warum ich nicht wie Hermann Broch schreibe," in *Fünfzehn Autoren suchen sich selbst*, edited by Uwe Schultz (Munich: List, 1967), pp. 64-71.

TRANSLATIONS: Joyce Cary, *Des Pudels Kern: Roman* (Hamburg: Krüger, 1949);

Gerald Hanley, *Dunkler Wind: Roman* (Hamburg: Krüger, 1957);

Sherwood Anderson, *Winesburg, Ohio: Roman um eine kleine Stadt* (Berlin & Frankfurt am Main: Suhrkamp, 1958);

Harold Nicolson, *Die Kunst der Biographie und andere Essays: Vier Essays* (Berlin & Frankfurt am Main: Suhrkamp, 1958).

PERIODICAL PUBLICATIONS: "Der Tod des Pegasus," *Die Zeit*, 30 May 1946;

"Rat an eine Leserin," *Welt am Sonntag*, 5 June 1949;

"Empören Sie sich! Gedanken zu Hans Henny Jahnns Romantrilogie *Fluß ohne Ufer*," *Welt am Sonntag*, 7 May 1950;

"Die Antwort ist Schweigen," *Die Welt*, 28 January 1951;

"Der Dichter als biologisches Phänomen," *Die Neue Zeitung*, 1 August 1951;

"Der Unbekannte wird gebeten . . . ," *Die Neue Zeitung*, 13 March 1952;

"Warum ich protestiere: Zum Gesetz über den Vertrieb jugendgefährdender Schriften," *Die Neue Zeitung*, 8 October 1952;

"Vorbemerkung des Autors zur *Hauptprobe*," *Blätter des Hessischen Staatstheaters Wiesbaden*, no. 8 (1952/1953);

"Die dichterische Substanz im Menschen," *Jahrbuch der Akademie der Wissenschaften und der Literatur Mainz* (1954): 315-321;

"Kurze Autobiographie," as Berthold Möncken, *Das Einhorn: Jahrbuch der Freien Akademie der Künste in Hamburg* (1957): 132-134;

"Nachruf auf Hans Henny Jahnn," *Jahresring* (1960/1961): 323-328;

"So lebte er hin. . . . Rede zur Verleihung des Georg-Büchner-Preises," *Merkur* (1961): 1001-1008;

"Strickwaren für Neger: Ist unsere Literatur arbeiterfremd?," *Merkur* (1962): 993-996;

"Der Mensch in der heutigen Literatur," *Jahresring* (1962/1963): 44-60;

"Die Furcht vor dem selbständigen Denken," *Christ und Welt*, 11 October 1963;

"Stimme und Verstummen," *Jahresring* (1965/1966): 236-242;

"Bitte kein literarisches Geschwätz," *Die Welt der Literatur*, 6 January 1966;

" 'Er wurde zuletzt ganz durchsichtig': Erinnerungen an Hermann Kasack," *Parabeln: Jahrbuch der Freien Akademie der Künste in Hamburg* (1966): 228-235;

"Dieses lebenlose Leben: Versuch über den NS-Alltag," *Merkur* (1967): 134-149;

"Ameisen brauchen keine Literatur," *Süddeutsche Zeitung*, 21-22 December 1968;

"Gedanken zur Rebellion: Religionsersatz und Revolutionsersatz," *neutralität* (December 1969): 35-37;

"Die Frage nach dem Gegenüber," *Jahresring* (1973/1974): 127-129.

Hans Erich Nossack was a characteristic voice of German literature after World War II;

yet he saw himself as a loner, unaligned with any group or movement. Most critics agree with this self-assessment. While the idea of the lonely voice was typical for a whole generation of writers, it was reinforced in Nossack's case by the fact that he started publishing late in life and that recognition was slow in coming.

Nossack was born in Hamburg in 1901 to Eugen and Elita Kröhnke Nossack. His family owned an import-export company which Nossack was expected to take over. After his Abitur (school-leaving examination) in 1919 he went on to study philosophy and law at the University of Jena to prepare himself for his future duties. But after three years he broke with his family, refused any further financial support from them, and became a manual laborer. He joined the Communist party and became active in politics. In 1925 he married Gabriele Knierer and started working for a bank. The increasing danger of National Socialism drove him back into active work for the Communist party. In 1933, branded a Communist, he took refuge in the family firm and soon became its managing director. His first manuscript was to have been published in 1933; instead, he was forbidden to write and was kept under surveillance by the Gestapo. The bombing of Hamburg from 24 July to 3 August 1943 destroyed his apartment and part of his office building; most of his manuscripts and all of his diaries were burned, forcing him to make a fresh start as a writer. Nossack found his voice as an author in response to the destruction of his native city and his life's work.

After World War II he continued his double existence as writer and businessman until 1956, when he was able to dissolve the company and devote his last twenty years exclusively to writing. While this decision involved some financial hardships, he did not make compromises in his writing and continued to bear the cross of being called a "difficult" author. Only his novel *Spätestens im November* (Not Later than November, 1955; translated as *Wait for November*, 1982) was at all successful, although some of his last books were more accessible. He was discovered in France much earlier than in Germany when Jean-Paul Sartre published translations of his work in 1947; the connection with Sartre led some critics to consider him an existentialist, although Nossack rejected the label. He has also been called a surrealist and a nihilist. He received several literary awards, notably the Büchner Prize in 1961 and the Wilhelm Raabe Prize in 1963.

Nossack lived in Aystetten, near Augsburg, from 1956 to 1962; in Darmstadt from 1962 to 1965; in Frankfurt from 1965 to 1969. In 1969 he returned to Hamburg, where he died in 1977.

After the traumatic air raid on Hamburg Nossack wrote down his experiences in a short report which was published in 1948 as *Der Untergang* (The Destruction). He and his wife had been on vacation fifteen kilometers from Hamburg, had witnessed the destruction of the city from a distance, and had returned into the burning ruins to search for friends. *Der Untergang* established the basic structure of Nossack's narrative works: each of them is a report on a past event which had a decisive impact on the narrator's life and continues to haunt the narrator in the present.

The narrator sees himself or herself as an isolated being, different from the crowd of "normal" people. The narrators and their friends are on their way to an unknown goal, to new frontiers beyond the prescribed limits. While on occasion they are able to disappear physically into unknown lands, they feel completely alienated. They "camouflage" themselves as normal persons, follow their daily routines, and perform their professional and family duties. But they are always aware that they are playing a role and really do not belong.

Nossack tries to avoid specific ideological labels; his position—and that of the narrator-protagonists—is that of the minority of "humanists" against the masses who are influenced by political ideologies, commercial suggestions, and conventional goals. Frequently he describes the problems of communication between these two types of people and the fruitless efforts of the humanists to make themselves understood.

Before 1943 Nossack's ambition had been to be a playwright, and a good part of his stories is taken up by dialogue. The really dramatic situations, however, are not those which could be shown on a stage: they occur within the human psyche. In his works of the immediate postwar period, the themes of death and the end of the human race predominate. *Nekyia: Bericht eines Überlebenden* (Sacrifice for the Dead: Report of a Survivor, 1947), one of Nossack's first publications, is the report of the leader of a band of half-human creatures called Lemuren (ghosts), who survive the end of civilization. The unnamed narrator goes back to his city, which is now a city of the dead, and relives in his memory the time before the catastrophe. Reality and memory become hard to distinguish. The story ends with a variation of the Orestes myth when the narrator remembers an encounter with his overpowering mother.

A catchy title made the story "Interview mit dem Tode" (Interview with Death) the title story of Nossack's first collection, published in 1948. The narrator is invited to meet Death, who wants to have a complimentary article written about him. Death lives in a small apartment with his mother, a domineering bourgeois woman, and his sister, a prostitute who brings home real coffee and cigarettes from her nightly assignations with black-market traders in pubs. Death explains that his enterprise is organized with bureaucratic perfection so that he can handle the many people who stand in line. On a stroll through the city with the narrator, the cynical Death nonchalantly causes the death of a little girl running after her ball. Disturbed by this event, the narrator ends up in a pub, where he meets Death's sister; she, however, refuses to become intimate with him. The story depicts the pervasiveness of death after the war.

Not all of Nossack's earlier stories are gloomy, and his special type of irony is visible in some of them. "Der Jüngling aus dem Meer" (The Young Man from the Sea), also contained in the collection *Interview mit dem Tode*, is a playful reversal of the myth of the sea nymph in love with a mortal man: here a young woman, alone in a cabin on the seashore, has a brief encounter with a beautiful young man from the depths of the sea. Encounters with "angels," who represent the world beyond the limits of normal human understanding, are common in Nossack's works.

Most of Nossack's novels are made up of episodes, some of which are unconnected with the main plot; the difference between these novels and collections of stories is only one of degree. He has a limited number of situations and character types: the domineering mother, the super-rationalistic intellectual, the unfulfilled wife, and the alienated father who wants to retire from society are recurrent figures in his works. A typical constellation occurs in *Spätestens im November*, one of his most closely structured novels. The narrator, Marianne Helldegen, the alienated wife of a successful entrepreneur, meets Berthold Möncken, a writer to whom the association of industrialists has just awarded a prize. They recognize instantly that they belong together and leave the same night. After they spend several happy weeks in a remote village, Marianne, tired of

Berthold's promises of a new departure and a new life in the fall–"not later than November"–when he completes the play he is writing, returns to her family. But in November the play is performed, as he had promised, and turns out to be a success. He buys an old Volkswagen, drives to Marianne's palatial house, and takes her with him after a grotesque encounter with her husband. Slightly drunk from celebrating his success, and urged by Marianne to speed on a wet road, Berthold has an accident in which both of them are killed. The new departure has become one beyond the limits of life. The dead woman, liberated from a confining and useless existence, makes this report on her life from the beyond.

Also in 1955 Nossack published *Der Neugierige* (The Curious One), a curious story about curiosity. The protagonist is a fish who escapes from the sea and drags himself from pond to pond, scarcely surviving. He realizes who he is when he sees his wet traces in the sand. It is only outside his element that he becomes aware of his true nature.

Spirale: Roman einer schlaflosen Nacht (Spiral: Novel of a Sleepless Night, 1956) is only a novel of sorts; its five constituent parts have been published separately or in different collections. Its framework is provided by a foreword: a man remembers an event from the past, and a spiral of memories is set in motion which keeps him awake until dawn. The five episodes are spirals, each of which returns to the point of departure, but with a new level of consciousness. In the first spiral, "Am Ufer" (On the River Bank), a young man tells of his dream of crossing the river and escaping the corrupt environment of his domineering mother; her illicit trading involves the entire family except for the father, who retreats into seeming insanity. "Die Schalttafel" (The Switchboard) contrasts two students: one has abruptly left the university, like Nossack himself; the other wants to live a life of mimicry in order to keep his inner freedom and humanity. The bulk of the book is taken up by "Unmögliche Beweisaufnahme" (The Impossible Proof), a trial in which an insurance broker is asked about the disappearance of his wife. The lawyers never understand what he means when he explains that his wife has departed for a place where one cannot be insured. He had provided all possible insurance for her life, but he knew that she had to go beyond his protection. He reproaches himself for not having followed her with enough determination, so that he lost her in the snow–which, according to the lawyers, did not occur in September. The story breaks off; conventional law cannot explain or judge her departure. In "Die Begnadigung" (The Amnesty) a prisoner is to be liberated, but at first he does not want to reenter society; he has to go through an involved inner process before he is ready to do so. Finally, "Das Mal" (The Monument) tells of an expedition to the Arctic which finds a man frozen in an upright position, thereby providing a landmark visible for long distances in the flat landscape. The narrator detects a smile in the face of the frozen man; he has found happiness in his death.

Der jüngere Bruder (The Younger Brother, 1958) is purportedly taken from a manuscript of one Stefan Schneider; the manuscript has been transmitted to a writer, Breckwaldt, who adds an account of Schneider's death and funeral. Schneider returns from Brazil to Hamburg in search of his "younger brother" whom he calls Carlos Heller, who has disappeared. He does not find him, and an encounter with a "Carlos" in a St. Pauli bar leads to his death. But first he confronts his past: his weak, sly, and subversive father; his domineering mother; and his submissive older brother. He also comes in contact with people who knew Carlos Heller, all of them searching for the impossible, trying to escape from the prison of ordinary life. These characters are habitués of the pub "Aporée," a word which Nossack uses in later books for a continent for escapees, for those who want to live differently. The word is never explained; it is an anagram of "Europa," but it is also close to *Aporia*, the Greek word for a problem without a solution.

Nach dem letzten Aufstand (after the Last Revolt, 1961) operates on two time levels. In the past, a dictatorial regime in an unnamed country creates a young "god" who is to be sacrificed after nine months. The narrator is chosen to be the guardian of the "god," and he becomes close to the young man and his woman companion. The "god" is sacrificed shortly before the state is overthrown and replaced by a secular, outwardly humanistic democracy. The narrator reproaches himself for not having saved him—but it seems that the "god" wanted to die. The new regime does not bring a real liberation, only a change of the people in power. In the present, the narrator is a night clerk in a Munich hotel and the companion of the "god" is a famous actress. The two form the nucleus of a group of alienated people who try to survive in the "democratic" new Germany.

Nossack in 1966 (Ullstein–dpa)

Das kennt man (Everybody Knows That, 1964) is the monologue of a Hamburg prostitute, written down by a student who watches her die during the night. This story raises the doubt whether the departure to unknown lands, the trip beyond the limits, is really justified or beneficial. The prostitute speaks of the "land on the other side of the river" as if it were just another trap in which she will be caught again.

In *Das Testament des Lucius Eurinus* (1965) the title character is a Roman official in the late second century A.D. who is in charge of enforcing the laws against Christians. A humane person, he is baffled by the Christians' fanaticism and their refusal to accept rational argument. He implies that their religion stems from social and personal resentments. Lucius Eurinus represents the aristocratic attitude toward vulgar and ugly revolt. When he finds out that his own wife has become a Christian, he decides that the only honorable way out is suicide.

Der Fall d'Arthez (1968; translated as *The d'Arthez Case*, 1971), one of Nossack's more controversial books, had a favorable response in various foreign countries but did not sit well with West German critics. The book implies that the Fed-

Nossack in 1974 (Ullstein–Christa Kujath)

eral Republic is a police state and links the West German police with the Gestapo. It also posits an alliance of government with the corporate world in all political systems. The main character, who calls himself D'Arthez after a minor character in a Balzac novel, is a well-known pantomimist. D'Arthez embarrassed his wealthy family when he left the university and became an actor, and even more when a satirical pantomime on the Nazis caused his imprisonment in a concentration camp. After his liberation he disappeared for three months, and later he refused to cooperate with either the Soviets or the Americans. The story begins when d'Arthez is questioned by the West German police because of a criminal case in Paris involving someone using his name. The narrator, the assistant interrogator, becomes intrigued by d'Arthez and falls in love with Edith Nasemann, d'Arthez's daughter. She, like d'Arthez, tries to find an independent way through life, breaking off an advantageous engagement with a career-minded student and declining a huge inheritance from the family corporation. The narrator finally chooses to give up his government career to work in the Third World instead of entering an alliance with Edith.

The narrator of *Dem unbekannten Sieger* (1969; translated as *To the Unknown Hero*, 1974) is a gymnasium teacher who wrote his dissertation on the 1918 German revolution. One of the revolution leaders was a military genius who disappeared as suddenly as he had emerged. A monument was erected to him as the "unknown hero" in a small town west of Berlin. The narrator gives a copy of the dissertation to his father, a shrewd businessman who has transformed the family grocery store into a modern supermarket. The father offers a humorous critique of the book, making the narrator aware that his father knows more about the revolution than the academically trained son. But only after the father's death, when he discovers a jacket worn by his father during the 1918 events, does the narrator realize that his father was the unknown hero.

Die gestohlene Melodie (The Stolen Melody, 1972) is a complex and baffling work about a popular tune that was stolen from its real composer on "the other side"–a land beyond the ordinary– and the group of misfits who tried to prevent its exploitation. The novel deals with the incompatibility of true art and commerce.

The narrator of *Bereitschaftsdienst: Bericht über eine Epidemie* (Emergency Duty: Report on an Epidemic, 1973) is a chemist who volunteers for emergency duty when a suicide epidemic grips the world. This "disease" does not spare his own family: his young wife takes her life and those of their two children. The authorities and the media try to control the proportions of the epidemic, which claims more than two million victims worldwide. The narrator moves to another city, takes an inconspicuous job, and remarries, but he is obsessed by the past. He realizes that there are no explanations for the suicides: they happened in all climates, under all political systems, in big cities and in villages; they cannot be accounted for in medical or in sociopolitical terms. Humanity has lost the will to face the horror of life on earth. The book is an indictment of modern society and a radical rejection of any religion or ideology.

Nossack's last novel, *Ein glücklicher Mensch: Erinnerungen an Aporée* (A Happy Person: Memories of Aporée, 1975), recounts the history of the lost continent of Aporée. The narrator, a retired government official living in Washington, D.C., tells the reader that Aporée does not exist anymore: the Americans have settled and developed it and renamed it Newropa. Previously, after a nuclear disaster, it had been uninhabitable; but after many years a small zone of green appeared along the coast where sheep could survive, although there were neither birds nor fish. The continent, which was left off of official maps, was kept under surveillance by the American navy. Rumor had it that on the other side of Aporée, the "Eastern" peoples were slowly starting to repopulate the border lands. But it seemed impossible to get across to the other side, and many inhabitants of Aporée disappeared trying to do so. Forty years ago the narrator immigrated to Aporée; but when he reached the shore, he found that the people were as unhappy as they had been elsewhere. Indeed, they spent their time retelling the memories of their former lives. Aporée is a country that lies between life and death: women who become pregnant die before childbirth; those who tire of the past disappear into the vast plains. The woman who lives with the narrator, however, bears a child before she dies. The narrator and his daughter return to the United States. Ramsic, the narrator's friend, says to him while they walk toward the helicopter: "You are a happy person." The reader is left to ponder what he means. The narrator's daughter becomes completely integrated into American society; the narrator waits for his death.

Nossack also wrote poems, a small selection of which was published in 1947, and plays, including *Die Rotte Kain* (The Cain Gang, 1949), *Die Hauptprobe* (The Dress Rehearsal, 1956), and *Ein Sonderfall* (A Special Case, 1963). The isolated performances of the plays have not been successful. Nossack was also an essayist who advocated the independence of literature from political and commercial considerations. He also made some translations from English into German, among them *Winesburg, Ohio* (1958) by Sherwood Anderson and Harold Nicolson's *The English Sense of Humour*, which he translated as *Die Kunst der Biographie und andere Essays* (The Art of Biography and Other Essays, 1958).

Nossack's importance, however, rests with the stories and novels in which his narrators probe into a painful past or try to explain extraordinary experiences not easily accessible to rationalism or common sense. He is an adversary of all political ideologies and of organized religion. He addresses a small group of readers who, like the characters in his books, see through the pretenses of "normal" people and who, while desperate, continue to face life until their time comes to die. There is even some hope in his position, a somewhat skeptical hope for a future when a

true humanism will be possible. Nossack's outlook is marked by his years of "camouflage" between 1933 and 1945; by his experience of the destruction of Hamburg in 1943; and by his disappointment with the course of German reconstruction after 1945, in which he could see only a repetition of old conditions and problems. He expresses his radical position in a lively idiomatic language and with an irony that may amuse even readers who disagree with him. Communication problems and parodies of popular literature play an important role in his works; he often plays with the view society has of writers and literature. There are many writer figures in Nossack's works who feel an urge to leave an account of themselves, although they are not sure that they have any potential readers. Nossack's depictions of reality are always convincing; he is less impressive when rendering his imaginary countries–the land on the other side of the river, Aporée, or the country before the last revolt. They seem to be states between death and rebirth, and Nossack infuses them with lifelessness. Nossack is more memorable when he describes modern apartment complexes as buildings housing people who wait for death, or who live a dead life. Like the painter in one of his stories, he almost prefers buildings without people.

Nossack's characters find no way to change society; all they can do is to parody society's conventions. Nossack's books try to draw the reader in and transform him. Nossack refuses to offer a program; he speaks with the voice of a prophet, while admitting that his message cannot be expressed in words, only by silence. An increasing number of critics and readers acknowledge the literary merits of Nossack's texts, but his audience remains divided as to the validity of his message.

Interviews:

"Werkstattgespräch mit Uwe Schultz," in *Selbstanzeige: Schriftsteller im Gespräch,* edited by Werner Koch (Frankfurt am Main: Fischer, 1971), pp. 17-25;

"Literatur und Biographie: Werkstattgespräch mit Christof Schmid," in *Literarische Werkstatt: Interviews,* edited by Gertrud Simmerding and Christof Schmid (Munich: Oldenbourg, 1972), pp. 40-50;

Horst Bienek, "Hans Erich Nossack," in his *Werkstattgespräche mit Schriftstellern* (Munich: Deutscher Taschenbuch Verlag, 1976), pp. 71-84;

Manfred Durzak, "Die intensivste Form des Lebens ist für mich ein Buch zu schreiben" and "Epische Rechenschaftsberichte: Das Erzählwerk von Hans Erich Nossack," in his *Gespräche über den Roman* (Frankfurt am Main: Suhrkamp, 1976), pp. 369-399.

References:

Günther Busch, "Bruchstücke eines Gesprächs," *Stuttgarter Zeitung*, 28/29 January 1961;

Karl G. Esselborn, *Gesellschaftskritische Literatur nach 1945: Politische Resignation und konservative Kulturkritik, besonders am Beispiel Hans Erich Nossacks* (Munich: Fink, 1977);

Hans Geulen, "Hans Erich Nossack," in *Deutsche Literatur seit 1945 in Einzeldarstellungen*, edited by D. Weber (Stuttgart: Kröner, 1968), pp. 197-220;

Hans Henny Jahnn, "Kleine Rede auf Hans Erich Nossack," *Sinn und Form*, 7 (1955): 313-319;

Joseph Kraus, *Hans E. Nossack* (Munich: Beck, 1981);

Kraus, *The Missing Link of the Quiet Rebellion of Hans Erich Nossack* (Bonn: Bouvier, 1976);

Hans Mayer, "Der totale Ideologieverdacht," in his *Deutsche Literatur seit Thomas Mann* (Reinbek: Rowohlt, 1967);

Peter Prochnik, "First Words: The Poetry of Hans Erich Nossack," *Modern Language Review*, 64 (1969): 100-110;

Marcel Reich-Ranicki, "Hans Erich Nossack: Das kennt man" and "Hans Erich Nossack: Die schwache Position der Literatur," in his *Literatur der kleinen Schritte: Deutsche Schriftsteller heute* (Munich: Piper, 1967), pp. 96-102, 207-215;

Christof Schmid, *Monologische Kunst: Untersuchungen zum Werk von Hans Erich Nossack* (Stuttgart: Kohlhammer, 1968);

Schmid, ed., *Über Hans Erich Nossack* (Frankfurt am Main: Suhrkamp, 1970).

Theodor Plievier

(17 February 1892-12 March 1955)

Dieter Sevin
Vanderbilt University

BOOKS: *Weltwende* (Berlin: Verlag der Zwölf, 1923);

Des Kaisers Kulis: Roman der deutschen Kriegsflotte (Berlin: Malik, 1929; revised edition, Constance: Asmus, 1949); translated by Margaret Green as *The Kaiser's Coolies* (New York: Knopf, 1931); translated by William F. Clarke as *The Kaiser's Coolies* (London: Faber & Faber, 1932);

Zwölf Mann und ein Kapitän: Novellen (Leipzig & Berlin: Neff, 1929);

Über seine Arbeit (Berlin: Malik, 1932);

Der Kaiser ging, die Generäle blieben: Ein deutscher Roman (Berlin: Malik, 1932); translated by A. W. Wheen as *The Kaiser Goes, the Generals Remain* (London: Faber & Faber, 1933; New York: Macmillan, 1933);

Der zehnte November 1918: Ein Kapitel aus dem gleichnamigen Roman, revised by A. Wenediktow (Moscow & Leningrad: Verlagsgenossenschaft ausländischer Arbeiter, 1935);

Das große Abenteuer: Roman (Amsterdam: de Lange, 1936); translated by Charles Ashleigh as *Revolt on the Pampas* (London: Joseph, 1937); translated by Robert Pick as *Revolt on the Pampas* (New York: Appleton-Century-Crofts, 1951);

Im Wald von Compiègne (Moscow: Iskra revoljucii, 1939);

Nichts als Episode (Moscow: Meshdvnarodnaja Kniga, 1941);

Der Igel: Die Geschichte vom Untergang einer Nazi-Bastion an der Ostfront (London: Freier Deutscher Kulturbund in Großbritannien, 1942);

Stalingrad: Roman (Berlin: Aufbau, 1945); translated by H. Langmead Robinson as *Stalingrad: The Death of an Army* (London: Athenaeum, 1948); translated by Richard and Clara Winston as *Stalingrad* (New York: Appleton-Century-Crofts, 1948);

Haifische: Roman (Weimar: Kiepenheuer, 1946);

Im letzten Winkel der Erde: Roman (Weimar: Kiepenheuer, 1946);

Theodor Plievier in 1955 (Ullstein–Fritz Eschen)

Generale unter sich (Mainz: Ehglücksfurtner Verlag, 1946);

Das gefrorene Herz: Erzählungen (Weimar: Kiepenheuer, 1947);

Eine deutsche Novelle (Weimar: Kiepenheuer, 1947);

Einige Bemerkungen über die Bedeutung der Freiheit: Rede (Nuremberg: Nest, 1948);

Der Seefahrer Wenzel und die Töchter der Casa Isluga (Zurich: Büchergilde Gutenberg, 1951);

The World's Last Corner, adapted from a translation by Pick of *Im letzten Winkel der Erde* and

Haifische (New York: Appleton-Century-
    Crofts, 1951);
Moskau: Roman (Munich: Desch, 1952); translated
    by Stuart Hood as *Moscow* (London: Muller,
    1953; New York: Ace Books, 1953);
Berlin: Roman (Munich, Vienna & Basel: Desch,
    1954); translated by Louis Hagen and Vi-
    vian Milroy as *Berlin: A Novel* (London: Ham-
    mond & Hammond, 1956; Garden City:
    Doubleday, 1957).

OTHER: Bernhard Kellermann, *Was sollen wir
    tun?*, with a contribution by Plievier (Berlin:
    Aufbau-Verlag, 1945).

Theodor Plievier captivated his readership
with intense prose, combining autobiographical
material with depictions of major historical
events of the twentieth century. His novels have
been extremely popular not only in Germany but
worldwide, with more than three million copies
sold of the German originals as well as translations. In West Germany new editions of his works
have been republished or are planned. His novel
Stalingrad (1945; translated, 1948) has also had a
new edition in the German Democratic Republic
(GDR).

Born in Berlin in 1892 to Theodorus Rudolf Plievier and Albertine Luise Augusta Thing
Plievier, Theodor Plievier had to start contributing to the livelihood of his large working-class family when he was twelve years old. At seventeen he
rebelled against the strict authority of his father,
who showed no understanding or sympathy for
the literary interests of his son, by running away
from home. Plievier worked his way across Europe, educating himself by reading every book
available to him. A job as a sailor took him to
South America, where he spent a considerable
length of time. The experiences and adventures
of these years later found their literary expression in *Das große Abenteuer* (The Great Adventure, 1936; translated as *Revolt on the Pampas*,
1937). Returning to Germany shortly before
World War I, he was drafted into the navy. In November 1918 he participated in the "Kiel Mutiny," writing pamphlets against the war. He was
discharged from the navy that year.

During the early 1920s Plievier wrote political essays in which he attacked social injustices
and warned of the danger of a new war. He continued to read intensively: "Die sich bis ins
Metaphysische erhebende Revolte lehrte mich
lesen und half mir, Schriftsteller auszuwählen,

angefangen mit den Propheten des Alten
Testamentes, über die Mystiker des Mittelalters,
auch über Lao-tse und die alten Chinesen bis zu
Philosophen wie Friedrich Nietzsche und
Autoren wie Heine, Ibsen, Gorky, Dostojewski,
Tolstoi und den lebenden Schriftstellern ..."
(My inner, almost metaphysical revolt taught me
to read and helped me to select authors beginning with the prophets of the Old Testament,
through the mystics of the Middle Ages, also
through Lao-tse and the old Chinese writers, to
philosophers such as Friedrich Nietzsche and authors such as Heine, Ibsen, Gorky, Dostoyevski,
and Tolstoy as well as contemporary writers ...).
His youthful feeling of revolt never diminished
but was transformed into an intense belief in
man's right to individual liberty and freedom
from want. This transformation explains Plievier's attraction to socialism during the 1920s. He
hoped that a socialist order would both end the
economic enslavement he saw all around him
and prevent another war.

Plievier achieved his first success as a novelist with *Des Kaisers Kulis* (1929; translated as *The
Kaiser's Coolies*, 1931). Dedicated to two sailors
who were sentenced to death for mutiny by an imperial war tribunal in 1917, the novel depicts
some of the major naval battles of World War I
from the perspective of the sailors and reflects
their fear and despair in the face of the constant
possibility of death. With its emphasis on a realistic documentary account, the book belongs to the
"Neue Sachlichkeit" (New Realism) movement of
the 1920s. There is no continuous plot; the style
is dominated by short and even incomplete sentences. The brutality and inhumanity of the commanding officers are contrasted with the
suffering and willingness to sacrifice of the en-
listed men, who are degraded to mere machines
and cannon fodder. This kind of outcry against
the abuse man suffers from man remained a
basic theme throughout Plievier's literary career.

The Nazis interpreted the novel as slander
against the German military; they were also antag-
onized by speeches in which Plievier openly expressed his pacifist and antinationalist views. As a
result his books were burned on 10 May 1933
and were no longer permitted to be sold in Germany. Narrowly avoiding arrest, he escaped to
Paris via Prague and Vienna.

In Paris he could barely survive on the meager advance his publisher had given him for two almost completed manuscripts–a novel, "Demokratie," and a play, "Koka"–which were lost

in his hasty departure and were never rewritten. An invitation to attend the Soviet Literary Convention in Moscow in August 1934, with all expenses paid, provided temporary relief from his financial problems. But since his German passport had been revoked, Plievier found that he had to stay in the Soviet Union. All attempts to obtain a passport from a neutral country, such as Sweden, were in vain. Consequently, Plievier remained in the Soviet Union for eleven years, until the defeat of Nazi Germany allowed his return home.

Living in the Soviet Union during the 1930s turned out to be quite different from what Plievier had expected. The royalties from his books had little purchasing power, so he moved from Moscow to Leningrad, where rents were lower. Although he actually lived rather well in comparison to many Soviet writers, the general drabness of life in the Soviet Union was all too evident.

Plievier started to write again. Drawing on the experiences of his years in South America, he produced *Das große Abenteuer*. While it is primarily an autobiographical adventure novel, the book does incorporate Plievier's social concerns and anti-Nazi convictions. Plievier portrays the evils of the social and racial demagogy of National Socialism in the character of the Chilean dictator Ibanez and shows the necessity of a united proletariat. This need is recognized by the protagonist, Atschassos, a revolutionary who attempts to organize a democratic opposition to Ibáñez. The political dimension is, however, certainly not the dominant level of this suspenseful story. Although the exile press welcomed the book as an antifascist adventure novel with high artistic and convincing political qualities, Plievier was not pleased with the work. His plans to completely revise it never materialized, however, during the subsequent turbulent years.

With the beginning of the great purges in early 1935, which Plievier considered a Soviet version of Robespierre's Reign of Terror, he was ready to flee over the Finnish border. But his preparation must have been noticed by the Soviet secret police because he was asked to move to Paulskoje, a tiny village in the Republic of the Volga Germans. The reason given was that he was to help develop an indigenous culture for the Volga Germans. The move turned out to be a blessing in disguise; Plievier survived, while many of the German immigrants in Leningrad fell victim to the purges.

Plievier became a farmer and lived comfortably on royalties from his books. From a literary standpoint, however, the time was quite barren. He tried to write, and he took notes on the fate of the Volga Germans; but he destroyed all of his work for security reasons as the purges reached even this remote area of the Soviet empire. Life became unpredictable for Plievier during this period, especially because he had never been a Communist party member. Little is known about Plievier's life from 1935 until he was permitted to return to Moscow in 1939.

Johannes R. Becher, a fellow German exile author, had interceded with the authorities on Plievier's behalf. Back in the Soviet capital Plievier spent his time building a house with his own hands. He wrote two novellas, *Im letzten Winkel der Erde* (In the Last Corner of the Earth, 1946) and *Haifische* (Sharks, 1946), again drawing on politically safe experiences in South America. (Parts of both works were combined and translated as *The World's Last Corner*, 1951.) With the German attack on Russia in June 1941, Plievier was unable to write, but his keen observations of those dramatic events would come to literary fruition in his novel *Moskau* (1952; translated as *Moscow*, 1953). As the German armies advanced Plievier and other foreign authors were moved in a special train to the distant city of Tashkent.

The capitulation of the German Sixth Army at Stalingrad early in 1943 signaled the turning point of the war, and Plievier was allowed to return to the capital. Plievier prepared radio broadcasts to be transmitted to Germany, urging the Germans to stop this senseless war; some of these programs were also broadcast into Germany by British and American stations. Plievier was given access to many letters of German soldiers at Stalingrad which had fallen into Russian hands; from these letters he was supposed to determine the mood of the German armed forces and the German people. The tragic plight of the soldiers soon aroused his compassion and his dormant creative powers. In December 1943 he finally received permission from the Soviet government to write *Stalingrad* (1945; translated, 1948), the novel which was to become his greatest international success.

One year later the manuscript was finished. Plievier recalled the circumstances of its writing: "Der Roman war fertig, bevor ich auch nur eine Zeile geschrieben hatte. Kein einziges meiner Bücher lag so klar vor mir wie *Stalingrad*. Das ungeheure Briefmaterial schrie nach Gestaltung,

Plievier in 1946 (Ullstein–Fritz Eschen)

und das Problem für mich war . . . das Recht zu haben, die Kriegsgefangenenlager zu besuchen, um die noch frischen Eindrücke der Stalingradkämpfer festzuhalten" (The novel was finished before I wrote even the first line. None of my other books did I see so clearly in front of me as *Stalingrad*. The immense number of letters was just begging to be utilized. My problem at the time was . . . to be granted permission to visit the prisoner of war camps in order to obtain the fresh and unfaded impressions of the men who fought at Stalingrad). Plievier was allowed to speak with German prisoners of war of all ranks. That their fate captivated him completely is reflected in the intensity of his writing.

The battle of Stalingrad began in November 1942 and ended with the unconditional surrender of General Field Marshal Paulus and the remnants of the Sixth Army on 2 February 1943. Plievier skillfully uses modern film techniques, such as rapid sequences of short scenes, and interweaves a large variety of analyses, monologues, and dialogues into his prose. Smoothly combining and blending documentation and fiction, the novel is not divided into chapters but, like a

Greek tragedy, presses on with increasing momentum toward the final climax.

The common soldier is represented by August Gnotke, who is totally disillusioned with the war and German leadership. He is nevertheless able to uphold his values throughout the brutal battle and siege. He finds meaning for his existence and preserves his sense of humanity by caring for a fellow soldier who would otherwise not have survived. Through the portrayal of Gnotke, with his keen sense of justice, his vitality, and his adaptability, Plievier reaffirms his belief in the common man.

Another main protagonist is Major Vilshoven, an idealized German officer who is capable of a change of character. Starting as an enthusiastic tank commander, Vilshoven eventually stands in opposition to the commanding officers, who refuse to act according to the dictates of their consciences and instead abide by Hitler's command to fight to the bitter end, thus sacrificing thousands of lives. Those officers repeatedly refused the Russian demand for capitulation, even though they were aware that their men were dying not only from enemy bullets but of hunger and disease. Plievier believed that this catastrophic defeat, in which 200,000 German soldiers lost their lives, could have been avoided if, during the initial stages of the encirclement, the German army had been permitted to make a concentrated effort to break through the Russian lines. Hitler's orders, however, defying all military logic, were to stay and defend their positions. He persisted in this militarily untenable directive until it was too late, sealing the fate of the encircled army. Plievier concludes that the highest German leaders actually wanted a total defeat in order to create a national myth which would unify the Germans behind the Nazis and inspire them to continue to fight.

Plievier always insisted that he had given a historically accurate and unbiased portrayal of the battle, even though he had to write under the watchful eye of Soviet censorship. An artistic description of the German defeat seemed to be useful to the authorities. The mere presentation of the facts was so horrifying that it satisfied the Soviet censors, who were anxious to have the German command shown in a bad light. No propagandistic additions were necessary. Plievier limited himself to the fall of the German Sixth Army, omitting the victorious Russian advance almost completely because, as a realist, he could not have glorified the Russian army to the satisfaction of the censors. The Red Army remains faceless–it has merely the function of nemesis.

With the collapse of the Third Reich Plievier returned to Germany with the nucleus of what was to constitute the new government of the Eastern Zone. Since Plievier was not a party member, his presence was not desired in Berlin; he was transferred to Weimar, where he became a member of the Thuringian parliament. He was furnished with a villa and a chauffeured car. His experiences and impressions of that period are reflected in the second half of his last novel, *Berlin* (1954; translated, 1956).

The eastern part of the divided Germany failed to provide Plievier with the creative freedom he had hoped for, and he left for the West on 28 July 1947. In the Eastern Zone he was accused of selling out to capitalism. The truth is, however, that he had exchanged a secure and comfortable life for a future full of uncertainty. His departure from East Germany began a new period of creativity. Free from censorship, Plievier revived an old plan of writing a novel on the German invasion of Russia. Since he intended to include both the Russian and the German sides, he explained, such a work could not have been written in the Soviet sphere of influence: "Es wäre niemals gestattet worden, die Rote Armee im Zustand der Desorganisation und die Bevölkerung in ihrer passiven Resistenz gegen das Regime darzustellen" (They would have never given permission to depict the Red Army in its state of confusion and disorganization, nor would they have allowed the description of the Russian people in their passive resistance against the regime).

Plievier settled in the small town of Wallhausen in southern Germany and started giving lectures. He refused to give up his ideological freedom by committing himself to either side in the cold war, emphasizing the need for independent thinking during dangerous times. In a speech in Paris in late 1948 he became one of the first Germans to advocate reconciliation between France and Germany. Plievier was an able orator who could hold his audiences spellbound; wherever he spoke he was received enthusiastically as the author of *Stalingrad*. The lectures, however, as well as his unsettled personal life–he divorced his second wife and remarried–did not allow him the peace and concentration he needed for the major works he had planned until 1951, when he began to write *Moskau* and *Berlin*.

Moskau, *Stalingrad*, and *Berlin* make up a trilogy that depicts the war on the Eastern front in an encompassing panorama. Unity of the three volumes is provided by the reappearance of certain characters. *Moskau* constitutes the rising action of the three novels, depicting the German invasion of Russia and the advance to the gates of Moscow; *Stalingrad* represents the climax of the story; *Berlin* is the denouement, showing the final defeat of Germany, the Russian invasion of the German capital, and the immediate postwar period.

In spite of this basic unity there are important differences between the volumes. For instance, when *Stalingrad* was written, the immediacy of the historical events dominated its style, structure, and language. In contrast *Moskau*, written ten years after the events it depicts, is characterized by strict control and skillful organization. While *Stalingrad* is an uninterrupted narrative, *Moskau* is divided into three main parts.

The first part of *Moskau* deals with the suspense among the German military just before and during the early stages of the invasion. The reader is introduced to the vastness of Russian space by means of a reconnaissance flight deep into the country, allowing the author to show the madness of this undertaking by the Nazi rulers. The second part is devoted to the chaos caused in the Soviet army by the German attack and its rapid advance. Plievier masterfully portrays the catastrophic Russian retreat. He describes the Russian people as he had known them during his eleven years in exile, depicting their customs and traits, their hopes and melancholy nature. Plievier felt compassion for the simple people of this vast country, who for centuries had been exploited by autocratic systems and had suffered through famines and wars; he also knew the culture of the old Russia, and Tolstoy was one of his favorite authors. His feelings are reflected in the second part of *Moskau*; in addition, it is probable that he was deliberately trying to counter the viciously degrading Nazi propaganda regarding the Russian people and their culture. The last part of the novel comprises the huge German offensive, which was turned back at the gates of the capital by the resistance of the people and the extremity of the Russian winter, for which the Germans were totally unprepared. Plievier gives the main credit for stopping the German advance not to Stalin or his regime but to the Russian people, who were fighting not out of loyalty to their government but were simply defending their country against foreign invaders. The criticism of the Communist regime in the novel is not significantly less intense than that of the Nazis.

While *Stalingrad* and *Moskau* focus on relatively short phases of the war, *Berlin* encompasses a much longer span of time. The first three parts are devoted to the invasion and occupation of Berlin in 1945, while the last two parts deal with postwar East Germany up to the Berlin workers' rebellion in 1953. Plievier shows great empathy for the city of his childhood; he particularly bemoans the destruction of great art treasures. In vivid and realistic language he describes brutal fighting as the Russian armies move slowly into the heart of Berlin while young boys and old men are pressed into defense units by the desperate Nazis, and Hitler, in his bunker, continues to sacrifice them and his last troops, only to commit suicide at the end.

In some sections of this last novel it is evident that Plievier's creative powers were diminishing. At times the delineation of events becomes blurred by too many parallel scenes, all of which try to capture the horrendous destruction and suffering which occurred simultaneously throughout the city. The workers' rebellion of 1953 concludes the novel and the trilogy. Private Gnotke, the major protagonist of the trilogy, his vitality unbroken despite all deprivations during the war, is killed by a stray bullet while marching in protest with the workers. Gnotke's participation in the re-bellion reaffirms the author's belief in the integrity of the common man, while Gnotke's pointless death represents a protest against injustice and the suffering inflicted on humanity by those in power.

Having received threats after *Moskau* was published, Plievier moved in June 1953 to the village of Avegno in Switzerland. He was planning a book about his youth and a novel about the new German democracy (tentatively titled "Bonn") when he died of a heart attack during a walk with his five-year-old daughter on 12 March 1955. He is buried in Avegno.

Bibliography:

Marc Schryer, "Theodor Plievier im Exil: Bibliographie seiner Schriften (1933-1945)," *Recherches Germaniques*, 2 (1972): 163-203.

References:

Ingrid E. Lotze, "Theodor Plieviers Kriegstrilogie *Moskau, Stalingrad, Berlin*," Ph.D. dissertation, Columbia University, 1969;

Dieter Sevin, *Individuum und Staat in Plieviers Romantrilogie* (Bonn: Bouvier, 1972);

Harry Wilde, *Theodor Plievier: Nullpunkt der Freiheit. Eine Biographie* (Munich: Desch, 1965).

Papers:

Due to his turbulent life, almost all of Plievier's personal papers and manuscripts were lost.

Hans Werner Richter

(12 November 1908-)

Heike A. Doane
University of North Carolina at Chapel Hill

BOOKS: *Die Geschlagenen* (Munich: Desch, 1949); translated by Robert Kee as *Beyond Defeat* (New York: Putnam's, 1950); translation republished as *The Odds against Us* (London: MacGibbon & Kee, 1950);

Sie fielen aus Gottes Hand (Munich: Desch, 1951); translated by Geoffrey Sainsbury as *They Fell from God's Hand* (New York: Dutton, 1956; London: Harrap, 1956);

Spuren im Sand: Roman einer Jugend (Vienna, Munich & Basel: Desch, 1953);

Du sollst nicht töten (Vienna, Munich & Basel: Desch, 1955);

Linus Fleck oder Der Verlust der Würde (Vienna, Munich & Basel: Desch, 1959);

Wer will einen Esel? (Munich: Lentz, 1962);

Euterpe von den Ufern der Newa oder die Ehrung Anna Achmatowas in Toarmina: Bericht (Berlin: Friedenauer Presse, 1965);

Menschen in freundlicher Umgebung: Sechs Satiren (Berlin: Wagenbach, 1965);

Karl Marx in Samarkand: Eine Reise an die Grenzen Chinas (Neuwied & Berlin: Luchterhand, 1967);

Deutschland, deine Pommern: Wahrheiten, Lügen und schlitzohriges Gerede (Hamburg: Hoffmann & Campe, 1970);

Blinder Alarm: Geschichten aus Bansin (Frankfurt am Main: Suhrkamp, 1970);

Rose weiß, Rose rot (Hamburg: Hoffmann & Campe, 1971);

Rache für den Ziegenbock (Heidelberg & Vienna: Ueberreuter, 1973);

Briefe an einen jungen Sozialisten, preface by Leonhard Reinisch (Hamburg: Hoffmann & Campe, 1974);

Kinderfarm Ponyhof: Von Gletta, Berci, Garina, Cecil, von Pferden, Hunden, Eseln, von Minna, der Katze und Felix, dem Bernhardiner und von allen anderen (Munich: Bertelsmann, 1976);

Bärbel Hoppsala: Neue Abenteuer auf der Kinderfarm Ponyhof (Munich: Bertelsmann, 1979);

Die Flucht nach Abanon: Erzählung (Munich: Nymphenburger Verlagshandlung, 1980);

Die Stunde der falschen Triumphe (Munich: Nymphenburger Verlagshandlung, 1981);

Von Erfahrungen und Utopien (Frankfurt am Main: Eichborn, 1981);

Ein Julitag (Munich: Nymphenburger Verlagshandlung, 1982);

Im Etablissement der Schmetterlinge: 21 Porträts aus der Gruppe 47 (Munich: Hanser, 1986).

OTHER: *Deine Söhne, Europa: Gedichte deutscher Kriegsgefangener*, edited by Richter (Munich: Nymphenburger Verlagshandlung, 1947);

Die Mauer oder Der 13. August, edited by Richter (Reinbek: Rowohlt, 1961);

Bestandsaufnahme: Eine deutsche Bilanz 1962, edited by Richter (Munich: Desch, 1962);

Almanach der Gruppe 47, 1947-1962, edited by Richter and Walter Mannzen (Reinbek: Rowohlt, 1962);

Hans Schwab-Felisch, ed., *Der Ruf: Eine deutsche Nachkriegszeitschrift*, contributions by Richter (Munich: Deutscher Taschenbuch Verlag, 1962);

Walter Rathenau: Schriften und Reden, edited by Richter (Frankfurt am Main: Fischer, 1964);

Plädoyer für eine neue Regierung oder Keine Alternative, edited by Richter (Reinbek: Rowohlt, 1965);

"Warum ich kein Tagebuch schreibe," in *Das Tagebuch und der moderne Autor*, edited by Uwe Schultz (Munich: Hanser, 1965), pp. 95-109;

"Brief an den Herausgeber," in *außerdem: Deutsche Literatur minus Gruppe 47 = wieviel?*, edited by Hans Dollinger (Munich: Scherz, 1967), pp. 5-8;

"Warum fliegt der Vogel?," in *Motive: Deutsche Autoren zur Frage: Warum schreiben Sie?*, edited by Richard Salis (Tübingen & Basel: Erdmann, 1971), pp. 300-305;

"Alle literarischen Formen kehren immer wieder," in *Die Literatur und ihre Medien*, edited by Ingeborg Drewitz (Düsseldorf & Cologne: Diederichs, 1972), pp. 99-102;

Hans Werner Richter (photograph copyright © by Isolde Ohlbaum, Munich)

Erzählungen aus Pommern, edited by Richter (Tübingen: Erdmann, 1973);

Der Ruf: Unabhängige Blätter der jungen Generation, edited by Richter and Alfred Andersch, with contributions by Andersch (Nendeln, Liechtenstein: Kraus, 1975);

"Wie entstand und was war die Gruppe 47?," in *Hans Werner Richter und die Gruppe 47,* edited by Hans A. Neunzig (Munich: Nymphenburger Verlagshandlung, 1979), pp. 41-176;

Berlin, ach Berlin, edited by Richter (Berlin: Severin & Siedler, 1981);

"Verhaltung am Schienenstrang" and "Skizzen von einer Reise in die östliche Zone," in *In Deutschland unterwegs: Reportagen, Skizzen, Berichte,* edited by Klaus R. Scherpe (Stuttgart: Reclam, 1982), pp. 96-101, 185-201.

PERIODICAL PUBLICATIONS: "Ta-tü-ta-ta: Ein Selbstporträt," *Welt und Wort,* 6 (1951): 387-388;

"Courage," *Die Literatur: Blätter für Literatur, Film, Funk und Bühne,* 1 (15 March 1952): 1;

"Wiedersehen mit Balzac," *Die Literatur: Blätter für Literatur, Film, Funk und Bühne,* 1 (1 April 1952): 4;

"Curzio Malaparte," *Die Literatur: Blätter für Literatur, Film, Funk und Bühne,* 1 (1 May 1952): 1;

"*Kampf um Moskau:* Gespräch mit Theodor Plivier *[sic],*" *Die Literatur: Blätter für Literatur, Film, Funk und Bühne,* 1 (15 May 1952): 1;

"Der Prozeßumein Buch," *Die Literatur: Blätter für Literatur, Film, Funk und Bühne,* 1 (15 May 1952): 2;

"Links, wo das Herz ist: Interview mit Leonhard Frank," *Die Literatur: Blätter für Literatur, Film, Funk und Bühne,* 1 (1 July 1952):1 ;

"*Der Kampf um Moskau:* Zu dem neuen Buch von Theodor Plivier," *Die Literatur: Blätter für Literatur, Film, Funk und Bühne,* 1 (1 September 1952): 3;

"Die Restauration lähmt ihre Kinder," *Die Kultur* (Munich), 153 (1960);

"Zum politischen Engagement der Schriftsteller," *Die neue Rundschau,* 78 (1967): 290-298;

"Aus der Niederlage lernen! Alter und Jugend sind keine Qualitätsbegriffe," *Die Welt der Arbeit* (Cologne), 26 May 1972;

"Straßensänger 1931/32," *Merkur,* 36 (1982): 984-990.

Hans Werner Richter's place in German literature is secured by the role he played for the Gruppe (Group) 47, a loosely knit association of aspiring writers whose first meeting he called in 1947, when Germany still lay in ruins. As the father of this legendary group, Richter helped bring to prominence many of Germany's literary talents. Writers such as Heinrich Böll, Günter Grass, Uwe Johnson, Hermann Lenz, and Martin

Walser, all of whom later gained international fame, were first recognized by the group and its mentor, Richter.

Although Richter made a name for himself in the 1950s as a writer of fiction, his literary career gradually took second place to his service to the group. He had returned from World War II as a spokesman for the "verlorene Generation" (lost generation; analogous to America's lost generation of World War I), with whom he shared the vision of a new democratic Germany. This political orientation was reflected in a writing style devoid of ornamentation. The writers of the lost generation wanted to avoid links to established literary tradition and to demonstrate a commitment to democratic socialism. All of the founding members of the group adhered to these principles, and soon a new realism began to flourish in short stories, poetry, novels, dramas, and radio plays. Richter, a political journalist, had helped establish the political roots from which West German literature evolved as the conscience of the nation.

In his own fiction Richter portrays ordinary people against the backdrop of some of Germany's greatest upheavals–through the years of the Weimar Republic, through war and defeat, and into the prosperity of the postwar German Wirtschaftswunder (economic miracle). Thematically he draws from his own life; stylistically he relies on a stark prose influenced by the American realists of the 1920s and 1930s and the German realists of the Weimar years.

Richter was born on 12 November 1908 in Bansin, a small town on the Baltic island of Usedom, the fifth of seven children of Richard and Anna Knuth Richter. Like many in the small community of fishermen, craftsmen, and small-scale farmers, Richter's family worked hard to survive. During the tourist season his father served as a lifeguard while his mother took in the laundry of Bansin's aristocratic summer resorters; the rest of the year the family depended on fishing and the occasional poaching of pike. World War I had left its mark on the family: Richard Richter had gone into the war a monarchist and returned a socialist, and Richter's two older brothers had become pacifists.

Richter discovered literature in 1924, at the age of fifteen, when he began a three-year apprenticeship with a book dealer in Swinemünde. After a short stint as a seaman in 1927 he became a bookseller in Berlin, where he joined the Communist party in 1930. Two years later he was

expelled from the party for Trotskyism, but through his continued socialist activities he attracted the attention of the National Socialist party. In 1933 he fled to Paris, where, he said later, he and others planned Hitler's assassination, drank a lot of coffee, and nearly starved. The following year Richter returned to Berlin to work at odd jobs, sell books, and continue his political activities. In 1940 he was accused of leading a pacifist youth ring, but the charges were forgotten when he was drafted into the army. In 1942 he married Antonie Lesemann. He was captured in the battle of Monte Cassino in 1943 and transported to Camp Ellis, Illinois, where he wrote for, and later edited, a POW newspaper called *Die Lagerstimme* (Voice of the Camp). In September 1945 he was transferred to Camp Kearney, Rhode Island, where he joined Walter Mannzen and others as coeditor of *Der Ruf* (The Call), a paper founded a few months earlier by the War Department General Staff, the Department of State, and the Office of War Information for the political reeducation of German prisoners.

Upon their release in 1946 Richter and Alfred Andersch, who had also been a prisoner at Camp Kearney, returned to Germany and started their own version of *Der Ruf* in Munich, with a new subtitle: *Unabhängige Blätter der jungen Generation* (Independent Paper of the Young Generation). It advocated, according to Siegfried Mandel, "freedom and unity of Germany, a social-humanistic foundation for the new political structure of Germany, a unified socialist Europe, no imposition of the idea of collective guilt upon the German people, and no unnecessary humiliation of Germans." These proposals were not entirely acceptable to the American Information Control Division (ICD). In April 1947, after resisting several attempts at censorship, Richter and Andersch resigned as editors. Richter tried to found a more literary journal, *Der Skorpion*, but the ICD detected nihilistic tendencies in the introductory issue and refused his application for a license. His idea of inviting the paper's contributors to read and discuss their writing, however, gave birth to the Gruppe 47, which was to leave an indelible mark on German literature.

The small group of literary hopefuls that gathered in early September 1947 shared beliefs in humanistic socialism, in politically committed literature, and in a realistic language devoid of "Kalligraphie" (aestheticized style). Richter took on all organizational responsibilities from the start: he chose the meeting places, sent handwritten invitations to participants, and led the critiquing sessions. His unique gift for moderating and his flair for socializing and improvising earned him the respect of the group. In the words of Jürgen von Hollander, one of the early members, Richter "beherrscht die geheime Kunst, starre Gegnerschaft zu fruchtbaren Meinungen zu entschärfen" (mastered the secret art of transforming rigid oppositions into productive ideas). Richter's unpretentious manner set the tone for the meetings; as Walser put it, "Snobs, arrogante Literaten und intellektuelle Zungenkünstler und Wortakrobaten werden nicht mehr eingeladen" (Snobs, arrogant literati and intellectual artists of the tongue and word acrobats are not invited back). Richter at his best was immortalized by the novelist Günter Grass as Simon Dach in *Das Treffen in Telgte* (1979; translated as *The Meeting at Telgte*, 1981).

One of the first books to demonstrate the simplicity and clarity of style to which the group initially aspired is *Deine Söhne, Europa* (Your Sons, Europe, 1947), a small volume of poetry written by prisoners of war and edited by Richter. It included three of his own poems written in 1945. These, like his first novel, *Die Geschlagenen* (The Defeated, 1949; translated as *Beyond Defeat*, 1950), display the frugality and directness of expression that became the hallmark of Trümmerliteratur (literature from the rubble). Richter's years at the front and in prison camps provide the background for the events of the novel. The protagonist, Gühler, is captured after the grueling battle of Monte Cassino and begins a long journey into the depths of defeat. His ordeal is orchestrated not so much by his captors as by his fellow prisoners. Even in the eleventh hour of the war they regard anyone who questions Hitler's aims as a traitor. Amid this reign of terror by his peers, Gühler's struggle for self-preservation becomes a struggle for truth. With a few comrades he eventually forces the other prisoners to acknowledge the army's defeat on all fronts and to accept as fact the news of the dead, the homeless, the devastation of Germany.

Like Hemingway, whose prose he admired, Richter in *Die Geschlagenen* occasionally contrasts austere description with an almost lyrical depiction of a natural phenomenon. The anguish of a generation torn between patriotism and guilt is reflected in the book's dedication: "Meinen vier Brüdern, die Gegner und Soldaten dieses Krieges waren, die ein System haßten und doch dafür kämpfen mußten und die weder sich selbst, ihren Glauben, noch ihr Land verrieten" (To my four brothers, who were opponents of this war and soldiers in it, who hated a system but had to fight for it, and who betrayed neither themselves, their beliefs, nor their country). In 1950 the book was awarded the Fontane Prize of the City of Berlin.

In his second novel, *Sie fielen aus Gottes Hand* (1951; translated as *They Fell from God's Hand*, 1956), Richter uses a technique similar to a John Dos Passos montage, depicting war-torn Europe from various vantage points. Basing his story on interviews with refugees, he traces the lives of thirteen inmates of a camp for displaced persons. These characters are caught up in a war machine gone out of control. The motif of relentless destruction is mirrored in every facet of their lives: in their loss of home and family, of moral choices, and finally of hope. A secondary plot describes the history of the camp, accentuating the discrepancy between an ideology perceived as exemplary and its practice, which led to endless human suffering.

Although the narrative scope of this novel is broader than that of the first, it does not surpass it artistically. Predictability, trendy love scenes, and too many clichés (most of which have been eliminated in the English translation) flaw Richter's prose. Thomas Mann objected to the book's "Gleichmacherei" (moral equalization), and other critics found fault with its structure. Notwithstanding the criticisms, the novel won the René Schickele Prize in 1952.

Richter's third novel, *Spuren im Sand* (Footprints in the Sand, 1953), is a gentle parody of the traditional bildungsroman in which the author recounts his youth with understatement and political satire. Focusing on the changes in his family and hometown, he recaptures history with childlike simplicity. His love for the working class is always apparent, even though he exposes that class's political delusions.

Richter's last war novel, *Du sollst nicht töten* (Thou Shalt Not Kill, 1955), was a response to Germany's rearmament. It focuses on a Pomeranian family whose three sons perish while fighting on different fronts, and whose only daughter, crippled by the war, is lost on the refugees' trek west. The book closes with a scene reminiscent of Brecht: the mother pulling a cart loaded with her few remaining possessions, accompanied by the grandson for whom she will have to provide during the flight. Even though Richter's topic was timely and his prose free of the platitudes and sentimentality that had marred his earlier novels, the book was not enthusiastically received by a nation that wanted to leave its past behind.

Richter's most productive decade concluded with *Linus Fleck oder Der Verlust der Würde* (Linus Fleck or the Loss of Dignity), a satirical novel published in 1959. Like Richter, Linus runs a paper dedicated to the reeducation of the younger generation; but unlike the author, he is eager to cooperate with the American military government. He readily modifies his convictions to the needs of the hour, but he does so in a blunt manner; consequently, more cunning opportunists easily push him aside once he is no longer useful to them. *Linus Fleck* is one of the many satires that were popular in the 1950s but have since lost their sting. Its criticism never reaches beyond the realm of Richter's personal experience, so that it paints a one-sided picture of prevailing conditions.

During the next decade most of Richter's interest was divided between the Gruppe 47 and politics. The group had gained great influence in the publishing world and had grown considerably in number. Its membership included Germany's most important critics and publishers, and its meetings had been transformed from literary workshops into cultural events. In 1956 Richter, Hans Jochen Vogel, and Gerhard Szczesny, in response to the increasing political awareness of the group, created the Grünwalder Kreis (circle). The circle was to be a political forum for the "homeless left," German intellectuals who feared that their political interests were threatened by the resurfacing of fascist elements in the young German state. Two years later, after holding rallies in several major West German cities, the Kreis disbanded. Richter cites lack of respect among political opponents, lack of money, and his own lack of organizational talent as reasons for its demise. The Komitee gegen Atomrüstung (Committee against Nuclear Arms), with Richter as its president from 1958 to 1961, was more significant, since it marked the beginning of an era of great political involvement for many German intellectuals. By 1965 Richter had edited four collections of political writings: *Die Mauer oder Der 13. August* (The Wall; or, The 13th of August, 1961), *Bestandsaufnahme* (Inventory, 1962), *Walter Rathenau: Schriften und Reden* (Walter Rathenau: Writings and Speeches, 1964), and *Plädoyer für eine neue Regierung oder Keine Alternative* (Plea for a New Government; or, No Alternative, 1965). All of these books document his efforts to initi-

Richter in 1971 (Ullstein–Ursula Röhnert)

ate political change through the continued regeneration of democratic principles. After the 1961 Berlin crisis and the ensuing debate between intellectuals from East and West, Richter, like several other writers, established residence in West Berlin. With the support of the Literarische Colloquium, spearheaded by Walter Höllerer, and Sender Freies Berlin (Broadcasting System of Free Berlin), he presided over a salon which produced a series of radio and television programs until 1972. He and his associates–the "Literatur-Mafia," as opponents called them–came under attack in 1966 for alleged cronyism between members of the Senate of Berlin, which allocated prize and grant money; the Colloquium, which chose the recipients; the Berlin Academy of Arts, and Sender Freies Berlin, which provided publicity. Nevertheless, Richter's salon managed to maintain the legacy of the Gruppe 47, which met for the last time in 1967. In *Im Etablissement der Schmetterlinge* (In the Salon of Butterflies, 1986) Richter presents his personal recollections of the group's most important members and of the literary turbulence they provoked over the years. In 1972 he received the Cultural Prize of the German Federation of Trade Unions. In 1975 he returned to Munich to concentrate on his writing.

Richter's years in Berlin resulted in two autobiographical works: a collection of stories, *Blinder Alarm: Geschichten aus Bansin* (False Alarm: Stories from Bansin, 1970), and a novel, *Rose weiß, Rose rot* (Rose White, Rose Red, 1971). In *Rose weiß, Rose rot*, the more noteworthy of the two, Richter explains his youthful radicalism and political disillusionment with the detachment of a man who is on his way to becoming what one literary critic termed a "leftist conservative." The novel was written after the political atmosphere had briefly appeared open to change and Richter's hope for a socialistic democracy in West Germany had been rekindled; with the Soviet invasion of Prague in 1968 and the radicalization of the student movement in Germany, however, Richter had had to face old disappointments anew. Trips to the Eastern bloc countries during the 1950s and 1960s had already increased his doubts about a socialist utopia, which culminated in *Briefe an einen jungen Sozialisten* (Letters to a Young Socialist, 1974). In 1978 he was awarded an honorary doctorate of liberal arts by the University of Karlsruhe.

Richter's later works are his most acclaimed. They include a long short story, *Die Flucht nach Abanon* (Flight to Abanon, 1980), and two novels, *Die Stunde der falschen Triumphe* (The Hour of False Triumphs, 1981) and *Ein Julitag* (A July Day, 1982). *Die Flucht nach Abanon* tells of two people who meet late in life. The protagonist is a man who has allowed aging, routine, and loneliness to limit his responses. As he observes the inner turmoil of his neighbor, an actress who struggles to retain the emotional intensity of her youth, the distance he maintains between them seems justified by a lifetime of experience and her retreat behind many masks. Only after her suicide does he realize that this loss of compassion is but a sign of his slow departure from life.

Die Stunde der falschen Triumphe is also characterized by psychological detail. In tracing the lives of two brothers-in-law Richter tells the same story twice, from different perspectives. One protagonist, a barber, has made his shop the center of the world. It is the place to which everyone who matters to him comes, it is tangible proof of his success, and in times of political uncertainty it is his refuge. His schoolteacher brother-in-law, on the other hand, is politically minded. He rushes to arms in World War I, returns a pacifist, and subsequently opposes the Nazi movement. By 1945, however, the lives of the two have become quite similar. Their fears, hopes, and errors have led them into submission and left them with the same sense of personal defeat.

Similarly, Christian Wolf of *Ein Julitag* has led a life of few choices, but he fares better than most of Richter's characters. At his brother's funeral in Sweden he meets his lover of almost fifty years earlier, who is now his brother's widow. The day of mourning becomes a day dedicated to the past. Together they explore memories, rebuilding an understanding they once shared. Their recollections provide cues upon which the narrator expands in flashbacks. Whereas the thinking of the protagonists is colored by the fatalism of old age–"Alles wird bestimmt von den Umständen, den Ereignissen, den Zufällen, niemand hat sein Schicksal in eigenen Händen" (Everything is determined by circumstance, by events, and by coincidence. No one holds his fate in his own hands)–the flashback chapters reconstruct the optimism of youth.

Richter's language has never been as unassuming or disciplined, yet displayed such psychological depth, as in these last two novels. In *Ein Julitag*, for the first time, he masters an artistically demanding structure. By subjecting Germany's past to his characters' power of recollection, the author highlights the distance between events and the way they are perceived. Throughout his prose Richter traces many lives through difficult times, seeking to record Germany's recent history in all its complexity. As a single work devoted to this aim, *Ein Julitag* is Richter's most significant success.

In 1980 Richter received an Honorary Professorship from the Senate of Berlin, and in 1982 he was given the Cultural Award of the Federal Union of German Industry. In 1986 he was awarded the Grand Prize for Literature of the Bavarian Academy of the Free Arts and the Alexander Gryphius Prize.

Interviews:

Toni Meissner, "Orden passen nicht auf Rollkragenpullis: AZ-Gespräch mit Hans Werner Richter, dem Vater der Gruppe 47," *Abendzeitung* (Munich), 10 November 1978;

Karl Stocker, "Autor-Werk-Rezeption: Fragen an Hans Werner Richter," in *Literatur der Moderne im Deutschunterricht*, edited by Stocker (Königsstein: Scriptor, 1982), pp. 60-69.

Bibliography:

Walter Schmitz, "Hans Werner Richter," in *Kritisches Lexikon zur deutschsprachigen Gegenwarts-*

literatur, edited by Heinz Ludwig Arnold (Munich: Edition text + kritik, 1978).

References:

Heinz Ludwig Arnold, ed., *Die Gruppe 47: Ein kritischer Grundriß* (Munich: Edition text + kritik, 1980);

Karl Esselborn, *Gesellschaftskritische Literatur nach 1945* (Munich: Fink, 1977);

Gerd-Rüdiger Helbig, *Die politischen Äußerungen aus der Gruppe 47: Eine Fallstudie über das Verhältnis von politischer Macht und intellektueller Kritik* (Erlangen: Hogel, 1967), pp. 66-91;

Klaus Jarmatz, "Die pseudorealistische Charakterdarstellung in Hans Werner Richters Kriegsromanen," *Weimarer Beiträge*, 3 (1958): 326-347;

Karl Heinz Kramberg, "Hans Werner Richter," in *Schriftsteller der Gegenwart*, edited by Klaus Nonnenmann (Olten & Freiburg im Breisgau: Walter, 1963), pp. 250-263;

Friedhelm Kröll, *Gruppe 47* (Stuttgart: Metzler, 1979);

Herbert Lehnert, "Die Gruppe 47: Ihre Anfänge und ihre Gründungsmitglieder," in *Die deutsche Literatur der Gegenwart: Aspekte und Tendenzen*, edited by Manfred Durzak, third edition (Stuttgart: Reclam, 1976), pp. 31-62;

Rudolf Walter Leonhardt, "Aufstieg und Niedergang der Gruppe 47," in *Deutsche Gegenwartsliteratur: Ausgangspositionen und aktuelle Entwicklungen*, edited by Durzak (Stuttgart: Reclam, 1981), pp. 61-76;

Reinhard Lettau, ed., *Die Gruppe 47: Bericht, Kritik, Polemik* (Neuwied & Berlin: Luchterhand, 1967);

Siegfried Mandel, *Group 47: The Reflected Intellect* (Carbondale & Edwardsville: Southern Illinois University Press/London & Amsterdam: Feffer & Simons, 1973);

H. Martell, "Ein Weg ohne Kompaß: Neubeginn am Beispiel der Zeitschrift *Der Ruf*," *Kürbiskern*, 2 (1975): 109-119;

Hans A. Neunzig, ed., *Hans Werner Richter und die Gruppe 47* (Munich: Nymphenburger, 1979);

Jochen Pfeifer, *Der deutsche Kriegsroman 1945-1960: Ein Versuch zur Vermittlung von Literatur und Sozialgeschichte* (Königsstein: Scriptor, 1981);

Hans Schwab-Felisch, "Ein linker Konservativer: Hans Werner Richter wird 75," *Merkur*, 37 (1983): 852-853;

Friedrich Sieburg, "Die gute Absicht," in his *Zur Literatur 1957-1963*, edited by Fritz Raddatz (Stuttgart: Deutsche Verlags-Anstalt, 1981), pp. 174-177;

Sieburg, "Das Kriegsbuch," in his *Zur Literatur 1924-1956*, edited by Raddatz (Stuttgart: Deutsche Verlags-Anstalt, 1981), pp. 225-228;

Karl Stocker, "*Die Stunde der falschen Triumphe*—auch ein Buch für die Jugend?," *Wirkendes Wort*, 5 (1981): 335-349;

Jérôme Vaillant, *Der Ruf, Unabhängige Blätter der jungen Generation (1945-1949): Eine Zeitschrift zwischen Illusion und Anpassung*, translated by Heidrun Hofmann (Munich, New York, London & Paris: Saur, 1978);

Heinrich Vormweg, "Deutsche Literatur 1945-1960: Keine Stunde Null," in *Die deutsche Literatur der Gegenwart: Aspekte und Tendenzen*, edited by Durzak, third edition (Stuttgart: Reclam, 1976), pp. 13-30;

Jürgen P. Wallmann, "Hans Werner Richter und die Gruppe 47," *Neue deutsche Hefte*, 27 (1980): 156-159;

Volker Christian Wehdeking, *Der Nullpunkt: Über die Konstituierung der deutschen Nachkriegsliteratur (1945-1948) in den amerikanischen Kriegsgefangenenlagern* (Stuttgart: Metzler, 1971);

Brigitte Weymann, "Hans Werner Richter: Die Flucht nach Abanon," *Neue deutsche Hefte*, 27 (1980): 612-613;

Weymann, "Hans Werner Richter: Die Stunde der falschen Triumphe," *Neue deutsche Hefte*, 28 (1981): 372-374;

Urs Widmer, *1945 oder die "Neue Sprache": Studien zur Prosa der "Jungen Generation"* (Düsseldorf: Schwann, 1966);

Horst Ziermann, *Gruppe 47: Die Polemik um die deutsche Gegenwartsliteratur* (Frankfurt am Main: Wolter, 1966).

Papers:

The Seminar für Deutsche Philologie at the Georg-August-Universität, Göttingen, Nikolausberger Weg 15, has the manuscripts of two important interviews with Richter, both conducted in 1967. The Library of Congress, Washington, D.C., has a few issues of *Die Lagerstimme*; Richter owns all issues on which he collaborated. He has bequeathed his papers to the city of Munich.

Luise Rinser
(30 April 1911-   )

Elke Frederiksen
University of Maryland at College Park

BOOKS: *Die gläsernen Ringe: Eine Erzählung* (Berlin: Fischer, 1941); translated by Richard and Clara Winston as *Rings of Glass* (Chicago: Regnery, 1958);

Tiere in Haus und Hof (Berlin: Atlantis, 1942);

Gefängnis-Tagebuch (Munich: Zinnen, 1946);

Das Ohlstadter Kinder-Weihnachtsspiel (Munich: Buchner, 1946);

Erste Liebe (Munich: Desch, 1946);

Pestalozzi und wir: Der Mensch und das Werk (Stuttgart: Günther, 1947);

Hochebene: Ein Unterhaltungsroman (Kassel: Schleber, 1948);

Jan Lobel aus Warschau: Erzählung (Kassel: Schleber, 1948);

Die Stärkeren: Roman (Kassel: Schleber, 1948);

Martins Reise (Zurich & Freiburg im Breisgau: Atlantis, 1949);

Mitte des Lebens: Roman (Frankfurt am Main: Fischer, 1950); translated by Richard and Clara Winston as *Nina* (Chicago: Regnery, 1956);

Sie zogen mit dem Stern: Eine Buben-Weihnacht (Munich: Don Bosco-Verlag, 1952);

Daniela: Roman (Frankfurt am Main: Fischer, 1953);

Eine Weihnachtsgeschichte (Heilbronn: Salzer, 1953);

Die Wahrheit über Konnersreuth: Ein Bericht (Einsiedeln, Zurich & Cologne: Benziger, 1954);

Erste Liebe: Erzählung (Zurich: Arche, 1954);

Der Sündenbock: Roman (Frankfurt am Main: Fischer, 1954);

Ein Bündel weißer Narzissen: Erzählungen (Frankfurt am Main: Fischer, 1956);

Abenteuer der Tugend: Roman (Frankfurt am Main: Fischer, 1957);

Magische Argonautenfahrt: Eine Einführung in die gesammelten Werke von Elisabeth Langgässer (Hamburg: Claassen, 1959);

Geh' fort, wenn du kannst: Erzählung (Frankfurt am Main: Fischer, 1959);

Der Schwerpunkt (Frankfurt am Main: Fischer, 1960);

Luise Rinser (photograph copyright © by Isolde Ohlbaum, Munich)

Nina: Mitte des Lebens; Abenteuer der Tugend (Frankfurt am Main: Fischer, 1961);

Vom Sinn der Traurigkeit (Felix Tristitia) (Zurich: Arche, 1962);

Die vollkommene Freude: Roman (Frankfurt am Main: Fischer, 1962);

Ich weiß deinen Namen: Dreiundsiebzig Fotografien, gedeutet von Luise Rinser (Würzburg: Echter, 1962);

Weihnachts-Triptychon (Zurich: Arche, 1963);

Septembertag (Frankfurt am Main: Fischer, 1964);

Über die Hoffnung (Zurich: Arche, 1964);

Hat Beten einen Sinn? (Zurich: Arche, 1966);

Ich bin Tobias (Frankfurt am Main: Fischer, 1966);

Gespräche über Lebensfragen (Würzburg: Echter, 1966);

Laie, nicht ferngesteuert (Zurich: Arche, 1967);

Jugend unserer Zeit (Würzburg: Echter, 1967);

Gespräch von Mensch zu Mensch (Würzburg: Echter/ Zurich: NZN-Buchverlag, 1967);

Von der Unmöglichkeit und der Möglichkeit, heute Priester zu sein (Würzburg: Echter, 1968);

Fragen, Antworten (Würzburg: Echter, 1968);

Zölibat und Frau: Essay (Würzburg: Echter, 1968);

Nach seinem Bild, by Rinser and Oswald Kettenberger (Zurich: NZN-Buchverlag/Würzburg: Echter, 1969);

Baustelle: Eine Art Tagebuch 1967-1970 (Frankfurt am Main: Fischer, 1970);

Unterentwickeltes Land Frau: Untersuchungen, Kritik, Arbeitshypothesen (Würzburg: Echter/Zurich: NZN-Buchverlag, 1970);

Grenzübergänge: Tagebuch-Notizen (Frankfurt am Main: Fischer, 1972);

Hochzeit der Widersprüche (Percha & Kempfenhausen: Schulz, 1973);

Dem Tode geweiht? Lepra ist heilbar! (Percha & Kempfenhausen: Schulz, 1974);

Der schwarze Esel: Roman (Frankfurt am Main: Fischer, 1974);

Wie, wenn wir ärmer würden oder Die Heimkehr des verlorenen Sohnes (Percha & Kempfenhausen: Schulz, 1974);

Bruder Feuer (Stuttgart: Thienemann, 1975);

Leiden, sterben, auferstehen (Würzburg: Echter, 1975);

Hallo Partner. Zeige mir, wie du dein Auto lenkst, und ich sage dir, wie (wer) du bist! (Percha & Kempfenhausen: Schulz, 1975);

Wenn die Wale kämpfen: Portrait eines Landes, Süd-Korea (Percha: Schulz, 1976);

Der verwundete Drache: Dialog über Leben und Werk des Komponisten Isang Yun, by Rinser and Isang Yun (Frankfurt am Main: Fischer, 1977);

Kriegsspielzeug: Tagebuch 1972-1978 (Frankfurt am Main: Fischer, 1978);

Khomeini und der islamische Gottesstaat: Eine große Idee—ein großer Irrtum? (Percha: Schulz, 1979);

Mein Lesebuch (Frankfurt am Main: Fischer, 1980);

Mit wem reden (Stuttgart: Thienemann, 1980);

Den Wolf umarmen: Autobiographie (Frankfurt am Main: Fischer, 1981);

Die rote Katze (Frankfurt am Main: Fischer, 1981);

Nordkoreanisches Reisetagebuch (Frankfurt am Main: Fischer, 1981; revised, 1983);

Winterfrühling 1979-1982 (Frankfurt am Main: Fischer, 1982);

Mirjam: Roman (Frankfurt am Main: Fischer, 1983);

Das Squirrel (Stuttgart: Thienemann, 1985);

Die Erzählungen (Frankfurt am Main: Fischer, 1985);

Im Dunkeln singen 1982-1985 (Frankfurt am Main: Fischer, 1985);

Wer wirft den Stein? (Stuttgart: Edition Weitbrecht, 1985);

Geschichten aus der Löwengrube (Frankfurt am Main: Fischer, 1986);

Silberschuld: Roman (Frankfurt am Main: Fischer, 1987).

OTHER: Johann Heinrich Pestalozzi, *Pestalozzi: Eine Auswahl für die Gegenwart*, edited by Rinser (Stuttgart: Günther, 1948);

"Antwort an Hermann Hesse," in *Vaterland, Muttersprache: Deutsche Schriftsteller und ihr Staat seit 1945*, edited by Klaus Wagenbach and others (Berlin: Wagenbach, 1979), pp. 53-54;

" 'Ein Mädchen ist doch nichts Ernsthaftes': Frauengestalten in der Literatur der vergangenen hundert Jahre," in *Frauen heute*, edited by Willy Brandt (Reinbek: Rowohlt, 1981), pp. 129-145.

Luise Rinser is one of the most successful contemporary West German authors. Her works span more than forty years: she experienced Germany under National Socialism, during World War II, and after 1945; she witnessed political and economic developments and changes in the 1950s, 1960s, and 1970s and is still writing in the late 1980s.

Rinser's name has appeared several times on the best-seller list: in the 1950s and early 1960s for her novels *Mitte des Lebens* (In the Middle of Life, 1950; translated as *Nina*, 1956) and *Die vollkommene Freude* (The Complete Joy, 1962), for her autobiography, *Den Wolf umarmen* (To Embrace the Wolf, 1981), and for her novel *Mirjam* (1983). Many of her books have been translated, primarily into French and Dutch; *Mitte des Lebens* has sold more than 500,000 copies in the German edition and has appeared in twenty-two languages, including Japanese and Hindi.

Luise Rinser

Baustelle	**Ich bin Tobias**
Eine Art Tagebuch 1967-70	315 Seiten, Leinen
390 Seiten, Leinen	
Ein Bündel	**Jan Lobel**
weißer Narzissen	**aus Warschau**
Erzählungen	Erzählung
264 Seiten, Leinen	80 Seiten, Leinen
Daniela	**Nina**
Roman	(Mitte des Lebens.
319 Seiten, Leinen	Abenteuer der Tugend.)
	Roman
Die gläsernen Ringe	(S. Fischer
Eine Erzählung	Sonderausgabe).
188 Seiten, Leinen	480 Seiten, Leinen
Grenzübergänge	**Der schwarze Esel**
Tagebuch-Notizen	Roman
349 Seiten, Leinen	271 Seiten, Leinen

S. Fischer

Luise Rinser

Luise Rinser
Ein Bündel
weißer
Narzissen

Erzählungen

Ein Bündel weißer
Narzissen. Erzählungen.
Band 1612

Abenteuer der Tugend.
Roman.
Band 1027

Daniela. Roman.
Band 1116

Gefängnistagebuch.
Band 1327

Die gläsernen Ringe
Eine Erzählung.
Band 393

Hochebene. Roman.
Band 532

Ich bin Tobias.
Band 1551

Mitte des Lebens.
Band 256

Der Sündenbock.
Roman.
Band 469

Die vollkommene
Freude. Roman.
Band 1235

FISCHER
TASCHENBÜCHER

Publisher's advertisement for Rinser's works

If Rinser has gained popularity through her books, she is just as well known–at least in German-speaking countries–for her political engagement and her colorful personality. In spite of her age–she was seventy-seven years old in 1988–she participates in peace demonstrations, appears in televised debates, and conducts lecture tours to read from her books and to address political issues. She is actively involved in the peace movement in Germany and has demonstrated against the nuclear arms race along with authors such as Günter Grass and Heinrich Böll. In May 1984 the Green party chose her as its candidate for the presidency of the Federal Republic of Germany.

Rinser has many admirers but also many crit-ics and even enemies. Some are irritated by her blunt personality. She is criticized for enjoying the limelight too much and for being too prolific a writer. But whatever one may think of her personally, nobody can deny her lifelong courageous fight for humankind in her books and in her continuous support of the politically oppressed and the economically disadvantaged.

The American literary scholar Annis Pratt, after closely examining more than 300 novels by women, maintains in her *Archetypal Patterns in Women's Fiction* (1981) that all women writers "create narratives manifesting an acute tension between what any normal human being might desire and what a woman must become. Women's fiction reflects an experience radically different from men's because [their] drive towards growth as persons is thwarted by [their] prescriptions concerning gender." This analysis holds true for Rinser: her work reflects the female conflict of being part of a patriarchal society and of being an outsider at the same time.

Rinser was born on 30 April 1911 in the small town of Pitzling in Upper Bavaria, the only child of strict Catholic parents, Josef and Luise Sailer Rinser. In *Den Wolf umarmen* she describes a difficult relationship with her distant mother, who did not understand Rinser's desire to write, and her domineering father, who envisioned his daughter's future to be that of a respected teacher, perhaps a high-school principal. In 1930 Rinser finished grammar school in Munich and studied psychology and pedagogy at the University of Munich, received her teaching diploma in 1934, and spent four years as an elementary-school teacher. During these years she became acquainted with the works of Sigmund Freud and Carl Gustav Jung; her fascination with Jung's work is reflected in the carefully developed psychological motivations of her characters. Rinser was strongly influenced by the Baroque-Catholic tradition of her native Bavaria, although she has always been critical of power politics within the church.

Rinser began to write in the 1930s. The conductor Horst-Günther Schnell, whom she married in 1939, encouraged her and insisted that she publish the story "Die Lilie" (The Lily); it appeared in 1938 in the journal *Neue Rundschau*. She later incorporated this story in her first longer narrative, *Die gläsernen Ringe* (1941; translated as *Rings of Glass*, 1958), which was a tremendous success; a second edition was scheduled to come out a few months after the first, but the Nazis prohibited any further publication of her works. Rinser attributes the success of the book in part to the need of readers at that time for fiction that differed from the "Blut- und Bodenliteratur" (Blood and Fatherland literature) that was nurtured by the Nazi regime. Hermann Hesse, who had left Nazi Germany for Switzerland, sent Rinser an enthusiastic letter of congratulations in May 1941 in which he praised her polished style and commitment to a different set of values than those that characterized many German works of the time: "Ich bin durch Ihre Geschichte wie durch einen Garten gegangen, jedem Bilde dankbar, mit jedem einverstanden, und es wird nicht lange dauern, bis ich es zum zweiten Mal lese" (I wandered through your story as if it were a garden, appreciating every image, in agreement with each of them, and it will not be long before I read it for the second time).

The action of the narrative is set during a war that could be World War I or II. But the war remains in the background; the book does not express a direct political message. Instead–and this constitutes its uniqueness–it shows a young girl's development toward independence. The girl *succeeds*–a deviation from most previous works with female protagonists. Rinser uses the traditional form of the bildungsroman, which had been the domain of the male protagonist from Goethe in the late eighteenth and early nineteenth centuries to Thomas Mann in the twentieth century, but breaks out of "prescribed" norms by placing at the center of the action a heroine who must overcome obstacles which are aggravated because she is a woman.

The main character's search for identity develops in several stages through conflicts with her largely hostile surroundings. This process is a struggle that is painful and joyous at the same time. She encounters particular difficulties in her relationships with her strict mother and the school authorities, who represent narrow bourgeois norms against which she rebels. Other characters–her grandfather, her favorite teacher, Erinna, and the farm girl Vicki–play a positive role in her development. These figures confront the protagonist with alternative ways of life, creating tension and conflict within her. This multiperspectivity reveals Rinser's concept of polarities, which are not viewed as hostile opposites but necessary parts of life which fertilize each other. In her later works Rinser, who was strongly influenced by Eastern philosophies, developed the concept of necessary polarities more intensively.

Nature plays an essential role in *Die gläsernen Ringe*; it offers escape and protection from hostile surroundings and provides the heroine with strength and strategies for survival. Rinser portrays convincingly the young girl's growth and development in the midst of chaos and conflict. She sees the future direction of her life in the metaphor of the glass rings which appear when a stone is thrown into water. The glass rings represent the clarity and order awaiting her in her adult life. This female bildungsroman occupies a unique position in German literature of the Nazi period.

Although the Nazis prohibited her from publishing after 1942, Rinser continued to write. She had given up her position as a schoolteacher when she married Schnell; she probably would have lost it in any event because she refused to join the National Socialist party. Her husband died on the eastern front in 1943, leaving her with two sons.

In 1944 Rinser was sentenced to death for high treason; she was accused of undermining military morale. She had tried to convince friends of the uselessness of continuing the war and had been betrayed by them. Rinser was held in a women's prison in Traunstein for several months, and only the end of the war prevented her execution.

It was in prison that she wrote one of her most significant books, which was one of the first German works to be published after the war and one of the few narrations of women's war experiences from a woman's perspective. *Gefängnis-Tagebuch* (Prison Diary, 1946) is a fascinating account of Rinser's prison experiences and of the lives of the other inmates. In this diary two of Rinser's characteristics are clearly discernible: her strong political engagement, which was unusual for a woman writer at that time, and her awareness of the plight of the oppressed–in this case, women.

In the introduction Rinser emphasizes that her account is "Tatsache, nicht Literatur" (fact, not fiction) and that she intends to portray "ein völlig wahres, ein photographisch genaues Bild des Lebens in einem Gefängnis" (a completely true, photographically exact picture of life in a prison). She far exceeds that goal. By skillfully combining descriptions of the prisoners' experiences and her own inner change, Rinser engages readers "die nichts dergleichen sahen und erlebten, die kaum oder gar nicht gelitten haben unter den teuflischen Methoden, die Freiheit des Menschen auszurotten" (who have never seen or experienced anything like this, who have probably never suffered from such diabolical methods aimed at annihilating human freedom). She explicitly addresses those who do not understand that nationalism and militarism must lead to destruction.

Gefängnis-Tagebuch is also significant because of its form. Rinser wrote it in fragmentary form as a diary because that was the only possible means of expression for her. She had nothing to write on but scraps of toilet paper, which she hid in her straw mattress; and she had only frag-

Dust jacket designed by Hannes Jähn for Rinser's 1981 collection of short stories

ments of time for writing because her days were occupied with prison duties, and in the evenings her cell was only dimly lighted. But writing gave her the strength to survive. With the diary form, Rinser continued a tradition that was especially important for German women writers in the nineteenth century. It was not until the late 1960s and early 1970s that the diary developed into one of the most popular German literary genres for both female and male writers.

The end of the war meant political freedom as well as new possibilities for Rinser's professional life. She joined the *Neue Zeitung* in Munich as a literary critic and columnist. During her years with the newspaper Rinser wrote some of her finest short stories, which can be compared with those by Böll and Wolfgang Borchert; Ernest Hemingway's influence is obvious.

The novel *Mitte des Lebens* brought Rinser worldwide fame; it is still her best-known book.

The form of the novel is as intriguing as its theme: fictional diary entries and letters interrupt and confuse the action, but at the same time they create, from various perspectives, a fascinating, intricate picture of Nina, the protagonist. The novel portrays a woman struggling against middle-class norms to emancipate herself in all areas of life; it shows the desperate search for identity of an intelligent, strong-willed woman, who, in spite of social pressures, achieves professional success and personal independence by freeing herself from unhappy love relationships. Nina's political commitment, which reflects Rinser's own philosophy, is revealed in her selfless attitude toward a number of persecuted Jews whom she helps to escape across the border at risk to her own life.

The 1957 sequel to *Mitte des Lebens*, *Abenteuer der Tugend*, presents a reversal of the emancipatory ideas developed in its predecessor. Nina gives up her independence and devotes herself to her demanding husband and, after his death, to God. Love as total sacrifice of one's self and love as religion are also the central themes in the third book of the cycle, *Die vollkommene Freude*. The book received devastating reviews by literary critics, including Marcel Reich-Ranicki, and it marks a low point in Rinser's career. She was labeled a "Catholic woman writer," a reputation she struggled for years to overcome.

Rinser left the *Neue Zeitung* in 1953 to devote herself to her writing. She married the composer and artist Carl Orff in 1954; they were divorced in 1959. Although she still admires Orff, she feels that their difficult relationship had a suffocating effect on her creative development. After her separation from Orff, Rinser moved to Italy. She also maintains a residence in Munich.

The late 1960s and early 1970s constitute a turning point in Rinser's writings. Political events climaxing in the 1968 student uprisings and the demand by many German authors for a more politically engaged literature had an impact on her. She had always been aware of the plight of the oppressed; now it became her main focus. She wrote essays and also returned to the diary form she had used in *Gefängnis-Tagebuch*. She demanded equal rights for women more explicitly and more actively than she had before and sought to raise the consciousness of women in patriarchal society. Her essay *Unterentwickeltes Land Frau* (Underdeveloped Country: Woman, 1970) criticizes gender discrimination but holds women

partly responsible for their own oppression. Using the Christian church as a model of an authoritarian-patriarchal social structure and documenting her thesis with texts from the earliest church fathers to Karl Barth, she demonstrates that women have been treated throughout history as underdeveloped beings. Rinser pleads for a gradual reform that would replace male superiority with a partnership of women and men.

For Rinser, the women's movement is part of a larger, irreversible process of emancipation of all humankind. She has spoken out against violence, war, and oppression in six volumes of diaries: *Baustelle* (Construction Site, 1970), *Grenzübergänge* (Border Crossings, 1972), *Kriegsspielzeug* (Toy of War, 1978), *Nordkoreanisches Reisetagebuch* (North Korean Travel Diary, 1981; revised, 1983), *Winterfrühling* (Winterspring, 1982), and *Im Dunkeln singen* (Singing in the Dark, 1985). These diaries, which present a fascinating mixture of firsthand descriptions of and reflections on political events and social situations in Europe, the United States, South America, East Asia, and India, are equaled in contemporary German literature only by the diaries of the Swiss-German author Max Frisch. With them Rinser finally rid herself of the label "Catholic woman writer" by vehemently turning against the expectations of a church-oriented bourgeois audience. She also sharply criticized the prejudices of established critics. Communication with readers from all social backgrounds is her goal; the immediacy and directness of the diary form, with the frequent use of dialogue, draw in the readers and invite them to think critically. In their attempt to overcome gender polarities and bridge ideological differences between East and West, the diaries are important documents of worldwide cultural, political, and social developments in the 1970s and 1980s.

In 1974 Rinser published the novel *Der schwarze Esel* (The Black Donkey) and in 1981 her best-selling autobiography, *Den Wolf umarmen*, appeared. Both books focus on the Nazi period; they are her contributions to the problem of *Vergangenheitsbewältigung* (dealing with the past), which has been attempted by many contemporary German writers, including Böll, Grass, and Siegfried Lenz. Oddly, reviews of *Der schwarze Esel*, which Rinser considers her best book, have been scarce in West Germany and Austria; in contrast, it has been highly praised in France and Italy and was awarded the Italian National Prize for Literature (Premio Europa,

Rinser in 1987 (Ullstein–Detlev Moos)

1980). The novel portrays the lives of six women, each of whom must cope with the terrible events of the past in her own way. As in *Mitte des Lebens* and *Gefängnis-Tagebuch*, Rinser uses a multiple perspective, viewing each of the six women through the eyes of the first-person narrator and of the protagonist herself. The most impressive figure is Klara, a hunchback, who deals calmly and courageously with the prejudices of a small middle-class Bavarian town. Rinser convincingly interweaves the lives of the six women with the history of the time.

Den Wolf umarmen represents Rinser's attempt to express her political, literary, and religious ideas through her personal experiences. It is an account of Rinser's life from 1911 to 1950, focusing on her ordeal with the Hitler regime. It also deals with her emancipation from her father, who becomes a figure in a Greek tragedy. He is Creon; Rinser appears as Antigone, who in the ancient tragedy was sacrificed by Creon because she disobeyed his law in obedience to a higher moral law. In contrast to Sophocles' female hero, however, Rinser does not die; she overcomes inferiority complexes and insecurities and fights for intellectual freedom.

Rinser's commitment to the survival of humanity is particularly evident in her novel *Mirjam*, which she calls a "Utopie vom Friedensreich" (utopia of a peaceful world). The novel presents a revision of the Christian myth of Mary Magdalene, who has traditionally been presented as a sinner and a whore. Rinser creates an "anti-Magdalene," whose image does not at all agree with that of Christian tradition: she is educated, independent, full of questions and doubts, a loner who does not fit the role expectations of a Jewish woman. Mirjam becomes a disciple of Jeschua (Jesus) of Nazareth, who tells her, "Lehre die Einheit alles Lebendigen, lehre die Liebe" (Teach the unity of all living things, teach love).

Rinser's main concern in this novel is the humanization of the Christian world based on a feminine principle which she defines as hope, love, and peace. The book can be read on three levels: it is a feminist novel describing the emancipation of Mirjam; it is a religious work portraying Jesus Christ from Mirjam's perspective; finally, it is a work of political philosophy which asks whether the world can be changed without violence and war. Jeschua and Jehuda (Judas) represent two opposing views: Jeschua demands complete nonviolence, whereas Jehuda sees the liberation of the Jewish people from the Romans as being possible only through war. Jeschua is an androgynous character who has preserved the female element within himself; he is a man who represents love. Jehuda is no longer portrayed merely as the betrayer of Jesus; instead, he appears as a fanatical freedom fighter who loves his country and his people. Rinser achieves with this novel a synthesis of many of her political and literary ideas. In spite of occasional stylistic weaknesses—her narrative style clings too much to the Bible—the book invites the reader to rethink traditional myths.

Rinser has largely been ignored by literary critics; she has always had more impact on the political scene, most recently as the presidential candidate for the Green party. She deserves more recognition as a writer, particularly for her early works, *Die gläsernen Ringe*, *Gefängnis-Tagebuch*, and *Jan Lobel aus Warschau* (Jan Lobel from Warsaw, 1948), but also for her diaries of the 1970s and 1980s.

References:

Hans Ester, "Gespräch mit Luise Rinser," *Deutsche Bücher*, 8 (1978): 237-246;

Elke Frederiksen, "Luise Rinser," *Neue Literatur der Frauen: Deutschsprachige Autorinnen der Ge-*

genwart, edited by Heinz Puknus (Munich: Beck, 1980), pp. 55-61, 316-318;

Frederiksen, "Luise Rinser's Autobiographical Prose: Political *Engagement* and Feminist Awareness," in *Faith of a (Woman) Writer,* edited by Alice Kessler-Harris and William McBrien (Westport, Conn.: Greenwood, 1988), pp. 165-171;

Marianne Konzag, "Gespräch mit Luise Rinser," *Sinn und Form,* 36 (1984): 815-825;

Luise Rinser: Zu ihrem 65. Geburtstag am 30. April 1976 (Frankfurt am Main: Fischer, 1976);

Edward McInnes, "Luise Rinser and the Religious Novel," *German Life and Letters,* 32 (Spring 1978): 40-45;

Rudolf Riedler, *Drei Gespräche: Luise Rinser, Peter Bamm, Johannes Mario Simmel. Fragen zur Person, zum Werk und zur Zeit* (Donauwörth: Auer, 1974), pp. 6-25;

Albert Scholz, *Luise Rinsers Leben und Werk: Eine Einführung* (Syracuse, N.Y.: Peerless Press, 1968);

Hans-Rüdiger Schwab, ed., *Luise Rinser: Materialien zu Leben und Werk* (Frankfurt am Main: Fischer, 1986);

Jürgen Serke, "Luise Rinser: 'Es gibt nur eine Schuld im Leben der Menschen: Lieblosigkeit,'" in *Frauen schreiben: Ein neues Kapitel deutschsprachiger Literatur,* edited by Serke (Hamburg: Gruner & Jahr, 1979), pp. 76-89;

Sigrid Weigel and Jürgen Koepp, "Luise Rinser," in *Kritisches Lexikon zur deutschsprachigen Gegenwartsliteratur,* edited by Heinz Ludwig Arnold, volume 3 (Munich: Edition text + kritik, 1982).

Heinz Risse
(30 March 1898-   )

Valentine C. Hubbs
University of Michigan

BOOKS: *Soziologie des Sports* (Berlin & Leipzig: Quelle & Meyer, 1921; revised edition, Hamburg: Merlin, 1964);

Die Flucht hinter das Gitter (Hamburg: Verlag Mein Roman, 1948);

Irrfahrer: Novelle (Hamburg: Deutscher Literatur-Verlag, 1948);

Das letzte Kapitel der Welt: Chaos oder Einheit als Ende der menschlichen Geschichte? (Stuttgart: Mittelbach, 1949);

Wenn die Erde bebt: Roman (Munich, Leipzig & Freiburg im Breisgau: List, 1950; revised edition, Berlin & Darmstadt: Deutsche Buchgemeinschaft, 1955); translated by Rita Eldon as *The Earthquake* (London: Secker & Warburg, 1953; New York: Farrar, Straus & Young, 1953);

Schlangen in Genf (Krefeld: Scherpe, 1951; revised edition, Munich: Langen-Müller, 1955);

Fledermäuse: Erzählung (Bremen: Schünemann, 1951);

So frei von Schuld: Roman (Munich: List, 1951);

Die Fackel des Prometheus: Essay (Munich: List, 1952);

Dann kam der Tag: Roman (Munich: List, 1953);

Die Grille: Erzählungen (Bremen: Schünemann, 1953);

Belohne dich selbst: Fabeln (Bremen: Schünemann, 1953);

Simson und die kleinen Leute (Munich: Langen-Müller, 1954);

Der schmale Grat, bound with Herbert Kaufmann, *Der Tod des Elefanten* (Hamburg: Agentur des Rauhen Hauses, 1955);

Sören der Lump: Roman (Munich: Langen-Müller, 1955; revised edition, Darmstadt & Berlin: Deutsche Buchgemeinschaft, 1964);

Fördert die Kultur! (Munich: Langen-Müller, 1955);

Große Fahrt und falsches Spiel: Roman (Munich: Langen-Müller, 1956; revised edition, Berlin & Darmstadt: Deutsche Buchgemeinschaft, 1957);

Heinz Risse in 1959 (Ullstein)

Wuchernde Lianen: Erzählung (Munich: Langen-Müller, 1956);

Immermannpreis-Reden 1957, by Risse and Erwin Laaths (Munich: Langen-Müller, 1957);

Das Duell mit dem Teufel (Hamburg: Agentur des Rauhen Hauses, 1957);

Einer Zuviel: Roman (Munich: Langen-Müller, 1957);

Gestein der Weisen: Essays (Munich: Langen-Müller, 1957);

Paul Cézanne und Gottfried Benn: Eine Studie (Munich: Langen-Müller, 1957);

Die Stadt ohne Wurzeln: Erzählung (Munich: Langen-Müller, 1957);

Die Insel der Seligen: Ein Gespräch (Munich: Langen-Müller, 1958);

Buchhalter Gottes: Erzählungen (Munich: Langen-Müller, 1958);

Die Schiffschaukel (Munich: Langen-Müller, 1959);

Über das Melancholische in der Kunst: Ein Gespräch (Krefeld: Scherpe, 1961);

Die letzte Instanz: Zwei Erzählungen (Berlin: Evangelische Verlags-Anstalt, 1961);

Der Diebstahl: Erzählungen und Fabeln (Lübeck & Hamburg: Matthiesen, 1962);

Fort geht's wie auf Samt: Erzählungen und Gespräche (Munich: Langen-Müller, 1962);

Ringelreihen oder Die Apologie des Verbleibs im Zimmer: Roman (Munich & Vienna: Langen-Müller, 1963);

Feiner Unfug auf Staatskosten: 12 Essays (Hamburg: Merlin, 1963);

Public Relations: Zwei Gespräche (Hamburg: Merlin, 1964);

Macht und Schicksal einer Leiche und andere Erzählungen (Krefeld: Scherpe, 1967);

Selected Readings, edited by Valentine C. Hubbs (New York: Holt, Rinehart & Winston, 1973);

Solingen, so wie es war (Düsseldorf: Droste, 1975);

Heinz Risse 80 Jahre (Krefeld: Scherpe, 1978);

Skepsis ohne Trauerflor: Impressionen und Illusionen (Hamburg: Merlin, 1980);

Berkeley und der Demiurg: Requiem auf das Spiel in der Sackgasse (Gifkendorf: Merlin, 1983);

Hinter ihm schlagen die Sträuche zusammen (Krefeld: Scherpe, 1986).

OTHER: "Das unzerbrechliche und das zerbrochene Christentum," in *Was halten Sie vom Christentum? 18 Antworten auf eine Umfrage* (Munich: List, 1957), pp. 124-134;

"Zur Vorgeschichte der Kammergründung und dieser Schrift" and "Weltverbesserer," in *Reflexe*, published by the Industrie- und Handelskammer zu Solingen (Cologne & Opladen: Westdeutscher Verlag, 1966), pp. 7-18, 69-80;

"Wozu leben wir?," in *Schriftsteller antworten jungen Menschen auf die Frage: Wozu leben wir?*, edited by Hans Peter Richter (Freiburg im Breisgau, Colmar & Paris: Alsatia, 1968);

"Jahrgang 1898," in *Jahr und Jahrgang 1898*, edited by Joachim Karsten (Hamburg: Hoffmann & Campe, 1968), pp. 133-180.

PERIODICAL PUBLICATIONS: "Die gute Tat," *Scala international*, 2 (February 1964): 30-32;

"Zur Verschleißfestigkeit der Kunst," *liberal: Beiträge zur Entwicklung einer freiheitlichen Ordnung*, 10 (June 1968): 443-449;

"Wer denkt heute noch an Verdun?," *liberal*, 11 (October 1969): 766-770.

Heinz Risse is a writer not by vocation but by avocation. He has earned a comfortable living as an independent certified accountant that frees him from the necessity of having to write according to the dictates of the literary marketplace or to please publishers and readers. In the early nineteenth century Joseph Görres, a German romanticist, decried the rationalism of the Age of Enlightenment and the Industrial Revolution it brought forth because these forces were turning the world into a workhouse and destroying the leisure necessary for a life of fulfillment; a spiritual descendant of romanticism, Risse has solved the problem—at least for himself—by gaining the independence required for the development of his spirit and intellect. His dual life is for him the ideal one, for he can guard his artistic integrity and need never prostitute his art for the sake of the necessities of life. During the week he devotes himself to accounting and on weekends he plunges into the irrational world of his art—each world nourishing the other in a kind of creative symbiosis.

Risse was born in Düsseldorf in 1898. His father, a physician, was descended from Westphalian farmers and his mother from a family of engineers and doctors. He attended the humanistic gymnasium (classical high school) of his native city from 1907 to 1915. Risse describes these years as "spartanisch" (Spartan) and criticizes the "sybaritische" (sybaritic) modern world. Graduating from the gymnasium during World War I, he voluntarily entered the army, although he was apolitical and believed that the war would last much longer than the initial enthusiasm and patriotic fervor. He was buried for four hours by shell fire, an experience that left him with a pronounced dislike of tight spaces. Shortly after his discharge from the army in 1918 he enrolled at the University of Marburg, but left after two semesters to study in Frankfurt am Main, where the athletics and the active cultural life attracted him. The opportunity to study the new science of sociology under Alfred Weber and philosophy under Heinrich Rickert induced him to transfer to Heidelberg after one semester; it was there that he completed his doctorate in sociology.

After working at various auditing and finance jobs, Risse saw an opportunity to become his own boss when a 1931 reform in the securities laws created the position of Wirtschaftsprüfer, an independent certified accountant whose task was to audit the financial records of public corporations. Risse passed the rigorous examination, obtained a license, and has been engaged in this profession ever since.

In 1940 Risse was inducted into the army, but was soon discharged for reasons of health. In 1945 he was detained by the British at a camp in Recklingshausen. Risse believes that a confusion of the term Wirtschaftsprüfer with Wirtschaftsführer (economic czar; a term referring to people such as the munitions magnate Alfred Krupp) was the main reason for his detention; he also thinks that he may have been suspected of being a member of the fifth column because of the many trips abroad he had made during the 1930s. But he was a member of the Nazi party and an officer in the reserves, and as an auditor he had examined the financial records of firms dealing in munitions and other war matériel; correspondence with these firms was found in his files. After nine months of investigation he was released.

Although Risse belongs chronologically to an earlier generation he must be regarded as a postwar writer, for virtually all of his literary production—with the exception of a few short stories and a book on the sociology of sports (1921)—was written and published after World War II. Like many of the characters in his novels and short stories, Risse is an outsider—at least in regard to the society of professional writers—for he has not broken with the literary traditions of the past, in spite of the fact that he is a modern writer. Perhaps the perspective of his years has enabled him to see more deeply into human society than some of the younger writers of the postwar era, many of whom are fashionably engaged in the pursuit of political change for its own sake. Risse is apolitical; his works deal with society's values and paradoxes, double and false standards, follies and contradictions. Only insofar as government agencies and policies affect the spiritual values of society do they fall under his critical pen. In his fable "Contrat social" in the volume Belohne dich selbst (Reward Yourself, 1953) he points out the folly of surrendering one's individuality to the government. But hindsight is a gift (or a curse) that comes too late, only after the pattern of life has led to its ultimate and un-

foreseeable consequences; nothing can then be changed. Risse admits that his own initial skepticism toward the National Socialist party was overcome by Hitler's early successes in dealing with economic problems. Man causes whatever results from his actions, but the individual does not know whether these actions are right or wrong until it is too late to change the course of events that they have produced. Thus Brocke in the novel Dann kam der Tag (Then Came the Day, 1953), who suddenly realizes at the age of seventy that he has wasted his life in the pursuit of false values, cannot save his son from the same fate—a fate he himself has unwittingly decreed by inculcating his own dubious values into his son, preventing the latter from developing healthy and generous traits of his own.

In 1950 Risse achieved recognition for his novel Wenn die Erde bebt (translated as The Earthquake, 1953), which was translated into several languages. Through a series of narratives, conversations, anecdotes, and philosophical discussions the reasons for the unnamed narrator's incarceration in a mental institution are revealed. The novel is a confession in a twofold sense: the psychiatrist urges the narrator to confess to the murder of his wife by writing of his motivations for the crime; at the same time, the narrator confesses his faith in his asocial and solipsistic credo of spiritual values. His attachment to the world of the spirit is symbolized by his ability to predict a person's death with uncanny accuracy, a talent that his employer, an insurance company, wishes to exploit. But this affinity with the nonmaterial world is destroyed by involvement with society and its material values. When the narrator accommodates himself to such values, he loses his clairvoyance; but it returns to him after he has repudiated materialism and become determined to build his own private spiritual world.

The struggle of the narrator with the corrupting influences of society is depicted in his relationship with his wife, Leonore, and with Gebsattel, a colleague at the insurance company whose ambition is to rise to the top of his profession. During the narrator's materialistic phase he accepts Gebsattel; only after an automobile accident, the result of Gebsattel's drunken driving, causes the death of Gebsattel's fiancée does a rift open between them. Gebsattel represents the realistic world of society with its false values, and the narrator's struggle against him is the struggle against the corrupting influence of materialism. In a clairvoyant conversation the dead girl tells the narrator that he is vulnerable and that there is no law beyond the one his conscience has created. This conversation represents a turning point in the narrator's life. He suddenly realizes that he is in danger of losing his soul to the materialism of society and resolves to protect the integrity of his spirit.

The destruction wrought by an earthquake uncovers the transience of the material world and the folly of technical progess. It also serves a function similar to that of the earthquake in Heinrich von Kleist's novella "Das Erdbeben in Chili" (The Earthquake in Chile, 1810) where this natural disaster destroys a corrupt and unjust society. Immediately after the quake the world becomes an innocent paradise; but the forces that had created the unjust society have only been temporarily set aside. Eventually the same corruption of conscience, the same folly, the same prejudices return. Ultimately the narrator must kill his wife to protect himself against her corrupting influence. The court which tries the narrator in absentia does not understand or even consider the reasons for the crime, and it condemns him to death.

From a realistic point of view the narrator is hopelessly paranoid. He sees society as an enemy of self-realization and the destroyer of the soul. But Risse is not interested in realism. His purpose is to uncover the potentially destructive forces of materialism by depicting an extreme point of view as a contrast to the "norm" of a realistic world whose progress is just as illusory as the narrator's quest for total and absolute independence. Risse considers any crime, whatever the motivation, to be reprehensible and believes that justice should be absolute. But society is imperfect and circumstances turn what should be absolute into something relative.

In Risse's second novel, *So frei von Schuld* (So Free of Guilt, 1951), the hero, Alexander Boethin, a simple, childlike carpenter, seeks to improve society by improving the individuals who make it up. But he fails because society is inwardly weak and dilapidated, like the buildings of the estate that Boethin tries in vain to rebuild. Society's foundation is materialistic and therefore ephemeral. Although Boethin is often sought out as an advisor on moral questions, he is generally considered misanthropic because he places his hopes in God and does not believe in the improvements that men invent to better their lives. The narrator of *Wenn die Erde bebt* was not just asocial but antisocial; he despised society and resented

its interference in his life. But Boethin is a Christlike figure, as his trade of carpentry implies, who wishes to convert the world to his own way of life. He is ultimately sacrificed for his efforts and for his belief in the supremacy of the spirit over matter. Like the narrator of *Wenn die Erde bebt* he commits a murder while in a state of unconsciousness and has no recollection of having done it. Both murders are symbolic of the violence that the outsider does to the complacency of society's faith in materialism, a violence of which the outsider is not even aware. Boethin's altruism, his concern for society, and his desire to improve the world require him to become involved; and involvement leads to conflict because of the incompatibility of his values with those of society. Ultimately this conflict leads to Boethin's downfall. He becomes a sacrifice to a society that is intrinsically unworthy of sacrifice.

Unlike the protagonists in Risse's other novels, Brocke in *Dann kam der Tag* is not an exponent of spiritual values; he is a complete materialist who amasses an unreasonable amount of wealth. On his seventieth birthday he returns to Hirschenblick, a hotel where he sold flowers to the guests when he was a boy. To the old man Hirschenblick represents the crossroads of his life, for it was here that he met the owner of a pottery factory who gave him the opportunity to learn the business. Eventually Brocke invented and patented an improved system of manufacture that greatly increased output without jeopardizing quality. He refused to allow his benefactor to use the system because he would not meet Brocke's terms. Brocke became a partner in a rival firm that, thanks to the invention, put his former employer out of business. Brocke blackmailed his partner into selling out to him, and in the course of fifty years he built a gigantic company by underselling his competitors and taking over their bankrupt factories. In the process he alienated his wife, molded the character of his son in his own image, and committed many deeds that now, toward the end of his life, weigh heavily upon his conscience. His attempts to undo the harm he has done–by contributing to the support of the destitute daughter of his former partner, for example–fail. When he attempts to burn down one of his factories, his son has him declared legally incompetent. The court does not understand Brocke's sense of guilt or his desire to repudiate his past life. The rational deliberations of a legal body cannot comprehend the irrational reasons for Brocke's actions.

The uselessness and insanity of technological progress are portrayed in the novel *Sören der Lump* (Sören the Rascal, 1955), in which the hero invents ingenious but useless machines as a commentary on progress; he calls his inventions, and indeed all inventions, "Verirrungen" (aberrations). Sören has been an outsider from birth. Because he was different from "normal" children, his parents did not trust him. He was said to have used his confirmation money, which was supposed to be donated to the church, to buy candy. Sören denied that he had done so, but his denial was interpreted as mendacity by his parents. Sören's guilt or innocence was never established; he was simply considered a "rascal." The complete lack of trust on the part of his parents determined Sören's fate. He was sent to live on a farm with a great-aunt who was to teach him the error of his ways. But she was a sadistic tyrant, and her treatment of him merely exacerbated his tendency to be an outsider. His innate pride and self-esteem were regarded as spite, leading to further misunderstanding of his character. Because of a prank that had more serious consequences than Sören had foreseen, he was banished from the farm and had to make his own way.

Years later the aunt summons her relatives, including Sören, to her deathbed. She has thousands of marks in cash which she intends to distribute among them, and Sören is to receive the largest share. To receive the money, however, each relative must stand mute and listen to the aunt's diatribe against him; if he interrupts in any way, the money is forfeited and will be distributed among the other relatives. When Sören's turn comes, he tears up the money and throws it into the fire, even though he is in dire need of it. Sören's action makes as much sense as life itself, as his inventions, and as his death: he is blown up by shell fire during World War I, a victim of technological progress.

In the struggle of the individual against society, society always wins. In the Kafkaesque tale *Die Stadt ohne Wurzeln* (The City without Roots, 1957) the state attempts to conceal from the people the fact that its materialistic policies are leading them to disaster. It cannot admit that the craters that appear mysteriously in various parts of the city are symptomatic of the decay of its cultural foundations. When attempts to fill the craters fail, the authorities fence them in and cover them over. The majority of the population goes about its business as usual, happy to be deluded, unheedful of the catastrophe which must inevita-

bly come. But one old man, an outsider and nonconformist, descends into one of the craters and discovers that the entire city is without roots. He is arrested and prevented from revealing the truth. Risse attributes man's apathy and willingness to be deluded to his intellectual indolence.

In the title story of the collection *Buchhalter Gottes* (God's Bookkeeper, 1958) a bookkeeper who has shut himself off from anything irrational in life is suddenly confronted by things of whose existence he had never dreamed. He becomes aware of the limitations and the loneliness of the petty life he has created in his small office cubicle—a life in which he had formerly been comfortable and content. Fever and delirium overcome him as he realizes what a waste his life has been. But Risse's heroes are almost never able to change anything; it is almost always too late. Chance, the shaper of one's fate, has led to circumstances that make it impossible to undo what has been done.

In the story "Der Diebstahl" (The Theft, 1962) a father's lack of faith in his son could have altered the son's life completely if a friend—who many years before had stolen from the father—had not replaced the money the son had stolen. This is one of the rare occasions in Risse's work where it is possible to make amends for past actions: by returning the money and taking the son under his wing the friend rights the wrong. Yet it was the original theft by this friend that had warped the personality of the father and made him unduly suspicious. Risse shows here that one's fate hangs on thin and remote threads of random occurrences.

The narrator of the novel *Ringelreihen oder Die Apologie des Verbleibs im Zimmer* (Ring-around-the-Rosy; or, The Apology of the Space in the Room, 1963) is another born outsider. He disassociates himself from society and denies that he is his brother's keeper. He is able to lead this life of absolute individualism because he is independently wealthy. When he realizes that he does not have enough money to continue living in this manner indefinitely, he decides to commit suicide when his funds are exhausted. Coincidence enables him, however, to collect an inheritance by fraud. Fundescu, the attorney who administers the estate, is also an outsider by virtue of the fact that he has only a year to live. Yet he considers the narrator a parasite on society who avoids all responsibility and risk.

During his travels the narrator finds himself in a country where a civil war breaks out, and he is forced to serve in the army as an interpreter. In this capacity he takes part in the interrogation of a prisoner who happens to be the son of Fundescu. The son is devoted to the establishment of economic equality through a redistribution of wealth. The narrator tells him that it has often been the ploy of the power establishment to evoke present sacrifice for the sake of a future happiness that is indefinite and, inasmuch as concepts of happiness differ, will probably not be considered such by all the people. The narrator also states that as soon as a person commits himself to a particular political group he has lost his intellectual freedom.

The latter half of the novel portrays the narrator's trial for helping Fundescu's son to escape, a deed of which he is innocent. The court discounts the narrator's argument that his refusal to become involved in the affairs of society would preclude his aiding a prisoner or anyone else. When the main witness against the narrator admits that he perjured himself, the court declares that the witness is now insane but was sane when he testified against the narrator. Eventually the witness is pushed out a window to his death. The court is an instrument of the state, and whatever benefits the state is considered to be justice. The narrator is condemned to death, but the General gives him the option of lending money to the state and going free. Because the narrator believes that he is already free, even if physically detained, he refuses. It is his own spiritual freedom that concerns him, not political freedom for himself or others. To become involved in a political cause, even to save his own life, would mean the loss of that spiritual freedom.

The General believes that freedom only exists within the group, in the state that the narrator despises as a community of termites. He offers the narrator the privilege of changing his mind about lending the money up to the moment he is standing before the firing squad. The novel ends before the narrator's execution; whether he chooses physical or spiritual death remains unstated, but one is inclined to believe that he opts for the former.

Risse's selfish, solipsistic individuals represent the antithesis of the totalitarian state. The state pursues materialism; the individual pursues the development of his spiritual attributes, such as intellect and feeling. The totalitarian state consists of masses of people, each with a particular function beneficial to the state; the individual is alone and beneficial to none but himself.

Through the contrast of state and individual the injustices and dangers inherent in the state are held up to criticism. Risse believes that mass society is a primitive stage of evolution, no different from the society of the ant or the termite. Change in the direction of individualism is the only progress he would recognize; what society regards as progress is for him an illusion.

Risse's works can be called didactic; they present a moral lesson, and character and plot are subordinated to that end. This does not lessen one's involvement in his stories or the tension which carries the reader along in furious haste to the inevitable end. His style is uncomplicated, his language correct and precise. Often he is ironic, and what is meant is the opposite of what is said. Thus praise becomes censure, apparent approval is really disapproval. He often uses dialogues to debate philosophical questions; frequently these take the form of the Socratic method. His works are sprinkled with aphorisms, many of which are contradicted by antithetical ones. There are subtle allusions to Heinrich von Kleist, Goethe, Friedrich von Schiller, Novalis, and other representatives of the German literary heritage. Risse enjoys having his characters reach logical conclusions that are based on false premises and are therefore false. Reason is the serpent in the garden of Eden and is responsible for a nihilistic technocracy that destroys the individual.

The questioning of generally accepted values makes Risse's work much more revolutionary than that of the political fanatic. He reveals the basic problems that threaten the very foundations of society: the folly of delegating power, power that always seems to be placed in the hands of the wrong people; the absurdity of governmental organizations; the consequences of neglecting one's spiritual nature; the corruptibility of mankind; the loss of contact with nature; the atrophying of the intellect produced by technological progress. In a world that seems to have lost contact with the spirituality of the past, a world hovering on the rim of the abyss of nihilism, the works of this unfanatical and undogmatic writer argue the essential indestructibility of the human spirit.

References:
Herbert Ahl, "Legitimität des Gewissens: Heinz Risse," in his *Literarische Portraits* (Munich & Vienna: Langen-Müller, 1962), pp. 52-60;
Karl August Horst, "Vor dem letzten Kapitel," *Merkur*, 6 (1952): 187-189;

Valentine C. Hubbs, "Obwohl es keine Vollkommenheit gibt: Zu Heinz Risses siebzigstem Geburtstag," *German Quarterly*, 41 (1968): 512-514;

Hubbs, "The World of Heinz Risse," *Books Abroad*, 37 (1963): 138-143;

W. Christian Schmitt, "Erstlingswerk sogar als 'Raubdruck': Der 87-jährige Autor Heinz Risse meldet sich zurück," *Börsenblatt für den deutschen Buchhandel* (Frankfurt edition), 41 (July 1985): 1868-1869;

Barbara Sigrid, "The Concept of Freedom in the Works of Heinz Risse," Ph.D. dissertation, University of Pittsburgh, 1972;

Helmut Uhlig, "Die Gefangenen Gottes: Zum Werk von Heinz Risse," *Monat*, 4 (June 1952): 319-323;

Johannes Urzidil, H. Gelsen, and others, *Heinz Risse 70 Jahre: Festschrift* (Krefeld: Scherpe, 1968).

Hans Sahl

(20 May 1902-   )

Sigrid Kellenter
Union College, Schenectady, New York

BOOKS: *Jemand: Ein Chorwerk* (Zurich: Oprecht, 1938);

Die hellen Nächte: Gedichte aus Frankreich (New York: Fles, 1942);

Die Wenigen und die Vielen: Roman einer Zeit (Frankfurt am Main: Fischer, 1959); translated by Richard and Clara Winston as *The Few and the Many* (New York: Harcourt, Brace & World, 1962);

Wir sind die Letzten: Gedichte (Darmstadt & Heidelberg: Schneider, 1976);

Memoiren eines Moralisten: Erinnerungen I (Zurich: Ammann, 1983);

Umsteigen nach Babylon: Erzählungen (Zurich: Ammann, 1987).

OTHER: "Das amerikanische Theater" and "Wilder, Miller, Williams," in *Welttheater: Bühnen, Autoren, Inszenierungen*, edited by Siegfried Melchinger and Henning Rischbieter (Braunschweig: Westermann, 1962), pp. 69-75, 515-537;

George Grosz: Heimatliche Gestalten, Zeichnungen, edited by Sahl (Frankfurt am Main: Fischer, 1966);

"Theater in den USA," in *Das Atlantisbuch des Theaters*, edited by Martin Hurlimann (Zurich: Atlantis, 1966), pp. 851-858;

Hans Sahl (photograph by Bert Torchia)

"Urlaub vom Tod," in *Deutsches Exildrama und Exil-*

theater: Jahrbuch für internationale Germanistik, series A, volume 3 (Bern: Lang, 1977), pp. 151-160.

TRANSLATIONS:· Thornton Wilder, *Unsere kleine Stadt* (Frankfurt am Main: Fischer, 1953);

Wilder, *Wir sind noch einmal davongekommen,* in Wilder, *Theater* (Frankfurt am Main: Fischer, 1955), pp. 83-178;

Tennessee Williams, *Die Katze auf dem heißen Dach* (Frankfurt am Main: Fischer, 1956);

Wilder, *Die Heiratsvermittlerin* (Frankfurt am Main: Fischer, 1957);

Williams, *Plötzlich letzten Sommer* (Frankfurt am Main: Fischer, 1960);

Williams, *Orpheus steigt herab* (Frankfurt am Main: Fischer, 1962);

Williams, *Süßer Vogel Jugend* (Frankfurt am Main: Fischer, 1962);

Arthur Miller, *Zwischenfall in Vichy* (Frankfurt am Main: Fischer, 1967);

Miller, *Nach dem Sündenfall* (Frankfurt am Main: Fischer, 1967);

Miller, *Der Preis* (Reinbek: Rowohlt, 1968);

Williams, *Der Milchzug hält hier nicht mehr* (Frankfurt am Main: Fischer, 1969);

Wilder, *Theophilus North* (Frankfurt am Main: Fischer, 1974).

Hans Sahl–poet, novelist, critic, and translator–is one of the many writers who had to wrest their works from the devastating experience of persecution, exile, and isolation. Though his career did not flourish in America as it might have in Germany, his talent has been recognized and his impressive, if relatively small, body of creative writing is belatedly receiving attention and appreciation.

Sahl was born in Dresden in 1902 to Paul David and Anna Maasz Sahl. He spent his youth in Berlin and studied literature and art history at the Universities of Leipzig and Breslau. After receiving his doctorate in Breslau in 1924 he returned to Berlin to begin a promising career as a writer and critic. His carefully drafted and well-received reviews of books and theatrical productions appeared in Berlin's leading newspapers. He also belonged to the avant-garde who tried to elevate film criticism to a discipline as respected as book and theater criticism. He had just signed a contract with Ernst Rowohlt for a book on the history of the silent film and was completing a volume of lyric poetry when Hitler came to power in 1933. He was forced to flee Germany because he was Jewish and, like many other rebellious and radical young intellectuals of the time, a Communist. He escaped via Prague, Zurich, and Paris, spent a year in French detention camps, and retreated to Marseilles with the French army.

Under the influence of Bertolt Brecht he wrote the oratorio *Jemand* (Someone) for the revolutionary workers' movement in Zurich in 1938. Performed by Swiss workers' choruses before cheering masses in Zurich the same year, this dramatic and emotional verse play depicts the rebellion of the proletariat as it breaks its chains, stands up for freedom and justice, and vows resistance to Hitler. He became a member of the Schutzverband deutscher Schriftsteller (Protective Association of German Writers), a group consisting mostly of young Communist authors in Paris, among them Anna Seghers, Egon Erwin Kisch, and Johannes R. Becher. After many disillusionments and a long battle with his conscience, Sahl finally broke with Marxist-Communist ideals, openly rejecting the Communist party in 1939. Having taken that step, he also distanced himself from his oratorio because of its simplistic ideology.

While in hiding in Marseilles in the summer of 1940 Sahl was approached by the Emergency Rescue Committee, which listed him as an artist to be saved. From August 1940 until April 1941 Sahl, ignoring the danger to himself, helped with the rescue work the committee had begun in Marseilles after the French-German peace treaty. When he finally escaped, he carried hidden in his toothpaste tube a list of endangered individuals which, on arrival in New York, he delivered to the government for immediate action.

In America Sahl became an ardent, though not uncritical, admirer of democracy and its ability to tolerate differences of opinion. He declined an invitation to join the Council for a Democratic Germany, founded in New York by Paul Tillich and supported by Brecht and other Communist writers. Like Thomas Mann, who had refused the chairmanship of the group, he did not believe that a pact with Stalin was the answer for the future of Germany. He did not share the illusion that a synthesis between communism and capitalism was possible, and he wanted to see the exiles prepare for a truly democratic Germany, immune to totalitarian ideologies of the left as well as the right. He became enthralled with publications such as the *Partisan Review,* the *New Leader,* and *Politics* and with unbiased discussions of Marxism by John Dewey, Sidney Hook, Max Eastman, Dwight McDonald, and other intellectuals. America, he said, with its willingness to compromise, spoiled him for the Old World alternatives of "either-or," "left or right." He is convinced that his literary career suffered because he was too far to the right for his radical friends in Germany and remained too far to the left for the conservatives.

During his first years in New York Sahl received financial support from various refugee committees and made a meager living from odd jobs, such as translating for the army air corps. Meanwhile, he prepared for publication poems he had written during his flight through Europe. The volume *Die hellen Nächte: Gedichte aus Frankreich* (The Bright Nights: Poems from France) was printed in New York in 1942 by Barthold Fles, a small exile press; it had a limited audience. Today the poems are recognized as authentic statements of the exile experience and as poetic reactions to an unpoetic era. Not always perfect, well-rounded, or polished, seemingly fragmentary and hastily written, and without pathos or deliberate ornamentation, they present a simple and urgent message. They are both testimony and moral judgment. In the best humanist tradition, they concentrate on timeless, positive human qualities which survive despite destructive historical forces. They display Sahl's conception of the artist as bearer of the moral opposition to his times and safekeeper of the eternal and indestructible in man. The traditional poetic forms of the sonnet, elegy, and ballad (which he was soon to abandon for a more open, unrhymed, "modern" form) and the allusions in form and content to Hölderlin, Heine, and Rilke mark his desire to place himself consciously in a literary tradition. But by "profaning" these traditional forms, by elevating the importance of the message, and by using simple, accessible, unidealized language, as Brecht demanded, he showed his connection to the present.

In 1942 Sahl wrote the radio play "Urlaub vom Tod" (translated as "Furlough from Death"), which was broadcast the same year in the series "We Fight Back," conceived by German writers and artists. The English version was also broadcast in 1942 as part of the "Treasury Star Parade," a series of twenty-minute plays to promote the sale of war bonds. It is remarkable that this drama was aired during the war, since it is not anti-German in the usual propagandistic sense. It is about a young man who, having been killed in battle on the Russian front, returns from the dead to accuse his family and friends and to question the validity of the war. It depicts the German tragedy as an entanglement which nobody except its instigators wanted. Sahl distinguishes here between Germans and Nazis, and he sees most Germans as forced accomplices to the crimes of their leaders. To the accusations of the son, the father replies, "Wir alle sind Gefangene. *Deutschland ist ein einziges Konzentrationslager*" (We are all prisoners. *All of Germany is a concentration camp*).

Progress on Sahl's novel *Die Wenigen und die Vielen* (1959; translated as *The Few and the Many*, 1962) was slow. Desperate for financial support, he entered two chapters–in German–in a novel contest for young authors sponsored by Houghton Mifflin in January 1944. The publishing house gave him an advance of $250, but he could not meet the deadline for completion. When he was finally satisfied with his manuscript he tried to find a publisher in Germany but was unable to do so until 1959. At that time interest in the Nazi period and in the exiles was small. Today the novel is considered one of the most representative of its times. It illuminates the years of Nazi terror and catches the image of an epoch through the consciousness of an "individualist between the fronts." The loose composition of the work–the narrative is interrupted by flashbacks, interior monologues, diary entries, and letters–is well suited to its theme. Although the protagonist, Kobbe, has experiences similar to Sahl's, the work is not an autobiography. Characters and events are elevated to the level of symbols, giving the reader a profound understanding of the overwhelming experience of totalitarianism.

Sahl's attempt to become an "American" writer failed, though he occasionally placed an article in the *New Leader*, *Politics*, or *Commonweal*. In 1958 he became a correspondent for the *Neue Zürcher Zeitung*, the *Süddeutsche Zeitung* (Munich), and *Die Welt* (Hamburg), reviewing literature, theater, art, and music in America. He continued this work until 1975. Material well-being came when he was sought out as a translator of American and British plays. The major American playwrights whose works were produced on German stages in Sahl's translations after the war were Thornton Wilder, Tennessee Williams, and Arthur Miller. Sahl also acquainted the German public with these authors through essays in books on world theater. He cherished the friendship and intellectual camaraderie of Wilder, which developed during their collaboration on the German versions of Wilder's plays. Sahl's translation skills and coverage of the American cultural scene were recognized in 1959 with the award of the Officers Cross of Merit by the Federal Republic of Germany and in 1979 by the Thornton Wilder Prize for Distinguished Translation, which was handed to him by Wilder's sister in a ceremony at Columbia University.

Although Sahl might have been able to carry out his work as a translator in Germany, his journalism tied him to America. Germany had not provided opportunity or professional security in the 1950s, when he had been willing to return home and assume a place in its literary life. His 1961 marriage to Melinda Albrechtova and the birth of two sons made it even more impractical to uproot himself again. In addition, the awareness expressed by the protagonist at the end of *Die Wenigen und die Vielen*–that exile would never cease as long as he lived, that it was no longer linked to any one country but had become a spiritual state, a way of life–had its rewards: it taught him to live between languages and cultures and instilled in him the pride of a world citizen enriched by an enlarged vision.

The most detrimental aspects of permanent exile for Sahl are the impeded contact with the literary life of Germany and the difficulties in bringing his projects to quick fruition there. His second volume of poetry, *Wir sind die Letzten* (We are the Last), was ready for publication for several years before it came out in 1976. It contains a selection of poems written since 1941 as well as a number of poems from his first volume. The new poems deal with postwar Germany as seen from a distance, with New York, and with postwar America. Sahl registers daily events and experiences and reacts to them. His gaze is frequently directed homeward, and as he reflects and tries to understand what happened during the Nazi period, he always exhibits tactfulness and awe toward the victims. His utterances tend toward understatements since Sahl knows that what he is saying would be inconsistent with exaggeration and sentimentality. At times sensitive and warm, at times distant and ironic, his tone and style renounce the "perfect," rhymed poem for unpretentious rhythmic prose, a form most appropriate to his message.

Negotiations over the production of his play *Hausmusik* (House-Music) also took several years. The play received a reading in Berlin in 1979; from 14 November to 20 December 1981 it was produced in English by the American Jewish Theatre in New York, and in April 1984 in the German cities of Landshut, Straubing, and Passau. It was enthusiastically received in both countries. A loosely connected succession of scenes, *Hausmusik* is the story of a painful homecoming, the return of a Jewish exile to his parents' house in Berlin. The house, now occupied by strangers, awakens memories of the past when the world was still whole, a time when the music of Schubert, Brahms, and Wagner played a central role in the cultural lives of German Jews, when Jews believed in the honor of their country, gave their lives for the Kaiser, and celebrated the Kaiser's birthday with the pride of truly "assimilated," enlightened Germans; it brings back recollections of their reluctance to believe in the destruction of their "perfect" world and the bitter consequences of that reluctance. The play avoids horror scenes; it shows accurately and sensitively the relationship of Jews and Germans before the war, poses ethical and religious questions, and opens the way to reconciliation.

Sahl's autobiography, *Memoiren eines Moralisten* (A Moralist's Memoirs), written in 1980 with the help of a tape recorder because of failing eyesight, was published in Zurich in 1983. Covering the years from 1902 until 1933, the book unmasks the people and events alluded to in his novel and makes palpable the cultural and political climate of Berlin, especially in the 1920s. The memoirs are the moving testimony of a last witness to a tumultuous time. In the year of the book's publication Sahl's literary achievements were recognized by the award of the Gryphius Prize. A second volume of the autobiography, "Der Lärm und die Stille" (The Noise and the Silence), as well as a third volume of poetry, "Der Mann im Stein" (The Man in Stone), were awaiting publication as of 1988.

Hans Sahl has created from his experiences a body of work that interprets the events of his time. The obligation to take a position and to intervene in the contest of ideas determines the form and content of all his works.

References:

Robert von Berg, "Deutschland–kein Wintermärchen: Uraufführung von Hans Sahls *Hausmusik* in New York," *Süddeutsche Zeitung*, 13 January 1982, p. 27;

Marianne Hauser, "Elegies on France," *Saturday Review of Literature*, 25 (29 August 1942): 12;

Hans Egon Holthusen, "Geschichte einer Emigration," *Merkur*, 14, no. 12 (1960): 1204-1208;

Sigrid Kellenter, "Alte und neue Heimat im Leben und Werk von Hans Sahl, Walter Sorell und Otto Zoff: Variationen über ein Thema," in *Kulturelle Wechselbeziehungen im Exil*, edited by Helmut Pfanner (Bonn: Bouvier, forthcoming);

Kellenter, "Charterflug in die Vergangenheit. Hans Sahl erinnert sich an seine Heimatstadt Berlin," *Exil: Forschung, Erkenntnisse, Ergebnisse* (1987): 5-14;

Kellenter, "Hans Sahl," afterword to Sahl's *Umsteigen nach Babylon: Erzählungen* (Zurich: Ammann, 1987), pp. 135-173;

Kellenter, "Hans Sahl," in *Deutsche Exilliteratur seit 1933: New York*, edited by John M. Spalek and Joseph P. Strelka (Bern: Francke, 1986), pp. 90-103;

Kellenter, "Hans Sahl's Exile Novel *The Few and the Many:* Recollections of the Past, Glimpses into the Future," *Studies in the Humanities*, 2 (June 1984): 23-30;

Kellenter, "Hans Sahls Roman *Die Wenigen und die Vielen*: 'Der Roman des Exils überhaupt?,'" *Exil: Forschung, Erkenntnisse, Ergebnisse* (1982): 26-38;

Kellenter, "Hans Sahl und das Problem der Rückkehr," in *Das Exilerlebnis*, edited by Donald G. Daviau and Ludwig M. Fischer (Columbia, S.C.: Camden House, 1982), pp. 411-423;

Klaus Mann, "Passion eines Menschen," *Das neue Tagebuch*, 6 (9 April 1938): 357-358;

Fritz Martini, Postscript to Sahl's, *Wir sind die Letzten* (Heidelberg: Schneider, 1976), pp. 70-83;

Kurt Pinthus, "Ein ungewöhnlicher Exilroman," *Aufbau* (New York), 25 December 1959, p. 10;

Wolfdietrich Schnurre, "Flucht in die Humanität: Zu Hans Sahls Zeitroman," *Der Monat*, 12 (December 1959): 75-77;

Richard F. Shephard, "*House Music* Studies German Attitudes," *New York Times*, 26 November 1981, p. 13;

Erich Wolfgang Skwara, *Hans Sahl: Leben und Werk* (Bern: Lang, 1986);

Jürgen Theobaldy, "Exil-Dichtung: Hans Sahls Gedichte *Wir sind die Letzten*," *Die Zeit*, 14 May 1982, p. 50;

Ulrich Weinzierl, "Ein melancholisches Abschiednehmen: Hans Sahl hat die *Memoiren eines Moralisten* verfaßt," *Frankfurter Allgemeine Zeitung*, 24 December 1983, p. 24.

Edzard Schaper

(30 September 1908-29 January 1984)

Virginia M. Anderson
Gordon College

BOOKS: *Der letzte Gast: Roman* (Stuttgart: Bonz, 1927);

Die Bekenntnisse des Försters Patrik Doyle: Roman (Stuttgart: Bonz, 1928);

Die Insel Tütarsaar: Roman (Leipzig: Insel, 1933);

Erde über dem Meer: Roman (Berlin: Die Buchgemeinde, 1934);

Die Arche, die Schiffbruch erlitt (Leipzig: Insel, 1935);

Die sterbende Kirche: Roman (Leipzig: Insel, 1935);

Das Leben Jesu (Leipzig: Insel, 1936); partially republished as *Die Weihnachtsgeschichte* (Zurich: Arche, 1950) and *Nikodemus: Eine Erzählung* (Zurich: Arche, 1952);

Das Lied der Väter (Leipzig: Insel, 1937);

Der Henker: Roman (Leipzig: Insel, 1940; revised edition, Zurich: Atlantis, 1949); republished as *Sie mähten gewappnet die Saaten: Roman* (Cologne & Olten: Hegner, 1956);

Semjon, der ausging, das Licht zu holen: Eine Weihnachtserzählung aus dem alten Estland (Basel: Reinhardt, 1947); republished as *Stern über der Grenze* (Cologne: Hegner, 1950); translated by Isabel and Florence McHugh as *Star over the Frontier* (Baltimore: Helicon Press, 1960);

Der letzte Advent: Roman (Zurich: Atlantis, 1949);

Der große, offenbare Tag: Die Erzählung eines Freundes (Cologne & Olten: Hegner, 1949);

Die Freiheit des Gefangenen: Roman (Cologne & Olten: Hegner, 1950); republished with *Die Macht der Ohnmächtigen* as *Macht und Freiheit: Ein Roman* (Cologne & Olten: Hegner, 1961);

Der Mensch in der Zelle: Dichtung und Deutung des gefangenen Menschen (Cologne & Olten: Hegner, 1951);

Die Macht der Ohnmächtigen: Roman (Cologne & Olten: Hegner, 1951); republished with *Die Freiheit des Gefangenen* as *Macht und Freiheit: Ein Roman* (Cologne & Olten: Hegner, 1961);

C. G. Mannerheim, Marschall von Finnland: Eine

Edzard Schaper (photograph by Oswald Ruppen)

Rede zu seinem Gedächtnis (Zurich: Arche, 1951);

Norwegische Reise (Zurich: Arche, 1951);

Finnisches Tagebuch (Zurich: Arche, 1951);

Hinter den Linien (Cologne & Olten: Hegner, 1951);

Vom Sinn des Alters: Eine Betrachtung (Zurich: Arche, 1952);

Untergang und Verwandlung: Betrachtungen und Reden (Zurich: Arche, 1952; revised edition, Berlin: Ullstein, 1956);

Um die neunte Stunde oder Nikodemus und Simon (Cologne & Olten: Hegner, 1953);

Der Mantel der Barmherzigkeit: Erzählung (Cologne & Olten: Hegner, 1953);

Die heiligen drei Könige (Zurich: Arche, 1953);

Der Gouverneur oder Der glückselige Schuldner: Roman (Cologne & Olten: Hegner, 1954);

Die letzte Welt: Ein Roman (Frankfurt am Main: Fischer, 1956);

Erkundungen in Gestern und Morgen (Zurich: Arche, 1956);

Bürger in Zeit und Ewigkeit: Antworten, edited by Lutz Besch (Hamburg: von Schröder, 1956);

Unschuld der Sünde (Frankfurt am Main: Fischer, 1957);

Attentat auf den Mächtigen: Roman (Frankfurt am Main: Fischer, 1957);

Das Wiedersehen und Der gekreuzigte Diakon (Cologne & Olten: Hegner, 1957);

Der Held: Weg und Wahn Karls XII. (Frankfurt am Main: Fischer, 1958);

Das Tier oder Die Geschichte eines Bären, der Oskar hieß: Roman (Frankfurt am Main: Fischer, 1958); translated by Norman Denny as *The Dancing Bear: A Novel* (London: Bodley Head, 1960; New York: Day, 1961);

Die Eidgenossen des Sommers (Cologne & Olten: Hegner, 1958);

Die Geisterbahn: Eine Erzählung (Cologne & Olten: Hegner, 1959);

Der Abfall vom Menschen: Du bist nicht allein; Das Martyrium der Lüge (Olten & Freiburg im Breisgau: Walter, 1961);

Der vierte König: Roman (Cologne & Olten: Hegner, 1961); partly republished as *Die Legende vom vierten König* (Cologne & Olten: Hegner, 1964);

Die Söhne Hiobs (Cologne & Olten: Hegner, 1962);

Verhüllte Altäre: Ansprachen (Cologne & Olten: Hegner, 1962);

Unser Vater Malchus (Olten: Vereinigung Oltner Bücherfreunde, 1962);

Heiligung der Opfer: Eine Rede zur Woche der Brüderlichkeit (Cologne & Olten: Hegner, 1963);

Der Aufruhr des Gerechten: Eine Chronik (Cologne & Olten: Hegner, 1963);

Dragonergeschichte: Novelle (Cologne & Olten: Hegner, 1963);

Strenger Abschied: Ein Hörspiel (Cologne & Olten: Hegner, 1964);

Der Gefangene der Botschaft: Drei Stücke (Cologne & Olten: Hegner, 1964);

Flucht und Bleibe: Ein Wort an die geflüchteten und ver- triebenen Deutschen (Cologne & Olten: Hegner, 1965);

Das Feuer Christi: Leben und Sterben des Johannes Hus in siebzehn dramatischen Szenen (Stuttgart & Berlin: Kreuz, 1965);

Einer trage des andern Last: Eine Elegie auf den letzten Gepäckträger (Zurich: Arche, 1965);

Wagnis der Gegenwart: An Kreuzwegen christlicher Geschichte (Stuttgart: Kreuz, 1965);

Die baltischen Länder im geistigen Spektrum Europas (Munich: Baltische Gesellschaft in Deutschland, 1965);

Gesammelte Erzählungen (Cologne & Olten: Hegner, 1965);

Über die Redlichkeit (Cologne & Olten: Hegner, 1967);

Schattengericht: Vier neue Erzählungen (Cologne & Olten: Hegner, 1967);

Schicksale und Abenteuer: Geschichten aus vielen Leben (Cologne & Olten: Hegner, 1968);

Die Heimat der Verbannten: Erzählung (Cologne & Olten: Hegner, 1968);

Dank an Edzard Schaper: Zu seinem 60. Geburtstag (Cologne & Olten: Hegner, 1968);

Gespräche mit Edzard Schaper, edited by Lutz Besch (Zurich: Arche, 1968);

Der letzte Advent (Cologne & Olten: Hegner, 1968);

Auf der Brücke der Hoffnung: Betrachtungen zur Weihnacht (Zurich: Arche, 1968);

Am Abend der Zeit: Ein Roman (Cologne & Olten: Hegner, 1970);

Taurische Spiele: Ein Roman (Cologne & Olten: Hegner, 1971);

Sperlingschlacht: Ein Roman (Cologne & Olten: Hegner, 1972);

Aufstand und Ergebung: Drei Romane (Cologne & Olten: Hegner, 1973);

Degenhall: Ein Roman (Zurich & Munich: Artemis, 1975);

Die Reise unter dem Abendstern: Ein Roman (Zurich: Artemis, 1976);

Geschichten aus vielen Leben: Sämtliche Erzählungen (Zurich & Munich: Artemis, 1977);

Grenzlinien: Ein Lesebuch, edited by Matthias Wörther (Zurich: Artemis, 1987).

OTHER: "Des Vaters Mühle: Erinnerungen," in *Mein Elternhaus* (Berlin: Warneck, 1937), pp. 221-231;

Thomas à Kempis, *Nachfolge Christi,* edited by Schaper (Frankfurt am Main: Fischer, 1957);

Paul Fleming, *Kein Landsmann sang mir gleich: Zwanzig seiner Gedichte,* introduction by Schaper (Cologne & Olten: Hegner, 1959);

R. A. Schröder, *Abendstunde,* edited by Lutz Besch, epilogue by Schaper (Zurich: Arche, 1960);

Altchristliche Erzählungen, edited by Schaper and Otto Karrer (Munich: Ars sacra, 1967).

TRANSLATIONS: Gudmundur Kamban, *Die Jungfrau auf Skalholt* (Leipzig: Insel, 1934);

Gabriel Scott, *Fant: Roman* (Leipzig: Insel, 1934);

Gunnar Gunnarsson, *Das Haus der Blinden* (Leipzig: Insel, 1935);

Kamban, *Ich seh ein großes, schönes Land: Roman* (Leipzig: Insel, 1937);

Sally Salminen, *Katrina: Roman* (Leipzig: Insel, 1937);

Kamban, *Der Herrscher auf Skalholt: Roman* (Leipzig: Insel, 1938);

Kaj Munk, *Dänische Predigten* (Stockholm: Neuer Verlag, 1945);

Harry Blomberg, *Eva: Der Roman einer tapferen Frau* (Basel: Reinhardt, 1947);

Efraim Briem, *Kommunismus und Religion in der Sowjetunion: Ein Ideenkampf* (Basel: Reinhardt, 1948);

Frans Eemil Sillanpää, *Das fromme Elend: Ein überstandenes Menschenschicksal in Finnland. Roman* (Zurich: Claassen, 1948);

Carl Herman Tillhagen, *Taikon erzählt: Zigeunermärchen und -geschichten, aufgezeichnet* (Zurich: Artemis, 1948);

Erik Hesselberg, *Kon-Tiki und ich* (Zurich: Arche, 1950);

Aleksis Kivi, *Die sieben Brüder: Roman* (Zurich: Manesse, 1950);

Pär Lagerkvist, *Barabbas: Roman* (Munich: Nymphenberger Verlagshandlung, 1950);

Ernst Manker, *Menschen und Götter in Lappland* (Zurich: Morgarten, 1950);

Petter Moen, *Der einsame Mensch: Petter Moens Tagebuch. Geschrieben im Gefängnis der Gestapo* (Zurich: Arche/Munich: Nymphenburger Verlagshandlung, 1950);

Nils-Eric Ringbom, *Jean Sibelius: Ein Meister und sein Werk* (Olten: Walter, 1950);

Thorfinn Solberg, *Die Wanderer im Norden: Roman aus dem Leben der norwegischen Lappen* (Basel: Reinhardt, 1950);

Lagerkvist, *Gast bei der Wirklichkeit: Roman* (Zurich: Arche, 1952);

Stanislaw Mackiewicz, *Der Spieler seines Lebens: F.M. Dostojewskij* (Zurich: Thomas, 1952);

Sillanpää, *Sonne des Lebens: Roman* (Zurich: Arche, 1952);

Harry Martinson, *Der Weg nach Glockenreich: Roman* (Munich: Nymphenburger Verlagshandlung, 1953);

Sillanpää, *Sterben und Auferstehen* (Frankfurt am Main: Fischer, 1956);

Charly Clerc, *Der Herbergswirt verteidigt sich* (Frankfurt am Main: Fischer, 1958).

PERIODICAL PUBLICATIONS: "Die Vogelinsel," *Velhagen & Klasings Monatshefte,* 47 (1932-1933): 416-425;

"Koit und Hämarik oder Morgenrot und Abendröte: Ein estnisches Märchen, nacherzählt," *Insel-Schiff,* 16 (1934): 25;

"G. F. Händel: Ein Bildnis," *Velhagen & Klasings Monatshefte,* 49 (1934-1935): 662-668;

"Antwort auf Fragen," *Insel-Schiff,* 17 (1936): 168;

"Semjon, der ausging, das Licht zu holen," *Insel-Schiff,* 18 (1936): 9;

"Baltische Lande und baltisches Volkstum im Bewußtsein der Deutschen," *Die Neue Rundschau,* 68 (1957): 673-690;

"Johannes Hus–Ketzer oder Märtyrer: Ein erdachtes Gespräch," *Schweizer Monatshefte für Politik und Kultur,* 45 (January 1966): 947-962.

Edzard Schaper was one of the leading German Christian novelists in the years immediately following World War II, a period when a number of German Christian writers enjoyed a wide readership. Schaper was not only known for his novels, short stories, and essays; his many lectures and appearances on radio and television also made him a familiar figure.

The scene in most of Schaper's works is eastern Europe, particularly the Baltic region, where he lived for many years. Three major themes of his works–borderlands, refugees, and prisoners–reflect his life experiences and his belief that these phenomena are symbolic of modern existence, both physically and spiritually. Beginning with his birth in a border region, Schaper experienced what it meant to live on the border, to live as a refugee in a strange land, and to be a hunted man who narrowly escaped imprisonment and death. Spiritually, Schaper saw man living in tension as a citizen of both time and eternity.

The youngest of eleven children, Edzard Hellmuth Schaper was born in 1908 in Ostrowo (now Ostrów Wielkopolski, Poland), a military

Schaper in 1956 (Ullstein–Fritz Eschen)

post on the Polish border where his father was stationed. World War I erupted when he was six; the streams of refugees he watched then haunted him through the years.

Following the war the family moved to Glogau in Silesia and then, in 1920, to the Hannover area, where Schaper's forefathers had been millers. There Schaper attended secondary school and began music studies. He worked as an assistant stage manager at theaters in Herford and Minden and then at an opera in Stuttgart. At the same time he began his writing career; by the age of twenty he had had two novels published, both of which he later repudiated.

His early success brought him into the social limelight, where he felt uncomfortable. In 1927 he suddenly left Stuttgart to spend almost three years on Christiansö, an isolated Danish island in the Baltic Sea, where he worked on a novel about Handel that was never completed. Next he worked as a gardener in Potsdam and then went to sea on a fishing boat.

While visiting friends in Berlin in 1931 Schaper met Alice Pergelbaum and proposed to her the same evening. She was a German who had

been born in St. Petersburg, Russia, and had later moved to Estonia. Schaper followed her to Estonia, and they were married in Reval in 1932. Alice became for him a bridge between his western European roots and his adopted homeland in the Baltic region. He began a settled period of creativity, working as a free-lance writer for the respected Insel publishers in Leipzig and also as a correspondent for the United Press.

Schaper's first novel of importance was *Die Insel Tütarsaar* (The Island Tütarsaar, 1933). The narrator, a young man estranged from his wife, spends the summer on an island with two shepherd boys who believe there is a treasure on the island that they must guard. This treasure becomes symbolic of the narrator's lost childhood faith. With his faith renewed, he decides to return to his wife and his responsibilities. The tone of the novel is lyrical, and the story is told with humor and typical Schaper sympathy toward those outside the mainstream of society. Schaper's theme of flight has no political dimension here; it is an escape from everyday routine to the isolation of nature where one finds inner strength.

Schaper's first mature novel, *Die sterbende Kirche* (The Dying Church, 1935), reflects his interest in the Russian Orthodox church. Although brought up a Lutheran, he came to a genuine faith through contact with Orthodox Christians whose simple piety impressed him. He later said, "Die Orthodoxie, das war und ist das personale Ereignis meines Lebens" (Orthodoxy was and is the personal event of my live).

The plot concerns the struggle of a small Russian Orthodox church in Estonia whose priest, Father Seraphim, is a refugee from the Bolsheviks. His faith is severely tested by family tragedies. Finally, during the celebration of the Easter Mass, the church dome collapses, killing the priest and ten of the parishioners. But the novel ends on a note of hope with the survival of a young man and a girl; the girl is a former Communist celebrating her first Easter as a believer. These two are a sign that the dying church has given birth to new life. The funeral is held in a Lutheran church, indicating that Christians of both confessions recognize their oneness—another favorite theme of Schaper's. In Germany both Protestants and Catholics, at that time in conflict with the Nazis, gave this novel about suffering Orthodox Christians a sympathetic reception.

Schaper's three main themes appear for the first time in this novel: the priest is a refugee living in a borderland who spends some time in prison; he also lives in the border region between time and eternity. The novel also reveals Schaper's skill in lifting the veil from life in the Baltic region following World War I, especially that of the Russian minority there. The literary critic Helmut Uhlig writes: "Es war das erste mal, daß russisches Wesen und russische Gläubigkeit von einem deutschen Dichter so tief und echt erfaßt und in beinahe russischer Diktion gestaltet wurden" (It was the first time that Russian character and faith were so deeply and genuinely grasped by a German novelist and expressed in almost Russian diction).

Two of Schaper's best short stories also appeared during this period: *Die Arche, die Schiffbruch erlitt* (The Ark That Suffered Shipwreck) in 1935 and "Semjon, der ausging, das Licht zu holen" (Semjon, Who Went Out To Fetch the Light) in 1936. The former is a superbly taut narrative of a circus caught in a storm while crossing the Baltic. The people survive, but almost all the animals freeze to death. Thus the ark, often a symbol of the church, brings the people to a safe haven, though valued possessions are lost. The idea that the church survives in its people despite outward loss and destruction is repeatedly expressed in Schaper's works. The other story, a modern-day Christmas legend, tells of a poor widower who is shot on Christmas Eve as he strays too near the Soviet border. Searching for him, his four children are led by a vision to a Christmas tree at the barracks of their own border guards, where they are welcomed and saved from freezing to death. The story was republished in 1950 as *Stern über der Grenze* (translated as *Star over the Frontier*, 1960).

Another major novel, *Der Henker* (The Executioner), was published in 1940. Again Schaper depicts the problems of ethnic groups in a border region, this time a revolt of Estonians against their German landowners in the early 1900s. The main character is a Russian officer of German background who inherits an estate from relatives killed in the revolt. Although he acts toward the rebels according to the law, he finally realizes there is a higher law of mercy leading to reconciliation. Several critics consider *Der Henker* to be Schaper's best novel in terms of plot, action, and character portrayal.

In 1939 Hitler had ordered the resettlement of Germans living in the Baltic area; but Schaper had refused to leave and had continued to file objective UP reports that pleased neither the Soviets nor the Nazis. Both suspected him of espionage and condemned him to death in absentia. When the Soviets annexed Estonia in 1940 Schaper, his wife, and their two daughters, Katharina and Elin Christiane, fled in an open fishing boat across the Baltic to Finland, where he became a Finnish citizen. Four years later the Soviets demanded his extradition and he was forced to flee to Sweden, where he worked as a woodcutter, a translator, and a social worker with war prisoners. In 1947 he settled in Zurich and was able to resume his literary career.

A sequel to *Die sterbende Kirche, Der letzte Advent* (The Last Advent) was published in 1949. The deacon Sabbas, who survived the collapse of the church dome, crosses the border into the Soviet Union and ministers to Christians in secret night services until he is caught and condemned to death. Sabbas realizes that worship is not dependent on the exterior symbols, such as buildings, icons, and altars, that he had once considered indispensable, but that the Spirit of Christ must "von Zeit zu Zeit seine Kirche abwerfen und in göttlicher Nacktheit sich nur in den Herzen Herberge suchen" (from time to time throw off his church and in divine nakedness seek his abode only in hearts).

In 1950 and 1951 Schaper published another novel and sequel, *Die Freiheit des Gefangenen* (The Freedom of the Prisoner) and *Die Macht der Ohnmächtigen* (The Power of the Powerless), stories of political prisoners at the time of Napoleon with obvious parallels to modern times. These novels were republished together in 1961 under the title *Macht und Freiheit* (Power and Freedom). An innocent officer is imprisoned, accused of a plot to overthrow the regime. Rebellious and angry, he eventually finds peace with God and inner freedom through conversations with a priest. The latter is also involved in discussions with an atheistic commissar which contrast the Weltanschauung of the totalitarian state with that of the church.

In 1951 Schaper became a Roman Catholic, but he made it clear that he still felt close to the Orthodox and Lutheran churches, especially to the Swedish Lutheran church that had been his spiritual home during the difficult refugee years. He chose to settle in 1952 in Brig, Switzerland, in the canton of Valais where the simple faith of the Alpine Catholics reminded him of Orthodox Christians.

Schaper's Christian views are clearly expressed in his works of this period, which tended at times to emphasize discussion and monologue

Schaper in 1983 (Ullstein–Horst Tappe)

more than action. One short story, *Der große, offenbare Tag* (The Great Day of Revelation, 1949), was criticized by Uhlig for being "mehr Traktat als Erzählung, mehr Predigt als Dichtung" (more tract than story, more sermon than literary work).

Schaper was extremely prolific; he continued to write novels, short stories, radio and television plays, and essays up to 1976, when his last novel, *Die Reise unter dem Abendstern* (Voyage under the Evening Star), was published. He also translated many works from Scandinavian languages and Finnish. He received five literary prizes, including the 1958 Berlin Fontane Prize, and an honorary doctorate from the University of Freiburg.

In interviews and lectures Schaper explained that his characters live not only on a geographical border but on the border between earth and heaven, between good and evil. They are not just refugees with no earthly home but spiritual refugees alienated from themselves and from God. His prisoners are not only confined to earthly cells but are prisoners of guilt whose true inner freedom can only come through faith in Christ.

A change is noticeable in Schaper's novels of the 1970s: they no longer express an overtly re-

ligious message, although Christian ideals are implicit in them. His skill as a storyteller, however, in no way diminishes; suspenseful plots, fine delineation of character, and richness of imagery characterize his fiction to the end. For example, *Am Abend der Zeit* (On the Evening of Time, 1970), set in Poland on the eve of World War I, is one of his best novels.

Schaper had always been an outsider in the literary world, but in his later years he was almost totally ignored. His Christian themes were no longer considered relevant, his Baltic settings were of little interest to a younger generation, and his classical style was deemed outmoded. Nevertheless, his unquestioned ability as a novelist has earned him a permanent niche in German literature. As Paul Konrad Kurz wrote on the occasion of Schaper's death of chronic heart disease in 1984: "Eine andere Generation wird ihn . . . eines Tages neu entdecken" (Another generation will . . . someday discover him anew).

References:
Heinz Beckmann, "Edzard Schaper ist wieder da," *Zeitwende*, 48 (1977): 119-120;
Alfons Bungert, "Gewalt bricht Glauben nicht," *Der Literat*, 25 (September 1983): 227-228;
Anneliese Dempf, "Untergegangene Welt," *Zeitwende*, 42 (May 1971): 213-214;
Wilhelm Grenzmann, "Edzard Schaper," *Welt und Wort*, 13 (October 1958): 299-300, 302;
Carl Helbling, "Neue Werke Edzard Schapers," *Schweizer Monatshefte für Politik und Kultur*, 41 (November 1961): 917-921;
J. E. Jepson, "Edzard Schaper's Image of Man and Society in the *Gesammelte Erzählungen*," *German Life and Letters*, 23 (July 1970): 323-331;
Gisbert Kranz, *Christliche Literatur der Gegenwart*, second edition (Aschaffenburg: Pattloch, 1963), pp. 45-50;
Irène Sonderegger Kummer, *Transparenze der Wirklichkeit: Edzard Schaper und die innere Spannung in der christlichen Literatur des 20. Jahrhunderts* (Berlin & New York: De Gruyter, 1971);
Ilse Leitenberg, "Autoren über Autoren," *Literatur und Kritik*, 197-198 (September-October 1985): 381-385;
Werner Ross, "Der verschollene Kontinent: Ein Versuch über christliche Literatur," in Schaper's *Grenzlinien: Ein Lesebuch* (Zurich: Artemis, 1987);

Erwin Tramer, "Gottsucher und Poet: Zum Tode Edzard Schapers," *Der Literat,* 26 (March 1984): 72;

Helmut Uhlig, "Edzard Schaper," in *Christliche Dichtung im 20. Jahrhundert,* edited by Otto Mann, second edition (Bern & Munich: Francke, 1968), pp. 421-431;

Max Wehrli, Afterword to Schaper, *Untergang und Verwandlung: Betrachtungen und Reden* (Zurich: Arche, 1952);

Wehrli, "Ein Leben, ein Werk 'hinter den Linien': Zum Tode von Edzard Schaper," *Jahrbuch Deutsche Akademie für Sprache und Dichtung* (1984): 151-152.

Papers:

The Deutsches Literaturarchiv in Marbach am Neckar has a collection of some of Edzard Schaper's manuscripts, letters, and photos.

Arno Schmidt
(18 January 1914-3 June 1979)

Friedrich Peter Ott
University of Massachusetts-Boston

BOOKS: *Leviathan* (Hamburg, Stuttgart, Berlin & Baden-Baden: Rowohlt, 1949);

Brand's Haide: Zwei Erzählungen (Hamburg: Rowohlt, 1951);

Aus dem Leben eines Fauns: Kurzroman (Hamburg: Rowohlt, 1953); translated by John E. Woods as *Scenes from the Life of a Faun* (London & New York: Boyars, 1983);

Die Umsiedler: 2 Prosastudien (Kurzformen zur Wiedergabe mehrfacher räumlicher Verschiebung der Handelnden bei festgehaltener Einheit der Zeit) (Frankfurt am Main: Frankfurter Verlagsanstalt, 1953);

Kosmas oder Vom Berge des Nordens (Krefeld & Baden-Baden: Agis, 1955);

Das steinerne Herz: Historischer Roman aus dem Jahre 1954 (Karlsruhe: Stahlberg, 1956);

Die Gelehrtenrepublik: Kurzroman aus den Roßbreiten (Karlsruhe: Stahlberg, 1957); translated by Michael Horovitz as *The Egghead Republic: A Short Novel from the Horse Latitudes,* edited by Ernst Krawehl and Marion Boyars (London & Boston: Boyars, 1979);

Fouqué und einige seiner Zeitgenossen: Biografischer Versuch (Darmstadt: Bläschke, 1958; enlarged, 1959);

Dya na sore: Gespräche in einer Bibliothek (Karlsruhe: Stahlberg, 1958);

Rosen & Porree (Karlsruhe: Stahlberg, 1959);

KAFF auch MARE CRISIUM (Karlsruhe: Stahlberg, 1960);

Belphegor: Nachrichten von Büchern und Menschen (Karlsruhe: Stahlberg, 1961);

Sitara und der Weg dorthin: Eine Studie über Wesen, Werk & Wirkung Karl Mays (Karlsruhe: Stahlberg, 1963);

Nobodaddy's Kinder: Trilogie (Hamburg: Rowohlt, 1963);

Kühe in Halbtrauer (Karlsruhe: Stahlberg, 1964);

Schwänze: Fünf Erzählungen (Frankfurt am Main: Fischer, 1964);

Die Ritter vom Geist: Von vergessenen Kollegen (Karlsruhe: Stahlberg, 1965);

Trommler beim Zaren (Karlsruhe: Stahlberg, 1966);

Tina oder Über die Unsterblichkeit (Darmstadt: Bläschke, 1966);

Seelandschaft mit Pocahontas: Erzählungen (Frankfurt am Main: Fischer Bücherei, 1966);

Der Triton mit dem Sonnenschirm: Großbritannische Gemütsergetzungen (Karlsruhe: Stahlberg, 1969);

Zettels Traum (Karlsruhe: Stahlberg, 1970);

Orpheus: Fünf Erzählungen (Frankfurt am Main: Fischer, 1970);

Nachrichten von Büchern und Menschen (Frankfurt am Main: Fischer, 1971);

Die Schule der Atheisten: Novellen-Comödie in 6 Aufzügen (Frankfurt am Main: Fischer, 1972);

Arno Schmidt (Stahlberg-Verlag, Karlsruhe)

Nachrichten aus dem Leben eines Lords (Frankfurt am Main: Fischer, 1975);

Krakatau: Erzählungen, edited by Heinz Schöffler (Stuttgart: Reclam, 1975);

Alexander oder Was ist Wahrheit: Drei Erzählungen (Frankfurt am Main: Fischer, 1975);

Abend mit Goldrand: Eine MärchenPosse. 55 Bilder aus der L$^{\ddot{a}}_{E}$ndlichkeit für Gönner der Verschreib-Kunst (Frankfurt am Main: Fischer, 1975); translated by John E. Woods as *Evening Edged in Gold: A FairytalefArse. 55 Scenes from the C$^{ou}_{u}$ntryside for Patrons of Er$^{ra}_{0}$ta* (New York & London: Harcourt Brace Jovanovich, 1980);

Aus julianischen Tagen (Frankfurt am Main: Fischer, 1979);

Vom Grinsen des Weisen (Leipzig: Kiepenheuer, 1982);

Julia, oder die Gemälde: Scenen aus dem Novecento (Zurich: Haffmans, 1983);

. . . denn 'wallflower' heißt ›Goldlack‹: Drei Nachtprogramme 1966-1974 (Zurich: Haffmans, 1984);

Deutsches Elend: 13 Erklärungen zur Lage der Nationen. Aufsätze zu Politik und Kunst 1956-1963 (Zurich: Haffmans, 1984);

Dichtergespräche im Elysium (Zurich: Haffmans, 1984).

TRANSLATIONS: Peter Fleming, *Die sechste Kolonne: Eine merkwürdige Geschichte aus unseren Tagen* (Hamburg: Rowohlt, 1953);

Neil Paterson, *Ein Mann auf dem Drahtseil; George Wilson: Zwei Erzählungen* (Hamburg: Rowohlt, 1953);

Hans Rüsch, *Rennfahrer: Roman* (Hamburg: Rowohlt, 1955);

Evan Hunter, *Aber wehe dem Einzelnen: Roman* (Vienna: Ullstein, 1957);

Hunter, *An einem Montagmorgen: Roman* (Hamburg: Nannen, 1959);

Stanislaus Joyce, *Meines Bruders Hüter* (Frankfurt am Main: Suhrkamp, 1960);

James Fenimore Cooper, *Conanchet oder Die Beweinte von Wish-Ton-Wish* (Stuttgart: Goverts, 1962);

William Faulkner, *New Orleans: Skizzen und Erzählungen* (Stuttgart: Goverts, 1962);

Joyce, *Das Dubliner Tagebuch des Stanislaus Joyce* (Frankfurt am Main: Suhrkamp, 1964);

Wilkie Collins, *Die Frau in Weiß* (Stuttgart: Goverts, 1965);

Edgar Allan Poe, *Werke,* translated by Schmidt, Hans Wollschläger, and others, 4 volumes (Olten & Freiburg im Breisgau: Walter, 1966-1973);

Edward Bulwer-Lytton, *Was wird er damit machen? Nachrichten aus dem Leben eines Lords* (Stuttgart: Goverts, Krüger, Stahlberg, 1971);

Bulwer-Lytton, *Dein Roman: 60 Spielarten Englischen Daseins* (Frankfurt am Main: Goverts, Krüger, Stahlberg, 1973);

Cooper, *Satanstoe: Bilder aus der amerikanischen Vergangenheit* (Frankfurt am Main: Goverts, Fischer, 1976);

Cooper, *Tausendmorgen: Bilder aus der amerikanischen Vergangenheit II* (Frankfurt am Main: Goverts, Fischer, 1977);

Cooper, *Die Roten: Bilder aus der amerikanischen Vergangenheit III* (Frankfurt am Main: Goverts, Fischer, 1978).

PERIODICAL PUBLICATIONS: "Seelandschaft mit Pocahontas," *Texte und Zeichen,* 1, no. 1 (1955): 9-53;

"Berechnungen I," *Texte und Zeichen,* 1, no. 1 (1955): 112-117;

"Berechnungen II," *Texte und Zeichen,* 2, no. 1 (1956): 95-102;

"Die Handlungsreisenden," *Texte und Zeichen,* 2, no. 3 (1956): 296-299;

"Eberhard Schlotter, das zweite Programm," *Akzente,* 2 (1967): 110-134;

"Dankadresse zum Goethe-Preis 1973," *Protokolle,* 1 (1976): 375-378;

"Berechnungen III," *Neue Deutsche Rundschau,* 1 (1980): 5-20.

In 1981, when Arno Schmidt made his posthumous debut in America, the critic Robert M. Adams found him to be a "Major European Novelist" in that he had extended the tradition of "cruel comedy" that had run from Rabelais, via Swift, to Joyce. Adams added regretfully: "He was a very great writer; we should have known his work sooner." It might have been some solace to Adams to know that the German audience, with its head start of thirty years, had not really known Schmidt either. Schmidt had early acquired a reputation for being quirky and esoteric. His frequently polemical and insular stance made it easy for him to gain opponents and hard for him to attract friends. Yet friends there were from the start, not only a small and often uncritical coterie of "fans" but also readers of sober judgment who recognized his talent, growth, and achievement. A considerable number of in-depth soundings of Schmidt's oeuvre appeared, but his reception has been hampered by a surfeit of journalistically superficial and even vicious reactions which have created the myth of Schmidt as an enfant terrible and a rogue elephant among the postwar German literary fauna. Schmidt still needs to be discovered, both in Germany and abroad, as a challenging stylistic innovator—especially in the application of psychological insight to prose structure and typography–and as a master storyteller whose command of language and metaphor results in evocations of reality that are ever fresh and unforgettable. Schmidt has expanded the expressive limits of realist prose.

Arno Otto Schmidt was born on 18 January 1914 in Hamburg into a lower-class family with petit-bourgeois ambitions and pride. His father, starting out as a Silesian glassblower, had risen by way of a military career to the status of police sergeant. In his last completed work, *Abend mit Goldrand* (1975; translated as *Evening Edged in Gold,* 1980), Schmidt bares autobiographical de-

Schmidt in his study (Stahlberg-Verlag, Karlsruhe– Foto Barth)

tails from these early years that are full of resentment against a father he perceived as tyrannical, shallow, coarse, and obscene. In this work Schmidt traces the themes and preoccupations of his oeuvre to the isolation of an emotionally and sensorially (he suffered from undetected extreme myopia) deprived childhood and a lonely youth. He compensated with voracious and eclectic reading, which he blames for the development of an imagination that ended up feeding almost exclusively on literature rather than on reality. The young Schmidt removed himself to "cerebral worlds"; later the writer did the same, turning neurotic necessity into creative method. Alienated from external reality, his "synthetic" imagination fed on books and paintings. His early reading of Friedrich Heinrich Karl de la Motte Fouqué, Edgar Allan Poe, Jules Verne, and Karl May stayed with him; he hardly ever invented new plots, preferring to use modern perspective and insight to develop traditional forms and fables.

Schmidt entered high school at age ten. Four years later, in 1928, his father died, and the family moved to Lauban, Silesia. In 1933 Schmidt graduated from the gymnasium in Görlitz, "wo ich den Expressionismus pries–was mich folglich im Frühjahr 33 das 'Sehr gut' im Abschlußzeugnis kostete" (where I praised expressionism–which in the spring of 1933 cost me my "A" in German literature). During these years Schmidt began to collect material for a biography of the German romantic Fouqué that was published in 1958. Little else has apparently survived of Schmidt's early literary efforts except for "Pharos," which is included in *Abend mit Goldrand*. It is a powerful sketch in lyrical prose in which a young man describes his sufferings at the hands of a sadistic paternal figure; he is freed only when the tyrant dies. Schmidt claimed to have entered the university to study mathematics and astronomy in 1933, leaving a year later due to Nazi pressures because his older sister Luzie had married a Jew. Recent evidence suggests that Schmidt's claims to even the buds of academic laurels were entirely mythical. What is certain is that in 1934 Schmidt took employment in a textile mill, rising from apprentice to bookkeeper. In 1937 he married Alice Murawski, the sister of a friend. They had no children–supposedly a conscious decision made to help thwart the self-realization of an evil Schopenhauerian world-will.

In 1940 Schmidt was drafted; his library and manuscripts were largely lost in the Russian advance in Silesia. He saw little military action, spending most of the war with a coast defense unit in occupied Norway. There he wrote *Dichtergespräche im Elysium* (Conversations of Authors in Elysium, 1984). Intended as a gift for his wife, its perspective is even more subjective than is usual for Schmidt. It is touching in its private emotions even where the language seems a bit overblown. Clearly, Schmidt possessed verbal power as a native gift; if he learned anything, it was discipline and economy. At the end of 1945 Schmidt was released from a British POW camp near Brussels.

Unable to return to Silesia because of the Soviet occupation, the Schmidts lived as refugees in Cordingen, a small town in the Lüneburg Heath; Schmidt eked out a precarious living, first as an interpreter, then as a free-lance writer. The ensuing years were miserable ones, not conducive to brightening a deeply pessimistic personal philosophy.

Schmidt's first published book, *Leviathan* (1949), comprises three stories in diary form; two of them, "Gadir oder Erkenne Dich Selbst" (Gadir; or, Know Thyself) and "Enthymesis oder W. I. E. H.," are set in antiquity; the title story takes place in 1945. "Gadir" is reminiscent of Ambrose Bierce's "An Occurrence at Owl Creek Bridge" (1891); it focuses on the last hours of Pytheas of Massilia, whom Schmidt admired for his early and isolated insistence that the Earth is a sphere. The protagonist of "Enthymesis" is Philostratos, a surveyor whose rejection of society–W. I. E. H. stands for "Wie Ich Euch Hasse" (How I Hate You)–leads him away from a desert expedition into a mythical world. The nameless protagonist of "Leviathan" leaves a diary in which he describes his escape from the advancing Soviets, up to the moment when he jumps to his death from a boxcar stuck on the remaining pillar of a blown-up bridge into the river far below. Thus all three stories present existential threshold situations in a cold, hostile world ruled by a diabolical principle, the Leviathan which encompasses all humanity. While Schmidt shared in the Mainz Academy Prize of 1950, apparently at the urging of Alfred Döblin, the small edition of his first book did not sell out for years. His next two books did not fare any better.

"Man is an island" could be the motto for *Leviathan* as well as for the next three novels, published in two volumes in 1951 and 1953. This trilogy echoes the preceding one in its insistence that human beings are the abandoned offspring of a hostile, diabolical father, the Blakean cosmic demon Nobodaddy. Schmidt's protagonists are middle-aged men, isolated and alienated from the world and themselves. They reject metaphysical speculation and hope as futile. One had better stick to one's own reason and senses; they at least are certain, if limited. Positivism, close realistic observation, empirical data, instinct, and sexuality form the elements of these early works, which shun the grand vision in favor of collagelike fragments held together by associative logic. To Schmidt statistics, lists of names, maps, and photos are seeds which blossom forth into metamorphosed reality through the writer's imagination. In these Schmidt meant to give that portrait of his own time that he thought every writer owes posterity.

The first two parts of the trilogy were published in 1951 in the volume *Brand's Haide* (Brand's Heath). "Brand's Haide" and "Schwarze

Spiegel" (Black Mirrors) are short novels in diary form. The protagonist of the former is a just-released POW named Schmidt, who is writing a Fouqué biography. He has been allotted a hole-in-the-wall in Cordingen, Lüneburg Heath, where he shares with the two girls in the adjoining room the misery of refugee existence among inhospitable natives. He falls in love, but the affair has an unhappy ending. It is a typical Schmidt story, evoking fragments of everyday life in pointillistic sketches. The story is intentionally banal, at times uncomfortably close to bathos, yet in the final analysis it is one of Schmidt's virtuoso demonstrations that for the true artist there are no trivial subjects. "Schwarze Spiegel" is located in what Schmidt regarded as a certain future: the world after the atomic holocaust which he believed would be the imminent and logical consequence of the militaristic, reactionary, and acultural society he saw arising in the "new" Germany. In the musings of the lone survivor among the skeletons and ruins, the main theme is that of a Robinson Crusoe in a tabula rasa world, free to start from scratch.

In 1953 the third part of the trilogy was added, covering the prewar and war years: *Aus dem Leben eines Fauns* (translated as *Scenes from the Life of a Faun*, 1983). The faun is Heinrich Düring, a minor civil servant as alienated from the Nazi state as he is from society and his family. Facets of Nazi fanaticism and cruelty appear briefly, the way they did to most Germans at the time: as isolated incidents, not too disquieting–an evil the less obvious for its banality. Düring keeps his own counsel; he is an example of the questionable reaction of "inner emigration." He tries to drop out into his own intellectual world, into a love affair, and into nature–like another faun before him, who, as the archives show, had haunted the heath as a deserter from the Napoleonic army. Düring, however, cannot escape; Arcadian retreats are not available under totalitarianism. The novel is pervaded by images of a frozen world illuminated by a gelid, hostile moon, with horrors lurking below the surface. In 1963 the trilogy was republished in one volume as *Nobodaddy's Kinder* (Nobodaddy's Children).

In the course of a refugee redistribution program the Schmidts were moved south to a village near Mainz. The experience was treated in *Die Umsiedler* (The Resettlers, 1953). Otto Kühl resettles with Katrin, a newfound love, fellow refugee, and war victim, in a modest corner amid the bigotry and provincialism of the natives. The vol-

Cover of Schmidt's 1970 magnum opus

ume contains another story, "Alexander oder Was ist Wahrheit" (Alexander; or, What Is Truth), set in the camp of Alexander the Great; intentional anachronisms make clear the parallels Schmidt saw between Alexandrianism and modern totalitarian decadence. The subtitle of the volume is *2 Prosastudien (Kurzformen zur Wiedergabe mehrfacher räumlicher Verschiebung der Handelnden bei festgehaltener Einheit der Zeit)* (2 Prose Studies [in Short Forms Designed to Reproduce Multiple Spatial Dislocation of the Protagonists, with Unity of Time Preserved]).

Kosmas oder Vom Berge des Nordens (Kosmas; or, From the Mountains of the North, 1955) is the last of Schmidt's stories set in antiquity, in this case late-Hellenistic Thrace at the time when enlightened paganism gives way to a bullying and bigoted Christianity. As in the other stories the evocation of a past world is convincing. At the same time the application to modern Germany, then ruled by Konrad Adenauer's Christian Democratic party, is clear. Also in 1955 the new and short-lived periodical *Texte und Zeichen*, edited by

Alfred Andersch, published the first of Schmidt's "Berechnungen" (Calculations), three essays in which he expounded his prose theory; the second appeared the following year. (The third was published in a different periodical in 1980.) The first issue also contained "Seelandschaft mit Pocahontas" (Lakescape with Pocahontas), which Günter Grass has called his favorite story. It is a touching tale of a brief summer affair between Joachim, a writer, and Selma Wientge, an awkward girl whose ugliness is transformed into exotic charm by his poetic-erotic vision. Bittersweet, gentle, yet unsentimental, the story resulted in indictments of Schmidt and the publisher for pornography and blasphemy.

Since 1951 the Schmidts had been living in Kastel on the Saar, a small town near Trier, in a strongly Catholic region. In 1955 they moved to the more liberal climate of Hesse, settling in Darmstadt. The charges against Schmidt and the magazine were dropped in 1956.

In the "Berechnungen" Schmidt gave what he had thought would be unnecessary explanations for the structure and typography of his works; these aspects had baffled and irritated readers and critics, to whom they had appeared as mere quirks and mannerisms. (Twenty-five years later the first English translations of Schmidt's works produced similar reactions.) Schmidt justified his techniques as ways of making literary expression conform more closely to the processes of mentation. According to Schmidt, carefully calculated typographic arrangement would trigger in the reader's mind the processes of recollecting and "mind gaming," making it seem as though the author's texts were the original productions or experiences of the reader. "Seelandschaft mit Pocahontas" is described as an experiment in reproducing the recollection of a somewhat distant past. Schmidt calls the story a "photo album"; reasoning that in recollecting a small complex of memories, such as a vacation, one relies on the snapshots one brought back to remember the whole context, Schmidt devised a graphic arrangement in which a series of short, bright verbal snapshots is followed by a "fleshed-out" text. The reader is guided along a chain of associations, each link of which is indicated by virgules which separate the individual fragments the way individual photos are framed on a filmstrip.

The dissociative structure of the Nobodaddy trilogy and the other novels from the 1950s follows from the attempt to modernize the diary form: even though the short-term memory remembers more details than the "photo album," it is still a sieve that retains only the more significant moments of a day. As Düring puts it in *Aus dem Leben eines Fauns: "Mein Leben?!: ist kein Kontinuum!"* (*My life?!: is not a continuum!*). Man's consciousness is an epic cataract "der von Stufe zu Stufe schäumt, Zerfall als Voraussetzung überlegenen Schauspiels, der aber, siehe da, eben so sicher unten ankommt, wie Ol' Man River" (foaming from ledge to ledge; dissociation as the prerequisite of a superior spectacle, yet the river reaches its level as surely as does Ol' Man River). Typographically, the stages of that cataract appear as paragraphs, a short, italicized introductory phrase serving as the ledge which disperses the verbal flow into a luminous spray of textual droplets that are striking and evocative, even where they seem accidental or gratuitous. Schmidt points out that the personality, as well as the world it "emanates," do not form a consistent order in any traditional sense. Order there is, but it is the hidden order of psychological association, which may superficially appear as the skip and jump of unfettered fancy. Thus close, active reading of Schmidt's works reveals the interdependence of the parts. Schmidt never *describes* what he wants the reader to feel; instead, he attempts to evoke the feeling itself. He activates the imagination through metaphorical intensity and economical concentration. That the resulting prose has the appeal of great immediacy and vividness, an appeal that does not wane with repeated readings, is indicative of the theory's aesthetic validity–even if the theory is not in agreement with recent theories of cognition.

Schmidt's next two novels also belong to the diary genre. *Das steinerne Herz* (A Heart of Stone) appeared in 1956. According to the author, it was intended as a character study of the "collector" personality, as a depiction of the decline and formation of interhuman relations, and as a depiction of East German reality. Walter Eggers ("alter ego") is a ruthless collector of Court calendars of the Hanoverian kingdom; he insinuates himself into the household of Frieda Thumann, whom he seduces because he rightly assumes that as a descendant of the compiler of the calendars she may have all that he is lusting after: "Schlüssel zu einer Bücherkammer *und* ein strammes weißes Weib: was will man mehr als Mann?!" (Key to a bookroom and a strapping white woman! What more can a man want?). A missing volume is stolen from the East Berlin State Library. In spite of the outrageous plot of the novel, it is one of the first serious West German literary depictions of the East German state.

Die Gelehrtenrepublik (1957; translated as *The Egghead Republic*, 1979) is another in that series of post-atomic-war negative utopias. The protagonist is George Winer, an American journalist from Kalamazoo and great-nephew of the writer Arno Schmidt. In the early years of the twenty-first century Winer travels through a radiation zone in the United States filled with mutants ranging from attractive centaur girls to horrible spider-people. Europe is gone; German is a dead language. Winer's destination is an artificial island jointly administered by the United States and the Soviet Union that is a cultural preserve for the world's creative geniuses, who loaf, whore, and indulge in the same cold war that led to the atomic holocaust in the first place. The novel combines Schmidt's cultural pessimism with biting, effective satire and a mystery story.

KAFF auch MARE CRISIUM (ONE-HORSE TOWN alias MARE CRISIUM, 1960) is probably the best thing Schmidt ever wrote. It is, once again, a banal story: two lovers take time off from work for an overnight visit to the countryside, where they walk, talk, make love, and sightsee. Deeper down, however, the novel operates on several skillfully interwoven levels, as suggested by its title and typographic structure. It is set both in the outer reality of the "Kaff " (one-horse town) Karl and Hertha visit–clearly based on Bargfeld, where Schmidt moved in 1958–and, via a story within the story, on the moon's Mare Crisium. Karl is filled with obsessions which he sublimates via the "mind game" he invents about an American and Soviet colony on the moon that came into being after atomic war has left Earth a dead and glowing orb. "Mare Crisium" also refers to the "sea of troubles" in Karl's mind. It is this deep sea of Karl's psyche which Schmidt meant when he referred to *KAFF auch MARE CRISIUM* as an attempt to present "das komplette Porträt eines Menschen in einem gegebenen Zeitraum x" (the complete portrait of a person within a certain period of time). The obvious debt to James Joyce is acknowledged indirectly: Karl carries a copy of *The Essential Joyce*. But Schmidt goes beyond his great precursor in that he makes psychological association as creative method both the subject and the technique of his book. Karl reveals himself both in the way in which he associatively reacts to the external

world and in what he actively does with these stimuli. The novel is a portrait of the subconscious of the artist as a middle-aged man: as a bookkeeper, Karl turns "senseless" facts into patterns imbued with sense–which is exactly what the positivist artist such as Schmidt does in his writings. In inventing the lunar fantasy Karl is also directly an artist, a parody of the creator who converts the accidental sounds he encounters into sounds signifying something. Schmidt uses two columns of print to distinguish between outer and inner reality. Because this portrait paints itself with those dots of time that are present-turning-past, this novel is richer than the "memory" novels. It reproduces in their visual immediacy ephemeral nonverbal gestures which words could only grasp in lumbering paraphrase: single or multiple question and exclamation marks express querying glances or triumphant gestures and the degree of their intensity; parentheses fix those fleeting moments in which face or motion betray reservation, doubt, or anticipation, or they contain preverbal insights, digressions, and asides. Such evocative economy demonstrates in a masterly fashion that less is more.

Throughout Schmidt's works the protagonists voice opinions, predilections, and peeves regarding all sorts of things, including literature, with a consistency and tenor that mark them as the author's own. Such judgments are usually unsupported by evidence, but they show how widely Schmidt was reading, especially writers of the late eighteenth and nineteenth centuries. He also wrote on literature. His Fouqué biography, *Fouqué und einige seiner Zeitgenossen* (Fouqué and Some of His Contemporaries), finally appeared in 1958. With exhaustive precision Schmidt had collected everything concerning his subject that he was able to find. His scholarship is unassailable; some Germanists felt that it should have merited at least an honorary doctorate. *Fouqué* is also a product of Schmidt's apocalyptic vision: convinced of imminent destruction, he felt that his effort might be an incentive to others to preserve irreplaceable documents through collection and inclusion in books. The preoccupation with Fouqué yielded much spin-off material that Schmidt presented in newspaper articles and in radio essays commissioned by Andersch. Several of these dramatized, conversational portraits of nearly forgotten literary figures were broadcast in 1957. Book publication of these efforts began in 1958 with *Dya na sore: Gespräche in einer Bibliothek*, consisting of nine "conversations in a li-

*Dust jacket designed by Franz Greno for Schmidt's 1972
novel about the survivors of a nuclear war*

brary" and a story, "Tina oder Über die
Unsterblichkeit" (Tina; or, Concerning Immortality). In 1961 there followed *Belphegor: Nachrichten
von Büchern und Menschen* (Belphegor: Tidings of
Books and Men), and in 1965 *Die Ritter vom Geist:
Von vergessenen Kollegen* (The Knighthood of the
Intellect: On Forgotten Colleagues). In all, there
are twenty-two essays ranging in subject from Goethe to Karl May and in tone from high praise to
iconoclastic polemics. Goethe is criticized for his
Olympian stance and presumed lack of talent for
prose structure, as is Adalbert Stifter for shirking
his social realist responsibilities and for plagiarizing James Fenimore Cooper. Ludwig Tieck is one
of Schmidt's heroes, for the realist component of
his work; so are Christoph Wieland and others
whose concern with prose form makes them forerunners of writers such as Schmidt. His pets are
the "Gehirntiere" (cerebral beasts) of the Enlightenment. This concern with "forgotten colleagues" earned him some sneers from Germanists who forgot that survival in a German seminar is not the type of immortality to which the art-

ist aspires. The essays are refreshing reading
even for experts; they inspire the reader to reexamine the canon, even where they are polemical
"acts of compensatory injustice"–as Schmidt
dubbed an essay on Stifter's *Der Nachsommer*
(1857), a work he thought overrated. The essays
place the books and personalities in the social context of their time. Several of Schmidt's rediscoveries have, as a result of his work, been published
anew.

The influence of Freud sets a caesura between Schmidt's work up to *KAFF auch MARE
CRISIUM* and his later work. His entire oeuvre is
concerned with developing prose structures conforming as much as possible to reality; in the late
work, however, it is a reality even more internal
than cognitive processes: the way in which the subconscious determines literary language. In 1963
Schmidt published *Sitara und der Weg dorthin*
(Sitara and the Road Thither), a study of the astounding success May's trivial stories had with generations of German youth, including the young
Schmidt. According to this study, the impact on
preadolescent readers is due to May's latent homosexuality, which Schmidt found evidenced in encoded words or phonemes as well as in recurrent
set-pieces Schmidt claimed are replete with anal
symbolism. Schmidt also found such conversion
of repressed sexual energy into artistic achievement in the words of Edgar Allan Poe, which he
was translating. Out of such discoveries he distilled the "Etym" theory, which claims that words
are stored in the brain in homophone order; supposedly, this procedure allows the subconscious to "sing along," if not in whole words
then in acoustic morphemes or "etyms," in a
lower voice beneath the surface meaning. While
Poe or May would have remained unaware of
what they were really saying, writers such as
Joyce and Schmidt were sufficiently aware of the
tricks of the subconscious to etymistically encode
their texts deliberately.

In 1964 Schmidt received the Berlin
Fontane Prize, with Günter Grass giving the laudation. In the same year, *Kühe in Halbtrauer* (Cows
in Semimourning) appeared. (The title refers to
the black and white Holsteins typical of northern
Germany.) This collection of ten stories, six of
which had been published in a student newspaper, showed little of the typographical experimentation of Schmidt's previous fiction and seemed
straightforward in content. Schmidt had always
maintained that it was the prose writer's job not
to describe great catastrophes but to make small

events and details interesting. Here he seemed to have succeeded completely in writing banally idyllic vignettes of bucolic life. Yet he also suggested that a considerable amount of artistic subtlety and complexity had gone into these stories. The verbal mastery, including phonetically faithful rendering of dialect, was obvious. But there were clearly intentional details, word choices, apparent non sequiturs, and deflections of attention which suggested that there had to be a deeper stratum below idyllic pointlessness. Eventually, critics decided that some of the stories were built on the logic of dreams, that they were utterances in which the protagonists were externalizing their fears of impotence or homosexuality. The stories can be read on several levels, including that of myth, and in intricate interrelation to one another.

In 1965 Schmidt received a prize sponsored by German industry, the Ehrengabe für Literatur des Kulturkreises der deutschen Industrie.

Another collection appeared the following year. *Trommler beim Zaren* (Drummer at the Court of the Tsar) consists of forty-two pieces which had appeared in newspapers as early as 1955. They range from the title story to literary discussions such as "Sylvie & Bruno," in which Schmidt says that Lewis Carroll's sensitivity to the multiple meanings of words makes him the "Father of the Church" of modern literature. The other pieces are anecdotal short stories and miscellanea of knowledge for the curious intellect, frequently debris from Schmidt's larger projects. They are always engaging because they, like all of Schmidt's writings, project the author's distinct and distorting perspective and challenge the reader to react, to become intellectually active.

Schmidt had a strong interest in English-language writers. Interest did not necessarily mean affection: he detested the works of William Faulkner, whose *New Orleans Sketches* (1958) he translated in 1962. He had little to say about writers of the twentieth century. In a review of a translation of *Tristram Shandy* (1760-1767) he included Laurence Sterne among "modernists" such as Carroll. In 1966 his cotranslation of the works of Poe began to appear; and he came to terms with Joyce, to whom he had been compared, concluding that there was not even an unconscious debt. Such preoccupations bore fruit in the volume *Der Triton mit dem Sonnenschirm: Großbritannische Gemütsergetzungen* (The Triton with the Parasol: Great Britannic Pleasures of the Mind, 1969), containing more radio features and essays on English-

language literary personalities: Cooper, the Brontë family, Wilkie Collins, Dickens, *Finnegans Wake* as an encoded tirade against Joyce's brother Stanislaus, a German model for Poe's "The Fall of the House of Usher," Edward Bulwer-Lytton.

In 1970 appeared a work that had been heralded as Schmidt's magnum opus, *Zettels Traum*. The title refers to the dream of Bottom the Weaver in Shakespeare's *A Midsummer Night's Dream* (Bottom is "Zettel" in the Schlegel-Tieck translation). *Bottom*, as the human posterior, is *Po* in German, which etymologically associates with *Poe*. Indeed the giant tome–1,352 pages of typescript, 13 inches by 17½ inches, photomechanically reproduced–could be termed an enormously enlarged and expanded radio essay on Poe. Here Schmidt expounds the theory of the etyms and uses it as the analytical tool to prove that great literary works result from less-than-noble impulses; he argues that repressed voyeurism, coprophilia, and impotence had been Poe's inspirations. Schmidt also attempts to demonstrate that art must speak not only with the voice of the ego but polyphonically, giving utterance to the id and superego, plus a humorous Schmidtian category, all at once. Under such theoretical weight, the skeletal story all but disappears: a married couple, both of them Poe translators, and their young daughter Franziska visit old Dän Pagenstecher, a Schmidt-like polyhistor in a Bargfeld-like village, to ask his advice. He holds forth, interrupted only by half-hearted demonstrations of love between himself and Franziska (an allusion to Poe's child bride) and by an excursion into the countryside in its earthly and mythical manifestations. Typographically the action proceeds down the middle of the page; the margins are reserved for Poe quotations and anonymous auctorial asides. Comprehension of their interdependence would demand a simultaneous reading of all three columns. Schmidt refers to this spatialization of time as a "Lese-Zylinder" (reading cylinder), visualizing the page curved back on itself so that the right and left margins would meet and mesh. Appraisals of the book have fluctuated between praise for "the book of the century" and comparison to a full-size replica of the Eiffel Tower, erected with matchsticks by a berserk hobbyist at the expense of his life.

The rest of Schmidt's books resemble *Zettels Traum* in format, structure, and linguistic technique, but are less complex. *Die Schule der Atheisten* (The Atheist's School, 1972) permits tra-

Arno Schmidt (photograph by Jörg Drews)

ditional reading, even though the plot is uncharacteristically intricate: the year is 2014; the locale is Tellingstedt near the Danish border, a reservation in which the few German survivors of the atomic war exist at the sufferance of the two world powers, a matriarchal United States and a patriarchal China. Envoys of the superpowers hold a summit at the house of William T. Kolderup and his granddaughter Suse. It turns out that there are connections between Kolderup and Isis, the man-devouring American secretary of state, dating back forty-five years when Kolderup was on board a ship also carrying the mother-to-be of Isis. His recollection becomes a story within the story—better, a play within the play, for the work is a "Lesedrama" (book-drama) subtitled *Novellen-Comödie in 6 Aufzügen* (Novella-Comedy in Six Acts). The title refers to the play within, in which a shipwreck turns out to be a test of the validity of the atheistic stance of certain characters. Yet in the end the plot seems unimportant. The work is enjoyable for readers

aspiring to a Schmidtian level of literacy: it is full of literary allusion, open and hidden; it is a collage of details, set pieces, motifs of works by Verne and Shakespeare, among others—more proof of a life spent in literature.

Schmidt's withdrawal from other reference points had become more and more evident in his hermeticism. A fence and trees shielded his house, into which he seemed to retreat hedgehog-like, launching defensive barbs against the world. But the world penetrated his retreat in the form of the Lord Mayor of Frankfurt am Main coming to ask if Schmidt would accept the city's prestigious Goethe Prize for 1973. The honoree sent his wife to Frankfurt to deliver an acceptance speech written by him that asserted that the poet must go his own way, isolated from king or ideology, and that the insistence on the forty-hour work week was a sign of decadence and laziness, at least in the eyes of a man whose work week had always had at least a hundred hours. In response, it was pointed out that there was little comparison between a production-line worker and someone who freely chose his way of life. Some also protested Schmidt's acceptance of a prize named for a figure he had never failed to attack. There can be no doubt that the Frankfurt affair confirmed Schmidt's insistence on isolation.

Abend mit Goldrand is set in what is clearly Bargfeld, in a house occupied by three old men, the wife and the stepdaughter of one of the men, and a housekeeper. It is a thorny idyll filled with discussions of books and reminiscences. Their life is interrupted by a group of orgiastic hippies who prove the pervasive and enduring power of sexuality, even over old fools. Only the most Schmidt-like of the figures, the improbably named A & O Gläser, is capable of a sublime love for the elfin leader of the hippies. The typography is reminiscent of that of *Zettels Traum*, for this work is also polyphonic; yet the various voices add up to a single person—the protagonists embody aspects of Schmidt's personality. A young Schmidt, called Martin, has convinced the three old men of his artistic talent with a piece called "Pharos"; he will be taken under their wings so that he will have it easier as a writer than they did. The book is clearly a stock-taking, an apologia; but Schmidt, like any true artist, goes beyond subjectivist eccentricity. *Abend mit Goldrand* is the artistic integration of a life spent in literature. This integration is the function of the fairy-tale dimension of the work. In a suspension of time, A & O is linked to the fairy-woman

Ann' Ev', his female alter ego, in an erotic though sexless love, not just in the here and now but in a sort of "eternal return"; they will meet again several hundred years from now, just as they are both present in the painting which is the secret center of the book, Bosch's *Garden of Delights*. According to A & O "Romane sind immer WunschErfüllungen" (all novels are fulfillments of wishes). All of this might be pathetic were it not for the beautiful aesthetic balance between acidly honest awareness of reality and the grace of an "old child" sovereignly playing with literary convention: the problems of aging and one writer's attempt at coming to terms with them have congealed in bittersweet and graceful synthesis, a ripeness one may attain only for moments. At the end of a "gold-rimmed" evening, A & O stands shuddering in the cold wind that has sprung up.

When Schmidt succumbed to a heart attack on 3 June 1979, he left a final work only one-third completed. The fragment, titled *Julia, oder die Gemälde: Scenen aus dem Novecento* (Julia; or, The Paintings: Scenes from the Novecento), was published in 1983 by Schmidt's widow in conjunction with the Arno Schmidt Stiftung, a foundation that became Schmidt's sole heir in 1983 when Alice Schmidt died. The foundation has been locked in a legal battle with Schmidt's publisher, the S. Fischer Verlag. An early resolution is in the interest not only of scholars and students in need of a critical edition but of the international reception of Arno Schmidt as an obscure yet major figure of world literature.

Letters:
Briefe an Werner Steinberg: 16 Briefe aus den Jahren 1954-1957 (Zurich: Haffmans, 1985);
Arno Schmidt: Der Briefwechsel mit Alfred Andersch: Die vollständige Korrespondenz 1952-1979 (Zurich: Arno Schmidt Stiftung im Haffmans Verlag, 1985).

Bibliographies:
Hans-Michael Bock, *Bibliographie Arno Schmidt 1949-1978* (Munich: Edition text + kritik, 1979);
Michael Matthias Schardt, *Bibliographie Arno Schmidt 1979-(?)1985: Mit Ergänzungen und Verbesserungen zur Arno-Schmidt-Bibliographie 1949-1978* (Aachen: Rader, 1985).

Biographies:
Porträt einer Klasse: Arno Schmidt zum Gedenken, edited by Ernst Krawehl (Frankfurt am Main: Fischer, 1982);
"Wu Hi?" Arno Schmidt in Görlitz Lauban Greiffenberg: Materialien für eine Biographie, Arno Schmidts Jahre 1928-1945, edited by Jan Philipp Reemtsma and Bernd Rauschenbach (Zurich: Haffmans, 1986).

References:
Robert M. Adams, "Devil's Brew," *New York Review of Books*, 28 (5 March 1981): 31-32;
Alfred Andersch, "Düsterhenns Dunkelstunde oder Ein längeres Gedankenspiel," *Merkur*, 26, no. 2 (1972): 133-144;
Hans-Michael Bock, ed., *Über Arno Schmidt: Rezensionen vom Leviathan bis zur Julia* (Zurich: Haffmans, 1984);
Wilfried von Bredow, "Der militante Eremit oder: Vom Schicksal eines westdeutschen Jakobiners," *Kürbiskern*, 4 (1970): 598-610;
Reimer Bull, *Bauformen des Erzählens bei Arno Schmidt: Ein Beitrag zur Poetik der Erzählkunst* (Bonn: Bouvier, 1970);
Horst Denkler, "Das heulende Gelächter des Gehirntiers: Vorläufiger Bericht über *Zettels Traum* von Arno Schmidt," *Basis*, 2 (1971): 246-259;
Denkler, "What will he do with it? Arno Schmidts Weg von *Zettels Traum* zur *Schule der Atheisten*," *Basis*, 4 (1973): 251-256;
Jörg Drews, "Caliban casts out Ariel: Zum Verhältnis von Mythos und Psychoanalyse in Arno Schmidts Erzählung 'Caliban über Setebos,'" *Protokolle*, 2 (1981): 145-160;
Drews and Bock, eds., *Der Solipsist in der Heide: Materialien zum Werk Arno Schmidts* (Munich: Edition text + kritik, 1974);
Werner Eggers, "Arno Schmidt," in *Deutsche Literatur der Gegenwart in Einzeldarstellungen*, edited by Dietrich Weber, volume 1 (Stuttgart: Kröner, 1976), pp. 312-337;
Ulrich Goerdten, "Symbolisches im Genitalgelände: Arno Schmidts 'Windmühlen' als Traumtext gelesen," *Protokolle*, 1 (1980): 3-28;
Goerdten, "Zeichensprache, Wurzelholz und Widerstand: Arno Schmidts Erzählung 'Kühe in Halbtrauer' als Vier-Instanzen-Prosa gelesen," *Protokolle*, 1 (1982): 61-80;
Jürgen Grambow, "Hinweis auf A.S.," *Sinn und Form*, 32, no. 4 (1980): 868-883;

Günter Häntzschel, "Arno Schmidt: Ein verkannter Idylliker. Schwierigkeiten beim Bewerten eines unbequemen Autors," *Germanisch-Romanische Monatsschrift,* 26, no. 3/4 (1976): 307-321;

David Hayman, "Some Writers in the Wake of the *Wake,*" in *In the Wake of the "Wake,"* edited by Hayman and Elliott Anderson (Madison: University of Wisconsin Press, 1978), pp. 3-38;

Helmut Heißenbüttel, "Annäherung an Arno Schmidt," in his *Über Literatur: Aufsätze* (Olten: Walter, 1966), pp. 56-70;

Boy Hinrichs, *Utopische Prosa als längeres Gedankenspiel: Untersuchungen zu Arno Schmidts Theorie der modernen Literatur und ihrer Konkretisierung in "Schwarze Spiegel," "Die Gelehrtenrepublik" und "Kaff auch Mare Crisium"* (Tübingen: Niemeyer, 1984);

Michael Minden, *Arno Schmidt: A Critical Study of His Prose* (Cambridge: Cambridge University Press, 1982);

Hans-Bernhard Moeller, "Perception, Word-Play, and the Printed Page: Arno Schmidt and His Poe Novel," *Books Abroad,* 45 (Winter 1971): 25-30;

Hugo J. Mueller, "Arno Schmidts Etymtheorie," *Wirkendes Wort,* 25 (1975): 37-44;

Friedrich Peter Ott, "Gedankenspiel als (Selbst-) Porträt: Arno Schmidts *Kaff auch Mare Crisium,*" *Protokolle,* 1 (1982): 35-48;

Ott, "Tradition and Innovation: An Introduction to the Prose Theory and Practice of Arno Schmidt," *German Quarterly,* 51 (January 1978): 19-38;

Tony Phelan, *Rationalist Narrative in Some Works of Arno Schmidt* (Coventry: University of Warwick, 1972);

Heiko Postma, *Aufarbeitung und Vermittlung literarischer Traditionen,* second edition (Frankfurt am Main: Bangert & Metzler, 1984);

Siegbert S. Prawer, " 'Bless Thee, Bottom! Bless Thee! Thou Art Translated': Typographical Parallelism, Word-Play and Literary Allusion in Arno Schmidt's *Zettels Traum,*" in *Essays in German and Dutch Literature,* edited by W. D. Scott-Robson (London: Institute of Germanic Studies, 1973), pp. 156-191;

Review of Contemporary Fiction, Arno Schmidt number, edited by Ott, 8 (Spring 1988);

Karl Heinz Schauder, "Arno Schmidts experimentelle Prosa," *Neue Deutsche Hefte,* 99 (1964): 39-62;

Gerhard Schmidt-Henkel, "Arno Schmidt," in *Deutsche Dichter der Gegenwart,* edited by Benno von Wiese (Berlin: Schmidt, 1973), pp. 261-276;

Schmidt-Henkel, "Arno Schmidt und seine *Gelehrtenrepublik,*" *Zeitschrift für deutsche Philologie,* 87, no. 4 (1968): 563-591;

Wolfram Schütte, "Das Bargfelder Ich: Reflexionen über das Werk Arno Schmidts," *Neue Rundschau,* 84, no. 3 (1973): 531-545;

Schütte, "Die unbekannte Größe: Arno Schmidt– unsere Gegenwart, seine Nachwelt," *Merkur,* 39, no. 7 (1981): 558-573;

Dieter H. Stündel, *Arno Schmidt: Zettels Traum* (Frankfurt am Main & Bern: Lang, 1982);

Heinrich Vormweg, "Der Fall Arno Schmidt," in *Die Literatur der Bundesrepublik Deutschland,* edited by Dieter Lattmann (Munich & Zurich: Kindler, 1973), pp. 270-279;

Vormweg, "Traum eines Babylonikers," *Merkur,* 25, no. 4 (1971): 354-361;

Robert Weninger, *Arno Schmidts Joyce-Rezeption 1957-1970* (Frankfurt am Main: Lang, 1982);

Hans Wollschläger, *Die Insel und einige andere Metaphern für Arno Schmidt: Rede zur Verleihung des Arno Schmidt Preises am 18. Januar 1982 in Bargfeld* (Bargfeld: Arno Schmidt Stiftung, 1982).

Papers:
Arno Schmidt's literary bequest and library are in the hands of the Arno Schmidt Stiftung, D-3101 Bargfeld, West Germany.

Wolfdietrich Schnurre

(22 August 1920-   )

Wulf Koepke

Texas A&M University

BOOKS: *Rettung des deutschen Films: Eine Streitschrift* (Stuttgart: Deutsche Verlags-Anstalt, 1950);

Die Rohrdommel ruft jeden Tag (Berlin & Witten: Ekkart, 1950);

Kalünz ist keine Insel: Eine Erzählung (Zurich: Arche, 1952);

Sternstaub und Sänfte: Aufzeichnungen des Pudels Ali (Berlin: Herbig, 1953); republished as *Die Aufzeichnungen des Pudels Ali* (Olten & Freiburg im Breisgau: Walter, 1962);

Die Blumen des Herrn Albin: Aus dem Tagebuch eines Sanftmütigen (Frankfurt am Main: Bärmeier & Nikel, 1955);

Kassiber (Frankfurt am Main: Suhrkamp, 1956);

Abendländler (Munich: Langen-Müller, 1957);

Protest im Parterre (Munich: Langen-Müller, 1957);

Als Vaters Bart noch rot war: Ein Roman in Geschichten (Zurich: Arche, 1958);

Die Flucht nach Ägypten: Geschichten (Zurich: Arche, 1958);

Eine Rechnung, die nicht aufgeht: Erzählungen (Olten & Freiburg im Breisgau: Walter, 1958);

Anaximanders Ende: Kammeroper in einem Akt, text by Schnurre, music by Werner Thärichen (Berlin & Wiesbaden: Bote & Bock, 1958);

Barfußgeschöpfe (Munich: Steinklopfer, 1958);

Das Los unserer Stadt: Eine Chronik (Olten & Freiburg im Breisgau: Walter, 1959; revised edition, Munich: Deutscher Taschenbuch Verlag, 1963);

Man sollte dagegen sein: Geschichten (Olten & Freiburg im Breisgau: Walter, 1960; edited by Roderick Watt and Ursula Smith, Portsmouth, N.H.: Heinemann Educational Books, 1982);

Jenö war mein Freund, edited by Fritz Bachmann (Frankfurt am Main: Hirschgraben-Verlag, 1960);

Berlin: Eine Stadt wird geteilt (Olten & Freiburg im Breisgau: Walter, 1962);

Ein Fall für Herrn Schmidt: Erzählungen (Stuttgart: Reclam, 1962);

Die Mauer des 13. August (Berlin: Stanek, 1962);

Funke im Reisig: Erzählungen (Olten & Freiburg im Breisgau: Walter, 1963);

Die Gläsernen: Hörspiel (Paderborn: Schöningh, 1963);

Die Tat: Erzählungen, Geschichten, Fabeln (Lübeck & Hamburg: Matthiesen, 1964);

Die Reise zur Babuschka (Groningen: Noordhoff, 1964); enlarged as *Die Reise zur Babuschka und andere Erzählungen*, by Schnurre and Peter Bichsel (Bern: Wagner, 1969);

Man muß auch mal Ferien machen: Fünf heitere Geschichten mit Bildern vom Verfasser (Freiburg im Breisgau: Hyperion, 1964);

Kassiber: Neue Gedichte. Formel und Dechiffrierung (Frankfurt am Main: Suhrkamp, 1964);

Ohne Einsatz kein Spiel (Olten & Freiburg im Breisgau: Walter, 1964);

Schreibtisch unter freiem Himmel: Polemik und Bekenntnis (Olten & Freiburg im Breisgau: Walter, 1964);

Die Erzählungen (Olten & Freiburg im Breisgau: Walter, 1966);

Freundschaft mit Adam (Baden-Baden: Signal, 1966);

Spreezimmer möbliert: Hörspiele (Munich: Deutscher Taschenbuch Verlag, 1967);

Was ich für mein Leben gern tue: Hand- und Fußnoten (Neuwied: Luchterhand, 1967);

Das Schwein, das zurückkam: Ein Spiel (Zurich: Arche, 1967);

Eine schöne Bescherung: Erzählung (Recklinghausen: Paulus, 1967);

Rapport des Verschonten: Geschichten (Zurich: Arche, 1968);

Richard kehrt zurück: Kurzroman einer Epoche (Zurich: Arche, 1970);

Die Wandlung des Hippipotamos, nachempfunden, gezeichnet und aufgeschrieben (Reutlingen: Ensslin & Laiblin, 1970);

Schnurre heiter (Olten & Freiburg im Breisgau: Walter, 1970);

Wolfdietrich Schnurre

Gocko, by Schnurre and Marina Schnurre (Munich: Parabel, 1970);

Wie der Koala-Bär wieder lachen lernte, by Schnurre and Marina Schnurre (Zurich & Freiburg im Breisgau: Atlantis, 1971);

Der Spatz in der Hand: Fabeln und Verse (Munich: Langen-Müller, 1971);

Meine Oasen; Meine fünf Schicksalsbücher (Basel: Realgymnasium, 1971);

Immer mehr Meerschweinchen (Recklinghausen: Bitter, 1971);

Der Meerschweinchendieb: Eine Bildgeschichte (Recklinghausen: Bitter, 1972);

Ich frag ja bloß (Munich: List, 1973);

Auf Tauchstation und 18 weitere Begebenheiten (Frankfurt am Main, Berlin & Vienna: Ullstein, 1973);

Die Weihnachtsmannaffäre: Erzählung (Zurich: Arche, 1974);

Schnurren und Murren: Ein Buch für Kinder (Recklinghausen: Bitter, 1974);

Der wahre Noah: Neuestes aus der Sintflutforschung, dargestellt in Bild und Bericht (Zurich: Arche, 1975);

Ich brauch dich (Munich: List, 1976);

Eine schwierige Reparatur: Erzählung (Düsseldorf: Eremiten-Presse, 1976);

Erzählungen 1945-1965 (Munich: List, 1977);

Der Schattenfotograf: Aufzeichnungen (Munich: List, 1978);

Klopfzeichen (Gütersloh: Gütersloher Verlagshaus Mohn, 1978);

Erfülltes Dasein: Aus der nachgelassenen Papieren des Oberverwaltungsinspektors Karlheinz Krenzke (Düsseldorf: Eremiten-Presse, 1979);

Peter Umlauf: Werkverzeichnis 1969-79 (Munich: Galerie & Editions A, 1980);

Ein Unglücksfall: Roman (Munich: List, 1981);

Twelve Stories, edited by Jack Stevenson and Bernfried Nugel (London: Bell & Hyman, 1982);

Climb, but Downward: Poems, translated by Jorn K. Bramann (Friendsville, Md.: Acheron Press, 1983);

Gelernt ist gelernt: Gesellenstücke (Frankfurt am Main & Berlin: Ullstein, 1984).

Wolfdietrich Schnurre, one of the original members of the writers' association Gruppe 47, writes successful short stories and novels with episodic structures. He has also written radio plays and poems. Many of his works are humorous or satirical and are illustrated with witty sketches by the author. His work does not aspire to be great literature, but he has a secure place as a representative of the first generation of German writers after World War II.

Schnurre was born in Frankfurt in 1920; his father, Otto Schnurre, was a librarian and scientist. In 1928 the family moved to Berlin, where Schnurre attended a socialist elementary school until 1934 and a humanistic secondary school from 1935 until 1939. The boy became familiar with the working-class neighborhoods of Berlin, where unemployment was high; where many types of people, including Jews and Gypsies, mingled; and where the political orientation was mostly Communist or social democrat. He was drafted into the armed forces when the war broke out in 1939 and became a reluctant fighter for his country. He was wounded several times; finally, he deserted and was taken prisoner by the Americans. The end of the war was followed by a nervous breakdown which incapacitated him until 1946. After recovering, he began his career as a writer in Berlin.

Schnurre worked as a theater and film critic from 1946 to 1949 and still occasionally writes literary criticism; but he has never been much given to theories and general statements. In the first years after World War II, the reaction against wartime propaganda prompted writers such as Walter Kolbenhoff to call for a literature of factual truth and realism. Schnurre countered with the concept of a Magischer Realismus (magical realism), a realism which would allow poetic imagination to run free. In a 1977 interview Schnurre credited his short story "Das Begräbnis" (The Funeral, 1946) with having generated the concept. The story is entirely realistic, except that "a certain Klott or Gott" is buried; the association with the idea that God is dead moves the action into a different sphere. In Schnurre's realism a light of symbolism or myth shines through the darkness of incomprehensible facts. In September 1947 Schnurre and Kolbenhoff attended the first meeting of the Gruppe 47, founded by Hans Werner Richter and Alfred Andersch; Schnurre left the group in 1951.

Compared to writers like Heinrich Böll or Günter Grass, Schnurre has remained within a rather narrow range of themes, styles, and narrative forms. Like Böll, he is plagued by the memory of the wrongs done during the Nazi period and of having fought the wrong war. More than

Schnurre in 1964 (Ullstein–Fritz Eschen)

most other writers, he continues to treat the plight of the victims of Nazi rule and criticizes the indifference with which much of postwar German society has treated these victims.

Some of Schnurre's works are collections of diarylike entries. He began this practice with *Sternstaub und Sänfte: Aufzeichnungen des Pudels Ali* (Stardust and Sedan Chair: The Notes of Ali the Poodle, 1953), in which a most human poodle who is a writer of esoteric sonnets and an aesthete records his love affairs, his literary successes and failures, and his political tribulations. Schnurre also used such short entries to compose *Der Schattenfotograf* (The Shadow Photographer, 1978), which offers hardly any story line but many observations on diverse subjects.

A typical Schnurre story is the radio play "Spreezimmer möbliert" (Furnished Room with View on the Spree, 1955), the title piece in a 1967 collection. A young scholar moves into a furnished room above the river Spree in East Berlin and begins to communicate with the voices of people who lived in the room before him, from the pre-World War I period through the war, the hard times of the 1920s, the Nazi period and World War II, and the postwar division of the city. The play is a short history in dialogues of Berlin in the twentieth century.

Schnurre makes fun of prejudices, such as those against modern art, and of the smugness with which most people regard the rest of the world. He sees things from unexpected perspectives. One of his short animal fables, from *Protest im Parterre* (Protest in the Orchestra Pit, 1957), illustrates these qualities:

Der Ausstellungsbesucher

Ein Affe entdeckte in einem zersplitterten Spiegel sein Konterfei. "Grauenhaft, diese Abstrakten," sagte er schaudernd.

(The Museum Visitor

A monkey discovered his image in a cracked mirror. "Horrible, these abstract painters," he said and shuddered.)

Als Vaters Bart noch rot war (When Father's Beard Was Still Red, 1958) is a novel about ten years in a boy's life with his father, narrated by the son. As each episode is a story in itself with a new cast of characters, except for father and son, the novel is subtitled *Roman in Geschichten* (Novel Composed of Stories). The father is a model of compassion and independent thinking: his refusal to put a sword into the claws of a stuffed eagle he restores results in his dismissal from his museum job and his persecution by the Gestapo. Most of the stories have a humorous twist, but humor turns into tragedy when one character dies for his anti-Nazi convictions and when the boy's Gypsy friend Jenö is deported. In the final episode father and son travel to Kalünz, an estate near the Polish border. Their host, a baron, tries to insulate himself and his relatives and friends from the outside world; but on New Year's Eve, 1938, the guests themselves rebel against their isolation. Kalünz, the last refuge, will be drawn into the catastrophic events of 1939.

Schnurre writes on the borderline between realism and surrealism; he also carries absurd propositions to their logical or illogical conclusions. In *Das Los unserer Stadt* (The Fate of Our Town, 1959), he describes the progressive destruction of a city and its way of life and the final escape of the narrator. The narration is split into small segments, and the connections between the paragraphs are by no means obvious. It is a strange world which emerges from these notes;

all of the details are realistic, but the whole is as bizarre and fantastic as the world of Kafka.

While humor is rarely absent from Schnurre's short stories, he also aspires to be a serious poet. Although Schnurre is a confirmed city dweller, most of his poems celebrate nature's victories over man's encroachment. An example is the poem "Wahrheit" (Truth), from the 1964 collection *Kassiber: Neue Gedichte* (Clandestine Communications between Prisoners: New Poems):

Ich war vierzehn, da sah ich,
im Holunder aß eine Amsel
von den Beeren der Dolde.

Gesättigt, flog sie zur Mauer
und strich sich an dem Gestein
einen Samen vom Schnabel.

Ich war vierzig, da sah ich,
auf der geborstnen Betonschicht
wuchs ein Holunder. Die Wurzeln

hatten die Mauer gesprengt,
ein Riß klaffte in ihr,
bequem zu durchschreiten.

Mit splitterndem Mörtel
schrieb ich daneben: "Die Tat
einer Amsel."

(I was fourteen, there I saw
A blackbird in the elder tree
Eating of the berries of the umbel.

Satisfied she flew to a wall
And on the rock she wiped
A seed from her bill.

I was forty, there I saw
On the cracked layer of concrete
An elder growing. The roots

Had cracked the wall,
A gap was opened in it,
Easy to march through.

With a piece of splintered mortar
I wrote next to it: "The deed
of a blackbird.")

Not all of Schnurre's poems are narrative: many are surrealistic. Still "Wahrheit" is typical in showing how the weak can conquer the strong, how what seems hard and durable may be vulnerable. Schnurre's poetry is without rhymes and fixed meters, mostly without regular stanzas, and is often

Schnurre in 1983, the year he won the Georg Büchner Prize
(Ullstein–Horst Tappe)

epigrammatic. Schnurre has said that he does not hurry his poetic production; his poems are rewritten many times, until the words and images are clear, sharp, and right.

Schnurre frequently writes about people on the fringes of society. *Ohne Einsatz kein Spiel* (No Game without Stakes, 1964), for example, shows how a police inspector tricks a family of professional thieves. It is a story in dialogues, in which the characters come alive and reveal their personalities and life stories through their own words. Another volume of dialogues, *Ich brauch dich* (I Need You, 1976), depicts lonely people who want to communicate, who long to share their lives with somebody, but do not know how. Schnurre is at his best when writing dialogues, especially in the Berlin dialect.

The novel *Ein Unglücksfall* (An Accident, 1981) is Schnurre's most ambitious attempt to come to grips with the Nazi period and its aftermath. The story is narrated by a rabbi. After World War II the small Jewish community in Berlin rebuilds its synagogue, which was destroyed in 1938. The glazier Goschnik outbids his competitors with ridiculously low prices. He does an excellent job until he comes to the Misrach window, a

huge round window which the committee wants installed without sections. After many objections Goschnik complies, but while trying to help set it in place he falls thirty meters to the ground. He is rushed to the hospital, where he survives for a short time. During this time, the rabbi stays with him, and a dialogue ensues in which Goschnik recapitulates his life. He had worked for a Jewish glazier and had become so friendly with him and his family that he became alienated from his own wife and son. He remained loyal to his friends during the Nazi period and hid them in his basement to keep them from being deported. When he was drafted into the army he left his friends in relative safety with a stockpile of food. When he deserted and made his way home from the front, however, he discovered that they had not remained in their hiding place but had left one night during the winter and had frozen to death in the Jewish cemetery. Goschnik survived by hiding in the same cellar; he realized, however, that his individual courage could not wipe out the guilt of all Germans–a guilt in which he shared. To atone for his guilt, he wanted to help restore the synagogue. But he now realizes that even this act of atonement and sacrifice was in vain. The rabbi implores Goschnik to consider himself absolved by his dead friends; after Goschnik's death, the rabbi even wants to have him buried in the Jewish cemetery. The other members of the synagogue object, however. Schnurre leaves the reader to decide whether a guilt like that of the Germans for the murder of the Jews can ever be expiated.

Schnurre's first wife, Eva Merz Schnurre, whom he married in 1952, committed suicide in 1965. The following year he married Marina Kamin, an illustrator. He received the Immermann Prize from the City of Düsseldorf in 1948, the Prize of the Young Generation of the City of Berlin in 1958, the Georg Mackensen Literature Prize in 1962, the Great Service Cross of the Federal Republic in 1981, the Cologne Literature Prize in 1982, and the Georg Büchner Prize in 1983.

Schnurre enables his readers to discover the humorous side of life and the basic goodness of human beings; he strengthens his readers' resolve to act according to the dictates of conscience and shows the relativity of what is considered important and unimportant. He is at his best when he portrays the people of Berlin, with their authentic language, in situations which reflect German history since 1930. His writing has a vein of surrealist fantasy, but it is most successful when it is saturated with realistic detail. Thus, he remains true to his ideal of "magic realism."

Interview:

Ekkehart Rudolph, *Protokoll zur Person: Autoren über sich und ihr Werk* (Munich: List, 1971), pp. 107-119.

References:

Reinhard Baumgart, "Schicksale gebündelt," *Neue Deutsche Hefte*, 6 (1959): 1028-1029;

Karl-Gert Kribben, "Wolfdietrich Schnurre," in *Deutsche Literatur der Gegenwart in Einzeldarstel-* *lungen*, edited by Dietrich Weber (Stuttgart: Kröner, 1968), pp. 279-296;

Rainer Lambrecht, *Wolfdietrich Schnurres "Kassiber": Eine systematische Interpretation* (Bonn: Bouvier, 1980);

Marcel Reich-Ranicki, "Der militante Kauz Wolfdietrich Schnurre," in his *Deutsche Literatur in West und Ost: Prosa seit 1945* (Munich: Piper, 1963), pp. 143-155;

Reich-Ranicki, "Wolfdietrich Schnurre," in *Schriftsteller der Gegenwart: Deutsche Literatur*, edited by Klaus Nonnenmann (Olten & Freiburg im Breisgau: Walter, 1963), pp. 286-293.

Anna Seghers
(Netty Reiling Radványi)
(19 November 1900–1 June 1983)

Gertraud Gutzmann
Smith College

BOOKS: *Der Aufstand der Fischer von St. Barbara: Eine Erzählung* (Berlin: Kiepenheuer, 1928); translated by Margret Goldsmith as *The Revolt of the Fishermen* (London: Mathews & Marrot, 1929; New York: Longmans, Green, 1930);

Auf dem Wege zur amerikanischen Botschaft und andere Erzählungen (Berlin: Kiepenheuer, 1930);

Die Gefährten: Roman (Berlin: Kiepenheuer, 1932);

Der Kopflohn: Roman aus einem deutschen Dorf im Spätsommer 1932 (Amsterdam: Querido, 1933); translated by Eva Wulff as "A Price on His Head," in *Two Novelettes* (Berlin: Seven Seas, 1960);

Ernst Thaelmann, What He Stands For, by Seghers and others, translated by Michael Davidson (London: Workers' Bookshop, 1934);

Der Weg durch den Februar: Roman (Paris: Editions du Carrefour, 1935; Moscow: Verlagsgenos- *senschaft Ausländischer Arbeiter in der UdSSR*, 1935);

Der letzte Weg des Koloman Wallisch: Erzählung (Paris: Editions du Carrefour, 1936);

Die Rettung: Roman (Amsterdam: Querido, 1937);

Die schönsten Sagen vom Räuber Wojnok (Moscow: Das Internationale Buch, 1940);

Das siebte Kreuz: Roman aus Hitlerdeutschland (Mexico City: El Libro Libre, 1942; Berlin: Aufbau, 1946); translated by James A. Galston as *The Seventh Cross* (Boston: Little, Brown, 1942; London: Hamish Hamilton, 1943);

Visado de tránsito, translated from German into Spanish by Angela Selke and Antonio Sánchez Barbudo (Mexico City: Nuevo Mundo, 1944); translated from the German by Galston as *Transit* (Boston: Little, Brown, 1944; London: Eyre & Spottiswoode, 1945); original German version published as *Transit: Roman* (Constance: Weller, 1948);

Der Ausflug der toten Mädchen und andere Erzählungen (New York: Aurora, 1946; enlarged edi-

Ullstein–Peter Probst

tion, Berlin: Aufbau, 1948); "Der Ausflug
der Toten Mädchen" translated by Elizabeth
R. Hermann and Edna H. Spitz as "The Excursion of the Dead Girls," in *German Women
Writers of the Twentieth Century*, edited by Hermann and Spitz (Oxford & New York: Pergamon Press, 1978);

*Sowjetmenschen: Lebensbeschreibungen nach ihren
Berichten* (Berlin: Kultur und Fortschritt,
1948);

Die Toten bleiben jung: Roman (Berlin: Aufbau,
1949); translated as *The Dead Stay Young* (Boston: Little, Brown, 1950; London: Eyre &
Spottiswoode, 1950);

Die Hochzeit von Haiti: Zwei Novellen (Berlin: Aufbau, 1949);

Die Linie: Drei Erzählungen (Berlin: Aufbau,
1950);

Die Schule des Kampfes (Moscow: Verlag für fremd-
sprachige Literatur, 1950);

Crisanta: Mexikanische Novelle (Leipzig: Insel,
1951);

Die Kinder: Drei Erzählungen (Berlin: Aufbau,
1951);

Erzählungen (Berlin: Aufbau, 1952);

Der Mann und sein Name: Erzählung (Berlin: Aufbau, 1952);

Der Bienenstock: Ausgewählte Erzählungen, 2 volumes
(Berlin: Aufbau, 1953);

Der Prozeß der Jeanne d'Arc zu Rouen 1431 (Berlin:
Aufbau-Bühnen-Vertrieb, 1953; adapted for
radio, Leipzig: Reclam, 1965);

*Frieden der Welt: Ansprachen und Aufsätze,
1947-1953* (Berlin: Aufbau, 1953);

*Über unsere junge Literatur: Diskussionsmaterial zur
Vorbereitung des vierten Deutschen Schriftsteller-
kongresses*, by Seghers and others (Berlin:
Aufbau, 1955);

*Die große Veränderung und unsere Literatur: Anspra-
che zum vierten Deutschen Schriftstellerkongreß,
Januar 1956* (Berlin: Aufbau, 1956);

*Hilfsmaterial für den Literaturunterricht an Ober- und
Fachschulen*, by Seghers, Hans Marchwitza,
and Willi Bredel (Berlin: Volk und Wissen,
1957);

Brot und Salz: Drei Erzählungen (Berlin: Aufbau,
1958);

Die Entscheidung: Roman (Berlin: Aufbau, 1959);

*Das Licht auf dem Galgen: Eine karibische Geschichte
aus der Zeit der Französischen Revolution* (Berlin: Aufbau, 1961);

Karibische Geschichten (Berlin: Aufbau, 1962);

Über Tolstoi, über Dostojewski (Berlin: Aufbau,
1963);

Die Kraft der Schwachen: Neun Erzählungen (Berlin:
Aufbau, 1965);

*Wiedereinführung der Sklaverei in Guadeloupe: Erzäh-
lung* (Frankfurt am Main: Suhrkamp, 1966);

Das wirkliche Blau: Eine Geschichte aus Mexiko (Berlin: Aufbau, 1967); translated by Joan Becker as "Benito's Blue," in *Benito's Blue and
Nine Other Stories* (Berlin: Seven Seas, 1973);

Das Vertrauen: Roman (Berlin & Weimar: Aufbau,
1968);

Ausgewählte Erzählungen (Hamburg: Rowohlt,
1969);

Glauben an Irdisches: Essays aus vier Jahrzehnten
(Leipzig: Reclam, 1969);

Briefe an Leser (Berlin: Aufbau, 1970);

Über Kunstwerk und Wirklichkeit, 4 volumes, edited
by Sigrid Bock (Berlin: Akademie, 1970-
1979);

Überfahrt: Eine Liebesgeschichte (Neuwied: Luchterhand, 1971);

Sonderbare Begegnungen (Berlin: Aufbau, 1973);

Fünf Erzählungen, edited by Doris and Hans-
Jürgen Schmitt (Stuttgart: Reclam, 1975);

Willkommen, Zukunft!: Reden, Essays und Aufsätze über Kunst und Wirklichkeit (Munich: Kürbiskern und Tendenzen Damnitz, 1975);

Steinzeit; Wiederbegegnung: 2 Erzählungen (Berlin & Weimar: Aufbau, 1977);

Die Macht der Worte: Reden, Schriften, Briefe, edited by Sina Witt (Leipzig & Weimar: Kiepenheuer, 1979);

Aufsätze, Ansprachen, Essays, 1927-1953 (Berlin: Aufbau, 1980);

Aufsätze, Ansprachen, Essays, 1954-1979 (Berlin: Aufbau, 1980);

Drei Frauen aus Haiti (Berlin: Aufbau/Darmstadt: Luchterhand, 1980);

Woher Sie kommen, wohin Sie gehen: Essays aus vier Jahrzehnten, edited by Manfred Behn (Darmstadt & Neuwied: Luchterhand, 1980);

Jude und Judentum im Werk Rembrandts (Leipzig: Reclam, 1981);

Bauern von Hruschowo und andere Erzählungen (Darmstadt: Luchterhand, 1982);

Überfahrt (Darmstadt & Neuwied: Luchterhand, 1982);

Ausgewählte Erzählungen, edited by Christa Wolf (Darmstadt: Luchterhand, 1983);

Vierzig Jahre der Margarete Wolf und andere Erzählungen (Darmstadt: Luchterhand, 1983);

Die Toten auf der Insel Djal: Sagen vom Unirdischen (Berlin: Aufbau, 1985).

OTHER: Nico Rost, *Goethe in Dachau,* translated from the Dutch by E. Rost-Blumberg, foreword by Seghers (Zurich: Universum, 1950);

Gustav Seitz, *Studienblätter aus China,* introduction by Seghers (Berlin: Aufbau, 1953);

L. N. Tolstoi: Bibliographie der Erstausgaben deutschsprachiger Übersetzungen und der seit 1945 in Deutschland, Österreich und der Schweiz in deutscher Sprache erschienenen Werke, introduction by Seghers (Leipzig: Deutsche Bücherei, 1958).

Anna Seghers is the most noted prose writer of the German Democratic Republic (GDR) and, according to many critics, one of the most important German writers of the modern period. Such novels as *Das siebte Kreuz* (1942; translated as *The Seventh Cross,* 1942) and *Transit* (1948; originally published as *Visado de tránsito,* 1944; translated into English, 1944) and her stories "Der Ausflug der toten Mädchen" (1946; translated as "The Excursion of the Dead Girls," 1978), "Die Kraft der Schwachen" (The Strength

Seghers in 1928 (Reclam Verlagsarchiv)

of the Weak, 1965), and *Das wirkliche Blau* (1967; translated as "Benito's Blue," 1973) have earned her a wide reading audience internationally as well, and the combined weight of her reputation at home and abroad has established her as one of the great literary figures of the twentieth century.

Seghers's life and career were committed to the ideals of socialist humanism and the struggle for social change. Considering the political orientation of her writing, it is not surprising that Seghers chose to settle in East Germany rather than her native Rhineland after she returned from exile in Mexico in 1947. As she said: "Weil ich hier die Resonanz haben kann, die sich ein Schriftsteller wünscht. . . . Weil ich hier ausdrükken kann, wozu ich gelebt habe" (Here there is the resonance that an author needs. . . . Because here I can express what I have lived for). As a cofounder of the GDR's Academy of the Arts and as the long-term president of the East German Writers' Union, Seghers played a decisive role in the cultural life of her country and influenced and promoted the careers of many established and emerging writers. Recalling Seghers's address to the International Writers' Conference, Christa Wolf–a major contemporary German literary voice in her own right–captures the aura that surrounded Seghers whenever she spoke in public: "Es war still in jenem Saal in Weimar im Mai des Jahres fünfundsechzig, als sie die Bühne betrat, und es blieb still, solange sie sprach" (There was total silence when she appeared on the platform in that hall in Weimar in May 1965 as long as she spoke). Wolf says that all the writers present, young and old, probably felt that they had before them the best possible mentor. A similar view was expressed in the many letters of admiration sent to Seghers by writers from the GDR and abroad on the occasion of her eightieth birthday.

During the immediate postwar years Seghers's novels and stories were published in the West as well as in the East; but during the cold war she fell into disgrace among Western critics. Her steadfast loyalty to the Communist party delayed the critical reception of her works in the West by more than two decades. But even then, while praised for her artistry, particularly in her exile writings, she was denounced for her official position in East German political and cultural life. Only recently has Seghers's substantial oeuvre received the critical attention it merits as a major body of writing on twentieth-century German social and political history.

Seghers was born Netty Reiling on 19 November 1900 to middle-class liberal Jewish parents in Mainz. Her youth was remarkably carefree and privileged, in contrast to those of many women of her generation. As the only daughter of Isidor Reiling, a well-known art dealer who was also the curator of the art collection of Mainz Cathedral, she grew up in a climate of cultural refinement and learning. At home she was encouraged to read fairy tales and legends as well as the works of Goethe, Schiller, Heine, Balzac, and Dostoyevski. Friends of her family, political refugees from czarist Russia, introduced her to *Crime and Punishment* and *The Brothers Karamazov*, which informed her own early literary efforts. She has also acknowledged the importance in her literary formation of John Dos Passos, Theodore Dreiser, Marcel Proust, Franz Kafka, and Fëdor Gladkov, as well as the cinema of Sergey Eisenstein.

In 1920, after receiving her diploma from a private secondary school for girls in Mainz, she left for Heidelberg, where she enrolled at Ruprechts-Karl University to study art, sinology, philology, and history. The years in Heidelberg, as well as a term at Cologne University, were hardly those of a carefree student existence, since they coincided with a period of intense political turmoil and economic instability. At Heidelberg Reiling came into contact with students from eastern and southeastern Europe who had been active in the revolutionary uprisings in their countries at the end of World War I. In her first novel, *Die Gefährten* (The Companions, 1932), she pays tribute to these young revolutionaries. One of them, the sociologist and political theorist László Radványi, was to become her husband in 1925. (Radványi later changed his name to Johann-Lorenz Schmidt.)

Reiling completed her four years at Heidelberg in 1924 with a doctoral dissertation entitled "Jude und Judentum im Werk Rembrandts" (The Jew and Judaism in the Works of Rembrandt). That year she wrote her first story, "Die Toten auf der Insel Djal" (The Dead of the Island of Djal), a fantastic tale about seafarers and their hero, a Dutch captain named Seghers. She signed the story with the pen name Anna Seghers. Wolf has called the adoption of this name an "undramatischer, doch nicht bedeutungsloser Akt einer Selbst-Taufe" (undramatic but not meaningless act of self-christening): in choosing Seghers, the name of a seventeenth-century Dutch etcher, as her pseudonym, the young author referred to her interest in Dutch art as well as to her childhood love for Holland. More important, she hoped that the unusual name would attract immediate attention to her stories and, at the same time, insure her anonymity.

In 1928, when her stories *Der Aufstand der Fischer von St. Barbara* (1928; translated as *The Revolt of the Fishermen*, 1929) and "Grubetsch" (published in the *Frankfurter Zeitung* in 1927) were awarded the Kleist Prize–the highest distinction a young writer could receive in the Weimar Republic–critics mistook Seghers for a man because the stories were written in a laconic, masculine style. But it soon became clear that the author was the twenty-eight-year-old Netty Reiling Radványi, a newly registered member of the Communist party of Germany and mother of two young children. After her literary debut Seghers followed her husband to Berlin, where Radványi directed the Marxistische Arbeiter-Schule (Marxist Institute for Workers' Education). By marrying Radványi, who had committed his life to the party and was ready to

Woodcut by Otfried Katschinka for Seghers's first book, Der Aufstand der Fischer von St. Barbara

carry out assignments wherever they might take him, Seghers had opted for a life of uncertainty and economic instability.

In 1929 Seghers joined the Bund Proletarisch-Revolutionärer Schriftsteller (BPRS [Association of Proletarian-Revolutionary Writers]). While she brought to her new associates a rich background in art and literature, they, in turn, introduced her to Marxist literary theory and included her in their debates about literature as an effective tool in politics.

In the fall of 1930 Seghers was a member of a delegation of the BPRS that traveled to Kharkov in the Soviet Union to attend the Second International Conference for Proletarian and Revolutionary Literature. During this trip Seghers visited major industrial sites and gained a firsthand impression of the country's efforts to strengthen its economy. She returned to Germany an admirer of the first socialist state and remained a staunch defender of the Soviet Union throughout her life, even refraining from commenting on the Stalinist purges in the late 1930s.

In the late 1920s and early 1930s Seghers made a name for herself with the publication of short stories such as *Der Aufstand der Fischer von St. Barbara,* "Grubetsch," "Die Ziegler" (The Ziegler Woman), and "Die Bauern von Hruschowo" (The Peasants of Hruschowo); the latter

three stories appeared in her first collection, *Auf dem Wege zur amerikanischen Botschaft und andere Erzählungen* (On the Road to the American Embassy and Other Stories, 1930). They are tales of ordinary people who gradually learn to rebel against their social milieu and their economic misery. Although they are members of the lower classes, Seghers's characters do not represent the class-conscious proletariat, the collective hero in many of her later works. These stories, with their sparse and charged language, reveal Seghers's talent for writing fiction which is richly symbolic and ardent in its humanitarian commitment.

When the National Socialists came to power in Germany in January 1933, Seghers was triply condemned for being a woman author, a Communist, and a Jew; her name appeared on the list of forbidden authors. In April 1933 she was arrested but was released shortly thereafter because of her husband's Hungarian citizenship. The Radványis fled to France, where they took up residence in Bellevue, a suburb of Paris.

By the time of her arrival in France, Seghers had completed two novels. *Die Gefährten,* which had been banned shortly after publication in Germany, is an account of revolutionaries from various parts of the world who fight for socialism. Seghers's second novel, *Der Kopflohn* (The Bounty, 1933; translated as "A Price on His

Seghers at work (Anna-Seghers-Archiv, Akademie der Künste der DDR)

Head," 1960), completed in Paris and published in Amsterdam, is the first literary response to German fascism. It tells of life in a village in Seghers's native region before the Nazi takeover.

Seghers's seven years of exile in France were among the most politically active and productive of her career. It was there that she wrote some of her most important works. *Der Weg durch den Februar* (The Way through February, 1935) deals with the revolt of the working class against the Dollfuß regime in Austria between November 1933 and February 1934. To gain firsthand impressions of the events, in the spring of 1934 Seghers traveled to cities in Austria where the fighting had been most violent. In her fictional account Seghers resorts to modernist techniques, such as simultaneity of events and frequent shifts in setting and narrative voice, to capture the frenzied quality of the uprising. *Die Rettung* (The Rescue, 1937) portrays life in a German mining town in the late 1920s and early 1930s, focusing on the economic and political crises that resulted in the gravitation of working-class people to the Na-

tional Socialists. Both novels readily found publishers, albeit in countries other than the author's own: *Der Weg durch den Februar* was published in Paris and Moscow, *Die Rettung* in Amsterdam.

Seghers regarded France as a second home, and frequently expressed her affection for the French people. As late as 1977, in a letter to her French publisher, she speaks of her admiration for the country that represented for her the best of Europe's progressive traditions. Most of her writing was done in the animated environment of Paris cafés, where friends and colleagues recall her sitting at an empty table filling page after page, oblivious to the confusion around her.

Much of Seghers's time in Paris was devoted to activities connected with the Schutzverband Deutscher Schriftsteller (Protective League of German Writers), where she met other exiles such as Rudolf Leonhard, Heinrich and Klaus Mann, and Ernst Bloch. She participated in lecture nights and contributed to political pamphlets and journals in hopes of enlightening the rest of Europe about National Socialism and encouraging the emergence of a resistance movement against Hitler in her homeland. Her faith in the potential for resistance against Nazism among the German people informs all of her writings of this period.

Through the Protective League of German Writers Seghers came into contact with famous French writers such as André Malraux and Louis Aragon. In August 1938 she published in the journal *Europe* excerpts from a diary in which she comments on her encounters with French writers and on her frustrated efforts to communicate to them her own artistic and political identity as well as that of other German exiles. In her speech on the theme of love for the fatherland at the First International Conference in the Defense of Culture in Paris in the fall of 1935, Seghers identified herself and her fellow exiles with a literary tradition represented by such figures as Gottfried Bürger, J. M. R. Lenz, Heinrich von Kleist, Friedrich Hölderlin, Karoline von Günderode, Heinrich Heine, and Georg Büchner. In her view they had risked artistic greatness, as well as their lives, by taking a decisive stance on the political and social issues of their times. In her closing remarks she pays tribute to these writers and their concern for their troubled fatherland: "Diese deutschen Dichter schrieben Hymnen auf ihr Land, an dessen gesellschaftlicher Mauer sie ihre Stirnen wund rieben. Sie liebten gleichwohl ihr Land" (These German poets wrote hymns to their coun-

Scene from the film version of Seghers's novel Das siebte Kreuz *(Staatlicher Filmarchiv der DDR)*

try on whose walls they beat their brows. But they loved their country nonetheless). Seghers's novels and stories written in exile are characterized by a similar commitment to Germany and its progressive traditions.

The late 1930s was also a time when Seghers freed herself from the aesthetic and theoretical dogmas that had characterized the debates on revolutionary art in leftist circles in the early years of the decade. When these issues once again became the focus of discussions among exiles such as Georg Lukács, Bertolt Brecht, and Hanns Eisler, Seghers came forth to articulate an independent position. In two letters to her friend Lukács she challenged his concept of realism and rejected the subordination of fiction writing to criteria based on a traditional literary canon and on scientific construction of reality. Instead, she advocated a realism that was open-ended and would allow for formal experimentation. Although Seghers later embraced Lukács's position on the social function of art, her exile writings show a closer affinity to the views of Brecht, Ernst Bloch, and Walter Benjamin than to those of her Hungarian mentor. In her novels *Das*

siebte Kreuz and *Transit* and in "Der Ausflug der toten Mädchen" Seghers uses many of the modernist techniques that Lukács found objectionable, such as multiple plots, stream of consciousness, and frequent shifts in voice and setting. As a result, as much as Lukács valued Seghers as a friend, he never cared for these works.

Seghers hoped that *Das siebte Kreuz* would signal her breakthrough as a major writer, but its publication was delayed by the chaos that erupted soon after she finished the manuscript in 1939. Before escaping from occupied Paris she left copies of the manuscript with friends, sending other copies to the United States. Franz C. Weiskopf, a German-Czech exile in New York and a close friend of Seghers, brought the manuscript to the attention of Maxim Lieber, who found an interested publisher in Little, Brown and Company of Boston. Before the book appeared in the fall of 1942, the publisher offered American readers a blurb comparing Seghers to Dos Passos and Ernest Hemingway. The book was received with almost unanimous acclaim among critics; some went so far as to compare

Seghers in May 1947, after her return from exile in Mexico (Ullstein)

Seghers to Thomas Mann and Hermann Broch. The novel became the choice of the Book-of-the-Month Club in October 1943.

Das siebte Kreuz is the story of the escape of seven inmates from the concentration camp Westhofen in southwestern Germany in the fall of 1937. The camp commander sets up seven crosses on which the escapees are to be executed when they are caught. Six of the men are captured and die a cruel death at the hands of their captors; the seventh, a young Communist named Georg Heisler, eludes his pursuers and flees the country. His escape demonstrates to the remaining captives that the Third Reich is not omnipotent. Those who come in contact with Heisler–workers, a Jewish doctor, a priest, a chemist, and others–are confronted with a difficult choice: to help Heisler, thereby risking their own lives, or to turn him over to the state. Through this cross section of Germans Seghers meant to identify the potential for resistance against Nazism in her

country. The idea of linking the flight motif with the panoramic depiction of German society had been suggested to her by Alessandro Manzoni's novel *I promesi sposi* (1827; translated as *The Betrothed*, 1834). An omniscient narrator functions as the collective voice of the camp inmates. It is he who, in a closing passage, articulates the faith in all that is "inviolable and unassailable" in mankind, echoing the author's lifelong credo.

With the advance of the German army the situation of exiles in Paris became untenable. Many of them fled overseas; others despaired and committed suicide. Seghers escaped to Pamiers, near Marseilles in unoccupied Southern France; her husband was in an internment camp in nearby Le Vernet. She found a café where she could write or study Racine and Balzac. There she began *Transit*, the Kafkaesque refugee story that she later completed in Mexico.

The narrator in *Transit*, an anonymous young worker, is a fugitive from Nazi Germany. Sitting in a harbor café in Marseilles in the spring of 1941, he tells the story of refugees from all parts of Europe who have come to southern France in the hope of leaving for a "promised land" abroad. They are caught in a nightmarish world of red tape, visas, functionaries, and consulates. Although he is initially not interested in leaving Europe, the worker's life begins to change when he finds a letter in a dead man's suitcase promising a visa to Mexico. He temporarily adopts the dead man's name, an act which becomes a threat to his very identity. But his friends–working-class people and other simple folk of Marseilles, none of whom has any intention of leaving the old world–tell him that he belongs with them and that he should share their fate. In his capacity as narrator, combining all the confusing stories into a coherent whole, he counts on the reader to participate in making sense out of the chaos. In telling his stories he captures the voice of the common people and their wisdom, and in so doing he conquers his feeling of isolation and displacement.

In contrast to the narrator of *Transit*, Seghers did leave Europe. With the help of the League of American Writers she obtained the papers and money necessary for her family's escape to their overseas exile. After a difficult journey, with holdovers in Martinique, Santo Domingo, and Ellis Island, they arrived in Mexico City in the summer of 1941. Speaking of the ordeal of that journey, Seghers confessed in a letter to her friend Bodo Uhse: "Ich habe das Gefühl, als wär

Seghers being inducted by Wilhelm Pieck into the Academy of Arts in 1950 (Frank Wagner, Anna Seghers *[Leipzig: VEB Bibliographisches Institut, 1980])*

ich ein Jahr lang tot gewesen" (I had the feeling of having been dead for a whole year).

In Mexico Seghers entered the company of a relatively large contingent of German-speaking Communists. Like Seghers, many of them had hoped for visas to the United States but were denied entry because of their affiliation with the Communist party. They joined together in an effort to establish a center for antifascist activity in Mexico City while maintaining contact with the leadership of the German Communist party in Moscow. Seghers was most active in her capacity as president of the Heinrich Heine Club, organizing cultural events for wider audiences. She also contributed extensively to the exile journal *Freies Deutschland*. The contact with a new continent and culture informed her subsequent writing, although she did not write about Mexico while living there. "Mexico is ideal for the artist," she stated in an interview with the American journal *New Masses* in February 1943. "The atmosphere is stimulating. But I don't believe that I shall ever write about it. I know so little about the country. . . . Everything is so youthful and I have not

quite absorbed it all." Later, after her return to East Germany, she paid tribute to Mexico in an essay on Mexican mural art and in the stories *Crisanta* (1951) and *Das wirkliche Blau*. The novels and essays Seghers wrote in Mexico deal almost exclusively with Germany. Wolf has characterized Seghers's exile writings as "Leiden an Deutschland" (grieving for Germany). In light of the news from Germany that reached the exile community in Mexico, such grieving was understandable. The war crimes, mass deportation of Jews, and the construction of death camps where Seghers's mother perished caused her to wonder: "Ein Volk, das sich auf die andren Völker wirft, um sie auszurotten, ist das noch unser Volk?" (A people that attacks other peoples to destroy them– is that still our people?). Throughout those years she reflected on the question of the exiled writer's national identity, on which she wrote repeatedly in essays such as "Deutschland und Wir" (Germany and We, 1941), "Volk und Schriftsteller" (A People and Its Writers, 1942), and "Aufgaben der Kunst" (The Duty of Art, 1944). The theme of love for the homeland is fur-

*Willi Bredel (left) and Seghers at the second Soviet Writers'
Congress, 1954 (Zentralbild)*

ther developed in "Der Ausflug der toten
Mädchen," a story she began writing while recovering from injuries sustained in a hit-and-run accident in 1943.

One of the most beautiful modern German
short stories, "Der Ausflug der toten Mädchen"
is perhaps Seghers's most experimental work. Set
in Mexico near the end of World War II, the
story begins with the narrator, an exiled German
woman writer, walking through the desolate, arid
Mexican countryside toward a white wall she has
seen in the distance. The wall turns out to be
part of a deserted ranch. As the narrator goes
through an open gate, the scenery changes and
she finds herself back in the lush, green Rhine
countryside in 1912 or 1913. It is the excursion
day of a Mainz girls' school, and the narrator recognizes companions from an earlier, happier life.

It is clear that she does not literally go back in
time but that the past surfaces from her memory.
As the title suggests, the schoolgirls are no longer
alive. But in the narrator's visionary return to
that day of her youth, the dead girls are resur-
rected out of her need to understand and communicate the meaning of their lives. As the narrator
brings forward each of her schoolmates in their
youthful innocence and promise in the idyllic setting on the Rhine, she interrupts with comments
on their fates. Most of them end tragically in
Nazi Germany, whether or not they supported
the state. For example, the narrator says of her
best friend Leni: "Ihr Gesicht war so glatt und
blank wie ein frischer Apfel, und nicht der
geringste Rest war darin, nicht die geringste
Narbe von den Schlägen, die ihr die Gestapo bei
der Verhaftung versetzt hatte, als sie sich
weigerte, über ihren Mann auszusagen" (Her
face was smooth and shiny and fresh as an apple,
and not the slightest sign or scar could be detected of the blows that the Gestapo had inflicted
on her at the time of her arrest, when she re-

Seghers in 1954 (Frank Wagner, Anna Seghers *[Leipzig:
VEB Bibliographisches Institut, 1980])*

4.

Es war schon so dunkel, dass man den Wald-
saum nicht mehr von den Wolken rügen unter
schied. Nur das Radio auge glänzte im Zimmer
hinter den Wänden, unendlich weit weg, summte
viele gebändigte Kinderstimmen.

Der Präsident Wilhelm Pieck hielt seine
Totenrede die Deutsche Demokratische
Republik war gegründet.

- - - - waren es die besten Vertreter der
Arbeiterklasse, die sich nicht von Verzweif-
lung überwältigen liessen. Oftmals buch-
stäblich mit nackten Händen, und ohne
Verzicht auf Belohnung griffen sie den
Trümmerbergen zu Leibe. - - -

hinter den Wänden verlor sich das
Summen wie in einem Bienenhaus. Es
machte die Stille noch stiller, den Schulleiter
legte den Kopf ans Radio. Es stellte es

Page from the manuscript for Seghers's novel Die Entscheidung *(Deutsche Fotothek)*

fused to give any information about her husband). In chronicling the lives of these women, Seghers shows the morally and physically devastating effects of Nazism on the entire German people.

In January 1947 Seghers began a journey to Germany by way of Sweden and France. In April she arrived in Berlin, where she was stunned by the devastation she saw. Within a few months she had settled in East Berlin and became involved in political and cultural activities. She joined the world peace movement, attended meetings in Paris and Warsaw, and represented her country at international conferences. Among her extensive travels, several trips to the Soviet Union, where she spent time in archives studying Tolstoy and Dostoyevski, were the most productive, resulting in publication of a 1963 collection of essays on the two Russian authors.

A novel with which she expected to contribute to the so-called antifascist reeducation program in postwar Germany was *Die Toten bleiben jung* (1949; translated as *The Dead Stay Young*, 1950), which treats German history from the November 1918 revolution to the defeat of Nazi Germany in 1945. The novel begins with the murder in a forest near Berlin of a young Communist worker by a group of officers and their subordinates. The killers represent various social groups and political interests of post-World War I Germany: the industrialists, the old nobility, the impoverished peasantry, and the lower middle class. Marie, the slain worker's bride, and her friends and neighbors speak for the working class and its concerns. Through the life stories and the personal and political choices of the characters Seghers points to the causes of the catastrophic course of recent German history. In shaping her vast subject matter into novel form, Seghers was probably influenced by Mexican mural art, which attracted her by its simultaneous simplicity and complexity. The novel has become a classic of socialist literature and history.

The novels *Die Entscheidung* (The Decision, 1959) and *Das Vertrauen* (Trust, 1968) deal with the choice many Germans faced in the immediate postwar era between the socialist society in the East and capitalist state in the West. Both novels revolve around the reconstruction of a steel mill in the Soviet Occupation Zone and the evolution of new social conditions in the GDR. The mill's former owners in the West and other enemies of the young socialist republic attempt to sabotage the rebuilding of the site—and by extension

Dust jacket for Seghers's 1959 novel about the reconstruction of a steel mill in East Germany

the entire East German economy—but the loyalty and efforts of many class-conscious socialists prevail in securing the future of the country. Seghers portrays the GDR as heir to all progressive German traditions and the West as a product of the capitalism and militarism of the past. Although these programmatic prosocialist novels are not Seghers's strongest pieces of fiction, they are more than mere political tracts, for they address the complexities of the post-World War II era and their impact on individual lives.

Shortly before her return from Mexico, Seghers had said that artists who had come in contact with other cultures had the responsibility of introducing them to reading audiences in their own countries. *Karibische Geschichten* (Caribbean Stories, 1962) is an attempt at such a cross-cultural dialogue, telling of the eighteenth-century slave revolutions in the Caribbean and the proclamation of the first black republic in Haiti. The collection of stories *Die Kraft der Schwachen* (The Strength of the Weak, 1965) concentrates on common people, among them women and children in cultures other than

Seghers at her home (Frank Wagner, Anna Seghers *[Leipzig: VEB Bibliographisches Institut, 1980])*

Seghers's own. In critical moments they come to recognize their inner strength for enduring hardship and injustice as well as their potential for social and political change. Seghers's last collection of stories, *Drei Frauen aus Haiti* (Three Women from Haiti, 1980), traces the lives of three women from the time of the Spanish conquest to the Duvalier regime. These women are lauded for their capacity to suffer and to retain the ability to resist, to survive, and to regenerate life.

Among Seghers's later writings are some pieces in which she reflects on fantasy, imagination, and the creative process. "Das wirkliche Blau" (Benito's Blue, 1967) is a story about art, creativity, and the social identity of the artist. During World War II Benito, a Mexican potter, runs out of a unique blue color imported from Germany. He journeys into Mexico's interior to find his own true "color" among his people. Benito's quest for his inimitable blue is a metaphor for the author's lifelong search for human fulfillment, social justice, and artistic authenticity.

"Reisebegegnung" (The Travel Encounter, 1973), which Seghers has called "Literatur-Geschichte" (a play on words suggesting a "story about literature" and "literary history"), depicts an encounter of E. T. A. Hoffmann, Nikolay Gogol, and Kafka, who engage in a dialogue about the relationship between fantasy, dreams, and historical time. Seghers makes a plea for infusing socialist literature with new visions and themes and articulates a concept of writing in which elements of the fantastic, of legends, and of fairy tales coexist with realistic settings.

Although Seghers was a prolific writer until her death, *Das siebte Kreuz, Transit,* and "Der Ausflug der toten Mädchen" stand out as her greatest literary achievements. These works have encouraged writers in the GDR—most notably Christa Wolf—to break with the narrow constraints of socialist realism and to explore new possibilities of writing.

On the occasion of Seghers's eightieth birthday, symposia and colloquia were held to honor her both in the GDR and in the Federal Republic of Germany, including a conference at the university of her native city of Mainz. A year later, after extensive political controversy, Seghers was awarded the status of honorary citizen of Mainz. After her death in June 1983 she was given a state burial at the Dorotheenstädtische Friedhof in East Berlin, the resting place of many high-ranking personages of the German Democratic Republic. Her life and works have been documented in several East and West German studies; chief among these are Kurt Batt's monograph *Anna Seghers: Versuch über Entwicklung und Werke* (1973), Klaus Sauer's *Anna Seghers* (1978) in the Beck series on modern authors, and Christiane Zehl Romero's richly documented monograph *Anna Seghers* (1987). The Academy of Arts of the GDR is preparing a comprehensive bibliography of her works. The novel that brought the author international acclaim, *The Seventh Cross*, appeared in a new edition in 1987 with a foreword by Kurt Vonnegut and an afterword by Dorothy Rosenberg. *Über Kunstwerk und Wirklichkeit* (On Artistic Production and Reality, 1970-1979), the four-volume edition of Seghers's letters, speeches, and essays edited by Sigrid Bock for the GDR Academy Publishing House, documents Seghers's life-long dedication to humanism and social change.

Letters:
Anna Seghers–Wieland Herzfelde: Ein Briefwechsel, edited by Ursula Emmerich and Erika Pick (Berlin: Aufbau, 1985);
"Anna Seghers: Briefe an F. C. Weiskopf," *Neue Deutsche Literatur,* 33, no. 11 (1985): 5-46.

References:
Anna Seghers, edited by Heinz Ludwig Arnold (Munich: Edition text + kritik, 1982);
"Anna Seghers: An interview by John Stuart with

the famous author of 'The Seventh Cross,'" *New Masses,* 46 (16 February 1943): 22-23;
Lowell Bangeter, *The Bourgeois Proletarian: A Study of Anna Seghers* (Bonn: Bouvier Verlag Herbert Grundmann, 1980);
Kurt Batt, *Anna Seghers: Versuch über Entwicklung und Werke* (Frankfurt am Main: Röderberg, 1973);
Batt, ed., *Über Anna Seghers: Ein Almanach zum 75. Geburtstag* (Berlin: Aufbau, 1975);
Kathleen J. LaBahn, *Anna Seghers' Exile Literature: The Mexican Years* (New York: Lang, 1986);
Christine Zehl Romero, *Anna Seghers* (Reinbek: Rowohlt, 1987);
Klaus Sauer, *Anna Seghers* (Munich: Beck & edition text + kritik, 1978);
Alexander Stephan, "Ein Exilroman als Bestseller: Anna Seghers' 'The Seventh Cross' in den USA," in *Exilforschung: Ein Internationales Jahrbuch,* edited by Thomas Koebner, Wulf Koepke, and Joachim Radkau (Munich: Edition text + kritik, 1985), pp. 238-259;
Christa Wolf, "Nachwort," in *Anna Seghers: Glauben an Irdisches (Essays aus vier Jahrzehnten),* edited by Wolf (Leipzig: Reclam, 1969), pp. 371-393; translated by Joan Becker as "Faith in the Terrestrial," in Wolf, *The Reader and the Writer: Essays, Sketches, Memories* (New York: International Publishers, 1977), pp. 111-137.

Papers:
The Akademie der Künste der DDR, East Berlin, and the Anna-Seghers-Archiv, East Berlin, hold the literary estate of Anna Seghers. The archives of Little, Brown and Company in Boston contain documents on the publication history of *The Seventh Cross.*

Johannes Mario Simmel
(7 April 1924-   )

Gerd K. Schneider
Syracuse University

BOOKS: *Begegnung im Nebel: Erzählungen* (Berlin, Vienna & Leipzig: Zsolnay, 1947);

Mich wundert, daß ich so fröhlich bin (Vienna: Zsolnay, 1949; Berlin: Verlag der Nation, 1955);

Von Drachen, Königskindern und guten Geistern (Vienna: Leuen-Verlag, 1950);

Der Mörder trinkt keine Milch (Linz: Demokratische Druck- und Verlagsgesellschaft, 1950);

Weinen ist streng verboten!: Eine Geschichte für kleine und große Mädchen (Vienna: Leuen, 1950);

Man lebt nur zweimal: Ein Kriminalroman (Linz: Demokratische Druck- und Verlagsgesellschaft, 1950);

Das geheime Brot (Vienna: Zsolnay, 1950);

Ein Autobus, groß wie die Welt: Ein Reiseerlebnis voll Spannung für Buben und Mädel (Vienna: Jungbrunnen-Verlag, 1951);

Meine Mutter darf es nie erfahren: Ein aufregendes Abenteuer rund um ein schlechtes Zeugnis (Vienna: Jungbrunnen-Verlag, 1952);

Ich gestehe alles: Roman (Hamburg: Zsolnay, 1953); translated by Catherine Hutter as *I Confess* (New York: Popular Library, 1977);

Wenn das nur gut geht, Paul: Ein aufregendes Abenteuer (Munich & Berlin: Weiss, 1953);

Der Hochstapler; Immer, wenn er Kuchen aß. . . , by Simmel and Hans Hartmann (Munich: Südverlag, 1954);

Gott schützt die Liebenden: Roman (Hamburg & Vienna: Zsolnay, 1957);

Affäre Nina B.: Roman (Hamburg & Vienna: Zsolnay, 1958); translated by Hutter as *The Affair of Nina B.* (New York: Popular Library, 1978);

Es muß nicht immer Kaviar sein: Die tolldreisten Abenteuer und auserlesenen Koch-Rezepte des Geheimagenten wider Willen Thomas Lieven (Zurich: Schweizer Druck- und Verlagshaus, 1960); translated by James Cleugh as *It Can't Always Be Caviar: The Fabulously Daring Adventures and Exquisite Cooking Recipes of the Involuntary Secret Agent Thomas Lieven* (Garden City: Doubleday, 1965); republished as *The Monte-Cristo Cover-Up: The Fabulously Dar-*

Johannes Mario Simmel (Ullstein–Ilona Jeismann-Schrumpf)

ing Adventures and Exquisite Cooking Recipes of the Involuntary Secret Agent Thomas Lieven (New York: Popular Library, 1977);

Bis zur bitteren Neige (Munich & Zurich: Droemer-Knaur, 1962); translated by Rosemarie Mays as *To the Bitter End* (New York: McGraw-Hill, 1970); republished as *The Berlin Connection* (New York: Popular Library, 1977);

Soldatensender Calais: Roman, as Michael Mohr (Vienna: Buchgemeinschaft Donauland, 1962);

Liebe ist nur ein Wort: Roman (Munich & Zurich: Droemer-Knaur, 1963); translated by Mays as *Love Is Just a Word* (New York: McGraw-Hill, 1969);

Der Schulfreund: Ein Schauspiel in 12 Bildern (Reinbek: Rowohlt, 1964);

Lieb Vaterland, magst ruhig sein: Roman (Munich & Zurich: Droemer-Knaur, 1965); translated by Richard and Clara Winston as *Dear Fatherland* (New York: Random House, 1969; London: Deutsch, 1969); republished as *Double Agent: Triple Cross* (New York: Popular Library, 1977);

Alle Menschen werden Brüder: Roman (Munich & Zurich: Droemer-Knaur, 1967); translated by Mays as *Cain '67* (New York: McGraw-Hill, 1971); republished as *The Cain Conspiracy* (New York: Popular Library, 1976);

Und Jimmy ging zum Regenbogen: Roman (Munich & Zurich: Droemer-Knaur, 1970); translated by Andrew White as *The Caesar Code* (New York: Popular Library, 1976);

Der Stoff, aus dem die Träume sind: Roman (Munich & Zurich: Droemer-Knaur, 1971);

Die Antwort kennt nur der Wind: Roman (Munich & Zurich: Droemer-Knaur, 1973); translated by Hutter as *The Wind and the Rain* (New York: Popular Library, 1978);

Niemand ist eine Insel: Roman (Munich: Droemer-Knaur, 1975);

Hurra, wir leben noch: Roman (Munich & Zurich: Droemer-Knaur, 1978);

Zweiundzwanzig Zentimeter Zärtlichkeit und andere Geschichten aus dreiunddreißig Jahren (Locarno: Droemer-Knaur, 1979);

Wir heißen euch hoffen (Ascona: Droemer-Knaur, 1980);

Die Erde bleibt noch lange jung und andere Geschichten aus fünfunddreißig Jahren (Ascona: Droemer-Knaur, 1981);

Bitte, laßt die Blumen leben (Munich: Droemer-Knaur, 1983);

Die im Dunkeln sieht man nicht (Munich: Droemer-Knaur, 1985).

OTHER: *Grüße und Wünsche zum sechzigsten Geburtstag (für Willy Droemer) und zum fünfundzwanzigsten Bestehen der Droemerschen Verlagsanstalt,* edited by Simmel (Munich: Droemer-Knaur, 1971).

Johannes Mario Simmel is one of the best-selling contemporary authors in German-speaking countries. According to the Allensbach Opinion Poll of September 1983, he is almost as well known as Heinrich Böll and better known than Günter Grass; eighty-five percent of the West German population has heard of Simmel.

His œuvre includes nineteen novels, three children's books, and a play. More than sixty million copies of his books have been sold worldwide, and translations of his novels have appeared in twenty-six languages in twenty-eight countries. Films based on his literary output have enjoyed the same success as his books, not only in the German-speaking countries but also in Egypt, Indonesia, Iran, Iraq, South America, Thailand, and the West Indies.

Simmel was born in Vienna in 1924 to Walter Simmel, a chemist, and Lisa Schneider Simmel. He studied chemistry during World War II and worked as a chemist in 1944-1945. He was an interpreter and translator in Vienna for the United States government until 1947; between 1947 and 1962 he was a reporter and editor for German and Austrian newspapers. From 1950 to 1962 he wrote thirty-six film scripts, some based on his own works; between 1951 and 1961 he was chief reporter and also worked as ghost writer for *Quick* magazine. As Simmel describes this phase of his career in a biographical statement put out by his publisher: "1950 übersiedle ich nach Deutschland und lebe in München, Berlin und Hamburg. In München werde ich von einer großen Illustrierten angeheuert und schreibe, als 'Mädchen für alles,' oft bis 2/3 des Textteils–Romanbearbeitungen, Tatsachenberichte, historische, kriminalistische, wissenschaftliche Serien, Kurzgeschichten, etc. Ich habe sieben Pseudonyme. Die Redaktion schickt mich auf weite Reisen in die weite Welt" (In 1950 I moved to Germany and lived in Munich, Berlin, and Hamburg. In Munich I am hired to work for a big illustrated magazine and write, as "Jack-of-all-trades," often up to 2/3 of the text–revisions of novels, documentary reports, historical, criminal, and scientific series, short stories, etc. I have seven pseudonyms. The editors send me away on long trips throughout the entire world). In 1963 Simmel decided to devote himself entirely to creative writing: "Journalismus ist die beste Schule für jeden Schriftsteller, aber es kommt der Moment, an dem man mit dem Journalismus aufhören muß" (Journalism is the best training for any writer, but the time comes when one has to quit journalism). From 1972 to 1983 he lived in Cannes and Monte Carlo; since 1983 he has resided in Zug, Switzerland. He has been married and divorced three times and has a grown daughter by his second marriage.

Simmel received the first prize from the Mannheim National Theater in 1959 for his play

Der Schulfreund (The Schoolpal, published in 1964); in 1980 he was given the Kulturpreis der Deutschen Freimaurer (Cultural Award of the German Freemasons) for his novel *Wir heißen euch hoffen* (We Bid You to Hope, 1980); and in 1985 he was awarded the Goldene Ehrenzeichen (Gold Medal of Merit) of the City of Vienna. Simmel is a member of the Austrian P.E.N. Club, the Guild of German Writers, and the Authors' Guild of America. A Johannes-Mario-Simmel-Club has existed in Düsseldorf since 1962.

Almost all of Simmel's novels are 500 to 600 pages in length, and all are based on actual current events which Simmel treats with poetic license. Topics treated by him include, he says, "immer und immer wieder die ungeheueren Verbrechen der Nazis und die ewig latente Gefahr der Neonazis; das zweigeteilte Deutschland; die im Stich gelassene Jugend; skrupellose Manipulationen durch Massenmedien; Drogenseuche und Drogenhandel; Rechtsradikalismus und Fremdenhaß; Elend des Alkoholismus; der Schrecken eines neuen großen Krieges mit seinen furchtbaren Waffen; der mörderische Kindergarten der internationalen Geheimdienste; das verderbliche Treiben multinationaler Gesellschaften; 'Weiße-Kragen-Verbrechen' bei internationalen Währungsverschiebungen; das Drama geistig behinderter Kinder, etc." (again and again the atrocious crimes of the Nazis and the perpetual latent danger of the neo-Nazis; divided Germany; abandoned youth; unscrupulous manipulation by the mass media; drug addiction and drug traffic; right-wing radicalism and the hatred of foreigners; the misery of alcoholism; the horror of a new world war with its frightful weapons; the murderous kindergarten of international espionage; the ruinous actions of multinational companies; "white collar crimes" in international currency transfers; the tragedy of retarded children, etc.).

Simmel's intent is to show the truth; he likes to quote Böll's statement, "Das Aktuelle ist immer der Schlüssel des Wirklichen" (Current affairs are always the key to reality), and Bertolt Brecht's view that "man ... die Wahrheit nur mit List schreiben kann" (one can only write the truth through cunning). Like Brecht, Simmel wants to compel readers to use their reasoning powers to create a new world free from war, racial prejudice, neofascism, and terror–in short, a world that is sane and healthy. Politically, Simmel considers himself a social democrat.

A pacifist-humanitarian message can be found in all of Simmel's novels. In his first best-seller, *Es muß nicht immer Kaviar sein* (1960; translated as *It Can't Always Be Caviar*, 1965), the hero, Thomas Lieven, formulates it this way: "Ich stelle mir gern vor, daß einmal eine Zeit kommen wird, in welcher alle Menschen auf dieser Erde ... harmonisch zusammenleben.... Es wird dann nicht einmal mehr Kriege geben.... Und so hebe ich denn mein Glas auf die menschliche Vernunft. Möge sie uns hinausgeleiten aus dem Schattentale der Furcht und hinein in ein Paradies voll Frieden und Fröhlichkeit" (I like to imagine that a time will come when all human beings in this world ... live together in harmony.... A time that knows no more wars.... And thus I raise my glass to toast human reason. May it lead us out of the valley of fear into a paradise of peace and happiness). Lieven, an agent working simultaneously for and against the German, French, and British secret services, joins a gang of criminals so that he can fight crime more effectively. This colorful agent follows the Machiavellian rule that the end justifies all means; the various roles Lieven plays are for the noble purpose of saving the lives of the innocent and punishing the guilty. Several erotic passages, as well as the many recipes Simmel gives for Lieven's exotic dishes, contributed to the novel's success. In an interview quoted by Jürgen Koepp, Simmel deprecates the work: "Es ist im Grunde aber nur eine Spielerei gewesen, garniert mit Kochrezepten, geschrieben für eine Illustrierte, von Woche zu Woche. Es mußte jedesmal geliebt werden, es mußte jedesmal gefressen werden, und es mußte jedesmal ein Abenteuer geben" (It was, fundamentally, only a game, garnished with recipes, written for an illustrated magazine, from week to week. In every episode one had to make love, one had to stuff oneself, and one had to have an adventure). The novel sold more than 2.2 million copies in the first ten years after its appearance; a thirteen-episode television series based on it was also successful. Outside of Germany the reception of the novel has been mixed; some critics liked its fast-moving pace, but others, such as Kenneth Allsop, did not: "See the Tall, Bronzed Man, Children, with Close-Cropped Black Hair a Little Grey at the Temples. This is the German James Bond, Invented by a German Len Deighton, and Written in Basic Wallace, Children. The Hero's name is Thomas Lieven. His Dossier, in *It Can't Always Be Caviar*, says that Tom, Tom, 007's Son, Loves 'beautiful women,

Simmel in 1978 (Ullstein–Binder/Thiele)

smart clothes, antique furniture, fast cars'. What is this Book meant to be, Children? It is meant to be a Sophisticated Send-Up. It is a Jovial Teutonic Joke. It is, Children, about as Amusing as Cold Sauerkraut. Colour it Mouldy."

In *Bis zur bitteren Neige* (1962; translated as *To the Bitter End*, 1970), the thirty-seven-year-old former child star Peter Jordan wants to make a comeback in a new film. Among the problems he faces are disenchantment with his wife, Joan, who is ten years his senior, and a love affair with his nineteen-year-old stepdaughter, Shirley, who is expecting a baby by him. Shirley has an abortion and later marries someone else, then dies in an accident. Jordan is guilt-ridden, but, with the help of alcohol and drugs, he finishes the movie. He then has a breakdown and is committed to an asylum, where he is treated by the Russian physician Natascha Petrowna. She helps him to escape from the asylum and arranges for him to be cured by a psychotherapist in Rome. When Jordan recovers he will go back to Hamburg with

Natascha and her deaf-and-dumb daughter Misa; they will wait for him while he serves a jail sentence for insurance fraud. The novel is narrated by Jordan on tapes made during his sessions with his psychotherapist. Its moral is stated by Natascha: "Wenn jeder Mensch auf der Welt nur einen einzigen glücklich machen würde, [wäre] die ganze Welt glücklich" (If everyone in the world would make only one person happy, then the whole world would be happy).

The critical reception of the work was cool. According to Judson LaHaye, "the simple plot line is bitter and decadent. It is a simple tale basically, but like so much of the 'now' generation's fun, it doesn't prove to be of much fun. It is worrisome, fussy, replete with problems demanding more than a psychiatrist's couch and, even with a happy ending, the problems remain." The reviewer in *Choice* called the work an "old-fashioned potboiler" and predicted that "serious readers of modern fiction will be disappointed by the uneven quality of the dialogue and the predictability of Simmel's stylistic dramatics. The translation by Rosemarie Mays is adequate, but the book remains slight, if diverting, fare."

Liebe ist nur ein Wort (1963; translated as *Love Is Just a Word*, 1969) is also told in flashbacks, this time in the form of a manuscript which the twenty-one-year-old protagonist, Oliver Mansfield, sent to a German publishing house in December 1961, just prior to his suicide or murder. The manuscript's title, which is the same as that of Simmel's novel, is based on the favorite song of Verena Lord, Oliver's thirty-two-year-old lover. The passionate love between the two is the main theme of the novel, in which Simmel criticizes postwar German society. His main targets are wealthy, influential former Nazis such as Oliver's father, a banker who defrauded the government and had to leave Germany; he now lives in Luxembourg with his sadistic mistress, Lizzy. Verena, the daughter of a wealthy industrialist, becomes the girlfriend of a high-ranking American officer, who leaves her when he finds out that she is expecting his child. After the birth of her daughter, Verena lives in poverty until the older, wealthy businessman Manfred Lord marries her. He tolerates her occasional infidelities but fights back violently when he finds out about her affair with Oliver. At the end, Oliver dies mysteriously, and Verena decides to remain in the bonds of matrimony, which provide her not with bliss but with security. The novel can be read on two levels: on one, it is a romantic tearjerker filled with suspense, blackmail, and electronic eavesdropping; on the other, it contains sharp criticism of conditions in the Federal Republic of Germany, especially the continued employment of former Nazis. The *Publishers Weekly* reviewer praised the book: "Under the guise of relating a student's day-to-day experiences, the novel touches on modern Germany and its reactions to memories of the Third Reich. Most disturbing is the acceptance of an unspeakable evil present in most of the characters, in fact, in all except the young man. This raises the novel from a simple love-mystery story to a serious treatise on the real nature of people. . . . It is a classic Teutonic message delivered here with thoughtfulness, taste, and skill." But Eugene J. Linehan did not find the novel to be totally convincing: "The heavy drinking, expensive living, almost total disregard for the ordinary discipline of healthy life makes one wonder if the author has not proven his case with mind-dulling logic. There is an air of unreality. And yet, even as we visit Dachau on a field trip with the school children, there is that nagging doubt that such

happenings are part of our factual history." The book's title perfectly describes Verena's view on life, but at the same time the novel suggests that love is a basic human need.

Behind the realistic spy novel *Lieb Vaterland, magst ruhig sein* (1965; translated as *Dear Fatherland*, 1969), C. Bryan noted in the *New York Times Book Review*, is "the barely restrained anger of its author." The novel centers on the power struggle between East and West following the erection of the Berlin Wall. The protagonist is a former waiter, Bruno Knolle, whose prison term for a break-in is reduced when he agrees to kidnap the West Berlin banker Otta Fanzelau and bring him to the East. Knolle is smuggled into West Berlin–ironically, through a tunnel which had been built with funds supplied by Fanzelau, a humanitarian who wanted to help his fellow Germans escape from East Berlin. The West believes the existence of the tunnel to be a secret, but the East knows about it and uses it for its own purposes. Knolle informs the West German authorities of the kidnapping plan, but the West uses him just as the East did. At the end, Knolle is put into prison again, and Fanzelau will spend the rest of his life in a psychiatric clinic after an unsuccessful attempt to take his own life. The message is that there is little difference between the dirty politics of the East and the West, and that the little man is used and abused under both systems.

Alle Menschen werden Brüder (All Men Become Brothers, 1967; translated as *Cain '67* 1971) has a double focus: on the personal level it deals with the Cain-Abel relationship between two estranged brothers, Richard and Werner Mark; on the social level it is about the emergence of neo-Nazi groups. Werner, the older brother, has joined a neo-Nazi group, "The Spider," together with the former concentration-camp physician Kamploh. With Richard's permission Werner publishes novels under his brother's name; Richard has given up his writing career and become co-owner of a nightclub. Werner blackmails Richard and steals his beautiful girlfriend, Lillian Lombard, who later becomes involved with Kamploh. Werner and Kamploh flee to Cairo, forcing Richard to be an accomplice in their escape. Werner tries to have his brother killed, but the hired assassin kills Werner by mistake. To escape death from "The Spider," Richard surrenders to the authorities. In the end he emerges victorious over his brother; but he cannot free himself from the passionate attachment to Lillian, who operates by the motto "Love is just a word." According to *Publishers Weekly*, the novel is a "potboiler almost without literary value yet compulsive reading." *Kirkus Reviews* describes it as an "extravagant adventure with all the clatter and wild unpredictability of a pinball machine," while Charles Keffer observes: "This is a rather difficult book to read. It is much, much too long. The story is told in a whole series of flashbacks to various time periods, all interwoven. The result is that the reader is not quite sure of what period he is reading and he needs to recall exactly where this part of the story left off previously. There are times throughout the novel when suspense is there, but finally these particular instances appear swamped by the excess verbiage of the remainder of the story. In summary, nothing more than a modest effort by Mr. Simmel."

Social criticism and personal revenge are also interwoven in *Und Jimmy ging zum Regenbogen* (And Jimmy went to the Rainbow, 1970; translated as *The Caesar Code*, 1976). The German title, which is based on a line from a Kipling poem, is also the key to deciphering a coded manuscript containing the formula for poison gas that could destroy all life on earth. The manufacturer of the gas, Raphaelo Aranda, offers it to the Russians and the Americans. Aranda, who is really the former Nazi chemist Dr. Friedjung, is killed by his sixty-five-year-old clerk, Valerie Steinfeld, who then commits suicide. Valerie's life is reconstructed by Aranda's son Manuel and the pharmacist Irene Waldegg from information given to them by Gross, the chief of the Viennese police, and Nora Hill, the owner of a bordello. With the assassination of Manuel, Simmel illustrates that the evils of life in the 1930s—the hatred of the Jews, political intrigue, and human suffering—did not end in 1945 but continue into the present. The *New York Times Book Review* said of the novel: "Mr. Simmel shifts loosely back and forth in time—1969, 1966, 1936, 1969—and muddles things further with irrelevant information. He goes in for some nicely detailed description of black-bagging, safe-cracking, electronic communication and other accessories of the spy business. But for the big crunch he relies on pure coincidence, a million-to-one shot. Disappointing."

Der Stoff, aus dem die Träume sind (The Stuff Dreams Are Made Of, 1971) is set in Neurode, a camp for young political refugees from the East situated in the middle of a moor. The journalist Walter Roland visits the camp with his photographer Bernie Engelhardt to put together a series on the inmates of the camp. These include the beautiful Irina Indigo, who left Czechoslovakia to join her fiancé, and eleven-year-old Karel, whose father had been shot during their escape. Karel is accidentally killed by a man who is trying to kidnap Irina. The murderer is pursued and caught by the sixty-two-year-old social worker Luise Gottschalk, who receives supernatural assistance from eleven friendly spirits. Roland—whose discovery of a spy ring has led to a murder attempt against him that resulted in the death of his friend Bernie—marries Irina and starts a new life with her abroad. The apparent happy ending is marred by the novel's failure to offer a way out of the conflict between the individual who wants to publish the truth and the mass media which want to suppress it.

The novel *Die Antwort kennt nur der Wind* (The Answer Is Only Known to the Wind, 1973; translated as *The Wind and the Rain*, 1978) is set in hotels and the stately residences of the super-rich on the French Riviera around 1972. The yacht of Herbert Hellmann, a wealthy German banker, has exploded, killing him and almost everyone else on board. The insurance investigator Robert Lucas discovers that the yacht was blown up by a powerful group of international businessmen in collusion with Hellmann's sister Hilda. Before Lucas can disclose his findings he is fired from his job because of his affair with the beautiful painter Angela Delpierre, who was the only survivor of the explosion. Lucas forces Hilda to sign a statement confessing to the murder of her brother; her accomplices make various attempts on Lucas's life but succeed only in murdering Angela. Life having lost all meaning for Lucas, he commits suicide. The unscrupulous world of international finance has the last word: Hilda Hellmann's confession is destroyed by her lawyer. The question posed by an old woman at the beginning of the novel—why the rich get richer and the poor get poorer—is answered in the German title of the work. This novel was well received in the United States, *Publishers Weekly* remarking: "This well-crafted novel by a best selling German suspense writer is admirably thoughtful in its attack on the unscrupulous world of the super-rich.... Capturing an array of corrupt characters in a violent episode in the world of international finance, Simmel brings this story to a disturbing, frightening finish."

The narrator of the novel *Niemand ist eine Insel* (No One Is an Island, 1975) is the handsome playboy Philipp Kaven, who is supported by the Hollywood star Sylvia Moran. Before Sylvia lies the greatest challenge of her career, the role of Grusche in the film version of Brecht's *Caucasian Chalk Circle*. As filming is about to commence she discovers that her daughter Babs has a severe brain disorder. A flashback reveals that several years earlier Sylvia did a benefit performance for mentally retarded children. On stage she professed love and understanding for these children, saying that "niemand ist eine Insel, ganz für sich allein, jeder von uns ist ein Teil des Ganzen, ein Teil der Menschheit" (no one is an island, entirely to oneself; everyone is a part of the whole, a part of humanity). But she reveals her true feelings when she shouts to Kaven: "Die armen, kleinen Kinder! Diese Stotterheinis! Diese Sabbermäulchen! Diese Kretins, die keine Menschen, die nicht einmal Tiere sind! Und dafür habe ich meinen Namen hergegeben! Strom des Lebens! das heißt: erfolgreich sein und schön sein und stark sein! Das Leben genießen! Dem Schwächeren einen Tritt in den Hintern; das ist der Strom des Lebens!" (These poor, small children! These stuttering imbeciles! These slobbermouths! These cretins which are not humans, not even animals! And to this cause I lent my good name. Current of life! that is: to be successful and to be beautiful and to be strong! To enjoy life! To give the weaker ones a kick in the pants; that is the current of life!). Her role as the mother figure Grusche in the Brecht play is a constant reminder of her family problems. Like her character in the play, Sylvia has an antagonist in real life: the altruistic physician Ruth Reinhardt, who loves and treats mentally retarded and brain-damaged children. Under Ruth's treatment, Babs has a chance to recover, and Kaven changes from a playboy to a caring father. Sylvia also changes, but too late. Shortly before her death, she professes her love for her daughter: "Heute liebe ich Babs noch viel mehr als damals.... Aber mit meiner Liebe ist nichts getan.... Die Liebe muß ... [sie stirbt]" (Today I love Babs even more than before.... But my love accomplishes nothing.... Love has to be ... [she dies]). Contrary to Brecht's view, Simmel shows that a rich and powerful woman can change even though conditions remain constant.

Change effected through love is also a theme in the novel *Bitte, laßt die Blumen leben* (Please, Let the Flowers Live, 1983). After he survives a plane crash Charles Duhamel, a Parisian lawyer for the rich, adopts a new name and a

more meaningful life in Hamburg. In addition to altruistic love, the novel deals with missiles, the Green party, and warmongers. Simmel does not offer solutions to any of the problems he raises; Hans-Christoph Blumenberg quotes him as saying: "Mein Weltbild ist unendlich düster, weil ich keinen Ausweg aus dem Konflikt sehe: Entweder wir lassen uns abschlachten, oder wir leisten bewaffneten Widerstand und schlagen die Großen tot. Man kann sagen, daß dieses Buch ebenso engagiert wie in größter Ratlosigkeit geschrieben worden ist" (My view of life is infinitely dark, because I can see no way out of this conflict: Either we allow ourselves to be slaughtered, or we take up armed resistance and kill the ones in power. One can say that the greatest helplessness as well as commitment motivated me to write this book).

Most German critics regard Simmel as a journalistic writer who knows his craft well and can play on the emotions of his readers. The result is an "Ersatzbefriedigung" (substitute satisfaction) that robs the readers of their incentive to critically analyze the issues and work for social and political change. Other critics point out that Simmel offers people things they hardly ever find in contemporary German literature: faith, love, and hope as countermeasures against pessimism and despair. Blumenberg touches on this aspect of Simmel's work: "Johannes Mario Simmel ist kein Revolutionär. Aus seinen Büchern spricht eine gewaltige Sehnsucht nach Harmonie, nach ordentlichen Verhältnissen, in denen anständige Menschen anständig leben können" (Johannes Mario Simmel is no revolutionary. Out of his books speaks a powerful desire for harmony, for law and order, in which decent people can lead a decent life).

Simmel believes in evolution rather than in revolution. He wants his readers to see the shortcomings of the world in which they live and to do something about these imperfections. He holds the readers' interest in his lengthy novels by weaving melodrama around fact. In this didactic intent Simmel resembles Brecht. Simmel's 1985 novel *Die im Dunkeln sieht man nicht* (Those in the Dark Can't Be Seen) takes its title from a phrase in Brecht's *Die Dreigroschenoper* (1929; translated as *The Threepenny Opera*, 1964). Other titles are borrowed from passages in classical literature that have a certain rhythm and convey emotional or enigmatic messages. In choosing such titles Simmel is attempting to bridge the gap between "serious" literature and the literature of entertainment.

References:

Kenneth Allsop, "Johannes Mario Simmel: *It Can't Always Be Caviar*," *Spectator* (31 December 1965): 869;

Mario Angelo, "Aus Gesprächen mit Johannes Mario Simmel," *Kürbiskern*, 2 (1977): 96-99;

Hans-Christoph Blumenberg, "Die Geständnisse des Froschkönigs," *Die Zeit*, 14 January 1983, pp. 17-18;

Heinz Brüggemann, "Johannes Mario Simmel– Deutsche Ideologie als Roman," in *Deutsche Bestseller–Deutsche Ideologie: Ansätze zu einer Verbraucherpoetik*, edited by Heinz Ludwig Arnold (Stuttgart: Klett, 1975), pp. 62-89;

C. Bryan, "Johannes Mario Simmel: Dear Fatherland," *New York Times Book Review*, 13 April 1969, p. 4;

Marlis Gerhardt, "Stoff für Träume," *Kürbiskern*, 2 (1977): 100-107;

"Johannes Mario Simmel: *Cain '67*," *Kirkus Reviews*, 39 (1971): 1175;

"Johannes Mario Simmel: *Cain '67*," *Publishers Weekly*, 210 (13 September 1976): 84;

"Johannes Mario Simmel: *Love Is Just a Word*," *Publishers Weekly*, 195 (7 April 1969): 53;

"Johannes Mario Simmel: *The Caesar Code*," *New York Times Book Review*, 23 May 1976, p. 47;

"Johannes Mario Simmel: *The Wind and the Rain*," *Publishers Weekly*, 213 (27 March 1978): 69;

"Johannes Mario Simmel: *To the Bitter End*," *Choice*, 8, nos. 5-6 (1971): 680;

Joachim Kaiser, "Johannes Mario Simmels Kunst der tragischen Operette," *Süddeutsche Zeitung*, 31 January-1 February 1976, p. 85;

Charles Keffer, "Johannes Mario Simmel," *Best Sellers*, 31, no. 22 (1972): 517;

Juergen Koepp, "Johannes Mario Simmel," in *Kritisches Lexikon zur deutschsprachigen Gegenwartsliteratur*, edited by Arnold (Munich: Edition text kritik, 1 August 1982): 1-10;

Judson LaHaye, "Johannes Mario Simmel: To the Bitter End," *Best Sellers*, 30, no. 6 (1970): 120;

Eugene Linehan, "Johannes Mario Simmel," *Best Sellers*, 29, no. 6 (1969): 115;

Bernd Neumann, "Rebellion und Unterwerfung: Versuch, Johannes Mario Simmel und seinen Erfolg zu verstehen," in *Basis: Jahrbuch für deutsche Gegenwartsliteratur*, edited by Reinhold Grimm and Jost Hermand, volume 7 (Frankfurt am Main: Suhrkamp, 1977), pp. 156-241;

Claudio Pozzoli, " 'Chronicler of Our Times,' " *World Press Review*, 30 (March 1983): 62;

Günther Rühle, "Die Welt des Johannes Mario Simmel," *Frankfurter Allgemeine Zeitung*, 26 September 1970, p. 1;

Albrecht Weber, *Das Phänomen Simmel: Zur Rezeption eines Bestseller-Autors unter Schülern im Literaturunterricht. Mit 7 Modellinterpretationen* (Freiburg im Breisgau: Herder, 1977).

Papers:

The Johannes Mario Simmel Collection of the Mugar Memorial Library, Boston University, contains manuscripts, typescripts, drafts, and source material for several of Simmel's works, as well as a large part of his correspondence.

Erwin Strittmatter

(14 August 1912-)

Herbert A. Arnold
Wesleyan University

BOOKS: *Ochsenkutscher* (Berlin & Weimar: Aufbau, 1950);

Der Wald der glücklichen Kinder (Berlin: Kinderbuchverlag, 1951);

Eine Mauer fällt: Erzählungen (Berlin & Weimar: Aufbau, 1953);

Katzgraben: Szenen aus dem Bauernleben (Berlin & Weimar: Aufbau, 1953); enlarged as *Katzgraben: Szenen aus dem Bauernleben. Mit einem Nachspiel, "Katzgraben 1958"* (Berlin: Aufbau, 1960);

Tinko: Roman (Berlin: Kinderbuchverlag, 1954);

Paul und die Dame Daniel: Eine Liebesgeschichte (Berlin: Das Neue Berlin, 1956);

Der Wundertäter: Roman, 3 volumes (Berlin & Weimar: Aufbau, 1957, 1973, 1980);

Pony Pedro (Berlin: Kinderbuchverlag, 1959);

Die Holländerbraut: Schauspiel in fünf Akten (Berlin & Weimar: Aufbau, 1959);

Ole Bienkopp: Roman (Berlin & Weimar: Aufbau, 1963); translated by Jack and Renate Mitchell as *Ole Bienkopp* (Berlin: Seven Seas, 1966);

Schulzenhofer Kramkalender (Berlin & Weimar: Aufbau, 1966);

Der entminte Acker (Berlin: Deutscher Militärverlag, 1967);

Ein Dienstag im September: 16 Romane im Stenogramm (Berlin & Weimar: Aufbau, 1969);

¾ hundert Kleingeschichten (Berlin & Weimar: Aufbau, 1971);

Die blaue Nachtigall oder Der Anfang von etwas (Berlin & Weimar: Aufbau, 1972);

Damals auf der Farm und andere Geschichten (Leipzig: Reclam, 1974);

Sulamith Mingedö, der Doktor und die Laus: Geschichten vom Schreiben (Berlin & Weimar: Aufbau, 1977);

Meine Freundin Tina Babe: Drei Nachtigall-Geschichten (Berlin & Weimar: Aufbau, 1977);

Selbstermunterungen (Berlin & Weimar: Aufbau, 1981);

Wahre Geschichten aller Ard(t): Aus Tagebüchern (Berlin & Weimar: Aufbau, 1982);

Als ich noch ein Pferderäuber war (Neuwied: Luchterhand, 1982);

Der Laden (Berlin & Weimar: Aufbau, 1983).

OTHER: Edith Rimkus, *Erntesommer: Mit der Kamera auf einem Volksgut*, foreword by Strittmatter (Dresden: Sachsenverlag, 1954).

Erwin Strittmatter is one of the most significant authors of the German Democratic Republic (GDR). According to Bertolt Brecht, he rose not so much *from* the proletariat as *with* it. Strittmatter is that rarest of authors who manages to be just far enough ahead of his time to stretch his audience but not enough to leave them behind or alienate them. Few writers have provoked as many discussions involving all levels of society, from farmers' letters published in local newspapers to members of the upper echelons of the Socialist Unity Party (SED) expressing themselves in specialized journals with limited circulation. Most of the responses have been positive, and Strittmatter's popularity is reflected in national prizes, translations, and a critical interest which has accompanied his publications since the early 1950s. He has proven himself a sympathetic and perceptive critic of his own evolving society in many genres. His strength lies in his prose, especially in his major novels; his two early plays received widespread recognition. He is equally successful as an author of children's books and of short prose in which he experiments with an earthy, quirky style that is appropriate for the speech expression of his central figures. These salt-of-the-earth types frequently display more wisdom than formal education, and their ties to the land, the seasons, and the strengths and limitations of country life are pronounced. Strittmatter is the chief chronicler of the major changes in German country life and agriculture since the Weimar Republic, especially in the eastern part of Germany, with a particular emphasis on land and social reforms in the German Democratic Republic since the late 1940s.

Erwin Strittmatter in 1983 (Ullstein–ADN/ZB)

Strittmatter was born in 1912 in Spremberg in the southeastern part of Germany. His father owned a bakery in a small village in the Lusatia region; Strittmatter had to move to a nearby town for his limited formal education. He left school in 1928 and worked in a variety of jobs, including baker, animal keeper, chauffeur, waiter, and factory worker. His membership in the Young Socialist Workers party led to a brief imprisonment in 1934. He was drafted into the army, from which he deserted toward the end of World War II. In 1945, while working as a baker, Strittmatter began writing for a local newspaper; later he became editor of a newspaper in Senftenberg. He joined the Socialist Unity Party in 1947 and became chief administrator for seven villages, overseeing land reform and agricultural nationalization efforts. His first novel, *Ochsenkutscher* (Oxcart Driver), appeared in 1950. The hero is a young boy named Lope Kleinermann, the illegitimate son of a village aesthete and a peasant girl, whose naive experiences expose the social and economic conditions of rural Wilhelminian Germany. Strittmatter uses techniques of the picaresque novel and the Dorfgeschichte (village tale) to depict the difficulties of understanding and changing the village mentality.

The need, as Strittmatter saw it, for socializing agriculture and the difficulties encountered in this revolution are the topics of the play *Katzgraben* (Cat's Ditch, 1953), named for the fictional village in which scenes from rural life present a poetic-didactic panorama of social and political reality from 1947 to 1949. Written for the Third World Festival of Youth in 1951 and initially rejected, the play was resuscitated by Brecht, who saw in it an opportunity to show how the consciousness of people depends on and often lags behind their social existence. Strittmatter also shows how sheer economic need can force people to act against their own best interests, and he highlights many of the political and social conflicts in East Germany after 1945. Protests against the play by simpleminded party functionaries who wanted only ideal heroes of socialism without internal contradictions or dialectical complexities stirred up much public controversy.

Strittmatter at work (photograph by Gerhard Kiesling, Berlin)

Strittmatter's ability to stimulate widespread popular debate and thus contribute to the consciousness-raising of both the party functionary and the man in the street is demonstrated in several of his subsequent publications.

Katzgraben centers on a progressive farmer, Kleinschmidt, who advocates the construction of a road to link his village to the city and the greater world beyond. The project is opposed not only by the old power structure of rich peasants but also by the other small farmers, who are as yet unaccustomed to making their own decisions. Gradually Kleinschmidt, with the help of the party functionary Steinert and the support of nearby miners, overcomes all obstacles, and the road is built. A similar conflict, typical of early GDR literature, between old and new values unfolds in Strittmatter's second play, *Die Holländerbraut* (The Dutchman's Bride), published in 1959 and first staged in 1960. Toward the end of World War II Hanna Tainz, the daughter of a poor farmhand, becomes pregnant; her lover,

Heinrich Erdmann, a lieutenant and the son of the most prominent family in the village, wants her to get an abortion. When she refuses, he spreads the rumor that the child was fathered by a Dutch POW; she is sent to a concentration camp, where she loses the child. After 1945 Hanna becomes the new village mayor. When Erdmann returns and causes trouble for her she finally decides to stop shielding him and exposes his past and present treachery. While critical and official reaction to both plays was positive, public enthusiasm was limited.

Strittmatter's children's book *Tinko* (1954) still enjoys unabated success and has led to film and theater sequels. Tinko is a ten-year-old boy from whose perspective the new postwar situation in a small village in Lusatia is told; the years after land reform bring new problems. Tinko's grandfather, August Kraske, fails to understand the need for cooperation and the joint use of the new land. In the end he isolates himself and alienates his grandson, who turns to his father for

Scene from the premiere of Strittmatter's comedy Katzgraben, *performed by the Berliner Ensemble, 1953 (photograph by A. Pisarek, Berlin)*

new directions. The story is told in laconic, humorous prose of deceptive simplicity, forcing the reader to make moral and political judgments the youthful hero is not equipped to make.

With the success of his early novels and his first play, Strittmatter became a full-time writer, rising to the position of first secretary of the German Writers' Union in 1959 and deputy chairman in 1961. A recipient of the GDR's National Prize for Art and Literature in 1953, 1955, 1956, and 1976, he was also honored with the Lessing Prize in 1960 and the Fontane Prize in 1966. Since 1958 he has lived with his wife, the poet Eva Strittmatter, and their sons on an agricultural cooperative in Dollgow.

The first volume of the trilogy *Der Wundertäter* (The Miracle Worker, 1957) uses the format of the Entwicklungsroman (novel of development) to trace the life of Stanislaus Büdner from his childhood before World War I to the end of World War II. Stanislaus is at first the traditional naif, unable to see through any of the forces oppressing him and others; but in the course of his experiences he finds the strength to

withdraw from the structures that have always thwarted the search for human happiness, and his first stage of awakening ends with his desertion from the army.

The novel most closely associated with Strittmatter in many readers' minds is *Ole Bienkopp* (1963). Ole Hansen, nicknamed "Bienkopp" (Bee Bonnet), the attractively headstrong hero, is committed to creating a better world in the framework of a socialism which he supports, although his interpretation does not always coincide with the official one. A practical dreamer, Ole is always a step ahead of his time and his contemporaries, whether in creating a farming cooperative before the villagers are ready for one or in developing new products without waiting for instructions from the local party representatives. His restless creativity and impatience always put him on—and sometimes over—the fine line that separates the innovator from the crank, the progressive socialist from the self-willed outsider. Ole finally dies in an impetuous and individualistic attempt to prove by example that his latest project would work. The book, with its portrait of party

Scene from the premiere in 1969 of a play based on Strittmatter's novel Tinko *at the Theater der jungen Welt, Leipzig (photograph by A. Pisarek, Berlin)*

functionaries impeding rather than aiding progress, caused a furor in the German Democratic Republic. It also led to the acceptance by Communist critics of the idea of the flawed socialist hero.

In the second volume of *Der Wundertäter* (1973) Stanislaus Büdner tries to make his way through postwar Germany, West and East, while retaining all his old uncertainties of judgment in social life, art, and love. Strittmatter's new emphasis on the nature and purpose of writing finds expression in several figures, most prominently the "Meisterfaun" (master faun) with whom Stanislaus debates the problems inherent in the dialectical oppositions of life and poetry, happiness and people, writing and living. At the end of the volume the hero is still searching for answers, but he has now found help.

The third volume of *Der Wundertäter* (1980) brings the story up to the present. The novel ends ambiguously, leaving the reader uncertain whether Stanislaus has been killed or whether

another sequel is possible. A continuation of *Der Wundertäter* would be fascinating, since in the third volume Strittmatter just begins to touch on a whole series of taboos, including Stalinism, the realism debate, and Brecht's ambivalence about the GDR. In the figure of Rosa, Stanislaus's great love, he fuses aspects of both art critic and social critic, indicating how some of the contradictions and problems of the earlier volumes might be resolved.

The years 1981 and 1982 saw the publication of aphorisms written in the 1960s in *Selbstermunterungen* (Cheering Oneself Up, 1981), diary entries written between April 1967 and December 1969 in *Wahre Geschichten aller Ard(t)* (All Sorts of True Stories, 1982), and a new collection of earlier short prose in *Als ich noch ein Pferderäuber war* (When I Was Still a Horse Thief, 1982). In 1983 a major novel, *Der Laden* (The Store), was published. Here Strittmatter returns to his native village in Lusatia, and many readers will recognize characters and events from the ear-

Strittmatter in his study (photograph by Edith Rimkus, Hinzenhagen/Güstrow)

lier short prose and novels. There is a sense of completion and closure in the way this story of Esau Matt and his parents connects with Strittmatter's first novel, *Ochsenkutscher*. But this time the emphasis is on nostalgia and the smile is more benign, even though the critical stance is still present. Once again Strittmatter is in the forefront of the most recent literary trend, a kind of socialist romanticism with a new emphasis on the psychic needs of the individual.

Throughout his career Strittmatter has thus been either leading or significantly contributing to changes in society and literature in the GDR and can, therefore, be regarded as one of the most representative figures in East German literature. It is high time for more of his major works to be made available in English.

References:

Leif Ludwig Albertsen, "Was Strittmatters *Katzgraben* will und nicht will," *Amsterdamer Beiträge zur neueren Germanistik*, 5 (1976): 25-40;

R. C. Andrews, "Re-education through Literature: Erwin Strittmatter's *Tinko*," *German Life and Letters*, 14 (1960-1961): 204-209;

Jürgen Bonk and others, *Adam Scharrer/Erwin Strittmatter* (Berlin: Volk und Wissen, 1962);

Kurt Böttcher and others, eds., *Erwin Strittmatter: Analysen, Erörterungen, Gespräche* (Berlin: Volk und Wissen, 1980);

Bertolt Brecht, "'Katzgraben'-Notate," in his *Gesammelte Werke*, volume 16 (Frankfurt am Main: Suhrkamp, 1967), pp. 773-840;

Werner Brettschneider, "Erwin Strittmatter," in *Deutsche Dichter der Gegenwart*, edited by Benno von Wiese (Berlin: Schmidt, 1973), pp. 250-260;

Barbara Einhorn, *Der Roman in der DDR, 1949-1969* (Kronberg: Scriptor, 1978), pp. 178-211, 273-317;

Wolfgang Emmerich, *Kleine Literaturgeschichte der DDR* (Darmstadt: Luchterhand, 1981), pp. 101-107, 146-149;

Cover for Strittmatter's 1966 collection of prose sketches

G. Fischborn, "The Drama of the German Democratic Republic since Brecht," *Modern Drama*, 23 (1981): 422-434;

Horst Haase, "Komisches und Tragisches in Erwin Strittmatters *Ole Bienkopp*," *Neue Deutsche Literatur*, 12 (1964): 130-141;

Haase and others, *Geschichte der deutschen Literatur: Literatur der DDR* (Berlin: Volk und Wissen, 1977), pp. 259-265, 376-382, 524-531;

Monika Hahnel, "Volksverbundenheit und Volkstümlichkeit im poetologischen Denken Erwin Strittmatters," *Weimarer Beiträge*, 26 (1980): 139-145;

Reinhard Hillich, "Erzählweise und Figurengestaltung in Strittmatters *Ochsenkutscher*," *Weimarer Beiträge*, 23 (1977): 79-109;

Klaus Jarmatz, "Natur in der Dichtung Erwin Strittmatters," *Weimarer Beiträge*, 20 (1974): 29-57;

Klaus Kandler, "Vom Schreiben und dem Schreibenden," *Weimarer Beiträge*, 30 (1984): 575-592;

Marcel Reich-Ranicki, *Deutsche Literatur in West und Ost: Prosa seit 1945* (Munich: Piper, 1963), pp. 411-421;

Eva Strittmatter, *Briefe aus Schulzenhoff* (Berlin: Aufbau, 1977);

V. Trauth, "Strittmatter: *Die Holländerbraut*," *Theater der Zeit*, 40 (1985): 46-49;

Frank Wagner, "Erwin Strittmatter: *Der Wundertäter. Zweiter Band*," *Weimarer Beiträge*, 19 (1973): 142-150;

William Walker, "Satire and Societal Criticism in the GDR Picaresque Novel," in *Studies in GDR Culture and Society*, edited by Margy Gerber (Lanham, Md.: University Press of America, 1981), pp. 155-166.

Bodo Uhse
(12 March 1904-2 July 1963)

Kathleen J. LaBahn
University of Wisconsin-Eau Claire

and

Gunther Weimann
Freie Universität Berlin

BOOKS: *Söldner und Soldat* (Paris: Éditions du Carrefour, 1935; Moscow: Verlagsgenossenschaft ausländischer Arbeiter in der UdSSR, 1935; Berlin: Aufbau, 1956);

Die erste Schlacht: Vom Werden und den ersten Kämpfen des Bataillons Edgar André (Strasbourg: Éditions Prométhée, 1938);

Leutnant Bertram: Roman (Mexico: El Libro Libre, 1943; Berlin: Volk und Welt, 1947); translated by Catherine Hutter as *Lieutenant Bertram: A Novel of the Nazi Luftwaffe* (New York: Simon & Schuster, 1944; Berlin: Seven Seas, 1961); translation republished as *The Shadow Throwers* (London: Hamilton, 1945);

Nous les fils, translated by Paul Roche (Paris: Éditions du Bateau ivre, 1947); original German version published as *Wir Söhne: Roman* (Berlin: Aufbau, 1948);

Die heilige Kunigunde im Schnee und andere Erzählungen (Berlin: Aufbau, 1949);

Die Brücke: Drei Erzählungen (Berlin: Aufbau, 1952);

Die Patrioten: Roman Erstes Buch: Abschied und Heimkehr (Berlin: Aufbau, 1954); enlarged as *Die Patrioten: Erstes Buch und Fragment des zweiten Buches,* edited by Günter Schubert (Berlin: Aufbau, 1965);

Tagebuch aus China (Berlin: Aufbau, 1956);

Mexikanische Erzählungen (Berlin: Aufbau, 1957);

Die Aufgabe: Eine Kollwitz-Erzählung (Dresden: Verlag der Kunst, 1958);

Gestalten und Probleme (Berlin: Verlag der Nation, 1959);

Reise in einem blauen Schwan: Erzählungen (Berlin: Aufbau, 1959);

Sonntagsträumerei in der Alameda und andere Erzählungen (Berlin: Henschel, 1961);

Bodo Uhse (Reclam Verlagsarchiv)

Abriß der Spanienliteratur, by Uhse and Edward Claudius (Berlin: Volk und Wissen, 1961);

Im Rhythmus der Conga: Ein kubanischer Sommer (Berlin: Aufbau, 1962);

Der Weg zum Rio Grande: Zwei Erzählungen (Leipzig: Insel, 1964);

Gesammelte Werke in Einzelausgaben, edited by Günter Caspar, 6 volumes (Berlin: Aufbau, 1974-1983);

Bamberg-Erzählungen, edited by Gerhard C. Krischker (Bamberg: Krischker, 1979).

OTHER: *Gekabelt aus Moskau: Schriftsteller und Krieg*, edited by Uhse (London: Freier deutscher Kulturbund in Großbritannien, 1943);

Vicente Lombardo-Toledano, *Johann Wolfgang von Goethe*, translated by Uhse (Mexico: Freies Deutschland, 1944);

Egon Erwin Kisch, *Schreib das auf, Kisch!*, edited by Uhse (Leipzig: Reclam, 1951);

Kisch, *Gesammelte Werke in Einzelausgaben*, edited by Uhse and Gisela Kisch, 8 volumes (Berlin: Aufbau, 1961-1986).

Bodo Uhse's career as a writer was marked by the rise of National Socialism in Germany; by exile in France, Spain, the United States, and Mexico; and by the division of postwar Germany into two political and cultural entities. While Uhse was a well-known cultural and political figure in the early years of the German Democratic Republic (GDR), his literary work received little critical attention in the GDR and remained virtually unknown in the West. Interest in East German literature and in the exile experiences of authors who fled Nazi Germany has recently helped to stimulate interest in Uhse in both the West and the East.

Uhse was born on 12 March 1904 in Rastatt. He was the son of a Prussian officer and, as a youth, took part in the activities of reactionary political groups in the Weimar Republic. He joined the Nazi party in 1927 but was expelled in 1930. Shortly thereafter he joined the German Communist party. From 1921 until his exile in 1933 he was active as a journalist and political organizer among the farmers and workers of Germany.

Although Uhse tried his hand at both poetry and prose before his flight from Germany, his first serious attempts at a literary career began in exile. The autobiographical novel *Söldner und Soldat* (Mercenary and Soldier, 1935) portrays the experiences of a young man between the years 1921 and 1930, experiences which mirror Uhse's own activities as a journalist and member of the right-wing Bund Oberland (Highland League) and later the Nazi party. Without excusing his own misguided and often brutal attempts to find both an individual and national identity in the reactionary political circles of the Weimar Republic, Uhse describes the irrational, nationalistic, and opportunistic motives which led many to National Socialism. Even after the main character has become disillusioned with the Nazis, he does not break with them immediately

but goes through a period of fatalistic, cynical resignation because he sees no alternative.

Critical response to *Söldner und Soldat* has been positive, although the juxtaposition of literary motifs and political journalism often mar the style of the novel. The immediacy and honesty with which Uhse describes his participation in nationalistic and reactionary organizations provide invaluable insight into the attraction such organizations had for unemployed workers, impoverished farmers, and restless, dissatisfied youths.

Shortly after the publication of *Söldner und Soldat* Uhse began work on a second novel in which he intended to warn against the remilitarization of Germany and an impending war. In *Leutnant Bertram* (1943; translated as *Lieutenant Bertram*, 1944) he portrays three different types of German officer. Major Jost believes that the military can and must remain unpolitical, but his distaste for the Nazis does not protect him from becoming a tool of the regime. Oberleutnant Harteneck represents the fanaticism and moral degeneration of the Nazi officer; his obsession with Nazi ideology makes him seem ridiculous at first, but his ability to seduce young officers to his beliefs makes him a new and dangerous element in Germany's already dubious military tradition. Leutnant Bertram is a young opportunist for whom a military career is the only chance to become part of a society which would otherwise have no place for him; his development from opportunism and cynicism to skepticism and finally to criticism of the Nazi regime is the main focus of the novel. When he is shot down over Republican lines in Spain, Bertram has traveled a long and difficult path; but Uhse makes it clear that the young officer still has a long journey ahead of him.

Uhse's portrayal of figures from the German resistance is indicative of a problem that would plague many German literary figures living in exile: they had lost personal contact with events in their homeland, as well as their native audience. Uhse's depiction of the Communist, Hein Sommerwand, and others who oppose the Nazis is vague and weak because he had not experienced firsthand the difficulties of organized resistance to National Socialism.

With the outbreak of the civil war in Spain Uhse's work on the novel came to a halt, not only because he was fighting in one of the international brigades but also because his purpose in writing the book seemed to have become superfluous. After his return to Paris in the winter of

Uhse (left) with Lion Feuchtwanger and Anna Seghers at the International Writers' Congress for the Defense of Culture, Paris, 1935 (Marta Feuchtwanger, Pacific Palisades, California)

1938 he decided to add a second part to the novel showing the involvement of the German military machine in the Spanish civil war. Uhse was not fully able to deal with the complexities involved in this expansion; characters from the first part of the novel are eliminated in the second part, which contains a good deal of propagandistic bravado and pathos regarding the heroic defense of Madrid.

In 1939 Uhse left France in response to an invitation from the P.E.N. Club of the United States. While in the United States he took part in exile activities and established contacts with many other German politicians and intellectuals who had fled Europe. His stay, however, was brief: in December 1939 he was denied permission to remain in the United States. After much uncertainty and delay he was granted a visa for Mexico, one of the few countries that accepted Communist exiles from Europe. From 1940 to 1948 he played a key role in the political and cultural activities of the Communist exile group in Mexico City.

Uhse's first months in Mexico were spent in obtaining visas and tickets for friends in Europe.

In 1941 he helped found a German cultural organization–the Heinrich Heine Club–and the newspaper *Freies Deutschland*, for which he wrote many articles on literature and culture. He was active in the political organization Bewegung Freies Deutschland (Movement for a Free Germany), and in 1942 he helped to found the German publishing house El Libro Libre, which published *Leutnant Bertram* in 1943. While in Mexico he married Alma Agee, who had been married to the American author William Agee.

As the end of the Nazi regime drew nearer, Uhse began work on his third novel, *Wir Söhne* (We Sons; published in French translation as *Nous les fils*, 1947; original German version published in 1948). Uhse drew on his own experiences after World War I to find parallels to the situation in Germany after World War II. He hoped that the disillusionment and failures of an earlier postwar generation would help a defeated Germany deal with the devastation and despair that years of National Socialism and war were bound to leave behind.

Wir Söhne focuses on the last year of World War I and the November 1918 revolution in Ger-

Uhse (right) and the actor Ernst Busch as soldiers in the International Brigades during the Spanish Civil War. The man on the left is unidentified (Ullstein–ADN/ZB).

many. A group of fifteen-year-olds, sons of officers at the front, have banded together in one of the romantic and reactionary youth groups of the period. During an outing in the mountains they become hopelessly lost but are found and led to safety by an older boy, Peter Exner. Exner becomes the leader of the group and begins to challenge the notions that the boys have learned in school and from their families. After Exner is drafted the boys try to keep the group together, but new ideas and conflicts drive them in opposite directions. While most of the boys join the reactionary forces that will lead to the next war, the unnamed narrator takes the side of revolutionary change. The revelation that Exner has not died in battle but has been shot for his opposition to the war makes a dramatic turning point for the narrator. Uhse indicates that the failed November revolution of 1918 must not be repeated; he also emphasizes that the youth of postwar Germany must receive special attention, lest the lies and legends of the defeated Third Reich become the seeds of new wars.

Because he drew on his own experiences and wrote without major interruptions, Uhse was

able to avoid many of the problems which mar *Leutnant Bertram*. Despite some problematical aspects, such as the somewhat mystical role of Peter Exner as a "Führer" figure, *Wir Söhne* is one of Uhse's best pieces of prose fiction; unfortunately, it has never received the critical attention it deserves.

After fifteen years in political exile, Uhse returned to Germany in September 1948 with his wife and two sons. He was consumed by relentless activity almost from the moment of his arrival in East Berlin. Beginning with the January 1949 issue, he took charge of the influential cultural and political monthly *Aufbau*. During his nine-year tenure as editor in chief important authors such as Günter Kunert and Heiner Kipphardt were introduced in the journal. In comparison with other East German publications in the 1950s, *Aufbau* under Uhse's leadership had an almost liberal profile. In 1958, however, he was dismissed as editor, and the journal was discontinued. This decision by the Socialist Unity Party (SED) was prompted, at least in part, by reviews of works by Ernest Hemingway, Jean-Paul Sartre, and Wolfgang Koeppen that went too far in their praise of these bourgeois authors.

In addition to his duties as editor, Uhse was active in various political and cultural organizations in the German Democratic Republic. From 1950 to 1954 he was a member of the Volkskammer, the East German parliament. From 1950 to 1952 he was the first president of the Writers' Union; from 1955 until his death he was a member of the German Academy of Arts, and between 1956 and 1960 he was secretary of the academy's Division of Poetry and Cultivation of the Language. In 1961 he was elected deputy-chairperson of the Union for Cultivation of German Culture and Language, and he was also a member of the executive committee of the P.E.N. Club.

After doing extensive research on German resistance to National Socialism, Uhse began writing his final and most successful novel, *Die Patrioten* (The Patriots), in 1952. Two years later the first volume of the novel, subtitled *Abschied und Heimkehr* (Farewell and Homecoming), was published. The novel was well received by critics in the GDR and became an immediate best-seller. The first edition of 10,000 copies sold out within weeks, and two further editions of 10,000 copies each were published in the same year. More than 110,000 copies of *Die Patrioten* have been published to date, and the novel has been translated into many languages, including Russian and Japanese. *Neues Deutschland*, the official organ of the SED, also published *Die Patrioten* in installments from 9 April to 21 October 1954; and on 7 October of that year, the fifth anniversary of the founding of the GDR, Uhse received the National Prize for Art and Literature for his novel.

Although the Aufbau publishing house announced the second volume of *Die Patrioten* several times in the following years, it was not until 1962 that Uhse began working seriously on it. He was constantly plagued by the feeling that he would not be able to shape the vast material he had accumulated. In January 1963 Uhse was named Peter Huchel's successor as editor of *Sinn und Form*, but only two issues appeared under his editorship. Following a stroke, Uhse died on 2 July 1963 without finishing the novel. In 1965 the Aufbau publishing house published the first volume together with the fragment of the second, edited by Günter Schubert.

Die Patrioten portrays the resistance to National Socialism within Germany. Uhse chose to write a war novel rather than an Aufbauroman (industrial novel about reconstruction) because the story of lives and deaths of those who fought in the resistance deeply moved him, and because he was convinced that this topic, rendered from a socialist perspective, could help "unser deutsches Volk von den letzten Schlacken des Nazismus zu befreien" (to free our German people from the last dregs of Nazism). In the essay "Der Autor und sein Leser" (The Author and His Reader), published in the final volume of his collected works (1983), Uhse underscored the pedagogical task of the author: "Ich halte mich an das Wort Stalins, daß Schriftsteller Ingenieure der menschlichen Seele sind" (I am guided by the words of Stalin, that writers are engineers of the human soul). To Uhse, this notion implied that East German literature of the 1950s should facilitate the process of denazification. He also hoped that the novel's focus on true patriotism, based on universal democratic humanism, could help in overcoming the division of Germany.

Die Patrioten is a many-stranded chronicle of loosely linked episodes. The first volume portrays the activities of a small group of courageous fighters who return to Germany from the Soviet Union in 1943. In traditional and realistic prose narration Uhse presents several model protagonists who do not waiver in their determination: Peter Wittkamp builds a resistance group among miners in the Ruhr area; Maria Holthusen orga-

nizes the escape of a Communist leader from a concentration camp near Hamburg; Helmut Wiegler sets up an illegal radio station near Berlin. Other characters, such as Käte Steinweg, who is the daughter of a Nazi professor and wife of a German officer, join the struggle against Hitler. Uhse's primary concern is how the antifascist struggle transforms these activists, how they mature politically and morally in the face of constant danger.

In *Die Patrioten* Uhse believed that he had rendered the historical truth about the final war years in Germany, but a central conceptual weakness of the novel results from his narrow understanding of fascism. When Helmut Wiegler remarks, "Hitler und Deutschland sind nicht eins, wie auch der Blutegel und der Mensch an dem er haftet, nicht eins sind" (Hitler and Germany are not the same, just as the leech and the human being whose blood it is sucking are not the same), he is espousing the definition of fascism formulated by the Communist International in 1933. Fascism is deemed to be the terrorist dictatorship of the most reactionary, chauvinistic, imperialistic segments of the capitalist class. Uhse saw the German proletariat as the victim of National Socialism, misled by Hitler's propaganda. But this interpretation cannot explain Hitler's rise to power in 1933 nor the mass psychological appeal of the National Socialist movement. By supporting the thesis of widespread resistance to Nazism among the German proletariat, *Die Patrioten* not only fails to illuminate the past but also contributes to myths which impede a deeper understanding of National Socialism.

While working on his last novel Uhse also published several collections of stories written in Mexican exile or using Latin American motifs, stories about the Spanish civil war and Germany under the Nazis, books on his travels to China and Cuba, a story about Käthe Kollwitz, and essays on Thomas and Heinrich Mann, Ernst Toller, Bertolt Brecht, Johannes R. Becher, and Egon Erwin Kisch.

Uhse's life and work were profoundly influenced by the political events that shook Germany and Europe in the twentieth century. No treatment of German exile literature or cultural and political developments in the early years of the German Democratic Republic would be complete without a discussion of him. In its strengths as well as its weaknesses his literary production reflects significant moments in the turmoil and tragedy that characterize German history from the end of the Weimar Republic to the establishment of two German states after World War II.

References:

Hans Peter Anderle, "Bodo Uhse: Porträt," in his *Mitteldeutsche Erzähler* (Cologne: Wissenschaft und Politik, 1965), pp. 125-127;

Bodo Uhse; Eduard Claudius: Abriß der Spanienliteratur, volume 5 of *Schriftsteller der Gegenwart*, by an editorial collective (Berlin: Volk und Wissen, 1960), pp. 7-51;

Günter Caspar, "Erinnerungen an Bodo Uhse," *Neue deutsche Literatur*, 32 (1984): 100-136;

Caspar, *Über Bodo Uhse: Ein Almanach* (Berlin & Weimar: Aufbau, 1984);

"Diskussion zu Bodo Uhses Roman 'Die Patrioten,' " *Neue deutsche Literatur*, 1 (1953): 126-141;

Franz Hammer, "Bodo Uhse der Schriftsteller," *Der Bibliothekar*, 27 (1973): 483-486;

Wolfgang Kießling, *Exil in Lateinamerika* (Frankfurt am Main: Röderberg, 1981);

Jürgen Kuczynski, "Alltagsfragen in Bodo Uhses 'Patrioten,' " *Neue deutsche Literatur*, 2 (1954): 137-139;

Literatur der Deutschen Demokratischen Republik, volume 2 of *Geschichte der deutschen Literatur von den Anfängen bis zur Gegenwart*, by an editorial collective (Berlin: Volk und Wissen, 1976);

Marcel Reich-Ranicki, *Auch dort erzählt Deutschland: Prosa von "drüben"* (Munich: List, 1960), pp. 80-88;

Reich-Ranicki, "Bodo Uhse," in his *Deutsche Literatur in West und Ost: Prosa seit 1945* (Munich: Piper, 1963), pp. 443-449;

Reich-Ranicki, "Probleme des deutschen Gegenwartsromans," *Neue deutsche Literatur*, 3 (1955): 112-113;

Doris and Hans-Jürgen Schmidt, eds., *Die großen sozialistischen Erzähler* (Frankfurt am Main: Fischer Taschenbuch Verlag, 1976);

Rolf Schneider, "Unvollkommene Versuche, einen Schriftsteller zu beschreiben," *Sinn und Form*, 24 (1972): 798-807;

Max Schroeder, "Der Weg zum Patriotismus: Bodo Uhse 50 Jahre alt," *Neue deutsche Literatur*, 2 (1954): 124-129;

Klaus Walter, "Bodo Uhse," in his *Literatur der Deutschen Demokratischen Republik*, volume 2 (Berlin: Volk und Wissen, 1979), pp. 354-365;

Walter, *Bodo Uhse: Leben und Werk* (Berlin: Volk und Wissen, 1984);

Walter, "Das patriotische Thema," *Neue deutsche Literatur*, 13 (1965): 82-94.

Papers:
The Akademie der Künste in East Berlin houses the Bodo Uhse archive.

Günther Weisenborn
(10 July 1902-26 March 1969)

Wulf Koepke
Texas A&M University

BOOKS: *Amerikanische Tragödie der sechs Matrosen von "S 4"* (Freiburg im Breisgau: Reichard, 1928);

Barbaren: Roman einer studentischen Tafelrunde (Berlin: Sieben-Stäbe-Verlag, 1931);

Das Mädchen von Fanö (Berlin: Kiepenheuer, 1935);

Die Furie: Roman aus der Wildnis (Berlin: Rowohlt, 1937); translated by Richard and Clarissa Graves as *The Fury* (London: Hutchinson, 1956);

Die einsame Herde: Buch der wilden, blühenden Pampa, as Christian Munk (Dresden: Heyne, 1937);

Traum und Tarantel: Buch von der unruhigen Kreatur, as Munk (Dresden: Heyne, 1938);

Die Silbermine von Santa Sabina: Roman aus Südamerika, as Munk (Berlin: Curtius, 1940);

Die Illegalen: Drama aus der deutschen Widerstandsbewegung (Berlin: Aufbau, 1946);

Babel: Schauspiel in drei Akten (Berlin: Aufbau, 1947);

Die guten Feinde (Berlin: Aufbau, 1947);

Historien der Zeit, enthaltend die Dramen Babel, Die guten Feinde, Die Illegalen (Berlin: Aufbau, 1947);

Memorial (Berlin: Aufbau, 1948);

Ballade vom Eulenspiegel, vom Federle und von der dicken Pompanne: Auf dem Theater dargestellt mit Prolog und Chören nach alten Schwänken (Berlin: Aufbau, 1949);

Spanische Hochzeit: Ein kleines Schauspiel (Berlin: Aufbau, 1949);

Die Neuberin: Komödiantenstück (Berlin: Henschel, 1950);

Spiel vom Thomaskantor: Aufzuführen zur Ehre des Meisters aller Musik. Nach alten Berichten verfaßt (Berlin: Henschel, 1950);

Drei ehrenwerte Herren: Komödie (Emsdetten: Lechte, 1953);

Der dritte Blick: Roman (Munich, Vienna & Basel: Desch, 1956);

Auf Sand gebaut: Roman (Munich, Vienna & Basel: Desch, 1956);

Günther Weisenborn

Das verlorene Gesicht: Die Ballade vom lachenden Mann (Munich, Vienna & Basel: Desch, 1956); revised as *"Lofter" oder Das verlorene Gesicht: Die Theater-Ballade vom lachenden Mann* (Berlin: Henschel, 1959); translated by Gabrielle Bingham as *The Man without a Face* (University Park: University of Pennsylvania Press, 1969);

Göttinger Kantate (Berlin: Arani, 1958);

Schiller und das moderne Theater (Düsseldorf: Verband der deutschen Volksbühnenvereine, 1959);

Die Familie von Nevada und ihre Darstellung auf dem Theater (Berlin: Henschel, 1959);

Die Familie von Makabah: Schauspiel (Munich, Vienna & Basel: Desch, 1960);

Der Verfolger: Die Niederschrift des Daniel Brendel (Munich, Vienna & Basel: Desch, 1961); translated by Paul Selver as *The Pursuer* (London: Heinemann, 1962);

Am Yangtse steht ein Riese auf: Notizbuch aus China (Munich: List, 1961);

Theater in China und Europa (Dortmund: Kulturamt der Stadt Dortmund, 1962);

Der gespaltene Horizont: Niederschriften eines Außenseiters (Munich, Vienna & Basel: Desch, 1964);

Theater, 4 volumes (Berlin: Henschel, 1964-1967);

Die Clowns von Avignon; Klopfzeichen: Zwei nachgelassene Stücke, edited by H. D. Tschörtner (Berlin: Henschel, 1982).

OTHER: *Die Mutter*, by Weisenborn and Bertolt Brecht, in Brecht, *Versuche*, volume 7 (Berlin: Kiepenheuer, 1933); translated by Lee Baxandall as *The Mother* (New York: Grove Press, 1965);

Der lautlose Aufstand: Bericht über die Widerstandsbewegung des deutschen Volkes 1933-1945, edited by Weisenborn (Hamburg: Rowohlt, 1953; revised and enlarged, 1954);

Chu Su-Ch'en, *Fünfzehn Schnüre Geld*, translated and adapted by Weisenborn (Berlin: Henschel, 1960).

PERIODICAL PUBLICATIONS: "An die deutschen Dichter im Ausland: Aus einer Gedächtnisrede für Ernst Toller," *Autor* (April 1947): 1-6;

"Von den literarischen Fraktionen," *Welt und Wort*, 7 (1952): 39-40;

"Von der Wahrhaftigkeit des Realismus," *Neue Deutsche Literatur*, 2 (1954): 122-126.

Günther Weisenborn is mainly remembered not as a writer but as a resistance fighter during the Nazi period and as the editor of a standard work on the German resistance, *Der lautlose Aufstand* (The Silent Rebellion, 1953), based on materials collected by the writer Ricarda Huch. Weisenborn was, however, a noted playwright; a friend of Bertolt Brecht, with whom he collaborated on *Die Mutter* (1933; translated as *The Mother*, 1965); and a major figure on the German literary scene in the years after 1945. He may have been overestimated then, but his almost total neglect in recent years is certainly undeserved. He wrote several noteworthy plays and some novels with interesting plots, and his autobio-

graphical novel *Memorial* (1948) stands out as a unique document. His works are hard to find, and there is little critical literature on him; even the information on his life is sketchy.

Weisenborn was born in 1902 in Velbert in the Rhineland. Like Brecht, Erich Kästner, and Ernst Glaeser, he belonged to the generation that grew up during World War I but was too young to be sent to the front. Weisenborn became a student of medicine at the University of Bonn but wanted to be a writer. The great success of his anti-war play *U-Boot S 4* (Submarine S-4; published as *Amerikanische Tragödie der sechs Matrosen von "S 4"* [American Tragedy of the Six Sailors of the "S 4"], 1928) in 1928 motivated him to abandon his studies, move to Berlin, and become a free-lance writer. He became involved in politics and moved in socialist circles. His second play, *SOS oder Die Arbeiter von Jersey* (SOS or the Workers from Jersey), was written in 1929; right-wing groups demonstrated against it when it was first performed in Coburg in 1932. His novel *Barbaren* (Barbarians, 1931) describes student life in the Rhineland under the Allied occupation after World War I and shows how the protagonist becomes an active Communist. It was banned when the Nazis came to power in 1933. In 1931 Weisenborn collaborated with Brecht on the adaptation of Maksim Gorky's novel *Mother* (1907) for the theater. With Brecht and other contemporary authors, such as Carl Zuckmayer, Weisenborn shared a preference for the ballad and the balladesque tone and form.

Weisenborn had an adventurous nature. At some point before 1933 he moved to Argentina, where he is said to have worked as a mail rider and farmer or rancher. In 1935 he published the novel *Das Mädchen von Fanö* (The Girl from Fanö), which was made into a successful film in 1937. It is a story of love, friendship, rivalry, and jealousy among German fishermen living near the Danish border. There are storms, dangers, and harsh conflicts, but there is also humor. These are "real" people from the country, not decadent city dwellers; they are also "Nordic." Thus the novel seemed to express the Nazi clichés. But the similarities with the Nazi Blut und Boden (blood and soil) ideology are only superficial. There is no racial conflict, no prejudice against the city or against foreigners. The protagonist is not a "leader," although he is the best and the most daring of the fishermen; he is a loner, an individualist. Weisenborn's novel shows the influence of hard-boiled American novels of the

Albert Garbe in a scene from Weisenborn's play Die Illegalen *(Bildredaktionsarchiv)*

1920s, an influence which is also prevalent in Brecht's works; it is a novel of the "tough guy," the lonely, daring hero with the right attitudes and emotions.

Weisenborn's play *Die Neuberin* (published, 1950) premiered in Berlin in 1935 and ran for more than 250 performances. It is the story of Caroline Neuber, an actress and theater director whose name is associated with the reform of the German theater in the eighteenth century. In the play she appears as a morally upright person defending her principles against opportunists; her stand is supported by the young Lessing. There are obvious parallels to the 1930s in the play, especially in Weisenborn's condemnation of the opportunists who support the Nazis out of fear and ambition rather than conviction.

Weisenborn left Germany during the Nazi period and worked for a time as a newspaper reporter in New York but returned in 1937 and accepted a position as Dramaturg (dramatic advisor) at the Schiller-Theater in Berlin. South

America had left a deep impression on him, and in 1937 he published the novel *Die Furie* (translated as *The Fury*, 1956), transplanting his "tough guy" to Argentina and Paraguay. The hero, Christian Munk, is a doctor who is doing research on how the Indians cope with pain. This seemingly detached man becomes emotionally involved and feels pain himself, to the point of being unable to publish his scientific studies and pursue an academic career. He decides to stay in South America, participates as a reporter and doctor in the Chaco War between Bolivia and Paraguay, and falls in love with Mary Peyton, the North American wife of a powerful Paraguayan politician. He finds out there are two wars going on at the same time: not only the senseless war between the two countries but also a civil war within Paraguay of the poor Indians against the rich landowners and foreign capitalists. The author's sympathy for the Indians is unmistakable. The love story has a tragic ending: Munk and Mary flee from her husband, but she is killed in a car accident while driving through the wild countryside to be reunited with her child. *Die Furie* is an action novel with some memorable episodes, especially Munk's exploits with the rebellious troops; but other parts, the love story among them, border on the trivial. Weisenborn accentuates the exotic element, both in the scenery and in the characterizations of people: the Latin Americans are hot-blooded and dangerous almost to the point of cliché.

Weisenborn used the name Christian Munk as a pseudonym for three more books on South America: *Die einsame Herde* (The Lonely Herd, 1937) and *Traum und Tarantel* (Dream and Tarantula, 1938) describe the Argentinian prairie and the life of the gauchos; the novel *Die Silbermine von Santa Sabina* (The Silver Mine of Santa Sabina, 1940) is another adventure story set in the north of Argentina. These were the last books Weisenborn published during the Nazi period.

While working for the Schiller-Theater Weisenborn became involved with the resistance group of Harro Schulze-Boysen and Arvid Harnack, nicknamed "Die rote Kapelle" (The Red Band) by the Nazis. The group was arrested in 1942 by the Gestapo, and most of its leading members were executed. Weisenborn spent the rest of the war in forced labor. Liberated in 1945 by the Soviet army, he was made mayor of the village of Luckau but soon returned to Berlin to become Dramaturg of the Hebbel-Theater and an editor of the satirical magazine *Ulenspiegel*; he was also elected president of the *Schutzverband deutscher Schriftsteller* (Protective Association of German Writers).

Weisenborn never ceased to deplore the scant attention paid to the German resistance movement and was also concerned by the reemergence in West German life of Nazis and opportunists who had collaborated with the Nazis. In 1946 he published the play *Die Illegalen* (The Illegals), which dramatizes the doubts, anxieties, and dangerous lives of the members of a Berlin resistance group and the conflicts they endure between private concerns, such as love, and their self-imposed duty. The authenticity of the tone and the background is beyond question, although the plot is a bit too obvious and, again, sometimes borders on the trivial.

Weisenborn published two plays in 1947. *Die guten Feinde* (The Good Enemies) dramatizes a conflict between the eminent scientists Max Pettenkofer and Robert Koch. *Babel* is an anticapi-

Weisenborn in 1962 (Ullstein–Harry Croner)

talist play set somewhere in Latin America, depicting the "glory and downfall" of the fabulously rich "meat king" Gamboa. The play bears similarities to Brecht's *Die Dreigroschenoper* (1929; translated as *The Threepenny Opera*, 1964) and *Die Heilige Johanna der Schlachthöfe* (1932; translated as *Saint Joan of the Stockyards*, 1969) and Lion Feuchtwanger's *Die Petroleuminseln* (1927; translated as *Oil Islands*, 1928) in its depiction of an early entrepreneurial capitalism of gigantic and heroic proportions, a mythical "Babel," a rebellion of humankind against a divine order; it is a high-risk speculative capitalism with a colonialist flavor. Weisenborn was obviously familiar with the writings of Upton Sinclair, John Dos Passos, and Sinclair Lewis.

In retrospect, Weisenborn's main achievement of these years is *Memorial*, an autobiographical report–although called a novel–on his years in prison, interlaced with memories of his student days in Bonn, life in Berlin, and adventures in America. It is a book of suffering and happiness, of despair and hope, of greatness and failure. It expresses the widespread hope of the time that the liberation of 1945 would be the beginning of a new life not only for German society but for the world–a life of freedom, of participatory government, of goodwill, of concern for the poor and the helpless, of socialism, of humanism, and of human rights. *Memorial* was written before the disillusionment of the cold war; it presents the hopeful spirit of 1945. It reminds the reader that all of the suffering should not be in vain: after such a catastrophe, life has to take on new meaning. These were short-lived hopes to be sure, but they make *Memorial* a special document.

Ballade vom Eulenspiegel, vom Federle und von der dicken Pompanne (Ballad of Eulenspiegel, of Federle, and of the Fat Pompanne, 1949), first performed in Hamburg in 1949, was to become Weisenborn's best-known play of the postwar years. Again, the play is close–perhaps too close–to Brecht, especially *Mutter Courage und ihre Kinder* (1949; translated as *Mother Courage and Her Children*, 1966). At that time Weisenborn saw himself as a rival of Brecht, and he tried in vain to prevent Brecht's plays and theories about the theater from overshadowing his work. While adopting some of Brecht's techniques in *Eulenspiegel*, Weisenborn developed his own theory of the "ortlose Bühne" (stage with a universal presence). Although *Eulenspiegel* ostensibly takes place during the Peasants' Wars in the sixteenth century, it is not a historical play; it is not limited by time or place. The intellectual Owlglass tries to raise the consciousness of the peasants, but the peasants do not understand their own long-term interests. Eulenspiegel and his love Federle pay the price for the people's stupidity and for the betrayal of the peasants by opportunists. Weisenborn's message is that oppression and exploitation will go on as long as the people allow them to. His leitmotif is justice, just as it was Brecht's in *Der kaukasische Kreisekreis* (1954; translated as the *The Caucasian Chalk Circle*, 1948); but the disillusioned Weisenborn does not believe in people's ability to change their conditions.

Weisenborn seems to have been desperate to regain his former popular appeal. He lost his touch both in his plays and his novels and sometimes made use of the techniques of trivial literature in order to be published. The comedy *Drei ehrenwerte Herren* (Three Honorable Gentlemen, 1953) treats the serious topic of the end of Nazi power in 1945 in the form of a slapstick farce, a most surprising choice for a politically committed author like Weisenborn.

Another dramatic ballad, *Das verlorene Gesicht* (1956; translated as *The Man without a Face*,

1969), is Weisenborn's best play of this period. Set in London in the early eighteenth century, it is the story of the "laughing man" whose face was disfigured when he was kidnapped and sold as a slave. The hero is suddenly elevated to the nobility, but he cannot live among the rich and powerful and returns to his world of actors, dancers, and jugglers. He does not even try to take revenge against those who disfigured and sold him: society cannot be changed.

The generally negative reception of Weisenborn's later works by the critics, while it correctly assesses their literary deficiencies, also has an ideological motivation. A novel dealing with political conditions in Bonn, *Auf Sand gebaut* (Built on Sand, 1956), expresses doubts about the legitimacy and durability of the new democracy in the Federal Republic. *Der dritte Blick* (The Third Eye, 1956) uses divided Berlin and the corruption and activities of the Wirtschaftswunder (economic miracle) period as its background. The protagonist, Viktor, has the gift of the "third eye": he can read people's thoughts. A young doctor back from the war who has a hard time finding his place in society, he would like to work for the good of humankind; but he is tempted by the many opportunities of the economic boom. Viktor gives in to these temptations and uses his extraordinary gift for financial gain. The novel is a dark picture of the 1950s, exaggerated at times, with a generous mixture of trivial elements that would be typical for an Illustriertenroman (serial novel printed in an illustrated magazine). Viktor's final change of heart comes too late; he is the tragic victim of the brutal capitalist society and his own misguided greed. The most authentic chapters are those dealing with prison conditions and the crimes of the Nazi period.

A much shorter and more convincing narrative is *Der Verfolger* (1961; translated as *The Pursuer*, 1962). During the Nazi years the narrator, Daniel Brendel, played in a dance band that was also secretly printing anti-Nazi leaflets and helping Jews. The pianist betrays the group; they are arrested and sentenced to death, but some escape when the files are destroyed in an air raid. Long after the war Daniel finds the informer and tries unsuccessfully to bring him to trial. In hatred and despair, he plans to run over the pianist with his car. While he waits, he remembers the past. Finally, at four o'clock in the morning, the man appears; but at the last moment the pursuer decides not to kill him. He will try to bring the trai-

Weisenborn in 1967 (Ullstein–Ursula Röhnert)

tor to justice legally, in spite of the odds against success.

Weisenborn wrote several radio plays, collaborated on the scenario for a 1955 film about the 20 July 1944 attempt to assassinate Hitler, and wrote other screenplays. He entered the struggle against nuclear war in his *Göttinger Kantate* (1958), which was produced for the annual meeting of the West German Social Democratic party, and in his play *Die Familie von Nevada und ihre Darstellung auf dem Theater* (The Family from Nevada and Their Presentation in the Theater, 1959).

Weisenborn's autobiographical reflections, *Der gespaltene Horizont: Niederschriften eines Außenseiters* (The Split Horizon: Notations of an Outsider, 1964), show that he remained true to his leftist positions from before 1933, modifying them somewhat in the light of his experience in the Rote Kapelle. Although the organization is generally considered a Communist group, the Schulze-Boysen and Harnack cells had members of various persuasions working together against the Nazis. These common goals and activities convinced Weisenborn that society at large could overcome ideological differences. His popularity fell victim to the cold war distrust of anyone who

would not take a definite pro- or anti-Communist stance.

Weisenborn's death in 1969 ended a career characterized by missed opportunities. Its promising beginning was cut short by political events in 1933. His attempts to survive as a serious writer in Nazi Germany and abroad failed, and his period of success after 1945 was short. His plays paled in comparison with those of Brecht, and ideological considerations limited the distribution of his books in both East and West. To reach an audience, most of his later works accentuate the features of popular literature which had been present, but less pronounced, in some of his earlier writings. He lost his touch for matching subject matter and style. *Das verlorene Gesicht* and *Der Verfolger* are the most memorable of his later works, but they have neither the vigor and vitality of his prewar novels and plays nor the authenticity and humanism of *Memorial*. They still reveal traces of Weisenborn's considerable talent, but they show that he lost his orientation after 1950. Still, his work deserves better than the almost total neglect into which it has fallen.

Letters:

Einmal laß mich traurig sein: Briefe, Lieder, Kassiber 1942-1943, edited by Joy Weisenborn (Zurich: Arche, 1984).

Bibliography:

Ingeborg Drewitz and Walther Huder, eds., *Günther Weisenborn* (Hamburg: Christians, 1985).

References:

Walther Huder, "Partisan der Menschlichkeit: Über Günther Weisenborn," *Welt und Wort*, 25 (1970): 45-46;

Marcel Reich-Ranicki, "Günther Weisenborn: *Der Verfolger*," in his *Deutsche Literatur in West und Ost: Prosa nach 1945* (Munich: Piper, 1963), pp. 294-298;

Josef-Hermann Sauter, "Gespräch mit Günther Weisenborn," *Sinn und Form*, 20 (1968): 714-725;

Gody Suter, "Weisenborn ad portas! Zu zwei Gegenwartsromanen," *Der Monat*, 9, no. 100 (1956-1957): 73-77;

Gerhardt Weissbach, "Günther Weisenborns 'Dramatische Balladen,'" *Aufbau*, 12 (1956): 469-471.

Peter Weiss

(8 November 1916-10 May 1982)

Michael Winkler
Rice University

BOOKS: *Från ö till ö* (Stockholm: Bonnier, 1947); translated f.om Swedish into German by Heiner Gimmler as *Von Insel zu Insel* (Berlin: Frölich & Kaufmann, 1984);

De besegrade (Stockholm, 1948); translated from Swedish into German by Beat Marzenauer as *Die Besiegten* (Frankfurt am Main: Suhrkamp, 1985);

Dokument I (Stockholm, 1949);

Duellen (Stockholm: Tryckeri Björkmans, 1953); translated from Swedish into German by J. C. Görsch as *Das Duell* (Frankfurt am Main: Suhrkamp, 1960);

Avantgardefilm (Stockholm: Wahlström & Widstrand, 1956);

Der Schatten des Körpers des Kutschers (Frankfurt am Main: Suhrkamp, 1960); translated by E. B. Garside and Rosemarie Waldrop as "The Shadow of the Coachman's Body," in *Bodies and Shadows: Two Short Novels* (New York: Delacorte, 1969); translated by S. M. Cupitt as "The Shadow of the Coachman's Body," in *The Conversation of the Three Walkers; and, The Shadow of the Coachman's Body* (London: Calder & Boyars, 1972);

Abschied von den Eltern: Erzählung (Frankfurt am Main: Suhrkamp, 1961); translated by Christopher Levenson as *The Leavetaking* (New York: Harcourt, Brace & World, 1962); translation republished in *Leavetaking; Vanishing Point* (London: Calder & Boyars, 1966);

Fluchtpunkt: Roman (Frankfurt am Main: Suhrkamp, 1962); translated by Levenson as "Vanishing Point," in *Leavetaking; Vanishing Point* (London: Calder & Boyars, 1966);

Das Gespräch der drei Gehenden (Frankfurt am Main: Suhrkamp, 1963); translated by Garside and Waldrop as "Conversation of the Three Wayfarers," in *Bodies and Shadows: Two Short Novels* (New York: Delacorte, 1969); translated by Cupitt as "The Conversation of the Three Walkers," in *The Conversation of the Three Walkers; and, The Shadow of*

Peter Weiss (Suhrkamp-Verlag, Frankfurt am Main)

the Coachman's Body (London: Calder & Boyars, 1972);

Die Verfolgung und Ermordung Jean Paul Marats, dargestellt durch die Schauspielgruppe des Hospizes zu Charenton unter Anleitung des Herrn de Sade: Drama in zwei Akten (Frankfurt am Main: Suhrkamp, 1964; revised, 1966); edited by Volkmar Sander, (New York: Harcourt, Brace & World, 1968); translated by Geoffrey Skelton and adapted into verse by Adrian Mitchell as *The Persecution and Assassination of Jean-Paul Marat as Performed by the Inmates of the Asylum of Charenton under the Direction of the Marquis de Sade* (New York:

Atheneum, 1965); translation republished as *The Persecution and Assassination of Marat as Performed by the Inmates of the Asylum of Charenton under the Direction of the Marquis of Sade* (London: Calder, 1965);

Die Ermittlung: Oratorium in 11 Gesängen (Frankfurt am Main: Suhrkamp, 1965); translated by Alexander Gross as *The Investigation: Oratorio in 11 Cantos* (London: Calder & Boyars, 1966); translated by Jon Swan and Ulu Grosbard as *The Investigation: A Play* (New York: Atheneum, 1966);

Nacht mit Gästen: Eine Moritat (Wiesbaden: Offizin Parvus, 1966); republished with *Wie dem Herrn Mockinpott das Leiden ausgetrieben wird* as *Nacht mit Gästen; Wie dem Herrn Mockinpott das Leiden ausgetrieben wird: Zwei Stücke* (Frankfurt am Main: Suhrkamp, 1969);

Sangen om Skrapuken (Stockholm: Seelig, 1967); German version published as *Gesang vom Lusitanischen Popanz: Stück mit Musik in zwei Akten* (Berlin: Rütten & Loening, 1968); translated by Lee Baxandall as *Song of the Lusitanian Bogey*, in *Two Plays* (New York: Atheneum, 1970);

Vietnam (Berlin: Voltaire, 1967);

Diskurs über die Vorgeschichte und den Verlauf des lang andauernden Befreiungskrieges in Viet Nam als Beispiel für die Notwendigkeit des bewaffneten Kampfes der Unterdrückten gegen ihre Unterdrücker, sowie über die Versuche der Vereinigten Staaten von Amerika die Grundlagen der Revolution zu vernichten (Frankfurt am Main: Suhrkamp, 1967); translated by Skelton as *Discourse on the Progress of the Prolonged War of Liberation in Vietnam . . .*, in *Two Plays* (New York: Atheneum, 1970); translation republished as *Discourse on Vietnam* (London: Calder & Boyars, 1970);

Der Turm (Stuttgart: Reclam, 1968); translated by Michael Benedikt and Michael Heine as *The Tower*, in *Postwar German Theatre: An Anthology of Plays*, edited by Benedikt and George E. Wellwarth (New York: Dutton, 1967), pp. 316-348;

Notizen zum kulturellen Leben in der Demokratischen Republik Viet Nam (Frankfurt am Main: Suhrkamp, 1968); translated as *Notes on the Cultural Life of the Democratic Republic of Vietnam* (London: Calder & Boyars, 1970; New York: Dell, 1970);

Rapporte, 2 volumes (Frankfurt am Main: Suhrkamp, 1968-1971);

Dramen, 2 volumes (Frankfurt am Main: Suhrkamp, 1968);

Bericht über die Angriffe der US-Luftwaffe und -Marine gegen die Demokratische Republik Viet Nam, nach der Erklärung Präsident Johnsons über die "begrenzte Bombardierung" am 31. März 1968, by Weiss and Gunilla Palmstierna-Weiss (Frankfurt am Main: Edition Voltaire, 1968); translated by Anna Björkwall and Davis Jones as *"Limited Bombing" in Vietnam: Report on the Attacks against the Democratic Republic of Vietnam by the U.S. Air Force and the Seventh Fleet, after the Declaration of "Limited Bombing" by President Lyndon B. Johnson on March 31, 1968* (London: Bertrand Russell Peace Foundation, 1969);

Trotzki im Exil: Stück in zwei Akten (Frankfurt am Main: Suhrkamp, 1970); translated by Skelton as *Trotsky in Exile* (London: Methuen, 1971; New York: Atheneum, 1972);

Hölderlin: Stück in zwei Akten (Frankfurt am Main: Suhrkamp, 1971);

American Presence in South East Asia (Singapore: Island Publishers, 1971);

Die Ästhetik des Widerstands: Roman, 3 volumes (Frankfurt am Main: Suhrkamp, 1975-1981);

Stücke (Berlin: Henschel, 1977);

Aufsätze, Journale, Arbeitspunkte: Schriften zu Kunst und Literatur, edited by Manfred Haiduk (Berlin: Henschel, 1979);

Notizbücher 1971-1980, 2 volumes (Frankfurt am Main: Suhrkamp, 1981);

Notizbücher 1960-1971, 2 volumes (Frankfurt am Main: Suhrkamp, 1982);

Peter Weiss im Gespräch, edited by Rainer Gerlach and Matthias Richter (Frankfurt am Main: Suhrkamp, 1984).

OTHER: August Strindberg, *Ein Traumspiel*, translated by Weiss (Frankfurt am Main: Suhrkamp, 1963);

Die Versicherung, in *Deutsches Theater der Gegenwart I*, edited by Karlheinz Braun (Frankfurt am Main: Suhrkamp, 1967), pp. 83-146;

Russelltribunalen, edited by Weiss and Peter Limqueco (Stockholm: PAN/Norstedt, 1968); translated as *Prevent the Crime of Silence: Reports from the Sessions of the International War Crimes Tribunal Founded by Bertrand Russell, London, Stockholm, Roskilde* (London: Lane, 1971);

Hermann Hesse, *Kindheit des Zauberers: Eine Autobiographie,* foreword and illustrations by Weiss (Leipzig: Insel, 1974);

Franz Kafka, *Der Prozeß: Stück in zwei Akten,* adapted by Weiss (Frankfurt am Main: Suhrkamp, 1974);

Strindberg, *Drei Stücke,* translated by Weiss (Frankfurt am Main: Suhrkamp, 1981).

Peter Weiss was a writer whose entire life was dominated by feelings of alienation and deep-seated insecurity. As a youth he made frequent attempts to escape from the social conventions into which he was born and to free himself from his parents' demands that he prepare himself for a career in business. In early adulthood he retreated more and more from the increasingly hostile world around him until he found–however vulnerable and uncertain it may have been–a sense of identity in artistic expression. This sense helped him to survive the anguish and feeling of helplessness with which he reacted to the Nazi dictatorship. His family's financial resources and his withdrawal into a private search for existential orientation saved him from the horrors of war and of the extermination camps. Yet the place to which he felt most intensely bound all his life was not one of the many cities in which he lived as an exile but Auschwitz, the point of reference that, in 1965, he chose to call "meine Ortschaft" (my township).

By this time he had gained public recognition as a playwright that soon developed into an international reputation. The spectacular public response to the first performances in Berlin in 1964 of his extraordinary drama *Die Verfolgung und Ermordung Jean Paul Marats, dargestellt durch die Schauspielgruppe des Hospizes zu Charenton unter Anleitung des Herrn de Sade* (1964; translated as *The Persecution and Assassination of Jean-Paul Marat as Performed by the Inmates of the Asylum of Charenton under the Direction of the Marquis de Sade,* 1965; usually referred to as *Marat/Sade*) was to make him during the next decade one of the most prominent spokesmen for socialism. There was ever stronger indication that in his espousal of revolutionary socialism's rebellious idealism and self-sacrificing pragmatism the hesitant, insecure, isolated, experimental artist Weiss had finally found a political cause that gave him a sense of meaningful commitment.

But critics objected that Weiss too often traded artistic subtlety for the short-lived effects of aggressive rhetoric and reduced the complexi-

ties of political life to the single-mindedness of a pugnaciously self-righteous dogmatism. It is likely, however, that Weiss was fully aware of how severely he had limited the expressive range of his "documentary plays" and that he intentionally sacrificed his earlier principles of unremitting exploration and carefully balanced judgment. He returned to an extensive fictional discussion of the many questions raised by the interdependence of art and politics in his magnum opus, the novel *Die Ästhetik des Widerstands* (The Aesthetics of Resistance, 1975-1981), a work which occupied him for more than a decade until shortly before his death.

Weiss left a wealth of information about himself in his diaries, notebooks, and autobiographical novels. But there is little reliable evidence to corroborate his self-representations. This is not to say that Weiss was overly secretive or deceptive about the years before he became a public figure; but many of his statements convey a perspective of one-sided, exaggerated hindsight. They emphasize the image he had of himself as an uprooted outsider, reared under pathogenic family circumstances, never belonging anywhere, always frustrated and rejected in his quest for at least a transitory sense of appreciation among his artistic peers. It is advisable not to accept all the statements he makes about himself as the literal truth; but they do reveal the impulses behind his prevailing attitudes and moods.

Peter Ulrich Weiss spent his childhood in the ambience of the wealthy bourgeoisie, both in the exclusive Berlin suburb of Nowawes, where he was born in 1916, and in the patrician neighborhoods of Bremen, where he went to school. His father, Eugen Weiss, a textile manufacturer, was a native of Czechoslovakia who had converted from Judaism to Lutheranism. His mother, Frieda Hummel Weiss, a Swiss Gentile, had been an actress before her second marriage and had sacrificed her artistic aspirations for solid respectability and the care of her six children. It was especially disappointing to Weiss, who felt ill at ease in the business world of his father, that not even she would support his search for self-realization through art. He remembered his youth as a time of stifling frustration when he was forced to conform to the notions of propriety, work, and success that to him characterized the mentality of the upper classes.

In 1929 his family returned from Bremen to Berlin. He attended the prestigious Heinrich-Kleist-Gymnasium, a traditional academic high school for prospective university students in Schmargendorf, and briefly enrolled at the art school of Eugen Spiro. In 1933 he transferred to the Rackow Trade School in Berlin, where he learned typing and stenography. A year later the Weisses immigrated to London, a disruption of their lives that was further complicated by the death of Weiss's youngest sister, Margit Beatrice, after an automobile accident. The traumatic experience was to haunt him for many years. His father's business in England did not succeed, and late in the summer of 1936 the family moved to Warnsdorf, a small industrial town in northern Bohemia. Weiss wrested from his parents permission to attend the Academy of Art in Prague and enrolled on 1 October 1937.

At the Prague academy, where one of his paintings was awarded a first prize, Weiss met the socialist writer Max Barth, who was twenty years his senior and became his intellectual mentor. His most helpful contact was with the novelist Hermann Hesse, to whom he had written for advice in January 1937 and whom he visited in Montagnola, Switzerland, during the summers of 1937 and 1938. Weiss saw Hesse as a gently guiding father figure, exemplary but not overpowering in his superior craftsmanship and artistry; he revered Hesse for his pacific independence as a writer of psychologically incisive fiction and admired him for his serene, reclusive devotion to a romantic ideal of humane individualism.

Weiss fled to Zurich on 1 October 1938 in the wake of the German occupation of the Sudetenland. He left Zurich on 29 January 1939 and traveled by way of Berlin to Sweden, where his family had found asylum and where his father had taken over a small textile mill in Alingsas, near Göteborg. Weiss worked at the mill until 1942 as a designer of prints in the photographic department; he also found seasonal employment as a lumberman and a farm laborer, but his income was never high enough for him to afford an apartment and studio of his own.

Weiss stayed with his parents, even though his mother had destroyed most of his paintings–especially the ones she considered too gloomy–as she was preparing to move their belongings from Czechoslovakia. He decided to become a Swedish artist and writer, but the years in Sweden were difficult for him. He encountered hostility toward foreigners, above all Germans, and met with indifference to his personal problems as he was learning a new language and trying to find some reassurance for his artistic endeavors. In 1944 he

married a Swedish painter with whom he had a daughter, but the marriage was dissolved without rancor in 1947. He became a Swedish citizen in 1945. He underwent psychoanalysis until 1951. He had his work exhibited in single and group shows and sold one painting to the National Museum. This suggests that Weiss's life in Sweden during the war years was not quite as isolated and without encouragement and successes as he later remembered.

Weiss returned to Berlin in the summer of 1947 as a special reporter for the newspaper *Stockholms Tidningen* and sent back terse, unemotional observations on life in the divided city. He remained an outsider, rejecting any suggestion that he move back to Germany.

Surrealistic images dominate Weiss's early work as a writer in Swedish. His first collection of short prose, *Från ö till ö* (From Island to Island; translated into German as *Von Insel zu Insel*, 1984), published in 1947 by the prestigious firm of Albert Bonnier in Stockholm, was received with critical acclaim and, along with *De besegrade* (The Vanquished, 1948; translated into German as *Die Besiegten*, 1985), *Dokument I* (1949), and *Duellen* (The Duel, 1953; translated into German as *Das Duell*, 1960), established his reputation among the postwar avant-garde of his host country. In his search for a lost coherence and purpose, for something firm and dependable that would impart direction and security to a seriously damaged existence, Weiss limits himself to sequences of forceful short scenes and symbolic situations. They are variations on his principal theme of mortal despair, using images of isolation and enclosure–prison walls and cells, darkened hallways in empty houses, vacant streets–and fantastic, dreamlike evocations of erotic lust, torture, and murder that reveal a perverse bond between victim and executioner.

From 1948 until the mid 1950s Weiss supervised adult education classes in art and film theory at the university in Stockholm and taught painting as a form of therapy at the Långholmen prison. In 1949 he joined a small group of amateurs who had started an experimental cinema studio at the university. Between 1952 and 1960 he made fourteen films, most of them short documentaries that reveal the strong influence of surrealism. His longest film, the eighty-minute *Hägringen* (The Mirage, 1959), is a stark portrait of loneliness and alienation.

In 1952 Weiss began to live with Gunilla Palmstierna, a divorced artist with two children

Weiss in 1963 (Ullstein–Heinz Köster)

who shared his affinity for the bohemian life of the artistic avant-garde; they were married in 1964. Gunilla became his collaborator and designed the stage settings and costumes for most of his plays.

Around 1950 Weiss returned to the German language, which he henceforth used exclusively in his literary writings. That the transition was not a quick and easy one but a laborious and determined effort is reflected in the tortured complexities of his grammar, which stand in marked contrast to his simple vocabulary. His writing of this time is characterized both by careful attention to the details of daily experience and by an inventive surrealistic re-creation of dream images and the unconscious. This breakthrough into a realistically evoked world of the grotesque and comically bizarre was supported by his use of the language of psychoanalysis, which encouraged his invention of explosive situations and encounters and of sadomasochistic conflicts among small groups of men and women who seek release, through orgiastic experiences of liberation and rebirth, from the mechanical controls imposed

upon their lives. Weiss experimented with various forms of the popular stage, such as the harlequinade, the Punch-and-Judy show, parodistic reversals of the morality play, and the mockheroic social drama. His aim was to show the bourgeois world as a ghoulish Grand Guignol and the circus world of the clown and acrobat as fraught with libidinous tensions and with the constant potential for self-destructive violence.

In his early plays Weiss found new metaphors to express his sociopsychological analysis of the postwar world, a language that was in agreement with literary modernism. This style did not, however, make him known beyond the small number of readers and theatergoers who felt an emotional and intellectual kinship with radical art. Even to them, Weiss's most challenging break with traditional linear and mimetic narrative, his "micro-novel" *Der Schatten des Körpers des Kutschers* (translated as "The Shadow of the Coachman's Body," 1969), became available only after the techniques of the "nouveau roman" had been firmly established. Written in 1952, his manuscript was turned down by several publishers and did not appear until 1960.

Scene from a performance of Weiss's Die Ermittlung *(photograph by A. Pisarek, Berlin)*

His last two books of prose, before he devoted the next ten years exclusively to writing for the stage, reached a larger readership and began to secure his position in German letters. The autobiographical novels *Abschied von den Eltern* (Departure from the Parents, 1961; translated as *The Leavetaking*, 1962) and *Fluchtpunkt* (1962; translated as "Vanishing Point," 1966), both written after the deaths of his parents in 1959, retrace the first thirty years of his life and describe his search for artistic autonomy until the spring of 1947. It is in Paris that the narrator begins to feel reconciled to the miseries of his past and the contradictions of his existence and accepts his exile as a challenge to participate in a supranational exchange of ideas that is taking place all around him. At the gathering of the Gruppe (Group) 47 in the fall of 1963 Weiss presented his first recitation–beating on a drum he held between his knees as he read–from *Marat/Sade*. This, his most original, provocative, and successful drama, was to establish him along with Günter Grass as the international voice of German literature during the 1960s.

The play about Marat's assassination by Charlotte Corday in 1793 had undergone several revisions since its inception in the fall of 1962, during which Weiss's initial sympathy for the hesitant intellectual Sade gave way to partisanship for the radical revolutionary Marat. A basic antagonism exists between two different temperaments that are nonetheless bound to each other: the libidinous, hedonistic individual, playfully self-indulgent in his amoral pursuit of sensual pleasure and yet in full intellectual control of his imagination, and the self-denying politician as rational idealist, unflinching in his professedly altruistic devotion to the "purity" of a world-historical cause. There is a profusion of subsidiary characters and a constant assault upon the spectators' senses as the audience is drawn into the confined, explosive world of the lunatic asylum that provides the setting of the play. Blending a variety of stylistic devices that range from carnivalesque buffoonery to stilted pathos and highly charged rhetorical exchanges, Weiss subjects his audience to a barrage of intellectual and sensory stimuli that both excite their sympathy and challenge their tolerance for the action on the stage. They are made part of a historical spectacle that reflects events of 1793 in the mirror of a performance in 1808 and at the same time relates the 1960s fervor for personal and societal liberation to a nineteenth-century consciousness that craved release from Napoleonic repression. An English version of the play, directed by Peter Brook, opened in London in the summer of 1965 and in New York, where it won the Drama Critics Circle Award in December of that year; it was released as a film in 1967.

To counterbalance his originality Weiss made sure that he knew the facts of history. By the end of his life he had accumulated a library of boxes and drawers of notes, excerpts, and clippings that show the extent of his research to familiarize himself with the issues he raised in his plays. His scrupulous respect for accuracy and the demands he made upon himself as a "reporter" of history inform his dramatic reconstruction of the processes of memory and self-exculpatory evasion that are a central concern of his next major play, *Die Ermittlung* (1965; translated as *The Investigation*, 1966).

During the early summer of 1964 Weiss was a private observer at the so-called Auschwitz-Prozeß (Auschwitz Trial) before a Frankfurt court in which twenty-two defendants stood trial for their roles in the administration of the death camp. He took extensive notes and made use of the detailed reports by the journalist Bernd Naumann, who was writing for the daily newspaper *Frankfurter Allgemeine Zeitung*. The trial, which lasted from 20 December 1963 until 19 August 1965, was still in progress at the start of rehearsals for Weiss's play. His "oratorio in eleven cantos" concentrates on the process of gathering evidence through the testimony of witnesses and cross-examinations of the accused; it leaves out such legal aspects as the experts' opinions, the pleas by the attorneys, and the justifications of the verdicts. Weiss does not attempt a naturalistic re-creation of the courtroom procedures; rather, he subjects the factual material to a strict, almost formulaic stylization. It was his intention to present a contemporary version of Dante's *Inferno*. The play premiered in both East and West Germany in October 1965; Ingmar Bergman directed a Swedish performance in early 1966; and an English version, cut from the original five hours to two, opened in New York in October 1966.

Weiss's play reconstructs operating procedures in the camp from the arrival of the inmates until their cremation, leading the audience like a Virgilian guide from the periphery through ever more horrifying stages into the vortex of an infernal system of mass murder. It is a world of total depersonalization and anonymity in which the victims, who are now the witnesses, have lost their individual identity, while the accused are represented as "authentic persons." But they are people with neither remorse nor willingness and capacity to see their deeds as anything but the work of loyal, though somewhat reluctant functionaries for a firmly controlled state bureaucracy. The prosecuting attorney, a composite role that represents several different legal authorities, is a little too obtrusively modeled after the East German lawyer Kaul, whose strategy throughout the trial was to make one point at every opportunity: that Auschwitz was an integral part of a system of mass destruction that was operated for the benefit of German industry, and the apparatus of fascist exploitation was the ultimate outcome of a capitalist social order. The attorney for the defense, likewise a role that combines several legal voices, consistently seeks to portray his clients as misused and dutiful civil servants who ought to be treated leniently. A comparison with Hannah Arendt's analysis of the Adolf Eichmann trial, *Eichmann in Jerusalem: A Report on the Banality of Evil* (1964), may put the ideological stance of Weiss's play into sharper perspective: Arendt emphasized the ordinary and altogether nondiabolical stature of an ambitious, devoted careerist who worked his way into a position of power by serving the administrative authorities of a modern totalitarian state. In contrast to the Israeli chief prosecutor, she saw Eichmann not as the personification of demonic evil but as a person with the normal characteristics of the ordinary citizen who functions according to the dictates of his sense of duty and of his need to please his superiors. Weiss points to a recent reemergence of the Nazi mentality as part of the capitalist restoration of West German society. At the same time he represents the death camp as an isolated hell, a small world with its own distinctive modes of behavior. His most personal intrusion into the "documentary" reconstruction of Auschwitz occurs when witness 3 in canto 4 suggests that the machinery of terror made even its victims a perversely fascinated part of its efficiency because both guards and inmates had grown up under the same system of ideals and conventions.

Weiss's decision, announced in a programmatic declaration published on 27 October 1965 in the conservative *Frankfurter Allgemeine*, to come out unequivocally in support of the Communist world movement did not come entirely as a surprise to the literary world. But the intensity with which he contributed to the public discussion of colonialism, militarism, and economic imperialism was unusual for a German writer. His plays about the struggle against Portuguese rule in Angola, *Sangen om Skrapuken* (1967; German version published as *Gesang vom Lusitanischen Popanz*, 1968; translated into English as *Song of the Lusitanian Bogey*, 1970), and the fight against foreign domination in Vietnam, *Diskurs über die Vorgeschichte und den Verlauf des lang andauernden Befreiungskrieges in Viet Nam als Beispiel für die Notwendigkeit des bewaffneten Kampfes der Unterdrückten gegen ihre Unterdrücker, sowie über die Versuche der Vereinigten Staaten von Amerika die Grundlagen der Revolution zu vernichten* (1967; translated as *Discourse on the Progress of the Prolonged War of Liberation in Vietnam . . .* , 1970), were performed to mixed reactions in the West. They employed a straightforward language to create simple situations within an uncomplicated plot that allowed for a clear distinction between good and evil and showed the enemy to be easily defeatable. Most critics, while acknowledging the sincerity of Weiss's intentions, lamented the progressive loss of subtlety in his characterizations and in his grasp of political realities. His analysis of world politics in the age of highly advanced technologies and international corporate power tends toward a naive moralism. He propagates simple solutions and proclaims a monotonous righteousness that cannot do justice to the complexities of modern global conflicts. His erstwhile supporters on the left, who had opted for the more flexible attitudes of ironic intellectualism, accused Weiss of a well-intentioned dogmatism; the right vilified him as a lackey of Moscow's subversive machinations; and the East came to denounce him as an unreliable ally and eventually as a traitor.

Weiss was never a rigorously trained proponent of communist ideology. His reading of Marx was selective, and his familiarity with neo-Marxist philosophy and aesthetics was unsystematic. His forays into Marxist social theory reflect a deep-seated need for some mental construct that would counterbalance his doubts, uncertainties, and hesitations. The original source of his commitment to artistic expression, at any rate, was not the kind of abstract dogmatism that goes with orthodox convictions; it was, rather, a com-

Weiss in 1982, the year of his death (Ullstein–AP)

passionate heart and the emotions of a moralist who was looking for some firm ground in a world of overpowering contradictions. As a result, Weiss, who had become a member of Sweden's Communist party in 1965, was torn between conflicting loyalties: he realized that his involvement in the issues of the day made him prey to ideological abuse and self-deception; yet he was unwilling to discard that deluding assurance of communality which sustained his public activities.

Although Weiss had abandoned the cognitive and artistic subtleties which inform *Marat/Sade* in favor of a simplified ideological model, he had not gained the kind of intellectual perspective that would allow him to reconcile his need for an unambiguous position in political matters with the demands of his aesthetic conscience. The result was the failure of the play *Trotzki im Exil* (1970; translated as *Trotsky in Exile*, 1971), which premiered in Düsseldorf on 20 January 1970. This failure intensified Weiss's old feeling of vulnerability and brought about, on 6 June 1970, a physical collapse. After a slow recovery, with frequent interruptions caused by his fragile health, he tried to come to terms with the course of his life in its relation to recent world history. He wrote a novel that turned into a comprehensive fictional re-creation of socialist resistance to fascist oppression, *Die Ästhetik des Widerstands* (1981).

Weiss wrote the three volumes of this prose epic between 9 July 1972 and 27 August 1980 in spite of many obstacles, both aesthetic and personal, in a supreme effort of sustained determination. The book blends autobiographical elements with a utopian concept of political self-education and thus stands within the tradition of the German bildungsroman. It also incorporates prominent as well as little-known personages and events from the history of the European struggle for proletarian emancipation. The entire heritage of resistance movements and of the working-class fight for self-determination is evoked to lend historical substance to the young protagonist's initiation into the worlds of art and politics. Weiss's book is written in a terse and at times excessively somber style, with passages of intense pathos and of lyrical introspection and long stretches of dispassionate, dry didacticism. It is an account of noble intent and self-sacrifice and a record of perpetual defeats, full of ordinary heroism, of faith in the righteous causes to which good people dedicate their lives, and of sadness and despair over the course of human affairs. It is a work of historical fiction that is irreconcilably at odds with itself, for each of its two fundamental premises–that of art's utopian promise of autonomy and that of the need of politics to devise ever new systems of coercion–constantly contradict each other.

Weiss died of a heart attack less than a year after the final volume of his trilogy appeared. In 1982 he was awarded the prestigious Georg Büchner Prize of the German Academy of Language and Literature. Shortly before his death he had accepted the prize for literature which the City of Bremen bestows annually. His other awards include the Charles Veillon Prize for *Fluchtpunkt* in 1963, the Lessing Prize of the Free and Hanseatic City of Hamburg in 1965, the Heinrich Mann Prize of the East German Academy of the Arts in 1966, the Carl Albert Anderson Prize in 1967, the Thomas Dehler Prize in 1978, and the Prize for Literature of the City of Cologne in 1981. But such a listing of the official recognition of his work can be deceptive. After his critical successes during the early 1960s, which were largely the result of his avant-garde experiments, Weiss was ever more often embroiled in journalistic controversies and disputes. When the activist consensus of the New Left began to disintegrate after the events of 1968 and gave way to fractional hostilities during the early 1970s, he was frequently denigrated for his refusal to give up his "old"–which were really quite recent–loyalties. Because it had taken him so long to make a political commitment, he was unable to retreat into an attitude of ironic disillusionment or apolitical self-examination. His works, as even his supportive critics pointed out with regretful annoyance, were not attuned to the new literary preoccupation with the reclusive self, and his attempts to mediate between art and politics were no longer convincing. While his commitment to socialist ideals was acknowledged by some in the West to constitute a valuable testimony on behalf of a long-suppressed cultural tradition, it provoked the scorn of the more flexible partisans of the left. In the East he was an "undesirable" during the last decade of his life. It is premature to render a conclusive judgment on his oeuvre, with its ideological aporias, imaginative brilliance, intellectual honesty, and provocative challenge to the bourgeois conscience. But there is good reason to expect that Weiss's best work–his two autobiographical novels, *Marat/Sade*, *Die Ermittlung*, and *Die Ästhetik des Widerstands*–will be remembered not only as significant documents of their time but as an exemplary part of postwar German literature.

Biographies:

Otto F. Best, *Peter Weiss* (New York: Ungar, 1976);

Heinrich Vormweg, *Peter Weiss* (Munich: Beck, 1981).

References:

Karlheinz Braun, comp., *Materialien zu Peter Weiss Marat/Sade* (Frankfurt am Main: Suhrkamp, 1967);

Volker Canaris, ed., *Über Peter Weiss* (Frankfurt am Main: Suhrkamp, 1970);

Donald Free, "Peter Weiss and the Theatre of the Future," *Drama Survey*, 6 (1967/1968): 119-171;

Rainer Gerlach, ed., *Peter Weiss* (Frankfurt am Main: Suhrkamp, 1984);

Manfred Haiduk, *Der Dramatiker Peter Weiss* (Berlin: Henschel, 1977);

Ian Hilton, *Peter Weiss: A Searching for Affinities* (London: Wolff, 1970);

Brigitte Keller-Schumacher, *Dialog und Mord: Eine Interpretation des Marat/Sade von Peter Weiss* (Frankfurt am Main: Athenäum, 1973);

Leslie L. Miller, "Peter Weiss, Marat and Sade: Comments on an Author's Commentary," *Symposium,* 25 (1971): 39-58;

Fred Müller, *Peter Weiss, drei Dramen: Interpretationen* (Munich: Oldenbourg, 1973);

R. C. Perry, "Weiss' *Der Schatten des Körpers des Kutschers,* a Forerunner of the Nouveau Roman?," *Germanic Review,* 47 (1972): 203-219;

Peter J. Raleigh, "Hölderlin: Peter Weiss's Artist in Revolt," *Colloquia Germanica,* 7 (1973): 193-213;

Erika Salloch, "The Divine Comedy as Model and Anti-model for *The Investigation* by Peter Weiss," *Modern Drama,* 14 (1971): 1-12;

Genia Schulz, "Die Ästhetik des Widerstands"– Versionen des Indirekten in Peter Weiss' Roman (Stuttgart: Metzler, 1986);

Gideon Shunami, "The Mechanism of Revolution in the Documentary Theatre of the Play *Trotzki im Exil* by Peter Weiss," *German Quarterly,* 44 (1971): 503-518;

Alexander Stephan, ed., *Die Ästhetik des Widerstands* (Frankfurt am Main: Suhrkamp, 1983);

John J. White, "History and Cruelty in Peter Weiss' *Marat/Sade,*" *Modern Language Review,* 63 (1968): 437-448.

Papers:
The papers of Peter Weiss have been donated to the Akademie der Künste, West Berlin, where they will be cataloged.

Books for Further Reading

Arnold, Heinz Ludwig. *Geschichte der deutschen Literatur aus Methoden: Westdeutsche Literatur von 1945-1971*, 3 volumes. Frankfurt am Main: Athenäum/Fischer Taschenbuch Verlag, 1972.

Bachmann, Dieter, ed. *Fortschreiben: 98 Autoren der deutschen Schweiz*. Zurich & Munich: Artemis, 1977.

Berg, Jan, and others. *Sozialgeschichte der deutschen Literatur von 1918 bis zur Gegenwart*. Frankfurt am Main: Fischer Taschenbuch Verlag, 1981.

Berman, Russell A. *The Rise of the Modern German Novel: Crisis and Charisma*. Cambridge: Harvard University Press, 1986.

Brettschneider, Werner. *Zwischen literarischer Autonomie und Staatsdienst: Die Literatur in der DDR*. Berlin: Schmidt, 1972.

Durzak, Manfred. *Die deutsche Kurzgeschichte der Gegenwart: Autorenporträts, Werkstattgespräche, Interpretationen*. Stuttgart: Reclam, 1980.

Durzak. *Der deutsche Roman der Gegenwart: Entwicklungsvoraussetzungen und Tendenzen*, third edition. Stuttgart, Berlin, Cologne & Mainz: Kohlhammer, 1979.

Durzak, ed. *Deutsche Gegenwartsliteratur: Ausgangspositionen und aktuelle Entwicklungen*. Stuttgart: Reclam, 1981.

Duwe, Wilhelm. *Ausdrucksformen deutscher Dichtung vom Naturalismus bis zur Gegenwart: Eine Stilgeschichte der Moderne*. Berlin: Schmidt, 1965.

Eisele, Ulf. *Die Struktur des modernen deutschen Romans*. Tübingen: Niemeyer, 1984.

Emmerich, Wolfgang. *Kleine Literaturgeschichte der DDR*, third edition. Darmstadt & Neuwied: Luchterhand, 1985.

Garland, H. B. *A Concise Survey of German Literature*. London: Macmillan, 1971; Coral Gables, Fla.: University of Miami Press, 1971.

Hohendahl, Peter Uwe, ed. *Literatur der DDR in den siebziger Jahren*. Frankfurt am Main: Suhrkamp, 1983.

Horst, Karl August. *Kritischer Führer durch die deutsche Literatur der Gegenwart: Roman, Lyrik, Essay*. Munich: Nymphenburger Verlagshandlung, 1962.

Jurgensen, Manfred. *Deutsche Frauenautoren der Gegenwart*. Bern: Francke, 1983.

Koebner, Thomas, ed. *Tendenzen der deutschen Gegenwartsliteratur*. Stuttgart: Kröner, 1984.

Kröll, Friedhelm. *Gruppe 47*. Stuttgart: Metzler, 1979.

Kunisch, Hermann. *Die deutsche Gegenwartsdichtung.* Munich: Nymphenburger Verlagshandlung, 1968.

Kunisch. *Handbuch der deutschen Gegenwartsliteratur,* second edition, edited by Herbert Wiesner, Helge Kähler, and others, 2 volumes. Munich: Nymphenburger Verlagshandlung, 1969-1970.

Langer, Lawrence. *The Holocaust and the Literary Imagination.* New Haven: Yale University Press, 1975.

Natan, Alex, ed. *Swiss Men of Letters: Twelve Literary Essays.* London: Wolff, 1970.

Nonnenmann, Klaus. *Schriftsteller der Gegenwart: Deutsche Literatur. Dreiundfünfzig Porträts.* Olten & Freiburg im Breisgau: Walter, 1963.

Pfeifer, Jochen. *Der deutsche Kriegsroman 1945-60: Ein Versuch zur Vermittlung von Literatur und Sozialgeschichte.* Königstein: Scriptor, 1981.

Raddatz, Fritz J. *Traditionen und Tendenzen: Materialien zur Literatur der DDR.* Frankfurt am Main: Suhrkamp, 1972.

Reed, Donna K. *The Novel and the Nazi Past.* New York, Bern & Frankfurt am Main: Lang, 1985.

Reich-Ranicki, Marcel. *Deutsche Literatur in West und Ost: Prosa seit 1945.* Munich: Piper, 1963.

Robertson, J. G. *A History of German Literature,* sixth edition, edited by Dorothy Reich. Edinburgh & London: Blackwood, 1970.

Rothmann, Kurt. *Deutschsprachige Schriftsteller seit 1945 in Einzeldarstellungen.* Stuttgart: Reclam, 1985.

Ryan, Judith. *The Uncompleted Past: Postwar German Novels and the Third Reich.* Detroit: Wayne State University Press, 1983.

Soergel, Albert, and Curt Hohoff. *Dichtung und Dichter der Zeit,* 2 volumes. Düsseldorf: Bagel, 1961-1963.

Wagener, Hans, ed. *Gegenwartsliteratur und Drittes Reich: Deutsche Autoren in der Auseinandersetzung mit der Vergangenheit.* Stuttgart: Reclam, 1977.

Waidson, H. M. *The Modern German Novel: A Mid-Twentieth Century Survey.* London & New York: Oxford University Press, 1959.

Wiesner, Herbert, ed. *Lexikon der deutschsprachigen Gegenwartsliteratur.* Munich: Nymphenburger Verlagshandlung, 1981.

Contributors

Virginia M. Anderson ....*Gordon College*
Herbert A. Arnold ....*Wesleyan University*
Mark E. Cory ....*University of Arkansas at Fayetteville*
Richard Critchfield ....*Texas A&M University*
Roger A. Crockett ....*Texas A&M University*
David B. Dickens ....*Washington and Lee University*
Heike A. Doane ....*University of North Carolina at Chapel Hill*
Inge Dube ....*Northwestern University*
Elke Frederiksen ....*University of Maryland at College Park*
Penrith Goff ....*Wayne State University*
Gertraud Gutzmann ....*Smith College*
Gunther J. Holst ....*University of South Carolina*
Ritta Jo Horsley ....*University of Massachusetts-Boston*
Valentine C. Hubbs ....*University of Michigan*
Ruth-Ellen B. Joeres ....*University of Minnesota*
Sigrid Kellenter ....*Union College, Schenectady, New York*
Wulf Koepke ....*Texas A&M University*
Egbert Krispyn ....*University of Georgia*
Kathleen J. LaBahn ....*University of Wisconsin-Eau Claire*
James K. Lyon ....*University of California, San Diego*
Erika A. Metzger ....*State University of New York at Buffalo*
Friedrich Peter Ott ....*University of Massachusetts-Boston*
Jochen Richter ....*Allegheny College*
Gerd K. Schneider ....*Syracuse University*
Dieter Sevin ....*Vanderbilt University*
Patricia H. Stanley ....*Florida State University*
H. M. Waidson ....*University College of Swansea (University of Wales)*
Franz-Joseph Wehage ....*Appalachian State University*
Gunther Weimann ....*Freie Universität Berlin*
Alfred D. White ....*University of Wales, College of Cardiff*
Michael Winkler ....*Rice University*
Reinhard K. Zachau ....*University of the South*
Nancy Anne McClure Zeller ....*Albany, New York*

Cumulative Index

Dictionary of Literary Biography, Volumes 1-69
Dictionary of Literary Biography Yearbook, 1980-1987
Dictionary of Literary Biography Documentary Series, Volumes 1-4

Cumulative Index

DLB before number: *Dictionary of Literary Biography*, Volumes 1-69
Y before number: *Dictionary of Literary Biography Yearbook*, 1980-1987
DS before number: *Dictionary of Literary Biography Documentary Series*, Volumes 1-4

A

F

G

H

Cumulative Index

L

Q

Dictionary of Literary Biography

1: *The American Renaissance in New England*, edited by Joel Myerson (1978)

2: *American Novelists Since World War II*, edited by Jeffrey Helterman and Richard Layman (1978)

3: *Antebellum Writers in New York and the South*, edited by Joel Myerson (1979)

4: *American Writers in Paris, 1920-1939*, edited by Karen Lane Rood (1980)

5: *American Poets Since World War II*, 2 parts, edited by Donald J. Greiner (1980)

6: *American Novelists Since World War II*, Second Series, edited by James E. Kibler, Jr. (1980)

7: *Twentieth-Century American Dramatists*, 2 parts, edited by John MacNicholas (1981)

8: *Twentieth-Century American Science-Fiction Writers*, 2 parts, edited by David Cowart and Thomas L. Wymer (1981)

9: *American Novelists, 1910-1945*, 3 parts, edited by James J. Martine (1981)

10: *Modern British Dramatists, 1900-1945*, 2 parts, edited by Stanley Weintraub (1982)

11: *American Humorists, 1800-1950*, 2 parts, edited by Stanley Trachtenberg (1982)

12: *American Realists and Naturalists*, edited by Donald Pizer and Earl N. Harbert (1982)

13: *British Dramatists Since World War II*, 2 parts, edited by Stanley Weintraub (1982)

14: *British Novelists Since 1960*, 2 parts, edited by Jay L. Halio (1983)

15: *British Novelists, 1930-1959*, 2 parts, edited by Bernard Oldsey (1983)

16: *The Beats: Literary Bohemians in Postwar America*, 2 parts, edited by Ann Charters (1983)

17: *Twentieth-Century American Historians*, edited by Clyde N. Wilson (1983)

18: *Victorian Novelists After 1885*, edited by Ira B. Nadel and William E. Fredeman (1983)

19: *British Poets, 1880-1914*, edited by Donald E. Stanford (1983)

20: *British Poets, 1914-1945*, edited by Donald E. Stanford (1983)

21: *Victorian Novelists Before 1885*, edited by Ira B. Nadel and William E. Fredeman (1983)

22: *American Writers for Children, 1900-1960*, edited by John Cech (1983)

23: *American Newspaper Journalists, 1873-1900*, edited by Perry J. Ashley (1983)

24: *American Colonial Writers, 1606-1734*, edited by Emory Elliott (1984)

25: *American Newspaper Journalists, 1901-1925*, edited by Perry J. Ashley (1984)

26: *American Screenwriters*, edited by Robert E. Morsberger, Stephen O. Lesser, and Randall Clark (1984)

27: *Poets of Great Britain and Ireland, 1945-1960*, edited by Vincent B. Sherry, Jr. (1984)

28: *Twentieth-Century American-Jewish Fiction Writers*, edited by Daniel Walden (1984)

29: *American Newspaper Journalists, 1926-1950*, edited by Perry J. Ashley (1984)

30: *American Historians, 1607-1865*, edited by Clyde N. Wilson (1984)

31: *American Colonial Writers, 1735-1781*, edited by Emory Elliott (1984)

32: *Victorian Poets Before 1850*, edited by William E. Fredeman and Ira B. Nadel (1984)

33: *Afro-American Fiction Writers After 1955*, edited by Thadious M. Davis and Trudier Harris (1984)

34: *British Novelists, 1890-1929: Traditionalists*, edited by Thomas F. Staley (1985)

35: *Victorian Poets After 1850*, edited by William E. Fredeman and Ira B. Nadel (1985)

36: *British Novelists, 1890-1929: Modernists*, edited by Thomas F. Staley (1985)

37: *American Writers of the Early Republic*, edited by Emory Elliott (1985)

38: *Afro-American Writers After 1955: Dramatists and Prose Writers*, edited by Thadious M. Davis and Trudier Harris (1985)

39: *British Novelists, 1660-1800*, 2 parts, edited by Martin C. Battestin (1985)

40: *Poets of Great Britain and Ireland Since 1960*, 2 parts, edited by Vincent B. Sherry, Jr. (1985)

41: *Afro-American Poets Since 1955*, edited by Trudier Harris and Thadious M. Davis (1985)

42: *American Writers for Children Before 1900*, edited by Glenn E. Estes (1985)

43: *American Newspaper Journalists, 1690-1872*, edited by Perry J. Ashley (1986)

44: *American Screenwriters*, Second Series, edited by Randall Clark, Robert E. Morsberger, and Stephen O. Lesser (1986)

45: *American Poets, 1880-1945*, First Series, edited by Peter Quartermain (1986)

46: *American Literary Publishing Houses, 1900-1980: Trade and Paperback*, edited by Peter Dzwonkoski (1986)

47: *American Historians, 1866-1912*, edited by Clyde N. Wilson (1986)